The *Instant* NATIONAL LOCATOR GUIDE

Publisher's Cataloging in Publication
(Prepared by Quality Books Inc.)

The instant national locator guide --
p. cm.

ISBN 0-9620096-5-2

1. Telephone--United States--Area codes--Directories. 2. Telephone--United States--Area codes--Maps. 3. Zip code--United States--Directories. 4. Zip code--United States--Maps. 5. Cities and towns--United States--Directories. 6. Cities and towns--United States--Maps.

HE8721   384.6'025'73
                                 QBI91-317

ISBN 0-9620096-5-2

Creighton-Morgan Publishing Group
P.O. Box 470862 San Francisco CA 94147 (415) 922-6684

HOW TO USE THIS BOOK

1

CITY & TOWN DIRECTORY

Section 1 / Pages 1-172

Use to find Zip & Area Codes, Counties & Populations of over 8,500 Cities & Towns. (All Incorporated Municipalities with Populations over 2,500 - Plus all County Seats, regardless of Population.)

This is a national directory, so there is no need to look up the state first. A real time-saver!

And, because all this information is located on just one line, you can find out at least six things about a city by looking it up just once; including if it is a County Seat (*); an Independent City (IC); a STATE CAPITAL (all caps); **over 15,000 in Population (bold);** and how many Counties the City spans (+#). The last column lists the page number where you can find the State Map.

2

STATE & CITY MAPS

Section 2 / Pages 1- 85

Use the 3-digit Zip Code Maps to Locate Cities & Towns Instantly.

First, look up the city in Section 1. (If you already know it's zip code, you can skip this step.) Note the first three digits of its Zip Code, and the Map Page Number in the last column.

Second, open to the State Map in Section 2.

Third, glance down the map until you spot the city's Zip Code Prefix. There, beside it, you will find the city you are looking for.

That's it! The bold lines running through states with multiple area codes indicate where the Area Code changes.

3

COUNTIES & COUNTY SEATS

Section 3 / Pages 1-20

Use to find State Capitals, Counties & County Seats.

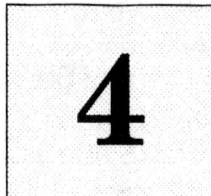

4

ZIP CODE REVERSE DIRECTORY

Section 4 / Pages 1- 32

Use to identify Cities & Towns by their Zip Codes.

5

AREA CODE DIRECTORY

Section 5 / Pages 1-2

Use to indentify States by their Area Codes.

U.S.A. AREA CODE MAP

(Inside back cover) Time Zones, Area Codes and Major Cities are shown on this at-a-glance U.S.A. map.

Use to find Zip & Area Codes, Counties & Populations of over 8,500 Cities & Towns.

Cities & Towns

City Column: Because Cities and Towns are listed alphabetically on a nationwide basis, there is no need to look up the State first. Every incorporated U.S. City and Town over 2,500 people is listed in this directory, plus all County Seats regardless of population.

Cities are alphabetized by the first word and then the second word, rather than the traditional letter-by-letter method. As an example, Red Wings, Minnesota is listed before Redding, Connecticut because Red comes before Redding.

County Seats are indicated by an *; STATE CAPITALs are in ALL CAPS; and cities with **populations over 15,000** are in **bold.**

State Column: Cities with identiical names are listed alphabetically by the abbreviation of the state. For example, Bedford, Iowa is listed before Bedford, Indiana because IA comes before IN.

Area Code Column: A # or ## indicates an Area Code change within the current year. For the new Code, see the Legend.

Zip Code Column: When a City has more than one Zip Code, this column indicates the Zip Code Range. For the specific Zip Code, call your local Post Office. Use the first three digits of the Zip Code to locate the City in Section 2.

County Column: When a city spans several Counties, they are listed as space permits. Any additional counties are indicated by the symbol (+). When the City is a County Seat, (indicated by * in the City Column) the first County listed is the one where the City acts as the County Seat. Any additional Counties are listed in parentheses.

(IC) indicates the City is governed independently of the County where it is located. When the City also acts as a County Seat, there is an * after the City's name in the City Column, and the County is listed in the County Column.

Population is listed in thousands. When the City is part of a larger metropolitan area (as Queens is to New York City) the Population is listed as NAV (Not available.)

Page Number of the State Map. When a State spans two pages, both pages may be noted here.

CITY	STATE	AREA CODE	ZIP CODE	COUNTY	POPULATION (in thousands)	MAP PAGE
Abbeville*	AL	205	36310	Henry	3	2-2&3
Abbeville*	GA	912	31001	Wilcox	1	2-16&17
Abbeville*	LA	318	70510-11	Vermilion	13	2-30
Abbeville*	SC	803	29620	Abbeville	6	2-70
Aberdeen	MD	301	21001	Harford	12	2-34&35
Aberdeen*	MS	601	39730	Monroe	7	2-42&43
Aberdeen	NJ	201	07747	Monmouth	17	2-50
Aberdeen*	SD	605	57401-02	Brown	25	2-71
Aberdeen	WA	206	98520	Grays Harbor	17	2-80
Abernathy	TX	806	79311	Hale/Lubbock	3	2-74
Abilene*	KS	913	67410	Dickinson	6	2-26&27
Abilene*	TX	915	79601-99	Taylor	112	2-74&75
Abingdon	IL	309	61410	Knox	4	2-20
Abington	MA	617	02351	Plymouth	13	2-36&37
Abingdon*	VA	703	24210	Washington	4	2-78&79
Abington Twp.	PA	215	19001	Montgomery	60	2-68
Absecon	NJ	609	08201	Atlantic	7	2-51
Accomac*	VA	804	23301	Accomack	1	2-78&79
Ackerman*	MS	601	39735	Choctaw	1	2-42&43
Acton	MA	508	01720	Middlesex	17	2-36&37
Acushnet	MA	508	02743	Bristol	6	2-36&37
Acworth	GA	404	30101	Cobb	4	2-16&17
Ada	OH	419	45810	Hardin	6	2-60
Ada*	OK	405	74820-21	Pontotoc	17	2-64&65
Ada*	MN	218	56510	Norman	2	2-40
Adams	MA	413	01220	Berkshire	10	2-36
Adamsville	AL	205	35005	Jefferson	5	2-2&3
Addison	IL	708	60101	Du Page	32	2-19
Addison	TX	214	75001	Dallas	7	2-74
Adel*	GA	912	31620	Cook	6	2-16&17
Adel*	IA	515	50003	Dallas	3	2-24&25
Adrian*	MI	517	49221	Lenawee	20	2-38&39
Afton	MN	612	55001	Washington	3	2-41
Agawam	MA	413	01001	Hampden	10	2-36
Agoura Hills	CA	818	91301	Los Angeles	12	2-7
Ahoskie	NC	919	27910	Hertford	5	2-58&59
Aiken*	SC	803	29801-02	Aiken	18	2-70
Ainsworth*	NE	402	69210	Brown	1	2-47
Aitkin*	MN	218	56431	Aitkin	1	2-40
Ajo	AZ	602	85321	Pima	5	2-5
Akron*	CO	303	80720	Washington	1	2-10&11
Akron	NY	716	14001	Erie	3	2-54
Akron*	OH	216	44301-99	Summit	222	2-62
Akron	PA	717	17501	Lancaster	3	2-67
Alabaster	AL	205	35007-144	Shelby	10	2-2&3
Alachua	FL	904	32615-16	Alachua	4	2-14
Alameda	CA	415	94501	Alameda	72	2-7
Alamo	CA	415	94507	Contra Costa	7	2-7

Bold = Over 15,000......ALL CAPS = STATE CAPITAL......* = County Seat......# = Changes to 510 in 9/91.....## = Changes to 410 in 11/91.....(+) = City located in additional counties......NAV = Population not available......C.H.= Court House......(IC)=Independent City

CITY	STATE	AREA CODE	ZIP CODE	COUNTY	POPULATION (in thousands)	MAP PAGE
Alamo*	GA	912	30411	Wheeler	1	2-16&17
Alamo*	TN	901	38001	Crockett	2	2-72
Alamo	TX	512	78516	Hidalgo	6	2-75
Alamo Heights	TX	512	78209	Bexar	6	2-75
Alamogordo*	NM	505	88310-11	Otero	27	2-53
Alamosa*	CO	303	81101	Alamosa	7	2-10&11
Albany	CA	415	94706	Alameda	15	2-7
Albany*	GA	912	31701-08	Dougherty	85	2-16&17
Albany	IN	317	47320	Delaware (+1)	3	2-22&23
Albany*	KY	606	42602	Clinton	2	2-29
Albany*	MO	816	64402	Gentry	1	2-44
ALBANY*	NY	518	12201-99	Albany	97	2-55
Albany*	OR	503	97321	Linn	29	2-63
Albany*	TX	915	76430	Shackelford	1	2-74&75
Albemarle*	NC	704	28001-02	Stanly	14	2-58
Albert Lea*	MN	507	56007	Freeborn	18	2-41
Albia*	IA	515	52531	Monroe	5	2-24&25
Albion*	IL	618	62806	Edwards	2	2-21
Albion*	IN	219	46701	Noble	2	2-22
Albion	MI	517	49224	Calhoun	12	2-38&39
Albion*	NE	402	68620	Boone	1	2-47
Albion*	NY	716	14411	Orleans	4	2-54
Albuquerque*	NM	505	87101-99	Bernalillo	366	2-53
Alcoa	TN	615	37701	Blount	7	2-72&73
Aldan	PA	215	19018	Delaware	5	2-68
Alden	NY	716	14004	Erie	3	2-54
Alderwood Manor	WA	206	98011&36	Snohomish	8	2-80
Aledo*	IL	309	61231	Mercer	3	2-20
Alexander City	AL	205	35010	Tallapoosa	14	2-2&3
Alexandria	IN	317	46001	Madison	6	2-22&23
Alexandria*	KY	606	41001	Campbell	5	2-29
Alexandria*	LA	318	71301-15	Rapides	51	2-30
Alexandria*	MN	612	56308	Douglas	8	2-41
Alexandria*	SD	605	57311	Hanson	1	2-71
Alexandria	VA	703	22301-99	(IC)	112	2-79
Alfred	NY	607	14802	Allegany	4	2-54&55
Alfred*	ME	207	04002	York	1	2-32&33
Algona*	IA	515	50511	Kossuth	6	2-24&25
Algoma	WI	414	54201	Kewaunee	4	2-85
Algonac	MI	313	48001	St. Clair	4	2-39
Algonquin	IL	708	60102	McHenry/Kane	8	2-20
Alhambra	CA	818	91800-99	Los Angeles	71	2-7
Alice*	TX	512	78332-42	Jim Wells	22	2-75
Aliceville	AL	205	35442	Pickens	3	2-2&3
Aliquippa	PA	412	15001	Beaver	17	2-66
Allegan*	MI	616	49010	Allegan	4	2-38&39
Allegany	NY	716	14706	Cattaraugus	8	2-54
Allen	TX	214	75002	Collin	8	2-74

Bold = Over 15,000......ALL CAPS = STATE CAPITAL......* = County Seat......# = Changes to 510 in 9/91..... ## = Changes to 410 in 11/91......(+) = City located in addional counties......NAV= Population not available......C.H.= Court House......(IC) = Independent City

CITY	STATE	AREA CODE	ZIP CODE	COUNTY	POPULATION (in thousands)	MAP PAGE
Allen Park	MI	313	48101	Wayne	31	2-39
Allendale	NJ	201	07401	Bergen	6	2-52
Allendale*	SC	803	29810	Allendale	4	2-70
Allentown*	PA	215	18100-99	Lehigh	104	2-67
Alliance*	NE	308	69301	Box Butte	10	2-47
Alliance	OH	216	44601	Mahoning/Stark	24	2-60
Allison*	IA	319	50602	Butler	1	2-25
Allison Park	PA	412	15101	Allegheny	6	2-68
Allouez	WI	414	54301	Brown	15	2-85
Alma	AR	501	72921	Crawford	3	2-6
Alma*	GA	912	31510	Bacon	4	2-16&17
Alma*	KS	913	66401	Wabaunsee	1	2-26&27
Alma	MI	517	48801	Gratiot	10	2-38&39
Alma*	NE	308	68920	Harlan	1	2-47
Alma*	WI	608	54610	Buffalo	1	2-85
Alpena*	MI	517	49707	Alpena	11	2-38&39
Alpha	NJ	201	08865	Warren	3	2-50
Alpharetta	GA	404	30201	Fulton	4	2-16&17
Alpine*	TX	915	79830-31	Brewster	6	2-74&75
Alpine	UT	801	84004	Utah	3	2-76
Alsip	IL	708	60658	Cook	17	2-19
Altadena	CA	818	91001-02	Los Angeles	43	2-7
Altamont*	TN	615	37301	Grundy	1	2-72&73
Altamonte Springs	FL	305	32714-15	Seminole	26	2-15
Altavista	VA	804	24517	Campbell	4	2-78&79
Alton	IL	618	62002	Madison	33	2-21
Alton*	MO	417	65606	Oregon	1	2-44
Alton	TX	512	78572	Hidalgo	3	2-75
Altoona	IA	515	50009	Polk	6	2-24&25
Altoona	PA	814	16601-03	Blair	55	2-66
Altoona	WI	715	54720	Eau Claire	4	2-84&85
Alturas*	CA	916	96101	Modoc	3	2-8
Altus*	OK	405	73521-23	Jackson	23	2-64&65
Alum Rock	CA	408	95127	Santa Clara	17	2-7
Alva*	OK	405	73717	Woods	6	2-64&65
Alvarado	TX	817	76009	Johnson	3	2-74
Alvin	TX	713	77511-12	Brazoria	18	2-74&75
Amarillo*	TX	806	79101-99	Potter	165	2-74
Amberley	OH	513	43227	Hamilton	3	2-62
Ambler	PA	215	19002	Montgomery	6	2-68
Amboy	IL	815	61310	Lee	2	2-20
Ambridge	PA	412	15003	Beaver	9	2-66
Amelia C.H.*	VA	804	23002	Amelia	1	2-78&79
American Falls*	ID	208	83211	Power	4	2-18
American Fork	UT	801	84003	Utah	14	2-76
Americus*	GA	912	31709	Sumter	13	2-16&17
Amesbury	MA	508	01913	Essex	13	2-36&37
Amherst	MA	413	01002-04	Hampshire	34	2-36

Bold = Over 15,000......ALL CAPS = STATE CAPITAL......* = County Seat......# = Changes to 510 in 9/91.....## = Changes to 410 in 11/91.....(+) = City located in additional counties......NAV = Population not available......C.H.= Court House......(IC)=Independent City

CITY	STATE	AREA CODE	ZIP CODE	COUNTY	POPULATION (in thousands)	MAP PAGE
Amherst	NY	716	14226	Erie	45	2-54
Amherst	OH	216	44001	Lorain	10	2-60
Amherst*	VA	804	24521	Amherst	1	2-78&79
Amidon*	ND	701	58620	Slope	1	2-57
Amite*	LA	504	70422	Tangipahoa	4	2-30&31
Amity Gardens	PA	215	19518	Berks	3	2-67
Amityville	NY	516	11701	Suffolk	10	2-56
Ammon	ID	208	83401	Bonneville	5	2-18
Amory	MS	601	38821	Monroe	7	2-42&43
Amsterdam	NY	518	12010	Montgomery	21	2-55
Anaconda*	MT	406	59711	Deer Lodge	10	2-46
Anacortes	WA	206	98221-22	Skagit	7	2-80
Anadarko*	OK	405	73005	Caddo	6	2-64&65
Anaheim	CA	714	92801-25	Orange	240	2-7
Anahuac*	TX	409	77514	Chambers	1	2-75
Anamosa*	IA	319	52205	Jones	5	2-25
Anchorage	AK	907	99501-40	Anchorage	239	2-4
Andalusia*	AL	205	36420	Covington	10	2-2&3
Anderson	CA	916	96007	Shasta	7	2-8
Anderson*	IN	317	46011-18	Madison	60	2-22&23
Anderson*	SC	803	29621	Anderson	28	2-70
Anderson*	TX	713	77830	Grimes	1	2-74&75
Andover	KS	316	67002	Butler	3	2-26&27
Andover	MA	508	01810	Essex	26	2-36&37
Andover	MN	612	55304	Anoka	9	2-41
Andover	NJ	201	07821 &60	Sussex	5	2-50
Andrews	SC	803	29510	Georgetown (+1)	3	2-70
Andrews*	TX	915	79714	Andrews	13	2-74&75
Angleton*	TX	409	77515	Brazoria	15	2-75
Angola*	IN	219	46703	Steuben	5	2-22
Ankeny	IA	515	50021	Polk	16	2-24&25
Ann Arbor*	MI	313	48103-08	Washtenaw	107	2-39
Anna	IL	618	62906	Union	5	2-21
Annandale	VA	703	22003	Fairfax	35	2-78&79
ANNAPOLIS*	MD	301	21401-99	Anne Arundel (IC)	34	2-35
Anniston*	AL	205	36201-06	Calhoun	30	2-2&3
Anoka*	MN	612	55303	Anoka	15	2-41
Anson*	TX	915	79501	Jones	3	2-74&75
Ansonia	CT	203	06401	New Haven	19	2-12&13
Anthony	TX	915	79821	El Paso	3	2-74&75
Anthony*	KS	316	67003	Harper	3	2-26&27
Antigo*	WI	715	54409	Langlade	8	2-84&85
Antioch	CA	415	94509	Contra Costa	50	2-7
Antioch	IL	708	60002	Lake	4	2-20
Antlers*	OK	405	74523	Pushmataha	3	2-64&65
Apache Junction	AZ	602	85217-19	Pinal (&1)	10	2-5
Apalachicola*	FL	904	32320	Franklin	3	2-14
Apex	NC	919	27502	Wake	3	2-58&59

Bold = Over 15,000......ALL CAPS = STATE CAPITAL......* = County Seat......# = Changes to 510 in 9/91..... ## = Changes to 410 in 11/91......(+) = City located in additional counties......NAV= Population not available......C.H.= Court House......(IC) = Independent City

CITY	STATE	AREA CODE	ZIP CODE	COUNTY	POPULATION (in thousands)	MAP PAGE
Apopka	FL	407	32703-4	Orange	6	2-14&15
Apple Valley	CA	619	92301	San Bernardino	14	2-9
Apple Valley	MN	612	55124	Dakota	22	2-41
Appleton*	WI	414	54911-15	Outagamie	64	2-85
Appling*	GA	404	30802	Columbia	1	2-16&17
Appomattox*	VA	804	24522	Appomattox	1	2-78&79
Aptos	CA	408	95003	Santa Cruz	7	2-7
Arab	AL	205	35016	Marshall	6	2-2&3
Aransas Pass	TX	512	78336	San Patricio (+2)	7	2-75
Arapaho*	OK	405	73620	Custer	1	2-64&65
Arcade	NY	716	14009	Wyoming	4	2-54
Arcade-Arden	CA	916	95821	Sacramento	90	2-8
Arcadia	CA	818	91006	Los Angeles	48	2-7
Arcadia*	FL	813	33821	De Soto	6	2-14&15
Arcadia*	LA	318	71001	Bienville	3	2-30
Arcata	CA	707	95521	Humboldt	14	2-8
Archbald	PA	717	18403	Lackawanna	6	2-67
Archbold	OH	419	43502	Fulton	10	2-60
Archdale	NC	919	27263	Guilford (+1)	5	2-58&59
Archer City*	TX	214	76351	Archer	1	2-74
Arco*	ID	208	83213	Butte	1	2-18
Arcola	IL	217	61910	Douglas	3	2-20&21
Arden	CA	916	95825	Sacramento	54	2-8
Arden Hills	MN	612	55112	Ramsey	8	2-41
Ardmore	IN	219	46628	St. Joseph	3	2-22
Ardmore*	OK	405	73401-03	Carter	25	2-64&65
Ardsley	NY	914	10502	Westchester	4	2-56
Arkadelphia*	AR	501	71923	Clark	10	2-6
Arkansas City*	AR	501	71630	Desha	1	2-6
Arkansas City	KS	316	67005	Cowley	13	2-26&27
Arlington	MA	617	02174	Middlesex	45	2-36&37
Arlington	NY	914	12603	Dutchess	11	2-56
Arlington	TX	817	76003-18	Tarrant	233	2-74
Arlington*	VA	703	22201-99	Arlington	154	2-78&79
Arlington	WA	206	98223	Snohomish	3	2-80
Arlington Heights	IL	708	60004-09	Cook/Lake	9	2-19
Arlyn Oaks	NY	516	11758	Nassau	3	2-56
Armona	CA	209	93202	Kings	3	2-8&9
Armour*	SD	605	57313	Douglas	1	2-71
Arnett*	OK	405	73832	Ellis	1	2-64&65
Arnold	MO	314	63010	Jefferson	20	2-44&45
Arnold	PA	412	15806	Westmooreland	7	2-68
Arroyo Grande	CA	805	93420-21	San Luis Obispo	13	2-9
Artesia	CA	213	90701	Los Angeles	14	2-7
Artesia	NM	505	88210-11	Eddy	10	2-53
Arthur*	NE	308	69121	Arthur	1	2-47
Arvada	CO	303	80001-05	Jefferson/Adams	94	2-10&11
Arvin	CA	805	93203	Kern	8	2-9

Bold = Over 15,000......ALL CAPS = STATE CAPITAL......* = County Seat......# = Changes to 510 in 9/91.....## = Changes to 410 in 11/91.....(+) = City located in additional counties......NAV = Population not available......C.H.= Court House......(IC)=Independent City

CITY	STATE	AREA CODE	ZIP CODE	COUNTY	POPULATION (in thousands)	MAP PAGE
Asbury Park	NJ	201	07712	Monmouth	17	2-50
Ash Flat*	AR	501	72513	Sharp	1	2-6
Ashburn*	GA	912	31714	Turner	9	2-16&17
Ashburnham	MA	508	01430	Worcester	4	2-36&37
Ashdown*	AR	501	71822	Little River	5	2-6
Asheboro*	NC	919	27203	Randolph	15	2-58&59
Asheville*	NC	704	28801-99	Buncombe	60	2-58
Ashland*	AL	205	36251	Clay	1	2-2&3
Ashland*	KS	316	67831	Clark	1	2-26&27
Ashland	KY	606	41101-05	Boyd	26	2-29
Ashland	MA	508	01721	Middlesex	9	2-36&37
Ashland*	MS	601	38603	Benton	1	2-42&43
Ashland*	OH	419	44805	Ashland	19	2-60
Ashland	OR	503	97520	Jackson	15	2-63
Ashland	PA	717	17921	Schuykill (+1)	4	2-67
Ashland	VA	804	23005	Hanover	5	2-78&79
Ashland*	WI	715	54806	Ashland	8	2-84&85
Ashland City*	TN	615	37015	Cheatham	1	2-72&73
Ashley*	ND	701	58413	McIntosh	1	2-57
Ashley	PA	717	18706	Luzerne	4	2-67
Ashtabula	OH	216	44004	Ashtabula	23	2-60
Ashville*	AL	205	35953	St. Clair	1	2-2&3
Ashwaubenon	WI	414	54304	Brown	15	2-85
Asotin*	WA	509	99402	Asotin	1	2-81
Aspen*	CO	303	81611-15	Pitkin	4	2-10&11
Aspermont*	TX	817	79502	Stonewall	1	2-74
Aspin Hill	MD	301	20906	Montgomery	10	2-34&35
Aspinwall	PA	412	15215	Allegheny	3	2-68
Aston	PA	215	19014	Delaware	14	2-68
Astoria*	OR	503	97103	Clatsop	9	2-63
Atantic Beach	FL	904	32233	Duval	8	2-14
Atascadero	CA	805	93422-23	San Luis Obispo	16	2-9
Atchison*	KS	913	66002	Atchison	12	2-26&27
Athens*	AL	205	35611	Limestone	15	2-2&3
Athens*	GA	404	30601-13	Clarke	44	2-16&17
Athens*	OH	614	45701	Athens	20	2-61
Athens	PA	717	18810	Bradford	4	2-67
Athens*	TN	615	37303	McMinn	12	2-72&73
Athens*	TX	214	75751	Henderson	11	2-74
Atherton	CA	415	94025	San Mateo	7	2-7
Atkins	AR	501	72823	Pope	3	2-6
Atkinson	NH	603	03811	Rockingham	4	2-49
ATLANTA*	GA	404	30042-199	Fulton	445	2-16&17
Atlanta*	MI	517	49709	Montmorency	1	2-38&39
Atlanta	TX	214	75551	Cass	6	2-74
Atlantic City	NJ	609	08401-99	Atlantic	38	2-51
Atlantic Highlands	NJ	201	07716	Monmouth	5	2-50
Atlantic*	IA	712	50022	Cass	8	2-24

Bold = Over 15,000......ALL CAPS = STATE CAPITAL......* = County Seat......# = Changes to 510 in 9/91..... ## = Changes to 410 in 11/91......(+) = City located in additional counties......NAV= Population not available......C.H. = Court House......(IC) = Independent City

CITY	STATE	AREA CODE	ZIP CODE	COUNTY	POPULATION (in thousands)	MAP PAGE
Atmore	AL	205	36502&4	Escambia	9	2-2&3
Atoka*	OK	405	74525	Atoka	3	2-64&65
Attalla	AL	205	35954	Etowah	8	2-2&3
Attica	IN	317	47918	Fountain	4	2-22&23
Attica	NY	716	14011	Wyoming (+1)	3	2-54
Attleboro	MA	508	02703	Bristol	39	2-36&37
Atwater	CA	209	95301	Merced	20	2-8&9
Atwood*	KS	913	67730	Rawlins	2	2-26&27
Auburn	AL	205	36830-49	Lee	29	2-2&3
Auburn*	CA	916	95603-04	Placer	8	2-8
Auburn	IL	217	62615	Sangamon	4	2-20&21
Auburn*	IN	219	46706	De Kalb	8	2-22
Auburn	MA	508	01501	Worcester	14	2-36&37
Auburn*	ME	207	04210-12	Androscoggin	22	2-32&33
Auburn*	NE	402	68305	Nemaha	3	2-47
Auburn	NH	603	03032	Rockingham	3	2-49
Auburn*	NY	315	13021	Cayuga	31	2-54&55
Auburn	WA	206	98001-03	King	30	2-80
Auburn Heights	MI	313	48057	Oakland	15	2-39
Auburndale	FL	813	33823	Polk	7	2-14&15
Audubon*	IA	712	50025	Audubon	3	2-24
Audubon	NJ	609	08106	Camden	10	2-51
Audubon	PA	215	19407	Montgomery	6	2-68
Augusta*	AR	501	72006	Woodruff	3	2-6
Augusta*	GA	404	30901-19	Richmond	47	2-16&17
Augusta	KS	316	67010	Butler	6	2-26&27
AUGUSTA*	ME	207	04330	Kennebec	20	2-32&33
Augusta	MI	313	49012	Kalamazoo	5	2-39
Aurora	CO	303	80010-45	Arapahoe (+1)	208	2-10&11
Aurora	IL	708	60504-07	Kane/Du Page	86	2-19
Aurora	IN	812	47001	Dearborn	4	2-23
Aurora	MN	218	55705	St. Louis	3	2-40
Aurora	MO	417	65605	Lawrence	6	2-44
Aurora	OH	216	44202	Portage	8	2-60
Aurora*	NE	402	68818	Hamilton	4	2-47
Austell	GA	404	30001	Cobb/Douglas	3	2-16&17
Austin	IN	812	47102	Scott	5	2-23
Austin*	MN	507	55912	Mower	21	2-41
AUSTIN*	TX	512	78701-99	Travis	446	2-75
Austintown	OH	216	44512	Mahoning	23	2-60
Ava*	MO	417	65608	Douglas	1	2-44
Avalon	PA	412	15202	Allegheny	6	2-68
Avenal	CA	209	93204	Kings	4	2-8&9
Avoca	PA	717	18641	Luzerne	3	2-67
Avon	MA	508	02322	Norfolk	5	2-36&37
Avon	NY	716	14414	Livingston	3	2-54
Avon	OH	216	44011	Lorain	7	2-60
Avon Lake	OH	216	44012	Lorain	13	2-60

Bold = Over 15,000......ALL CAPS = STATE CAPITAL......* = County Seat......# = Changes to 510 in 9/91.....## = Changes to 410 in 11/91.....(+) = City located in additional counties......NAV = Population not available......C.H.= Court House......(IC)=Independent City

CITY	STATE	AREA CODE	ZIP CODE	COUNTY	POPULATION (in thousands)	MAP PAGE
Avon Park	FL	813	33825	Highlands	8	2-14&15
Avondale	AZ	602	85323	Maricopa	8	2-5
Ayden	NC	919	28513	Pitt	4	2-58&59
Ayer	MA	508	01432-33	Middlesex	6	2-36&37
Azle	TX	817	76020	Tarrant/Parker	6	2-74
Aztec*	NM	505	87410	San Juan	7	2-53
Azusa	CA	818	91702	Los Angeles	35	2-7
Babylon	NY	516	11702-04	Suffolk	12	2-56
Bad Axe*	MI	517	48413	Huron	3	2-38&39
Baden	PA	412	15005	Beaver	5	2-66
Bagley*	MN	218	56621	Clearwater	1	2-40
Baileys Crossroads	VA	703	22041	Fairfax	4	2-78&79
Bainbridge*	GA	912	31717	Decatur	10	2-16&17
Bainbridge	NY	607	13733	Chenango	3	2-54&55
Baird*	TX	915	79504	Callahan	1	2-74&75
Baker	LA	504	70704	East Baton Rouge	13	2-30&31
Baker*	MT	406	59313	Fallon	1	2-46
Baker*	OR	503	97814	Baker	9	2-63
Bakersfield*	CA	805	93300-89	Kern	150	2-9
Bakersville*	NC	704	28705	Mitchell	1	2-58
Bal Harbour	FL	305	33154	Dade	5	2-15
Balch Springs	TX	214	75180	Dallas	14	2-74
Balcones Heights	TX	512	78201	Bexar	3	2-75
Bald Knob	AR	501	72010	White	3	2-6
Baldwin	FL	904	32234	Duval	2	2-14
Baldwin	LA	318	70514	St. Mary	2	2-30
Baldwin*	MI	616	49304	Lake	1	2-38&39
Baldwin	PA	412	15234	Allegheny	24	2-68
Baldwin Park	CA	818	91706	Los Angeles	63	2-7
Baldwinsville	NY	315	13027	Onondaga	6	2-54&55
Baldwyn	MS	601	38824	Lee/Prentiss	3	2-42&43
Ball	LA	318	71405	Rapides	4	2-30
Ballinger*	TX	915	76821	Runnels	4	2-74&75
Ballston Spa*	NY	518	12020	Saratoga	5	2-55
Ballwin	MO	314	63011-22	St. Louis	13	2-44&45
Balsam Lake*	WI	715	54810	Polk	1	2-84&85
Baltimore	OH	614	43105	Fairfield	3	2-61
Baltimore*	MD	301	21201-99	Baltimore (I)	760	2-34&35
Bamberg*	SC	803	29003	Bamberg	3	2-70
Bandera*	TX	512	78003	Bandera	1	2-75
Bangor*	ME	207	04401	Penobscot	30	2-32&33
Bangor	MI	616	48706	Bay	17	2-38&39
Bangor	PA	215	18013-50	Northampton	5	2-67
Banning	CA	714	92220	Riverside	16	2-8
Bar Harbor	ME	207	04609	Hancock	4	2-32&33
Baraboo*	WI	608	53913	Sauk	8	2-85
Barberton	OH	216	44203	Summit	30	2-62
Barboursville	WV	304	25504	Cabell	3	2-82

Bold = Over 15,000......ALL CAPS = STATE CAPITAL......* = County Seat......# = Changes to 510 in 9/91..... ## = Changes to 410 in 11/91......(+) = City located in addional counties......NAV= Population not available......C.H.= Court House......(IC) = Independent City

CITY	STATE	AREA CODE	ZIP CODE	COUNTY	POPULATION (in thousands)	MAP PAGE
Barbourville*	KY	606	40906	Knox	3	2-29
Bardstown*	KY	502	40004	Nelson	6	2-28&29
Bardwell*	KY	502	42023	Carlisle	1	2-28&29
Barling	AR	501	72923	Sebastian	4	2-6
Barnesboro	PA	814	15714	Cambria	3	2-66
Barnesville	OH	614	43713	Belmont	5	2-61
Barnesville*	GA	404	30204	Lamar	5	2-16&17
Barnstable*	MA	508	02630	Barnstable	36	2-36&37
Barnum Island	NY	516	11558	Nassau	4	2-56
Barnwell*	SC	803	29812	Barnwell	5	2-70
Barre	VT	802	05641	Washington	10	2-77
Barrington	IL	708	60010	Cook/Lake	9	2-19
Barrington	NH	603	03825	Strafford	4	2-49
Barrington	NJ	609	08007	Camden	7	2-51
Barrington	RI	401	02806	Bristol	16	2-69
Barron*	WI	715	54812	Barron	3	2-84&85
Barrow	AK	907	99723	North Slope	2	2-4
Barstow	CA	619	92310-12	San Bernardino	20	2-9
Bartlesville*	OK	918	74003-06	Washington	30	2-65
Bartlett	IL	708	60103	Du Page/Cook	15	2-19
Bartlett*	NE	308	68622	Wheeler	1	2-47
Bartlett	TN	901	38134	Shelby	21	2-72
Bartonville	IL	309	61607	Peoria	6	2-20
Bartow*	FL	813	33830	Polk	15	2-14&15
Basile	LA	318	70515	Evangeline	2	2-30
Basin*	WY	307	82410	Big Horn	1	2-83
Bassett*	NE	402	68714	Rock	1	2-47
Bastrop*	LA	318	71220-21	Morehouse	17	2-30
Bastrop*	TX	512	78602	Bastrop	5	2-75
Batavia	IL	708	60510	Kane/Du Page	13	2-19
Batavia*	NY	716	14020-21	Genesee	16	2-54
Batavia*	OH	513	45103	Clermont	1	2-61
Batesburg	SC	803	29006	Lexington/Saluda	4	2-70
Batesville*	AR	501	72501-03	Independence	9	2-6
Batesville	IN	812	47006	Ripley/Franklin	4	2-23
Batesville*	MS	601	38606	Panola	5	2-42&43
Bath*	ME	207	04530	Sagadahoc	10	2-32&33
Bath*	NY	607	14810	Steuben	5	2-54&55
BATON ROUGE*	LA	504	70801-99	East Baton Rouge	369	2-31
Battle Creek	MI	616	49015-17	Calhoun	54	2-38&39
Battle Ground	WA	206	98604	Clark	3	2-80
Battle Mountain	NV	702	89820	Lander	3	2-48
Baudette*	MN	218	56623	Lake of Woods	1	2-40
Baxley*	GA	912	31513	Appling	4	2-16&17
Baxter	MN	218	56401	Crow Wing	3	2-40
Baxter Springs	KS	316	66713	Cherokee	5	2-26&27
Bay City*	MI	517	48706-08	Bay	39	2-38&39
Bay City*	TX	409	77414	Matagorda	19	2-75

Bold = Over 15,000......ALL CAPS = STATE CAPITAL......* = County Seat......# = Changes to 510 in 9/91......## = Changes to 410 in 11/91......(+) = City located in additional counties......NAV = Population not available......C.H.= Court House......(IC)=Independent City

CITY	STATE	AREA CODE	ZIP CODE	COUNTY	POPULATION (in thousands)	MAP PAGE
Bay Harbor Islands	FL	305	33154	Dade	5	2-15
Bay Minette*	AL	205	36507	Baldwin	7	2-2&3
Bay St. Louis*	MS	601	39520-29	Hancock	10	2-42&43
Bay Shore	NY	516	11706	Suffolk	10	2-56
Bay Springs*	MS	601	39422	Jasper	2	2-42&43
Bay Village	OH	216	44140	Cuyahoga	18	2-62
Bayard	NM	505	88023	Grant	3	2-53
Bayberry	NY	315	13088	Onondaga	6	2-54&55
Bayboro*	NC	919	28515	Pamlico	1	2-58&59
Bayonne	NJ	201	07002	Hudson	64	2-52
Bayport	MN	612	55003	Washington	3	2-41
Bayport	NY	516	11705	Suffolk	9	2-56
Bayside	WI	414	53217	Milwaukee (+1)	5	2-85
Baytown	TX	713	77520-22	Harris (+1)	61	2-74&75
Bayville	NY	516	11709	Nassau	3	2-56
Baywood Park	CA	805	93402	San Luis Obispo	3	2-9
Beach*	ND	701	58621	Golden Valley	1	2-57
Beachwood	NJ	201	08722	Ocean	8	2-50&51
Beachwood	OH	216	44122	Cuyahoga	9	2-62
Beacon	NY	914	12508	Dutchess	13	2-56
Beardstown	IL	217	62618	Cass	6	2-20&21
Beatrice*	NE	402	68310	Gage	12	2-47
Beattyville*	KY	606	41311	Lee	1	2-29
Beaufort*	NC	919	28516	Carteret	4	2-58&59
Beaufort*	SC	803	29901-03	Beaufort	9	2-70
Beaumont	CA	714	92223	Riverside	8	2-9
Beaumont*	TX	409	77701-99	Jefferson	119	2-75
Beaver City*	NE	308	68926	Furnas	1	2-47
Beaver Dam	KY	502	42320	Ohio	3	2-28&29
Beaver Dam	WI	414	53916	Dodge	15	2-85
Beaver Falls	PA	412	15010	Beaver	13	2-66
Beaver*	OK	405	73932	Beaver	1	2-64&65
Beaver*	PA	412	15009	Beaver	4	2-66
Beaver*	UT	801	84713	Beaver	1	2-76
Beavercreek	OH	513	45401	Greene	33	2-61
Beaverton	OR	503	97075-76	Washington	35	2-63
Beckley*	WV	304	25801-02	Raleigh	20	2-82
Bedford*	IA	712	50833	Taylor	2	2-24
Bedford*	IN	812	47421	Lawrence	14	2-23
Bedford*	KY	502	40006	Trimble	1	2-28&29
Bedford	MA	617	01730	Middlesex	13	2-36&37
Bedford	NH	603	03102	Hillsborough	9	2-49
Bedford	OH	216	44146	Cuyahoga	15	2-62
Bedford*	PA	814	15522	Bedford	3	2-66
Bedford	TX	817	76021-22	Tarrant	21	2-74
Bedford*	VA	703	24523	Bedford (IC)	6	2-78&79
Bedford Heights	OH	216	44146	Cuyahoga	13	2-62
Beebe	AR	501	72012	White	4	2-6

Bold = Over 15,000......ALL CAPS = STATE CAPITAL......* = County Seat......# = Changes to 510 in 9/91..... ## = Changes to 410 in 11/91......(+) = City located in addional counties......NAV= Population not available......C.H.= Court House......(IC) = Independent City

CITY	STATE	AREA CODE	ZIP CODE	COUNTY	POPULATION (in thousands)	MAP PAGE
Beech Grove	IN	317	46107	Marion	13	2-22&23
Beeville*	TX	512	78102-04	Bee	15	2-75
Bel Air*	MD	301	21014	Harford	158	2-34&35
Bel-Ridge	MO	314	63133	St. Louis	3	2-44&45
Belchertown	MA	413	01007	Hampshire	8	2-36
Belding	MI	616	48809	Ionia	6	2-38&39
Belen	NM	505	87002	Valencia	5	2-53
Belfast*	ME	207	04915	Waldo	6	2-32&33
Belford	NJ	201	07718	Monmouth	7	2-50
Bell	CA	213	90201	Los Angeles	29	2-7
Bell Gardens	CA	213	90201	Los Angeles	36	2-7
Bella Vista	AR	501	72712	Benton	3	2-6
Bellair	FL	813	34616	Clay	5	2-14&15
Bellair	TX	713	77401-02	Harris	15	2-74&75
Bellaire	OH	614	43906	Belmont	8	2-61
Bellaire*	MI	616	49615	Antrim	1	2-38&39
Bellbrook	OH	513	45305	Greene	5	2-61
Belle Fourche*	SD	605	57717	Butte	4	2-71
Belle Glade	FL	407	33430	Palm Beach	17	2-14&15
Belle Isle	FL	305	32809	Orange	3	2-15
Belle Plaine	IA	319	52208	Benton	3	2-25
Belle Plaine	MN	612	56011	Scott	3	2-41
Belleair Bluffs	FL	813	34635	Pinellas	3	2-14&15
Bellefontaine Nbrs	MO	314	63137	St. Louis	11	2-45
Bellefontaine*	OH	513	43311	Logan	12	2-61
Bellefonte*	PA	814	16823&80	Centre	6	2-66
Belleview	FL	904	32620	Escambia	8	2-14
Belleville*	IL	618	62220-25	St. Clair	42	2-21
Belleville*	KS	913	66935	Republic	2	2-26&27
Belleville	MI	313	48111	Wayne	4	2-39
Belleville	NJ	201	07109	Essex	39	2-52
Bellevue	KY	606	41073	Campbell	7	2-29
Bellevue	NE	402	68005	Sarpy	33	2-47
Bellevue	OH	419	44811	Huron/Sandusky	8	2-60
Bellevue	PA	412	15202	Allegheny	10	2-68
Bellevue	VA	703	23227	Fairfax	4	2-78&79
Bellevue	WA	206	98004-09	King	32	2-80
Bellflower	CA	213	90706-07	Los Angeles	58	2-7
Bellingham	MA	508	02019	Norfolk	14	2-36&37
Bellingham*	WA	206	98225-27	Whatcom	47	2-80
Bellmawr	NJ	609	08031	Camden	14	2-51
Bellmead	TX	817	76705	McLennan	8	2-74
Bellmore	NY	516	11710	Nassau	18	2-56
Bellows Falls	VT	802	05101	Windham	3	2-77
Bellport	NY	516	11713	Suffolk	3	2-56
Bellville*	TX	409	77418	Austin	3	2-75
Bellwood	IL	708	60025 &104	Cook	19	2-19
Belmar	NJ	201	07719	Monmouth	7	2-50

Bold = Over 15,000......ALL CAPS = STATE CAPITAL......* = County Seat......# = Changes to 510 in 9/91.....## = Changes to 410 in 11/91.....(+) = City located in additional counties......NAV = Population not available......C.H.= Court House......(IC)=Independent City

CITY	STATE	AREA CODE	ZIP CODE	COUNTY	POPULATION (in thousands)	MAP PAGE
Belmond	IA	515	50421	Wright	3	2-24&25
Belmont	CA	415	94002	San Mateo	24	2-7
Belmont	MA	617	02178	Middlesex	25	2-36&37
Belmont	NC	704	28012	Gaston	5	2-58
Belmont	NH	603	03220	Belknap	4	2-49
Belmont*	NY	716	14813	Allegany	1	2-54
Beloit*	KS	913	67420	Mitchell	7	2-26&27
Beloit	WI	608	53511	Rock	34	2-85
Belpre	OH	614	45714	Washington	7	2-61
Belton	MO	816	64012	Cass	14	2-44
Belton	SC	803	29627	Anderson	5	2-70
Belton*	TX	817	76513	Bell	11	2-74
Belvidere*	IL	815	61008	Boone	15	2-20
Belvidere*	NJ	201	07823	Warren	1	2-50
Belzoni*	MS	601	39038	Humphreys	2	2-42&43
Bemidji*	MN	218	56601-19	Beltrami	10	2-40
Benbrook	TX	817	76126	Tarrant	14	2-74
Bend*	OR	503	97701-09	Deschutes	19	2-63
Benicia	CA	707	94510	Solano	21	2-8
Benjamin*	TX	817	79505	Knox	1	2-74
Benkelman*	NE	308	69021	Dundy	1	2-47
Bennettsville*	SC	803	29512	Marlboro	9	2-70
Bennington*	VT	802	05201	Bennington	16	2-77
Bensalem	PA	215	19020	Bucks	59	2-68
Bensley	VA	804	23234	Chesterfield	4	2-78&79
Benson	AZ	602	85602	Cochise	3	2-5
Benson	NC	919	27504	Johnston	3	2-58&59
Benson*	MN	612	56215	Swift	3	2-41
Bentleyville	PA	412	15314	Washington	3	2-66
Benton*	AR	501	72015	Saline	19	2-6
Benton*	IL	618	62812	Franklin	7	2-21
Benton*	KY	502	42025	Marshall	4	2-28&29
Benton*	LA	318	71006	Bossier	1	2-30
Benton*	MO	314	63736	Scott	1	2-44&45
Benton*	TN	615	37307	Polk	1	2-72&73
Benton Harbor	MI	616	49022	Berrien	15	2-38&39
Bentonville*	AR	501	72712-14	Benton	10	2-6
Benzinger	PA	814	15857	Elk	8	2-66
Berea	KY	606	40403	Madison	9	2-29
Berea	OH	216	44017	Cuyahoga	20	2-62
Bergenfield	NJ	201	07621	Bergen	26	2-52
Berkeley	CA	415	94701-10	Alameda	104	2-7
Berkeley	IL	708	60163	Cook	5	2-19
Berkeley	MO	314	63134	St. Louis	16	2-44&45
Berkeley Heights	NJ	201	07922	Union	12	2-52
Berkeley Springs*	WV	304	25411	Morgan	1	2-82
Berkley	MA	508	02780	Bristol	3	2-36&37
Berkley	MI	313	48072	Oakland	19	2-39

Bold = Over 15,000......ALL CAPS = STATE CAPITAL......* = County Seat......# = Changes to 510 in 9/91...... ## = Changes to 410 in 11/91......(+) = City located in addional counties......NAV= Population not available......C.H.= Court House......(IC) = Independent City

CITY	STATE	AREA CODE	ZIP CODE	COUNTY	POPULATION (in thousands)	MAP PAGE
Berlin	CT	203	06037	Hartford	16	2-12&13
Berlin	NH	603	03570	Coos	13	2-49
Berlin	NJ	609	08009	Camden	6	2-51
Berlin	WI	414	54923	Green Lake (+)	5	2-85
Bernalillo*	NM	505	87004	Sandoval	3	2-53
Bernards	NJ	201	07920	Somerset	12	2-50
Bernardsville	NJ	201	07924	Somerset	7	2-50
Berne	IN	219	46711	Adams	3	2-22
Berryville*	AR	501	72616	Carroll	3	2-6
Berryville*	VA	703	22611	Clarke	1	2-78&79
Berthoud	CO	303	80513	Larimer	2	2-10&11
Bertrand	MI	616	49120	Berrien	5	2-38&39
Berwick	LA	504	70342	St. Mary	5	2-30&31
Berwick	ME	207	03901	York	4	2-32&33
Berwick	PA	717	18603	Columbia	12	2-67
Berwyn	IL	708	60402	Cook	46	2-19
Berwyn Heights	MD	301	20740	Prince Georges	3	2-34&35
Bessemer	AL	205	35020-23	Jefferson	32	2-2&3
Bessemer*	MI	906	49911	Gogebic	3	2-38
Bessemer City	NC	704	28016	Gaston	5	2-58
Bethany	CT	203	06525	New Haven	4	2-12&13
Bethany	OK	405	73008	Oklahoma	22	2-64&65
Bethany*	MO	816	64424	Harrison	2	2-44
Bethel	AK	907	99559	Bethel	4	2-4
Bethel	CT	203	06801	Fairfield	9	2-12&13
Bethel Park	PA	412	15102	Allegheny	33	2-68
Bethesda	MD	301	20813-17	Montgomery	70	2-34&35
Bethlehem	CT	203	06751	Litchfield	3	2-12&13
Bethlehem	PA	215	18015-18	Lehigh (+1)	71	2-67
Bethpage	NY	516	11714	Nassau	17	2-56
Bettendorf	IA	319	52722	Scott	29	2-25
Beulah*	MI	616	49617	Benzie	1	2-38&39
Beulah	ND	701	58523	Mercer	3	2-57
Beverly	MA	508	01915	Essex	38	2-36&37
Beverly	NJ	609	08010	Burlington	3	2-51
Beverly Hills	CA	213	90209-13	Los Angeles	33	2-7
Beverly Hills	MI	313	48009	Oakland	12	2-39
Bexley	OH	614	43209	Franklin	13	2-61
Bicknell	IN	812	47512	Knox	5	2-23
Biddeford	ME	207	04005-07	York	21	2-32&33
Big Bear Lake	CA	714	92315	San Bernardino	5	2-9
Big Beaver	PA	412	15010	Beaver	3	2-66
Big Lake*	TX	915	76932	Reagan	4	2-74&75
Big Rapids*	MI	616	49307	Mecosta	14	2-38&39
Big Spring*	TX	915	79720-21	Howard	26	2-74&75
Big Stone Gap	VA	703	24219	Wise	5	2-78&79
Big Timber*	MT	406	59011	Sweet Grass	1	2-46
Billerica	MA	508	01821-22	Middlesex	25	2-36&37

Bold = Over 15,000......ALL CAPS = STATE CAPITAL......* = County Seat.....# = Changes to 510 in 9/91.....## = Changes to 410 in 11/91.....(+) = City located in additional counties......NAV = Population not available......C.H.= Court House......(IC)=Independent City

CITY	STATE	AREA CODE	ZIP CODE	COUNTY	POPULATION (in thousands)	MAP PAGE
Billings*	MT	406	59101-99	Yellowstone	80	2-46
Biloxi	MS	601	39530-35	Harrison	50	2-42&43
Binghamton*	NY	607	13901-99	Broome	54	2-54&55
Birchwood City	MD	301	20745	Prince Georges	8	2-35
Birdsboro	PA	215	19508	Berks	4	2-67
Birmingham*	AL	205	35200-59	Jefferson	283	2-2&3
Birmingham	MI	313	48008-12	Oakland	21	2-39
Bisbee*	AZ	602	85603	Cochise	8	2-5
Biscayne Park	FL	305	33161	Dade	3	2-15
Bishop	CA	619	93512	Inyo	3	2-9
Bishop	TX	512	78343	Nueces	4	2-75
Bishopville*	SC	803	29010	Lee	3	2-70
BISMARCK*	ND	701	58501	Burleigh	48	2-57
Bison*	SD	605	57620	Perkins	1	2-71
Bixby	OK	918	74008	Tulsa/Wagoner	7	2-65
Black Jack	MO	314	63031	St. Louis	5	2-44&45
Black Mountain	NC	704	28711	Buncombe	4	2-58
Black Oak	IN	219	46406	Lake	10	2-22
Black River Falls*	WI	715	54615	Jackson	3	2-84&85
Blackfoot*	ID	208	83221	Bingham	10	2-18
Blacksburg	VA	703	24060-63	Montgomery	32	2-78&79
Blackshear*	GA	912	31516	Pierce	3	2-16&17
Blackstone	MA	508	01504	Worcester	6	2-36&37
Blackstone	VA	804	23824	Nottoway	4	2-78&79
Blackville	SC	803	29817	Barnwell	3	2-70
Blackwell	OK	405	74631	Kay	8	2-64&65
Blackwood	NJ	609	08012	Camden	5	2-51
Bladensburg	MD	301	20710	Prince Georges	8	2-34&35
Blaine	MN	612	55434	Anoka/Ramsey	34	2-41
Blair*	NE	402	68008	Washington	7	2-47
Blairsville*	GA	404	30512	Union	1	2-16&17
Blairsville	PA	412	15717	Indiana	4	2-66
Blakely	PA	717	18447	Lackawanna	7	2-67
Blakely*	GA	912	31723	Early	6	2-16&17
Blanchester	OH	513	45107	Clinton/Warren	3	2-61
Bland*	VA	703	24315	Bland	1	2-78&79
Blanding	UT	801	84511	San Juan	3	2-76
Blasdell	NY	716	14219	Erie	3	2-54
Blauvelt	NY	914	10913	Rockland	5	2-56
Blissfield	MI	517	49228	Lenawee	3	2-38&39
Bloomer	WI	715	54724	Chippewa	3	2-84&85
Bloomfield	CT	203	06002	Hartford	7	2-12&13
Bloomfield	NJ	201	07003	Essex	48	2-52
Bloomfield	NM	505	87413	San Juan	5	2-53
Bloomfield Hills	MI	313	48302-04	Oakland	4	2-39
Bloomfield*	IA	515	52537	Davis	3	2-24&25
Bloomfield*	IN	812	47424	Greene	3	2-23
Bloomfield*	MO	314	63825	Stoddard	1	2-44&45

Bold = Over 15,000......ALL CAPS = STATE CAPITAL......* = County Seat......# = Changes to 510 in 9/91..... ## = Changes to 410 in 11/91......(+) = City located in addional counties......NAV= Population not available......C.H.= Court House......(IC) = Independent City

CITY	STATE	AREA CODE	ZIP CODE	COUNTY	POPULATION (in thousands)	MAP PAGE
Bloomingdale	IL	708	60108	Du Page	12	2-19
Bloomingdale	NJ	201	07403	Passaic	8	2-52
Bloomington	CA	714	92316	San Bernardino	19	2-9
Bloomington*	IL	309	61701-04	McLean	48	2-20
Bloomington*	IN	812	47401-08	Monroe	52	2-23
Bloomington	MN	612	55420	Hennepin	89	2-41
Bloomsburg*	PA	717	17815	Columbia	11	2-67
Blountstown*	FL	904	32424	Calhoun	3	2-14
Blountville*	TN	615	37617	Sullivan	1	2-72&73
Blue Ash	OH	513	45242	Hamilton	10	2-62
Blue Earth*	MN	507	56013	Faribault	3	2-41
Blue Island	IL	708	60406	Cook	22	2-19
Blue Point	NY	516	11715	Suffolk	4	2-56
Blue Ridge*	GA	404	30513	Fannin	1	2-16&17
Blue Springs	MO	816	64013-15	Jackson	33	2-44
Bluefield	VA	703	24605	Tazewell	6	2-78&79
Bluefield	WV	304	24701	Mercer	15	2-82
Bluff Park	AL	205	35226	Jefferson	8	2-2&3
Bluffton	OH	419	45817	Allen/Hancock	3	2-60
Bluffton*	IN	219	46714	Wells	9	2-22
Blythe	CA	619	92225-26	Riverside	7	2-9
Blytheville*	AR	501	72315-19	Mississippi	23	2-6
Boardman	OH	216	44512	Mahoning	38	2-60
Boaz	AL	205	35957	Marshall/Etowah	8	2-2&3
Boca Raton	FL	407	33427-99	Palm Beach	61	2-14&15
Boerne*	TX	512	78004-06	Kendall	5	2-75
Bogalusa	LA	504	70427	Washington	17	2-30&31
Bogota	NJ	201	07603	Bergen	8	2-52
Bohemia	NY	516	11716	Suffolk	9	2-56
Boise City*	OK	405	73933	Cimarron	1	2-64&65
BOISE*	ID	208	83701-99	Ada	115	2-18
Bolingbrook	IL	708	60439	Will/Du Page	41	2-20
Bolivar*	MO	417	65613	Polk	6	2-44
Bolivar*	TN	901	38008	Hardeman	1	2-72
Bolivia	NC	919	28422	Brunswick	1	2-58&59
Bolton	CT	203	06043	Tolland	4	2-12&13
Bolton	MA	508	01740	Worcester	3	2-36&37
Bon Air	VA	804	23235	Chesterfield	16	2-78&79
Bonham*	TX	214	75418	Fannin	7	2-74
Bonifay*	FL	904	32425	Holmes	3	2-14
Bonne Terre	MO	314	63628	St. Francois	4	2-44&45
Bonner Springs	KS	913	66012	Wyandotte (+1)	6	2-26&27
Bonners Ferry*	ID	208	83805	Boundary	1	2-18
Bonney Lake	WA	206	98390	Pierce	5	2-80
Boone*	IA	515	50036	Boone	13	2-24&25
Boone*	NC	704	28607	Watauga	10	2-58
Booneville	AR	501	72927	Logan	4	2-6
Booneville*	KY	606	41314	Owsley	1	2-29

Bold = Over 15,000......**ALL CAPS** = STATE CAPITAL......***** = County Seat......**#** = Changes to 510 in 9/91.....**##** = Changes to 410 in 11/91.....**(+)** = City located in additional counties......**NAV** = Population not available......**C.H.** = Court House......**(IC)** = Independent City

CITY	STATE	AREA CODE	ZIP CODE	COUNTY	POPULATION (in thousands)	MAP PAGE
Booneville*	MS	601	38829	Prentiss	6	2-42&43
Boonton	NJ	201	07005	Morris	6	2-52
Boonville*	IN	812	47601	Warrick	6	2-23
Boonville*	MO	816	65233	Cooper	7	2-44
Boothbay	ME	207	04537	Lincoln	2	2-32&33
Boothbay Harbor	ME	207	04538	Lincoln	2	2-32&33
Bordentown	NJ	609	08505	Burlington	5	2-51
Borger	TX	806	79007-08	Hutchinson	16	2-74
Boscawen	NH	603	03301	Merrimack	3	2-49
Boscobel	WI	608	53805	Grant	3	2-85
Bosque Farms	NM	505	87068	Valencia	3	2-53
Bossier City	LA	318	71171-72	Bossier	58	2-30
BOSTON*	MA	617	02101-99	Suffolk	573	2-36&37
Boston*	TX	214	75557	Bowie	5	2-74
Bothell	WA	206	98011-12	King/Snohomish	5	2-80
Bottineau*	ND	701	58318	Bottineau	2	2-57
Boulder City	NV	702	89005-06	Clark	10	2-48
Boulder*	CO	303	80301-99	Boulder	80	2-10&11
Boulder*	MT	406	59632	Jefferson	1	2-46
Bound Brook	NJ	201	08805	Somerset	10	2-50
Bountiful	UT	801	84010-11	Davis	36	2-76
Bourbonnais	IL	815	60914	Kankakee	6	2-20
Bourne	MA	508	02532	Barnstable	15	2-36&37
Bow	NH	603	03301	Merrimack	4	2-49
Bowbells*	ND	701	58721	Burke	1	2-57
Bowdoinham	ME	207	04008	Sagadahoc	2	2-32&33
Bowdon	GA	404	30108	Carroll	2	2-16&17
Bowie	MD	301	20715-16	Prince Georges	35	2-34&35
Bowie	TX	817	76230	Montague	6	2-74
Bowling Green	FL	813	33834	Hardee	2	2-14&15
Bowling Green*	KY	502	42101-04	Warren	49	2-28&29
Bowling Green*	MO	314	63334	Pike	2	2-44&45
Bowling Green*	OH	419	43402	Wood	25	2-60
Bowling Green*	VA	804	22427	Caroline	1	2-78&79
Bowman*	ND	701	58623	Bowman	1	2-57
Box Elder	SD	605	57719	Pennington	3	2-71
Boxborough	MA	508	01719	Middlesex	3	2-36&37
Boxford	MA	508	01921	Essex	5	2-36&37
Boydton*	VA	804	23917	Mecklenburg	1	2-78&79
Boyertown	PA	215	19512	Berks	4	2-67
Boylston	MA	508	01505	Worcester	4	2-36&37
Boyne City	MI	616	49712	Charlevoix	4	2-38&39
Boynton Beach	FL	407	33424-37	Palm Beach	42	2-14&15
Bozeman*	MT	406	59715-16	Gallatin	23	2-46
Brackenridge	PA	412	15014	Allegheny	4	2-68
Brackettville*	TX	512	78832	Kinney	1	2-75
Braddock	PA	412	15104	Allegheny	5	2-68
Braddock Hills	PA	412	15221	Allegheny	3	2-68

Bold = Over 15,000......ALL CAPS = STATE CAPITAL......* = County Seat......# = Changes to 510 in 9/91..... ## = Changes to 410 in 11/91......(+) = City located in addional counties......NAV= Population not available......C.H.= Court House......(IC) = Independent City

CITY	STATE	AREA CODE	ZIP CODE	COUNTY	POPULATION (in thousands)	MAP PAGE
Bradenton*	FL	813	34201-10	Manatee	38	2-14&15
Bradford	PA	814	16701	McKean	10	2-66
Bradley	IL	815	60915	Kankakee	12	2-20
Bradley Beach	NJ	201	07720	Monmouth	5	2-50
Brady*	TX	915	76825	McCulloch	6	2-74&75
Braidwood	IL	815	60408	Will	4	2-20
Brainerd*	MN	218	56401	Crow Wing	11	2-40
Braintree	MA	617	02184	Norfolk	37	2-36&37
Brandenburg*	KY	502	40108	Meade	2	2-28&29
Brandon	FL	813	33509-11	Hillsborough	33	2-14&15
Brandon*	MS	601	39042-43	Rankin	14	2-42&43
Brandon	SD	605	57005	Minnehaha	3	2-71
Brandon	VT	802	05733	Rutland	4	2-77
Branford	CT	203	06405	New Haven	5	2-12&13
Branson	MO	417	65616	Taney	3	2-44
Brattleboro	VT	802	05301	Windham	12	2-77
Brawley	CA	619	92227	Imperial	17	2-9
Brazil*	IN	812	47834	Clay	8	2-23
Brazoria	TX	409	77422	Brazoria	3	2-75
Brea	CA	714	92621-22	Orange	32	2-7
Breaux Bridge	LA	318	70517	St. Martin	6	2-30
Breckenridge*	CO	303	80424	Summit	1	2-10&11
Breckenridge*	MN	218	56520	Wilkin	3	2-40
Breckenridge*	TX	817	76024	Stephens	7	2-74
Breckenridge Hills	MO	314	63114	St. Louis	5	2-44&45
Brecksville	OH	216	44141	Cuyahoga	10	2-62
Breese	IL	618	62230	Clinton	4	2-21
Bremen	GA	404	30110	Haralson/Carroll	4	2-16&17
Bremen	IN	219	46506	Marshall	4	2-22
Bremerton	WA	206	98310-15	Kitsap	36	2-80
Brenham*	TX	409	77833	Washington	13	2-75
Brentwood	CA	415	94513	Contra Costa	5	2-7
Brentwood	MD	301	20722	Prince Georges	3	2-34&35
Brentwood	MO	314	63144	St. Louis	8	2-44&45
Brentwood	NY	516	11717	Suffolk	28	2-56
Brentwood	PA	412	15227	Allegheny	12	2-68
Brentwood	TN	615	37027	Williamson	13	2-72&73
Brevard*	NC	704	28712	Transylvania	6	2-58
Brewer	ME	207	04412	Penobscot	9	2-32&33
Brewster	MA	508	02631	Barnstable	5	2-36&37
Brewster*	NE	308	68821	Blaine	1	2-47
Brewton*	AL	205	36426-27	Escambia	7	2-2&3
Briarcliff Manor	NY	914	10510	Westchester	7	2-56
Brick	NJ	201	08723-24	Ocean	64	2-50&51
Bridge City	TX	409	77611	Orange	7	2-75
Bridge View	IL	708	60455	Cook	4	2-19
Bridgeport	AL	205	35740	Jackson	3	2-2&3
Bridgeport*	CA	619	93517	Mono	1	2-9

**Bold = Over 15,000......ALL CAPS = STATE CAPITAL......* = County Seat......# = Changes to 510 in 9/91.....## = Changes to 410 in 11/91.....(+) = City located in additional counties......NAV = Population not available......C.H. = Court House......(IC)=Independent City

CITY	STATE	AREA CODE	ZIP CODE	COUNTY	POPULATION (in thousands)	MAP PAGE
Bridgeport*	CT	203	06601-99	Fairfield	144	2-12&13
Bridgeport	MI	517	48722	Saginaw	13	2-38&39
Bridgeport*	NE	308	69336	Morrill	1	2-47
Bridgeport	OH	614	43912	Belmont	3	2-61
Bridgeport	PA	215	19405	Montgomery	5	2-68
Bridgeport	TX	817	76026	Wise	4	2-74
Bridgeport	WV	304	26330	Harrison	7	2-82
Bridgeton	MO	314	63044	St. Louis	18	2-44&45
Bridgeton*	NJ	609	08302	Cumberland	18	2-51
Bridgetown	OH	513	45211	Hamilton	12	2-62
Bridgeville	DE	302	19933	Sussex	1	2-35
Bridgeville	PA	412	15017	Allegheny	6	2-68
Bridgewater	MA	508	02324	Plymouth	7	2-36&37
Bridgewater	NJ	201	08807	Somerset	6	2-50
Bridgewater	VA	703	22812	Rockingham	3	2-78&79
Bridgton	ME	207	04009	Cumberland	4	2-32&33
Brielle	NJ	201	08730	Monmouth	4	2-50
Brier	WA	206	98036	Snohomish	3	2-80
Brigantine	NJ	609	08203	Atlantic	8	2-51
Brigham City*	UT	801	84302	Box Elder	1	2-76
Brighton	AL	205	35020	Jefferson	5	2-2&3
Brighton*	CO	303	80601	Adams	12	2-10&11
Brighton	MI	313	48116	Livingston	5	2-39
Brighton	PA	412	15009	Beaver	8	2-66
Brillion	WI	414	54110	Calumet	3	2-85
Brinkley	AR	501	72021	Monroe	5	2-6
Brisbane	CA	415	94005	San Mateo	3	2-7
Bristol	CT	203	06010	Hartford	60	2-12&13
Bristol*	FL	904	32321	Liberty	1	2-14
Bristol	PA	215	19007	Bucks	10	2-68
Bristol*	RI	401	02809	Bristol	20	2-69
Bristol	TN	615	37620-25	Sullivan	24	2-72&73
Bristol	VA	703	24201-03	(IC)	18	2-78&79
Bristol	VT	802	05443	Addison	3	2-77
Bristow	OK	918	74010	Creek	5	2-65
Britton*	SD	605	57430	Marshall	1	2-71
Broadus*	MT	406	59317	Powder River	1	2-46
Broadview	IL	708	60153	Cook	8	2-19
Broadview Heights	OH	216	44141	Cuyahoga	10	2-62
Brockport	NY	716	14420	Monroe	9	2-54
Brockton	MA	508	02401-99	Plymouth	97	2-36&37
Brodhead	WI	608	53520	Green	3	2-85
Broken Arrow	OK	918	74012-14	Tulsa/Wagoner	48	2-65
Broken Bow*	NE	308	68822	Custer	4	2-47
Broken Bow	OK	405	74728	McCurtain	4	2-64&65
Bronson*	FL	904	32621	Levy	1	2-14
Bronx*	NY	212	10401-99	Bronx	NAV	2-56
Bronxville	NY	914	10708	Westchester	6	2-56

Bold = Over 15,000......ALL CAPS = STATE CAPITAL......* = County Seat......# = Changes to 510 in 9/91..... ## = Changes to 410 in 11/91......(+) = City located in addional counties......NAV= Population not available......C.H.= Court House......(IC) = Independent City

CITY	STATE	AREA CODE	ZIP CODE	COUNTY	POPULATION (in thousands)	MAP PAGE
Brook Park	OH	216	44142	Cuyahoga	25	2-62
Brookfield	CT	203	06804	Fairfield	6	2-12&13
Brookfield	IL	708	60513	Cook	19	2-19
Brookfield	MO	816	64628	Linn	5	2-44
Brookfield	WI	414	53005	Waukesha	34	2-85
Brookhaven	NY	516	11719	Suffolk	3	2-56
Brookhaven*	MS	601	39601	Lincoln	10	2-42&43
Brookhaven	PA	215	19015	Delaware	8	2-68
Brookings	OR	503	97415	Curry	3	2-63
Brookings*	SD	605	57006	Brookings	15	2-71
Brookline	MA	617	02146	Norfolk	54	2-36&37
Brooklyn	CT	203	06234	Windham	6	2-12&13
Brooklyn*	NY	718	11201-99	Kings	NAV	2-56
Brooklyn	OH	216	44144	Cuyahoga	12	2-62
Brooklyn Center	MN	612	55429	Hennepin	31	2-41
Brooklyn Park	MN	612	55443	Hennepin	53	2-41
Brookside	DE	302	19713	New Castle	8	2-35
Brooksville*	FL	904	34601-14	Hernando	5	2-14
Brooksville*	KY	606	41004	Bracken	1	2-29
Brookville*	IN	317	47012	Franklin	3	2-22&23
Brookville	NY	716	11545	Nassau	3	2-54
Brookville	OH	513	45309	Montgomery	4	2-61
Brookville*	PA	814	15825	Jefferson	4	2-66
Brookwood	NJ	201	08527	Ocean	6	2-50&51
Broomfield	CO	303	80020-21	Boulder (+2)	20	2-10&11
Broughton	PA	412	15236	Allegheny	3	2-68
Broussard	LA	318	70518	Lafayette	3	2-30
Brown Deer	WI	414	53223	Milwaukee	13	2-85
Brownfield*	TX	806	79316	Terry	10	2-74
Brownsburg	IN	317	46112	Hendricks	6	2-22&23
Brownstown*	IN	812	47220	Jackson	3	2-23
Brownsville*	KY	502	42210	Edmonson	1	2-28&29
Brownsville	PA	412	15417	Fayette	4	2-66
Brownsville*	TN	901	38012	Haywood	10	2-72
Brownsville*	TX	512	78520-26	Cameron	102	2-75
Browntown	NJ	201	08857	Middlesex	3	2-50
Brownwood*	TX	915	76801-04	Brown	18	2-74&75
Broyhill Park	VA	703	22042	Fairfax	4	2-78&79
Brunswick*	GA	912	31520-22	Glynn	19	2-16&17
Brunswick	MD	301	21716	Frederick	5	2-34&35
Brunswick	ME	207	04011	Cumberland	19	2-32&33
Brunswick	OH	216	44212	Medina	30	2-60
Brush	CO	303	80723	Morgan	4	2-10&11
Bryan*	OH	419	43506	Williams	8	2-60
Bryan*	TX	409	77801-06	Brazos	62	2-75
Bryant	AR	501	72022	Saline	4	2-6
Bryson City*	NC	704	28713	Swain	1	2-58
Buchanan*	GA	404	30113	Haralson	1	2-16&17

Bold = Over 15,000......ALL CAPS = STATE CAPITAL......* = County Seat......# = Changes to 510 in 9/91.....## = Changes to 410 in 11/91.....(+) = City located in additional counties......NAV = Population not available......C.H.= Court House......(IC)=Independent City

CITY	STATE	AREA CODE	ZIP CODE	COUNTY	POPULATION (in thousands)	MAP PAGE
Buchanan	MI	616	49107	Berrien	5	2-38&39
Buckeye	AZ	602	85326	Maricopa	3	2-5
Buckeye Lake	OH	614	43008	Licking	3	2-61
Buckhannon*	WV	304	26201	Upshur	7	2-82
Buckingham	PA	215	18912	Bucks	9	2-68
Buckingham*	VA	804	23921	Buckingham	1	2-78&79
Buckley	WA	206	98321	Pierce	3	2-80
Buckner	MO	816	64016	Jackson	3	2-44
Bucksport	ME	207	04416	Hancock	4	2-32&33
Bucyrus*	OH	419	44820	Crawford	13	2-60
Buechel	KY	502	40218	Jefferson	7	2-28
Buena	NJ	609	08310	Atlantic	8	2-51
Buena Park	CA	714	90620	Orange	66	2-7
Buena Vista	CO	303	81211	Chaffee	2	2-10&11
Buena Vista*	GA	912	31803	Marion	1	2-16&17
Buena Vista	MI	517	48601	Saginaw	12	2-38&39
Buena Vista	VA	703	24416	(IC)	6	2-78&79
Buffalo*	MN	612	55313	Wright	5	2-41
Buffalo*	MO	417	65622	Dallas	1	2-44
Buffalo*	NY	716	14201-99	Erie	324	2-54
Buffalo*	OK	405	73834	Harper	1	2-64&65
Buffalo*	SD	605	57720	Harding	1	2-71
Buffalo*	WY	307	82834	Johnson	3	2-83
Buffalo Grove	IL	708	60090	Cook/Lake	26	2-19
Buford	GA	404	30518	Gwinnett/Hall	8	2-16&17
Buhl	ID	208	83316	Twin Falls	4	2-18
Bullhead City	AZ	602	86430	Mohave	17	2-5
Bunkie	LA	318	71322	Avoyelles	5	2-30
Bunnell*	FL	904	32110	Flagler	2	2-14
Burbank	CA	818	91500-10	Los Angeles	89	2-7
Burbank	IL	708	60459	Cook	28	2-19
Burgaw*	NC	919	28425	Pender	1	2-58&59
Burkburnett	TX	817	76354	Wichita	11	2-74
Burke*	SD	605	57523	Gregory	1	2-71
Burke	VA	703	22015	Fairfax	21	2-78&79
Burkesville*	KY	502	42717	Cumberland	2	2-28&29
Burleson	TX	817	76028	Johnson/Tarrant	13	2-74
Burley*	ID	208	83318	Cassia	9	2-18
Burlingame	CA	415	94010-11	San Mateo	26	2-7
Burlington*	CO	719	80807	Kit Carson	7	2-11
Burlington	CT	203	06085	Hartford	6	2-12&13
Burlington*	IA	319	52601	Des Moines	28	2-25
Burlington*	KS	316	66839	Coffey	2	2-26&27
Burlington*	KY	606	41005	Boone	1	2-29
Burlington	MA	617	01803	Middlesex	23	2-36&37
Burlington	NC	919	27215-17	Alamance	38	2-58&59
Burlington	NJ	609	08016	Burlington	11	2-51
Burlington	WA	206	98233	Skagit	4	2-80

Bold = Over 15,000......ALL CAPS = STATE CAPITAL......* = County Seat......# = Changes to 510 in 9/91..... ## = Changes to 410 in 11/91......(+) = City located in addional counties......NAV= Population not available......C.H.= Court House......(IC) = Independent City

CITY	STATE	AREA CODE	ZIP CODE	COUNTY	POPULATION (in thousands)	MAP PAGE
Burlington	WI	414	53105	Racine (+1)	8	2-85
Burlington*	VT	802	05401-07	Chittenden	37	2-77
Burnet*	TX	512	78611	Burnet	3	2-75
Burnham	IL	708	60633	Cook	4	2-19
Burns*	OR	503	97720	Harney	2	2-63
Burnsville	MN	612	55337	Savage	40	2-41
Burnsville*	NC	704	28714	Yancey	1	2-58
Burr Ridge	IL	708	60521	Du Page/Cook	5	2-19
Burrilville	RI	401	02830	Providence	13	2-69
Burton	MI	313	48509	Genesse	30	2-39
Burwell*	NE	308	68823	Garfield	1	2-47
Bushnell*	FL	904	33513	Sumter	1	2-14
Bushnell	IL	309	61422	McDonough	4	2-20
Butler*	AL	205	36904	Choctaw	1	2-2&3
Butler*	GA	912	31006	Taylor	1	2-16&17
Butler	IN	219	46721	De Kalb	3	2-22
Butler*	MO	816	64730	Bates	4	2-44
Butler	NJ	201	07405	Morris	8	2-52
Butler*	PA	412	16001-03	Butler	16	2-66
Butte*	MT	406	59701-03	Silver Bow	33	2-46
Butte*	NE	402	68722	Boyd	1	2-47
Buxton	ME	207	04093	York	6	2-32&33
Byesville	OH	614	43723	Guernsey	3	2-61
Byram	NJ	201	07821	Sussex	8	2-50
Byrdstown*	TN	615	38549	Pickett	1	2-72&73
Cabot	AR	501	72023	Lonoke	5	2-6
Cadillac*	MI	616	49601	Wexford	10	2-38&39
Cadiz*	KY	502	42211	Trigg	2	2-28&29
Cadiz*	OH	614	43907	Harrison	3	2-61
Cahaba Heights	AL	205	35243	Jefferson	4	2-2&3
Cahokia	IL	618	62023	St. Clair	18	2-21
Cairo*	GA	912	31728	Grady	9	2-16&17
Cairo*	IL	618	62914	Alexander	6	2-21
Cairo	NY	518	12413	Greene	4	2-55
Calais	ME	207	04619	Washington	4	2-32&33
Caldwell*	ID	208	83605-06	Canyon	18	2-18
Caldwell	NJ	201	07006-07	Essex	8	2-52
Caldwell*	OH	614	43724	Noble	11	2-61
Caldwell*	TX	409	77836	Burleson	3	2-75
Caledonia*	MN	507	55921	Houston	2	2-41
Calexico	CA	619	92231-32	Imperial	18	2-9
Calhoun*	GA	404	30701	Gordon	6	2-16&17
Calhoun*	KY	502	42327	McLean	1	2-28&29
California*	MO	314	65018	Moniteau	3	2-44&45
California	PA	412	15419	Washington	6	2-66
California City	CA	619	93505	Kern	3	2-9
Calimesa	CA	714	92320	Riverside	3	2-9
Calipatria	CA	619	92233	Imperial	3	2-9

Bold = Over 15,000......ALL CAPS = STATE CAPITAL......* = County Seat......# = Changes to 510 in 9/91.....## = Changes to 410 in 11/91.....(+) = City located in additional counties......NAV = Population not available......C.H.= Court House......(IC)=Independent City

CITY	STATE	AREA CODE	ZIP CODE	COUNTY	POPULATION (in thousands)	MAP PAGE
Calistoga	CA	707	94515	Napa	4	2-8
Callaway	FL	904	32401-40	Bay	7	2-14
Calumet City	IL	708	60409	Cook	39	2-19
Calumet Park	IL	708	60643	Cook	9	2-19
Calverton	NY	516	11933	Suffolk	4	2-56
Calwa	CA	209	93725	Fresno	7	2-8&9
Camanche	IA	319	52730	Clinton	5	2-25
Camarillo	CA	805	93010-11	Ventura	44	2-9
Camas	WA	206	98607	Clark	6	2-80
Cambridge*	IL	309	61238	Henry	2	2-20
Cambridge*	MA	617	02138-42	Middlesex	91	2-36&37
Cambridge*	MD	301	21613	Dorchester	11	2-34&35
Cambridge*	MN	612	55008	Isanti	3	2-41
Cambridge*	OH	614	43725	Guernsey	12	2-61
Camden*	AL	205	36726	Wilcox	1	2-2&3
Camden*	AR	501	71701	Ouachita	17	2-6
Camden	ME	207	04843	Knox	4	2-32&33
Camden*	NC	919	27921	Camden	1	2-58&59
Camden*	NJ	609	08101-99	Camden	82	2-51
Camden	NY	315	13316	Onondaga	3	2-54&55
Camden*	SC	803	29020	Kershaw	7	2-70
Camden*	TN	901	38320	Benton	3	2-72
Camdenton*	MO	314	65020	Camden	1	2-44&45
Camelot	WA	206	98002	King	5	2-80
Cameron*	LA	318	70631	Cameron	1	2-30
Cameron	MO	816	64429	Clinton/De Kalb	4	2-44
Cameron*	TX	817	76520	Milam	5	2-74
Camilla*	GA	912	31730	Mitchell	5	2-16&17
Camp Hill	PA	717	17011	Cumberland	8	2-67
Camp Verde	AZ	602	86322	Yavapai	6	2-5
Campbell	CA	408	95008-09	Santa Clara	34	2-7
Campbell	OH	216	44405	Mahoning	12	2-60
Campbellsville*	KY	502	42718	Taylor	9	2-28&29
Campton*	KY	606	41301	Wolfe	1	2-29
Canadian*	TX	806	79014	Hemphill	3	2-74
Canal Fulton	OH	216	44614	Stark	4	2-60
Canal Winchester	OH	614	43110	Fairfield (+1)	3	2-61
Canandaigua*	NY	716	14424-25	Ontario	12	2-54
Canastota	NY	315	13032	Madison	5	2-54&55
Canby	OR	503	97013	Clackamas	8	2-63
Candia	NH	603	03034	Rockingham	3	2-49
Cando*	ND	701	58324	Towner	1	2-57
Canfield	OH	216	44406	Mahoning	6	2-60
Canisteo	NY	607	14823	Steuben	3	2-54&55
Cannelton*	IN	812	47520	Perry	2	2-23
Cannon Falls	MN	507	55009	Goodhue	2	2-41
Canoga Park	CA	818	91303-09	Los Angeles	NAV	2-7
Canon City*	CO	719	81212	Fremont	13	2-11

Bold = Over 15,000......ALL CAPS = STATE CAPITAL......* = County Seat......# = Changes to 510 in 9/91..... ## = Changes to 410 in 11/91......(+) = City located in addional counties......NAV= Population not available......C.H.= Court House......(IC) = Independent City

CITY	STATE	AREA CODE	ZIP CODE	COUNTY	POPULATION (in thousands)	MAP PAGE
Canonsburg	PA	412	15317	Washington	10	2-66
Canterbury	CT	203	06331	Windham	3	2-12&13
Canton	CT	203	06019	Hartford	2	2-12&13
Canton*	GA	404	30114	Cherokee	4	2-16&17
Canton	IL	309	61520	Fulton	13	2-20
Canton	MA	617	02021	Norfolk	18	2-36&37
Canton	MI	313	48187	Wayne	5	2-39
Canton*	MS	601	39046	Madison	11	2-42&43
Canton	NC	704	28716	Haywood	5	2-58
Canton*	NY	315	13617	St. Lawrence	7	2-54&55
Canton*	OH	216	44701-99	Stark	89	2-60
Canton*	SD	605	57013	Lincoln	2	2-71
Canton*	TX	214	75103	Van Zandt	3	2-74
Canyon City*	OR	503	97820	Grant	1	2-63
Canyon*	TX	806	79015-16	Randall	11	2-74
Cape Canaveral	FL	407	32920	Brevard	6	2-14&15
Cape Coral	FL	813	33904	Lee	49	2-14&15
Cape Elizabeth	ME	207	04107	Cumberland	8	2-32&33
Cape Girardeau	MO	314	63701-02	Cape Girardeau	34	2-44&45
Cape May*	NJ	609	08204	Cape May	5	2-51
Cape May C.H.	NJ	609	08210	Cape May	4	2-51
Capistrano Beach	CA	714	92624	Orange	6	2-7
Capitol Heights	MD	301	20743	Prince Georges	3	2-35
Capitola	CA	408	95010	Santa Cruz	9	2-7
Carbon Hill	AL	205	35549	Walker	3	2-2&3
Carbondale	CO	303	81623	Garfield	2	2-10&11
Carbondale	IL	618	62901-03	Jackson	26	2-21
Carbondale	PA	717	18407	Lackawanna	12	2-67
Carencro	LA	318	70520	Lafayette	4	2-30
Carey	OH	419	43316	Wyandot	4	2-60
Caribou	ME	207	04736	Aroostook	10	2-32&33
Carl Junction	MO	417	64834	Jasper	4	2-44
Carle Place	NY	516	11514	Nassau	5	2-56
Carleton	MI	313	48117	Monroe	3	2-39
Carlinville*	IL	217	62626	Macoupin	6	2-20&21
Carlisle	AR	501	72024	Lonoke	3	2-6
Carlisle	IA	515	50047	Polk/Warren	3	2-24&25
Carlisle*	KY	606	40311	Nicholas	1	2-29
Carlisle	MA	508	01741	Middlesex	3	2-36&37
Carlisle*	PA	717	17013	Cumberland	19	2-67
Carlsbad	CA	619	92008-09	San Diego	50	2-9
Carlsbad*	NM	505	88220-21	Eddy	27	2-53
Carlstadt	NJ	201	07072	Bergen	7	2-52
Carlton*	MN	218	55718	Carlton	1	2-40
Carlyle*	IL	618	62231	Clinton	3	2-21
Carmel	CA	408	93921-23	Monterey	5	2-9
Carmel	IN	317	46032	Hamilton	20	2-22&23
Carmel*	NY	914	10512	Putnam	3	2-56

Bold = Over 15,000......ALL CAPS = STATE CAPITAL......* = County Seat......# = Changes to 510 in 9/91.....## = Changes to 410 in 11/91.....(+) = City located in additional counties......NAV = Population not available......C.H.= Court House......(IC)=Independent City

CITY	STATE	AREA CODE	ZIP CODE	COUNTY	POPULATION (in thousands)	MAP PAGE
Carmel Valley	CA	408	93924	Monterey	4	2-9
Carmi*	IL	618	62821	White	6	2-21
Carmichael	CA	916	95608-09	Sacramento	49	2-8
Carnegie	PA	412	15106	Allegheny	10	2-68
Carnesville*	GA	404	30521	Franklin	1	2-16&17
Carneys Point	NJ	609	08069	Salem	8	2-51
Caro*	MI	517	48723	Tuscola	4	2-38&39
Carol City	FL	305	33055	Dade	50	2-15
Carol Stream	IL	708	60188	Du Page	21	2-19
Caroline	NY	607	14817	Tompkins	3	2-54&55
Carpentersville	IL	708	60110	Kane	25	2-19
Carpinteria	CA	805	93013	Santa Barbara	11	2-9
Carrboro	NC	919	27510	Orange	8	2-58&59
Carrington*	ND	701	58421	Foster	2	2-57
Carrizo Springs*	TX	512	78834	Dimmit	7	2-75
Carrizozo*	NM	505	88301	Lincoln	1	2-53
Carroll*	IA	712	51401	Carroll	10	2-24
Carrollton*	AL	205	35447	Pickens	1	2-2&3
Carrollton*	GA	404	30117	Carroll	18	2-16&17
Carrollton*	IL	217	62206	Greene	3	2-20&21
Carrollton*	KY	502	41008	Carroll	4	2-28&29
Carrollton	MI	517	48724	Saginaw	7	2-38&39
Carrollton*	MO	816	64633	Carroll	4	2-44
Carrollton*	MS	601	38917	Carroll	1	2-42&43
Carrollton*	OH	216	44615	Carroll	3	2-60
Carrollton	TX	214	75006-11	Dallas (+2)	57	2-74
Carson	CA	213	90745	Los Angeles	87	2-7
Carson*	ND	701	58529	Grant	1	2-57
CARSON CITY*	NV	702	89701-21	Carson City	35	2-48
Carter Lake	IA	712	51510	Pottawattamie	3	2-24
Carteret	NJ	201	07008	Middlesex	21	2-50
Cartersville*	GA	404	30120	Bartow	10	2-16&17
Carterville	IL	618	62918	Williamson	4	2-21
Carthage*	IL	217	62321	Hancock	3	2-20&21
Carthage*	MO	417	64836	Jasper	11	2-44
Carthage*	MS	601	39051	Leake	3	2-42&43
Carthage*	NC	919	28327	Moore	1	2-58&59
Carthage	NY	315	13619	Jefferson	4	2-54&55
Carthage*	TN	615	37030	Smith	2	2-72&73
Carthage*	TX	214	75633	Panola	6	2-74
Caruthersville*	MO	314	63830	Pemiscot	7	2-44&45
Carver	MA	508	02330	Plymouth	2	2-36&37
Cary	IL	708	60013	McHenry	6	2-20
Cary	NC	919	27511-13	Wake	22	2-58&59
Casa Grande	AZ	602	85222	Pinal	15	2-5
Cascade Vista	WA	206	98055	King	8	2-80
Cascade*	ID	208	83611	Valley	1	2-18
Casey	IL	217	62420	Clark (+1)	3	2-20&21

**Bold = Over 15,000......ALL CAPS = STATE CAPITAL......* = County Seat......# = Changes to 510 in 9/91..... ## = Changes to 410 in 11/91......(+) = City located in addional counties......NAV= Population not available....C.H.= Court House......(IC) = Independent City

CITY	STATE	AREA CODE	ZIP CODE	COUNTY	POPULATION (in thousands)	MAP PAGE
Caseyville	IL	618	62232	St. Clair	4	2-21
Casper*	WY	307	82601-15	Natrona	47	2-83
Casselberry	FL	407	32707-8	Seminole	15	2-14&15
Cassopolis*	MI	616	49031	Cass	1	2-38&39
Cassville*	MO	417	65625	Barry	1	2-44
Castle Dale*	UT	801	84513	Emery	1	2-76
Castle Hills	TX	512	78213	Bexar	5	2-75
Castle Point	MO	314	63136	St. Louis	8	2-44&45
Castle Rock*	CO	303	80104	Douglas	4	2-10&11
Castle Shannon	PA	412	15234	Allegheny	10	2-68
Castleton	VT	802	05735	Rutland	4	2-77
Castro Valley	CA	415	94546	Alameda	45	2-7
Castroville	CA	408	95012	Monterey	4	2-9
Catasauqua	PA	215	18032	Lehigh	7	2-67
Cathedral City	CA	619	92234-35	Riverside	20	2-9
Cathlamet*	WA	206	98612	Wahkiakum	1	2-80
Catlettsburg*	KY	606	41129	Boyd	3	2-29
Catonsville Manor	MD	301	21207	Baltimore	3	2-35
Catskill*	NY	518	12414	Greene	5	2-55
Cavalier*	ND	701	58220	Pembina	1	2-57
Cave Spring	VA	703	24018	Roanoke	15	2-78&79
Cayce	SC	803	29033	Lexington	11	2-70
Cayuga Heights	NY	607	14850	Tompkins	3	2-54&55
Cazenovia	NY	315	13035	Madison	3	2-54&55
Cedar City	UT	801	84720-22	Iron	10	2-76
Cedar Falls	IA	319	50613	Black Hawk	33	2-25
Cedar Grove	NJ	201	07009	Essex	12	2-52
Cedar Hill	TX	214	75104	Dallas/Ellis	7	2-74
Cedar Lake	IN	219	46303	Lake	8	2-22
Cedar Rapids*	IA	319	52401-99	Linn	110	2-25
Cedar Springs	MI	616	49319	Kent	3	2-38&39
Cedarburg	WI	414	53012	Ozaukee	9	2-85
Cedarhurst	NY	516	11516	Nassau	6	2-56
Cedartown*	GA	404	30125	Polk	9	2-16&17
Cedarville	OH	513	45314	Greene	3	2-61
Celina*	OH	419	45822	Mercer	9	2-60
Celina*	TN	615	38551	Clay	1	2-72&73
Center*	ND	701	58530	Oliver	1	2-57
Center*	NE	402	68724	Knox	1	2-47
Center*	TX	409	75935	Shelby	5	2-75
Center City*	MN	612	55012	Chisago	1	2-41
Center Line	MI	313	48015	Macomb	9	2-39
Center Point	AL	205	35215	Jefferson	22	2-2&3
Centereach	NY	516	11720	Suffolk	31	2-56
Centerport	NY	315	11721	Suffolk	4	2-54&55
Centerville*	IA	515	52544	Appanoose	6	2-24&25
Centerville*	MO	314	63633	Reynolds	1	2-44&45
Centerville	OH	513	45459	Montgomery	18	2-61

Bold = Over 15,000......ALL CAPS = STATE CAPITAL......* = County Seat......# = Changes to 510 in 9/91.....## = Changes to 410 in 11/91.....(+) = City located in additional counties......NAV = Population not available......C.H.= Court House......(IC)=Independent City

CITY	STATE	AREA CODE	ZIP CODE	COUNTY	POPULATION (in thousands)	MAP PAGE
Centerville	PA	412	15417	Washington	4	2-66
Centerville*	TN	615	37033	Hickman	2	2-72&73
Centerville*	TX	214	75833	Leon	1	2-74
Centerville	UT	801	84014	Davis	8	2-76
Central City*	CO	303	80427	Gilpin	2	2-10&11
Central City	KY	502	42330	Munlenberg	5	2-28&29
Central City*	NE	308	68826	Merrick	3	2-47
Central Falls	RI	401	02863	Providence	17	2-69
Central Islip	NY	516	11722	Suffolk	20	2-56
Central Point	OR	503	97502	Jackson	6	2-63
Central Valley	CA	916	96019	Shasta	3	2-8
Centralia	IL	618	62801	Marion/Clinton	15	2-21
Centralia	MO	314	65240	Audrain/Boone	3	2-44&45
Centralia	WA	206	98531	Lewis	12	2-80
Centre*	AL	205	35960	Cherokee	1	2-2&3
Centreville*	AL	205	35042	Bibb	3	2-2&3
Centreville*	MD	301	21617	Queen Anne's	1	2-34&35
Centreville*	MI	616	49032	St. Joseph	1	2-38&39
Centreville	VA	703	22020	Fairfax	4	2-78&79
Ceres	CA	209	95307	Stanislaus	17	2-8&9
Cerritos	CA	213	90701	Los Angeles	57	2-7
Chadron*	NE	308	69337	Dawes	6	2-47
Chadwick Manor	MD	301	21207	Baltimore	3	2-34&35
Chaffee	MO	314	63740	Scott	3	2-44&45
Chagrin Falls	OH	216	44022	Cuyahoga	4	2-62
Challis*	ID	208	83226	Custer	1	2-18
Chalmette*	LA	504	70043-44	St. Bernard	37	2-30&31
Chamberlain*	SD	605	57325	Brule	1	2-71
Chambersburg*	PA	717	17201	Franklin	16	2-67
Chamblee	GA	404	30341	De Kalb	6	2-16&17
Champaign	IL	217	61820-21	Champaign	60	2-20&21
Champion	OH	216	44481	Trumbull	5	2-60
Champlain	NY	518	12919	Clinton	6	2-55
Champlin	MN	612	55316	Hennepin	9	2-41
Chandler	AZ	602	85224-49	Maricopa	65	2-5
Chandler	IN	812	47610	Warrick	3	2-23
Chandler*	OK	405	74834	Lincoln	3	2-64&65
Chanhassen	MN	612	55317	Carver (+1)	6	2-41
Channahon	IL	815	60410	Will	4	2-20
Channing*	TX	806	79018	Hartley	1	2-74
Chantilly	VA	703	22021	Fairfax	4	2-78&79
Chanute	KS	316	66720	Neosho	10	2-26&27
Chapel Hill	NC	919	27514-16	Durham/Orange	36	2-58&59
Chappaqua	NY	914	10514	Westchester	6	2-56
Chappell*	NE	308	69129	Deuel	1	2-47
Chardon*	OH	216	44024	Geauga	4	2-60
Chariton*	IA	515	50049	Lucus	5	2-24&25
Charleroi	PA	412	15022	Washington	5	2-66

Bold = Over 15,000......ALL CAPS = STATE CAPITAL......* = County Seat......# = Changes to 510 in 9/91..... ## = Changes to 410 in 11/91......(+) = City located in addional counties......NAV= Population not available......C.H.= Court House......(IC) = Independent City

CITY	STATE	AREA CODE	ZIP CODE	COUNTY	POPULATION (in thousands)	MAP PAGE
Charles City*	IA	515	50616	Floyd	9	2-24&25
Charles City*	VA	804	23030	Charles City	1	2-78&79
Charles Town*	WV	304	25414	Jefferson	3	2-82
Charlestown	IN	812	47111	Clark	6	2-23
Charleston*	IL	217	61920	Coles	20	2-20&21
Charleston*	MO	314	63834	Mississippi	5	2-44&45
Charleston*	MS	601	38921	Tallahatchie	2	2-42&43
Charlestown	NH	603	03603	Sullivan	4	2-49
Charlestown	RI	401	02813	Washington	5	2-69
Charleston*	SC	803	29401-23	Charleston	68	2-70
CHARLESTON*	WV	304	25301-99	Kanawha	57	2-82
Charleswood	KY	502	40229	Jefferson	4	2-28
Charlevoix*	MI	616	49720	Charlevoix	3	2-38&39
Charlotte*	MI	517	48813	Eaton	8	2-38&39
Charlotte*	NC	704	28201-99	Mecklenburg	352	2-58
Charlotte*	TN	615	37036	Dickson	1	2-72&73
Charlotte	VT	802	05445	Chittenden	3	2-77
Charlotte C.H.*	VA	804	23923	Charlotte	1	2-78&79
Charlottesville*	VA	804	22901-08	Albemarle (IC)	40	2-79
Charlton	MA	508	01507	Worcester	7	2-36&37
Chase City	VA	804	23924	Mecklenburg	3	2-78&79
Chaska*	MN	612	55318	Carver	9	2-41
Chatham	IL	217	62629	Sangamon	6	2-20&21
Chatham	MA	508	02633	Barnstable	6	2-36&37
Chatham	NJ	201	07928	Morris	9	2-52
Chatham*	VA	804	24531	Pittsylvania	1	2-78&79
Chatom*	AL	205	36518	Washington	1	2-2&3
Chatsworth*	GA	404	30705	Murray	1	2-16&17
Chattahoochee	FL	904	32324	Gadsden	5	2-14
Chattanooga*	TN	615	37401-99	Hamilton	162	2-72&73
Chautauqua	NY	716	14722	Chautauqua	4	2-54
Cheboygan*	MI	616	49721	Cheboygan	4	2-38&39
Checotah	OK	918	74426	McIntosh	4	2-65
Cheektowaga	NY	716	14225	Erie	90	2-54
Chehalis*	WA	206	98532	Lewis	6	2-80
Chelan	WA	509	98816	Chelan	3	2-81
Chelmsford	MA	508	01824	Middlesex	30	2-36&37
Chelsea	MA	617	02150	Suffolk	26	2-36&37
Chelsea	ME	207	04345	Kennebec	2	2-32&33
Chelsea	MI	313	48118	Washtenaw	4	2-39
Chelsea*	VT	802	05038	Orange	1	2-77
Cheltenham	PA	215	19012	Montgomery	34	2-68
Cheney	WA	509	99004	Spokane	8	2-81
Cheraw	SC	803	29520	Chesterfield	6	2-70
Cherokee Village	AR	501	72525	Sharp	3	2-6
Cherokee*	IA	712	51012	Cherokee	7	2-24
Cherokee*	OK	405	73728	Alfalfa	1	2-64&65
Cherry Hill	NJ	609	08002-03	Camden	70	2-51

Bold = Over 15,000......ALL CAPS = STATE CAPITAL......* = County Seat......# = Changes to 510 in 9/91.....## = Changes to 410 in 11/91.....(+) = City located in additional counties......NAV = Population not available......C.H.= Court House......(IC)=Independent City

CITY	STATE	AREA CODE	ZIP CODE	COUNTY	POPULATION (in thousands)	MAP PAGE
Cherry Hills Village	CO	303	80110	Arapahoe	5	2-11
Cherryvale	KS	316	67335	Montgomery	3	2-26&27
Cherryville	NC	704	28021	Gaston	5	2-58
Chesaning	MI	517	48616	Saginaw	3	2-38&39
Chesapeake City	VA	804	23320-25	(IC)	135	2-78&79
Cheshire	CT	203	06410	New Haven	6	2-12&13
Cheshire	MA	413	01225	Berkshire	3	2-36
Chester*	IL	618	62233	Randolph	8	2-21
Chester*	MT	406	59522	Liberty	1	2-46
Chester	NJ	201	07930	Morris	5	2-52
Chester	PA	215	19013-16	Delaware	44	2-68
Chester*	SC	803	29706	Chester	6	2-70
Chester	VA	804	23831	Chesterfield	12	2-78&79
Chester	VT	802	05143	Windsor	3	2-77
Chester	WV	304	26034	Hancock	3	2-82
Chesterfield	NH	603	03443	Cheshire	3	2-49
Chesterfield*	SC	803	29709	Chesterfield	1	2-70
Chesterfield*	VA	804	23832	Chesterfield	1	2-78&79
Chesterton	IN	219	46304	Porter	9	2-22
Chestertown*	MD	301	21620	Kent	3	2-34&35
Chestnut Ridge	NY	914	10952	Rockland	8	2-56
Cheverly	MD	301	20785	Prince Georges	3	2-34&35
Cheviot	OH	513	45211	Hamilton	10	2-62
Chevy Chase	MD	301	20815	Montgomery	3	2-34&35
Chewelah	WA	509	99109	Stevens	2	2-81
Cheyenne*	OK	405	73628	Roger Mills	1	2-64&65
CHEYENNE*	WY	307	82001-09	Laramie	53	2-83
Cheyenne Wells*	CO	719	80810	Cheyenne	2	2-11
Chicago*	IL	312	60601-99	Cook/Du Page	3020	2-19
Chicago Heights	IL	708	60411	Cook	35	2-19
Chicago Ridge	IL	708	60415	Cook	13	2-19
Chickasaw	AL	205	36611	Mobile	7	2-2&3
Chickasha*	OK	405	73018	Grady	17	2-64&65
Chico	CA	916	95926-29	Butte	32	2-8
Chicopee	MA	413	01013-22	Hampden	57	2-36
Childersburg	AL	205	35044	Talladega	5	2-2&3
Childress*	TX	817	79201	Childress	6	2-74
Chili Corner	NY	716	14624	Monroe	4	2-54
Chillicothe	IL	309	61523	Peoria	6	2-20
Chillicothe*	MO	816	64601	Livingston	8	2-44
Chillicothe*	OH	614	45601	Ross	23	2-61
Chillum	MD	301	20783	Prince Georges	15	2-34
Chilton*	WI	414	53014	Calumet	2	2-85
China	ME	207	04926	Kennebec	3	2-32&33
Chino	CA	714	91708-10	Riverside	50	2-9
Chino Valley	AZ	602	86323	Yavapai	5	2-5
Chinook*	MT	406	59523	Blaine	1	2-46
Chipley*	FL	904	32428	Washington	3	2-14

Bold = Over 15,000......ALL CAPS = STATE CAPITAL......* = County Seat......# = Changes to 510 in 9/91..... ## = Changes to 410 in 11/91......(+) = City located in addional counties......NAV= Population not available......C.H.= Court House......(IC) = Independent City

CITY	STATE	AREA CODE	ZIP CODE	COUNTY	POPULATION (in thousands)	MAP PAGE
Chippewa	PA	412	15010	Beaver	7	2-66
Chippewa Falls*	WI	715	54729	Chippewa	12	2-84&85
Chisholm	MN	218	55719	St. Louis	6	2-40
Chittenango	NY	315	13037	Madison	4	2-54&55
Choctaw	OK	405	73020	Oklahoma	8	2-64&65
Choteau*	MT	406	59422	Teton	1	2-46
Chowchilla	CA	209	93610	Madera	5	2-8&9
Christiansburg*	VA	703	24073	Montgomery	1	2-78
Christopher	IL	618	62822	Franklin	3	2-21
Chubbuck	ID	208	83202	Bannock	7	2-18
Chula Vista	CA	619	92010-13	San Diego	118	2-9
Church Hill	TN	615	37642	Hawkins	4	2-72&73
Church Point	LA	318	70525	Acadia	5	2-30
Churchill	PA	412	15235	Allegheny	4	2-68
Cicero	IL	708	60650	Cook	61	2-19
Cicero	IN	317	46034	Hamilton	3	2-22&23
Cimarron*	KS	316	67835	Gray	5	2-26&27
Cincinnati*	OH	513	45201-99	Hamilton	369	2-62
Cinnaminson	NJ	609	08077	Burlington	16	2-51
Circle*	MT	406	59215	McCone	1	2-46
Circle Pines	MN	612	55014	Anoka	20	2-41
Circleville*	OH	614	43113	Pickaway	11	2-61
Cisco	TX	817	76437	Eastland	5	2-74
Citronelle	AL	205	36522	Mobile	3	2-2&3
Citrus Heights	CA	916	95610-11	Sacramento	97	2-8
Clairton	PA	412	15025	Allegheny	12	2-68
Clanton*	AL	205	35045	Chilton	7	2-2&3
Clare	MI	517	48617	Clare/Isabella	3	2-38&39
Claremont	CA	714	91711	Los Angeles	34	2-7
Claremont	NH	603	03743	Sullivan	14	2-49
Claremore*	OK	918	74017	Rogers	16	2-65
Clarendon*	AR	501	72029	Monroe	2	2-6
Clarendon*	TX	806	79226	Donley	1	2-74
Clarendon Hills	IL	708	60514	Du Page	6	2-19
Clarinda*	IA	712	51632	Page	5	2-24
Clarion*	IA	515	50525	Wright	3	2-24&25
Clarion*	PA	814	16214	Clarion	5	2-66
Clark	NJ	201	07066	Union	16	2-52
Clark*	SD	605	57225	Clark	1	2-71
Clarkesville*	GA	404	30523	Habersham	1	2-16&17
Clarks Summit	PA	717	18411	Lackawanna	5	2-67
Clarksburg*	WV	304	26301-02	Harrison	19	2-82
Clarksdale*	MS	601	38614	Coahoma	21	2-42&43
Clarkston	GA	404	30021	De Kalb	5	2-16&17
Clarkston	WA	509	99403	Asotin	7	2-81
Clarksville*	AR	501	72830	Johnson	5	2-6
Clarksville	IN	317	46060	Hamilton	25	2-22&23
Clarksville	IN	812	47130	Clark	15	2-23

Bold = Over 15,000......ALL CAPS = STATE CAPITAL......* = County Seat......# = Changes to 510 in 9/91.....## = Changes to 410 in 11/91.....(+) = City located in additional counties......NAV = Population not available......C.H.= Court House......(IC)=Independent City

CITY	STATE	AREA CODE	ZIP CODE	COUNTY	POPULATION (in thousands)	MAP PAGE
Clarksville*	TN	615	37040-43	Montgomery	60	2-72&73
Clarksville*	TX	214	75426	Red River	4	2-74
Claude*	TX	806	79019	Armstrong	1	2-74
Clawson	MI	313	48017	Oakland	12	2-39
Claxton*	GA	912	30417	Evans	3	2-16&17
Clay*	WV	304	25043	Clay	1	2-82
Clay Center*	KS	913	67432	Clay	5	2-26&27
Clay Center*	NE	402	68933	Clay	1	2-47
Claymont	DE	302	19703	New Castle	10	2-35
Clayton*	AL	205	36016	Barbour	1	2-2&3
Clayton	CA	415	94517	Contra Costa	4	2-7
Clayton*	GA	404	30525	Rabun	1	2-16&17
Clayton*	MO	314	63105	St. Louis	13	2-44&45
Clayton*	NM	505	88415	Union	33	2-53
Clayton	NC	919	27520	Johnston	4	2-58&59
Clayton	NJ	609	08312	Gloucester	6	2-51
Clear Lake	IA	515	50428	Cerro Gorgo	7	2-24&25
Clear Lake*	SD	605	57226	Deuel	1	2-71
Clearfield*	PA	814	16830	Clearfield	7	2-66
Clearfield	UT	801	84015	Davis	18	2-76
Clearlake	CA	707	95422	Lake	10	2-8
Clearwater*	FL	813	34615-30	Pinellas	100	2-14&15
Cleburne*	TX	817	76031-33	Johnson	21	2-74
Clementon	NJ	609	08021	Camden	6	2-51
Clemson	SC	803	29631-33	Anderson/Pickens	3	2-70
Clermont	FL	904	34711-12	Lake	4	2-14
Cleveland	OK	918	74020	Pawnee	3	2-65
Cleveland	TX	713	77327-28	Liberty	6	2-74&75
Cleveland*	GA	404	30528	White	1	2-16&17
Cleveland*	MS	601	38732-33	Bolivar	14	2-42&43
Cleveland*	OH	216	44101-99	Cuyahoga	535	2-62
Cleveland*	TN	615	37311-12	Bradley	26	2-72&73
Cleveland Heights	OH	216	44118	Cuyahoga	56	2-62
Clewiston	FL	813	33440	Hendry	5	2-14&15
Cliffside Park	NJ	201	07010	Bergen	22	2-52
Clifton*	AZ	602	85533	Greenlee	4	2-5
Clifton	NJ	201	07011-15	Passaic	76	2-52
Clifton	TX	817	76634	Bosque	3	2-74
Clifton Forge	VA	703	24422	(IC)	5	2-78&79
Clifton Heights	PA	215	19018	Delaware	7	2-68
Clifton Park	NY	518	12065	Saratoga	23	2-55
Clinton*	AR	501	72031	Van Buren	1	2-6
Clinton	CT	203	06413	Middlesex	11	2-12&13
Clinton*	IA	319	52732	Clinton	31	2-25
Clinton*	IL	217	61727	De Witt	9	2-20&21
Clinton	IN	317	47842	Vermillion	10	2-22&23
Clinton*	KY	502	42031	Hickman	2	2-28&29
Clinton*	LA	504	70722	East Feliciana	1	2-30&31

Bold = Over 15,000......ALL CAPS = STATE CAPITAL......* = County Seat......# = Changes to 510 in 9/91......## = Changes to 410 in 11/91......(+) = City located in addional counties......NAV= Population not available......C.H.= Court House......(IC) = Independent City

CITY	STATE	AREA CODE	ZIP CODE	COUNTY	POPULATION (in thousands)	MAP PAGE
Clinton	MA	508	01510	Worcester	13	2-36&37
Clinton	ME	207	04427	Kennebec	3	2-32&33
Clinton*	MO	816	64735	Henry	8	2-44
Clinton	MS	601	39056-60	Hinds	17	2-42&43
Clinton*	NC	919	28328	Sampson	7	2-58&59
Clinton	OK	405	73601	Custer/Washita	9	2-64&65
Clinton	SC	803	29325	Laurens	9	2-70
Clinton*	TN	615	37716	Anderson	1	2-72&73
Clinton	UT	801	84015	Davis	7	2-76
Clintonville	WI	715	54929	Waupaca	5	2-84&85
Clintwood*	VA	703	24228	Dickenson	1	2-78&79
Clio	MI	313	48420	Genesee	3	2-39
Clive	IA	515	50053	Polk	7	2-24&25
Cloquet	MN	218	55720	Carlton	11	2-40
Closter	NJ	201	07624	Bergen	8	2-52
Clover	SC	803	29710	York	4	2-70
Cloverdale	CA	707	95425	Sonoma	4	2-8
Clovis	CA	209	93612-13	Fresno	41	2-8&9
Clovis*	NM	505	88101-03	Curry	3	2-53
Clute	TX	713	77531	Brazoria	10	2-74&75
Clyde	OH	419	43410	Sandusky	5	2-60
Clyde	TX	915	79510	Callahan	3	2-74&75
Clyde Hill	WA	206	98004	King	3	2-80
Coachella	CA	619	92236	Riverside	13	2-9
Coal City	IL	815	60416	Grundy	4	2-20
Coal Grove	OH	614	45638	Lawrence	3	2-61
Coal Valley	IL	309	61240	Rock Island/Henry	4	2-20
Coalgate*	OK	405	74538	Coal	1	2-64&65
Coaldale	PA	717	18218	Schuylkill	3	2-67
Coalinga	CA	209	93210	Fresno	7	2-8&9
Coalville*	UT	801	84017	Summit	1	2-76
Coatesville	PA	215	19320	Chester	10	2-67
Cobleskill	NY	518	12043	Schoharie	5	2-55
Cochran*	GA	912	31014	Bleckley	5	2-16&17
Cockrell Hill	TX	214	75211	Dallas	3	2-74
Cocoa	FL	407	32922-27	Brevard	21	2-14&15
Cocoa Beach	FL	407	32931-32	Brevard	11	2-14&15
Coconut Creek	FL	407	33060-63	Broward	8	2-14&15
Cody*	WY	307	82414	Park	9	2-83
Coeburn	VA	703	24230	Wise	3	2-78&79
Coeur d'Alene*	ID	208	83814	Kootenai	27	2-18
Coffeeville*	MS	601	39822	Yalobusha	1	2-42&43
Coffeyville	KS	316	67337	Montgomery	14	2-26&27
Cohasset	MA	617	02025	Norfolk	7	2-36&37
Cohoes	NY	518	12047	Albany	18	2-55
Colby*	KS	913	67701	Thomas	6	2-26&27
Colchester	CT	203	06415	New London	3	2-12&13
Colchester	VT	802	05446	Chittenden	13	2-77

Bold = Over 15,000......ALL CAPS = STATE CAPITAL......* = County Seat......# = Changes to 510 in 9/91.....## = Changes to 410 in 11/91.....(+) = City located in additional counties......NAV = Population not available......C.H.= Court House......(IC)=Independent City

CITY	STATE	AREA CODE	ZIP CODE	COUNTY	POPULATION (in thousands)	MAP PAGE
Cold Spring Harbor	NY	516	11724	Suffolk	5	2-56
Coldspring*	TX	409	77331	San Jacinto	1	2-75
Coldwater	OH	419	45828	Mercer	4	2-60
Coldwater*	KS	000	67029	Comanche	1	2-26&27
Coldwater*	MI	517	49036	Branch	9	2-38&39
Coleman*	TX	915	76834	Coleman	5	2-74&75
Colfax*	LA	318	71417	Grant	1	2-30
Colfax*	WA	509	99111	Whitman	3	2-81
College Park	GA	404	30340	Fulton/Clayton	28	2-16&17
College Park	MD	301	20740	Prince Georges	23	2-34&35
College Place	WA	509	99324	Walla Walla	6	2-81
College Station	TX	409	77840	Brazos	50	2-75
Collegeville	PA	215	19426	Montgomery	3	2-68
Colleyville	TX	817	76034	Tarrant	7	2-74
Collierville	TN	901	38017	Shelby	12	2-72
Collingdale	PA	215	19023	Delaware	10	2-68
Collingswood	NJ	609	08108	Camden	15	2-51
Collins*	MS	601	39428	Covington	1	2-42&43
Collins Park	DE	302	19720	New Castle	3	2-35
Collinsville	IL	618	62234	Madison/St. Clair	19	2-21
Collinsville	OK	918	74021	Rogers/Tulsa	4	2-65
Colonial Heights	VA	804	23834	(IC)	17	2-79
Colonie	NY	518	12212	Albany	8	2-55
Colorado City*	TX	915	79512	Mitchell	5	2-74&75
Colorado Springs*	CO	719	80901-99	El Paso	265	2-11
Colquitt*	GA	912	31737	Miller	1	2-16&17
Colton	CA	714	92324	San Bernardino	29	2-9
Columbia	CT	203	06237	Tolland	3	2-12&13
Columbia	IL	618	62236	Monroe	4	2-21
Columbia*	KY	502	42728	Adair	4	2-28&29
Columbia*	LA	318	71418	Caldwell	1	2-30
Columbia	MD	301	21045-46	Howard	68	2-34&35
Columbia*	MO	314	65201-05	Boone	63	2-44&45
Columbia*	MS	601	39429	Marion	8	2-42&43
Columbia*	NC	919	27925	Tyrrell	1	2-58&59
Columbia	PA	717	17512	Lancaster	10	2-67
COLUMBIA*	SC	803	29201-99	Richland	93	2-70
Columbia*	TN	615	38401-02	Maury	28	2-72&73
Columbia City*	IN	219	46725	Whitley	5	2-22
Columbia Falls	MT	406	59912	Flathead	4	2-46
Columbia Heights	MN	612	55421	Anoka	20	2-41
Columbiana*	AL	205	35051	Shelby	3	2-2&3
Columbiana	OH	216	44408	Columbiana (+1)	5	2-60
Columbus*	GA	404	31901-95	Muscogee (+1)	178	2-17
Columbus*	IN	812	47201-03	Bartholomew	31	2-23
Columbus*	KS	316	66725	Cherokee	3	2-26&27
Columbus*	MS	601	39701-05	Lowndes	28	2-42&43
Columbus*	MT	406	59019	Stillwater	1	2-46

Bold = Over 15,000......ALL CAPS = STATE CAPITAL......* = County Seat......# = Changes to 510 in 9/91..... ## = Changes to 410 in 11/91......(+) = City located in addional counties......NAV= Population not available......C.H.= Court House......(IC) = Independent City

CITY	STATE	AREA CODE	ZIP CODE	COUNTY	POPULATION (in thousands)	MAP PAGE
Columbus*	NC	704	28722	Polk	1	2-58
Columbus*	NE	402	68601-02	Platte	19	2-47
Columbus*	TX	409	78934-43	Colorado	4	2-75
COLUMBUS*	OH	614	43201-99	Franklin	566	2-61
Columbus	WI	414	53925	Columbia (+1)	4	2-85
Colusa*	CA	916	95932	Colusa	4	2-9
Colville*	WA	509	99114	Stevens	5	2-81
Colwyn	PA	215	19023	Delaware	3	2-68
Comanche*	TX	915	76442	Comanche	4	2-74&75
Combined Locks	WI	414	54113	Outagamie	3	2-85
Commack	NY	516	11725	Suffolk	36	2-56
Commerce	CA	213	90040	Los Angeles	11	2-7
Commerce	GA	404	30529	Jackson	4	2-16&17
Commerce	MI	313	48085	Oakland	4	2-39
Commerce	OK	918	74339	Ottawa	3	2-65
Commerce	TX	214	75428	Hunt	8	2-74
Commerce City	CO	303	80022	Adams	16	2-10&11
Compton	CA	213	90221-24	Los Angeles	93	2-7
Comstock	MI	616	49041	Kalamazoo	5	2-38&39
Concord	CA	415	94518-24	Contra Costa	105	2-7
Concord	MA	508	01742	Middlesex	5	2-36&37
Concord*	NC	704	28025-26	Cabarrus	20	2-58
CONCORD*	NH	603	03301-04	Merrimack	32	2-49
Concordia*	KS	913	66901	Cloud	7	2-26&27
Condon*	OR	503	97823	Gilliam	1	2-63
Conejos*	CO	303	81129	Conejos	1	2-10&11
Conneaut	OH	216	44030	Ashtabula	14	2-60
Connellsville	PA	412	15425	Fayette	10	2-66
Connersville*	IN	317	47331	Fayette	17	2-22&23
Conover	NC	704	28613	Catawba	4	2-58
Conrad*	MT	406	59425	Pondera	2	2-46
Conroe*	TX	409	77301-85	Montgomery	20	2-75
Conshohocken	PA	215	19428	Montgomery	7	2-68
Convent*	LA	504	70723	St. James	1	2-30&31
Converse	TX	512	78109	Bexar	5	2-75
Conway	PA	412	15027	Beaver	3	2-66
Conway*	AR	501	72032	Faulkner	23	2-6
Conway*	SC	803	29526	Horry	13	2-70
Conyers*	GA	404	30207-08	Rockdale	7	2-16&17
Cookeville*	TN	615	38501-03	Putman	23	2-72&73
Coolidge	AZ	602	85228	Pinal	7	2-5
Coon Rapids	MN	612	55433	Anoka	43	2-41
Cooper*	TX	214	75432	Delta	1	2-74
Cooper City	FL	407	33328	Broward	10	2-14&15
Cooper Road	LA	318	71107	Caddo	10	2-30
Coopersburg	PA	215	18036	Lehigh	3	2-67
Cooperstown*	ND	701	58425	Griggs	1	2-57
Cooperstown*	NY	607	13326	Otsego	2	2-54&55

Bold = Over 15,000......ALL CAPS = STATE CAPITAL......* = County Seat......# = Changes to 510 in 9/91.....## = Changes to 410 in 11/91.....(+) = City located in additional counties......NAV = Population not available......C.H.= Court House......(IC)=Independent City

CITY	STATE	AREA CODE	ZIP CODE	COUNTY	POPULATION (in thousands)	MAP PAGE
Coopersville	MI	616	49404	Ottawa	5	2-38&39
Coos Bay	OR	503	97420	Coos	15	2-63
Copiague	NY	516	11726	Suffolk	20	2-56
Coplay	PA	215	18037	Lehigh	3	2-67
Copley	OH	216	44321	Summit	5	2-62
Coppell	TX	214	75019	Dallas/Denton	4	2-74
Copperas Cove	TX	817	76522	Coryell (+1)	19	2-74
Coquille*	OR	503	97423	Coos	4	2-63
Coral Gables	FL	305	33134	Dade	43	2-15
Coral Hills	MD	301	20743	Prince Georges	6	2-35
Coral Springs	FL	305	33065	Broward	59	2-15
Coralville	IA	319	52241	Johnson	8	2-25
Coraopolis	PA	412	15108	Allegheny	7	2-68
Corbin	KY	606	40701-02	Knox/Whitley	9	2-29
Corcoran	CA	209	93212	Kings	7	2-8&9
Corcoran	MN	612	55340	Hennepin	4	2-41
Cordele*	GA	912	31015	Crisp	11	2-16&17
Cordell*	OK	405	73632	Washita	1	2-64&65
Cordova	AK	907	99574	Valdez-Cordova	2	2-4
Cordova	AL	205	35550	Walker	3	2-2&3
Corinna	ME	207	04928	Penobscot	1	2-32&33
Corinth*	MS	601	38834	Alcorn	12	2-42&43
Corinth	NY	518	12822	Saratoga	3	2-55
Cornelia	GA	404	30531	Habersham	3	2-16&17
Cornelius	OR	503	97113	Washington	5	2-63
Corning*	AR	501	72422	Clay	4	2-6
Corning	CA	916	96120-21	Tehama	5	2-8
Corning*	IA	515	50841	Adams	2	2-24&25
Corning	NY	607	14830	Steuben	13	2-54&55
Cornwall	NY	914	12518	Orange	4	2-56
Cornwall	PA	717	17016&83	Lebanon	3	2-67
Corona	CA	714	91718-20	Riverside	46	2-9
Coronado	CA	619	92118	San Diego	20	2-9
Corpus Christi*	TX	512	78401-99	Nueces	263	2-75
Corrales	NM	505	87048	Bernalillo (+1)	3	2-53
Corry	PA	814	16407	Erie	7	2-66
Corsicana*	TX	214	75110	Navarro	1	2-74
Corte Madera	CA	415	94925	Marin	8	2-7
Cortez*	CO	303	81321	Montezuma	7	2-10&11
Cortland*	NY	607	13045	Cortland	19	2-54&55
Cortland	OH	216	44410	Trumbull	5	2-60
Corunna*	MI	517	48817	Shiawassee	2	2-38&39
Corvallis*	OR	503	97330-33	Benton	39	2-63
Corydon*	IA	515	50060	Wayne	2	2-24&25
Corydon*	IN	812	47112	Harrison	3	2-23
Coshocton*	OH	614	43812	Coshocton	13	2-61
Costa Mesa	CA	714	92626-28	Orange	88	2-7
Cotati	CA	707	94931	Sonoma	4	2-8

Bold = Over 15,000......ALL CAPS = STATE CAPITAL......* = County Seat......# = Changes to 510 in 9/91..... ## = Changes to 410 in 11/91......(+) = City located in addional counties......NAV= Population not available......C.H.= Court House......(IC) = Independent City

CITY	STATE	AREA CODE	ZIP CODE	COUNTY	POPULATION (in thousands)	MAP PAGE
Cottage Grove	MN	612	55016	Washington	19	2-41
Cottage Grove	OR	503	97424	Lane	7	2-63
Cottonwood	AZ	602	86326	Yavapai	5	2-5
Cottonwood Falls*	KS	316	66845	Chase	1	2-26&27
Cotulla*	TX	512	78014	La Salle	4	2-75
Coudersport*	PA	814	16915	Potter	2	2-66
Council Bluffs*	IA	712	51501-03	Pottawattamie	56	2-24
Council Grove*	KS	316	66846	Morris	2	2-26&27
Council*	ID	208	83612	Adams	1	2-18
Country Club Hills	IL	708	60477	Cook	15	2-19
Countryside	IL	708	60525	Cook	7	2-19
Coupeville*	WA	206	98239	Island	1	2-80
Courtland*	VA	804	23837	Southampton	1	2-78&79
Coushatta*	LA	318	71019	Red River	1	2-30
Coventry	CT	203	06238	Tolland	9	2-12&13
Coventry	RI	401	02816	Kent	7	2-69
Covina	CA	818	91722-24	Los Angeles	40	2-7
Covington*	GA	404	30209	Newton	10	2-16&17
Covington*	IN	317	47932	Fountain	3	2-22&23
Covington	KY	606	41011-18	Kenton	47	2-29
Covington*	LA	504	70433-34	St. Tammany	7	2-30&31
Covington	OH	513	45318	Miami	3	2-61
Covington*	TN	901	38019	Tipton	6	2-72
Covington*	VA	703	24426	Alleghany (IC)	7	2-78&79
Coweta	OK	918	74429	Wagoner	5	2-65
Coxsackie	NY	518	12051	Greene	3	2-55
Cozad	NE	308	69130	Dawson	4	2-47
Crafton	PA	412	15205	Allegheny	8	2-68
Craig*	CO	303	81625-26	Moffat	9	2-10&11
Crandon*	WI	715	54520	Forest	1	2-84&85
Crane*	TX	915	79731	Crane	3	2-74&75
Cranford	NJ	201	07016	Union	24	2-52
Cranston	RI	401	02910	Providence	73	2-69
Crawfordsville*	IN	317	47933	Montgomery	13	2-22
Crawfordville*	FL	904	32327	Wakulla	1	2-14
Crawfordville*	GA	404	30631	Taliaferro	1	2-16&17
Creede*	CO	303	81130	Mineral	1	2-10&11
Crescent City*	CA	707	95531	Del Norte	3	2-8
Cresco*	IA	319	52136	Howard	4	2-25
Cresskill	NJ	201	07626	Bergen	7	2-52
Crest Hill	IL	815	60435	Will	10	2-20
Crestline	OH	419	44827	Crawford (+1)	5	2-60
Creston*	IA	515	50801	Union	8	2-24&25
Crestview*	FL	904	32536	Okaloosa	7	2-14
Crestwood	IL	708	60445	Cook	11	2-19
Crestwood	MO	314	63126	St. Louis	12	2-44&45
Crete	IL	708	60417	Will	6	2-20
Crete	NE	402	68333	Saline	5	2-47

Bold = Over 15,000......ALL CAPS = STATE CAPITAL......* = County Seat......# = Changes to 510 in 9/91.....## = Changes to 410 in 11/91.....(+) = City located in additional counties......NAV = Population not available......C.H.= Court House......(IC)=Independent City

CITY	STATE	AREA CODE	ZIP CODE	COUNTY	POPULATION (in thousands)	MAP PAGE
Creve Coeur	IL	309	61611	Tazewell	6	2-20
Creve Coeur	MO	314	63141	St. Louis	9	2-44&45
Cripple Creek*	CO	303	80813	Teller	1	2-10&11
Crisfield	MD	301	21817	Somerset	3	2-34&35
Crockett*	TX	409	75835	Houston	7	2-75
Cromwell	CT	203	06416	Middlesex	10	2-12&13
Crookston*	MN	218	56716	Polk	7	2-40
Crooksville	OH	614	43731	Perry	3	2-61
Crosby*	ND	701	58730	Divide	1	2-57
Crosbyton*	TX	806	79322	Crosby	1	2-74
Cross City*	FL	904	32628	Dixie	2	2-14
Crossett	AR	501	71635	Ashley	7	2-6
Crossville*	TN	615	38555	Cumberland	7	2-72&73
Croton-on-Hudson	NY	914	10520-21	Westchester	7	2-56
Crowell*	TX	817	79227	Foard	1	2-74
Crowley	TX	817	76036	Tarrant	6	2-74
Crowley*	LA	318	70526-27	Acadia	16	2-30
Crown Point*	IN	219	46307	Lake	16	2-22
Crystal	MN	612	55428	Hennepin	25	2-41
Crystal City	MO	314	63019	Jefferson	3	2-44&45
Crystal City*	TX	512	78839	Zavala	8	2-75
Crystal Falls*	MI	906	49920	Iron	2	2-38
Crystal Lake	IL	815	60014	McHenry	21	2-20
Crystal River	FL	904	32629	Citrus	3	2-14
Crystal Springs	MS	601	39059	Copiah	5	2-42&43
Cudahy	CA	213	90201	Los Angeles	20	2-7
Cudahy	WI	414	53110	Milwaukee	20	2-85
Cuero*	TX	512	77954	De Witt	7	2-75
Cullman*	AL	205	35055-56	Cullman	13	2-2&3
Culmore	VA	703	22041	Fairfax	3	2-78&79
Culpeper*	VA	703	22701	Culpeper	6	2-78&79
Culver City	CA	213	90230-33	Los Angeles	39	2-7
Cumberland	IN	317	46229	Marion/Hancock	3	2-22&23
Cumberland	KY	606	40823	Harlan	4	2-29
Cumberland*	MD	301	21501-05	Allegany	23	2-34&35
Cumberland	RI	401	02864	Providence	5	2-69
Cumberland*	VA	804	23040	Cumberland	1	2-78&79
Cumberland Ctr	ME	207	04021	Cumberland	5	2-32&33
Cumming*	GA	404	30130	Forsyth	1	2-16&17
Cumru	PA	215	19540	Berks	11	2-67
Cupertino	CA	408	95014-16	Santa Clara	38	2-7
Currituck*	NC	919	27929	Currituck	1	2-58&59
Curwensville	PA	814	16833	Clearfield	3	2-66
Cushing	OK	918	74023	Payne	7	2-65
Cusseta*	GA	404	31805	Chattahoochee	1	2-16&17
Custer*	SD	605	57730	Custer	1	2-71
Cut Bank*	MT	406	59427	Glacier	3	2-46
Cuthbert*	GA	912	31740	Randolph	5	2-16&17

Bold = Over 15,000......ALL CAPS = STATE CAPITAL......* = County Seat.....# = Changes to 510 in 9/91..... ## = Changes to 410 in 11/91......(+) = City located in addional counties......NAV= Population not available......C.H.= Court House......(IC) = Independent City

CITY	STATE	AREA CODE	ZIP CODE	COUNTY	POPULATION (in thousands)	MAP PAGE
Cutler	CA	209	93615	Tulare	3	2-8&9
Cutler Ridge	FL	305	33157	Dade	20	2-15
Cutlerville	MI	616	49508	Kent	9	2-38&39
Cuyahoga Falls	OH	216	44221-24	Summit	42	2-62
Cynthiana*	KY	606	41031	Harrison	5	2-29
Cypress	CA	714	90630	Orange	43	2-7
Dade City*	FL	904	33525-26	Pasco	5	2-14
Dadeville*	AL	205	36853	Tallapoosa	3	2-2&3
Dahlonega*	GA	404	30533	Lumpkin	3	2-16&17
Daingerfield*	TX	214	75638	Morris	2	2-74
Dakota City*	IA	515	50529	Humboldt	1	2-24&25
Dakota City*	NE	402	68731	Dakota	2	2-47
Daleville	AL	205	36322	Dale	4	2-2&3
Dalhart*	TX	806	79022	Dallam	6	2-74
Dallas*	GA	404	30132	Paudling	3	2-16&17
Dallas	NC	704	28034	Gaston	3	2-58
Dallas*	OR	503	97338	Polk	8	2-63
Dallas	PA	717	18612&90	Luzerne	3	2-67
Dallas*	TX	214	75201-399	Dallas	1003	2-74
Dallastown	PA	717	17313	York	4	2-67
Dalton	MA	413	01226-27	Berkshire	6	2-36
Dalton*	GA	404	30720-22	Whitfield	22	2-16&17
Daly City	CA	415	94014-17	San Mateo	83	2-7
Danbury	CT	203	06810-13	Fairfield	60	2-12&13
Danbury*	NC	919	27016	Stokes	1	2-58&59
Dandridge*	TN	615	37725	Jefferson	5	2-72&73
Dania	FL	305	33004	Broward	12	2-15
Danielson	CT	203	06239	Windham	5	2-12&13
Danielsville*	GA	404	30633	Madison	1	2-16&17
Dannemora	NY	518	12929	Clinton	4	2-55
Danvers	MA	508	01923	Essex	24	2-36&37
Danville*	AR	501	72833	Yell	1	2-6
Danville	CA	415	94526	Alameda	28	2-7
Danville*	IL	217	61832-34	Vermilion	37	2-20&21
Danville*	IN	317	46122	Hendricks	4	2-22&23
Danville*	KY	606	40422	Boyle	13	2-29
Danville*	PA	717	17821	Montour	5	2-67
Danville	VA	804	24540-43	(IC)	45	2-78&79
Daphne	AL	205	36526	Baldwin	3	2-2&3
Darby	PA	215	19023	Delaware	11	2-68
Dardanelle	AR	501	72834	Yell	4	2-6
Darien	CT	203	06820	Fairfield	19	2-12&13
Darien*	GA	912	31305	McIntosh	1	2-16&17
Darien	IL	708	60559	Du Page	16	2-19
Darlington*	SC	803	29532	Darlington	8	2-70
Darlington*	WI	608	53530	Lafayette	1	2-85
Dartmouth	MA	508	02714	Bristol	24	2-36&37
Davenport*	IA	319	52801-99	Scott	103	2-25

Bold = Over 15,000......ALL CAPS = STATE CAPITAL......* = County Seat......# = Changes to 510 in 9/91.....## = Changes to 410 in 11/91.....(+) = City located in additional counties......NAV = Population not available......C.H. = Court House......(IC)=Independent City

CITY	STATE	AREA CODE	ZIP CODE	COUNTY	POPULATION (in thousands)	MAP PAGE
Davenport*	WA	509	99122	Lincoln	1	2-81
David City*	NE	402	68632	Butler	3	2-47
Davidson	NC	704	28036	Mecklenburg	3	2-58
Davie	FL	305	33314	Broward	36	2-15
Davis	CA	916	95616-18	Yolo	41	2-8
Davis	OK	405	73030	Murray	3	2-64&65
Davison	MI	313	48423	Genesee	13	2-39
Dawson Springs	KY	502	42408	Hopkins	3	2-28&29
Dawson*	GA	912	31742	Terrell	6	2-16&17
Dawsonville*	GA	404	30534	Dawson	1	2-16&17
Dayton	KY	606	41074	Campbell	7	2-29
Dayton	MN	612	55303	Hennepin/Wright	4	2-41
Dayton*	OH	513	45401-99	Montgomery	181	2-61
Dayton*	TN	615	37321	Rhea	5	2-72&73
Dayton	TX	409	77535	Liberty	5	2-75
Dayton*	WA	509	99328	Columbia	3	2-81
Daytona Beach	FL	904	32114-24	Volusia	61	2-14
De Forest	WI	608	53532	Dane	3	2-85
De Funiak Springs*	FL	904	32433	Walton	5	2-14
De Kalb	IL	815	60115	De Kalb	31	2-20
De Kalb*	MS	601	39328	Kemper	1	2-42&43
De Land*	FL	904	32720-24	Volusia	20	2-14
De Pere	WI	414	54115	Brown	15	2-85
De Queen*	AR	501	71832	Sevier	5	2-6
De Quincy	LA	318	70633	Calcasieu	4	2-30
De Ridder	LA	318	70634	Beauregard	11	2-30
De Smet*	SD	605	57231	Kingsbury	1	2-71
De Soto	MO	314	63020	Jefferson	6	2-44&45
De Soto	TX	214	75115	Dallas	16	2-74
De Witt	AR	501	72042	Arkansas	4	2-6
De Witt	IA	319	52742	Clinton	4	2-25
De Witt	MI	517	48820	Clinton	3	2-38&39
De Witt	NY	315	13214	Onondaga	9	2-54&55
Deadwood*	SD	605	57732	Lawrence	1	2-71
Dearborn	MI	313	48120-28	Wayne	87	2-39
Dearborn Heights	MI	313	48127	Wayne	62	2-39
Decatur*	AL	205	35601-03	Morgan (+1)	45	2-2&3
Decatur*	GA	404	30030-38	De Kalb	529	2-16&17
Decatur*	IL	217	62521-26	Macon	91	2-20&21
Decatur*	IN	219	46733	Adams	8	2-22
Decatur*	MS	601	39327	Newton	19	2-42&43
Decatur*	TN	615	37322	Meigs	1	2-72&73
Decatur*	TX	817	76234	Wise	5	2-74
Decaturville*	TN	901	38329	Decatur	1	2-72
Decorah*	IA	319	52101	Winneshiek	103	2-25
Dedham*	MA	617	02026	Norfolk	23	2-36&37
Deep River	CT	203	06417	Middlesex	4	2-12&13
Deephaven	MN	612	55391	Hennepin	4	2-41

Bold = Over 15,000......ALL CAPS = STATE CAPITAL......* = County Seat......# = Changes to 510 in 9/91..... ## = Changes to 410 in 11/91......(+) = City located in addional counties......NAV= Population not available......C.H.= Court House......(IC) = Independent City

CITY	STATE	AREA CODE	ZIP CODE	COUNTY	POPULATION (in thousands)	MAP PAGE
Deer Lodge*	MT	406	59722	Powell	4	2-46
Deer Park	NY	516	11729	Suffolk	31	2-56
Deer Park	OH	513	45236	Hamilton	7	2-62
Deer Park	TX	713	77536	Harris	23	2-74&75
Deerfield	IL	708	60015	Lake/Cook	57	2-19
Deerfield	MA	413	01342	Franklin	5	2-36
Deerfield Beach	FL	305	33441-43	Broward	45	2-15
Defiance*	OH	419	43512	Defiance	17	2-60
Del City	OK	405	73115	Oklahoma	27	2-64&65
Del Mar	CA	619	92014	San Diego	5	2-9
Del Norte*	CO	719	81132	Rio Grande	1	2-11
Del Rio*	TX	512	78840-42	Val Verde	34	2-75
Delafield	WI	414	53018	Waukesha	5	2-85
Delair	NJ	609	08110	Camden	4	2-51
Delanco	NJ	609	08075	Burlington	4	2-51
Delano	CA	805	93215-06	Kern	20	2-9
Delavan	WI	414	53115	Walworth	6	2-85
Delaware*	OH	614	43015	Delaware	19	2-61
Delhi	LA	318	71232	Richland	3	2-30
Delhi Hills	OH	513	45238	Hamilton	27	2-62
Delhi*	NY	607	13753	Delaware	3	2-54&55
Dellwood	MO	314	63136	St. Louis	6	2-44&45
Delmar	NY	518	12054	Albany	3	2-55
Delphi*	IN	317	46923	Carroll	3	2-22&23
Delphos	OH	419	45833	Allen/Van Wert	7	2-60
Delran	NJ	609	08075	Burlington	15	2-51
Delray Beach	FL	407	33444-84	Palm Beach	67	2-14&15
Delta	MI	517	48906	Eaton	23	2-38&39
Delta*	CO	303	81416	Delta	4	2-10&11
Delta	OH	419	43515	Fulton	3	2-60
Demarest	NJ	201	07627	Bergen	5	2-52
Deming*	NM	505	88030-31	Luna	11	2-53
Demopolis	AL	205	36732	Marengo	8	2-2&3
Demotte	IN	219	46310	Jasper	3	2-22
Denham Springs	LA	504	70726-27	Livingston	10	2-30&31
Denison	TX	214	75020-21	Grayson	25	2-74
Denison*	IA	712	51442	Crawford	6	2-24
Denmark	SC	803	29042	Bamberg	4	2-70
Dennis	MA	508	02638	Barnstable	12	2-36&37
Dennison	OH	614	44621	Tuscarawas	3	2-61
Denton*	MD	301	21629	Caroline	24	2-34&35
Denton*	TX	817	76201-06	Denton	46	2-74
Denver City	TX	806	79323	Yoakum	5	2-74
DENVER*	CO	303	80201-95	Denver	508	2-10&11
Denville	NJ	201	07834	Morris	14	2-52
Depew	NY	716	14043	Erie	20	2-54
Deptford	NJ	609	08096	Gloucester	24	2-51
Derby	CT	203	06418	New Haven	12	2-12&13

Bold = Over 15,000......ALL CAPS = STATE CAPITAL......* = County Seat......# = Changes to 510 in 9/91.....## = Changes to 410 in 11/91.....(+) = City located in additional counties......NAV = Population not available......C.H.= Court House......(IC)=Independent City

CITY	STATE	AREA CODE	ZIP CODE	COUNTY	POPULATION (in thousands)	MAP PAGE
Derby	KS	316	67037	Sedgwick	9	2-26&27
Derby	VT	802	05829	Orleans	4	2-77
Dermott	AR	501	71634 &38	Chicot	5	2-6
Derry	NH	603	03038	Rockingham	18	2-49
Derry	PA	717	15627	Westmooreland	3	2-68
Des Arc*	AR	501	72040	Prairie	1	2-6
DES MOINES*	IA	515	50301-99	Polk	193	2-24&25
Des Moines	WA	206	98188	King	10	2-80
Des Peres	MO	314	63131	St. Louis	8	2-44&45
Des Plaines	IL	708	60016-17	Cook	57	2-19
Desert Hot Springs	CA	619	92240	Riverside	8	2-9
Desloge	MO	314	63601	St. Francois	3	2-44&45
Destin	FL	904	32541	Okaloosa	4	2-14
Detroit*	MI	313	48201-99	Wayne	1086	2-39
Detroit Lakes*	MN	218	56501-02	Becker	6	2-40
Devils Lake*	ND	701	58301	Ramsey	7	2-57
Devine	TX	512	78016	Medina	4	2-75
Devon	PA	215	19333	Chester	6	2-67
Dewey	OK	918	74029	Washington	4	2-65
Dexter	ME	207	04930	Penobscot	4	2-32&33
Dexter	MO	314	63841	Stoddard	7	2-44&45
Diamond Bar	CA	714	91765	Los Angeles	30	2-7
Diboll	TX	409	75941	Angelina	5	2-75
Dickens*	TX	806	79229	Dickens	1	2-74
Dickinson*	ND	701	58601-02	Stark	17	2-57
Dickinson	TX	713	77539	Galveston	7	2-74&75
Dickson	TN	615	37055	Dickson	7	2-72&73
Dickson City	PA	717	18519	Lackawanna	7	2-67
Dighton	MA	508	02715	Bristol	5	2-36&37
Dighton*	KS	316	67839	Lane	1	2-26&27
Dilley	TX	512	78017	Frio	3	2-75
Dillingham	AK	907	99576	Dillingham	2	2-4
Dillon*	MT	406	59725	Beaverhead	4	2-46
Dillon*	SC	803	29536	Dillon	7	2-70
Dilworth	MN	218	56529	Clay	3	2-40
Dimmitt*	TX	806	79027	Castro	4	2-74
Dinuba	CA	209	93618	Tulare	11	2-8&9
Dinwiddie*	VA	804	23841	Dinwiddie	1	2-78&79
Dist Ht-Forestville	MD	301	20747	Prince Georges	7	2-35
Dixfield	ME	207	04224	Oxford	2	2-32&33
Dixmoor	IL	708	60406	Cook	4	2-19
Dixon	CA	916	95620	Solono	10	2-8
Dixon*	IL	815	61021	Lee	16	2-20
Dixon*	KY	502	42409	Webster	1	2-28&29
Dobbs Ferry	NY	914	10522	Westchester	10	2-56
Dobson*	NC	919	27017	Surry	1	2-58&59
Dodge City*	KS	316	67801	Ford	20	2-26&27
Dodgeville*	WI	608	53533	Iowa	3	2-85

Bold = Over 15,000......ALL CAPS = STATE CAPITAL......* = County Seat....# = Changes to 510 in 9/91..... ## = Changes to 410 in 11/91......(+) = City located in addional counties......NAV= Population not available......C.H.= Court House......(IC) = Independent City

CITY	STATE	AREA CODE	ZIP CODE	COUNTY	POPULATION (in thousands)	MAP PAGE
Dolgeville	NY	315	13329	Herkimer/Fulton	3	2-55
Dolomite	AL	205	35061	Jefferson	3	2-2&3
Dolton	IL	708	60419	Cook	24	2-19
Donaldsonville*	LA	504	70346	Ascension	8	2-30&31
Donalsonville*	GA	912	31745	Seminole	3	2-16&17
Doniphan*	MO	314	63935	Ripley	1	2-44&45
Donna	TX	512	78537	Hidalgo	10	2-75
Donora	PA	412	15033	Washington	7	2-66
Doraville	GA	404	30340	De Kalb	7	2-16&17
Dormont	PA	412	15216	Allegheny	12	2-68
Dos Palos	CA	209	93620	Fresno	3	2-8&9
Dothan*	AL	205	36301-04	Houston/Dale	55	2-2&3
Double Springs*	AL	205	35553	Winston	1	2-2&3
Douglas	AZ	602	85607-08	Cochise	14	2-5
Douglas*	GA	912	31533	Coffee	11	2-16&17
Douglas	MA	508	01516	Worcester	4	2-36&37
Douglas*	WY	307	82633	Converse	6	2-83
Douglass Hills	KY	502	40243	Jefferson	4	2-28
Douglasville*	GA	404	30133-35	Douglas	8	2-16&17
Dove Creek*	CO	303	81324	Dolores	1	2-10&11
DOVER*	DE	302	19901-03	Kent	23	2-35
Dover	MA	508	02030	Norfolk	5	2-36&37
Dover*	NH	603	03820	Strafford	23	2-49
Dover	NJ	201	07801-02	Morris	75	2-52
Dover	OH	216	44622	Tuscarawas	3	2-60
Dover	PA	717	17315	York	13	2-67
Dover*	TN	615	37058	Stewart	1	2-72&73
Dover-Foxcroft*	ME	207	04426	Piscataquis	4	2-32
Dowagiac	MI	616	49047	Cass	6	2-38&39
Downers Grove	IL	708	60515-17	Du Page	44	2-19
Downey	CA	213	90240-42	Los Angeles	85	2-7
Downieville*	CA	916	95936	Sierra	1	2-8
Downingtown	PA	215	19335	Chester	7	2-67
Doylestown*	PA	215	18901	Bucks	7	2-68
Dracut	MA	508	01826	Middlesex	21	2-36&37
Draper	UT	801	84020	Salt Lake	5	2-76
Dravosburg	PA	412	15034	Allegheny	3	2-68
Drayton Plains	MI	313	48020	Oakland	18	2-39
Dresden*	TN	901	38225	Weakley	1	2-72
Drew	MS	601	38737-38	Sunflower	3	2-42&43
Driggs*	ID	208	83422	Teton	1	2-18
Drumright	OK	918	74030	Creek	3	2-65
Du Bois	PA	814	15801	Clearfield	9	2-66
Du Quoin	IL	618	62832	Perry	6	2-21
Duarte	CA	818	91010	Los Angeles	20	2-7
Dublin	CA	415	94568	Alameda	19	2-7
Dublin*	GA	912	31021	Laurens	17	2-16&17
Dublin	OH	614	43017	Delaware/Franklin	4	2-61

Bold = Over 15,000......ALL CAPS = STATE CAPITAL......* = County Seat......# = Changes to 510 in 9/91.....## = Changes to 410 in 11/91.....(+) = City located in additional counties......NAV = Population not available......C.H.= Court House......(IC)=Independent City

CITY	STATE	AREA CODE	ZIP CODE	COUNTY	POPULATION (in thousands)	MAP PAGE
Dublin	TX	817	76446	Erath	3	2-74
Dubois*	ID	208	83423	Clark	1	2-18
Dubuque*	IA	319	52001-04	Dubuque	60	2-25
Duchesne*	UT	801	84021	Duchesne	1	2-76
Dudley	MA	508	01570	Worcester	4	2-36&37
Duluth	GA	404	30136	Gwinnett	3	2-16&17
Duluth*	MN	218	55801-99	St. Louis	82	2-40
Dumas	AR	501	71639	Desha	6	2-6
Dumas*	TX	806	79029	Moore	13	2-74
Dumfries	VA	703	22026	Prince William	3	2-78&79
Dumont	NJ	201	07628	Bergen	18	2-52
Dunbar	WV	304	25064	Kanawha	9	2-82
Duncan*	OK	405	73533-34	Stephens	22	2-64&65
Duncanville	TX	214	75137-38	Dallas	34	2-74
Dundee	IL	708	60118	Kane	4	2-19
Dundee	MI	313	48131	Monroe	3	2-39
Dunedin	FL	813	33698	Pinellas	33	2-14&15
Dunellen	NJ	201	08812	Middlesex	6	2-50
Dunkirk	IN	317	47336	Jay/Blackford	3	2-22&23
Dunkirk	NY	716	14048	Chautauqua	15	2-54
Dunlap*	TN	615	37327	Sequatchie	3	2-72&73
Dunmore	PA	717	18512	Lackawanna	17	2-67
Dunn	NC	919	28334	Harnett	9	2-58&59
Dunsmuir	CA	916	96025	Siskiyou	2	2-8
Dupo	IL	618	62239	St. Clair	3	2-21
Dupont	PA	717	18641	Luzerne	3	2-67
Dupree*	SD	605	57623	Ziebach	1	2-71
Duquesne	PA	412	15110	Allegheny	10	2-68
Durand	MI	517	48429	Shiawassee	4	2-38&39
Durand*	WI	715	54736	Pepin	1	2-84&85
Durango*	CO	303	81301-02	La Plata	13	2-10&11
Durant	MS	601	39063	Holmes	3	2-42&43
Durant*	OK	405	74701-02	Bryan	13	2-64&65
Durham	CT	203	06422	Middlesex	3	2-12&13
Durham*	NC	919	27701-99	Durham	113	2-58&59
Durham	NH	603	03824	Strafford	8	2-49
Duryea	PA	717	18642	Luzerne	5	2-67
Duxbury	MA	617	02331-32	Plymouth	11	2-36&37
Dwight	IL	815	60420	Livingston/Grundy	4	2-20
Dyer	IN	219	46311	Lake	10	2-22
Dyersburg*	TN	901	38024-25	Dyer	15	2-72
Dyersville	IA	319	52040	Delaware (+1)	4	2-25
Eads*	CO	719	81036	Kiowa	1	2-11
Eagan	MN	612	55120	Dakota	31	2-41
Eagle	ID	208	83616	Ada	3	2-18
Eagle Grove	IA	515	50533	Wright	4	2-24&25
Eagle Lake	TX	409	77434	Colorado	4	2-75
Eagle Pass*	TX	512	78852-53	Maverick	4	2-75

Bold = Over 15,000......ALL CAPS = STATE CAPITAL......* = County Seat......# = Changes to 510 in 9/91..... ## = Changes to 410 in 11/91......(+) = City located in addional counties......NAV= Population not available......C.H.= Court House......(IC) = Independent City

CITY	STATE	AREA CODE	ZIP CODE	COUNTY	POPULATION (in thousands)	MAP PAGE
Eagle Point	OR	503	97524	Jackson	3	2-63
Eagle River*	MI	906	49924	Keweenaw	1	2-38
Eagle River*	WI	715	54521	Vilas	1	2-84&85
Eagle*	CO	303	81631	Eagle	1	2-10&11
Earle	AR	501	72331	Crittenden	4	2-6
Earlimart	CA	805	93219	Tulare	5	2-9
Easley	SC	803	29640-41	Pickens	4	2-70
East Alton	IL	618	62024	Madison	7	2-21
East Aurora	NY	716	14052	Erie	7	2-54
East Bakersfield	CA	805	93305	Kern	19	2-9
East Bethel	MN	612	55005	Anoka	6	2-41
East Brewton	AL	205	36426	Escambia	3	2-2&3
East Bridgewater	MA	508	02333	Plymouth	4	2-36&37
East Brunswick	NJ	201	08816	Middlesex	40	2-50
East Chicago	IN	219	46312	Lake	37	2-22
East Cleveland	OH	216	44112	Cuyahoga	36	2-62
East Detroit	MI	313	48021	Macomb	36	2-39
East Dublin	GA	912	31021	Laurens	3	2-16&17
East Dundee	IL	708	60118	Kane/Cook	2	2-19
East Goshen	PA	215	19380	Chester	10	2-67
East Granby	CT	203	06026	Hartford	4	2-12&13
East Grand Forks	MN	218	56721	Polk	9	2-40
East Grand Rapids	MI	616	49506	Kent	11	2-38&39
East Greenbush	NY	518	12061	Rensselaer	3	2-55
East Greenwich*	RI	401	02818	Kent	10	2-69
East Haddam	CT	203	06423	Middlesex	6	2-12&13
East Half Hollow Hills	NY	516	11746	Suffolk	7	2-56
East Hampton	CT	203	06424	Middlesex	9	2-12&13
East Hanover	NJ	201	07936	Morris	9	2-52
East Hartford	CT	203	06108	Hartford	53	2-12&13
East Haven	CT	203	06512	New Haven	25	2-12&13
East Hills	NY	516	11576	Nassau	7	2-56
East Huntington	NY	516	11743	Suffolk	4	2-56
East Islip	NY	516	11730	Suffolk	13	2-56
East Lansdowne	PA	215	19050	Delaware	3	2-68
East Lansing	MI	517	48823-26	Ingham	47	2-38&39
East Liverpool	OH	216	43920	Columbiana	16	2-60
East Longmeadow	MA	413	01028	Hampden	12	2-36
East Los Angeles	CA	213	90022	Los Angeles	117	2-7
East Lyme	CT	203	06333	New London	14	2-12&13
East Massapequa	NY	516	11758	Nassau	4	2-56
East McKeesport	PA	412	15035	Allegheny	3	2-68
East Meadow	NY	516	11554	Nassau	40	2-56
East Midvale	UT	801	84047	Salt Lake	6	2-76
East Moline	IL	309	61244	Rock Island	20	2-20
East Naples	FL	813	33939	Collier	9	2-14&15
East Norriton	PA	215	19401	Montgomery	13	2-68
East Northport	NY	516	11731	Suffolk	20	2-56

Bold = Over 15,000......ALL CAPS = STATE CAPITAL......* = County Seat......# = Changes to 510 in 9/91.....## = Changes to 410 in 11/91.....(+) = City located in additional counties......NAV = Population not available......C.H.= Court House......(IC)=Independent City

CITY	STATE	AREA CODE	ZIP CODE	COUNTY	POPULATION (in thousands)	MAP PAGE
East Orange	NJ	201	07017-19	Essex	78	2-52
East Palestine	OH	216	44413	Columbiana	5	2-60
East Palo Alto	CA	415	94303	Santa Clara	18	2-7
East Patchogue	NY	516	11772	Suffolk	14	2-56
East Pennsboro	PA	717	17025	Cumberland	4	2-67
East Peoria	IL	309	61611	Tazewell	22	2-20
East Petersburg	PA	717	17520	Lancaster	4	2-67
East Point	GA	404	30344	Fulton	40	2-16&17
East Prairie	MO	314	63845	Mississippi	3	2-44&45
East Providence	RI	401	02914	Providence	52	2-69
East Quoque	NY	516	11942	Suffolk	3	2-56
East Ridge	TN	615	37412	Hamilton	22	2-72&73
East Rochester	NY	716	14445	Monroe	7	2-54
East Rockaway	NY	516	11518	Nassau	11	2-56
East Rutherford	NJ	201	07073	Bergen	8	2-52
East St. Louis	IL	618	62201-08	St. Clair	51	2-21
East Stroudsburg	PA	717	18301	Monroe	8	2-67
East Syracuse	NY	315	13057	Onondaga	3	2-54&55
East Tawas	MI	517	48730	Iosco	3	2-38&39
East Vestal	NY	607	13902	Broome	6	2-54&55
East Whiteland	PA	215	19355	Chester	8	2-67
East Williston	NY	516	11596	Nassau	3	2-56
East Windsor	CT	203	06088	Hartford	9	2-12&13
East Windsor	NJ	609	08520	Mercer	15	2-50
Eastampton	NJ	609	08060	Burlington	4	2-51
Eastham	MA	508	02642	Barnstable	1	2-36&37
Easthampton	MA	413	01027	Hampshire	16	2-36
Eastlake	OH	216	44094-95	Lake	22	2-62
Eastland*	TX	817	76448	Eastland	4	2-74
Eastman*	GA	912	31023	Dodge	16	2-16&17
Easton	CT	203	06612	Fairfield	6	2-12&13
Easton	MA	508	02334	Bristol	17	2-36&37
Easton*	MD	301	21601	Talbot	8	2-34&35
Easton*	PA	215	18042-44	Northampton	26	2-67
Eastville*	VA	804	23347	Northampton	1	2-78&79
Eaton	CO	303	80615	Weld	2	2-10&11
Eaton*	OH	513	45320	Preble	7	2-61
Eaton Rapids	MI	517	48827	Eaton	5	2-38&39
Eatonton*	GA	912	31024	Putnam	5	2-16&17
Eatontown	NJ	201	07724	Monmouth	14	2-50
Eau Claire*	WI	715	54701-03	Eau Claire	54	2-84&85
Ebensburg*	PA	814	15931	Cambria	3	2-66
Economy	PA	412	15003-05	Beaver	10	2-66
Ecorse	MI	313	48229	Wayne	15	2-39
Edcouch	TX	512	78538	Hidalgo	3	2-75
Eddystone	PA	215	19013	Delaware	3	2-68
Eddyville*	KY	502	42038	Lyon	1	2-28&29
Eden	NC	919	27288	Rockingham	16	2-58&59

Bold = Over 15,000......ALL CAPS = STATE CAPITAL......* = County Seat......# = Changes to 510 in 9/91..... ## = Changes to 410 in 11/91......(+) = City located in addional counties......NAV= Population not available......C.H.= Court House......(IC) = Independent City

CITY	STATE	AREA CODE	ZIP CODE	COUNTY	POPULATION (in thousands)	MAP PAGE
Eden Prairie	MN	612	55344	Hennepin	24	2-41
Edenton*	NC	919	27932	Chowan	6	2-58&59
Edgard*	LA	504	70049	St. John/Baptist	1	2-30&31
Edgartown*	MA	508	02539	Dukes	2	2-36&37
Edgecliff	TX	817	76134	Tarrant	3	2-74
Edgefield*	SC	803	29824	Edgefield	2	2-70
Edgemoor	DE	302	19802 &09	New Castle	5	2-35
Edgerton	WI	608	53534	Rock	4	2-85
Edgewater	CO	303	80214	Jefferson	5	2-10&11
Edgewater	FL	904	32132	Volusia	7	2-14
Edgewater	NJ	201	07020	Bergen	5	2-52
Edgewood	KY	606	41017	Kenton	8	2-29
Edgewood	PA	412	15218	Allegheny	4	2-68
Edina	MN	612	55410	Hennepin	49	2-41
Edina*	MO	816	63537	Knox	1	2-44
Edinboro	PA	814	16412	Erie	6	2-66
Edinburg*	TX	512	78539-40	Hidalgo	1	2-75
Edinburgh	IN	812	46124	Johnson (+1)	5	2-23
Edison	NJ	201	08817-20	Middlesex	79	2-50
Edmond	OK	405	73034	Oklahoma	48	2-64&65
Edmonds	WA	206	98020	Snohomish	30	2-80
Edmonton*	KY	502	42129	Metcalfe	2	2-28&29
Edna*	TX	512	77957	Jackson	5	2-75
Edwardsville	KS	913	66113	Wyandotte	3	2-26&27
Edwardsville*	IL	618	62025	Madison	13	2-21
Edwardsville	PA	717	18704	Luzerne	6	2-67
Effingham*	IL	217	62401	Effingham	12	2-20&21
Egg Harbor City	NJ	609	08215	Atlantic	19	2-51
Ekalaka*	MT	406	59324	Carter	1	2-46
El Cajon	CA	619	92019-22	San Diego	84	2-9
El Campo	TX	409	77437	Wharton	11	2-75
El Centro*	CA	619	92243-44	Imperial	27	2-9
El Cerrito	CA	415	94530	Contra Costa	22	2-7
El Dorado Springs	MO	417	64744	Cedar	3	2-44
El Dorado*	AR	501	71730-31	Union	26	2-6
El Dorado*	KS	316	67042	Butler	11	2-26&27
El Lago	TX	713	77586	Harris	3	2-74&75
El Mirage	AZ	602	85335	Maricopa	4	2-5
El Monte	CA	818	91731-34	Los Angeles	96	2-7
El Paso	IL	309	61738	Woodford	3	2-20
El Paso*	TX	915	79901-99	El Paso	491	2-74&75
El Portal	FL	305	33138	Dade	2	2-15
El Reno*	OK	405	73036	Canadian	16	2-64&65
El Rio	CA	805	93030	Ventura	6	2-9
El Segundo	CA	213	90245	Los Angeles	15	2-7
El Sobrante	CA	415	94803	Contra Costa	10	2-7
Elba*	AL	205	36323	Coffee	4	2-2&3
Elberton*	GA	404	30635	Elbert	6	2-16&17

Bold = Over 15,000.....ALL CAPS = STATE CAPITAL......* = County Seat......# = Changes to 510 in 9/91.....## = Changes to 410 in 11/91.....(+) = City located in additional counties......NAV = Population not available......C.H.= Court House......(IC)=Independent City

CITY	STATE	AREA CODE	ZIP CODE	COUNTY	POPULATION (in thousands)	MAP PAGE
Elbow Lake*	MN	218	56531	Grant	2	2-40
Eldon	MO	314	65026	Miller	4	2-44&45
Eldora*	IA	515	50627	Hardin	3	2-24&25
Eldorado	IL	618	62930	Saline	5	2-21
Eldorado*	TX	915	76936	Schleicher	1	2-74&75
Eldridge	IA	319	52748	Scott	3	2-25
Electra	TX	817	76360	Wichita	4	2-74
Elgin	IL	708	60120-23	Kane/Cook	71	2-19
Elgin	TX	512	78621	Bastrop	5	2-75
Eliot	ME	207	03903	York	2	2-32&33
Elizabeth*	NJ	201	07201-99	Union	107	2-52
Elizabeth*	WV	304	26143	Wirt	1	2-82
Elizabeth City*	NC	919	27906-09	Pasquotank	14	2-59
Elizabethton*	TN	615	37643-44	Carter	12	2-72&73
Elizabethtown*	IL	618	62931	Hardin	1	2-21
Elizabethtown*	KY	502	42701-02	Hardin	18	2-28&29
Elizabethtown*	NC	919	28337	Bladen	3	2-58&59
Elizabethtown*	NY	518	12932	Essex	1	2-55
Elizabethtown	PA	717	17022	Lancaster	8	2-67
Elk City	OK	405	73644	Beckham	13	2-64&65
Elk Grove Village	IL	708	60007	Cook/Du Page	31	2-19
Elk Point*	SD	605	57025	Union	1	2-71
Elk River*	MN	612	55330	Sherburne	7	2-41
Elkader*	IA	319	52043	Clayton	2	2-25
Elkhart	IN	219	46514-17	Elkhart	43	2-22
Elkhart*	KS	316	67950	Morton	2	2-26&27
Elkhorn*	WI	414	53121	Walworth	4	2-85
Elkin	NC	919	28621	Surry/Wilkes	3	2-58&59
Elkins*	WV	304	26241	Randolph	8	2-82
Elko*	NV	702	89801	Elko	11	2-48
Elkton*	KY	502	42220	Todd	2	2-28&29
Elkton*	MD	301	21921	Cecil	7	2-34&35
Ellaville*	GA	912	31806	Schley	1	2-16&17
Ellendale*	ND	701	58436	Dickey	1	2-57
Ellensburg*	WA	509	98926	Kittitas	12	2-81
Ellenville	NY	914	12428	Ulster	4	2-56
Ellettsville	IN	812	47429	Monroe	3	2-23
Ellicott City*	MD	301	21043	Howard	4	2-34&35
Ellijay*	GA	404	30540	Gilmer	1	2-16&17
Ellington	CT	203	06029	Tolland	2	2-12&13
Ellinwood	KS	316	67526	Barton	3	2-26&27
Ellisville	MO	314	63011	St. Louis	7	2-44&45
Ellisville*	MS	601	39437	Jones	5	2-42&43
Ellsworth*	KS	913	67439	Ellsworth	2	2-26&27
Ellsworth*	ME	207	04605	Hancock	5	2-32&33
Ellsworth*	WI	715	54010-11	Pierce	1	2-84&85
Ellwood City	PA	412	16117	Beaver/Lawrence	10	2-66
Elm Grove	WI	414	53122	Waukesha	7	2-85

Bold = Over 15,000......ALL CAPS = STATE CAPITAL......* = County Seat......# = Changes to 510 in 9/91..... ## = Changes to 410 in 11/91......(+) = City located in addional counties......NAV = Population not available......C.H.= Court House......(IC) = Independent City

CITY	STATE	AREA CODE	ZIP CODE	COUNTY	POPULATION (in thousands)	MAP PAGE
Elma	WA	206	98541	Grays Harbor	3	2-80
Elmhurst	IL	708	60126	Du Page	46	2-19
Elmira*	NY	607	14901-99	Chemung	7	2-54&55
Elmira Heights	NY	607	14903	Chemung	4	2-54&55
Elmont	NY	516	11003	Nassau	29	2-56
Elmsford	NY	914	10523	Westchester	3	2-56
Elmwood Park	NJ	201	07407	Bergen	19	2-52
Elmwood Place	OH	513	45216	Hamilton	3	2-62
Elon College	NC	919	27244	Alamance	3	2-58&59
Eloy	AZ	602	85231	Pinal	6	2-5
Elsa	TX	512	78543	Hidalgo	5	2-75
Elsmere	DE	302	19805	New Castle	6	2-35
Elsmere	KY	606	41018	Kenton	7	2-29
Elsmere	NY	518	12054	Albany	4	2-55
Elwood	IN	317	46036	Madison/Tipton	10	2-22&23
Elwood*	NE	308	68937	Gosper	1	2-47
Ely	MN	218	55731	St. Louis	5	2-40
Ely*	NV	702	89301	White Pine	4	2-48
Elyria*	OH	216	44035-39	Lorain	57	2-60
Emerson	NJ	201	07630	Bergen	8	2-52
Emeryville	CA	415	94608	Alameda	4	2-7
Eminence*	MO	314	65466	Shannon	1	2-44&45
Emmaus	PA	215	18049	Lehigh	11	2-67
Emmetsburg*	IA	712	50536	Palo Alto	4	2-24
Emmett*	ID	208	83617	Gem	5	2-18
Emory*	TX	214	75440	Raines	1	2-74
Emporia*	KS	316	66801	Lyon	26	2-26&27
Emporia*	VA	804	23847	Greensville (IC)	4	2-78&79
Emporium*	PA	814	15834	Cameron	2	2-66
Encinitas	CA	619	92024	San Diego	83	2-9
Endicott	NY	607	13760	Broome	15	2-54&55
Endwell	NY	607	13760	Broome	14	2-54&55
Enfield	CT	203	06082	Hartford	8	2-12&13
Enfield	NC	919	27823	Halifax	3	2-58&59
Enfield	NH	603	03748	Grafton	3	2-49
England	AR	501	72046	Lonoke	4	2-6
Englewood	CO	303	80110-55	Arapahoe	32	2-10&11
Englewood	FL	813	34223-24	Sarasota (+1)	10	2-14&15
Englewood	NJ	201	07631-32	Bergen	24	2-52
Englewood	OH	513	45322	Montgomery	12	2-61
Englewood Cliffs	NJ	201	07632	Bergen	6	2-52
English*	IN	812	47118	Crawford	1	2-23
Enid*	OK	405	73701-06	Garfield	50	2-64&65
Ennis	TX	214	75119-20	Ellis	12	2-74
Enon	OH	513	45323	Clark	3	2-61
Enterprise	AL	205	36330-31	Coffee/Dale	20	2-2&3
Enterprise*	OR	503	97828	Wallowa	2	2-63
Enumclaw	WA	206	98022	King	5	2-80

Bold = Over 15,000......ALL CAPS = STATE CAPITAL......* = County Seat......# = Changes to 510 in 9/91.....## = Changes to 410 in 11/91.....(+) = City located in additional counties......NAV = Population not available......C.H.= Court House......(IC)=Independent City

CITY	STATE	AREA CODE	ZIP CODE	COUNTY	POPULATION (in thousands)	MAP PAGE
Ephraim	UT	801	84627	Sanpete	3	2-76
Ephrata	PA	717	17522	Lancaster	11	2-67
Ephrata*	WA	509	98823	Grant	5	2-81
Epping	NH	603	03042	Rockingham	3	2-49
Epsom	NH	603	03234	Merrimack	3	2-49
Erie*	KS	316	66733	Neosho	1	2-26&27
Erie*	PA	814	16501-99	Erie	115	2-66
Erin*	TN	615	37061	Houston	1	2-72&73
Erlanger	KY	606	41018	Kenton	15	2-29
Errol Heights	OR	503	97266	Multnomah	8	2-63
Erwin	NC	919	28339	Harnett	3	2-58&59
Erwin*	TN	615	37650	Unicoi	4	2-72&73
Escalon	CA	209	95320	San Joaquin	3	2-8&9
Escanaba*	MI	906	49829	Delta	13	2-38
Escondido	CA	619	92025-27	San Diego	83	2-9
Espanola	NM	505	87532	Rio Arriba (+1)	7	2-53
Essex	CT	203	06426	Middlesex	6	2-12&13
Essex	MA	508	01929	Essex	3	2-36&37
Essex	VT	802	05452	Chittenden	14	2-77
Essex Junction	VT	802	05452	Chittenden	7	2-77
Essexville	MI	517	48732	Bay	5	2-38&39
Estancia*	NM	505	87016	Torrance	1	2-53
Estes Park	CO	303	80517	Larimer	3	2-10&11
Estherville*	IA	712	51334	Emmet	7	2-24
Etna	PA	412	15223	Allegheny	4	2-68
Etowah	TN	615	37331	McMinn	4	2-72&73
Euclid	OH	216	44117	Cuyahoga	57	2-62
Eudora	AR	501	71640	Chicot	4	2-6
Eudora	KS	913	66025	Douglas	3	2-26&27
Eufaula	AL	205	36027	Barbour	12	2-2&3
Eufaula*	OK	918	74432	McIntosh	3	2-65
Eugene*	OR	503	97401-05	Lane	105	2-63
Euless	TX	817	76039-40	Tarrant	30	2-74
Eunice	LA	318	70535	St. Landry/Acadia	12	2-30
Eunice	NM	505	88231	Lea	7	2-53
Eureka	MO	314	63025	St. Louis	4	2-44&45
Eureka Springs	AR	501	72632	Carroll	2	2-6
Eureka*	CA	707	95501-02	Humboldt	24	2-8
Eureka*	IL	309	61530	Woodford	5	2-20
Eureka*	KS	316	67045	Greenwood	3	2-26&27
Eureka*	NV	702	89316	Eureka	1	2-48
Eustis	FL	904	32726-27	Lake	9	2-14
Eutaw*	AL	205	35462	Greene	1	2-2&3
Evans	CO	303	80620	Weld	5	2-10&11
Evansdale	IA	319	50707	Black Hawk	5	2-25
Evanston	IL	708	60201-99	Cook	72	2-19
Evanston*	WY	307	82930-31	Uinta	12	2-83
Evansville*	IN	812	47701-99	Vanderburgh	130	2-23

Bold = Over 15,000......ALL CAPS = STATE CAPITAL......* = County Seat......# = Changes to 510 in 9/91...... ## = Changes to 410 in 11/91......(+) = City located in addional counties......NAV= Population not available......C.H.= Court House......(IC) = Independent City

CITY	STATE	AREA CODE	ZIP CODE	COUNTY	POPULATION (in thousands)	MAP PAGE
Evansville	WI	608	53536	Rock	3	2-85
Evansville	WY	307	82636	Natrona	2	2-83
Eveleth	MN	218	55734	St. Louis	5	2-40
Everett	MA	617	02149	Middlesex	37	2-36&37
Everett*	WA	206	98201-08	Snohomish	59	2-80
Evergreen*	AL	205	36401	Conecuh	4	2-2&3
Evergreen Park	IL	708	60642	Cook	22	2-19
Everman	TX	817	76140	Tarrant	5	2-74
Evesham	NJ	609	08053	Burlington	21	2-51
Ewa Beach	HI	808	96706-07	Honolulu	15	2-19
Ewing	NJ	609	08618	Mercer	36	2-50
Excelsior	MN	612	55331	Hennepin	3	2-41
Excelsior Springs	MO	816	64024	Clay/Ray	10	2-44
Exeter	CA	209	93221	Tulare	6	2-8&9
Exeter*	NH	603	03833	Rockingham	12	2-49
Exeter	PA	717	18643	Luzerne	5	2-67
Exeter	RI	401	02822	Washington	4	2-69
Fair Haven	NJ	201	07701-04	Monmouth	6	2-50
Fair Haven	VT	802	05743	Rutland	3	2-77
Fair Lawn	NJ	201	07410	Bergen	32	2-52
Fair Oaks	CA	916	95628	Sacramento	23	2-8
Fairbanks	AK	907	99701-16	Fairbanks North Star	30	2-4
Fairborn	OH	513	45324	Greene	29	2-61
Fairburn	GA	404	30213	Fulton	3	2-16&17
Fairbury	IL	815	61739	Livingston	4	2-20
Fairbury*	NE	402	68352	Jefferson	5	2-47
Fairdale	KY	502	40118	Jefferson	3	2-28
Fairfax	CA	415	94930	Marin	7	2-7
Fairfax*	VA	703	22030-39	Fairfax (IC)	20	2-78&79
Fairfield	AL	205	35064	Jefferson	13	2-2&3
Fairfield*	CA	707	94533	Solano	68	2-8
Fairfield	CT	203	06430-32	Fairfield	54	2-12&13
Fairfield*	IA	515	52556	Jefferson	9	2-24&25
Fairfield*	ID	208	83322	Camas	1	2-18
Fairfield*	IL	618	62837	Wayne	6	2-21
Fairfield	ME	207	04937	Somerset	6	2-32&33
Fairfield	NJ	201	07006	Essex	8	2-52
Fairfield	OH	513	45014	Butler	39	2-61
Fairfield*	TX	214	75840	Freestone	4	2-74
Fairhaven	MA	508	02719	Bristol	17	2-36&37
Fairhope	AL	205	36532-33	Baldwin	7	2-2&3
Fairlawn	OH	216	44313	Summit	6	2-62
Fairmont*	MN	507	56031	Martin	11	2-41
Fairmont	NC	919	28340	Robeson	3	2-58&59
Fairmont*	WV	304	26554-55	Marion	22	2-82
Fairmount	IN	317	46928	Grant	3	2-22&23
Fairmount	NY	315	13031 &219	Onondaga	9	2-54&55
Fairplay*	CO	303	80440	Park	1	2-10&11

Bold = Over 15,000......ALL CAPS = STATE CAPITAL......* = County Seat......# = Changes to 510 in 9/91.....## = Changes to 410 in 11/91.....(+) = City located in additional counties......NAV = Population not available......C.H.= Court House......(IC)=Independent City

CITY	STATE	AREA CODE	ZIP CODE	COUNTY	POPULATION (in thousands)	MAP PAGE
Fairport	NY	716	14450	Monroe	6	2-54
Fairport Harbor	OH	216	44077	Lake	3	2-62
Fairview	NJ	201	07022	Bergen	10	2-52
Fairview	NJ	201	07701	Monmouth	4	2-50
Fairview Heights	IL	618	62208	St. Clair	12	2-21
Fairview Park	OH	216	44126	Cuyahoga	19	2-62
Fairview*	OK	405	73737	Major	3	2-64&65
Fairway	KS	913	66205	Johnson	5	2-26&27
Falcon Heights	MN	612	55108	Ramsey	5	2-41
Falconer	NY	716	14733	Chautauqua	3	2-54
Falfurrias*	TX	512	78355	Brooks	6	2-75
Fall River	MA	508	02720-26	Bristol	94	2-36&37
Fallbrook	CA	619	92028	San Diego	14	2-9
Fallon*	NV	702	89406	Churchill	4	2-48
Falls Church	VA	703	22040-48	(IC)	9	2-78&79
Falls City*	NE	402	68355	Richardson	5	2-47
Fallsburg	NY	914	12733	Sullivan	10	2-56
Falmouth*	KY	606	41040	Pendleton	3	2-29
Falmouth	MA	508	02540-41	Barnstable	5	2-36&37
Falmouth	ME	207	04105	Cumberland	6	2-32&33
Fanwood	NJ	201	07023	Union	10	2-52
Far Rockaway	NY	516	11601-99	Queens	NAV	2-56
Fargo*	ND	701	58102-99	Cass	65	2-57
Faribault*	MN	507	55021	Rice	16	2-41
Farmers Branch	TX	214	75234	Dallas	28	2-74
Farmersville	CA	209	93222-23	Tulare	6	2-8&9
Farmerville*	LA	318	71241	Union	3	2-30
Farmingdale	ME	207	04345	Kennebec	3	2-32&33
Farmingdale	NY	516	11735	Nassau	7	2-56
Farmington	CT	203	06032	Hartford	2	2-12&13
Farmington	IL	309	61531	Fulton	3	2-20
Farmington*	ME	207	04938	Franklin	6	2-32&33
Farmington	MI	313	48018	Oakland	11	2-39
Farmington	MN	612	55024	Dakota	4	2-41
Farmington*	MO	314	63640	St. Francois	8	2-44&45
Farmington	NH	603	03835	Strafford	3	2-49
Farmington	NM	505	87401	San Juan	38	2-53
Farmington*	UT	801	84025	Davis	1	2-76
Farmington Hills	MI	313	48018	Oakland	64	2-39
Farmville	NC	919	27828	Pitt	5	2-58&59
Farmville*	VA	804	23901	Prince Edward	6	2-78&79
Farragut	TN	615	37922	Knox	8	2-72&73
Farrell	PA	412	16121	Mercer	9	2-66
Farwell*	TX	806	79325	Parmer	1	2-74
Faulkton*	SD	605	57438	Faulk	1	2-71
Fayette*	AL	205	35555	Fayette	7	2-2&3
Fayette*	MO	816	65248	Howard	2	2-44
Fayette*	MS	601	39069	Jefferson	1	2-42&43

Bold = Over 15,000......ALL CAPS = STATE CAPITAL......* = County Seat......# = Changes to 510 in 9/91...... ## = Changes to 410 in 11/91......(+) = City located in addional counties......NAV= Population not available......C.H.= Court House......(IC) = Independent City

CITY	STATE	AREA CODE	ZIP CODE	COUNTY	POPULATION (in thousands)	MAP PAGE
Fayetteville*	AR	501	72701-03	Washington	40	2-6
Fayetteville*	GA	404	30214	Fayette	3	2-16&17
Fayetteville*	NC	919	28301-14	Cumberland	66	2-58&59
Fayetteville	NY	315	13066	Onondaga	5	2-54&55
Fayetteville*	TN	615	37334	Lincoln	7	2-72&73
Fayetteville*	WV	304	25840	Fayette	2	2-82
Federal Heights	CO	303	80221	Adams	8	2-10&11
Feeding Hills	MA	413	01030	Hampden	5	2-36
Fellowship	NJ	609	08057	Burlington	4	2-51
Felton	CA	408	95041	Santa Cruz	4	2-7
Fenton	MI	313	48430	Genesee	9	2-39
Fergus Falls*	MN	218	56537	Otter Tail	12	2-40
Ferguson	MO	314	63135	St. Louis	23	2-44&45
Fern Creek	KY	502	40291	Jefferson	10	2-28
Fernandina Beach*	FL	904	32034	Nassau	8	2-14
Ferndale	MD	301	21061	Anne Arundel	3	2-34&35
Ferndale	MI	313	48220	Oakland	25	2-39
Ferndale	WA	206	98248	Watcom	4	2-80
Ferriday	LA	318	71334	Concordia	5	2-30
Fessenden*	ND	701	58438	Wells	1	2-57
Festus	MO	314	63028	Jefferson	8	2-44&45
Fillmore	CA	805	93015	Ventura	10	2-9
Fillmore*	UT	801	84631	Millard	1	2-76
Fincastle*	VA	703	24090	Botetourt	1	2-78&79
Finderne	NJ	201	08807	Somerset	4	2-50
Findlay*	OH	419	45839-40	Hancock	36	2-60
Finley*	ND	701	58230	Steele	1	2-57
Finneytown	OH	513	45224	Hamilton	4	2-62
Fircrest	WA	206	98466	Pierce	6	2-80
Firebaugh	CA	209	93622	Fresno	4	2-8&9
Fitchburg	MA	508	01420	Worcester	40	2-36&37
Fitchburg	WI	608	53575	Dane	12	2-85
Fitzgerald*	GA	912	31750	Ben Hill	11	2-16&17
Flagstaff*	AZ	602	86001-18	Coconino	41	2-5
Flandreau*	SD	605	57028	Moody	1	2-71
Flat River	MO	314	63601	St. Francois	4	2-44&45
Flat Rock	MI	313	48134	Wayne	6	2-39
Flatwoods	KY	606	41139	Greenup	9	2-29
Fleetwood	PA	215	19522	Berks	4	2-67
Flemingsburg*	KY	606	41041	Fleming	3	2-29
Flemington*	NJ	201	08822	Hunterdon	4	2-50
Flint*	MI	313	48501-32	Genesee	149	2-39
Flora	IL	618	62839	Clay	6	2-21
Floral Park	NY	516	11001-05	Nassau	17	2-56
Florence*	AL	205	35630-33	Lauderdale	37	2-2&3
Florence*	AZ	602	85232	Pinal	5	2-5
Florence	CA	213	90001	Los Angeles	40	2-7
Florence	CO	303	81226	Fremont	3	2-10&11

Bold = Over 15,000......ALL CAPS = STATE CAPITAL......* = County Seat......# = Changes to 510 in 9/91.....## = Changes to 410 in 11/91.....(+) = City located in additional counties......NAV = Population not available......C.H.= Court House......(IC)=Independent City

CITY	STATE	AREA CODE	ZIP CODE	COUNTY	POPULATION (in thousands)	MAP PAGE
Florence	KY	606	41042	Boone	18	2-29
Florence	NJ	609	08518	Burlington	4	2-51
Florence	OR	503	97439	Lane	5	2-63
Florence*	SC	803	29501-04	Florence	31	2-70
Florence*	WI	715	54121	Florence	1	2-84&85
Floresville*	TX	512	78114	Wilson	5	2-75
Florham Park	NJ	201	07932	Morris	9	2-52
Florida City	FL	305	33034	Dade	6	2-15
Florin	CA	916	95828	Sacramento	17	2-8
Florissant	MO	314	63031-34	St. Louis	59	2-44&45
Flossmoor	IL	708	60422	Cook	8	2-19
Flower Hill	NY	516	11050	Nassau	5	2-56
Flower Mound	TX	214	75067	Denton	4	2-74
Floyd*	VA	703	24091	Floyd	1	2-78&79
Floydada*	TX	806	79235	Floyd	3	2-74
Flushing	MI	313	48433	Genesee	8	2-39
Flushing	NY	718	11301-99	Queens	NAV	2-56
Folcroft	PA	215	19032	Delaware	8	2-68
Foley	AL	205	36535-36	Baldwin	4	2-2&3
Foley*	MN	612	56329	Benton	1	2-41
Folkston*	GA	912	31537	Charlton	1	2-16&17
Follansbee	WV	304	26037	Brooke	4	2-82
Folsom	CA	916	95630	Sacramento	18	2-8
Fond du Lac*	WI	414	54935	Fond du Lac	36	2-85
Fonda*	NY	518	12068	Montgomery	1	2-55
Fontana	CA	714	92334-36	San Bernardino	55	2-9
Ford City	PA	412	16226	Armstrong	4	2-66
Fordyce*	AR	501	71742	Dallas	5	2-6
Forest Acres	SC	803	29206	Richland	6	2-70
Forest City*	IA	515	50436	Winnebago (+1)	4	2-24&25
Forest City	NC	704	28043	Rutherford	8	2-58
Forest Grove	OR	503	97116	Washington	12	2-63
Forest Heights	MD	301	20745	Prince Georges	3	2-35
Forest Hills	PA	412	15221	Allegheny	8	2-68
Forest Lake	MN	612	55025	Washington	5	2-41
Forest Park	GA	404	30050-51	Clayton	19	2-16&17
Forest Park	IL	708	60130	Cook	15	2-19
Forest Park	OH	513	45240	Hamilton	19	2-62
Forest*	MS	601	39074	Scott	5	2-42&43
Forestdale	AL	205	35214	Jefferson	4	2-2&3
Forks	WA	206	98331	Clallam	3	2-80
Forman*	ND	701	58032	Sargent	1	2-57
Forrest City*	AR	501	72335	St. Francis	14	2-6
Forsyth*	GA	912	31029	Monroe	5	2-16&17
Forsyth*	MO	417	65653	Taney	1	2-44
Forsyth*	MT	406	59327	Rosebud	2	2-46
Fort Atkinson	WI	414	53538	Jefferson	10	2-85
Fort Benton*	MT	406	59442	Chouteau	1	2-46

Bold = Over 15,000......ALL CAPS = STATE CAPITAL......* = County Seat......# = Changes to 510 in 9/91..... ## = Changes to 410 in 11/91......(+) = City located in addional counties......NAV= Population not available......C.H.= Court House......(IC) = Independent City

CITY	STATE	AREA CODE	ZIP CODE	COUNTY	POPULATION (in thousands)	MAP PAGE
Fort Bragg	CA	707	95437	Mendocino	5	2-8
Fort Branch	IN	812	47648	Gibson	3	2-23
Fort Collins*	CO	303	80521-26	Larimer	77	2-10&11
Fort Davis*	TX	915	79734	Jeff Davis	1	2-74&75
Fort Dodge*	IA	515	50501	Webster	28	2-24&25
Fort Edward	NY	518	12828	Washington	4	2-55
Fort Fairfield	ME	207	04742	Aroostook	4	2-32&33
Fort Gaines*	GA	912	31751	Clay	1	2-16&17
Fort Kent	ME	207	04743	Aroostook	5	2-32&33
Fort Knox	KY	502	40121	Hardin/Meade	31	2-28&29
Fort Lauderdale*	FL	305	33301-99	Broward	155	2-15
Fort Lee	NJ	201	07024	Bergen	33	2-52
Fort Lupton	CO	303	80621	Weld	4	2-10&11
Fort Madison*	IA	319	52627	Lee	13	2-25
Fort McKinley	OH	513	45426	Montgomery	10	2-61
Fort Meade	FL	813	33841	Polk	5	2-14&15
Fort Mill	SC	803	29715	York	4	2-70
Fort Mitchell	KY	606	41017	Kenton	7	2-29
Fort Morgan*	CO	303	80701	Morgan	9	2-10&11
Fort Myers*	FL	813	33901-19	Lee	41	2-14&15
Fort Oglethorpe	GA	404	30742	Catoosa/Walker	6	2-16
Fort Payne*	AL	205	35967	De Kalb	11	2-2&3
Fort Pierce*	FL	407	34945-88	St. Lucie	38	2-14&15
Fort Pierre*	SD	605	57532	Stanley	1	2-71
Fort Plain	NY	518	13339	Montgomery	3	2-55
Fort Scott*	KS	316	66701	Bourbon	9	2-26&27
Fort Shawnee	OH	419	45806	Allen	5	2-60
Fort Smith*	AR	501	72901-17	Sebastian	75	2-6
Fort Stockton*	TX	915	79735	Pecos	9	2-74&75
Fort Sumner*	NM	505	88119	De Baca	1	2-53
Fort Thomas	KY	606	41075	Campbell	16	2-29
Fort Valley*	GA	912	31030	Peach	9	2-16&17
Fort Walton Beach	FL	904	32548-49	Okaloosa	24	2-14
Fort Wayne*	IN	219	46801-99	Allen	171	2-22
Fort Worth*	TX	817	76101-99	Tarrant	414	2-74
Fort Wright	KY	606	41011	Kenton	49	2-29
Fort Yates*	ND	701	58538	Sioux	1	2-57
Fort Yukon	AK	907	99740	Yukon-Koyukuk	1	2-4
Fortuna	CA	707	95540	Humboldt	8	2-8
Forty Fort	PA	717	18704	Luzerne	6	2-67
Fossil*	OR	503	97830	Wheeler	1	2-63
Foster	RI	401	02825	Providence	3	2-69
Foster City	CA	415	94404	San Mateo	26	2-7
Fostoria	OH	419	44830	Hancock (+2)	15	2-60
Fountain	CO	719	80817	El Paso	8	2-11
Fountain Hill	PA	215	18015	Lehigh	5	2-67
Fountain Inn	SC	803	29644	Greenville (+1)	4	2-70
Fountain Place	LA	504	70811	East Baton Rouge	9	2-31

Bold = Over 15,000......ALL CAPS = STATE CAPITAL......* = County Seat......# = Changes to 510 in 9/91.....## = Changes to 410 in 11/91.....(+) = City located in additional counties......NAV = Population not available......C.H.= Court House......(IC)=Independent City

CITY	STATE	AREA CODE	ZIP CODE	COUNTY	POPULATION (in thousands)	MAP PAGE
Fountain Valley	CA	714	92708	Orange	55	2-7
Fowler*	IN	317	47944	Benton	2	2-22&23
Fox Chapel	PA	412	15238	Allegheny	5	2-68
Fox Lake	IL	708	60020	Lake/McHenry	7	2-20
Fox Point	WI	414	53217	Milwaukee	7	2-85
Fox River Grove	IL	708	60021	McHenry	3	2-20
Foxborough	MA	508	02035	Norfolk	15	2-36&37
Frackville	PA	717	17931	Schuylkill	5	2-67
Framingham	MA	508	01701	Middlesex	65	2-36&37
Frankenmuth	MI	517	48734	Saginaw	4	2-38&39
Frankfort	IL	815	60423	Will	4	2-20
Frankfort*	IN	317	46041	Clinton	15	2-22&23
FRANKFORT*	KY	502	40601-22	Franklin	26	2-28&29
Frankfort	NY	315	13340	Herkimer	3	2-54&55
Franklin*	GA	404	30217	Heard	1	2-16&17
Franklin*	IN	317	46131	Johnson	12	2-22&23
Franklin*	KY	502	42134-35	Simpson	8	2-28&29
Franklin*	LA	318	70538	St Mary	9	2-30
Franklin	MA	508	02038	Norfolk	18	2-36&37
Franklin	MI	313	48025	Oakland	3	2-39
Franklin*	NC	704	28734	Macon	1	2-58
Franklin	NH	603	03235	Merrimack	8	2-49
Franklin	NJ	201	07416	Sussex	5	2-50
Franklin*	NE	308	68939	Franklin	1	2-47
Franklin	OH	513	45005	Warren	10	2-61
Franklin*	PA	814	16323	Venango	8	2-66
Franklin*	TN	615	37064-65	Williamson	18	2-72&73
Franklin	VA	804	23851	(IC)	7	2-78&79
Franklin*	TX	409	77856	Robertson	1	2-75
Franklin	WI	414	53132	Milwaukee	17	2-85
Franklin*	WV	304	26807	Pendleton	1	2-82
Franklin Lakes	NJ	201	07417	Bergen	9	2-52
Franklin Park	IL	708	60131	Cook	18	2-19
Franklin Park	NY	315	13057	Onondaga	3	2-54&55
Franklin Park	PA	412	15143	Allegheny	6	2-68
Franklinton*	LA	504	70438	Washington	4	2-30&31
Frederick*	MD	301	21701	Frederick	34	2-34&35
Frederick*	OK	405	73542	Tillman	5	2-64&65
Fredericksburg	VA	703	22401-05	(IC)	19	2-79
Fredericksburg*	TX	512	78624	Gillespie	7	2-75
Fredericktown*	MO	314	63645	Madison	4	2-44&45
Fredonia	NY	716	14063	Chautauqua	11	2-54
Fredonia*	KS	316	66736	Wilson	3	2-26&27
Freeburg	IL	618	62243	St. Clair	3	2-21
Freehold*	NJ	201	07728	Monmouth	21	2-50
Freeland	PA	717	18224	Luzerne	4	2-67
Freeport*	IL	815	61032	Stephenson	26	2-20
Freeport	ME	207	04032	Cumberland	6	2-32&33

Bold = Over 15,000......ALL CAPS = STATE CAPITAL......* = County Seat......# = Changes to 510 in 9/91..... ## = Changes to 410 in 11/91......(+) = City located in addional counties......NAV= Population not available......C.H.= Court House......(IC) = Independent City

CITY	STATE	AREA CODE	ZIP CODE	COUNTY	POPULATION (in thousands)	MAP PAGE
Freeport	NY	516	11520	Nassau	40	2-56
Freeport	TX	409	77541	Brazoria	14	2-75
Freer	TX	512	78357	Duval	18	2-75
Freetown	MA	508	02702	Bristol	8	2-36&37
Fremont	CA	415	94536-39	Alameda	153	2-7
Fremont	MI	616	49412	Newaygo	4	2-38&39
Fremont*	NE	402	68025	Dodge	24	2-47
Fremont*	OH	419	43420	Sandusky	17	2-60
Frenchburg*	KY	606	40322	Menifee	1	2-29
Fresno*	CA	209	93701-99	Fresno	284	2-8&9
Friday Harbor*	WA	206	98250	San Juan	1	2-80
Fridley	MN	612	55432	Anoka	30	2-41
Friendship*	WI	608	53934	Adams	1	2-85
Friendswood	TX	713	77546	Galveston (+1)	22	2-74&75
Friona	TX	806	79035	Parmer	3	2-74
Frisco	TX	214	75034	Collin/Denton	4	2-74
Front Royal*	VA	703	22630	Warren	11	2-78&79
Frontenac	MO	314	63131	St. Louis	3	2-44&45
Frostburg	MD	301	21532	Allegany	8	2-34&35
Frostproof	FL	813	33843	Polk	3	2-14&15
Fruit Heights	UT	801	84037	Davis	3	2-76
Fruita	CO	303	81521	Mesa	3	2-10&11
Fruitland	MD	301	21826	Wicomico	3	2-34&35
Fruitland Park	FL	904	34731	Lake	2	2-14
Fruitville	FL	813	34232	Sarasota	3	2-14&15
Fryeburg	ME	207	04037	Oxford	3	2-32&33
Fullerton	CA	714	92631-35	Orange	108	2-7
Fullerton*	NE	308	68638	Nance	1	2-47
Fulton	IL	815	61252	Whiteside	4	2-20
Fulton	KY	502	42041	Fulton	3	2-28&29
Fulton*	MO	314	65251	Callaway	10	2-44&45
Fulton*	MS	601	38843	Itawamba	3	2-42&43
Fulton	NY	315	13069	Oswego	13	2-54&55
Fultondale	AL	205	35068	Jefferson	6	2-2&3
Fuquay-Varina	NC	919	27526	Wake	3	2-58&59
Gadsden*	AL	205	35901-05	Etowah	46	2-2&3
Gaffney*	SC	803	29340-42	Cherokee	13	2-70
Gahanna	OH	614	43230	Franklin	18	2-61
Gail*	TX	915	79738	Bordon	1	2-74&75
Gainesboro*	TN	615	38562	Jackson	1	2-72&73
Gainesville*	FL	904	32601-13	Alachua	85	2-14
Gainesville*	GA	404	30501-06	Hall	16	2-16&17
Gainesville*	MO	417	65655	Ozark	1	2-44
Gainesville*	TX	817	76240	Cooke	14	2-74
Gaithersburg	MD	301	20877-79	Montgomery	31	2-34&35
Galax	VA	703	24333	(IC)	7	2-78&79
Galena	AK	907	99741	Yukon-Koyukuk	1	2-4
Galena*	IL	815	61036	Jo Daviess	4	2-20

Bold = Over 15,000......ALL CAPS = STATE CAPITAL......* = County Seat......# = Changes to 510 in 9/91.....## = Changes to 410 in 11/91.....(+) = City located in additional counties......NAV = Population not available......C.H.= Court House......(IC)=Independent City

CITY	STATE	AREA CODE	ZIP CODE	COUNTY	POPULATION (in thousands)	MAP PAGE
Galena	KS	316	66739	Cherokee	4	2-26&27
Galena*	MO	417	65656	Stone	1	2-44
Galena Park	TX	713	77547	Harris	10	2-74&75
Galesburg*	IL	309	61401-02	Knox	33	2-20
Galion	OH	419	44833	Crawford	12	2-60
Gallatin*	MO	816	64640	Daviess	1	2-44
Gallatin*	TN	615	37066	Sumner	19	2-72&73
Gallipolis*	OH	614	45631	Gallia	4	2-61
Galloway	NJ	609	08213	Atlantic	12	2-51
Gallup*	NM	505	87301-10	McKinley	22	2-53
Galt	CA	209	95632	Sacramento	6	2-8&9
Galva	IL	309	61434	Henry	3	2-20
Galveston*	TX	409	77550-54	Galveston	62	2-75
Gamewell	NC	704	28645	Caldwell	3	2-58
Gann Valley*	SD	605	57341	Buffalo	1	2-71
Garden City	GA	912	31408	Chatham	7	2-16&17
Garden City	ID	208	83704	Ada	4	2-18
Garden City*	KS	316	67846	Finney	22	2-26&27
Garden City	MI	313	48135	Wayne	5	2-39
Garden City	NY	516	11530	Nassau	23	2-56
Garden City*	TX	915	79739	Glasscock	1	2-74&75
Garden Grove	CA	714	92640-45	Orange	134	2-7
Gardena	CA	213	90247-49	Los Angeles	49	2-7
Gardendale	AL	205	35071	Jefferson	8	2-2&3
Gardiner	ME	207	04345	Kennebec	6	2-32&33
Gardner	MA	508	01440	Worcester	18	2-36&37
Garfield	NJ	201	07026	Bergen	26	2-52
Garfield Heights	OH	216	44125	Cuyahoga	33	2-62
Garland	TX	214	75040-48	Dallas (+2)	169	2-74
Garner	NC	919	27529	Wake	10	2-58&59
Garner*	IA	515	50438	Hancock	3	2-24&25
Garrett	IN	219	46738	De Kalb	5	2-22
Garnett*	KS	913	66032	Anderson	3	2-26&27
Garwood	NJ	908	07027	Union	5	2-52
Gary	IN	219	46401-99	Lake	143	2-22
Gas City	IN	317	46933	Grant	6	2-22&23
Gastonia*	NC	704	28052-55	Gaston	52	2-58
Gate City*	VA	703	24251	Scott	1	2-78&79
Gates	NY	716	14624	Monroe	30	2-54
Gatesville*	NC	919	27938	Gates	1	2-58&59
Gatesville*	TX	817	76528	Coryell	6	2-74
Gatlinburg	TN	615	37738	Sevier	4	2-72&73
Gautier	MS	601	39553	Jackson	10	2-42&43
Gaylord*	MI	517	49735	Otsego	3	2-38&39
Gaylord*	MN	612	55334	Sibley	2	2-41
Geistown	PA	814	15904	Cambria	3	2-66
Geneseo	IL	309	61254	Henry	6	2-20
Geneseo*	NY	716	14454	Livingston	7	2-54

Bold = Over 15,000......ALL CAPS = STATE CAPITAL......* = County Seat......# = Changes to 510 in 9/91..... ## = Changes to 410 in 11/91......(+) = City located in addional counties......NAV= Population not available......C.H.= Court House......(IC) = Independent City

CITY	STATE	AREA CODE	ZIP CODE	COUNTY	POPULATION (in thousands)	MAP PAGE
Geneva*	AL	205	36340	Geneva	5	2-2&3
Geneva*	IL	708	60134	Kane	10	2-19
Geneva*	NE	402	68361	Fillmore	3	2-47
Geneva	NY	315	14456	Ontario (+1)	15	2-54&55
Geneva	OH	216	44041	Ashtabula	6	2-60
Genoa	IL	815	60135	De Kalb	3	2-20
George West*	TX	512	78022	Live Oak	3	2-75
Georgetown*	CO	303	80444	Clear Creek	1	2-10&11
Georgetown*	DE	302	19947	Sussex	2	2-35
Georgetown*	GA	912	31754	Quitman	1	2-16&17
Georgetown	IL	217	61846	Vermilion	4	2-20&21
Georgetown*	KY	502	40324	Scott	10	2-28&29
Georgetown	MA	508	01833	Essex	2	2-36&37
Georgetown*	OH	513	45121	Brown	3	2-61
Georgetown*	SC	803	29440	Georgetown	10	2-70
Georgetown*	TX	512	78626-28	Williamson	12	2-75
Georgia	VT	802	05478	Franklin	3	2-77
Gering*	NE	308	69341	Scotts Bluff	8	2-47
Germantown	OH	513	45327	Montgomery	5	2-61
Germantown	TN	901	38138	Shelby	31	2-72
Germantown	WI	414	53022	Washington	11	2-85
Gettysburg*	PA	717	17325	Adams	8	2-67
Gettysburg*	SD	605	57442	Potter	1	2-71
Gibbsboro	NJ	609	08026	Camden	3	2-51
Gibbstown	NJ	609	08027	Gloucester	5	2-51
Gibraltar	MI	313	48173	Wayne	5	2-39
Gibson City	IL	217	60936	Ford	3	2-20&21
Gibson*	GA	404	30810	Glascock	1	2-16&17
Gibsonton	FL	813	33534	Hillsborough	4	2-14&15
Gibsonville	NC	919	27249	Alamance (+1)	3	2-58
Giddings*	TX	409	78942	Lee	4	2-75
Gifford	FL	407	32960	Indian River	6	2-14&15
Gilbert	AZ	602	85234	Maricopa	7	2-5
Gilbert	MN	218	55741	St. Louis	3	2-40
Gilford	NH	603	03246	Belknap	5	2-49
Gilford Park	NJ	908	08753	Ocean	5	2-50&51
Gillespie	IL	217	62033	Macoupin	4	2-20&21
Gillette*	WY	307	82716-17	Campbell	23	2-83
Gilmer*	TX	903	75644	Upshur	5	2-74
Gilroy	CA	408	95020-21	Santa Clara	27	2-7
Girard*	KS	316	66743	Crawford	2	2-26&27
Girard	OH	216	44420	Trumbull	12	2-60
Girard	PA	814	16417	Erie	3	2-66
Gladewater	TX	903	75647	Gregg (+1)	7	2-74
Gladstone	MI	906	49837	Delta	5	2-38
Gladstone	MO	816	64118	Clay	26	2-44
Gladstone	OR	503	97027	Clackamas	10	2-63
Gladwin*	MI	517	48624	Gladwin	3	2-38&39

Bold = Over 15,000......ALL CAPS = STATE CAPITAL......* = County Seat......# = Changes to 510 in 9/91.....## = Changes to 410 in 11/91.....(+) = City located in additional counties......NAV = Population not available......C.H.= Court House......(IC)=Independent City

CITY	STATE	AREA CODE	ZIP CODE	COUNTY	POPULATION (in thousands)	MAP PAGE
Glasgow*	KY	502	42141-42	Barren	13	2-28&29
Glasgow*	MT	406	59230	Valley	3	2-46
Glassboro	NJ	609	08028	Gloucester	14	2-51
Glassport	PA	412	15045	Allegheny	6	2-68
Glastonbury	CT	203	06033	Hartford	7	2-12&13
Glen Burnie	MD	301##	21061-32	A. Arundel	31	2-34&35
Glen Burnie Pk	MD	301##	21061	Anne Arundel	31	2-35
Glen Carbon	IL	618	62034	Madison	6	2-21
Glen Cove	NY	516	11542	Nassau	25	2-56
Glen Ellyn	IL	708	60137	Du Page	25	2-19
Glen Head	NY	516	11545	Nassau	7	2-56
Glen Ridge	NJ	201	07028	Essex	8	2-52
Glen Rock	NJ	201	07452	Bergen	12	2-52
Glen Rose*	TX	817	76043	Somervell	1	2-74
Glenarden	MD	301	20706	Prince Georges	5	2-34&35
Glencoe	AL	205	35905	Etowah (+1)	5	2-2&3
Glencoe	IL	708	60022	Cook	9	2-19
Glencoe*	MN	612	55336	McLeod	4	2-41
Glendale	AZ	602	85301-12	Maricopa	129	2-5
Glendale	CA	818	91201-99	Los Angeles	153	2-7
Glendale	CO	303	80222	Arapahoe	2	2-10&11
Glendale	MO	314	63122	St. Louis	6	2-44&45
Glendale	WI	414	53209	Milwaukee	14	2-85
Glendale Heights	IL	708	60137	Du Page	24	2-19
Glendive*	MT	406	59330	Dawson	5	2-46
Glendora	CA	818	91740	Los Angeles	41	2-7
Glendora	NJ	609	08029	Camden	5	2-51
Glennville	GA	912	30427	Tattnall	4	2-16&17
Glenolden	PA	215	19036	Delaware	7	2-68
Glenpool	OK	918	74033	Tulsa	3	2-65
Glenrock	WY	307	82637	Converse	2	2-83
Glens Falls	NY	518	12801	Warren	16	2-55
Glenview	IL	708	60025	Cook	34	2-19
Glenville*	WV	304	26351	Gilmer	1	2-82
Glenwood*	IA	712	51534	Mills	6	2-24
Glenwood	IL	708	60425	Cook	10	2-19
Glenwood*	MN	612	56334	Pope	3	2-41
Glenwood	PA	717	17109	Dauphin	3	2-67
Glenwood Springs*	CO	303	81601	Garfield	5	2-10&11
Globe*	AZ	602	85501-02	Gila	7	2-5
Glocester	RI	401	02814	Providence	7	2-69
Gloucester	MA	508	01930-31	Essex	29	2-36&37
Gloucester	NJ	609	08012	Camden	14	2-51
Gloucester*	VA	804	23061	Gloucester	1	2-78&79
Gloversville	NY	518	12078	Fulton	18	2-55
Godfrey	IL	618	62035	Madison	3	2-21
Goffstown	NH	603	03045	Hillsborough	11	2-49
Golconda*	IL	618	62938	Pope	1	2-21

Bold = Over 15,000......ALL CAPS = STATE CAPITAL......* = County Seat......# = Changes to 510 in 9/91..... ## = Changes to 410 in 11/91......(+) = City located in addional counties......NAV= Population not available......C.H.= Court House......(IC) = Independent City

CITY	STATE	AREA CODE	ZIP CODE	COUNTY	POPULATION (in thousands)	MAP PAGE
Gold Beach*	OR	503	97444	Curry	1	2-63
Golden*	CO	303	80401-19	Jefferson	12	2-10&11
Golden Valley	MN	612	55427	Hennepin	24	2-41
Goldendale*	WA	509	98620	Klickitat	4	2-81
Goldfield*	NV	702	89013	Esmeralda	1	2-48
Goldsboro*	NC	919	27530-34	Wayne	34	2-58&59
Goldthwaite*	TX	915	76844	Mills	1	2-74&75
Goleta	CA	805	93116	Santa Barbara	27	2-9
Golf Manor*	OH	513	45237	Hamilton	4	2-62
Goliad*	TX	512	77963	Goliad	1	2-75
Gonzales	CA	408	93926	Monterey	3	2-9
Gonzales	LA	504	70737	Ascension	7	2-30&31
Gonzales*	TX	512	78629	Gonzales	2	2-75
Goochland*	VA	804	23063	Goochland	1	2-78&79
Gooding*	ID	208	83330	Gooding	3	2-18
Goodland*	KS	913	67735	Sherman	2	2-26&27
Goodlettsville	TN	615	37072	Davidson (+1)	10	2-72
Goodview	MN	507	55987	Winona	3	2-41
Goodyear	AZ	602	85338	Maricopa	3	2-5
Goose Creek	SC	803	29445	Berkeley	17	2-70
Gordon	GA	912	31031	Wilkinson	3	2-16&17
Gorham	ME	207	04038	Cumberland	4	2-32&33
Gorham	NH	603	03581	Coos	3	2-49
Goshen*	IN	219	46526	Elkhart	21	2-22
Goshen*	NY	914	10924	Orange	5	2-56
Gosnell	AR	501	72319	Mississippi	4	2-6
Gothenburg	NE	308	69138	Dawson	3	2-47
Gouverneur	NY	315	13642	St. Lawrence	4	2-54&55
Gove*	KS	913	67736	Gove	1	2-26&27
Gowanda	NY	716	14070	Cattaraugus (+1)	3	2-54
Graceville	FL	904	32440	Jackson	3	2-14
Grafton	MA	508	01519	Worcester	11	2-36&37
Grafton*	ND	701	58237	Walsh	5	2-57
Grafton	WI	414	53024	Ozaukee	8	2-85
Grafton*	WV	304	26354	Taylor	6	2-82
Graham*	NC	919	27253	Alamance	8	2-58&59
Graham*	TX	817	76046	Young	9	2-74
Grambling	LA	318	71245	Lincoln	4	2-30
Gramercy	LA	504	70052	St. James	3	2-30&31
Granbury*	TX	817	76048	Hood	5	2-74
Granby	CT	203	06035	Hartford	8	2-12&13
Granby	MA	413	01033	Hampshire	5	2-36
Grand Bay	AL	205	36541	Mobile	3	2-2&3
Grand Blanc	MI	313	48439	Genesee	7	2-39
Grand Forks*	ND	701	58201-07	Grand Forks	45	2-57
Grand Haven*	MI	616	49417	Ottawa	12	2-38&39
Grand Island	NY	716	14072	Erie	17	2-54
Grand Island*	NE	308	68801-03	Hall	40	2-47

Bold = Over 15,000......ALL CAPS = STATE CAPITAL......* = County Seat......# = Changes to 510 in 9/91.....## = Changes to 410 in 11/91.....(+) = City located in additional counties......NAV = Population not available......C.H. = Court House......(IC)=Independent City

CITY	STATE	AREA CODE	ZIP CODE	COUNTY	POPULATION (in thousands)	MAP PAGE
Grand Junction*	CO	303	81501-06	Mesa	32	2-10&11
Grand Ledge	MI	517	48837	Eaton	7	2-38&39
Grand Marais*	MN	218	55604	Cook	1	2-40
Grand Prairie	TX	214	75050-53	Dallas (+2)	91	2-74
Grand Rapids*	MI	616	49501-99	Kent	186	2-38&39
Grand Rapids*	MN	218	55744	Itasca	7	2-40
Grand Saline	TX	903	75140	Van Zandt	3	2-74
Grand Terrace	CA	714	92324	San Bernardino	10	2-9
Grandview	MO	816	64030	Jackson	25	2-44
Grandview	WA	509	98930	Yakima	6	2-81
Grandview Heights	OH	614	43212	Franklin	7	2-61
Grandville	MI	616	49418	Kent	12	2-38&39
Grangeville*	ID	208	83530-31	Idaho	1	2-18
Granite City	IL	618	62040	Madison	36	2-21
Granite Falls	NC	704	28630	Caldwell	3	2-58
Granite Falls*	MN	612	56241	Yellow Medicine	3	2-41
Grant City*	MO	816	64456	Worth	1	2-44
Grant*	NE	308	69140	Perkins	1	2-47
Grants*	NM	505	87020	Cibola	12	2-53
Grants Pass*	OR	503	97526-27	Josephine	17	2-63
Grantsburg*	WI	715	54840	Burnett	1	2-84&85
Grantsville	UT	801	84029	Tooele	4	2-76
Grantsville*	WV	304	26147	Calhoun	1	2-82
Granville	NY	518	12832	Washington	3	2-55
Granville	OH	614	43023	Licking	4	2-61
Grapevine	TX	817	76051	Dallas (+1)	7	2-74
Grass Valley	CA	916	95945-46	Nevada	9	2-8
Gravel Ridge	AR	501	72075 &06	Pulaski	4	2-6
Gray	ME	207	04039	Cumberland	5	2-32&33
Gray*	GA	912	31032	Jones	1	2-16&17
Grayling*	MI	517	49738	Crawford	1	2-38&39
Graylyn Crest	DE	302	19810	New Castle	5	2-35
Grayslake	IL	708	60030	Lake	6	2-20
Grayson*	KY	606	41143	Carter	3	2-29
Graysville	AL	205	35073	Jefferson	3	2-2&3
Great Barrington	MA	413	01230	Berkshire	4	2-36
Great Bend*	KS	316	67530	Barton	16	2-26&27
Great Falls	SC	803	29055	Chester	3	2-70
Great Falls*	MT	406	59401-06	Cascade	57	2-46
Great Neck	NY	516	11020-27	Nassau	9	2-56
Great Neck Estates	NY	516	11021	Nassau	3	2-56
Greece	NY	716	14616	Monroe	16	2-54
Greeley*	CO	303	80631-39	Weld	57	2-10&11
Greeley*	NE	308	68842	Greeley	1	2-47
Green Bay*	WI	414	54301-99	Brown	93	2-85
Green Cove Springs*	FL	904	32043	Clay	4	2-14
Green Haven	MD	301##	21122	Anne Arundel	4	2-34&35
Green Island	NY	518	12183	Albany	3	2-55

Bold = Over 15,000......ALL CAPS = STATE CAPITAL......* = County Seat......# = Changes to 510 in 9/91..... ## = Changes to 410 in 11/91......(+) = City located in addional counties......NAV= Population not available......C.H.= Court House......(IC) = Independent City

CITY	STATE	AREA CODE	ZIP CODE	COUNTY	POPULATION (in thousands)	MAP PAGE
Green Knoll	NJ	908	08876	Somerset	5	2-50
Green Lake*	WI	414	54941	Green Lake	1	2-85
Green River*	WY	307	82935	Sweetwater	14	2-83
Green Rock	IL	309	61241	Henry	3	2-20
Green Tree	PA	412	15220	Allegheny	6	2-68
Greenacres	WA	509	99016	Spokane	4	2-81
Greenacres City	FL	407	33463	Palm Beach	9	2-15
Greenbelt	MD	301	20770	Prince Georges	17	2-35
Greenbrae	CA	415	94904	Marin	3	2-7
Greencastle*	IN	317	46135	Putnam	8	2-22&23
Greencastle	PA	717	17225	Franklin	4	2-67
Greendale	IN	812	47025	Dearborn	4	2-23
Greendale	WI	414	53129	Milwaukee	16	2-85
Greene	ME	207	04236	Androscoggin	3	2-32&33
Greeneville*	TN	615	37743-44	Greene	14	2-72&73
Greenfield	CA	408	93927	Monterey	5	2-9
Greenfield*	IA	515	50849	Adair	2	2-24&25
Greenfield*	IN	317	46140	Hancock	11	2-22&23
Greenfield	OH	513	45123	Highland	5	2-62
Greenfield*	MA	413	01301-02	Franklin	17	2-36
Greenfield*	MO	417	65661	Dade	1	2-44
Greenfield	WI	414	53220	Milwaukee	32	2-85
Greenhills	OH	513	45218	Hamilton	5	2-62
Greenlawn	NY	516	11740	Suffolk	14	2-56
Greensboro*	AL	205	36744	Hale	3	2-2&3
Greensboro*	GA	404	30642	Greene	3	2-16&17
Greensboro*	NC	919	27401-99	Guilford	159	2-58&59
Greensburg*	IN	812	47240	Decatur	9	2-23
Greensburg*	KS	316	67054	Kiowa	2	2-26&27
Greensburg*	KY	502	42743	Green	2	2-28&29
Greensburg*	LA	504	70441	St. Helena	1	2-30&31
Greensburg*	PA	412	15601	Westmoreland	16	2-68
Greenup*	KY	606	41144	Greenup	1	2-29
Greenvale	NY	914	11548	Westchester	9	2-56
Greenville*	AL	205	36037	Butler	7	2-2&3
Greenville*	GA	404	30222	Meriwether	1	2-16&17
Greenville*	IL	618	62246	Bond	6	2-21
Greenville*	KY	502	42345	Muhlenberg	4	2-28&29
Greenville	MI	616	48838	Montcalm	8	2-38&39
Greenville*	MO	314	63944	Wayne	1	2-44&45
Greenville*	MS	601	38701-04	Washington	70	2-42&43
Greenville*	NC	919	27834-36	Pitt	38	2-58&59
Greenville*	OH	513	45331	Darke	12	2-61
Greenville	PA	412	16125	Mercer	8	2-66
Greenville*	SC	803	29601-16	Greenville	57	2-70
Greenville*	TX	903	75401	Hunt	24	2-74
Greenwich	CT	203	06830-36	Fairfield	60	2-12&13
Greenwich	NY	518	12834	Washington	4	2-55

Bold = Over 15,000......ALL CAPS = STATE CAPITAL......* = County Seat......# = Changes to 510 in 9/91.....## = Changes to 410 in 11/91.....(+) = City located in additional counties......NAV = Population not available......C.H.= Court House......(IC)=Independent City

CITY	STATE	AREA CODE	ZIP CODE	COUNTY	POPULATION (in thousands)	MAP PAGE
Greenwood	AR	501	72936+49	Sebastian	4	2-6
Greenwood	IN	317	46142-43	Johnson	23	2-22&23
Greenwood*	MS	601	38930	Leflore	20	2-42&43
Greenwood*	SC	803	29646-49	Greenwood	22	2-70
Greenwood Lake	NY	914	10925	Orange	3	2-56
Greenwood Village	CO	303	80121	Arapahoe	6	2-10&11
Greenwood Village	TX	713	77093	Harris	3	2-74&75
Greer	SC	803	29650-52	Greenville (+1)	11	2-70
Gregory	TX	512	78359	San Patricio	3	2-75
Grenada*	MS	601	38901	Grenada	10	2-42&43
Gresham	OR	503	97030	Multnomah	38	2-63
Gretna*	LA	504	70053-54	Jefferson	20	2-30&31
Gridley	CA	916	95948	Butte	4	2-8
Griffin*	GA	404	30223-24	Spalding	23	2-16&17
Griffith	IN	219	46319	Lake	17	2-22
Grinnell	IA	515	50112	Poweshiek	9	2-24&25
Griswold	CT	203	06351	New London	9	2-12&13
Groesbeck*	TX	817	76642	Limestone	3	2-74
Grosse Ille	MI	313	48138	Wayne	9	2-39
Grosse Pointe	MI	313	48225	Wayne	6	2-39
Groton	CT	203	06340-49	New London	10	2-12&13
Groton	MA	508	01450	Middlesex	6	2-36&37
Grove	OK	918	74344	Delaware	3	2-65
Grove City	OH	614	43123	Franklin	17	2-61
Grove City	PA	412	16127	Mercer	9	2-66
Grove Hill*	AL	205	36451	Clarke	1	2-2&3
Groveland	MA	508	01834	Essex	5	2-36&37
Groveport	OH	614	43125	Franklin	3	2-61
Grover City	CA	805	93433	San Luis Obispo	10	2-9
Groves	TX	409	77619	Jefferson	17	2-75
Groveton	VA	703	22303 &06	Fairfax	6	2-78&79
Groveton Gardens	VA	703	22303	Fairfax	3	2-78&79
Grovetown	GA	404	30813	Columbia	3	2-16&17
Groveton*	TX	409	75845	Trinity	1	2-75
Grundy Center*	IA	319	50638	Grundy	3	2-25
Grundy*	VA	703	24614	Buchanan	1	2-78&79
Guadalupe	AZ	602	85283	Maricopa	5	2-5
Guadalupe	CA	805	93434	San Luis Obispo	4	2-9
Guildhall*	VT	802	05905	Essex	1	2-77
Guilford	CT	203	06437	New Haven	17	2-12&13
Guilford	ME	207	04443	Piscataquis	2	2-32&33
Gulf Breeze	FL	904	32561-62	Santa Rosa	5	2-14
Gulfport	FL	813	33707	Pinellas	11	2-14&15
Gulfport*	MS	601	39501-07	Harrison	43	2-42&43
Gunnison*	CO	303	81230	Gunnison	6	2-10&11
Guntersville*	AL	205	35976	Marshall	7	2-2&3
Gurdon	AR	501	71743	Clark	3	2-6
Gurnee	IL	708	60031	Lake	9	2-20

Bold = Over 15,000......ALL CAPS = STATE CAPITAL......* = County Seat......# = Changes to 510 in 9/91..... ## = Changes to 410 in 11/91......(+)
= City located in addional counties......NAV= Population not available......C.H.= Court House......(IC) = Independent City

CITY	STATE	AREA CODE	ZIP CODE	COUNTY	POPULATION (in thousands)	MAP PAGE
Gustine	CA	209	95322	Merced	3	2-8&9
Guthrie*	OK	405	73044	Logan	12	2-64&65
Guthrie*	TX	806	79236	King	1	2-74
Guthrie Center*	IA	515	50115	Guthrie	11	2-24&25
Guttenberg	NJ	201	07093	Hudson	7	2-52
Guymon*	OK	405	73942	Texas	8	2-64&65
Hacienda Heights	CA	818	91745	Los Angeles	52	2-7
Hackensack*	NJ	201	07601-08	Bergen	35	2-52
Hackettstown	NJ	908	07840	Warren	9	2-50
Haddon	NJ	609	08108	Camden	15	2-51
Haddon Heights	NJ	609	08035	Camden	9	2-51
Haddonfield	NJ	609	08033	Camden	12	2-51
Hadley	MA	413	01035	Hampshire	4	2-36
Hagerstown*	MD	301	21740-42	Washington	33	2-34&35
Hahnville*	LA	504	70057	St. Charles	2	2-30&31
Hailey*	ID	208	83333	Blaine	1	2-18
Haines City	FL	813	33844	Polk	11	2-14&15
Haledon	NJ	201	07508	Passaic	6	2-52
Hales Corners	WI	414	53130	Milwaukee	7	2-85
Haleyville	AL	205	35565	Winston	5	2-2&3
Half Hollow Hills	NY	516	11746	Suffolk	5	2-56
Half Moon Bay	CA	415	94019	San Mateo	7	2-7
Halifax	MA	617	02338	Plymouth	5	2-36&37
Halifax*	NC	919	27839	Halifax	1	2-58&59
Halifax*	VA	804	24558	Halifax	1	2-78&79
Hallandale	FL	305	33009-16	Broward (+1)	39	2-15
Hallettsville*	TX	512	77964	Lavaca	2	2-75
Hallock*	MN	218	56728	Kittson	1	2-40
Hallowell	ME	207	04347	Cumberland	4	2-32&33
Halsite	NY	516	11743	Suffolk	4	2-56
Haltom City	TX	817	76117	Tarrant	33	2-74
Ham Lake	MN	612	55304	Anoka	8	2-41
Hamburg*	AR	501	71646	Ashley	4	2-6
Hamburg	NY	716	14075	Erie	10	2-54
Hamburg	PA	215	19526	Berks	4	2-67
Hamden	CT	203	06514	New Haven	51	2-12&13
Hamilton Park	PA	717	17603	Lancaster	4	2-67
Hamilton Square	NJ	609	08690	Mercer	10	2-50
Hamilton*	AL	205	35570	Marion	6	2-2&3
Hamilton*	GA	404	31811	Harris	1	2-16&17
Hamilton	IL	217	62341	Hancock	4	2-20&21
Hamilton	MA	508	01936	Essex	7	2-36&37
Hamilton*	MT	406	59840	Ravalli	2	2-46
Hamilton	NY	315	13346	Madison	4	2-54&55
Hamilton*	OH	513	45011-15	Butler	63	2-61
Hamilton*	TX	817	76531	Hamilton	3	2-74
Hamlet	NC	919	28345	Richmond	5	2-58&59
Hamlin	TX	915	79520	Fisher (+1)	3	2-74&75

Bold = Over 15,000......ALL CAPS = STATE CAPITAL......* = County Seat......# = Changes to 510 in 9/91.....## = Changes to 410 in 11/91.....(+) = City located in additional counties......NAV = Population not available......C.H.= Court House......(IC)=Independent City

CITY	STATE	AREA CODE	ZIP CODE	COUNTY	POPULATION (in thousands)	MAP PAGE
Hamlin*	WV	304	25523	Lincoln	1	2-82
Hammond	IN	219	46320-27	Lake	90	2-22
Hammond	LA	504	70401-04	Tangipahoa	20	2-30&31
Hammonton	NJ	609	08037	Atlantic	12	2-51
Hampden	MA	413	01036	Hampden	5	2-36
Hampden	ME	207	04444	Penobscot	3	2-32&33
Hampden	PA	717	17055	Cumberland	17	2-67
Hampstead	NH	603	03841	Rockingham	3	2-49
Hampton*	AR	501	71744	Calhoun	2	2-6
Hampton*	IA	515	50441	Franklin	5	2-24&25
Hampton	NH	603	03842	Rockingham	7	2-49
Hampton*	SC	803	29924	Hampton	3	2-70
Hampton	VA	804	23661-70	(IC)	127	2-78&79
Hampton Bays	NY	516	11946	Suffolk	5	2-56
Hamtramck	MI	313	48212	Wayne	21	2-39
Hanahan	SC	803	29406	Berkeley	14	2-70
Hancock	MI	906	49930	Houghton	5	2-38
Hanford*	CA	209	93230-32	Kings	24	2-8&9
Hannibal	MO	314	63401	Marion (+1)	18	2-44&45
Hanover	IN	812	47243	Jefferson	4	2-23
Hanover	MA	617	02339	Plymouth	12	2-36&37
Hanover	NH	603	03755	Grafton	7	2-49
Hanover	NJ	201	07981	Morris	12	2-52
Hanover	PA	717	17331	York	15	2-67
Hanover*	VA	804	23069	Hanover	1	2-78&79
Hanover Park	IL	708	60103	Park (+1)	31	2-19
Hanson	MA	617	02341	Plymouth	8	2-36&37
Hapeville	GA	404	30354	Fulton	6	2-16&17
Harahan	LA	504	70123	Jefferson	12	2-30&31
Hardin*	IL	618	62047	Calhoun	1	2-21
Hardin*	MT	406	59034	Big Horn	3	2-46
Hardinsburg*	KY	502	40143	Breckinridge	2	2-28&29
Hardwick	GA	912	31034	Baldwin	8	2-16&17
Hardwick	VT	802	05843	Caledonia	3	2-77
Hardy	AR	501	72542	Sharp	1	2-6
Hardyston	NJ	201	07460	Sussex	5	2-50
Harker Heights	TX	817	76543	Bell	7	2-74
Harlan*	IA	712	51537	Shelby	5	2-24
Harlan*	KY	606	40831	Harlan	3	2-29
Harlingen	TX	512	78550-52	Cameron	54	2-75
Harlowton*	MT	406	59036	Wheatland	1	2-46
Harper Woods	MI	313	48225	Wayne	15	2-39
Harpswell	ME	207	04079	Cumberland	4	2-32&33
Harrah	OK	405	73045	Oklahoma	3	2-64&65
Harriman	TN	615	37748	Roane	8	2-72&73
Harrington	DE	302	19952	Kent	2	2-35
Harrington Park	NJ	201	07640	Bergen	5	2-52
Harris	PA	814	16827	Centre	4	2-66

Bold = Over 15,000......ALL CAPS = STATE CAPITAL......* = County Seat......# = Changes to 510 in 9/91.....## = Changes to 410 in 11/91......(+) = City located in addional counties......NAV= Population not available......C.H.= Court House......(IC) = Independent City

CITY	STATE	AREA CODE	ZIP CODE	COUNTY	POPULATION (in thousands)	MAP PAGE
Harrisburg*	AR	512	72432	Poinsett	1	2-6
Harrisburg*	IL	618	62946	Saline	10	2-21
Harrisburg*	NE	308	69345	Banner	1	2-47
HARRISBURG*	PA	717	17101-99	Dauphin	51	2-67
Harrison*	AR	501	72601-02	Boone	12	2-6
Harrison*	MI	517	48625	Clare	1	2-38&39
Harrison*	NE	308	69346	Sioux	1	2-47
Harrison	NJ	201	07029	Hudson	12	2-52
Harrison	NY	914	10528	Westchester	23	2-56
Harrison	OH	513	45030	Hamilton	6	2-62
Harrison	PA	412	15065	Allegheny	13	2-68
Harrisonburg*	LA	318	71340	Catahoula	1	2-30
Harrisonburg*	VA	703	22801	Rockingham (IC)	26	2-79
Harrisonville*	MO	816	64701	Cass	6	2-44
Harrisville*	MI	517	48741	Alcona	1	2-38&39
Harrisville*	WV	304	26362	Ritchie	1	2-82
Harrodsburg*	KY	606	40330	Mercer	7	2-29
Hart*	MI	616	49420	Oceana	1	2-38&39
Hartford	AL	205	36344	Geneva	3	2-2&3
Hartford	VT	802	05047	Windsor	8	2-77
Hartford	WI	414	53027	Washington	7	2-85
Hartford City*	IN	317	47348	Blackford	7	2-22&23
HARTFORD*	CT	203	06101-99	Hartford	138	2-12&13
Hartford*	KY	502	42347	Ohio	2	2-28&29
Hartington*	NE	402	68739	Cedar	1	2-47
Hartland	VT	802	05048	Windsor	2	2-77
Hartland	WI	414	53029	Waukesha	6	2-85
Hartsdale	NY	914	10530	Westchester	10	2-56
Hartselle	AL	205	35640	Morgan	9	2-2&3
Hartsville	SC	803	29550	Darlington	9	2-70
Hartsville*	TN	615	37074	Trousdale	2	2-72&73
Hartville*	MO	417	65667	Wright	1	2-44
Hartwell*	GA	404	30643	Hart	5	2-16&17
Harvard	IL	815	60033	McHenry	5	2-20
Harvard	MA	508	01451	Worcester	12	2-36&37
Harvey	IL	708	60426	Cook	35	2-19
Harvey	LA	504	70058	Jefferson	15	2-30&31
Harvey	ND	701	58341	Wells	2	2-57
Harwich	MA	508	02645	Barnstable	2	2-36&37
Harwinton	CT	203	06790-91	Litchfield	3	2-12&13
Harwood Heights	IL	708	60656	Cook	8	2-19
Hasbrouck Heights	NJ	201	07604	Bergen	13	2-52
Haskell*	TX	817	79521	Haskell	3	2-74
Hastings-on-Hudson	NY	914	10706	Westchester	8	2-56
Hastings*	MI	616	49058	Barry	6	2-38&39
Hastings*	MN	612	55033	Dakota (+1)	12	2-41
Hastings*	NE	402	68901-02	Adams	23	2-47
Hatboro	PA	215	19040	Montgomery	8	2-68

Bold = Over 15,000......ALL CAPS = STATE CAPITAL......* = County Seat......# = Changes to 510 in 9/91.....## = Changes to 410 in 11/91.....(+) = City located in additional counties......NAV = Population not available......C.H.= Court House......(IC)=Independent City

CITY	STATE	AREA CODE	ZIP CODE	COUNTY	POPULATION (in thousands)	MAP PAGE
Hatfield	MA	413	01038	Hampshire	3	2-36
Hatfield	PA	215	19440	Montgomery	3	2-68
Hattiesburg*	MS	601	39401-07	Forrest	40	2-42&43
Hauppauge	NY	516	11787-88	Suffolk	21	2-56
Havana	FL	904	32333	Gadsden	3	2-14
Havana*	IL	309	62644	Mason	4	2-20
Havelock	NC	919	28532	Craven	18	2-58&59
Haverford	PA	215	19083	Delaware	52	2-68
Haverhill	MA	508	01830-35	Essex	48	2-36&37
Haverhill	NH	603	03765	Grafton	3	2-49
Haverstraw	NY	914	10927	Rockland	8	2-56
Havre de Grace	MD	301##	21078	Harford	9	2-34&35
Havre*	MT	406	59501	Hill	10	2-46
Hawaiian Gardens	CA	213	90716	Los Angeles	12	2-7
Hawarden	IA	712	51023	Sioux	3	2-24
Hawesville*	KY	502	42348	Hancock	1	2-28&29
Hawkinsville*	GA	912	31036	Pulaski	5	2-16&17
Haworth	NJ	201	07641	Bergen	4	2-52
Hawthorne	CA	213	90250	Los Angeles	60	2-7
Hawthorne	NJ	201	07506	Passaic	18	2-52
Hawthorne	NY	914	10532	Westchester	5	2-56
Hawthorne*	NV	702	89415-16	Mineral	1	2-48
Hayden	ID	208	83835	Kootenai	3	2-18
Haydon	CO	303	81639	Routt	2	2-10&11
Hayes Center*	NE	308	69032	Hayes	1	2-47
Hayesville*	NC	704	28904	Clay	1	2-58
Haynesville	LA	318	71038	Claiborne	3	2-30
Hayneville*	AL	205	36040	Lowndes	1	2-2&3
Hays*	KS	913	67601	Ellis	17	2-26&27
Haysville	KS	316	67060	Sedgwick	8	2-26&27
Hayti	MO	314	63851	Pemiscot	3	2-44&45
Hayti*	SD	605	57241	Hamlin	1	2-71
Hayward	CA	415#	94540-46	Alameda	101	2-7
Hayward*	WI	715	54843	Sawyer	1	2-84&85
Hazard*	KY	606	41701	Perry	5	2-29
Hazel Crest	IL	708	60429	Cook	14	2-19
Hazel Del	WA	206	98660 &65	Clark	5	2-80
Hazel Park	MI	313	48030	Oakland	20	2-39
Hazelwood	MO	314	63042-45	St. Louis	16	2-44&45
Hazlehurst*	GA	912	31539	Jeff Davis	4	2-16&17
Hazlehurst*	MS	601	39083	Copiah	4	2-42&43
Hazlet	NJ	908	07730	Monmouth	23	2-50
Hazleton	PA	717	18201	Luzerne	26	2-67
Headland	AL	205	36345	Henry	3	2-2&3
Healdsburg	CA	707	95448	Sonoma	8	2-8
Healdton	OK	405	73438	Carter	4	2-64&65
Hearne	TX	409	77859	Robertson	5	2-75
Heath	OH	614	43056	Licking	7	2-61

Bold = Over 15,000......ALL CAPS = STATE CAPITAL......* = County Seat......# = Changes to 510 in 9/91..... ## = Changes to 410 in 11/91......(+)
= City located in addional counties......NAV= Population not available......C.H.= Court House......(IC) = Independent City

CITY	STATE	AREA CODE	ZIP CODE	COUNTY	POPULATION (in thousands)	MAP PAGE
Heathsville*	VA	804	22473	Northumberland	1	2-78&79
Heavener	OK	918	74937	Le Flore	3	2-65
Hebbronville*	TX	512	78361	Jim Hogg	1	2-75
Heber City*	UT	801	84032	Wasatch	1	2-76
Heber Springs*	AR	501	72543	Cleburne	5	2-6
Hebron	CT	203	06248	Tolland	5	2-12&13
Hebron	IN	219	46341	Porter	3	2-22
Hebron*	NE	402	68370	Thayer	1	2-47
Hedwig Village	TX	713	77024	Harris	3	2-74&75
Heflin*	AL	205	36264	Cleburne	3	2-2&3
Helena*	AR	501	72342	Phillips	10	2-6
Helena*	MT	406	59601-26	Lewis & Clark	24	2-46
Hellertown	PA	215	18055	Northampton	6	2-67
Helper	UT	801	84526	Carbon	3	2-76
Hemet	CA	714	92343-44	Riverside	26	2-9
Hemphill*	TX	409	75948	Sabine	1	2-75
Hempstead	NY	516	11550-54	Nassau	42	2-56
Hempstead*	TX	713	77445	Waller	3	2-74&75
Henderson*	KY	502	42420	Henderson	26	2-28&29
Henderson*	NC	919	27536	Vance	16	2-58&59
Henderson	NV	702	89014-16	Clark	26	2-48
Henderson*	TN	901	38340	Chester	4	2-72
Henderson*	TX	903	75652-55	Rusk	11	2-74
Hendersonville*	NC	704	28739	Henderson	8	2-58
Hendersonville	TN	615	37075	Sumner	30	2-72&73
Hennepin*	IL	815	61327	Putnam	1	2-20
Henniker	NH	603	03242	Merrimack	3	2-49
Henrietta*	TX	817	76365	Clay	3	2-74
Henry	IL	309	61537	Marshall	3	2-20
Henryetta	OK	918	74437	Okmulgee	6	2-65
Heppner*	OR	503	97836	Morrow	1	2-63
Hercules	CA	415#	94547	Contra Costa	10	2-7
Hereford*	TX	806	79045	Deaf Smith	14	2-74
Herington	KS	913	67449	Dickinson	3	2-26&27
Heritage Village	CT	203	06488	New Haven	10	2-12&13
Herkimer*	NY	315	13350	Herkimer	8	2-54&55
Hermann*	MO	314	65041	Gasconade	2	2-44&45
Hermantown	MN	218	55811	St. Louis	7	2-40
Hermiston	OR	503	97838	Umatilla	10	2-63
Hermitage	PA	412	16148	Mercer	17	2-66
Hermitage*	MO	417	65668	Hickory	1	2-44
Hermon	ME	207	04401	Penobscot	3	2-32&33
Hermosa Beach	CA	213	90254	Los Angeles	18	2-7
Hernando*	MS	601	38632	De Soto	3	2-42&43
Herndon	VA	703	22070-95	Fairfax	11	2-78&79
Herricks	NY	516	11040	Nassau	4	2-56
Herrin	IL	618	62948	Williamson	11	2-21
Hertford*	NC	919	27944	Perquimans	1	2-58&59

Bold = Over 15,000......ALL CAPS = STATE CAPITAL......* = County Seat......# = Changes to 510 in 9/91......## = Changes to 410 in 11/91.....(+) = City located in additional counties......NAV = Population not available......C.H.= Court House......(IC)=Independent City

CITY	STATE	AREA CODE	ZIP CODE	COUNTY	POPULATION (in thousands)	MAP PAGE
Hesperia	CA	619	92345	San Bernardino	14	2-9
Hesston	KS	316	67062	Harvey	3	2-26&27
Hettinger*	ND	701	58639	Adams	1	2-57
Hewitt	TX	817	76643	McLennan	5	2-74
Heyburn	ID	208	83336	Minidoka	3	2-18
Hialeah	FL	305	33010-16	Dade	167	2-15
Hialeah Gardens	FL	305	33016	Dade	3	2-15
Hiawassee*	GA	404	30546	Towns	1	2-16&17
Hiawatha	IA	319	52233	Linn	5	2-25
Hiawatha*	KS	913	66434	Brown	3	2-26&27
Hibbing	MN	218	55746-47	St. Louis	20	2-40
Hickman*	KY	502	42050	Fulton	3	2-28&29
Hickory	NC	704	28601-03	Burke (+1)	25	2-58
Hickory Hills	IL	708	60457	Cook	14	2-19
Hicksville	NY	516	11801-99	Nassau	43	2-56
Hicksville	OH	419	43526	Defiance	4	2-60
Higginsville	MO	816	64037	Lafayette	4	2-44
High Bridge	NJ	201	08829	Hunterdon	3	2-50
High Point	NC	919	27260-64	Guilford (+2)	68	2-58&59
Highland	CA	714	92346	San Bernardino	11	2-9
Highland	IL	618	62249	Madison	7	2-21
Highland	IN	219	46322	Lake	25	2-22
Highland Falls	NY	914	10928	Orange	4	2-56
Highland Heights	KY	606	41076	Campbell	4	2-29
Highland Heights	OH	216	44124	Cuyahoga	6	2-62
Highland Park	IL	708	60035	Lake	32	2-20
Highland Park	MI	313	48203	Wayne	25	2-39
Highland Park	NJ	908	08904	Middlesex	13	2-50
Highland Park	TX	214	75205	Dallas	9	2-74
Highland Springs	VA	804	23075	Henrico	8	2-78&79
Highland Village	TX	214	75067	Denton	3	2-74
Highlands	NJ	908	07732	Monmouth	5	2-50
Highmore*	SD	605	57345	Hyde	1	2-71
Highspire	PA	717	17034	Dauphin	3	2-67
Hightstown	NJ	609	08520	Mercer	5	2-50
Highwood	IL	708	60040	Lake	5	2-20
Hill City*	KS	913	67642	Graham	3	2-26&27
Hillcrest Center	CA	805	93306	Kern	25	2-9
Hilliard	OH	614	43026	Franklin	8	2-61
Hillsboro*	IL	217	62049	Montgomery	5	2-20&21
Hillsboro	KS	316	67063	Marion	3	2-26&27
Hillsboro*	MO	314	63050	Jefferson	1	2-44&45
Hillsboro*	NC	919	27278	Orange	3	2-58&59
Hillsboro*	ND	701	58045	Traill	1	2-57
Hillsboro*	OH	513	45133	Highland	6	2-62
Hillsboro*	OR	503	97123-24	Washington	30	2-63
Hillsboro*	TX	817	76645	Hill	7	2-74
Hillsborough	CA	415	94010	San Mateo	10	2-7

Bold = Over 15,000......ALL CAPS = STATE CAPITAL......* = County Seat......# = Changes to 510 in 9/91..... ## = Changes to 410 in 11/91......(+) = City located in addional counties......NAV= Population not available......C.H.= Court House......(IC) = Independent City

CITY	STATE	AREA CODE	ZIP CODE	COUNTY	POPULATION (in thousands)	MAP PAGE
Hillsborough	NH	603	03244	Hillsborough	3	2-49
Hillsdale	NJ	201	07642	Bergen	10	2-52
Hillsdale*	MI	517	49242	Hillsdale	7	2-38&39
Hillside	IL	708	60162	Cook	8	2-19
Hillside	MD	301	21157	Prince Georges	3	2-34&35
Hillside	NJ	908	07205	Union	21	2-52
Hillside Manor	NY	516	11040	Nassau	4	2-56
Hillsville*	VA	703	24343	Carroll	1	2-78&79
Hillview	KY	502	40229	Bullitt	7	2-28
Hilo*	HI	808	96720	Hawaii	42	2-19
Hilton	NY	716	14468	Monroe	4	2-54
Hilton Head Island	SC	803	29925-28	Beaufort	18	2-70
Hindman*	KY	606	41822	Knott	1	2-29
Hinesburg	VT	802	05461	Chittenden	3	2-77
Hinesville*	GA	912	31313	Liberty	11	2-16&17
Hingham	MA	617	02043	Plymouth	20	2-36&37
Hinsdale	IL	708	60521-22	Du Page (+1)	1	2-19
Hinsdale	NH	603	03451	Cheshire	4	2-49
Hinton*	WV	304	25951	Summers	3	2-82
Hitchcock	TX	409	77563	Galveston	6	2-75
Ho Ho Kus	NJ	201	07423	Bergen	4	2-52
Hobart	IN	219	46342	Lake	23	2-22
Hobart*	OK	405	73651	Kiowa	4	2-64&65
Hobbs	NM	505	88240-41	Lea	35	2-53
Hoboken	NJ	201	07030	Hudson	41	2-52
Hodgenville*	KY	502	42748	Larue	2	2-28&29
Hoffman Estates	IL	708	60196	Cook	41	2-19
Hogansville	GA	404	30230	Troup	3	2-16&17
Hohenwald*	TN	615	38462	Lewis	3	2-72&73
Hoisington	KS	316	67544	Barton	3	2-26&27
Hokendauqua	PA	215	18052	Lehigh	3	2-67
Hokes Bluff	AL	205	35903	Etowah	3	2-2&3
Holbrook*	AZ	602	86025-29	Navajo	6	2-5
Holbrook	MA	617	02343	Norfolk	11	2-36&37
Holden	MA	508	01520	Worcester	4	2-36&37
Holden	ME	207	04429	Penobscot	3	2-32&33
Holdenville*	OK	405	74848	Hughes	5	2-64&65
Holdrege*	NE	308	68949	Phelps	6	2-47
Holiday City/Berkeley	NJ	908	08753	Ocean	6	2-51
Holland	MI	616	49422-24	Allegan (+1)	30	2-38&39
Holland	PA	215	18966	Bucks	5	2-68
Hollandale	MS	601	38748	Washington	4	2-42&43
Hollidaysburg*	PA	814	16648	Blair	5	2-66
Hollin Hall Village	VA	703	22308	Fairfax	4	2-78&79
Hollis	NH	603	03049	Hillsborough	5	2-49
Hollis*	OK	405	73550	Harmon	2	2-64&65
Hollis Ctr.	ME	207	04042	York	3	2-32&33
Hollister*	CA	408	95023-24	San Benito	16	2-9

**Bold = Over 15,000......ALL CAPS = STATE CAPITAL......* = County Seat......# = Changes to 510 in 9/91.....## = Changes to 410 in 11/91.....(+) = City located in additional counties......NAV = Population not available......C.H.= Court House......(IC)=Independent City

CITY	STATE	AREA CODE	ZIP CODE	COUNTY	POPULATION (in thousands)	MAP PAGE
Holliston	MA	508	01746	Middlesex	12	2-36&37
Holly	MI	313	48442	Oakland	5	2-39
Holly Hill	FL	904	32117	Volusia	10	2-14
Holly Springs*	MS	601	38635	Marshall	8	2-42&43
Hollywood	FL	305	33020-84	Broward	127	2-15
Hollywood Park	TX	512	78232	Bexar	3	2-75
Holmdel	NJ	908	07733	Monmouth	8	2-50
Holmes Beach	FL	813	34218	Manatee	4	2-14&15
Holt	AL	205	35404	Tuscaloosa	3	2-2&3
Holton*	KS	913	66436	Jackson	3	2-26&27
Holtville	CA	619	92250	Imperial	4	2-9
Holyoke*	CO	303	80734	Phillips	1	2-10&11
Holyoke	MA	413	01040-41	Hampshire	43	2-36
Homer	AK	907	99603	Kenai Peninsula	2	2-4
Homer*	GA	404	30547	Banks	1	2-16&17
Homer*	LA	318	71040	Claiborne	4	2-30
Homer	NY	607	13077	Cortland	4	2-54&55
Homerville*	GA	912	31634	Clinch	3	2-16&17
Homestead	FL	305	33030-35	Dade	22	2-15
Homestead	PA	412	15120	Allegheny	5	2-68
Hometown	IL	708	60456	Cook	5	2-19
Homewood	AL	205	35209	Jefferson	21	2-2&3
Homewood	IL	708	60430	Cook	19	2-19
Hominy	OK	918	74035	Osage	3	2-65
Hondo*	TX	512	78861	Medina	6	2-75
Honea Path	SC	803	29654	Anderson (+1)	4	2-70
Honesdale*	PA	717	18431	Wayne	5	2-67
Honolulu*	HI	808	96801-99	Honolulu	396	2-19
Hood River*	OR	503	97031	Hood River	4	2-63
Hooksett	NH	603	03106	Merrimack	7	2-49
Hoopeston	IL	217	60942	Vermilion	6	2-20&21
Hoosick Falls	NY	518	12090	Rensselaer	4	2-55
Hoover	AL	205	35216	Jefferson (+1)	31	2-2&3
Hopatcong	NJ	201	07843	Sussex	15	2-50
Hope Mills	NC	919	28348	Cumberland	6	2-58&59
Hope*	AR	501	71801	Hemstead	10	2-6
Hopedale	MA	508	01747	Worcester	4	2-36&37
Hopewell	NJ	609	08302	Cumberland	14	2-51
Hopewell	NJ	609	08560	Mercer	10	2-50
Hopewell	VA	804	23860	(IC)	24	2-78&79
Hopkins	MN	612	55343-47	Hennepin	15	2-41
Hopkinsville*	KY	502	42240-41	Christian	27	2-28&29
Hopkinton	MA	508	01748	Middlesex	8	2-36&37
Hopkinton	NH	603	03301	Merrimack	4	2-49
Hopkinton	RI	401	02833	Washington	6	2-69
Hopwood Acres	MI	517	48912	Ingham	3	2-38&39
Hoquiam	WA	206	98550	Grays Harbor	10	2-80
Horicon	WI	414	53032	Dodge	4	2-85

Bold = Over 15,000......ALL CAPS = STATE CAPITAL......* = County Seat.....# = Changes to 510 in 9/91...... ## = Changes to 410 in 11/91......(+) = City located in addional counties......NAV= Population not available......C.H.= Court House......(IC) = Independent City

CITY	STATE	AREA CODE	ZIP CODE	COUNTY	POPULATION (in thousands)	MAP PAGE
Horn Lake	MS	601	38637	De Soto	4	2-42&43
Hornell	NY	607	14843	Steuben	10	2-54&55
Horseheads	NY	607	14844-45	Chemung	7	2-54&55
Horsham	PA	215	19044	Montgomery	15	2-68
Hot Springs*	SD	605	57747	Fall River	4	2-71
Hot Springs Ntl Pk*	AR	501	71901-14	Garland	38	2-6
Hot Sulphur Springs*	CO	303	80451	Grand	1	2-10
Houghton*	MI	906	49931	Houghton	7	2-38
Houlton*	ME	207	04730	Aroostook	6	2-32&33
Houma*	LA	504	70360-64	Terrebonne	101	2-30&31
Houston*	MO	417	65483	Texas	2	2-44
Houston*	MS	601	38851	Chickasaw	3	2-42&43
Houston*	TX	713	77001-299	Harris	1728	2-74&75
Howard*	KS	316	67349	Elk	1	2-26&27
Howard*	SD	605	57349	Miner	1	2-71
Howard	WI	414	54303	Brown	8	2-85
Howell*	MI	517	48843	Livingston	7	2-38&39
Hoxie	AR	501	72433	Lawrence	3	2-6
Hoxie*	KS	913	67740	Sheridan	2	2-26&27
Hoyt Lakes	MN	218	55750	St. Louis	3	2-40
Hubbard	OH	216	44425	Trumbull	9	2-60
Huber Heights	OH	513	45424	Montgomery	44	2-61
Hudson	MA	508	01749	Middlesex	16	2-36&37
Hudson	MI	517	49247	Lenawee	3	2-38&39
Hudson	NC	704	28638	Caldwell	3	2-58
Hudson	NH	603	03051	Hillsborough	14	2-49
Hudson*	NY	518	12534	Columbia	8	2-55
Hudson	OH	216	44236	Summit	12	2-62
Hudson*	WI	715	54016	St. Croix	5	2-84&85
Hudson Falls*	NY	518	12839	Washington	8	2-55
Hudsonville	MI	616	49426	Ottawa	5	2-38&39
Hueytown	AL	205	35023	Jefferson	16	2-2&3
Hughson	CA	209	95326	Stanislaus	3	2-8&9
Hugo*	CO	719	80821	Lincoln	1	2-11
Hugo*	OK	405	74743	Choctaw	6	2-64&65
Hugoton*	KS	316	67951	Stevens	3	2-26&27
Hugo	MN	612	55038	Washington	4	2-41
Hull	MA	617	02045	Plymouth	9	2-36&37
Humble	TX	713	77338-47	Harris	12	2-74&75
Humboldt	IA	515	50548	Humboldt	5	2-24&25
Humboldt	TN	901	38343	Gibson	10	2-72
Hummelstown	PA	717	17036	Dauphin	4	2-67
Hunters Creek Vlg.	TX	713	77024	Harris	4	2-74&75
Hunters Trace	KY	502	40216	Jefferson	5	2-28&29
Huntingburg	IN	812	47542	Dubois	5	2-23
Huntington	NY	516	11743	Suffolk	13	2-56
Huntingdon*	PA	814	16652	Huntingdon	6	2-66
Huntingdon*	TN	901	38344	Carroll	3	2-72

Bold = Over 15,000......ALL CAPS = STATE CAPITAL......* = County Seat......# = Changes to 510 in 9/91.....## = Changes to 410 in 11/91......(+) = City located in additional counties......NAV = Population not available......C.H.= Court House......(IC)=Independent City

CITY	STATE	AREA CODE	ZIP CODE	COUNTY	POPULATION (in thousands)	MAP PAGE
Huntington	VA	703	22303	Fairfax	5	2-78&79
Huntington*	IN	219	46750	Huntington	16	2-22
Huntington*	WV	304	25701-99	Cabell	59	2-82
Huntington Beach	CA	714	92646-49	Orange	183	2-7
Huntington Beach	NY	516	11721	Suffolk	3	2-56
Huntington Park	CA	213	90255	Los Angeles	55	2-7
Huntington Station	NY	516	11746	Suffolk	30	2-56
Huntington Woods	MI	313	48070	Oakland	9	2-39
Huntsville*	AL	205	35801-99	Madison	160	2-2&3
Huntsville*	AR	501	72740	Madison	1	2-6
Huntsville*	MO	816	65259	Randolph	1	2-44
Huntsville*	TN	615	37756	Scott	1	2-72&73
Huntsville*	TX	409	77340-42	Walker	33	2-75
Hurley*	WI	715	54534	Iron	1	2-84&85
Huron	CA	209	93234	Fresno	4	2-8&9
Huron	OH	419	44839	Erie	7	2-60
Huron*	SD	605	57350	Beadle	12	2-71
Hurricane	WV	304	25526	Putnam	4	2-82
Hurst	TX	817	76053-54	Tarrant	36	2-74
Hurstbourne	KY	502	40222	Jefferson	4	2-28
Hutchins	TX	214	75141	Dallas	3	2-74
Hutchinson*	KS	316	67501-05	Reno	42	2-26&27
Hutchinson	MN	612	55350	McLeod	9	2-41
Hyannis	MA	508	02601	Barnstable	10	2-36&37
Hyannis*	NE	308	69350	Grant	1	2-47
Hyannisport	MA	508	02647	Barnstable	10	2-36&37
Hyattsville	MD	301	20780-88	Prince Georges	13	2-35
Hybla Valley	VA	703	22306	Fairfax	4	2-78&79
Hyde Park*	VT	802	05655	Lamoille	1	2-77
Hyden*	KY	606	41749	Leslie	1	2-29
Hyrum	UT	801	84319	Cache	4	2-76
Hysham*	MT	406	59038	Treasure	1	2-46
Ida Grove*	IA	712	51445	Ida	2	2-24
Idabel*	OK	405	74745	McCurtain	7	2-64&65
Idaho City*	ID	208	83731	Boise	1	2-18
Idaho Falls*	ID	208	83401-15	Bonneville	43	2-18
Idaho Springs	CO	303	80452	Clear Creek	2	2-10&11
Ilion	NY	315	13357	Herkimer	9	2-54&55
Immokalee	FL	813	33934	Collier	11	2-14&15
Imperial	CA	619	92251	Imperial	3	2-9
Imperial Beach	CA	619	92032	San Diego	25	2-9
Imperial*	NE	308	69033	Chase	1	2-47
Independence*	CA	619	93526	Inyo	1	2-9
Independence*	IA	319	50644	Buchanan	6	2-25
Independence*	KS	316	67301	Montgomery	10	2-26&27
Independence*	KY	606	41051	Kenton	9	2-29
Independence	MN	612	55359	Hennepin	3	2-41
Independence*	MO	816	64050-58	Jackson	112	2-44

Bold = Over 15,000......ALL CAPS = STATE CAPITAL......* = County Seat......# = Changes to 510 in 9/91..... ## = Changes to 410 in 11/91......(+) = City located in addional counties......NAV = Population not available......C.H.= Court House......(IC) = Independent City

CITY	STATE	AREA CODE	ZIP CODE	COUNTY	POPULATION (in thousands)	MAP PAGE
Independence	OH	216	44131	Cuyahoga	6	2-62
Independence	OR	503	97351	Polk	4	2-63
Independence*	VA	703	24348	Grayson	1	2-78&79
Indialantic	FL	407	32902	Brevard	3	2-14&15
Indian Harbour Beach	FL	407	32937	Brevard	6	2-14
Indian Head Park	IL	708	60525	Cook	3	2-19
Indian Rocks Beach	FL	813	34635	Pinellas	4	2-14&15
Indiana*	PA	412	15701	Indiana	14	2-66
INDIANAPOLIS*	IN	317	46201-99	Marion	723	2-22&23
Indianola*	IA	515	50125	Warren	10	2-24&25
Indianola*	MS	601	38751	Sunflower	9	2-42&43
Indio	CA	619	92201-02	Riverside	29	2-9
Inez*	KY	606	41224	Martin	1	2-29
Ingleside	TX	512	78362	San Patricio	5	2-75
Inglewood	CA	213	90301-99	Los Angeles	102	2-7
Ingram	PA	412	15205	Allegheny	4	2-68
Inkster	MI	313	48141	Wayne	33	2-39
Intern'l Falls*	MN	218	56649	Koochiching	6	2-40
Inver Grove Heights	MN	612	55075	Dakota	17	2-41
Inverness*	FL	904	32650-52	Citrus	4	2-14
Inverness	IL	708	60067	Cook	5	2-19
Iola*	KS	316	66749	Allen	7	2-26&27
Ionia*	MI	616	48846	Ionia	5	2-38&39
Iorn Mountain*	MI	906	49801	Dickinson	8	2-38
Iornwood	MI	906	49938	Gogebic	8	2-38
Iowa City*	IA	319	52240-46	Johnson	52	2-25
Iowa Falls	IA	515	50126	Hardin	6	2-24&25
Iowa Park	TX	817	76367	Wichita	6	2-74
Ipswich	MA	508	01938	Essex	11	2-36&37
Ipswich*	SD	605	57451	Edmunds	1	2-71
Irmo	SC	803	29063	Lexington (+1)	4	2-70
Irondale	AL	205	35210	Jefferson	9	2-2&3
Irondequoit	NY	716	14617	Monroe	75	2-54
Ironton*	MO	314	63650	Iron	1	2-44&45
Ironton*	OH	614	45638	Lawrence	3	2-61
Irvine	CA	714	92713-18	Orange	88	2-7
Irvine*	KY	606	40336	Estill	3	2-29
Irving	TX	214	75060-63	Dallas	130	2-74
Irvington	NJ	201	07111	Essex	63	2-52
Irvington	NY	914	10533	Westchester	6	2-56
Irwin	PA	412	15642	Westmooreland	5	2-68
Irwinton*	GA	912	31042	Wilkinson	1	2-16&17
Ishpeming	MI	906	49849	Marquette	8	2-38
Isla Vista	CA	805	93117	Santa Barbara	17	2-9
Island Lake	IL	708	60042	Lake (+1)	3	2-20
Island Park	NY	516	11558	Nassau	5	2-56
Islandia	NY	516	11722	Suffolk	3	2-56
Isle of Palms	SC	803	29451	Charleston	3	2-70

Bold = Over 15,000......ALL CAPS = STATE CAPITAL......* = County Seat......# = Changes to 510 in 9/91.....## = Changes to 410 in 11/91......(+) = City located in additional counties......NAV = Population not available......C.H.= Court House......(IC)=Independent City

CITY	STATE	AREA CODE	ZIP CODE	COUNTY	POPULATION (in thousands)	MAP PAGE
Isle of Wight*	VA	804	23397	Isle of Wight	50	2-78&79
Islip	NY	516	11751	Suffolk	13	2-56
Issaquah	WA	206	98027	King	6	2-80
Itasca	IL	708	60143	Du Page	7	2-19
Ithaca*	MI	517	48847	Gratiot	2	2-38&39
Ithica*	NY	607	14850-53	Tompkins	27	2-54&55
Itta Bena	MS	601	38941	Leflore	3	2-42&43
Iuka*	MS	601	38852	Tishomingo	2	2-42&43
Ivanhoe	CA	209	93235	Tulare	3	2-8&9
Ivanhoe*	MN	507	56142	Lincoln	1	2-41
Jacinto City	TX	713	77029	Harris	9	2-74&75
Jacksboro*	TN	615	37757	Campbell	1	2-72&73
Jacksboro*	TX	817	76056	Jack	3	2-74
Jackson	AL	205	36545	Clarke	6	2-2&3
Jackson*	CA	209	95642	Amador	2	2-8&9
Jackson*	GA	404	30233	Butts	4	2-16&17
Jackson*	KY	606	41339	Breathitt	2	2-29
Jackson	LA	504	70748	East Feliciana	4	2-30&31
Jackson*	MI	517	49201-04	Jackson	37	2-38&39
Jackson*	MN	507	56143	Jackson	3	2-41
Jackson*	MO	314	63755	Cape Girardeau	8	2-44&45
JACKSON*	MS	601	39201-99	Hinds	208	2-42&43
Jackson*	NC	919	27845	Northampton	1	2-58&59
Jackson	NJ	908	08527	Ocean	26	2-50&51
Jackson*	OH	614	45640	Jackson	6	2-61
Jackson*	TN	901	38301-08	Madison	52	2-72
Jackson*	WY	307	83001	Teton	5	2-83
Jacksonville	AL	205	36265	Calhoun	10	2-2&3
Jacksonville	AR	501	72076	Pulaski	30	2-6
Jacksonville*	FL	904	32201-99	Duval (&Jackson)	608	2-14
Jacksonville*	IL	217	62650-51	Morgan	20	2-20&21
Jacksonville*	NC	919	28540-46	Onslow	28	2-58&59
Jacksonville	TX	903	75766	Cherokee	14	2-74
Jacksonville Beach	FL	904	32250	Duval	13	2-14
Jaffrey	NH	603	03452	Cheshire	4	2-49
Jal	NM	505	88252	Lea	3	2-53
Jamaica*	NY	718	11401-99	Queens	NAV	2-56
Jamesburg	NJ	908	08831	Middlesex	5	2-50
Jamestown*	KY	502	42629	Russell	1	2-28&29
Jamestown*	ND	701	58401-02	Stutsman	15	2-57
Jamestown	NY	716	14701-02	Chautauqua	35	2-54
Jamestown	RI	401	02835	Newport	4	2-69
Jamestown*	TN	615	38556	Fentress	1	2-72&73
Janesville*	WI	608	53545-47	Rock	51	2-85
Jasonville	IN	812	47438	Greene	2	2-23
Jasper*	AL	205	35501-02	Walker	12	2-2&3
Jasper*	AR	501	72641	Newton	1	2-6
Jasper*	FL	904	32052	Hamilton	2	2-14

Bold = Over 15,000......ALL CAPS = STATE CAPITAL......* = County Seat......# = Changes to 510 in 9/91..... ## = Changes to 410 in 11/91......(+) = City located in addional counties......NAV= Population not available......C.H.= Court House......(IC) = Independent City

CITY	STATE	AREA CODE	ZIP CODE	COUNTY	POPULATION (in thousands)	MAP PAGE
Jasper*	GA	404	30143	Pickens	1	2-16&17
Jasper*	IN	812	47546-47	Dubois	9	2-23
Jasper*	TN	615	37347	Marion	2	2-72&73
Jasper*	TX	409	75951	Jasper	7	2-75
Jay*	OK	918	74346	Delaware	1	2-65
Jay	ME	207	04239	Franklin	5	2-32&33
Jayton*	TX	806	79528	Kent	1	2-74
Jeanerette	LA	318	70544	Iberia	6	2-30
Jeannette	PA	412	15644	Westmooreland	13	2-68
Jefferson*	GA	404	30549	Jackson	1	2-16&17
Jefferson*	IA	515	50129	Greene	5	2-24&25
Jefferson*	NC	919	28640	Ashe	1	2-58&59
Jefferson	NJ	201	07849	Morris	16	2-52
Jefferson*	OH	216	44047	Ashtabula	3	2-60
Jefferson	PA	412	15344	Allegheny	7	2-68
Jefferson*	TX	903	75657	Marion	2	2-74
Jefferson*	WI	414	53549	Jefferson	5	2-85
JEFFERSON CITY*	MO	314	65101-10	Cole	36	2-44&45
Jefferson City	TN	615	37760	Jefferson	6	2-72&73
Jefferson Valley	NY	914	10535	Westchester	6	2-56
Jeffersontown	KY	502	40299	Jefferson	19	2-28
Jeffersonville*	GA	912	31044	Twiggs	1	2-16&17
Jeffersonville*	IN	812	47130-31	Clark	22	2-23
Jellico	TN	615	37762	Campbell	3	2-72&73
Jena*	LA	318	71342	La Salle	4	2-30
Jenison	MI	616	49428-n29	Ottawa	16	2-38&39
Jenkins	KY	606	41537	Letcher	3	2-29
Jenkintown	PA	215	19046	Montgomery	5	2-68
Jenks	OK	918	74037	Tulsa	6	2-65
Jennings*	LA	318	70546	Jefferson Davis	12	2-30
Jennings	MO	314	63136	St. Louis	14	2-44&45
Jensen Beach	FL	407	34957-58	Martin	7	2-14&15
Jericho	VT	802	05465	Chittenden	4	2-77
Jerome	AZ	602	86331	Yavapai	1	2-5
Jerome*	ID	208	83338	Jerome	7	2-18
Jersey City*	NJ	201	07301-99	Hudson	219	2-52
Jersey Shore	PA	717	17740	Lycoming	5	2-67
Jersey Village	TX	713	77040	Harris	4	2-74&75
Jerseyville*	IL	618	62052	Jersey	7	2-21
Jessup	PA	717	18434	Lackawanna	5	2-67
Jesup*	GA	912	31545	Wayne	22	2-16&17
Jetmore*	KS	316	67854	Hodgeman	1	2-26&27
Jewett City	CT	203	06351	New London	3	2-12&13
Jim Thorpe*	PA	717	18229	Carbon	5	2-67
Johnson	VT	802	05656	Lamoille	3	2-77
Johnson City	NY	607	13790	Broome	17	2-54&55
Johnson City	TN	615	37601-15	Washington (+1)	45	2-73
Johnson City*	TX	512	78636	Blanco	1	2-75

Bold = Over 15,000......ALL CAPS = STATE CAPITAL......* = County Seat......# = Changes to 510 in 9/91.....## = Changes to 410 in 11/91.....(+)
= City located in additional counties......NAV = Population not available......C.H.= Court House......(IC)=Independent City

CITY	STATE	AREA CODE	ZIP CODE	COUNTY	POPULATION (in thousands)	MAP PAGE
Johnson*	KS	316	67855	Stanton	1	2-26&27
Johnsonburg	PA	814	15845	Elk	4	2-66
Johnston	IA	515	50131	Polk	3	2-24&25
Johnston	RI	401	02919	Providence	26	2-69
Johnston	SC	803	29832	Edgefield	3	2-70
Johnston City	IL	618	62951	Williamson	4	2-21
Johnstown	PA	814	15901-09	Cambria	33	2-66
Johnstown*	NY	518	12095	Fulton	9	2-55
Joliet*	IL	815	60431-36	Will	79	2-20
Jones Creek	TX	409	77541	Brazoria	3	2-75
Jonesboro*	AR	501	72401-03	Craighead	32	2-6
Jonesboro*	GA	404	30236-37	Clayton	4	2-16&17
Jonesboro*	IL	618	62952	Union	2	2-21
Jonesboro	IN	317	46938	Grant	2	2-22&23
Jonesboro*	LA	318	71251	Jackson	5	2-30
Jonesboro*	TN	615	37659	Washington	2	2-72&73
Jonesville	LA	318	71343	Catahoula	3	2-30
Jonesville*	VA	703	24263	Lee	1	2-78&79
Joplin	MO	417	64801-04	Jasper (+1)	40	2-44
Jordan*	MT	406	59337	Garfield	1	2-46
Jordon	MN	612	55357	Scott	3	2-41
Jourdanton*	TX	512	78026	Atascosa	3	2-75
Juanita	WA	206	98011 &33	King	11	2-80
Julesburg*	CO	303	80737	Sedgwick	1	2-10&11
Junction*	TX	915	76849	Kimble	2	2-74&75
Junction*	UT	801	84740	Piute	1	2-76
Junction City*	KS	913	66441	Geary	21	2-26&27
Junction City	OR	503	97448	Lane	3	2-63
JUNEAU	AK	907	99801-03	Juneau	26	2-4
Juneau*	WI	414	53039	Dodge	1	2-85
Jupiter	FL	407	33468-79	Palm Beach	10	2-14&15
Justice	IL	708	60458	Cook	10	2-19
Kadoka*	SD	605	57543	Jackson	1	2-71
Kahoka*	MO	816	63445	Clark	1	2-44
Kalamazoo*	MI	616	49001-09	Kalamazoo	77	2-38&39
Kalispell*	MT	406	59901-03	Flathead	11	2-46
Kalkaska*	MI	616	49646	Kalkaska	1	2-38&39
Kanab*	UT	801	84741	Kane	2	2-76
Kane	PA	814	16735	McKean	5	2-66
Kankakee*	IL	815	60901	Kankakee	29	2-20
Kannapolis	NC	704	28081	Cabarrus (+1)	33	2-58
Kansas City*	KS	913	66101-99	Wyandotte	161	2-26&27
Kansas City	MO	816	64101-99	Jackson (+2)	441	2-44
Kaplan	LA	318	70548	Vermilion	5	2-30
Karnes City*	TX	512	78118	Karnes	3	2-75
Kasson	MN	507	55944	Dodge	3	2-41
Katy	TX	713	77449-94	Fort Bend (+2)	6	2-74&75
Kaufman*	TX	214	75142	Kaufman	5	2-74

Bold = Over 15,000......ALL CAPS = STATE CAPITAL......* = County Seat......# = Changes to 510 in 9/91..... ## = Changes to 410 in 11/91......(+) = City located in addional counties......NAV= Population not available......C.H.= Court House......(IC) = Independent City

CITY	STATE	AREA CODE	ZIP CODE	COUNTY	POPULATION (in thousands)	MAP PAGE
Kaukauna	WI	414	54130	Outagamie	12	2-85
Kaysville	UT	801	84037	Davis	10	2-76
Keams Canyon	AZ	602	86034	Navajo	1	2-5
Keansburg	NJ	908	07734	Monmouth	10	2-50
Kearney*	NE	308	68847-48	Buffalo	24	2-47
Kearny	AZ	602	85237	Pinal	3	2-5
Kearny	NJ	201	07032	Hudson	35	2-52
Keego Harbor	MI	313	48320	Oakland	3	2-39
Keene*	NH	603	03431	Cheshire	21	2-49
Keene	TX	817	76059	Johnson	3	2-74
Keizer	OR	503	97303	Marion	20	2-63
Keller	TX	817	76248	Tarrant	4	2-74
Kellogg	ID	208	83837	Shoshone	4	2-18
Kelso*	WA	206	98626	Cowlitz	11	2-80
Kemmerer*	WY	307	83101	Lincoln	4	2-83
Kemp Mill	MD	301	20902	Montgomery	4	2-34&35
Ken Rock	IL	815	61109	Winnebago	6	2-20
Kenai	AK	907	99611	Kenai Peninsula	4	2-4
Kenansville*	NC	919	28349	Duplin	1	2-58&59
Kendall	FL	305	33156	Dade	50	2-15
Kendallville	IN	219	46755	Noble	7	2-22
Kenedy	TX	512	78119&78125	Karnes	4	2-75
Kenhorst	PA	215	19607	Berks	3	2-67
Kenilworth	IL	708	60043	Cook	3	2-19
Kenilworth	NJ	908	07033	Union	8	2-52
Kenmore	NY	716	14217	Erie	18	2-54
Kennebec*	SD	605	57544	Lyman	1	2-71
Kennebunk	ME	207	04043	York	6	2-32&33
Kennebunkport	ME	207	04046	York	3	2-32&33
Kennedale	TX	817	76060	Tarrant	3	2-74
Kenner	LA	504	70062-65	Jefferson	73	2-30&31
Kennesaw	GA	404	30144	Cobb	5	2-16&17
Kenneth City	FL	813	33709	Pinellas	4	2-14&15
Kennett Square	PA	215	19348	Chester	5	2-67
Kennett*	MO	314	63857	Dunklin	9	2-44&45
Kennewick	WA	509	99336-37	Benton	4	2-81
Kenosha*	WI	414	53140-42	Kenosha	74	2-85
Kenova	WV	304	25530	Wayne	4	2-82
Kent	CT	203	06757	Litchfield	2	2-12&13
Kent	OH	216	44240	Portage	29	2-60
Kent	WA	206	98031-32	King	28	2-80
Kentfield	CA	415	94904	Marin	5	2-7
Kentland*	IN	219	47951	Newton	2	2-22
Kenton*	OH	419	43326	Hardin	8	2-60
Kentwood	LA	504	70444	Tangipahoa	3	2-30&31
Kentwood	MI	616	49508	Kent	35	2-38&39
Kenyon	MN	507	55946	Goodhue	2	2-41
Keokuk	IA	319	52632	Lee	14	2-25

Bold = Over 15,000......ALL CAPS = STATE CAPITAL......* = County Seat......# = Changes to 510 in 9/91.....## = Changes to 410 in 11/91.....(+) = City located in additional counties......NAV = Population not available......C.H.= Court House......(IC)=Independent City

CITY	STATE	AREA CODE	ZIP CODE	COUNTY	POPULATION (in thousands)	MAP PAGE
Keosauqua*	IA	319	52565	Van Buren	1	2-25
Kerman	CA	209	93630	Fresno	4	2-8&9
Kermit*	TX	915	79745	Winkler	1	2-74&75
Kernersville	NC	919	27284-85	Forsyth	8	2-58&59
Kerrville*	TX	512	78028-29	Kerr	19	2-75
Keshena*	WI	715	54135	Menominee	1	2-84&85
Ketchikan	AK	907	99901	Ketchikan Gateway	7	2-4
Kettering	OH	513	45429	Greene (+1)	60	2-61
Kewanee	IL	309	61443	Henry	15	2-20
Kewaunee*	WI	414	54216	Kewaunee	2	2-85
Key West*	FL	305	33040-41	Monroe	25	2-15
Keyport	NJ	908	07735	Monmouth	8	2-50
Keyser*	WV	304	26726	Mineral	6	2-82
Keytesville*	MO	816	65261	Chariton	1	2-44
Kiel	WI	414	53042	Calumet (+1)	3	2-85
Kilgore	TX	903	75662-63	Gregg (+1)	11	2-74
Killeen	TX	817	76540-44	Bell	60	2-74
Killingworth	CT	203	06417	Middlesex	4	2-12&13
Kimball*	NE	308	69145	Kimball	3	2-47
Kimberly	WI	414	54136	Outagamie	6	2-85
Kinder	LA	318	70648	Allen	3	2-30
King	NC	919	27021	Stokes	4	2-58&59
King & Queen C.H.*	VA	804	23085	King & Queen	1	2-79
King City	CA	408	93930	Monterey	7	2-9
King George*	VA	703	22485	King George	1	2-78&79
King William*	VA	804	23086	King William	1	2-78&79
Kingfisher*	OK	405	73750	Kingfisher	4	2-64&65
Kingman*	AZ	602	86401-45	Mohave	10	2-5
Kingman*	KS	316	67068	Kingman	4	2-26&27
Kings Mountain	NC	704	28086	Cleveland (+1)	9	2-58
Kings Park	NY	516	11754	Suffolk	8	2-56
Kings Park	VA	703	22151	Fairfax	6	2-78&79
Kings Park West	VA	703	22030	Fairfax	6	2-78&79
Kings Point	NY	516	11024	Suffolk	16	2-56
Kingsburg	CA	209	93631	Fresno	5	2-8&9
Kingsford	MI	906	49801	Dickinson	5	2-38
Kingsland	GA	912	31548	Camden	2	2-16&17
Kingsport	TN	615	37660-65	Hawkins (+1)	32	2-72&73
Kingston	MA	617	02364	Plymouth	8	2-36&37
Kingston*	MO	816	64650	Caldwell	1	2-44
Kingston	NH	603	03848	Rockingham	4	2-49
Kingston*	NY	914	12401	Ulster	25	2-56
Kingston	PA	717	18704&8	Luzerne	16	2-67
Kingston	RI	401	02881	Washington	6	2-69
Kingston*	TN	615	37763	Roane	4	2-72&73
Kingstree*	SC	803	29556	Williamsburg	4	2-70
Kingsville*	TX	512	78363-64	Kleberg	29	2-75
Kingwood*	WV	304	26537	Preston	2	2-82

Bold = Over 15,000......ALL CAPS = STATE CAPITAL......* = County Seat......# = Changes to 510 in 9/91..... ## = Changes to 410 in 11/91......(+) = City located in addional counties......NAV= Population not available......C.H.= Court House......(IC) = Independent City

CITY	STATE	AREA CODE	ZIP CODE	COUNTY	POPULATION (in thousands)	MAP PAGE
Kinloch	MO	314	63140	St. Louis	4	2-44&45
Kinnelon	NJ	201	07405	Morris	8	2-52
Kinsley*	KS	316	67547	Edwards	2	2-26&27
Kinston*	NC	919	28501-03	Lenoir	25	2-58&59
Kiowa*	CO	303	80117	Elbert	1	2-10&11
Kirby	TX	512	78219	Bexar	6	2-75
Kirkland	WA	206	98033-34	King	20	2-80
Kirksville*	MO	816	63501	Adair	17	2-44
Kirkwood	MO	314	63122	St. Louis	27	2-44&45
Kirtland	OH	216	44094	Lake	6	2-62
Kissimmee*	FL	305	34741-59	Osceola	26	2-15
Kittanning*	PA	412	16201	Armstrong	5	2-66
Kittery	ME	207	03904	York	9	2-32&33
Klamath Falls*	OR	503	97601-03	Klamath	18	2-63
Knox*	IN	219	46534	Starke	4	2-22
Knoxville*	GA	912	31050	Crawford	1	2-16&17
Knoxville*	IA	515	50138	Marion	8	2-24&25
Knoxville	IL	309	61448	Knox	3	2-20
Knoxville*	TN	615	37901-99	Knox	173	2-72&73
Kodiak	AK	907	99615	Kodiak Island	5	2-4
Kokomo*	IN	317	46901-04	Howard	47	2-22&23
Kosciusko*	MS	601	39090	Attala	7	2-42&43
Kotzebue	AK	907	99752	North Arctic	5	2-4
Kountze*	TX	409	77625	Hardin	2	2-75
Kulpmont	PA	717	17834	Northumberland	4	2-67
Kutztown	PA	215	19530	Berks	4	2-67
L'Anse*	MI	906	49946	Baraga	2	2-38
La Belle*	FL	813	33935	Hendry	2	2-14&15
La Canada	CA	818	91011	Los Angeles	20	2-7
La Crescent	MN	507	55947	Houston	4	2-41
La Crescenta	CA	818	91224	Los Angeles	13	2-7
La Crosse*	KS	913	67548	Rush	1	2-26&27
La Crosse*	WI	608	54601-03	La Crosse	47	2-85
La Feria	TX	512	78559	Cameron	3	2-75
La Follette	TN	615	37766	Campbell	8	2-72&73
La Grande*	OR	503	97850	Union	11	2-63
La Grange*	GA	404	30240-41	Troup	27	2-16&17
La Grange	IL	708	60525	Cook	15	2-19
La Grange*	KY	502	40031	Oldham	3	2-28&29
La Grange*	TX	409	78945	Fayette	4	2-75
La Grange Park	IL	708	60525	Cook	13	2-19
La Habra	CA	213	90631	Orange	48	2-7
La Habra Heights	CA	213	90631-33	Orange	5	2-7
La Jolla	CA	619	92037-38	San Diego	3	2-9
La Junta*	CO	719	81050	Otero	8	2-11
La Marque	TX	409	77568	Galveston	16	2-75
La Mesa	CA	619	92041-44	San Diego	51	2-9
La Mirada	CA	213	90637-39	Los Angeles	41	2-7

Bold = Over 15,000......ALL CAPS = STATE CAPITAL......* = County Seat......# = Changes to 510 in 9/91.....## = Changes to 410 in 11/91.....(+) = City located in additional counties......NAV = Population not available......C.H.= Court House......(IC)=Independent City

CITY	STATE	AREA CODE	ZIP CODE	COUNTY	POPULATION (in thousands)	MAP PAGE
La Moure*	ND	701	58458	La Moure	1	2-57
La Palma	CA	714	90623	Orange	15	2-7
La Plata*	MD	301	20646	Charles	3	2-34&35
La Porte*	IN	219	46350	La Porte	22	2-22
La Porte	TX	713	77571-72	Harris	19	2-74&75
La Puente	CA	818	91744-49	Los Angeles	33	2-7
La Quinta	CA	619	92253	Riverside	7	2-9
La Salle	CO	303	80645	Weld	2	2-10&11
La Salle	IL	815	61301	La Salle	10	2-20
La Vale	MD	301	21502	Allegany	5	2-34&35
La Vergne	TN	615	37086	Rutherford	7	2-72&73
La Verne	CA	714	91750	Los Angeles	28	2-7
La Vista	NE	402	68128	Sarpy	10	2-47
Lacey	WA	206	98503	Thurston	15	2-80
Lackawanna	NY	716	14218	Erie	22	2-54
Lacon*	IL	309	61540	Marshall	2	2-20
Laconia*	NH	603	03246-47	Belknap	16	2-49
Lacy-Lakeview	TX	817	76705	McLennan	3	2-74
Ladue	MO	314	63124	St. Louis	9	2-44&45
Ladysmith*	WI	715	54848	Rusk	3	2-84&85
Lafayette*	AL	205	36862	Chambers	3	2-2&3
Lafayette	CA	415#	94549	Contra Costa	22	2-7
Lafayette	CO	303	80026	Boulder	9	2-10&11
LaFayette*	GA	404	30728	Walker	7	2-16&17
Lafayette*	IN	317	47901-06	Tippecanoe	44	2-22&23
Lafayette*	LA	318	70501-09	Lafayette	94	2-30
Lafayette*	TN	615	37083	Macon	3	2-72&73
Lagrange*	IN	219	46761	Lagrange	2	2-22
Laguna Beach	CA	714	92651-54	Orange	18	2-7
Laguna Hills	CA	714	92653	Orange	16	2-7
Lahaina	HI	808	96761	Maui	6	2-19
Lake Alfred	FL	813	33850	Polk	3	2-14&15
Lake Andes*	SD	605	57356	Charles Mix	1	2-71
Lake Arthur	LA	318	70549	Jefferson	4	2-30
Lake Bluff	IL	708	60044	Lake	4	2-20
Lake Butler*	FL	904	32054	Union	2	2-14
Lake Charles*	LA	318	70601-29	Calcasieu	73	2-30
Lake City*	CO	303	81235	Hinsdale	1	2-10&11
Lake City*	FL	904	32055-56	Columbia	10	2-14
Lake City	GA	404	30260	Clayton	3	2-16&17
Lake City*	MI	616	49651	Missaukee	1	2-38&39
Lake City	MN	612	55041	Goodhue (+1)	4	2-41
Lake City	SC	803	29560	Florence	7	2-70
Lake Clarke Shores	FL	407	33406	Palm Beach	3	2-15
Lake Dallas	TX	817	75065	Denton	3	2-74
Lake Elmo	MN	612	55042	Washington	5	2-41
Lake Elsinore	CA	714	92330-31	Riverside	11	2-9
Lake Forest	IL	708	60045	Lake	15	2-20

Bold = Over 15,000......ALL CAPS = STATE CAPITAL......* = County Seat......# = Changes to 510 in 9/91..... ## = Changes to 410 in 11/91......(+) = City located in addional counties......NAV= Population not available......C.H.= Court House......(IC) = Independent City

CITY	STATE	AREA CODE	ZIP CODE	COUNTY	POPULATION (in thousands)	MAP PAGE
Lake Forest Estates	NE	402	68134	Douglas	3	2-47
Lake Geneva	WI	414	53147	Walworth	6	2-85
Lake George*	NY	518	12845	Warren	1	2-55
Lake Grove	NY	516	11755	Suffolk	9	2-56
Lake Havasu City	AZ	602	86403	Mohave	18	2-5
Lake In The Hills	IL	708	60102	McHenry	6	2-20
Lake Jackson	TX	409	77566	Brazoria	22	2-75
Lake Mary	FL	407	32746	Seminole	3	2-14&15
Lake Mills	WI	414	53551	Jefferson	4	2-85
Lake Orion	MI	313	48035	Oakland	3	2-39
Lake Oswego	OR	503	97034-5	Clackamas (+2)	23	2-63
Lake Park	FL	407	33403	Palm Beach	7	2-14&15
Lake Pleasant*	NY	518	12108	Hamilton	1	2-55
Lake Providence*	LA	318	71254	East Carroll	5	2-31
Lake St. Louis	MO	314	63367	St. Charles	5	2-44&45
Lake Station	IN	219	46405	Lake	15	2-22
Lake Village*	AR	501	71653	Chicot	4	2-6
Lake Wales	FL	813	33853-59	Polk	8	2-14&15
Lake Worth	FL	407	33460-67	Palm Beach	30	2-14&15
Lake Worth	TX	817	76135	Tarrant	4	2-74
Lake Zurich	IL	708	60047	Lake	11	2-20
Lakehurst	NJ	908	08733	Ocean	3	2-50&51
Lakeland	FL	813	33801-13	Polk	66	2-14&15
Lakeland*	GA	912	31635	Lanier	1	2-16&17
Lakeland	NY	315	13209	Onondaga	3	2-54&55
Lakemore	OH	216	44250	Summit	3	2-62
Lakeport*	CA	707	95453	Lake	4	2-8
Lakeside	CA	619	92040	San Diego	24	2-9
Lakeside	VA	804	23228	Henrico	12	2-78&79
Lakeside Park	KY	606	41017	Kenton	3	2-29
Lakeview*	OR	503	97630	Lake	2	2-63
Lakeville	MA	508	02346	Plymouth	6	2-36&37
Lakeville	MN	612	55044	Dakota	15	2-41
Lakewood	CA	213	90711-16	Los Angeles	75	2-7
Lakewood	CO	303	80215	Jefferson	124	2-10&11
Lakewood	NJ	908	08701	Ocean	23	2-50&51
Lakewood	NY	716	14750	Chautauqua	4	2-54
Lakewood	OH	216	44107	Cuyahoga	60	2-62
Lakin*	KS	316	67860	Kearny	1	2-26&27
Lakota*	ND	701	58344	Nelson	1	2-57
Lamar*	CO	719	81052	Prowers	7	2-11
Lamar*	MO	417	64759	Barton	131	2-44
Lambertville	NJ	609	08530	Hunterdon	4	2-51
Lamesa*	TX	806	79331	Dawson	12	2-74
Lamoni	IA	515	50140	Decatur	3	2-24&25
Lamont	CA	805	93241	Kern	1	2-9
Lampasas*	TX	512	76550	Lampasas	6	2-75
Lancaster	CA	805	93534-39	Los Angeles	63	9-7

Bold = Over 15,000......ALL CAPS = STATE CAPITAL......* = County Seat......# = Changes to 510 in 9/91.....## = Changes to 410 in 11/91.....(+) = City located in additional counties......NAV = Population not available......C.H.= Court House......(IC)=Independent City

CITY	STATE	AREA CODE	ZIP CODE	COUNTY	POPULATION (in thousands)	MAP PAGE
Lancaster*	KY	606	40444	Garrard	3	2-29
Lancaster	MA	508	01523	Worcester	6	2-36&37
Lancaster*	MO	816	63548	Schuyler	1	2-44
Lancaster*	NH	603	03584	Coos	3	2-49
Lancaster	NY	716	14086	Erie	30	2-54
Lancaster*	OH	614	43130	Fairfield	34	2-61
Lancaster*	PA	717	17601-99	Lancaster	56	2-67
Lancaster*	SC	803	29720	Lancaster	10	2-70
Lancaster	TX	214	75146	Dallas	5	2-74
Lancaster*	VA	804	22503	Lancaster	1	2-78&79
Lancaster*	WI	608	53813	Grant	4	2-85
Lander*	WY	307	82520	Fremont	7	2-83
Lanesboro	MA	413	01237	Berkshire	3	2-36
Lanett	AL	205	36863	Chambers	9	2-2&3
Langdon*	ND	701	58249	Cavalier	1	2-57
Langley Park	MD	301	20783	Prince Georges	12	2-35
Lanham	MD	301	20706	Prince Georges	7	2-34&35
Lansdale	PA	215	19446	Montgomery	17	2-68
Lansdowne	MD	301##	21227	Baltimore	10	2-34&35
Lansdowne	PA	215	19050	Delaware	12	2-68
Lansford	PA	717	18232	Carbon	4	2-67
Lansing	IL	708	60438	Cook	28	2-19
Lansing	KS	913	66043	Leavenworth	5	2-26&27
LANSING*	MI	517	48901-99	Ingham	128	2-38&39
Lansing	NY	607	14882	Tompkins	3	2-54&55
Lantana	FL	407	33462	Palm Beach	8	2-14&15
Lapeer*	MI	313	48446	Lapeer	5	2-39
Laporte*	PA	717	18626	Sullivan	1	2-67
Laramie*	WY	307	82057-71	Albany	24	2-83
Larchmont	NY	914	10538	Westchester	6	2-56
Laredo*	TX	512	78040-44	Webb	117	2-75
Largo	FL	813	34640-49	Pinellas	66	2-14&15
Larkspur	CA	415	94943	Marin	11	2-7
Larksville	PA	717	18704	Luzerne	4	2-67
Larned*	KS	316	67550	Pawnee	5	2-26&27
Las Animas*	CO	719	81054	Bent	5	2-11
Las Cruces*	NM	505	88001-08	Dona Ana	54	2-53
Las Vegas*	NM	505	87701	San Miguel	15	2-53
Las Vegas*	NV	702	89101-99	Clark	191	2-48
Latham	NY	518	12110	Albany	11	2-55
Lathrup Village	MI	313	48076	Oakland	5	2-39
Latrobe	PA	412	15650	Westmooreland	10	2-68
Lauderdale Lakes	FL	305	33313	Broward	28	2-15
Lauderdale-by-Sea	FL	305	33308	Broward	2	2-15
Lauderhill	FL	305	33313	Broward	44	2-15
Laurel	DE	302	19956	Sussex	3	2-35
Laurel	MD	301	20707-08	Prince Georges	12	2-34&35
Laurel*	MS	601	39440-42	Jones	20	2-42&43

Bold = Over 15,000......ALL CAPS = STATE CAPITAL......* = County Seat......# = Changes to 510 in 9/91..... ## = Changes to 410 in 11/91......(+) = City located in addional counties......NAV= Population not available......C.H. = Court House......(IC) = Independent City

CITY	STATE	AREA CODE	ZIP CODE	COUNTY	POPULATION (in thousands)	MAP PAGE
Laurel	MT	406	59044	Yellowstone	7	2-46
Laurel	VA	804	23060	Henrico	3	2-78&79
Laureldale	PA	215	19605	Berks	4	2-67
Laurens*	SC	803	29360	Laurens	10	2-70
Laurinburg*	NC	919	28352	Scotland	12	2-58&59
Laurium	MI	906	49913	Houghton	3	2-38
Lawndale	CA	213	90260	Los Angeles	26	2-7
Lawnside	NJ	609	08054	Camden	3	2-51
Lawrence	IN	317	46226	Marion	26	2-22&23
Lawrence*	KS	913	66044-46	Douglas	56	2-26&27
Lawrence	MA	508	01840-45	Essex	66	2-36&37
Lawrence	NJ	609	08638	Mercer	19	2-50
Lawrence	NY	516	11559	Nassau	6	2-56
Lawrenceburg*	IN	812	47025	Dearborn	4	2-23
Lawrenceburg*	KY	502	40342	Anderson	5	2-28&29
Lawrenceburg*	TN	615	38464	Lawrence	10	2-72&73
Lawrenceville*	GA	404	30243-46	Gwinnett	14	2-16&17
Lawrenceville*	IL	618	62439	Lawrence	6	2-21
Lawrenceville*	VA	804	23868	Brunswick	1	2-78&79
Lawton*	OK	405	73501-07	Comanche	85	2-64&65
Layton	UT	801	84040-41	Davis	34	2-76
Le Center*	MN	612	56057	Le Sueur	1	2-41
Le Claire	IA	319	52753	Scott	3	2-25
Le Mars*	IA	712	51031	Plymouth	8	2-24
Le Roy	IL	309	61752	McLean	3	2-20
Le Sueur	MN	612	56058	Le Sueur	4	2-41
Lead	SD	605	57754	Lawrence	4	2-71
Leadville*	CO	719	80461	Lake	4	2-11
League City	TX	713	77573-74	Galveston	16	2-74&75
Leakesville*	MS	601	39451	Greene	1	2-42&43
Leakey*	TX	512	78873	Real	1	2-75
Leavenworth*	KS	913	66048	Leavenworth	35	2-26&27
Leawood	KS	913	66206	Johnson	13	2-26&27
Lebanon	CT	203	06249	New London	5	2-12&13
Lebanon	IL	618	62254	St. Clair	4	2-21
Lebanon*	IN	317	46052	Boone	11	2-22&23
Lebanon*	KY	502	40033	Marion	6	2-28&29
Lebanon	ME	207	04027	York	3	2-32&33
Lebanon*	MO	417	65536	Laclede	10	2-44
Lebanon	NH	603	03766	Grafton	11	2-49
Lebanon	NJ	201	07830	Hunterdon	5	2-50
Lebanon*	OH	513	45036	Warren	9	2-61
Lebanon	OR	503	97355	Linn	10	2-63
Lebanon*	PA	717	17042	Lebanon	26	2-67
Lebanon*	TN	615	37087-88	Wilson	13	2-72&73
Lebanon*	VA	703	24266	Russell	3	2-78&79
Ledyard	CT	203	06339	New London	14	2-12&13
Lee	MA	413	01238	Berkshire	6	2-36

Bold = Over 15,000......ALL CAPS = STATE CAPITAL......* = County Seat......# = Changes to 510 in 9/91.....## = Changes to 410 in 11/91.....(+) = City located in additional counties......NAV = Population not available......C.H.= Court House......(IC)=Independent City

CITY	STATE	AREA CODE	ZIP CODE	COUNTY	POPULATION (in thousands)	MAP PAGE
Leechburg	PA	412	15656	Armstrong	3	2-66
Leeds	AL	205	35094	Jefferson (+2)	9	2-2&3
Lees Summit	MO	816	64063-64	Cass (+1)	36	2-44
Leesburg	FL	904	34748-89	Lake	14	2-14
Leesburg*	GA	912	31763	Lee	1	2-16&17
Leesburg*	VA	703	22075	Loudoun	10	2-78&79
Leesville*	LA	318	71446	Vernon	11	2-30
Lehi	UT	801	84043	Utah	7	2-76
Lehigh Acres	FL	813	33970-71	Lee	10	2-14&15
Lehighton	PA	215	18235	Carbon	6	2-67
Leicester	MA	508	01524	Worcester	3	2-36&37
Leitchfield*	KY	502	42754-55	Grayson	5	2-28&29
Leland*	MI	616	49654	Leelanau	1	2-38&39
Leland	MS	601	38756	Washington	7	2-42&43
Lemay	MO	314	63125	St. Louis	38	2-44&45
Lemon Grove	CA	619	92045	San Diego	22	2-9
Lemont	IL	708	60439	Cook	5	2-19
Lemoore	CA	209	93245	Kings	11	2-8&9
Lemoyne	PA	717	17043	Cumberland	4	2-67
Lenexa	KS	913	66215	Johnson	25	2-26&27
Lennox	CA	213	90304	Los Angeles	19	2-7
Lenoir City	TN	615	37771	Loudon	6	2-72&73
Lenoir*	NC	704	28645	Caldwell	13	2-58
Lenox	MA	413	01240	Berkshire	3	2-36
Lenwood	CA	619	92311	San Bernardino	3	2-9
Leola*	SD	605	57456	McPherson	1	2-71
Leominster	MA	508	01453	Worcester	35	2-36&37
Leon*	IA	515	50144	Decatur	2	2-24&25
Leon Valley	TX	512	78238	Bexar	9	2-75
Leonardtown*	MD	301	20650	St. Mary's	1	2-34&35
Leonia	NJ	201	07605	Bergen	8	2-52
Leoti*	KS	316	67861	Wichita	2	2-26&27
Levelland*	TX	806	79336-38	Hockley	14	2-74
Levittown	NY	516	11756	Nassau	57	2-56
Levittown	PA	215	19053-59	Bucks	17	2-68
Lewisburg*	PA	717	17837	Union	5	2-67
Lewisburg*	TN	615	37091	Marshall	9	2-72&73
Lewisburg*	WV	304	24901-02	Greenbrier	2	2-82
Lewisdale	MD	301	20783	Prince Georges	4	2-35
Lewiston*	ID	208	83501	Nez Perce	29	2-18
Lewiston	ME	207	04240-43	Androscoggin	37	2-32&33
Lewiston	NY	716	14092	Niagara	3	2-54
Lewistown*	IL	309	61542	Fulton	3	2-20
Lewistown*	MT	406	59457	Fergus	6	2-46
Lewistown*	PA	717	17044	Mifflin	9	2-67
Lewisville	TX	214	75067	Dallas (+1)	28	2-74
Lewisville*	AR	501	71845	Lafayette	1	2-6
Lexington*	GA	404	30648	Oglethorpe	1	2-16&17

Bold = Over 15,000......ALL CAPS = STATE CAPITAL......* = County Seat......# = Changes to 510 in 9/91..... ## = Changes to 410 in 11/91......(+) = City located in addional counties......NAV= Population not available......C.H.= Court House......(IC) = Independent City

CITY	STATE	AREA CODE	ZIP CODE	COUNTY	POPULATION (in thousands)	MAP PAGE
Lexington*	KY	606	40501-99	Fayette	213	2-29
Lexington	MA	617	02173	Middlesex	29	2-36&37
Lexington*	MO	816	64067	Lafayette	4	2-44
Lexington*	MS	601	39095	Holmes	2	2-42&43
Lexington*	NC	704	27292-93	Davidson	15	2-58
Lexington*	NE	308	68850	Dawson	7	2-47
Lexington	OH	419	44904	Richland	4	2-60
Lexington*	SC	803	29072	Lexington	1	2-70
Lexington*	TN	901	38351	Henderson	6	2-72
Lexington*	VA	703	24450	Rockbridge (IC)	6	2-79
Libby*	MT	406	59923	Lincoln	2	2-46
Liberal*	KS	316	67901-05	Seward	15	2-26&27
Liberty*	IN	317	47353	Union	2	2-22&23
Liberty*	KY	606	42539	Casey	2	2-29
Liberty*	MO	816	64068	Clay	17	2-44
Liberty*	MS	601	39645	Amite	1	2-42&43
Liberty	NY	914	12754	Sullivan	4	2-56
Liberty	PA	717	16930	Tioga	3	2-67
Liberty	SC	803	29657	Pickens	3	2-70
Liberty*	TX	409	77575	Liberty	8	2-75
Libertyville	IL	708	60048	Lake	18	2-20
Lido Beach	NY	516	11561	Nassau	3	2-56
Lighthouse Point	FL	305	33064	Broward	11	2-15
Ligonier	IN	219	46767	Noble	3	2-22
Lihue*	HI	808	96766	Kauai	5	2-19
Lilburn	GA	404	30247	Gwinnett	4	2-16&17
Lillington*	NC	919	27546	Harnett	1	2-58&59
Lima*	OH	419	45801-09	Allen	45	2-60
Limerick	PA	215	19468	Montgomery	5	2-68
Limestone	ME	207	04750-51	Aroostook	9	2-32&33
Limon	CO	719	80828	Lincoln	6	2-11
Lincoln	CA	916	95648	Placer	5	2-8
Lincoln*	IL	217	62656	Logan	16	2-20&21
Lincoln*	KS	913	67455	Lincoln	2	2-26&27
Lincoln	MA	617	01773	Middlesex	8	2-36&37
Lincoln	ME	207	04457	Penobscot	5	2-32&33
LINCOLN*	NE	402	68501-99	Lancaster	185	2-47
Lincoln	RI	401	02860	Providence	17	2-69
Lincoln City	OR	503	97367	Lincoln	5	2-63
Lincoln Heights	OH	513	45215	Hamilton	5	2-62
Lincoln Park	MI	313	48146	Wayne	43	2-39
Lincoln Park	NJ	201	07035	Morris	9	2-52
Lincolnshire	IL	708	60069	Lake	4	2-20&21
Lincolnton*	GA	404	30817	Lincoln	1	2-16&17
Lincolnton*	NC	704	28092-93	Lincoln	4	2-58
Lincolnwood	IL	708	60645	Cook	12	2-19
Linden*	AL	205	36748	Marengo	3	2-2&3
Linden	NJ	908	07036	Union	37	2-52

Bold = Over 15,000......ALL CAPS = STATE CAPITAL......* = County Seat......# = Changes to 510 in 9/91.....## = Changes to 410 in 11/91.....(+) = City located in additional counties......NAV = Population not available......C.H.= Court House......(IC)=Independent City

CITY	STATE	AREA CODE	ZIP CODE	COUNTY	POPULATION (in thousands)	MAP PAGE
Linden*	TN	615	37096	Perry	1	2-72&73
Linden*	TX	903	75563	Cass	1	2-74
Lindenhurst	IL	708	60046	Lake	7	2-20
Lindenhurst	NY	516	11757	Suffolk	27	2-56
Lindenwold	NJ	609	08021	Camden	18	2-51
Lindon	UT	801	84042 &62	Utah	3	2-76
Lindsay	CA	209	93247	Tulare	8	2-8&9
Lindsay	OK	405	73052	Garven	3	2-64&65
Lindsborg	KS	913	67456	McPherson	3	2-26&27
Linn*	MO	314	65051	Osage	1	2-44&45
Linneus*	MO	816	64653	Linn	1	2-44
Lino Lakes	MN	612	55014	Anoka	6	2-41
Linton	IN	812	47441	Greene	6	2-23
Linton*	ND	701	58552	Emmons	1	2-57
Linwood	NJ	609	08221	Atlantic	6	2-51
Lipscomb	AL	205	35020	Jefferson	3	2-2&3
Lipscomb*	TX	806	79056	Lipscomb	1	2-74
Lisbon	CT	203	06351	New London	3	2-12&13
Lisbon	ME	207	04250	Androscoggin	9	2-32&33
Lisbon*	ND	701	58054	Ransom	1	2-57
Lisbon*	OH	216	44432	Columbiana	2	2-60
Lisle	IL	708	60532	Du Page	16	2-19
Litchfield*	CT	203	06759	Litchfield	7	2-12&13
Litchfield	IL	217	62056	Montgomery	7	2-20&21
Litchfield	ME	207	04350	Kennebec	2	2-32&33
Litchfield*	MN	612	55355	Meeker	5	2-41
Litchfield	NH	603	03051	Hillsborough	4	2-49
Lithonia	GA	404	30058	De Kalb	3	2-16&17
Lititz	PA	717	17543	Lancaster	8	2-67
Little Canada	MN	612	55117	Ramsey	7	2-41
Little Chute	WI	414	54140	Outagamie	8	2-85
Little Compton	RI	401	02837	Newport	3	2-69
Little Falls*	MN	612	56345	Morrison	7	2-41
Little Falls	NJ	201	07424	Passaic	11	2-52
Little Falls	NY	315	13365	Herkimer	6	2-54&55
Little Ferry	NJ	201	07643	Bergen	10	2-52
LITTLE ROCK*	AR	501	72201-99	Pulaski	185	2-6
Little Silver	NJ	908	07739	Monmouth	6	2-50
Little Valley*	NY	716	14755	Cattaraugus	1	2-54
Littlefield*	TX	806	79339	Lamb	6	2-74
Littlestown	PA	717	17340	Adams	3	2-67
Littleton*	CO	303	80120-62	Arapahoe	34	2-10&11
Littleton	MA	508	01460	Middlesex	7	2-36&37
Littleton	NH	603	03561	Grafton	5	2-49
Live Oak	CA	916	95953	Sutter	3	2-8
Live Oak*	FL	904	32060	Suwannee	7	2-14
Live Oak	TX	512	78233	Bexar	9	2-75
Livermore	CA	415#	94550-51	Alameda	53	2-7

Bold = Over 15,000......ALL CAPS = STATE CAPITAL......* = County Seat......# = Changes to 510 in 9/91..... ## = Changes to 410 in 11/91......(+) = City located in addional counties......NAV= Population not available......C.H.= Court House......(IC) = Independent City

CITY	STATE	AREA CODE	ZIP CODE	COUNTY	POPULATION (in thousands)	MAP PAGE
Livermore Falls	ME	207	04254	Androscoggin	4	2-32&33
Liverpool	NY	315	13088-90	Onondaga	3	2-54&55
Livingston*	AL	205	35470	Sumter	3	2-2&3
Livingston	CA	209	95334	Merced	6	2-8&9
Livingston*	LA	504	70754	Livingston	1	2-30&31
Livingston*	MT	406	59047	Park	6	2-46
Livingston	NJ	201	07039	Essex	28	2-52
Livingston*	TN	615	38570	Overton	3	2-72&73
Livingston*	TX	409	77351	Polk	6	2-75
Livonia	MI	313	48150-54	Wayne	100	2-39
Llano*	TX	915	78643	Llano	3	2-74&75
Lloyd Harbor	NY	516	11743	Suffolk	3	2-56
Loa*	UT	801	84747	Wayne	1	2-76
Lochearn	MD	301##	21207	Baltimore	4	2-34&35
Lock Haven*	PA	717	17745	Clinton	8	2-66
Lockhart*	TX	512	78644	Caldwell	10	2-75
Lockland	OH	513	45215	Hamilton	4	2-62
Lockport	IL	815	60441	Will	9	2-20
Lockport*	NY	716	14094	Niagara	25	2-54
Locust Valley	NY	516	11560	Nassau	5	2-56
Lodi	CA	209	95240-42	San Joaquin	44	2-8&9
Lodi	NJ	201	07644	Bergen	24	2-52
Lodi	OH	216	44254	Medina	3	2-60
Logan*	IA	712	51546	Harrison	2	2-24
Logan*	OH	614	43138	Hocking	6	2-61
Logan*	UT	801	84321	Cache	1	2-76
Logan*	WV	304	25601	Logan	2	2-82
Logansport*	IN	219	46947	Cass	18	2-22
Loma Linda	CA	714	92354	San Bernardino	12	2-9
Lombard	IL	708	60148	Du Page	38	2-19
Lomita	CA	213	90717	Los Angeles	19	2-7
Lompoc	CA	805	93436-38	Santa Barbara	31	2-9
London*	KY	606	40741	Laurel	4	2-29
London*	OH	614	43140	Madison	7	2-61
Londonderry	NH	603	03053	Rockingham	14	2-49
Lone Grove	OK	405	73443	Carter	3	2-64&65
Long Beach	CA	213	90745-899	Los Angeles	396	2-7
Long Beach	MS	601	39560	Harrison	14	2-42&43
Long Beach	NY	516	11561	Nassau	34	2-56
Long Branch	NJ	908	07740	Monmouth	31	2-50
Long Prairie*	MN	612	56347	Todd	2	2-41
Longboat Key	FL	813	34228	Manatee (+1)	5	2-15
Longmeadow	MA	413	01106	Hampden	16	2-36
Longmont	CO	303	80501-02	Boulder	51	2-10&11
Longview	NC	704	28601	Burke (+1)	4	2-58
Longview*	TX	903	75601-15	Gregg	73	2-74
Longview	WA	206	98632	Cowlitz	30	2-80
Longwood	FL	407	32750	Seminole	10	2-14&15

Bold = Over 15,000......ALL CAPS = STATE CAPITAL......* = County Seat......# = Changes to 510 in 9/91......## = Changes to 410 in 11/91......(+) = City located in additional counties......NAV = Population not available......C.H.= Court House......(IC)=Independent City

CITY	STATE	AREA CODE	ZIP CODE	COUNTY	POPULATION (in thousands)	MAP PAGE
Lonoke*	AR	501	72086	Lonoke	5	2-6
Loogootee	IN	812	47553	Martin	3	2-23
Lorain	OH	216	44052-55	Lorain	74	2-60
Lordsburg*	NM	505	88045	Hidalgo	3	2-53
Lordstown	OH	216	44481	Trumbull	3	2-60
Los Alamitos	CA	213	90720-21	Orange	11	2-7
Los Alamos*	NM	505	87544	Los Alamos	11	2-53
Los Altos	CA	415	94022-24	Santa Clara	27	2-7
Los Altos Hills	CA	415	94022	Santa Clara	7	2-7
Los Angeles*	CA	213	90001-199	Los Angeles	3259	2-7
Los Banos	CA	209	93635	Merced	13	2-8&9
Los Gatos	CA	408	95030-32	Santa Clara	27	2-7
Los Lunas*	NM	505	87031	Valencia	5	2-53
Los Nietos	CA	213	90606	Los Angeles	7	2-7
Loudon*	TN	615	37774	Loudon	4	2-72&73
Loudonville	NY	518	12211	Albany	11	2-55
Loudonville	OH	419	44842	Ashland (+1)	3	2-60
Louisa*	KY	606	41230	Lawrence	2	2-29
Louisa*	VA	703	23093	Louisa	1	2-78&79
Louisburg*	NC	919	27549	Franklin	3	2-58&59
Louisiana	MO	314	63353	Pike	3	2-44&45
Louisville	CO	303	80027	Boulder	6	2-10&11
Louisville*	GA	912	30434	Jefferson	3	2-16&17
Louisville*	IL	618	62858	Clay	1	2-21
Louisville*	KY	502	40201-99	Jefferson	287	2-28
Louisville*	MS	601	39339	Winston	7	2-42&43
Louisville	OH	216	44641	Stark	8	2-60
Loup City*	NE	308	68853	Sherman	1	2-47
Loveland	CO	303	80537-39	Larimer	37	2-10&11
Loveland	OH	513	45140	Hamilton (+2)	9	2-61
Lovelock*	NV	702	89419	Pershing	1	2-48
Loves Park	IL	815	61111	Winnebago	13	2-20
Lovingston*	VA	804	22949	Nelson	1	2-78&79
Lovington*	NM	505	88260	Lea	11	2-53
Lowell	IN	219	46356	Lake	6	2-22
Lowell	MA	508	01850-54	Middlesex	94	2-36&37
Lowell	MI	616	49331	Kent	4	2-38&39
Lowell	NC	704	28098	Gaston	3	2-58
Lower	NJ	609	08204	Cape May	17	2-51
Lower Allen	PA	717	17011	Cumberland	14	2-67
Lower Burrell	PA	412	15068	Westmooreland	13	2-68
Lower Gwynedd	PA	215	19437	Montgomery	7	2-68
Lower Makefield	PA	215	19067	Bucks	17	2-68
Lower Merion	PA	215	19003	Montgomery	6	2-68
Lower Moreland	PA	215	19006	Montgomery	12	2-68
Lower Paxton	PA	717	17109	Dauphin	34	2-67
Lower Pottsgrove	PA	215	19464	Montgomery	8	2-68
Lower Providence	PA	215	19401	Montgomery	18	2-68

Bold = Over 15,000......ALL CAPS = STATE CAPITAL......* = County Seat......# = Changes to 510 in 9/91..... ## = Changes to 410 in 11/91.......(+) = City located in addional counties......NAV= Population not available......C.H.= Court House......(IC) = Independent City

CITY	STATE	AREA CODE	ZIP CODE	COUNTY	POPULATION (in thousands)	MAP PAGE
Lower Saucon	PA	215	18015	Northampton	7	2-67
Lower Southampton	PA	215	19047	Bucks	18	2-68
Lower Swatara	PA	717	17057	Dauphin	7	2-67
Lowville*	NY	315	13367	Lewis	3	2-54&55
Lubbock*	TX	806	79401-99	Lubbock	178	2-74
Lucedale*	MS	601	39452	George	1	2-42&43
Ludington*	MI	616	49431	Mason	8	2-38&39
Ludlow	KY	606	41016	Kenton	5	2-29
Ludlow	MA	413	01056	Hampden	18	2-36
Ludlow	VT	802	05149	Windsor	2	2-77
Ludowici*	GA	912	31316	Long	1	2-16&17
Lufkin*	TX	409	75901-15	Angelina	32	2-75
Luling	TX	512	78648	Caldwell	5	2-75
Lumberton*	NC	919	28358-59	Robeson	19	2-58&59
Lumberton	NJ	609	08048	Burlington	5	2-51
Lumpkin*	GA	912	31815	Stewart	1	2-16&17
Lunenburg	MA	508	01462	Worcester	8	2-36&37
Lunenburg*	VA	804	23952	Lunenburg	1	2-78&79
Luray*	VA	703	22835	Page	3	2-78&79
Lusk*	WY	307	82225	Niobrara	1	2-83
Lutcher	LA	504	70071	St. James	5	2-30&31
Lutz Hill	MD	301##	21237	Baltimore	3	2-34&35
Luverne*	AL	205	36049	Crenshaw	3	2-2&3
Luverne*	MN	507	56156	Rock	4	2-41
Luzerne	PA	717	18709	Luzerne	4	2-67
Lyman	ME	207	04005	York	3	2-32&33
Lyman	WY	307	82937	Uinta	2	2-83
Lynbrook	NY	516	11563	Nassau	20	2-56
Lynchburg	VA	804	24501-15	(IC)	69	2-78&79
Lynchburg*	TN	615	37352	Moore	1	2-72&73
Lynden	WA	206	98264	Watcom	4	2-80
Lyndhurst	NJ	201	07071	Bergen	20	2-52
Lyndhurst	OH	216	44124	Cuyahoga	18	2-62
Lyndon*	KS	913	67451	Osage	1	2-26&27
Lyndon	VT	802	05849	Caledonia	5	2-77
Lynn	MA	617	01901-08	Essex	80	2-36&37
Lynn Haven	FL	904	32444	Bay	6	2-14
Lynne Acres	MD	301##	21207	Baltimore	7	2-34&35
Lynnfield	MA	617	01940	Essex	12	2-36&37
Lynnwood	WA	206	98036-37	Snohomish	24	2-80
Lynwood	CA	213	90262	Los Angeles	55	2-7
Lyons*	GA	912	30436	Toombs	4	2-16&17
Lyons	IL	708	60534	Cook	9	2-19
Lyons*	KS	316	67554	Rice	4	2-26&27
Lyons*	NY	315	14489	Wayne	4	2-54&55
Mableton	GA	404	30059	Cobb	21	2-16&17
Macclenny*	FL	904	32063	Baker	4	2-14
Macedonia	OH	216	44056	Summit	6	2-62

Bold = Over 15,000......ALL CAPS = STATE CAPITAL......* = County Seat......# = Changes to 510 in 9/91.....## = Changes to 410 in 11/91.....(+) = City located in additional counties......NAV = Population not available......C.H.= Court House......(IC)=Independent City

CITY	STATE	AREA CODE	ZIP CODE	COUNTY	POPULATION (in thousands)	MAP PAGE
Machias*	ME	207	04654	Washington	2	2-32&33
Macomb*	IL	309	61455	McDonough	19	2-20
Macon*	GA	912	31201-99	Bibb	121	2-16&17
Macon*	MO	816	63552	Macon	5	2-44
Macon*	MS	601	39341	Noxubee	1	2-42&43
Madawaska	ME	207	04756	Aroostook	6	2-32&33
Madeira	OH	513	45243	Hamilton	9	2-62
Madeira Beach	FL	813	33708	Pinellas	4	2-14&15
Madera*	CA	209	93637-39	Madera	25	2-8&9
Madill*	OK	405	73446	Marshall	3	2-64&65
Madison	AL	205	35758	Madison	4	2-2&3
Madison	CT	203	06443	New Haven	14	2-12&13
Madison*	FL	904	32340	Madison	4	2-14
Madison*	GA	404	30650	Morgan	3	2-16
Madison	IL	618	62060	Madison (+1)	5	2-21
Madison*	IN	812	47250	Jefferson	12	2-23
Madison	ME	207	04950	Somerset	4	2-32&33
Madison*	MN	612	56256	Lac Qui Parle	2	2-41
Madison	NC	919	27025	Rockingham	3	2-58&59
Madison*	NE	402	68748	Madison	2	2-47
Madison	NJ	201	07940	Morris	16	2-52
Madison*	SD	605	57042	Lake	6	2-71
Madison*	VA	703	22727	Madison	1	2-78&79
MADISON*	WI	608	53701-99	Dane	170	2-85
Madison*	WV	304	25130	Boone	3	2-82
Madison Heights	MI	313	48071	Oakland	35	2-39
Madisonville*	KY	502	42431	Hopkins	17	2-28&29
Madisonville*	TN	615	37354	Monroe	3	2-72&73
Madisonville*	TX	409	77864	Madison	3	2-75
Madras*	OR	503	97741	Jefferson	1	2-63
Magee	MS	601	39111-12	Simpson	3	2-42&43
Magnolia	NJ	609	08049	Camden	5	2-51
Magnolia*	AR	501	71753	Columbia	11	2-6
Magnolia*	MS	601	39652	Pike	1	2-42&43
Mahanoy City	PA	717	17948	Schuylkill	6	2-67
Mahnomen*	MN	218	56557	Mahnomen	1	2-40
Mahtomedi	MN	612	55115	Washington	4	2-41
Mahwah	NJ	201	07430	Bergen	8	2-52
Maiden	NC	704	28650	Catawba (+1)	3	2-58
Maitland	FL	407	32751	Orange	9	2-14&15
Malad City*	ID	208	83252	Oneida	1	2-18
Malden	MA	617	02148	Middlesex	54	2-36&37
Malden	MO	314	63863	Dunklin	5	2-44&45
Malibu	CA	213	90264-65	Los Angeles	10	2-7
Malone*	NY	518	12953	Franklin	7	2-55
Malta*	MT	406	59538	Phillips	1	2-46
Malvern*	AR	501	72104-05	Hot Spring	10	2-6
Malvern	PA	215	19355	Chester	3	2-67

Bold = Over 15,000......ALL CAPS = STATE CAPITAL......* = County Seat......# = Changes to 510 in 9/91..... ## = Changes to 410 in 11/91......(+) = City located in addional counties......NAV= Population not available......C.H.= Court House......(IC) = Independent City

CITY	STATE	AREA CODE	ZIP CODE	COUNTY	POPULATION (in thousands)	MAP PAGE
Malverne	NY	516	11565	Nassau	9	2-56
Mamaroneck	NY	914	10543	Westchester	17	2-56
Mamou	LA	318	70554	Evangeline	3	2-30
Manahawkin	NJ	609	08050	Ocean	6	2-51
Manalapan	NJ	908	07728	Monmouth	19	2-50
Manasquan	NJ	908	08736	Monmouth	5	2-50
Manassas*	VA	703	22110-11	Prince William (IC)	17	2-78&79
Manassas Park	VA	703	22111	(IC)	5	2-79
Manchester	CT	203	06040-43	Hartford	50	2-12&13
Manchester	GA	404	31816	Meriwether (+1)	5	2-16
Manchester*	IA	319	52057	Delaware	5	2-25
Manchester*	KY	606	40962	Clay	2	2-29
Manchester	MA	508	01944	Essex	6	2-36&37
Manchester	MO	314	63011	St. Louis	6	2-44&45
Manchester	NH	603	03101-99	Hillsborough	100	2-49
Manchester	OH	216	44216	Summit	5	2-62
Manchester	PA	717	17345	York	8	2-67
Manchester*	TN	615	37355	Coffee	7	2-72&73
Manchester	VT	802	05255	Bennington	3	2-77
Mandan*	ND	701	58554	Morton	15	2-57
Mandeville	LA	504	70448	St. Tammany	6	2-30&31
Mangum*	OK	405	73554	Greer	3	2-64&65
Manhasset	NY	516	11030	Nassau	8	2-56
Manhattan*	KS	913	66502	Riley (+1)	33	2-26&27
Manhattan	NY	212	10027	New York	NAV	2-56
Manhattan Beach	CA	213	90266	Los Angeles	34	2-7
Manheim	PA	717	17545	Lancaster	5	2-67
Manila	AR	501	72442	Mississippi	3	2-6
Manila*	UT	801	84046	Daggett	1	2-76
Manistee*	MI	616	49660	Manistee	7	2-38&39
Manistique*	MI	906	49854	Schoolcraft	3	2-38
Manitou Springs	CO	719	80829	El Paso	5	2-11
Manitowoc*	WI	414	54220	Manitowoc	32	2-85
Mankato*	KS	913	66956	Jewell	1	2-26&27
Mankato*	MN	507	56001	Blue Earth	29	2-41
Manlius	NY	315	13104	Onondaga	5	2-54&55
Manning*	ND	701	58642	Dunn	1	2-57
Manning*	SC	803	29102	Clarendon	4	2-70
Mannington	WV	304	26582	Marion	3	2-82
Manor Woods	MD	301	20853	Montgomery	4	2-34&35
Manorhaven	NY	516	11050	Nassau	5	2-56
Mansfield*	LA	318	71052	De Soto	7	2-30
Mansfield	MA	508	02048	Bristol	7	2-36&37
Mansfield*	OH	419	44901-99	Richland	51	2-60
Mansfield	PA	717	16933	Tioga	3	2-67
Mansfield	TX	817	76063	Johnson (+1)	8	2-74
Manteca	CA	209	95336	San Joaquin	36	2-8&9
Manteno	IL	815	60950	Kankakee	3	2-20

Bold = Over 15,000......ALL CAPS = STATE CAPITAL......* = County Seat......# = Changes to 510 in 9/91.....## = Changes to 410 in 11/91.....(+) = City located in additional counties......NAV = Population not available......C.H.= Court House......(IC)=Independent City

CITY	STATE	AREA CODE	ZIP CODE	COUNTY	POPULATION (in thousands)	MAP PAGE
Manteo*	NC	919	27954	Dare	1	2-58&59
Manti*	UT	801	84642	Sanpete	1	2-76
Mantorville*	MN	507	55955	Dodge	1	2-41
Manvel	TX	713	77578	Brazoria	4	2-74&75
Manville	NJ	908	08835	Somerset	11	2-50
Many*	LA	318	71449	Sabine	4	2-30
Maple Grove	MN	612	55369	Hennepin	29	2-41
Maple Heights	OH	216	44137	Cuyahoga	28	2-62
Maple Shade	NJ	609	08052	Burlington	20	2-51
Mapleton	UT	801	84663	Utah	3	2-76
Maplewood	MN	612	55109	Ramsey	30	2-41
Maplewood	MO	314	63143	St. Louis	9	2-44&45
Maplewood	NJ	201	07040	Essex	22	2-52
Maquoketa*	IA	319	52060	Jackson	6	2-25
Marathon	FL	305	33050-52	Monroe	8	2-15
Marble Falls	TX	512	78654	Burnet	3	2-75
Marble Hill*	MO	314	63764	Bollinger	1	2-44&45
Marblehead	MA	617	01945	Essex	20	2-36&37
Marceline	MO	816	64658	Chariton (+1)	3	2-44
Marcus Hook	PA	215	19061	Delaware	3	2-68
Marengo*	IA	319	52301	Iowa	2	2-25
Marengo	IL	815	60152	McHenry	4	2-20
Marfa*	TX	915	79843	Presidio	1	2-74&75
Margate	FL	305	33063	Broward	36	2-15
Margate City	NJ	609	08402	Atlantic	9	2-51
Marianna*	AR	501	72360	Lee	7	2-6
Marianna*	FL	904	32446	Jackson	7	2-14
Mariemont	OH	513	45227	Hamilton	3	2-62
Marietta*	GA	404	30060-68	Cobb	42	2-16&17
Marietta*	OH	614	45750	Washington	64	2-61
Marietta*	OK	405	73448	Love	1	2-64&65
Marietta	PA	717	17547	Lancaster	3	2-67
Marina	CA	408	93933	Monterey	27	2-9
Marine City	MI	313	48039	St. Clair	5	2-39
Marinette*	WI	715	54143	Marinette	11	2-84&85
Marion*	AL	205	36756	Perry	4	2-2&3
Marion*	AR	501	72364	Crittenden	4	2-6
Marion	IA	319	52302	Linn	19	2-25
Marion*	IL	618	62959	Williamson	15	2-21
Marion*	IN	317	46952-53	Grant	36	2-22&23
Marion*	KS	316	66861	Marion	2	2-26&27
Marion*	KY	502	42064	Crittenden	3	2-28&29
Marion	MA	508	02738	Plymouth	4	2-36&37
Marion*	NC	704	28752	McDowell	4	2-58
Marion*	OH	614	43301-02	Marion	35	2-61
Marion*	SC	803	29571	Marion	7	2-70
Marion*	VA	703	24354	Smyth	7	2-78&79
Mariposa*	CA	209	95338	Mariposa	1	2-8&9

Bold = Over 15,000......ALL CAPS = STATE CAPITAL......* = County Seat......# = Changes to 510 in 9/91..... ## = Changes to 410 in 11/91......(+) = City located in addional counties......NAV= Population not available......C.H.= Court House......(IC) = Independent City

CITY	STATE	AREA CODE	ZIP CODE	COUNTY	POPULATION (in thousands)	MAP PAGE
Marissa	IL	618	62257	St. Clair	2	2-21
Marked Tree	AR	501	72365	Poinsett	3	2-6
Markham	IL	708	60426	Cook	15	2-19
Markleeville*	CA	916	96120	Alpine	1	2-8
Marks*	MS	601	38646	Quitman	1	2-42&43
Marksville*	LA	318	71351	Avoyelles	5	2-30
Marlborough	CT	203	06447	Hartford	5	2-12&13
Marlborough	MA	508	01752	Middlesex	32	2-36&37
Marlette	MI	517	48453	Sanilac	4	2-38&39
Marley	MD	301##	21061	Anne Arundel	5	2-34&35
Marlin*	TX	817	76661	Falls	6	2-74
Marlinton*	WV	304	24954	Pocahontas	3	2-82
Marlow	OK	405	73055	Stephens	5	2-64&65
Marlton	NJ	609	08053	Burlington	3	2-51
Marple	PA	215	19008	Delaware	23	2-68
Marquette Heights	IL	309	61554	Tazewell	3	2-20
Marquette*	MI	906	49855	Marquette	21	2-38
Marseilles	IL	815	61341	La Salle	5	2-20
Marshall*	AR	501	72650	Searcy	1	2-6
Marshall*	IL	217	62441	Clark	3	2-20&21
Marshall*	MI	616	49068	Calhoun	6	2-38&39
Marshall*	MN	507	56258	Lyon	11	2-41
Marshall*	MO	816	65340	Saline	2	2-44
Marshall*	NC	704	28753	Madison	1	2-58
Marshall*	TX	903	75670-71	Harrison	24	2-74
Marshallton	DE	302	19808 &09	New Castle	3	2-35
Marshalltown*	IA	515	50158	Marshall	26	2-24&25
Marshfield	MA	617	02050	Plymouth	21	2-36&37
Marshfield*	MO	417	65706	Webster	4	2-44
Marshfield	WI	715	54449	Marathon (+1)	20	2-84&85
Martha Lake	WA	206	98011	Snohomish	3	2-80
Martin*	SD	605	57551	Bennett	1	2-71
Martin	TN	901	38237	Weakley	9	2-72
Martinez*	CA	415#	94553	Contra Costa	27	2-7
Martins Ferry	OH	614	43935	Belmont	9	2-61
Martinsburg*	WV	304	25401	Berkeley	13	2-82
Martinsville*	IN	317	46151	Morgan	11	2-22&23
Martinsville*	VA	703	24112-15	Henry (IC)	18	2-78&79
Mary Esther	FL	904	32569	Okaloosa	4	2-14
Maryland City	MD	301##	20707	Anne Arundel	6	2-34&35
Maryland Heights	MO	314	63043	St. Louis	27	2-44&45
Marysville*	CA	916	95901	Yuba	10	2-8
Marysville*	KS	913	66508	Marshall	4	2-26&27
Marysville	MI	313	48040	St. Clair	6	2-39
Marysville*	OH	513	43040	Union	7	2-61
Marysville	WA	206	98270	Snohomish	6	2-80
Maryville*	MO	816	64468	Nodaway	9	2-44
Maryville*	TN	615	37801-04	Blount	18	2-72&73

Bold = Over 15,000......ALL CAPS = STATE CAPITAL......* = County Seat......# = Changes to 510 in 9/91.....## = Changes to 410 in 11/91.....(+)
= City located in additional counties......NAV = Population not available......C.H.= Court House......(IC)=Independent City

CITY	STATE	AREA CODE	ZIP CODE	COUNTY	POPULATION (in thousands)	MAP PAGE
Mascoutah	IL	618	62258	St. Clair	5	2-21
Mason	MI	517	48854	Ingham	6	2-38&39
Mason	OH	513	45040	Warren	9	2-61
Mason*	TX	915	76856	Mason	1	2-74&75
Mason City*	IA	515	50401	Cerro Gordo	30	2-24&25
Mason City	IL	217	62664	Mason	3	2-20&21
Masontown	PA	412	15461	Fayette	5	2-66
Massapequa	NY	516	11758	Nassau	24	2-56
Massapequa Park	NY	516	11762	Nassau	19	2-56
Massena	NY	315	13662	St. Lawrence	13	2-54&55
Massillon	OH	216	44646-48	Stark	32	2-60
Mastic	NY	516	11950	Suffolk	10	2-56
Matador*	TX	806	79244	Motley	1	2-74
Matawan	NJ	908	07747	Monmouth	8	2-50
Mathews*	VA	804	23109	Mathews	1	2-78&79
Mathis	TX	512	78368	San Patricio	6	2-75
Mattapan	MA	617	02126	Suffolk	6	2-36&37
Mattapoisett	MA	508	02739	Plymouth	4	2-36&37
Matteson	IL	708	60443	Cook	11	2-19
Mattoon	IL	217	61938	Coles	20	2-20&21
Mauldin	SC	803	29662	Greenville	8	2-70
Maumee	OH	419	43537	Lucus	16	2-60
Maumelle	AR	501	72118	Pulaski	5	2-6
Mauston*	WI	608	53948	Juneau	3	2-85
Maxton	NC	919	28364	Robeson (+1)	3	2-58&59
Mayersville*	MS	601	39113	Issaquena	1	2-42&43
Mayfield Heights	OH	216	44124	Cuyahoga	32	2-62
Mayfield*	KY	502	42066	Graves	10	2-28&29
Maynard	MA	508	01754	Middlesex	9	2-36&37
Maynardville*	TN	615	37807	Union	1	2-72&73
Mayo*	FL	904	32066	Lafayette	1	2-14
Mayodan	NC	919	27027	Rockingham	3	2-58&59
Mays Landing*	NJ	609	08330	Atlantic	1	2-51
Maysville*	KY	606	41056	Mason	7	2-29
Maysville*	MO	816	64469	De Kalb	1	2-44
Maysville	OK	405	73057	Garvin	1	2-64&65
Mayville*	NY	716	14757	Chautauqua	1	2-54
Mayville	WI	414	53050	Dodge	4	2-85
Maywood	CA	213	90270	Los Angeles	25	2-7
Maywood	IL	708	60153-54	Cook	27	2-19
Maywood	NJ	201	07607	Bergen	10	2-52
Maywood	NY	518	12205	Albany	3	2-55
McAdoo	PA	717	18237	Schuykill	3	2-67
McAlester*	OK	918	74501-02	Pittsburg	18	2-65
McAllen	TX	512	78501-04	Hidalgo	83	2-75
McArthur*	OH	614	45651	Vinton	11	2-61
McCandless	PA	412	15237	Allegheny	25	2-68
McClusky*	ND	701	58463	Sheridan	1	2-57

Bold = Over 15,000......ALL CAPS = STATE CAPITAL......* = County Seat......# = Changes to 510 in 9/91..... ## = Changes to 410 in 11/91......(+) = City located in addional counties......NAV = Population not available......C.H. = Court House......(IC) = Independent City

CITY	STATE	AREA CODE	ZIP CODE	COUNTY	POPULATION (in thousands)	MAP PAGE
McColl	SC	803	29570	Marlboro	3	2-70
McComb	MS	601	39648	Pike	13	2-42&43
McConnellsburg*	PA	717	17233	Fulton	1	2-67
McConnelsville*	OH	614	43756	Morgan	14	2-61
McCook*	NE	308	69001	Red Willow	9	2-47
McCormick*	SC	803	29835	McCormick	1	2-70
McCrory	AR	501	72101	Woodruff	2	2-6
McDonald	OH	216	44437	Trumbull	4	2-60
McDonald	PA	412	15057	Allegheny (+1)	3	2-66
McDonough*	GA	404	30253	Henry	3	2-16&17
McFarland	CA	805	93250	Kern	6	2-9
McFarland	WI	608	53558	Dane	4	2-85
McGehee	AR	501	71654	Desha	5	2-6
McHenry	IL	815	60050	McHenry	14	2-20
McIntosh*	SD	605	57641	Corson	1	2-71
McKee*	KY	606	40447	Jackson	1	2-29
McKees Rocks	PA	412	15136	Allegheny	9	2-68
McKeesport	PA	412	15130-35	Allegheny	28	2-68
McKenzie	TN	901	38201	Carroll (+2)	5	2-72
McKinney*	TX	214	75069-70	Collin	18	2-74
McLean	VA	703	22101-06	Fairfax	36	2-78&79
McLeansboro	IL	618	62859	Hamilton	2	2-21
McLoud	OK	405	74851	Pottawatomie	4	2-64&65
McMicken Heights	WA	206	98188	King	4	2-80
McMinnville*	OR	503	97128	Yamhill	15	2-63
McMinnville*	TN	615	37110	Warren	10	2-72&73
McPherson*	KS	316	67460	McPherson	2	2-26&27
McRae*	GA	912	31055	Telfair	3	2-16&17
McSherrystown	PA	717	17344	Adams	3	2-67
Meade*	KS	316	67864	Meade	2	2-26&27
Meadowbrook	IN	219	46774	Allen	4	2-22
Meadville*	MS	601	39653	Franklin	1	2-42&43
Meadville*	PA	814	16335	Crawford	14	2-66
Mebane	NC	919	27302	Alamance (+1)	3	2-58&59
Mechanic Falls	ME	207	04256	Androscoggin	3	2-32&33
Mechanicsburg	PA	717	17055	Perry	3	2-67
Mechanicville	NY	518	12118	Saratoga	6	2-55
Medfield	MA	508	02052	Norfolk	10	2-36&37
Medford	MA	617	02155	Middlesex	58	2-36&37
Medford*	OK	405	73759	Grant	1	2-64&65
Medford*	OR	503	97501-04	Jackson	43	2-63
Medford*	WI	715	54451	Taylor	4	2-84&85
Medford Lakes	NJ	609	08055	Burlington	5	2-51
Media*	PA	215	19063-65	Delaware	6	2-68
Medical Lake	WA	509	99022	Spokane	4	2-81
Medicine Lodge*	KS	316	67104	Barber	2	2-26&27
Medina	NY	716	14103	Orleans	6	2-54
Medina	WA	206	98039	King	3	2-80

Bold = Over 15,000......ALL CAPS = STATE CAPITAL......* = County Seat......# = Changes to 510 in 9/91.....## = Changes to 410 in 11/91.....(+) = City located in additional counties......NAV = Population not available......C.H.= Court House......(IC)=Independent City

CITY	STATE	AREA CODE	ZIP CODE	COUNTY	POPULATION (in thousands)	MAP PAGE
Medina*	OH	216	44256-59	Medina	16	2-60
Medora*	ND	701	58645	Billings	1	2-57
Medway	MA	508	02053	Norfolk	4	2-36&37
Meeker*	CO	303	81641	Rio Blanco	1	2-10&11
Melbourne*	AR	501	72565	Izard	1	2-6
Melbourne	FL	407	32901-40	Brevard	58	2-14&15
Melbourne Beach	FL	407	32951	Brevard	3	2-14&15
Melrose	MA	617	02176-77	Middlesex	30	2-36&37
Melrose Park	IL	708	60160-65	Cook	20	2-19
Melville	NY	516	11747	Suffolk	8	2-56
Melvindale	MI	313	48122	Wayne	12	2-39
Memphis*	MO	816	63555	Scotland	1	2-44
Memphis*	TN	901	38101-99	Shelby	652	2-72
Memphis*	TX	806	79245	Hall	2	2-74
Mena*	AR	501	71953	Polk	5	2-6
Menands	NY	518	12204	Albany	5	2-55
Menard*	TX	915	76859	Menard	1	2-74&75
Menasha	WI	414	54952	Calumet (+1)	15	2-85
Mendenhall*	MS	601	39114	Simpson	2	2-42&43
Mendham	NJ	201	07945	Morris	5	2-52
Mendon	MA	508	01756	Worcester	4	2-36&37
Mendota	CA	209	93640	Fresno	7	2-8&9
Mendota	IL	815	61342	La Salle	7	2-20
Mendota Heights	MN	612	55118	Dakota	7	2-41
Menlo Park	CA	415	94025-28	San Mateo	27	2-7
Menominee*	MI	906	49858	Menominee	9	2-38
Menomonee Falls	WI	414	53051	Waukesha	28	2-85
Menomonie*	WI	715	54751	Dunn	13	2-84&85
Mentone	CA	714	92359	San Bernardino	4	2-9
Mentor	OH	216	44060-61	Lake	43	2-62
Mentor-on-the-Lake	OH	216	44060	Lake	8	2-62
Mentrone*	TX	915	79754	Loving	1	2-74&75
Mequon	WI	414	53092	Ozaukee	16	2-85
Merced*	CA	209	95340-44	Merced	47	2-8&9
Mercedes	TX	512	78570	Hidalgo	12	2-75
Mercer Island	WA	206	98040	King	22	2-80
Mercer*	PA	412	16137	Mercer	2	2-66
Mercerville	NJ	609	08619	Mercer	15	2-50
Merchantville	NJ	609	08109	Camden	4	2-51
Meredith	NH	603	03253	Belknap	5	2-49
Meriden	CT	203	06450	New Haven	58	2-12&13
Meridian	ID	208	83642	Ada	7	2-18
Meridian	MI	517	48823	Ingham	29	2-38&39
Meridian*	MS	601	39301-09	Lauderdale	42	2-42&43
Meridian*	TX	817	76665	Bosque	1	2-74
Merriam	KS	913	66203	Johnson	10	2-26&27
Merrick	NY	516	11566	Nassau	24	2-56
Merrill*	WI	715	54452	Lincoln	10	2-84&85

Bold = Over 15,000......ALL CAPS = STATE CAPITAL......* = County Seat......# = Changes to 510 in 9/91..... ## = Changes to 410 in 11/91......(+) = City located in addional counties......NAV= Population not available......C.H.= Court House......(IC) = Independent City

CITY	STATE	AREA CODE	ZIP CODE	COUNTY	POPULATION (in thousands)	MAP PAGE
Merrillville	IN	219	46410	Lake	27	2-22
Merrimac	MA	508	01860	Essex	5	2-36&37
Merrimack	NH	603	03054	Hillsborough	15	2-49
Merritt Island	FL	407	32952-54	Brevard	38	2-14&15
Mertzon*	TX	915	76941	Irion	1	2-74&75
Mesa	AZ	602	85201-16	Maricopa	237	2-5
Mesquite	TX	214	75149-82	Dallas	82	2-74
Metairie	LA	504	70001-11	Jefferson	173	2-30&31
Methuen	MA	508	01844	Essex	39	2-36&37
Metropolis*	IL	618	62960	Massac	7	2-21
Metter*	GA	912	30439	Candler	4	2-16&17
Metuchen	NJ	908	08840	Middlesex	14	2-50
Mexia	TX	817	76667	Limestone	7	2-74
Mexico	ME	207	04257	Oxford	4	2-32&33
Mexico*	MO	314	65265	Audrain	11	2-44&45
Meyersdale	PA	814	15552	Somerset	3	2-66
Miami	AZ	602	85539	Gila	3	2-5
Miami*	FL	305	33101-269	Dade	386	2-15
Miami*	OK	918	74354-55	Ottawa	14	2-65
Miami*	TX	806	79059	Roberts	1	2-74
Miami Beach	FL	305	33139	Dade	98	2-15
Miami Shores	FL	305	33138	Dade	9	2-15
Miami Springs	FL	305	33166	Dade	12	2-15
Miamisburg	OH	513	45342-43	Montgomery	16	2-61
Michigan City	IN	219	46360	La Porte	36	2-22
Middleborough	MA	508	02346	Plymouth	16	2-36&37
Middlebourne*	WV	304	26149	Tyler	1	2-82
Middleburg*	PA	717	17842	Snyder	1	2-67
Middleburgh Heights	OH	216	44130	Cuyahoga	15	2-62
Middlebury	CT	203	06762	New Haven	6	2-12&13
Middlebury*	VT	802	05753	Addison	7	2-77
Middlefield	CT	203	06455	Middlesex	4	2-12&13
Middleport	OH	614	45760	Meigs	3	2-61
Middlesboro	KY	606	40965	Bell	12	2-29
Middlesex	NJ	908	08846	Middlesex	14	2-50
Middleton	MA	508	01949	Essex	4	2-36&37
Middleton	WI	608	53562	Dane	12	2-85
Middletown*	CT	203	06457	Middlesex	39	2-12&13
Middletown	DE	302	19709	New Castle	3	2-35
Middletown	IN	317	47356	Henry	3	2-22&23
Middletown	KY	502	40243	Jefferson	4	2-28
Middletown	NJ	908	07748	Monmouth	21	2-50
Middletown	NY	914	10940	Orange	23	2-56
Middletown	OH	513	45042-44	Butler (+1)	44	2-61
Middletown	PA	215	18017	Northampton	6	2-67
Middletown	PA	717	17057	Dauphin	10	2-67
Middletown	PA	215	19056	Bucks	34	2-68
Middletown	RI	401	02840	Newport	3	2-69

Bold = Over 15,000......ALL CAPS = STATE CAPITAL......* = County Seat......# = Changes to 510 in 9/91.....## = Changes to 410 in 11/91......(+) = City located in additional counties......NAV = Population not available......C.H.= Court House......(IC)=Independent City

CITY	STATE	AREA CODE	ZIP CODE	COUNTY	POPULATION (in thousands)	MAP PAGE
Middletown Twp.	PA	215	19037	Delaware	11	2-68
Midfield	AL	205	35228	Jefferson	6	2-2&3
Midland*	MI	517	48640-41	Midland	37	2-38&39
Midland	PA	412	15059	Beaver	4	2-66
Midland*	TX	915	79701-12	Midland	98	2-74&75
Midland	WA	206	98444	Pierce	3	2-80
Midland Park	NJ	201	07432	Bergen	7	2-52
Midlothian	IL	708	60445	Cook	14	2-19
Midlothian	TX	214	76065	Ellis	3	2-74
Midvale	UT	801	84047	Salt Lake	10	2-76
Midwest City	OK	405	73110	Oklahoma	54	2-64&65
Mifflinburg	PA	717	17844	Union	3	2-67
Mifflintown*	PA	717	17059	Juniata	1	2-67
Milaca*	MN	612	56353	Mille Lacs	1	2-41
Milan	IL	309	61264	Rock Island	6	2-20
Milan	MI	313	48160	Washtenaw (+1)	4	2-39
Milan*	MO	816	63556	Sullivan	1	2-44
Milan	NM	505	87021	Cibola	4	2-53
Milan	TN	901	38358	Gibson	8	2-72
Milbank*	SD	605	57252	Grant	4	2-71
Miles City*	MT	406	59301	Custer	9	2-46
Milford	CT	203	06460	New Haven	52	2-12&13
Milford	DE	302	19963	Sussex (+1)	5	2-35
Milford	MA	508	01757	Worcester	25	2-36&37
Milford	MI	313	48042	Oakland	6	2-39
Milford	NH	603	03055	Hillsborough	9	2-49
Milford	OH	513	45150	Clermont (+1)	6	2-61
Milford*	PA	717	18337	Pike	1	2-67
Milford Ridge	MD	301##	21207	Baltimore	4	2-34&35
Mill Valley	CA	415	94941-42	Marin	12	2-7
Millbrae	CA	415	94030	San Mateo	20	2-7
Millbrook	AL	205	36054	Elmore	8	2-2&3
Millburn	NJ	201	07041	Essex	20	2-52
Millbury	MA	508	01527	Worcester	5	2-36&37
Millcreek Twp.	PA	814	16506	Erie	45	2-66
Milledgeville*	GA	912	31061	Baldwin	14	2-16&17
Millen*	GA	912	30442	Jenkins	4	2-16&17
Miller*	SD	605	57362	Hand	1	2-71
Millersburg*	OH	216	44654	Holmes	3	2-60
Millersburg	PA	717	17061	Dauphin	3	2-67
Millersville	PA	717	17551	Lancaster	7	2-67
Millington	TN	901	38053-54	Shelby	20	2-72
Millinocket	ME	207	04462	Penobscot	7	2-32&33
Millis	MA	508	02054	Norfolk	7	2-36&37
Millstadt	IL	618	62260	St. Clair	3	2-21
Milltown	NJ	908	08850	Middlesex	7	2-50
Millvale	PA	412	15209	Allegheny	5	2-68
Millville	NJ	609	08332	Cumberland	26	2-51

**Bold = Over 15,000......ALL CAPS = STATE CAPITAL......* = County Seat......# = Changes to 510 in 9/91..... ## = Changes to 410 in 11/91......(+) = City located in addional counties......NAV= Population not available......C.H.= Court House......(IC) = Independent City

CITY	STATE	AREA CODE	ZIP CODE	COUNTY	POPULATION (in thousands)	MAP PAGE
Milo	ME	207	04463	Piscataquis	3	2-32&33
Milpitas	CA	408	95035-36	Santa Clara	44	2-7
Milton	DE	302	19968	Sussex	1	2-35
Milton	CA	408	95235	Santa Cruz	6	2-7
Milton*	FL	904	32570-71	Santa Rosa	7	2-14
Milton	MA	617	02186	Norfolk	26	2-36&37
Milton	PA	717	17847	Northumberland	7	2-67
Milton*	VT	802	05468	Chittenden	7	2-77
Milton	WA	206	98354	Pierce (+1)	3	2-80
Milton	WI	608	53563	Rock	4	2-85
Milton-Freewater	OR	503	97862	Umatilla	6	2-63
Milwaukie	OR	503	97222	Multnomah (+1)	18	2-63
Milwaukee*	WI	414	53201-99	Milwaukee (+1)	605	2-85
Minden*	LA	318	71055	Webster	15	2-30
Minden*	NE	308	68959	Kearney	3	2-47
Minden*	NV	702	89423	Douglas	1	2-48
Mineola*	NY	516	11501	Nassau	20	2-56
Mineola	TX	903	75773	Wood	4	2-74
Mineral Wells	TX	817	76067	Palo Pinto (+1)	15	2-74&75
Minersville	PA	717	17954	Schuykill	5	2-67
Minerva	OH	216	44657	Stark (+2)	5	2-60
Mingo Junction	OH	614	43938	Jefferson	5	2-61
Minneapolis*	KS	913	67467	Ottawa	2	2-26&27
Minneapolis*	MN	612	55401-99	Hennepin	358	2-41
Minnetonka	MN	612	55345	Hennepin	43	2-41
Minnewaukan*	ND	701	58351	Benson	1	2-57
Minoa	NY	315	13116	Onondaga	4	2-54&55
Minot*	ND	701	58701-04	Ward	35	2-57
Minster	OH	419	45865	Auglaize	2	2-60
Mint Hill	NC	704	28212	Mecklenburg	10	2-58
Mio*	MI	517	48647	Oscoda	1	2-38&39
Mira Loma	CA	714	91752	Riverside	9	2-9
Miramar	FL	305	33023	Broward	38	2-15
Mishawaka	IN	219	46544-45	St. Joseph	42	2-22
Mission	KS	913	66205	Johnson	9	2-26&27
Mission	TX	512	78572	Hidalgo	23	2-75
Mission Hills	KS	913	66205	Johnson	4	2-26&27
Mission Viejo	CA	714	92691	Orange	54	2-7
Missoula*	MT	406	59801-07	Missoula	33	2-46
Missouri City	TX	713	77459	Fort Bent	24	2-74&75
Missouri Valley	IA	712	51555	Harrison	30	2-24
Mitchell	IN	812	47446	Lawrence	5	2-23
Mitchell*	SD	605	57301	Davison	13	2-71
Moab*	UT	801	84532	Grand	5	2-76
Moberly	MO	816	65270	Randolph	13	2-44
Mobile*	AL	205	36601-99	Mobile	205	2-2&3
Mobridge	SD	605	57601	Walworth	4	2-71
Mocksville*	NC	704	27028	Davie	3	2-58

Bold = Over 15,000......ALL CAPS = STATE CAPITAL......* = County Seat......# = Changes to 510 in 9/91.....## = Changes to 410 in 11/91.....(+) = City located in additional counties......NAV = Population not available......C.H.= Court House......(IC)=Independent City

CITY	STATE	AREA CODE	ZIP CODE	COUNTY	POPULATION (in thousands)	MAP PAGE
Modesto*	CA	209	95350-56	Stanislaus	132	2-8&9
Mogadore	OH	216	44260	Portage (+1)	4	2-60
Mohall*	ND	701	58761	Renville	1	2-57
Mohawk	NY	315	13407	Herkimer	3	2-54&55
Mohegan Lake	NY	914	10547	Westchester	4	2-56
Mojave	CA	805	93501	Kern	3	2-9
Mokena	IL	708	60448	Will	5	2-20
Molalla	OR	503	97038	Clackamas	3	2-63
Moline	IL	309	61265	Rock Island	46	2-20
Momence	IL	815	60954	Kankakee	3	2-20
Monaca	PA	412	15061	Beaver	8	2-66
Monahans*	TX	915	79756	Ward	9	2-74&75
Moncks Corner*	SC	803	29461	Berkeley	5	2-70
Mondovi	WI	715	54755	Buffalo	3	2-84&85
Monessen	PA	412	15062	Westmooreland	10	2-68
Monett	MO	417	65708	Barry (+1)	6	2-44
Monmouth*	IL	309	61462	Warren	10	2-20
Monmouth	ME	207	04259	Kennebec	3	2-32&33
Monmouth	OR	503	97361	Polk	6	2-63
Monmouth Junction	NJ	908	08852	Middlesex	3	2-50
Monona	WI	608	53716	Dane	8	2-85
Monongahela	PA	412	15063	Washington	6	2-66
Monroe	CT	203	06468	Fairfield	14	2-12&13
Monroe*	GA	404	30655	Walton	9	2-16&17
Monroe*	LA	318	71201-12	Ouachita	56	2-30
Monroe*	MI	313	48161	Monroe	21	2-39
Monroe*	NC	704	28110	Union	17	2-58
Monroe	NY	914	10950	Orange	6	2-56
Monroe	OH	513	45050	Butler (+1)	4	2-61
Monroe	WA	206	98272	Snohomish	3	2-80
Monroe*	WI	608	53566	Green	10	2-85
Monroe City	MO	314	63456	Marion (+2)	2	2-44&45
Monroe Falls	OH	216	44262	Summit	5	2-62
Monroeville*	AL	205	36460-61	Monroe	6	2-2&3
Monroeville	PA	412	15146	Allegheny	29	2-68
Monrovia	CA	818	91016	Los Angeles	33	2-7
Monson	MA	413	01057	Hampden	2	2-36
Montague	MA	413	01351	Franklin	8	2-36
Montague*	TX	817	76251	Montague	1	2-74
Montclair	CA	714	91763	San Bernardino	25	2-9
Montclair	NJ	201	07042-44	Essex	39	2-52
Monte Sereno	CA	408	95030	Santa Clara	3	2-7
Monte Vista	CO	303	81144	Rio Grande	4	2-10&11
Montebello	CA	213	90640	Los Angeles	54	2-7
Montebello	NY	914	10901	Rockland	3	2-56
Montecito	CA	805	93108	Santa Barbara	9	2-9
Montello*	WI	608	53949	Marquette	1	2-85
Monterey	CA	408	93940-44	Monterey	30	2-9

Bold = Over 15,000......ALL CAPS = STATE CAPITAL......* = County Seat......# = Changes to 510 in 9/91...... ## = Changes to 410 in 11/91......(+) = City located in addional counties......NAV= Population not available......C.H.= Court House......(IC) = Independent City

CITY	STATE	AREA CODE	ZIP CODE	COUNTY	POPULATION (in thousands)	MAP PAGE
Monterey Park	CA	818	91754-56	Los Angeles	60	2-7
Monterey*	VA	703	24465	Highland	1	2-78&79
Montesano*	WA	206	98563	Grays Harbor	3	2-80
Montevallo	AL	205	35115	Shelby	4	2-2&3
Montevideo*	MN	612	56265	Chippewa	5	2-41
Montezuma	GA	912	31063	Macon	5	2-16&17
Montezuma*	IA	515	50171	Poweshiek	1	2-24&25
MONTGOMERY*	AL	205	36101-99	Montgomery	193	2-2&3
Montgomery	IL	708	60538	Kane (+1)	4	2-20
Montgomery	OH	513	45242	Hamilton	10	2-62
Montgomery	WV	304	25136	Fayette (+1)	3	2-82
Montgomery City*	MO	314	63361	Montgomery	2	2-45
Montgomery Village	MD	301	20879	Montgomery	17	2-34
Monticello*	AR	501	71655	Drew	9	2-6
Monticello*	FL	904	32344	Jefferson	3	2-14
Monticello*	GA	404	31064	Jasper	1	2-16&17
Monticello	IA	319	52310	Jones	3	2-25
Monticello*	IL	217	61856	Piatt	5	2-20&21
Monticello*	IN	219	47960	White	5	2-22
Monticello*	KY	606	42633	Wayne	6	2-29
Monticello	MN	612	55362	Wright	3	2-41
Monticello*	MO	314	63457	Lewis	1	2-44&45
Monticello*	MS	601	39654	Lawrence	1	2-42&43
Monticello*	NY	914	12701	Sullivan	6	2-56
Monticello*	UT	801	84535	San Juan	2	2-76
Montoursville	PA	717	17754	Lycoming	6	2-67
Montpelier	MD	301	20708	Prince Georges	4	2-34&35
Montpelier	OH	419	43543	Williams	4	2-60
MONTPELIER*	VT	802	05602	Washington	8	2-77
Montrose	CA	818	91020	Los Angeles	4	2-7
Montrose*	CO	303	81401	Montrose	9	2-10&11
Montrose*	PA	717	18801	Susquehanna	2	2-67
Montrose	VA	804	23231	Henrico	3	2-78&79
Montross*	VA	804	22520	Westmoreland	1	2-78&79
Montvale	NJ	201	07645	Bergen	7	2-52
Montville	CT	203	06353	New London	16	2-12&13
Montville	NJ	201	07045	Morris	3	2-52
Moon	PA	412	15108	Allegheny	20	2-68
Moonachie	NJ	201	07074	Bergen	3	2-52
Moore	OK	405	73160	Cleveland	43	2-64&65
Moore Haven*	FL	813	33471	Glades	1	2-14&15
Moorefield*	WV	304	26836	Hardy	1	2-82
Moorestown	NJ	609	08057	Burlington	16	2-51
Mooresville	IN	317	46158	Morgan	5	2-22&23
Mooresville	NC	704	28115	Iredell	9	2-58
Moorhead*	MN	218	56560	Clay	28	2-40
Moorpark	CA	805	93020-21	Ventura	15	2-9
Moosic	PA	717	18517	Lackawanna	6	2-67

Bold = Over 15,000......ALL CAPS = STATE CAPITAL......* = County Seat......# = Changes to 510 in 9/91.....## = Changes to 410 in 11/91.....(+) = City located in additional counties......NAV = Population not available......C.H.= Court House......(IC)=Independent City

CITY	STATE	AREA CODE	ZIP CODE	COUNTY	POPULATION (in thousands)	MAP PAGE
Mora*	MN	612	55051	Kanabec	2	2-41
Mora*	NM	505	87732	Mora	1	2-53
Moraga	CA	415#	94556	Contra Costa	15	2-7
Moraine	OH	513	45439	Montgomery	5	2-61
Morehead*	KY	606	40351	Rowan	8	2-29
Morehead City	NC	919	28557	Carteret	4	2-58&59
Moreland Hills	OH	216	44022	Cuyahoga	3	2-62
Morgan*	GA	912	31766	Calhoun	1	2-16&17
Morgan*	UT	801	84050	Morgan	2	2-76
Morgan City	LA	504	70380-81	St. Mary	17	2-30&31
Morgan Hill	CA	408	95037-38	Santa Clara	21	2-7
Morganfield*	KY	502	42437	Union	4	2-28&29
Morganton*	NC	704	28655	Burke	14	2-58
Morgantown*	KY	502	42261	Butler	2	2-28&29
Morgantown*	WV	304	26502-07	Monongalia	26	2-82
Morneno Valley	CA	714	92387-88	Riverside	68	2-9
Moro*	OR	503	97039	Sherman	1	2-63
Morrilton*	AR	501	72110	Conway	7	2-6
Morris*	IL	815	60450	Grundy	9	2-20
Morris*	MN	612	56267	Stevens	4	2-41
Morris Plains	NJ	201	07950	Morris	5	2-52
Morrison*	IL	815	61270	Whiteside	6	2-20
Morristown*	NJ	201	07960-63	Morris	16	2-52
Morristown*	TN	615	37813-16	Hamblen	19	2-72&73
Morrisville	PA	215	19067	Bucks	10	2-68
Morrisville	VT	802	05661	Lamoille	5	2-77
Morro Bay	CA	805	93442-43	San Luis Obispo	9	2-9
Morrow	GA	404	30260	Clayton	4	2-16&17
Morton	IL	309	61550	Tazewell	14	2-20
Morton	MS	601	39117	Scott	3	2-42&43
Morton*	TX	806	79346	Cochran	2	2-74
Morton Grove	IL	708	60053	Cook	23	2-19
Moscow*	ID	208	83843	Latah	17	2-18
Moses Lake	WA	509	98837	Grant	11	2-81
Mosinee	WI	715	54455	Marathon	3	2-84&85
Mosquero*	NM	505	87733	Harding	1	2-53
Moss Point	MS	601	39563	Jackson	19	2-42&43
Mott*	ND	701	58646	Hettinger	1	2-57
Moulton*	AL	205	35650	Lawrence	3	2-2&3
Moultrie*	GA	912	31768	Colquitt	16	2-16&17
Mound	MN	612	55364	Hennepin	4	2-41
Mound Bayou	MS	601	38762	Bolivar	3	2-42&43
Mound City*	IL	618	62963	Pulaski	1	2-21
Mound City*	KS	913	66056	Linn	8	2-26&27
Mound City*	SD	605	57646	Campbell	1	2-71
Mounds View	MN	612	55432	Ramsey	13	2-41
Moundsville*	WV	304	26041	Marshall	11	2-82
Mount Airy	NC	919	27030-31	Surry	7	2-58&59

Bold = Over 15,000......ALL CAPS = STATE CAPITAL......* = County Seat......# = Changes to 510 in 9/91..... ## = Changes to 410 in 11/91......(+) = City located in addional counties......NAV= Population not available......C.H.= Court House......(IC) = Independent City

CITY	STATE	AREA CODE	ZIP CODE	COUNTY	POPULATION (in thousands)	MAP PAGE
Mount Angel	OR	503	97362	Marion	3	2-63
Mount Arlington	NJ	201	07856	Morris	5	2-52
Mount Ayr*	IA	515	50854	Ringgold	2	2-24&25
Mount Carmel*	IL	618	62863	Wabash	10	2-21
Mount Carmel	PA	717	17851	Northumberland	8	2-67
Mount Carroll*	IL	815	61053	Carroll	17	2-20
Mount Clemens*	MI	313	48043-46	Macomb	18	2-39
Mount Desert	ME	207	04660	Hancock	2	2-32&33
Mount Dora	FL	904	32757	Lake	6	2-14
Mount Ephraim	NJ	609	08059	Camden	5	2-51
Mount Gilead*	OH	419	43338	Morrow	3	2-60
Mount Healthy	OH	513	45231	Hamilton	8	2-62
Mount Holly	NC	704	28120	Gaston	5	2-58
Mount Holly*	NJ	609	08060	Burlington	10	2-51
Mount Horeb	WI	608	53572	Dane	3	2-85
Mount Ida*	AR	501	71957	Montgomery	1	2-6
Mount Joy	PA	717	17552	Lancaster	6	2-67
Mount Juliet	TN	615	37122	Wilson	3	2-72&73
Mount Kisco	NY	914	10549	Westchester	7	2-56
Mount Laurel	NJ	609	08054	Burlington	17	2-51
Mount Lebanon	PA	412	15228	Allegheny	33	2-68
Mount Morris	IL	815	61054	Ogle	3	2-20
Mount Morris	MI	313	48458	Genesee	3	2-39
Mount Morris	NY	716	14510	Livingston	3	2-54
Mount Olive	NC	919	28365	Duplin (+1)	5	2-58&59
Mount Olive	NJ	201	07828	Morris	19	2-52
Mount Oliver	PA	412	15210	Allegheny	5	2-68
Mount Olivet*	KY	606	41064	Robertson	1	2-29
Mount Penn	PA	215	19606	Berks	3	2-67
Mount Pleasant*	IA	319	52641-42	Henry	7	2-25
Mount Pleasant	MI	517	48858-59	Isabella	22	2-38&39
Mount Pleasant	PA	412	15666	Westmooreland	5	2-68
Mount Pleasant	SC	803	29464-65	Charleston	18	2-70
Mount Pleasant	TN	615	38474	Maury	3	2-72&73
Mount Pleasant*	TX	903	75455	Titus	11	2-74
Mount Prospect	IL	708	60056	Cook	53	2-19
Mount Rainier	MD	301	20712	Prince Georges	7	2-34&35
Mount Shasta	CA	916	96067	Siskiyou	3	2-8
Mount Sterling*	IL	217	62353	Brown	2	2-20&21
Mount Sterling*	KY	606	40353	Montgomery	5	2-29
Mount Vernon*	GA	912	30445	Montgomery	1	2-16&17
Mount Vernon	IA	319	52314	Linn	3	2-25
Mount Vernon*	IL	618	62864	Jefferson	18	2-21
Mount Vernon*	IN	812	47620	Posey	8	2-23
Mount Vernon*	KY	606	40456	Rockcastle	2	2-29
Mount Vernon*	MO	417	65712	Lawrence	3	2-44
Mount Vernon	NY	914	10550-59	Westchester	67	2-56
Mount Vernon*	OH	614	43050	Knox	14	2-61

Bold = Over 15,000......ALL CAPS = STATE CAPITAL......* = County Seat......# = Changes to 510 in 9/91.....## = Changes to 410 in 11/91.....(+) = City located in additional counties......NAV = Population not available....C.H.= Court House......(IC)=Independent City

CITY	STATE	AREA CODE	ZIP CODE	COUNTY	POPULATION (in thousands)	MAP PAGE
Mount Vernon*	TX	903	75457	Franklin	1	2-74
Mount Vernon*	WA	206	98273	Skagit	15	2-80
Mount Washington	KY	502	40047	Bullitt	4	2-28
Mount Zion	IL	217	62549	Macon	5	2-20&21
Mountain Brook	AL	205	35223	Jefferson	20	2-2&3
Mountain City*	TN	615	37683	Johnson	1	2-72&73
Mountain Home*	AR	501	72653	Baxter	8	2-6
Mountain Home*	ID	208	83647	Elmore	7	2-18
Mountain Iron	MN	218	55768	St. Louis	4	2-40
Mountain Lakes	NJ	201	07046	Morris	4	2-52
Mountain View*	AR	501	72560	Stone	1	2-6
Mountain View	CA	415	94039-43	Santa Clara	60	2-7
Mountainside	NJ	908	07092	Union	7	2-52
Mountlake Terrace	WA	206	98043	Snohomish	17	2-80
Mukwonago	WI	414	53149	Waukesha	4	2-85
Mulberry	FL	813	33860	Polk	3	2-14&15
Muldrow	OK	918	74948	Sequoyah	3	2-65
Muleshoe*	TX	806	79347	Bailey	4	2-74
Mullen*	NE	308	69152	Hooker	1	2-47
Mullens	WV	304	25882	Wyoming	3	2-82
Mullins	SC	803	29574	Marion	6	2-70
Mulvane	KS	316	67110	Sedgwick (+1)	4	2-26&27
Muncie*	IN	317	47302-08	Delaware	74	2-22&23
Muncy	PA	717	17756	Lycoming	3	2-67
Mundelein	IL	708	60060	Lake	17	2-20
Munfordville*	KY	502	42765	Hart	2	2-28&29
Munhall	PA	412	15120	Allegheny	15	2-68
Munising*	MI	906	49862	Alger	2	2-38
Munsey Park	NY	516	11030	Nassau	3	2-56
Munster	IN	219	46321	Lake	20	2-22
Murdo*	SD	605	57559	Jones	1	2-71
Murfreesboro*	AR	501	71958	Pike	1	2-6
Murfreesboro	NC	919	27855	Hertford	3	2-58&59
Murfreesboro*	TN	615	37129-33	Rutherford	40	2-72
Murphy*	ID	208	83650	Owyhee	1	2-18
Mount Vernon*	KY	606	40456	Rockcastle	2	2-29
Mount Vernon*	MO	417	65712	Lawrence	3	2-44
Mount Vernon	NY	914	10550-59	Westchester	67	2-56
Mount Vernon*	OH	614	43050	Knox	14	2-61
Mount Vernon*	TX	903	75457	Franklin	1	2-74
Mount Vernon*	WA	206	98273	Skagit	15	2-80
Mount Washington	KY	502	40047	Bullitt	4	2-28
Mount Zion	IL	217	62549	Macon	5	2-20&21
Mountain Brook	AL	205	35223	Jefferson	20	2-2&3
Mountain City*	TN	615	37683	Johnson	1	2-72&73
Mountain Home*	AR	501	72653	Baxter	8	2-6
Mountain Home*	ID	208	83647	Elmore	7	2-18

Bold = Over 15,000......ALL CAPS = STATE CAPITAL......* = County Seat......# = Changes to 510 in 9/91..... ## = Changes to 410 in 11/91......(+) = City located in addional counties......NAV= Population not available......C.H.= Court House......(IC) = Independent City

CITY	STATE	AREA CODE	ZIP CODE	COUNTY	POPULATION (in thousands)	MAP PAGE
Mountain Iron	MN	218	55768	St. Louis	4	2-40
Mountain Lakes	NJ	201	07046	Morris	4	2-52
Mountain View*	AR	501	72560	Stone	1	2-6
Mountain View	CA	415	94039-43	Santa Clara	60	2-7
Mountainside	NJ	908	07092	Union	7	2-52
Mountlake Terrace	WA	206	98043	Snohomish	17	2-80
Mukwonago	WI	414	53149	Waukesha	4	2-85
Mulberry	FL	813	33860	Polk	3	2-14&15
Muldrow	OK	918	74948	Sequoyah	3	2-65
Muleshoe*	TX	806	79347	Bailey	4	2-74
Mullen*	NE	308	69152	Hooker	1	2-47
Mullens	WV	304	25882	Wyoming	3	2-82
Mullins	SC	803	29574	Marion	6	2-70
Mulvane	KS	316	67110	Sedgwick (+1)	4	2-26&27
Muncie*	IN	317	47302-08	Delaware	74	2-22&23
Muncy	PA	717	17756	Lycoming	3	2-67
Mundelein	IL	708	60060	Lake	17	2-20
Munfordville*	KY	502	42765	Hart	2	2-28&29
Munhall	PA	412	15120	Allegheny	15	2-68
Munising*	MI	906	49862	Alger	2	2-38
Munsey Park	NY	516	11030	Nassau	3	2-56
Munster	IN	219	46321	Lake	20	2-22
Murdo*	SD	605	57559	Jones	1	2-71
Murfreesboro*	AR	501	71958	Pike	1	2-6
Murfreesboro	NC	919	27855	Hertford	3	2-58&59
Murfreesboro*	TN	615	37129-33	Rutherford	40	2-72
Murphy*	ID	208	83650	Owyhee	1	2-18
Murphy*	NC	704	28906	Cherokee	2	2-58
Murphysboro*	IL	618	62966	Jackson	9	2-21
Murray*	KY	502	42071	Calloway	15	2-28&29
Murray	UT	801	84107	Salt Lake	27	2-76
Murrysville	PA	412	15668	Westmooreland	16	2-68
Muscatine*	IA	319	52761	Muscatine	24	2-25
Muscle Shoals	AL	205	35660-61	Colbert	9	2-2&3
Muskego	WI	414	53150	Waukesha	15	2-85
Muskegon*	MI	616	49440-45	Muskegon	40	2-38&39
Muskegon Hts	MI	616	49444	Muskegon	40	2-38&39
Muskogee*	OK	918	74401-03	Muskogee	42	2-65
Mustang	OK	405	73064	Canadian	7	2-64&65
Muttontown	NY	516	11791	Nassau	3	2-56
Myerstown	PA	717	17067	Lebanon	3	2-67
Myrtle Beach	SC	803	29572-87	Horry	28	2-70
Myrtle Creek	OR	503	97457	Douglas	3	2-63
Myrtle Grove	FL	904	32606	Escambia	14	2-14
Myrtle Point	OR	503	97458	Coos	3	2-63
Nacogdoches*	TX	409	75961-63	Nacogdoches	28	2-75
Nahant	MA	617	01908	Essex	4	2-36&37
Nahunta*	GA	912	31553	Brantley	1	2-16&17

Bold = Over 15,000.....ALL CAPS = STATE CAPITAL.....* = County Seat.....# = Changes to 510 in 9/91.....## = Changes to 410 in 11/91.....(+) = City located in additional counties......NAV = Population not available......C.H.= Court House......(IC)=Independent City

CITY	STATE	AREA CODE	ZIP CODE	COUNTY	POPULATION (in thousands)	MAP PAGE
Nampa	ID	208	83651-87	Canyon	28	2-18
Nanticoke	PA	717	18634	Luzerne	13	2-67
Nantucket*	MA	508	02554	Nantucket	5	2-36&37
Nanty Glo	PA	814	15943	Cambria	4	2-66
Napa*	CA	707	94558-59	Napa	56	2-8
Naperville	IL	708	60563-67	Du Page (+1)	67	2-19
Naples*	FL	813	33939-64	Collier	21	2-14&15
Napoleon*	ND	701	58561	Logan	1	2-57
Napoleon*	OH	419	43545	Henry	8	2-60
Napoleonville*	LA	504	70390	Assumption	16	2-30&31
Nappanee	IN	219	46550	Elkhart (+1)	5	2-22
Naranja	FL	305	33092	Dade	5	2-15
Narberth	PA	215	19072	Montgomery	5	2-68
Narragansett	RI	401	02882	Washington	3	2-69
Nashua*	NH	603	03060-63	Hillsborough	72	2-49
Nashville*	AR	501	71852	Howard	5	2-6
Nashville*	GA	912	31639	Berrien	5	2-16&17
Nashville*	IL	618	62263	Washington	3	2-21
Nashville*	IN	812	47448	Brown	1	2-23
Nashville*	NC	919	27856	Nash	3	2-58&59
NASHVILLE*	TN	615	37201-99	Davidson	462	2-72&73
Nassau Bay	TX	713	77058	Harris	5	2-74&75
Natchez*	MS	601	39120-22	Adams	22	2-42&43
Natchitoches*	LA	318	71457-58	Natchitoches	16	2-30
Natick	MA	508	01760	Middlesex	30	2-36&37
National City	CA	619	92050	San Diego	57	2-9
National Park	NJ	609	08063	Gloucester	4	2-51
Naugatuck	CT	203	06770	New Haven	29	2-12&13
Navasota	TX	409	77868	Grimes	6	2-75
Nazareth	PA	215	18064	Northampton	5	2-67
Nebraska City*	NE	402	68410	Otoe	7	2-47
Nederland	TX	409	77627	Jefferson	17	2-75
Needham	MA	617	02192	Norfolk	28	2-36&37
Needles	CA	619	92363	San Bernardino	4	2-9
Neenah	WI	414	54956	Winnebago	23	2-85
Negaunee	MI	906	49866	Marquette	5	2-38
Neillsville*	WI	715	54456	Clark	2	2-84&85
Nekoosa	WI	715	54457	Wood	3	2-84&85
Neligh*	NE	402	68756	Antelope	1	2-47
Nelson*	NE	402	68961	Nuckolls	1	2-47
Nelsonville	OH	614	45764	Athens	5	2-61
Neodesha	KS	316	66757	Wilson	3	2-26&27
Neosho*	MO	417	64850	Newton	9	2-44
Nephi*	UT	801	84648	Juab	3	2-76
Neptune	NJ	908	07753-54	Monmouth	30	2-50
Neptune Beach	FL	904	32233	Duval	5	2-14
Neptune City	NJ	908	07753	Monmouth	5	2-50
Nesquehoning	PA	717	18240	Carbon	3	2-67

Bold = Over 15,000......ALL CAPS = STATE CAPITAL......* = County Seat......# = Changes to 510 in 9/91..... ## = Changes to 410 in 11/91......(+) = City located in addional counties......NAV= Population not available......C.H.= Court House......(IC) = Independent City

CITY	STATE	AREA CODE	ZIP CODE	COUNTY	POPULATION (in thousands)	MAP PAGE
Ness City*	KS	913	67560	Ness	2	2-26&27
Netcong	NJ	201	07857	Morris	4	2-52
Nether Providence	PA	215	19086	Delaware	13	2-68
Nevada*	IA	515	50201	Story	6	2-24&25
Nevada*	MO	417	64772	Vernon	9	2-44
Nevada City*	CA	916	95959	Nevada	2	2-8
New Albany*	IN	812	47150	Floyd	38	2-23
New Albany*	MS	601	38652	Union	7	2-42&43
New Augusta*	MS	601	39462	Perry	4	2-42&43
New Baltimore	MI	313	48047	Macomb	5	2-39
New Bedford	MA	508	02740-48	Bristol	96	2-36&37
New Berlin	WI	414	53151	Waukesha	31	2-85
New Bern*	NC	919	28560-62	Craven	19	2-58&59
New Bloomfield*	PA	717	17068	Perry	1	2-67
New Boston	OH	614	45662	Scioto	3	2-61
New Braunfels*	TX	512	78130-33	Comal	27	2-75
New Brighton	MN	612	55112	Ramsey	23	2-41
New Brighton	PA	412	15066	Beaver	7	2-66
New Britain	CT	203	06050-53	Hartford	73	2-12&13
New Britain	PA	215	18914	Bucks	3	2-68
New Brooklyn	NJ	609	08081	Camden (+1)	4	2-51
New Brunswick*	NJ	908	08901-99	Middlesex	40	2-50
New Buffalo	MI	616	49117	Berrien	3	2-38&39
New Cannan	CT	203	06840	Fairfield	17	2-12&13
New Carlisle	OH	513	45344	Clark	6	2-61
New Carrollton	MD	301	20784	Prince Georges	13	2-35
New Castle	DE	302	19720	New Castle	4	2-35
New Castle*	IN	317	47362	Henry	19	2-22&23
New Castle*	KY	502	40050	Henry	13	2-28&29
New Castle*	PA	412	16101-08	Lawrence	32	2-66
New Castle*	VA	703	24127	Craig	1	2-78&79
New Chicago	IN	219	46342	Lake	3	2-22
New City*	NY	914	10956	Rockland	37	2-56
New Cumberland	PA	717	17070	Cumberland	8	2-67
New Cumberland*	WV	304	26047	Hancock	1	2-82
New Eagle	PA	412	15067	Washington	3	2-66
New Fairfield	CT	203	06810-12	Fairfield	5	2-12&13
New Gloucester	ME	207	04260	Cumberland	3	2-32&33
New Hampshire Est.	MD	301	20903	Montgomery	3	2-34
New Hampton*	IA	515	50659-61	Chickasaw	4	2-24&25
New Hanover	NJ	609	08511	Burlington	14	2-51
New Hanover	PA	215	19525	Montgomery	5	2-68
New Hartford	CT	203	06057	Litchfield	5	2-12&13
New Haven*	CT	203	06501-99	New Haven	126	2-12&13
New Haven	IN	219	46774	Allen	7	2-22
New Hempstead	NY	914	10977	Rockland	4	2-56
New Holland	PA	717	17557	Lancaster	5	2-67
New Holstein	WI	414	53061	Calumet	3	2-85

Bold = Over 15,000......ALL CAPS = STATE CAPITAL......* = County Seat......# = Changes to 510 in 9/91.....## = Changes to 410 in 11/91......(+) = City located in additional counties......NAV = Population not available......C.H.= Court House......(IC)=Independent City

CITY	STATE	AREA CODE	ZIP CODE	COUNTY	POPULATION (in thousands)	MAP PAGE
New Hope	MN	612	55428	Hennepin	24	2-41
New Hyde Park	NY	516	11040-43	Nassau	10	2-56
New Iberia*	LA	318	70560-62	Iberia	35	2-30
New Kensington	PA	412	15068	Westmooreland	17	2-68
New Kent*	VA	804	23124	New Kent	1	2-78&79
New Lenox	IL	815	60451	Will	6	2-20
New Lexington*	OH	614	43764	Perry	5	2-61
New London	CT	203	06320	New London	29	2-12&13
New London*	MO	314	63459	Ralls	1	2-44&45
New London	NH	603	03257	Merrimack	3	2-49
New London	WI	414	54961	Outagamie (+1)	6	2-85
New Madrid*	MO	314	63869	New Madrid	3	2-44&45
New Martinsville*	WV	304	26155	Wetzel	7	2-82
New Miami	OH	513	45011	Butler (+1)	3	2-61
New Milford	CT	203	06776	Litchfield	19	2-12&13
New Milford	NJ	201	07646	Bergen	16	2-52
New Orleans*	LA	504	70101-99	Orleans	554	2-30&31
New Paltz	NY	914	12561	Ulster	5	2-56
New Philadelphia*	OH	216	44663	Tuscarawas	17	2-60
New Port Richey	FL	813	34652-56	Pasco	14	2-14&15
New Prague	MN	612	56071	Le Sueur (+1)	3	2-41
New Providence	NJ	908	07974	Union	12	2-52
New Richmond	WI	715	54017	St. Croix	4	2-84&85
New Roads*	LA	504	70760	Pointe Coupee	3	2-30&31
New Rochelle	NY	914	10801-99	Westchester	72	2-56
New Rockford*	ND	701	58356	Eddy	1	2-57
New Smyrna Beach	FL	904	32168-70	Volusia	11	2-14
New Stanton	PA	412	15672	Westmooreland	3	2-68
New Ulm*	MN	507	56073	Brown	13	2-41
New Whiteland	IN	317	46184	Johnson	4	2-22&23
New Wilmington	PA	412	16142&72	Lawrence	3	2-66
New York Mills	NY	315	13417	Oneida	4	2-54&55
NEW YORK*	NY	212	10001-299	NY (+5)	7303	2-56
Newark	CA	415#	94560	Alameda	37	2-7
Newark	DE	302	19711-26	New Castle	24	2-35
Newark*	OH	614	43055-56	Licking	41	2-61
Newark*	NJ	201	07101-99	Essex	316	2-52
Newark	NY	315	14513	Wayne	10	2-54&55
Newberg	OR	503	97132	Yamhill	11	2-63
Newberry*	MI	906	49868	Luce	2	2-38
Newberry*	SC	803	29108	Newberry	9	2-70
Newburg	KY	502	40218	Jefferson	6	2-28
Newburgh	IN	812	47629-30	Warrick	3	2-23
Newburgh	NY	914	12550	Orange	25	2-56
Newburgh Heights	OH	216	44105	Cuyahoga	3	2-62
Newbury	MA	508	01950	Essex	99	2-36&37
Newburyport	MA	508	01950-52	Essex	16	2-36&37
Newcastle	OK	405	73065	McClain	3	2-64&65

Bold = Over 15,000......ALL CAPS = STATE CAPITAL......* = County Seat......# = Changes to 510 in 9/91..... ## = Changes to 410 in 11/91......(+)
= City located in addional counties......NAV= Population not available......C.H.= Court House......(IC) = Independent City

CITY	STATE	AREA CODE	ZIP CODE	COUNTY	POPULATION (in thousands)	MAP PAGE
Newcastle*	WY	307	82701	Weston	4	2-83
Newcomerstown	OH	614	43832	Tuscarawas	4	2-61
Newfane	NY	716	14108	Niagara	3	2-54
Newfane*	VT	802	05345	Windham	1	2-77
Newington	CT	203	06111	Hartford	30	2-12&13
Newkirk*	OK	405	74647	Kay	2	2-64&65
Newland*	NC	704	28657	Avery	1	2-58
Newman	CA	209	95360	Merced	3	2-8&9
Newmarket	NH	603	03857	Rockingham	4	2-49
Newnan*	GA	404	30263-65	Coweta	11	2-16&17
Newport*	AR	501	72112	Jackson	8	2-6
Newport	DE	302	19804	New Castle	1	2-35
Newport	KY	606	41071-76	Campbell	20	2-29
Newport*	IN	317	47966	Vermillion	1	2-22&23
Newport	ME	207	04953	Penobscot	3	2-32&33
Newport	MN	612	55055	Washington	3	2-41
Newport*	NH	603	03773	Sullivan	6	2-49
Newport*	OR	503	97365	Lincoln	8	2-63
Newport*	RI	401	02840	Newport	29	2-69
Newport*	TN	615	37821	Cocke	7	2-72&73
Newport*	VT	802	05855	Orleans	4	2-77
Newport*	WA	509	99156	Pend Oreille	1	2-81
Newport Beach	CA	714	92658-63	Orange	66	2-7
Newport Hills	WA	206	98002 &06	King	6	2-80
Newport News	VA	804	23601-07	(IC)	156	2-78&79
Newton*	GA	912	31770	Baker	1	2-16&17
Newton*	IA	515	50208	Jasper	15	2-24&25
Newton*	IL	618	62448	Jasper	3	2-21
Newton*	KS	316	67114	Harvey	16	2-26&27
Newton	MA	617	02158	Middlesex	82	2-36&37
Newton	MS	601	39345	Newton	4	2-42&43
Newton*	NC	704	28658	Catawba	8	2-58
Newton	NH	603	03858	Rockingham	3	2-49
Newton*	NJ	201	07860	Sussex	7	2-50
Newton*	TX	409	75966	Newton	1	2-75
Newtown	CT	203	06470	Fairfield	19	2-12&13
Newtown	PA	215	18940	Bucks	3	2-68
Newton Falls	OH	216	44444	Trumbull	5	2-60
Nezperce*	ID	208	83543	Lewis	1	2-18
Niagara Falls	NY	716	14301-99	Niagara	65	2-54
Niceville	FL	904	32578	Okaloosa	9	2-14
Nicholasville*	KY	606	40356	Jessamine	10	2-29
Nichols Hills	OK	405	73116	Oklahoma	4	2-64&65
Nicoma Park	OK	405	73066	Oklahoma	3	2-64&65
Niles	IL	708	60648	Cook	29	2-19
Niles	MI	616	49120	Berrien (+1)	13	2-38&39
Niles	OH	216	44446	Trumbull	23	2-60
Niskayuna	NY	518	12309	Schenectady	17	2-55

Bold = Over 15,000......ALL CAPS = STATE CAPITAL......* = County Seat......# = Changes to 510 in 9/91.....## = Changes to 410 in 11/91.....(+) = City located in additional counties......NAV = Population not available......C.H.= Court House......(IC)=Independent City

CITY	STATE	AREA CODE	ZIP CODE	COUNTY	POPULATION (in thousands)	MAP PAGE
Nitro	WV	304	25143	Kanawha (+1)	8	2-82
Nixa	MO	417	65714	Christian	4	2-44
Noble	OK	405	73068	Cleveland	3	2-64&65
Noblesville*	IN	317	46060	Hamilton	13	2-22&23
Nocona	TX	817	76255	Montague	3	2-74
Nogales*	AZ	602	85621	Santa Cruz	19	2-5
Nokomis	IL	217	62075	Montgomery	3	2-20&21
Nome	AK	907	99762	Nome	2	2-4
Norco	CA	714	91760	Riverside	22	2-9
Norcross	GA	404	30091-93	Gwinnett	3	2-16&17
Norfolk	MA	508	02056	Norfolk	7	2-36&37
Norfolk	NE	402	68701	Madison	21	2-47
Norfolk	VA	804	23501-99	(IC)	278	2-78&79
Normal	IL	309	61761	McLean	37	2-20
Norman*	OK	405	73069-72	Cleveland	78	2-64&65
Normandy	MO	314	63121	St. Louis	4	2-44&45
Normandy Park	WA	206	98166	King	4	2-80
Norridge	IL	708	60656	Cook	15	2-19
Norridgewock	ME	207	04957	Somerset	3	2-32&33
Norristown*	PA	215	19401-09	Montgomery	33	2-68
North Adams	MA	413	01247	Berkshire	17	2-36
North Andover	MA	508	01845	Essex	20	2-36&37
North Arlington	NJ	201	07032	Bergen	16	2-52
North Attleboro	MA	508	02760-63	Bristol	22	2-36&37
North Augusta	SC	803	29841-42	Aiken (+1)	14	2-70
North Aurora	IL	708	60542	Kane	5	2-19
North Baltimore	OH	419	45872	Wood	3	2-60
North Bay Village	FL	305	33141	Dade	5	2-15
North Bend	OR	503	97459	Coos	9	2-63
North Bergen	NJ	201	07047	Hudson	48	2-52
North Berwick	ME	207	03906	York	3	2-32&33
North Braddock	PA	412	15104	Allegheny	9	2-68
North Branford	CT	203	06471	New Haven	12	2-12&13
North Brookfield	MA	508	01535	Worcester	3	2-36&37
North Brunswick	NJ	908	08902	Middlesex	25	2-50
North Caldwell	NJ	201	07006	Essex	6	2-52
North Canton	OH	216	44720	Stark	14	2-60
North Catasauqua	PA	215	18032	Northampton	3	2-67
North Charleston	SC	803	29406	Charleston (+1)	67	2-70
North Chicago	IL	708	60064	Lake	41	2-20
North City	WA	206	98155	King	6	2-80
North College Hill	OH	513	45239	Hamilton	11	2-62
North Dartmouth	MA	508	02747	Bristol	8	2-36&37
North East	PA	814	16428	Erie	5	2-66
North Fond du Lac	WI	414	54935	Fond du Lac	4	2-85
North Haledon	NJ	201	07508	Passaic	8	2-52
North Hampton	NH	603	03862	Rockingham	3	2-49
North Haven	CT	203	06473	New Haven	22	2-12&13

Bold = Over 15,000......ALL CAPS = STATE CAPITAL......* = County Seat......# = Changes to 510 in 9/91..... ## = Changes to 410 in 11/91......(+) = City located in addional counties......NAV= Population not available......C.H.= Court House......(IC) = Independent City

CITY	STATE	AREA CODE	ZIP CODE	COUNTY	POPULATION (in thousands)	MAP PAGE
North Hero*	VT	802	05474	Grand Isle	1	2-77
North Highlands	CA	916	95660	Sacramento	43	2-8
North Huntingdon	PA	412	15642	Westmooreland	31	2-68
North Kansas City	MO	816	64116	Clay	4	2-44
North Kingstown	RI	401	02852-54	Washington	3	2-69
North Las Vegas	NV	702	89030	Clark	49	2-48
North Lauderdale	FL	305	33068	Broward	19	2-15
North Little Rock	AR	501	72114-19	Pulaski	63	2-6
North Londonderry	PA	717	17078	Lebanon	4	2-67
North Lynnwood	WA	206	98036	Snohomish	4	2-80
North Manchester	IN	219	46962	Wabash	6	2-22
North Mankato	MN	507	56001-02	Nicollet	10	2-41
North Miami	FL	305	33161	Dade	44	2-15
North Miami Beach	FL	305	33160-62	Dade	37	2-15
North Middleton	PA	717	17013	Cumberland	10	2-67
North Muskegon	MI	616	49445	Muskegon	4	2-38&39
North Myrtle Beach	SC	803	29582	Horry	7	2-70
North Oaks	MN	612	55127	Ramsey	3	2-41
North Ogden	UT	801	84404	Weber	10	2-76
North Olmsted	OH	216	44070	Cuyahoga	36	2-62
North Palm Beach	FL	407	33408	Palm Beach	11	2-15
North Park	IL	815	61111	Winnebago	15	2-20
North Plainfield	NJ	908	07060	Somerset	20	2-50
North Platte*	NE	308	69101-03	Lincoln	24	2-47
North Port	FL	813	34287	Sarasota	6	2-14&15
North Providence	RI	401	02911	Providence	31	2-69
North Reading	MA	508	01864	Middlesex	11	2-36&37
North Richland Hills	TX	817	76118	Tarrant	3	2-74&75
North Ridgeville	OH	216	44039	Lorain	22	2-60
North Riverside	IL	708	60546	Cook	6	2-19
North Royalton	OH	216	44133	Cuyahoga	17	2-62
North Salt Lake	UT	801	84054	Davis	6	2-76
North Smithfield	RI	401	02876	Providence	10	2-69
North Springfield	VA	703	22151	Fairfax	7	2-78&79
North St. Paul	MN	612	55109	Ramsey	12	2-41
North Stonington	CT	203	06359	New London	4	2-13
North Strabane	PA	412	15317	Washington	4	2-66
North Syracuse	NY	315	13212	Onondaga	8	2-54&55
North Tarrytown	NY	914	10591	Westchester	8	2-56
North Tonawanda	NY	716	14120	Niagara	8	2-54
North Vernon	IN	812	47265	Jennings	6	2-23
North Versailles	PA	412	15137	Allegheny	13	2-68
North Wales	PA	215	19454	Montgomery	4	2-68
North Wildwood	NJ	609	08260	Cape May	5	2-51
North Wilkesboro	NC	919	28659	Wilkes	3	2-58&59
North Woodley	VA	703	22046	Fairfax	3	2-78&79
Northampton*	MA	413	01060-63	Hampshire	28	2-36
Northampton	PA	215	18067	Northampton	8	2-67

Bold = Over 15,000......ALL CAPS = STATE CAPITAL......* = County Seat......# = Changes to 510 in 9/91.....## = Changes to 410 in 11/91.....(+) = City located in additional counties......NAV = Population not available......C.H.= Court House......(IC)=Independent City

CITY	STATE	AREA CODE	ZIP CODE	COUNTY	POPULATION (in thousands)	MAP PAGE
Northborough	MA	508	01532	Worcester	10	2-36&37
Northbridge	MA	508	01534	Worcester	12	2-36&37
Northbrook	IL	708	60062	Cook	31	2-19
Northfield	IL	708	60093	Cook	5	2-19
Northfield	MN	507	55057	Dakota (+1)	13	2-41
Northfield	NH	603	03276	Merrimack	3	2-49
Northfield	NJ	609	08225	Atlantic	7	2-51
Northfield	OH	216	44067	Summit	4	2-62
Northfield	VT	802	05663	Washington	5	2-77
Northford	CT	203	06472	New Haven	3	2-12&13
Northglenn	CO	303	80233	Adams	32	2-10&11
Northlake	IL	708	60164	Cook	12	2-19
Northport	AL	205	35476	Tuscaloosa	14	2-2&3
Northport	NY	516	11768	Suffolk	7	2-56
Northumberland	PA	717	17857	Northumberland	4	2-67
Northvale	NJ	201	07647	Bergen	6	2-52
Northville	MI	313	48167	Oakland (+1)	6	2-39
Northwood*	IA	515	50459	Worth	2	2-24&25
Northwoods	MO	314	63121	St. Louis	5	2-44&45
Norton*	KS	913	67654	Norton	3	2-26&27
Norton	MA	508	02766	Bristol	13	2-36&37
Norton	OH	216	44203	Summit	12	2-62
Norton	VA	703	24273	(IC)	5	2-78&79
Norton Shores	MI	616	49441	Muskegon	22	2-38&39
Norwalk	CA	213	90650	Los Angeles	90	2-7
Norwalk	CT	203	06850-56	Fairfield	79	2-12&13
Norwalk	IA	515	50211	Warren	3	2-24&25
Norwalk*	OH	419	44857	Huron	14	2-60
Norway	ME	207	04268	Oxford	4	2-32&33
Norway	MI	906	49870	Dickinson	3	2-38
Norwell	MA	617	02061	Plymouth	12	2-36&37
Norwich*	CT	203	06360	New London	79	2-12&13
Norwich*	NY	607	13815	Chenango	8	2-54&55
Norwood	MA	617	02062	Norfolk	29	2-36&37
Norwood	NJ	201	07648	Bergen	5	2-52
Norwood	OH	513	45212	Hamilton	25	2-62
Norwood	PA	215	19074	Delaware	6	2-68
Notre Dame	IN	219	46556	St. Joseph	10	2-22
Nottoway*	VA	804	23955	Nottoway	1	2-78&79
Novato	CA	415	94947-49	Marin	45	2-7
Novi	MI	313	48050	Oakland	26	2-39
Nowata*	OK	918	74048	Nowata	4	2-65
Nutley	NJ	201	07110	Essex	29	2-52
Nyack	NY	914	10960	Rockland	6	2-56
Nyssa	OR	503	97913	Malheur	3	2-63
O'Fallon	IL	618	62269	St. Clair	13	2-21
O'Fallon	MO	314	63366	St. Charles	12	2-44&45
O'Hara	PA	412	15238	Allegheny	9	2-68

Bold = Over 15,000......ALL CAPS = STATE CAPITAL......* = County Seat......# = Changes to 510 in 9/91..... ## = Changes to 410 in 11/91......(+) = City located in addional counties......NAV= Population not available......C.H.= Court House......(IC) = Independent City

CITY	STATE	AREA CODE	ZIP CODE	COUNTY	POPULATION (in thousands)	MAP PAGE
O'Neill*	NE	402	68763	Holt	4	2-47
Oak Brook	IL	708	60521	Du Page (+1)	8	2-19
Oak Creek	WI	414	53154	Milwaukee	17	2-85
Oak Forest	IL	708	60452	Cook	25	2-19
Oak Grove	MO	816	64075	Jackson (+1)	4	2-44
Oak Grove*	LA	318	71263	West Carroll	1	2-30
Oak Harbor	OH	419	43449	Ottawa	3	2-60
Oak Harbor	WA	206	98277-78	Island	12	2-80
Oak Hill	WV	304	25901	Fayette	7	2-82
Oak Lawn	IL	708	60453-59	Cook	58	2-19
Oak Park	IL	708	60301-99	Cook	55	2-19
Oak Park	MI	313	48237	Oakland	30	2-39
Oak Park Heights	MN	612	55082	Washington	3	2-41
Oak Ridge	TN	615	37830-31	Anderson (+1)	28	2-72&73
Oak Ridge North	TX	713	77302	Montgomery	3	2-75
Oak Valley	NJ	609	08090	Gloucester	5	2-51
Oak View	CA	805	93022	Ventura	5	2-9
Oak View	MD	301	20903	Montgomery	4	2-34&35
Oakdale	CA	209	95361	Stanislaus	9	2-8&9
Oakdale	LA	318	71463	Allen	8	2-30
Oakdale	MN	612	55128	Washington	12	2-41
Oakland	ME	207	04963	Kennebec	5	2-32&33
Oakland	NJ	201	07436	Bergen	14	2-52
Oakland*	CA	415#	94601-62	Alameda	356	2-7
Oakland*	MD	301	21550	Garrett	1	2-34&35
Oakland City	IN	812	47660	Gibson	3	2-23
Oakland Park	FL	305	33304	Broward	25	2-15
Oaklawn	KS	316	67216	Sedgwick	4	2-26&27
Oakley*	KS	913	67748	Logan (& Thomas)	2	2-26&27
Oaklyn	NJ	609	08107	Camden	5	2-51
Oakmont	PA	412	15139	Allegheny	7	2-68
Oakridge	OR	503	97463	Lane	4	2-63
Oakton	VA	703	22124	Fairfax	13	2-78&79
Oakville	CT	203	06779	Litchfield	9	2-12&13
Oakwood	OH	216	44146	Cuyahoga	9	2-62
Oakwood	OH	513	45873	Paulding	9	2-61
Oberlin*	KS	913	67749	Decatur	2	2-26&27
Oberlin*	LA	318	70655	Allen	2	2-30
Oberlin	OH	216	44074	Lorain	8	2-60
Obetz	OH	614	43207	Franklin	4	2-61
Ocala*	FL	904	32670-78	Marion	47	2-14
Ocean City	MD	301##	21842	Worcester	5	2-34&35
Ocean City	NJ	609	08226	Cape May	14	2-51
Ocean Springs	MS	601	39564-65	Jackson	15	2-42&43
Oceanport	NJ	908	07757	Monmouth	6	2-50
Oceanside	CA	619	92054-56	San Diego	99	2-9
Oceanside	NY	516	11572	Nassau	34	2-56
Ocilla*	GA	912	31774	Irwin	3	2-16&17

Bold = Over 15,000......ALL CAPS = STATE CAPITAL......* = County Seat......# = Changes to 510 in 9/91.....## = Changes to 410 in 11/91.....(+) = City located in additional counties......NAV = Population not available......C.H.= Court House......(IC)=Independent City

CITY	STATE	AREA CODE	ZIP CODE	COUNTY	POPULATION (in thousands)	MAP PAGE
Ocoee	FL	407	34761	Orange	8	2-14&15
Oconomowoc	WI	414	53066	Waukesha	9	2-85
Oconto*	WI	414	54153	Oconto	4	2-85
Odenton	MD	301##	21113	Anne Arundel	8	2-34&35
Odessa	MO	816	64076	Lafayette	3	2-44
Odessa*	TX	915	79760-68	Ector	101	2-74&75
Oelwein	IA	319	50662	Fayette	7	2-25
Ogallala*	NE	308	69153	Keith	6	2-47
Ogden*	UT	801	84401-99	Weber	70	2-76
Ogdensburg	NY	315	13669	St. Lawrence	12	2-54&55
Oglesby	IL	815	61348	La Salle	4	2-20
Oglethorpe*	GA	912	31068	Macon	1	2-16&17
Ohioville	PA	412	15059	Beaver	4	2-66
Oildale	CA	805	93308	Kern	23	2-9
Ojai	CA	805	93023	Ventura	7	2-9
Ojus	FL	305	33180	Dade	2	2-15
Okanogan*	WA	206	98840	Okanogan	1	2-80
Okeechobee*	FL	813	34972-74	Okeechobee	4	2-14&15
Okemah*	OK	918	74859	Okfuskee	3	2-65
OKLAHOMA CITY*	OK	405	73101-99	Oklahoma	446	2-64&65
Okmulgee*	OK	918	74447	Okmulgee	15	2-65
Okolona	KY	502	40219	Jefferson	20	2-28
Okolona*	MS	601	38860	Chickasaw	3	2-42&43
Olathe*	KS	913	66061-62	Johnson	50	2-26&27
Old Bridge	NJ	908	08857	Middlesex	6	2-50
Old Farm	MD	301	20852	Montgomery	3	2-34&35
Old Forge	PA	717	18518	Lackawanna	9	2-67
Old Lyme	CT	203	06371	New London	6	2-12&13
Old Orchard Beach	ME	207	04064	York	6	2-32&33
Old Saybrook	CT	203	06475	Middlesex	9	2-12&13
Old Tappan	NJ	201	07675	Bergen	4	2-52
Old Town	ME	207	04468	Penobscot	8	2-32&33
Old Westbury	NY	516	11568	Nassau	3	2-56
Oldsmar	FL	813	34677	Pinellas	3	2-14&15
Olean	NY	716	14760	Cattaraugus	18	2-54
Olive Hill	KY	606	41164	Carter	2	2-29
Oliver Springs	TN	615	37840	Morgan (+2)	4	2-72&73
Olivet*	SD	605	57052	Hutchinson	1	2-71
Olivette	MO	314	63132	St. Louis	7	2-44&45
Olivia*	MN	612	56277	Renville	3	2-41
Olmsted Falls	OH	216	44138	Cuyahoga	6	2-62
Olney*	IL	618	62450	Richland	9	2-21
Olney	MD	301	20832	Montgomery	10	2-34&35
Olney	TX	817	76374	Young	4	2-74
Olympia Fields	IL	708	60461	Cook	5	2-19
OLYMPIA*	WA	206	98501-07	Thurston	31	2-80
Olyphant	PA	717	18447	Lackawanna	5	2-67
Omaha*	NE	402	68101-99	Douglas	355	2-47

Bold = Over 15,000......ALL CAPS = STATE CAPITAL......* = County Seat......# = Changes to 510 in 9/91..... ## = Changes to 410 in 11/91......(+) = City located in addional counties......NAV= Population not available......C.H.= Court House......(IC) = Independent City

CITY	STATE	AREA CODE	ZIP CODE	COUNTY	POPULATION (in thousands)	MAP PAGE
Omak	WA	509	98841	Okanogan	4	2-81
Omro	WI	414	54963	Winnebago	3	2-85
Onalaska	WI	608	54650	La Crosse	9	2-85
Onawa*	IA	712	51040	Monona	3	2-24
Oneida	NY	315	13421	Madison	10	2-54&55
Oneida	TN	615	37841	Scott	4	2-72&73
Oneonta	NY	607	13820	Otsego	14	2-54&55
Oneonta*	AL	205	35121	Blount	5	2-2&3
Onida*	SD	605	57564	Sully	1	2-71
Ontario	CA	714	91761-62	San Bernardino	114	2-9
Ontario	OH	419	44862	Richland	4	2-60
Ontario	OR	503	97914	Malheur	10	2-63
Ontonagon*	MI	906	49953	Ontonagon	2	2-38
Opa Locka	FL	305	33054-56	Dade	15	2-15
Opelika*	AL	205	36801-03	Lee	26	2-2&3
Opelousas*	LA	318	70570-71	St. Landry	19	2-30
Opp	AL	205	36467	Covington	7	2-2&3
Opportunity	WA	509	99214	Spokane	21	2-81
Oquawka*	IL	309	61469	Henderson	2	2-20
Oradell	NJ	201	07649	Bergen	9	2-52
Orange	CA	714	92664-69	Orange	100	2-7
Orange	CT	203	06477	New Haven	13	2-12&13
Orange	MA	508	01364	Franklin	7	2-36&37
Orange	NJ	201	07050-52	Essex	32	2-52
Orange*	TX	409	77630	Orange	24	2-75
Orange*	VA	703	22960	Orange	2	2-78&79
Orange City	FL	904	32763	Volusia	3	2-14
Orange City*	IA	712	51041	Sioux	5	2-24
Orange Cove	CA	209	93646	Fresno	4	2-7
Orange Park	FL	904	32073	Clay	9	2-14
Orangeburg	NY	914	10962	Rockland	3	2-56
Orangeburg*	SC	803	29115-17	Orangeburg	15	2-70
Orangevale	CA	916	95662	Sacramento	21	2-8
Orchard Mesa	CO	303	81501	Mesa	5	2-10&11
Orchard Park	NY	716	14127	Erie	3	2-54
Ord*	NE	308	68862	Valley	3	2-47
Ordway*	CO	719	81063	Crowley	1	2-11
Oregon*	IL	815	61061	Ogle	4	2-20
Oregon*	MO	816	64473	Holt	1	2-44
Oregon	OH	419	43616	Lucas	18	2-60
Oregon	WI	608	53575	Dane	4	2-85
Oregon City*	OR	503	97045	Clackamas	14	2-63
Orem	UT	801	84057-59	Utah	62	2-76
Orinda	CA	415#	94563	Contra Costa	17	2-7
Orland	CA	916	95963	Glenn	4	2-8
Orland Park	IL	708	60462	Cook	26	2-19
Orlando*	FL	407	32801-99	Orange	149	2-14&15
Orleans	MA	508	02653	Barnstable	6	2-36&37

Bold = Over 15,000......ALL CAPS = STATE CAPITAL......* = County Seat......# = Changes to 510 in 9/91.....## = Changes to 410 in 11/91.....(+) = City located in additional counties......NAV = Population not available......C.H.= Court House......(IC)=Independent City

CITY	STATE	AREA CODE	ZIP CODE	COUNTY	POPULATION (in thousands)	MAP PAGE
Ormond Beach	FL	904	32174-76	Volusia	21	2-14
Oro Valley	AZ	602	85704	Pima	3	2-5
Orofino*	ID	208	83544	Clearwater	4	2-18
Orono	ME	207	04473	Penobscot	11	2-32&33
Orono	MN	612	55323	Hennepin	7	2-41
Oroville*	CA	916	95965-66	Butte	9	2-8
Orrington	ME	207	04474	Penobscot	3	2-32&33
Orrville	OH	216	44667	Wayne	7	2-60
Ortonville*	MN	612	56278	Big Stone	3	2-41
Orwigsburg	PA	717	17961	Schuykill	3	2-67
Osage City	KS	913	66523	Osage	2	2-26&27
Osage*	IA	515	50461	Mitchell	3	2-24&25
Osawatomie	KS	913	66064	Miami	4	2-26&27
Osborne*	KS	913	67473	Osborne	2	2-26&27
Osceola	AR	501	72370	Mississippi	8	2-6
Osceola*	IA	515	50213	Clarke	4	2-24&25
Osceola*	MO	417	64776	St. Clair	1	2-44
Osceola*	NE	402	68651	Polk	1	2-47
Oshkosh*	NE	308	69154	Garden	2	2-47
Oshkosh*	WI	414	54901-04	Winnebago	50	2-85
Oskaloosa*	IA	515	52577	Mahaska	10	2-24&25
Oskaloosa*	KS	913	66066	Jefferson	1	2-26&27
Osseo	MN	612	55369	Hennepin	3	2-41
Ossining	NY	914	10562	Westchester	20	2-56
Ossipee*	NH	603	03864	Carroll	1	2-49
Oswego	IL	708	60543	Kendall	3	2-20
Oswego*	KS	316	67356	Labette	2	2-26&27
Oswego*	NY	315	13126	Oswego	20	2-54&55
Othello	WA	509	99327	Adams	4	2-81
Otis Orchards	WA	509	99027	Spokane	4	2-81
Otsego	MI	616	49078	Allegan	4	2-38&39
Ottawa*	IL	815	61350	La Salle	18	2-20
Ottawa*	KS	913	66067	Franklin	11	2-26&27
Ottawa*	OH	419	45875	Putman	4	2-60
Ottawa Hills	OH	419	43606	Lucus	4	2-60
Ottumwa*	IA	515	52501	Wapello	26	2-24&25
Ouray*	CO	303	81427	Ouray	1	2-10&11
Overland	MO	314	63114	St. Louis	18	2-44&45
Overland Park	KS	913	66204	Johnson	94	2-26&27
Overlea	MD	301##	21206	Baltimore	6	2-34&35
Oviedo	FL	407	32765-66	Seminole	3	2-14&15
Owasso	OK	918	74055	Rogers (+1)	6	2-65
Owatonna*	MN	507	55060	Steele	18	2-41
Owego*	NY	607	13827	Tioga	5	2-54&55
Owensboro*	KY	502	42301-03	Daviess	56	2-28&29
Owenton*	KY	502	40359	Owen	1	2-28&29
Owingsville*	KY	606	40360	Bath	1	2-29
Owosso	MI	517	48867	Snlawassee	16	2-38&39

Bold = Over 15,000......ALL CAPS = STATE CAPITAL......* = County Seat......# = Changes to 510 in 9/91..... ## = Changes to 410 in 11/91......(+) = City located in addional counties......NAV= Population not available......C.H.= Court House......(IC) = Independent City

CITY	STATE	AREA CODE	ZIP CODE	COUNTY	POPULATION (in thousands)	MAP PAGE
Oxford	AL	205	36203	Calhoun (+1)	9	2-2&3
Oxford	MA	508	01540	Worcester	11	2-36&37
Oxford	ME	207	04270	Oxford	3	2-32&33
Oxford	OH	513	45056	Butler	17	2-61
Oxford*	MS	601	38655	Lafayette	9	2-42&43
Oxford*	NC	919	27565	Granville	8	2-58&59
Oxford	PA	215	19363	Chester	3	2-67
Oxnard	CA	805	93030-35	Ventura	126	2-9
Oxon Hill	MD	301	20745	Prince Georges	8	2-35
Oyster Bay	NY	516	11771	Nassau	6	2-56
Ozark*	AL	205	36360-61	Dale	14	2-2&3
Ozark*	AR	501	72949	Franklin	3	2-6
Ozark*	MO	417	65721	Christian	3	2-44
Ozona*	TX	915	76943	Crockett	1	2-74&75
Pacific	MO	314	63069	Franklin (+1)	5	2-44&45
Pacific Grove	CA	408	93950	Monterey	16	2-9
Pacifica	CA	415	94044	San Mateo	37	2-7
Paden City	WV	304	26159	Wetzel (+1)	4	2-82
Paducah*	KY	502	42001-03	McCracken	28	2-28&29
Paducah*	TX	806	79248	Cottle	1	2-74
Page	AZ	602	86040	Coconino	6	2-5
Pagedale	MO	314	63133	St. Louis	4	2-44&45
Pageland	SC	803	29728	Chesterfield	3	2-70
Pagosa Sprgs*	CO	303	81147	Archuleta	1	2-10&11
Pahokee	FL	407	33476	Palm Beach	6	2-14&15
Painesville*	OH	216	44077	Lake	16	2-62
Paint Rock*	TX	915	76866	Concho	1	2-74&75
Paintsville*	KY	606	41240	Johnson	4	2-29
Palacios	TX	512	77465	Matagorda	5	2-75
Palatine	IL	708	60067	Cook	33	2-19
Palatka*	FL	904	32177-78	Putnam	11	2-14
Palestine	TX	903	76351	Archer	1	2-74
Palestine*	TX	903	75801-02	Anderson	19	2-74
Palisades Park	NJ	201	07650	Bergen	14	2-52
Palm Bay	FL	407	32905	Brevard	19	2-14&15
Palm Beach	FL	407	33480	Palm Beach	12	2-14&15
Palm Beach Gdns	FL	407	33420	Palm Beach	15	2-15
Palm Desert	CA	619	92260-61	Riverside	12	2-9
Palm Harbor	FL	813	34682-85	Pinellas	5	2-14&15
Palm Springs	CA	619	92262-64	Riverside	31	2-9
Palm Springs	FL	407	33480	Palm Beach	5	2-14&15
Palmdale	CA	805	93550-51	Los Angeles	27	2-9
Palmer	AK	907	99645	Matanuska Susitna	2	2-4
Palmer	MA	413	01069	Hampden	4	2-36
Palmerton	PA	215	18071	Carbon	5	2-67
Palmetto	GA	404	30268	Fulton (+1)	2	2-16&17
Palmyra*	MO	314	63461	Marion	3	2-44&45
Palmyra	NJ	609	08065	Burlington	7	2-51

Bold = Over 15,000......ALL CAPS = STATE CAPITAL......* = County Seat......# = Changes to 510 in 9/91.....## = Changes to 410 in 11/91.....(+) = City located in additional counties......NAV = Population not available......C.H.= Court House......(IC)=Independent City

CITY	STATE	AREA CODE	ZIP CODE	COUNTY	POPULATION (in thousands)	MAP PAGE
Palmyra	NY	315	14522	Wayne	4	2-54&55
Palmyra	PA	717	17078	Lebanon	7	2-67
Palmyra*	VA	804	22963	Fluvanna	1	2-78&79
Palo Alto	CA	415	94301-09	Santa Clara	55	2-7
Palo Pinto*	TX	817	76072	Palo Pinto	26	2-74&75
Palos Heights	IL	708	60463	Cook	10	2-19
Palos Hills	IL	708	60465	Cook	16	2-19
Palos Park	IL	708	60464	Cook	3	2-19
Palos Verdes Est.	CA	213	90274	Los Angeles	14	2-7
Pampa*	TX	806	79065-66	Gray	21	2-74
Pana	IL	217	62557	Christian	6	2-20&21
Panama City*	FL	904	32401-13	Bay	37	2-14
Panguitch*	UT	801	84759	Garfield	1	2-76
Panhandle*	TX	806	79068	Carson	2	2-74
Paola*	KS	913	66071	Miami	5	2-26&27
Paoli*	IN	812	47454	Orange	4	2-23
Papillion*	NE	402	68046	Sarpy	7	2-47
Paradise	CA	916	95969	Butte	25	2-8
Paradise Valley	AZ	602	85253	Maricopa	12	2-5
Paragould*	AR	501	72450-51	Greene	16	2-6
Paramount	CA	213	90723	Los Angeles	42	2-7
Paramus	NJ	201	07652-53	Bergen	26	2-52
Paris*	AR	501	72855	Logan	4	2-6
Paris*	ID	208	83261	Bear Lake	1	2-18
Paris*	IL	217	61944	Edgar	9	2-20&21
Paris*	KY	606	40361	Bourbon	8	2-29
Paris	ME	207	04271	Oxford	4	2-32&33
Paris*	MO	816	65275	Monroe	1	2-44
Paris*	TN	901	38242	Henry	10	2-72
Paris*	TX	903	75460-61	Lamar	26	2-74
Park City	IL	708	60085	Lake	4	2-20
Park City	KS	316	67219	Sedgwick	4	2-26&27
Park City	UT	801	84060	Summit (+1)	3	2-76
Park Falls	WI	715	54552	Price	3	2-84&85
Park Forest	IL	708	60466	Cook (+1)	26	2-19
Park Hills	KY	606	41015	Kenton	4	2-29
Park Orchard	WA	206	98031	King	3	2-80
Park Rapids*	MN	218	56470	Hubbard	3	2-40
Park Ridge	IL	708	60068	Cook	37	2-19
Park Ridge	NJ	201	07656	Bergen	8	2-52
Parker*	AZ	602	85344	La Paz	3	2-5
Parker	FL	904	32401	Bay	4	2-14
Parker*	SD	605	57053	Turner	1	2-71
Parkersburg*	WV	304	26101-06	Wood	38	2-82
Parkesburg	PA	215	19365	Chester	3	2-67
Parkside	MD	301	20814	Montgomery	4	2-34&35
Parkwater	WA	509	99211	Spokane	5	2-81
Parlier	CA	209	93648	Fresno	6	2-8&9

Bold = Over 15,000......ALL CAPS = STATE CAPITAL......* = County Seat......# = Changes to 510 in 9/91..... ## = Changes to 410 in 11/91......(+) = City located in additional counties......NAV = Population not available......C.H.= Court House......(IC) = Independent City

CITY	STATE	AREA CODE	ZIP CODE	COUNTY	POPULATION (in thousands)	MAP PAGE
Parma	OH	216	44129	Cuyahoga	91	2-62
Parma Heights	OH	216	44130	Cuyahoga	6	2-62
Parowan*	UT	801	84761	Iron	2	2-76
Parsippany	NJ	201	07054	Morris	51	2-52
Parsons	KS	316	67357	Labette	3	2-26&27
Parsons*	WV	304	26287	Tucker	1	2-82
Pasadena	CA	818	91101-99	Los Angeles	129	2-7
Pasadena	MD	301##	21122	Anne Arundel	4	2-34&35
Pasadena	TX	713	77501-08	Harris	120	2-74&75
Pascagoula*	MS	601	39563-68	Jackson	30	2-42&43
Pasco*	WA	509	99301-02	Franklin	19	2-81
Paso Robles	CA	805	93446-47	San Luis Obispo	9	2-9
Pass Christian	MS	601	39571	Harrison	5	2-42&43
Passaic	NJ	201	07055	Passaic	52	2-52
Patchogue	NY	516	11772	Suffolk	12	2-56
Paterson*	NJ	201	07501-99	Passaic	139	2-52
Patterson	CA	209	95363	Stanislaus	5	2-8&9
Patterson	LA	504	70392	St. Mary	5	2-30&31
Patton	PA	814	16801	Centre	7	2-66
Paulding*	MS	601	39348	Jasper	1	2-42&43
Paulding*	OH	419	45879	Paulding	2	2-60
Pauls Valley*	OK	405	73075	Garvin	5	2-64&65
Paulsboro	NJ	609	08066	Gloucester	7	2-51
Paw Paw*	MI	616	49079	Van Buren	3	2-38&39
Pawcatuck	CT	203	06379	New London	5	2-12&13
Pawhuska*	OK	918	74056	Osage	5	2-65
Pawling	NY	914	12564	Dutchess	5	2-56
Pawnee*	OK	918	74058	Pawnee	1	2-65
Pawnee City*	NE	402	68420	Pawnee	1	2-47
Pawtucket	RI	401	02860-65	Providence	73	2-69
Paxton*	IL	217	60957	Ford	4	2-20&21
Paxton	MA	508	01612	Worcester	4	2-36&37
Payette*	ID	208	83661	Payette	6	2-18
Payson	AZ	602	85541	Gila	7	2-5
Payson	UT	801	84651	Utah	8	2-76
Peabody	MA	508	01960-61	Essex	47	2-36&37
Peachtree City	GA	404	30269	Fayette	6	2-16&17
Pearisburg	VA	703	24134	Giles	2	2-78&79
Pearl	MS	601	39208	Rankin	19	2-42&43
Pearl River	NY	914	10965	Rockland	16	2-56
Pearland	TX	713	77581	Brazoria (+1)	14	2-74&75
Pearsall*	TX	512	78061	Frio	7	2-75
Pearson*	GA	912	31642	Atkinson	4	2-16&17
Pecos*	TX	915	79772	Reeves	13	2-74&75
Peekskill	NY	914	10566	Westchester	19	2-56
Pekin*	IL	309	61554-55	Tazewell (+1)	33	2-20
Pelham	AL	205	35124	Shelby	7	2-2&3
Pelham	GA	912	31779	Mitchell	4	2-16&17

Bold = Over 15,000......ALL CAPS = STATE CAPITAL......* = County Seat......# = Changes to 510 in 9/91.....## = Changes to 410 in 11/91.....(+) = City located in additional counties......NAV = Population not available......C.H.= Court House......(IC)=Independent City

CITY	STATE	AREA CODE	ZIP CODE	COUNTY	POPULATION (in thousands)	MAP PAGE
Pelham	NH	603	03076	Hillsborough	8	2-49
Pelham	NY	914	10803	Westchester	7	2-56
Pelham Manor	NY	914	10803	Westchester	6	2-56
Pell City	AL	205	35125	St. Clair	6	2-2&3
Pella	IA	515	50219	Marion	8	2-24&25
Pembroke*	GA	912	31321	Bryan	1	2-16&17
Pembroke	MA	617	02359	Plymouth	14	2-36&37
Pembroke	NC	919	28372	Robeson	3	2-58&59
Pembroke	NH	603	03275	Merrimack	5	2-49
Pembroke Park	FL	305	33009	Broward	5	2-15
Pembroke Pines	FL	305	33034	Broward	47	2-15
Pen Argyl	PA	215	18072	Northampton	3	2-67
Penbrook	PA	717	17103	Dauphin	3	2-67
Pender*	NE	402	68047	Thurston	1	2-47
Pendleton	SC	803	29670	Anderson	3	2-70
Pendleton*	OR	503	97801	Umatilla	14	2-63
Penn Hills	PA	412	15235	Allegheny	55	2-68
Penn Yan*	NY	315	14527	Yates	5	2-54&55
Penndel	PA	215	19047	Bucks	3	2-68
Penns Grove	NJ	609	08069	Salem	6	2-51
Penns Park	PA	814	18943	Bucks	1	2-66
Pennsauken	NJ	609	08110	Camden	35	2-51
Pennsville	NJ	609	08070	Salem	12	2-51
Pensacola*	FL	904	32501-98	Escambia	65	2-14
Peoria	AZ	602	85345	Maricopa	13	2-5
Peoria*	IL	309	61601-99	Peoria	118	2-20
Peoria Heights	IL	309	61614	Peoria (+2)	7	2-20
Pepper Pike	OH	216	44124	Cuyahoga	6	2-62
Pepperell	MA	508	01463	Middlesex	8	2-36&37
Perkasie	PA	215	18944	Bucks	5	2-68
Perrine	FL	305	33157	Dade	16	2-15
Perris	CA	714	92370	Riverside	10	2-9
Perry*	FL	904	32347	Taylor	8	2-14
Perry*	GA	912	31069	Houston	9	2-16&17
Perry	IA	515	50220	Dallas	7	2-24&25
Perry	NY	716	14530	Wyoming	4	2-54
Perry*	OK	405	73077	Noble	5	2-64&65
Perrysburg	OH	419	43551	Wood	10	2-60
Perryton*	TX	806	79070	Ochiltree	9	2-74
Perryville*	AR	501	72126	Perry	1	2-6
Perryville*	MO	314	63775	Perry	7	2-44&45
Perth Amboy	NJ	908	08861-63	Middlesex	39	2-50
Peru	IL	815	61354	La Salle	10	2-20
Peru*	IN	317	46970-71	Miami	14	2-22&23
Peshtigo	WI	715	54157	Marinette	3	2-84&85
Petal	MS	601	39465	Forrest	9	2-42&43
Petaluma	CA	707	94952-54	Sonoma	38	2-8
Peterborough	NH	603	03458	Hillsborough	2	2-49

Bold = Over 15,000......ALL CAPS = STATE CAPITAL......* = County Seat......# = Changes to 510 in 9/91..... ## = Changes to 410 in 11/91......(+) = City located in addional counties......NAV= Population not available......C.H.= Court House......(IC) = Independent City

CITY	STATE	AREA CODE	ZIP CODE	COUNTY	POPULATION (in thousands)	MAP PAGE
Petersburg	AK	907	99833	Wrangell Ptrsbrg.	3	2-4
Petersburg*	IL	217	62675	Menard	2	2-20&21
Petersburg*	IN	812	47567	Pike	3	2-23
Petersburg	VA	804	23801-05	(IC)	41	2-78&79
Petersburg*	WV	304	26847	Grant	1	2-82
Petoskey*	MI	616	49770	Emmet	6	2-38&39
Pevely	MO	314	63070	Jefferson	3	2-44&45
Pewaukee	WI	414	53072	Waukesha	5	2-85
Pharr	TX	512	78577	Hidalgo	29	2-75
Phenix City*	AL	205	36867-68	Russell (+1)	28	2-2&3
Philadelphia*	MS	601	39350	Neshoba	7	2-42&43
Philadelphia*	PA	215	19101-99	Philadelphia	1642	2-68
Philip*	SD	605	57567	Haakon	1	2-71
Philippi*	WV	304	26416	Barbour	2	2-82
Philipsburg*	MT	406	59858	Granite	1	2-46
Phillips	ME	207	04966	Franklin	1	2-32&33
Phillips*	WI	715	54555	Price	1	2-84&85
Phillipsburg	NJ	908	08865	Warren	16	2-50
Phillipsburg*	KS	913	67661	Phillips	3	2-26&27
Philomath	OR	503	97370	Benton	3	2-63
Philpsburg	PA	814	16866	Centre	4	2-66
PHOENIX*	AZ	602	85001-99	Maricopa	934	2-5
Phoenix	IL	708	61254	Cook	3	2-19
Phoenixville	PA	215	19460	Chester	14	2-67
Picayune	MS	601	39466	Pearl River	10	2-42&43
Pickens*	SC	803	29671	Pickens	3	2-70
Pickerington	OH	614	43147	Fairfield (+1)	4	2-61
Pico Rivera	CA	213	90660-61	Los Angeles	54	2-7
Piedmont	AL	205	36272	Calhoun (+1)	16	2-2&3
Piedmont	CA	415#	94611	Alameda	10	2-7
Pierce*	NE	402	68767	Pierce	1	2-47
PIERRE*	SD	605	57501	Hughes	12	2-71
Pigeon Forge	TN	615	37863	Sevier	3	2-72&73
Piggott*	AR	501	72454	Clay	4	2-6
Pikeville*	KY	606	41501	Pike	6	2-29
Pikeville*	TN	615	37367	Bledsoe	1	2-72&73
Pinardville	NH	603	03045	Hillsborough	5	2-49
Pinckneyville*	IL	618	62274	Perry	3	2-21
Pine Bluff*	AR	501	71601-13	Jefferson	69	2-6
Pine Castle	FL	407	32809	Orange	10	2-14&15
Pine City*	MN	612	55063	Pine	2	2-41
Pine Hill	NJ	609	08021	Camden	9	2-51
Pine Hills	FL	407	32808	Orange	30	2-14&15
Pine Lawn	MO	314	63121	St. Louis	6	2-44&45
Pinedale*	WY	307	82941	Sublette	1	2-83
Pinehurst	TX	713	77362	Orange	3	2-74&75
Pinellas Park	FL	813	34664-66	Pinellas	40	2-14&15
Pineville*	KY	606	40977	Bell	2	2-29

Bold = Over 15,000......ALL CAPS = STATE CAPITAL......* = County Seat......# = Changes to 510 in 9/91.....## = Changes to 410 in 11/91.....(+) = City located in additional counties......NAV = Population not available......C.H.= Court House......(IC)=Independent City

CITY	STATE	AREA CODE	ZIP CODE	COUNTY	POPULATION (in thousands)	MAP PAGE
Pineville	LA	318	71360-61	Rapides	12	2-30
Pineville*	MO	417	64856	McDonald	1	2-44
Pineville*	WV	304	24874	Wyoming	1	2-82
Piney Point	TX	713	77024	Harris	3	2-74&75
Pinole	CA	415#	94564	Contra Costa	14	2-7
Pioche*	NV	702	89043	Lincoln	1	2-48
Pipestone*	MN	507	56164	Pipeston	4	2-41
Piqua	OH	513	45356	Miami	20	2-61
Piscataway	NJ	908	08854-55	Middlesex	43	2-50
Pismo Beach	CA	805	93448-49	S. L. Obispo	6	2-9
Pitcairn	PA	412	15140	Allegheny	4	2-68
Pitman	NJ	609	08071	Gloucester	10	2-51
Pittsboro*	MS	601	38951	Calhoun	1	2-42&43
Pittsboro*	NC	919	27312	Chatham	1	2-58&59
Pittsburg	CA	415#	94565	Contra Costa	41	2-7
Pittsburg	KS	316	66762	Crawford	18	2-26&27
Pittsburg*	TX	903	75686	Camp	9	2-74
Pittsburgh*	PA	412	15122-299	Allegheny	402	2-68
Pittsfield*	IL	217	62363	Pike	4	2-20&21
Pittsfield*	MA	413	01201-03	Berkshire	49	2-36
Pittsfield	ME	207	04967	Somerset	4	2-32&33
Pittsfield	NH	603	03263	Merrimack	2	2-49
Pittston	PA	717	18640-44	Luzerne	9	2-67
Placentia	CA	714	92670	Orange	38	2-7
Placerville*	CA	916	95667	El Dorado	7	2-8
Plainfield	CT	203	06374	Windham	3	2-12&13
Plainfield	IL	815	60544	Will	4	2-20
Plainfield	IN	317	46168	Hendricks	9	2-22&23
Plainfield	NJ	908	07060-63	Union	46	2-52
Plainfield Heights	MI	616	49505	Kent	5	2-38&39
Plains*	TX	806	79355	Yoakum	1	2-74
Plainview	NY	516	11803	Nassau	31	2-56
Plainview*	TX	806	79072-73	Hale	22	2-74
Plainville	CT	203	06062	Hartford	16	2-12&13
Plainville	MA	617	02762	Norfolk	6	2-36&37
Plainwell	MI	616	49080	Allegan	3	2-38&39
Plaistow	NH	603	03865	Rockingham	6	2-49
Planada	CA	209	95365	Merced	2	2-8&9
Plankinton*	SD	605	57368	Aurora	1	2-71
Plano	IL	708	60545	Kendall	5	2-20
Plano	TX	214	75023-75	Collin (+1)	107	2-74
Plant City	FL	813	33564-67	Hillsborough	17	2-14&15
Plantation*	FL	305	33036	Monroe	3	2-15
Plaquemine*	LA	504	70764-65	Iberville	7	2-30&31
Platte City*	MO	816	64079	Platte	1	2-44
Platteville	CO	303	80651	Weld	2	2-10&11
Platteville	WI	608	53818	Grant	10	2-85
Plattsburg*	MO	816	64477	Clinton	1	2-44

Bold = Over 15,000......ALL CAPS = STATE CAPITAL......* = County Seat......# = Changes to 510 in 9/91...... ## = Changes to 410 in 11/91......(+)
= City located in addional counties......NAV= Population not available......C.H.= Court House......(IC) = Independent City

CITY	STATE	AREA CODE	ZIP CODE	COUNTY	POPULATION (in thousands)	MAP PAGE
Plattsburgh*	NY	518	12901	Clinton	21	2-55
Plattsmouth*	NE	402	68048	Cass	7	2-47
Pleasant Grove	AL	205	35127	Jefferson	7	2-2&3
Pleasant Grove	UT	801	84062	Utah	11	2-76
Pleasant Hill	CA	415#	94523	Contra Costa	28	2-7
Pleasant Hill	IA	515	50301	Polk	4	2-24&25
Pleasant Hill	IL	708	60187	Du Page	4	2-19
Pleasant Hill	MO	816	64080	Cass	3	2-44
Pleasant Hills	PA	412	15236	Allegheny	9	2-68
Pleasant Ridge	MI	313	48069	Oakland	3	2-39
Pleasant View	UT	801	84404	Weber	4	2-76
Pleasanton	CA	415#	94566	Alameda	44	2-7
Pleasanton	TX	512	78064	Atascosa	6	2-75
Pleasantville	NJ	609	08232	Atlantic	14	2-51
Pleasantville	NY	914	10570-72	Westchester	7	2-56
Pleasure Ridge Pk	KY	502	40258	Jefferson	27	2-28&29
Plentywood*	MT	406	59254	Sheridan	1	2-46
Plover	WI	715	54467	Portage	5	2-84&85
Plum	PA	412	15239	Allegheny	25	2-68
Plymouth	CT	203	06782	Litchfield	10	2-12&13
Plymouth*	IN	219	46563	Marshall	8	2-22
Plymouth*	MA	508	02360	Plymouth	42	2-36&37
Plymouth	MI	313	48170	Wayne	10	2-39
Plymouth	MN	612	55441	Hennepin	43	2-41
Plymouth*	NC	919	27962	Washington	4	2-58&59
Plymouth	NH	603	03264	Grafton	6	2-49
Plymouth	PA	717	18651	Luzerne	7	2-67
Plymouth	WI	414	53073	Sheboygan	6	2-85
Plymouth Twp.	PA	215	19401	Montgomery	17	2-68
Pocahontas*	AR	501	72455	Randolph	6	2-6
Pocahontas*	IA	712	50574	Pocahontas	2	2-24
Pocatello*	ID	208	83201-06	Bannock	46	2-18
Pocola	OK	918	74902	Le Flore	3	2-65
Pocomoke City	MD	301##	21851	Worcester	4	2-34&35
Point Pleasant	NJ	908	08742	Ocean	17	2-50&51
Point Pleasant*	WV	304	25550	Mason	5	2-82
Pointe a la Hache*	LA	504	70082	Plaquemines	1	2-31
Poland	ME	207	04273	Androscoggin	4	2-32&33
Poland	OH	216	44514	Mahoning	3	2-60
Polo	IL	815	61064	Ogle	3	2-20
Polson*	MT	406	59860	Lake	3	2-46
Pomeroy*	OH	614	45769	Meigs	2	2-61
Pomeroy*	WA	509	99347	Garfield	1	2-81
Pomfret	CT	203	06258	Windham	3	2-12&13
Pomona	CA	714	91765-69	Los Angeles	115	9-7
Pompano Beach	FL	305	33060-75	Broward	69	2-15
Pompton Lakes	NJ	201	07442	Passaic	11	2-52
Ponca City	OK	405	74601-04	Kay (+1)	28	2-64&65

Bold = Over 15,000......ALL CAPS = STATE CAPITAL......* = County Seat......# = Changes to 510 in 9/91.....## = Changes to 410 in 11/91.....(+) = City located in additional counties......NAV = Population not available......C.H.= Court House......(IC)=Independent City

CITY	STATE	AREA CODE	ZIP CODE	COUNTY	POPULATION (in thousands)	MAP PAGE
Ponca*	NE	402	68770	Dixon	1	2-47
Ponchatoula	LA	504	70454	Tangipahoa	5	2-30&31
Pontiac*	IL	815	61764	Livingston	11	2-20
Pontiac*	**MI**	313	48053-59	Oakland	70	2-39
Pontoon Beach	IL	618	62040	Madison	3	2-21
Pontotoc*	MS	601	38863	Pontotoc	5	2-42&43
Pooler	GA	912	31322	Chatham	3	2-16&17
Poolesville	MD	301	20837	Montgomery	4	2-34&35
Poplar Bluff*	**MO**	314	63901	Butler	16	2-44&45
Poplarville*	MS	601	39470	Pearl River	2	2-42&43
Poquoson	VA	804	23662	(IC)	8	2-78&79
Port Allegany	PA	814	16743	McKean	3	2-66
Port Allen*	LA	504	70767	West Baton Rouge	6	2-31
Port Angeles*	**WA**	206	98362	Clallam	18	2-80
Port Arthur	**TX**	409	77640-43	Jefferson	64	2-75
Port Barre	LA	318	70577	St. Laundry	3	2-30
Port Carbon	PA	717	17965	Schuykill	3	2-67
Port Charlotte	**FL**	813	33952	Charlotte	36	2-14&15
Port Chester	**NY**	914	10573	Westchester	23	2-56
Port Clinton*	OH	419	43452	Ottawa	7	2-60
Port Gibson*	MS	601	39150	Claiborne	1	2-42&43
Port Hueneme	**CA**	805	93041-43	Ventura	20	2-9
Port Huron*	**MI**	313	48060-61	St. Clair	33	2-39
Port Isabel	TX	512	78578	Cameron	4	2-75
Port Jervis	NY	914	12771	Orange	8	2-56
Port Lavaca*	TX	512	77979	Calhoun	11	2-75
Port Monmouth	NJ	908	07758	Monmouth	4	2-50
Port Neches	TX	409	77651	Jefferson	14	2-75
Port Orange	**FL**	904	32127	Volusia	19	2-14
Port Orchard*	WA	206	98366	Kitsap	5	2-80
Port Richey	FL	813	34668-74	Pasco	2	2-14&15
Port Royal	SC	803	29935	Beaufort	3	2-70
Port St. Joe*	FL	904	32456	Gulf	11	2-14
Port St. Lucie	**FL**	407	34952 &92	St. Lucie	15	2-14&15
Port Townsend*	WA	206	98368	Jefferson	6	2-80
Port Vue	PA	412	15133	Allegheny	5	2-68
Port Washington	NY	516	11050	Nassau	14	2-56
Port Washington*	WI	414	53074	Ozaukee	8	2-85
Port Wentworth	GA	912	31407	Chatham	4	2-16&17
Portage	**IN**	219	46368	Porter	29	2-22
Portage	PA	814	15946	Cambria	4	2-66
Portage*	WI	608	53901	Columbia	8	2-85
Portage Lakes	OH	216	44319	Summit	11	2-62
Portageville	MO	314	63873	New Madrid (+1)	3	2-45
Portales*	NM	505	88130	Roosevelt	10	2-53
Porter	IN	219	46304	Porter	3	2-22
Porterville	**CA**	209	93257-58	Tulare	24	2-8&9
Portland	CT	203	06480	Middlesex	8	2-12&13

Bold = Over 15,000......ALL CAPS = STATE CAPITAL......* = County Seat......# = Changes to 510 in 9/91..... ## = Changes to 410 in 11/91......(+) = City located in addional counties......NAV= Population not available......C.H.= Court House......(IC) = Independent City

CITY	STATE	AREA CODE	ZIP CODE	COUNTY	POPULATION (in thousands)	MAP PAGE
Portland*	IN	219	47371	Jay	8	2-22
Portland*	ME	207	04101-99	Cumberland	63	2-32&33
Portland	MI	517	48875	Ionia	4	2-38&39
Portland*	OR	503	97201-99	Multnomah	387	2-63
Portland	TN	615	37148	Sumner	4	2-72&73
Portland	TX	512	78374	Nueces (+1)	12	2-75
Portola	CA	916	96122	Plumas	2	2-8
Portola Valley	CA	415	94025	San Mateo	4	2-7
Portsmouth	NH	603	03801	Rockingham	30	2-49
Portsmouth*	OH	614	45662	Scioto	23	2-61
Portsmouth	RI	401	02871	Newport	4	2-69
Portsmouth	VA	804	23701-99	(IC)	112	2-78&79
Posen	IL	708	60469	Cook	5	2-19
Post Falls	ID	208	83854	Kootenai	6	2-18
Post*	TX	806	79356	Garza	3	2-74
Poteau*	OK	918	74953	Le Flore	7	2-65
Poteet	TX	512	78065	Atascosa	3	2-75
Potomac	MD	301	20851	Montgomery	23	2-34&35
Potosi*	MO	314	63664	Washington	2	2-44&45
Potsdam	NY	315	13676	St. Lawrence	10	2-54&55
Pottstown	PA	215	19464	Montgomery	23	2-68
Pottsville*	PA	717	17901	Schuylkill	1	2-67
Poughkeepsie*	NY	914	12601-99	Dutchess	30	2-56
Poulsbo	WA	206	98370	Kitsap	4	2-80
Poultney	VT	802	05764	Rutland	3	2-77
Poway	CA	619	92064	San Diego	38	2-9
Powder Springs	GA	404	30073	Cobb	3	2-16&17
Powell	WY	307	82435	Park	6	2-83
Powhatan*	VA	804	23139	Powhatan	1	2-78&79
Powhattan Mill	MD	301##	21207	Baltimore	3	2-34&35
Pownal	VT	802	05261	Bennington	3	2-77
Prairie du Chien*	WI	608	53821	Crawford	5	2-85
Prairie View	TX	409	77446	Waller	4	2-75
Prairie Village	KS	913	66208	Johnson	26	2-26&27
Pratt*	KS	316	67124	Pratt	6	2-26&27
Prattville*	AL	205	36067	Autauga (+1)	19	2-2&3
Premont	TX	512	78375	Jim Wells	3	2-75
Prentiss*	MS	601	39474	Jefferson Davis	1	2-42&43
Prescott*	AR	501	71857	Nevada	4	2-6
Prescott*	AZ	602	86301	Yavapai	20	2-5
Prescott	WI	715	54021	Pierce	3	2-84&85
Prescott Valley	AZ	602	86314	Yavapai	3	2-5
Presque Isle	ME	207	04769	Aroostook	11	2-32&33
Preston	CT	203	06360	New London	5	2-12&13
Preston*	GA	912	31824	Webster	1	2-16&17
Preston*	ID	208	83263	Franklin	4	2-18
Preston*	MN	507	55965	Fillmore	2	2-41
Prestonsburg*	KY	606	41653	Floyd	4	2-29

Bold = Over 15,000......ALL CAPS = STATE CAPITAL......* = County Seat......# = Changes to 510 in 9/91.....## = Changes to 410 in 11/91.....(+) = City located in additional counties......NAV = Population not available......C.H.= Court House......(IC)=Independent City

CITY	STATE	AREA CODE	ZIP CODE	COUNTY	POPULATION (in thousands)	MAP PAGE
Price*	UT	801	84501	Carbon	10	2-76
Prichard	AL	205	36610	Mobile	40	2-2&3
Primghar*	IA	712	51245	O'Brien	1	2-24
Prince Frederick*	MD	301##	20678	Calvert	43	2-35
Prince George*	VA	804	23875	Prince George	1	2-78&79
Princess Anne*	MD	301##	21853	Somerset	1	2-34&35
Princeton*	IL	815	61356	Bureau	7	2-20
Princeton*	IN	812	47670	Gibson	9	2-23
Princeton*	KY	502	42445	Caldwell	7	2-28&29
Princeton	MN	612	55371	Mille Lacs (+1)	3	2-41
Princeton*	MO	816	64673	Mercer	1	2-44
Princeton	NJ	609	08540-44	Mercer	14	2-50
Princeton	TX	214	75077	Collin	3	2-74
Princeton*	WV	304	24740	Mercer	8	2-82
Prineville*	OR	503	97754	Crook	5	2-63
Prior Lake	MN	612	55372	Scott	10	2-41
Proctor	MN	218	55810	St. Louis	3	2-40
Prospect	CT	203	06712	New Haven	6	2-12&13
Prospect Heights	IL	708	60070	Cook	13	2-19
Prospect Park	NJ	201	07508	Passaic	5	2-52
Prospect Park	PA	215	19076	Delaware	7	2-68
Prosser*	WA	509	99350	Benton	4	2-81
Providence	KY	502	42450	Webster	4	2-28&29
PROVIDENCE*	RI	401	02901-40	Providence	157	2-69
Providence	UT	801	84332	Cache	3	2-76
Provincetown	MA	508	02657	Barnstable	4	2-36&37
Provo*	UT	801	84601-06	Utah	77	2-76
Pryor*	OK	918	74361-62	Mayes	8	2-65
Pueblo*	CO	719	81001-19	Pueblo	100	2-11
Pulaski*	TN	615	38478	Giles	7	2-72&73
Pulaski*	VA	703	24301	Pulaski	9	2-78&79
Pullman	WA	509	99163-65	Whitman	24	2-81
Pumphrey	MD	301##	21227	Anne Arundel	3	2-34&35
Punta Gorda*	FL	813	33948-83	Charlotte	7	2-14&15
Punxsutawney	PA	814	15767	Jefferson	4	2-66
Purcell*	OK	405	73080	McClain	4	2-64&65
Purvis*	MS	601	39475	Lamar	1	2-42&43
Putnam*	CT	203	06260	Windham	8	2-12&13
Puyallup	WA	206	98371-74	Pierce	19	2-80
Quakertown	PA	215	18951	Bucks	9	2-68
Quanah*	TX	817	79252	Hardeman	3	2-74
Queens	NY	718	11401	Queens	NAV	2-56
Queensborough	WA	206	98011	Snohomish	7	2-80
Quincy*	CA	916	95971	Plumas	1	2-8
Quincy*	FL	904	32351-52	Gadsden	8	2-14
Quincy*	IL	217	62301-06	Adams	41	2-20&21
Quincy	MA	617	02169	Norfolk	84	2-36&37
Quincy	WA	509	98848	Grant	4	2-81

Bold = Over 15,000......ALL CAPS = STATE CAPITAL......* = County Seat......# = Changes to 510 in 9/91..... ## = Changes to 410 in 11/91......(+) = City located in addional counties......NAV= Population not available......C.H.= Court House......(IC) = Independent City

CITY	STATE	AREA CODE	ZIP CODE	COUNTY	POPULATION (in thousands)	MAP PAGE
Quincy Manor	MD	301	20784	Prince Georges	3	2-35
Quitman*	GA	912	31643	Brooks	5	2-16&17
Quitman*	MS	601	39355	Clarke	2	2-42&43
Quitman*	TX	903	75783	Wood	1	2-74
Racine*	WI	414	53401-99	Racine	83	2-85
Radford	VA	703	24141-43	(IC)	14	2-78&79
Radnor	PA	215	19087	Delaware	27	2-68
Raeford*	NC	919	28376	Hoke	4	2-58&59
Rahway	NJ	908	07065-67	Union	27	2-52
Rainbow City	AL	205	35901	Etowah	7	2-2&3
Rainsville	AL	205	35986	De Kalb	4	2-2&3
Raleigh*	MS	601	39153	Smith	15	2-42&43
RALEIGH*	NC	919	27601-99	Wake	180	2-58&59
Ralston	NE	402	68127	Douglas	6	2-47
Ramona	CA	619	92065	San Diego	1	2-9
Ramsey	NJ	201	07446	Bergen	5	2-52
Rancho Cordova	CA	916	95670	Sacramento	48	2-8
Rancho Cucamonga	CA	714	91729-30	San Bern.	75	2-9
Rancho Mirage	CA	619	92270	Riverside	8	2-9
Rancho Palos Verdes	CA	213	90274	Los Angeles	46	2-7
Randallstown	MD	301##	21133	Baltimore	20	2-35
Randolph	MA	617	02368	Norfolk	29	2-36&37
Randolph	VT	802	05060	Orange	5	2-77
Randolph*	UT	801	84064	Rich	1	2-76
Rangely	CO	303	81648	Rio Blanco	2	2-10&11
Ranger	TX	817	76470	Eastland	3	2-74
Rankin	PA	412	15104	Allegheny	3	2-68
Rankin*	TX	915	79778	Upton	1	2-74&75
Ranson	WV	304	25438	Jefferson	2	2-82
Rantoul	IL	217	61866	Champaign	20	2-20&21
Rapid City*	SD	605	57701-09	Pennington	52	2-71
Raritan	NJ	908	08869	Somerset	6	2-50
Raton*	NM	505	87740	Colfax	8	2-53
Ravena	NY	518	12143	Albany	3	2-55
Ravenna*	OH	216	44266	Portage	11	2-60
Ravenswood	WV	304	26164	Jackson	4	2-82
Ravensworth	VA	703	22151	Fairfax	3	2-78&79
Ravenwood	VA	703	22044	Fairfax	2	2-78&79
Rawlins*	WY	307	82301	Carbon	10	2-83
Raymond*	MS	601	39154	Hinds	2	2-42&43
Raymond	NH	603	03077	Rockingham	5	2-49
Raymond	WA	206	98577	Pacific	3	2-80
Raymondville*	TX	512	78580	Willacy	10	2-75
Raymore	MO	816	64083	Cass	3	2-44
Rayne	LA	318	70578	Acadia	9	2-30
Raynham	MA	508	02767	Bristol	10	2-36&37
Raytown	MO	816	64133	Jackson	31	2-44
Rayville*	LA	318	71269	Richland	4	2-30

Bold = Over 15,000......ALL CAPS = STATE CAPITAL......* = County Seat......# = Changes to 510 in 9/91.....## = Changes to 410 in 11/91.....(+) = City located in additional counties......NAV = Population not available......C.H.= Court House......(IC)=Independent City

CITY	STATE	AREA CODE	ZIP CODE	COUNTY	POPULATION (in thousands)	MAP PAGE
Reading	MA	617	01867	Middlesex	23	2-36&37
Reading	OH	513	45215	Hamilton	13	2-62
Reading*	PA	215	19601-99	Berks	78	2-67
Red Bank	NJ	908	07701-04	Monmouth	12	2-50
Red Bank	TN	615	37415	Hamilton	13	2-72&73
Red Bay	AL	205	35582	Franklin	3	2-2&3
Red Bluff*	CA	916	96080	Tehama	12	2-8
Red Cloud*	NE	402	68970	Webster	1	2-47
Red Lake Falls*	MN	218	56750	Red Lake*	1	2-40
Red Lion	PA	717	17356	York	6	2-67
Red Lodge*	MT	406	59068	Carbon	1	2-46
Red Oak*	IA	712	51566	Montgomery	7	2-24
Red Springs	NC	919	28377	Robeson	4	2-58&59
Red Wing*	MN	612	55066	Goodhue	13	2-41
Redding*	CA	916	96001-03	Shasta	51	2-9
Redding	CT	203	06875	Fairfield	7	2-12&13
Redfield*	SD	605	57469	Spink	2	2-71
Redlands	CA	714	92373-75	San Bernardino	52	2-9
Redmond	OR	503	97756	Deschutes	6	2-63
Redmond	WA	206	98052-53	King	29	2-80
Redondo Beach	CA	213	90277-78	Los Angeles	63	2-7
Redwood City*	CA	415	94061-65	San Mateo	57	2-7
Redwood Falls*	MN	507	56283	Redwood	5	2-41
Reed City*	MI	616	49677	Osceola	2	2-38&39
Reedley	CA	209	93654	Fresno	13	2-8&9
Reedsburg	WI	608	53959	Sauk	5	2-85
Reedsport	OR	503	97467	Douglas	5	2-63
Refugio*	TX	512	78377	Refugio	3	2-75
Regency Estates	MD	301	20852	Montgomery	5	2-34
Rehoboth	MA	508	02769	Bristol	8	2-36&37
Rehoboth Beach	DE	302	19971	Sussex	2	2-35
Reidsville*	GA	912	30453	Tattnall	1	2-16&17
Reidsville	NC	919	27320-23	Rockingham	12	2-58&59
Reno*	NV	702	89501-99	Washoe	110	2-48
Rensselaer*	IN	219	47978	Jasper	5	2-22
Rensselaer	NY	518	12144	Rensselaer	9	2-55
Renton	WA	206	98055-58	King	35	2-80
Republic	MO	417	65738	Greene	6	2-44
Republic*	WA	509	99166	Ferry	1	2-81
Reserve*	NM	505	87830	Catron	1	2-53
Revere	MA	617	02151	Suffolk	84	2-36&37
Rexburg*	ID	208	83440	Madison	12	2-18
Reynoldsburg	OH	614	43068	Franklin (+2)	23	2-61
Reynoldsville	PA	814	15851	Jefferson	3	2-66
Rhinebeck	NY	914	12572	Dutchess	3	2-56
Rhinelander*	WI	715	54501	Oneida	7	2-84&85
Rialto	CA	714	92376-77	San Bernardino	53	2-9
Rice Lake	WI	715	54868	Barron	2	2-84&85

Bold = Over 15,000......ALL CAPS = STATE CAPITAL......* = County Seat......# = Changes to 510 in 9/91..... ## = Changes to 410 in 11/91......(+) = City located in addional counties......NAV= Population not available......C.H.= Court House......(IC) = Independent City

CITY	STATE	AREA CODE	ZIP CODE	COUNTY	POPULATION (in thousands)	MAP PAGE
Richardson	TX	214	75080-83	Dallas (+1)	82	2-74
Richfield	MN	612	55423	Hennepin	38	2-41
Richfield	OH	216	44286	Summit	4	2-62
Richfield*	UT	801	84701	Sevier	6	2-76
Richland	MS	601	39218	Rankin	4	2-42&43
Richland	WA	509	99352	Benton	31	2-81
Richland Center*	WI	608	53581	Richland	5	2-85
Richland Hills	TX	817	76118	Tarrant	8	2-74
Richlands	VA	703	24641	Tazewell	6	2-78&79
Richmond	CA	415#	94801-08	Contra Costa	77	2-7
Richmond*	IN	317	47374-75	Wayne	40	2-22&23
Richmond* KY	606	40475	Madison	22		2-29
Richmond	ME	207	04357	Sagadahoc	3	2-32&33
Richmond	MI	313	48062	Macomb	4	2-39
Richmond*	MO	816	64085	Ray	5	2-44
Richmond	RI	401	02812	Washington	4	2-69
Richmond*	TX	713	77469	Fort Bend	15	2-74&75
RICHMOND*	VA	804	23201-99	Henrico (IC)	219	2-78&79
Richmond	VT	802	05477	Chittenden	3	2-77
Richmond Hts	MO	314	63117	St. Louis	11	2-44&45
Richmond Hts	OH	216	44143	Cuyahoga	10	2-62
Richmont Beach	WA	206	98160	King	7	2-80
Richton Park	IL	708	60471	Cook	10	2-19
Richwood	TX	409	77530-31	Brazoria	3	2-75
Richwood	WV	304	26261	Nicholas	4	2-82
Ridge	NY	516	11961	Suffolk	7	2-56
Ridgecrest	CA	619	93555	Kern	24	2-9
Ridgecrest	WA	206	98155	King	7	2-80
Ridgefield	CT	203	06877	Fairfield	20	2-12&13
Ridgefield	NJ	201	07657	Bergen	10	2-52
Ridgefield Park	NJ	201	07660	Bergen	13	2-52
Ridgeland	MS	601	39157-58	Madison	5	2-42&43
Ridgeland*	SC	803	29936	Jasper	1	2-70
Ridgewood	NJ	201	07450-52	Bergen	25	2-52
Ridgway*	PA	814	15853	Elk	5	2-66
Ridley	PA	215	19033	Delaware	33	2-68
Ridley Park	PA	215	19078	Delaware	8	2-68
Rifle	CO	303	81650	Garfield	3	2-10&11
Rigby*	ID	208	83442	Jefferson	3	2-18
Rincon	GA	912	31326	Effingham	2	2-16&17
Rindge	NH	603	03461	Cheshire	3	2-49
Ringgold*	GA	404	30736	Catoosa	1	2-16&17
Ringwood	NJ	201	07456	Passaic	13	2-52
Rio Grande City*	TX	512	78582	Starr	1	2-75
Rio Linda	CA	916	95673	Sacramento	7	2-8
Rio Rancho	NM	505	87124	Sandoval	10	2-53
Rio Vista	CA	707	94571	Contra Costa	3	2
Ripley*	MS	601	38663	Tippah	4	2-42&43

Bold = Over 15,000......ALL CAPS = STATE CAPITAL......* = County Seat......# = Changes to 510 in 9/91.....## = Changes to 410 in 11/91.....(+) = City located in additional counties......NAV = Population not available......C.H.= Court House......(IC)=Independent City

CITY	STATE	AREA CODE	ZIP CODE	COUNTY	POPULATION (in thousands)	MAP PAGE
Ripley*	TN	901	38063	Lauderdale	6	2-72
Ripley*	WV	304	25271	Jackson	3	2-82
Ripon	CA	209	95366	San Joaquin	6	2-8&9
Ripon	WI	414	54971	Fond du Lac	7	2-85
Rising Sun*	IN	812	47040	Ohio	3	2-23
Rison*	AR	501	71665	Cleveland	1	2-6
Rittman	OH	216	44270	Wayne (+1)	6	2-60
Ritzville*	WA	509	99169	Adams	1	2-81
River Edge	NJ	201	07661	Bergen	11	2-52
River Falls	WI	715	54022	Pierce	9	2-84&85
River Forest	IL	708	60305	Cook	12	2-19
River Grove	IL	708	60171	Cook	10	2-19
River Oaks	TX	817	76114&77019	Tarrant	7	2-74
River Rouge	MI	313	48217	Wayne	13	2-39
River Vale	NJ	201	07675	Bergen	9	2-52
Riverbank	CA	209	95367	Stanislaus	6	2-8&9
Riverdale	GA	404	30274	Clayton	7	2-16&17
Riverdale	IL	708	60627	Cook	13	2-19
Riverdale	MD	301	20737	Prince Georges	4	2-34&35
Riverdale	NJ	201	07457	Morris	3	2-52
Riverdale	UT	801	84401	Weber	6	2-76
Riverdale Heights	MD	301	20737	Prince Georges	3	2-35
Riverhead*	NY	516	11901	Suffolk	7	2-56
Riverside*	CA	714	92501-99	Riverside	196	2-9
Riverside	IL	708	60546	Cook	9	2-19
Riverside	MO	816	64150	Platte	3	2-44
Riverside	NJ	609	08075	Burlington	8	2-51
Riverton	NJ	609	08077	Burlington	3	2-51
Riverton	UT	801	84065	Salt Lake	7	2-76
Riverton	WY	307	82501	Fremont	9	2-83
Riverview	MI	313	48192	Wayne	15	2-39
Riverview	MO	314	63137	St. Louis	3	2-44&45
Riviera Beach	FL	407	33404	Palm Beach	30	2-14&15
Riviera Beach	MD	301##	21122	A. Arundel	6	2-35
Roanoke	AL	205	36274	Randolph	6	2-2&3
Roanoke	VA	703	24001-38	(IC)	101	2-78&79
Roanoke Rapids	NC	919	27870	Halifax	15	2-58&59
Roaring Spring	PA	814	16673	Blair	3	2-66
Robbins	IL	708	60472	Cook	9	2-19
Robbinsdale	MN	612	55422	Hennepin	14	2-41
Robbinsville*	NC	704	28771	Graham	1	2-58
Robert Lee*	TX	915	76945	Coke	1	2-74&75
Robinson*	IL	618	62454	Crawford	7	2-21
Robstown	TX	512	78380	Nueces	12	2-75
Roby*	TX	915	79543	Fisher	1	2-74&75
Rochelle	IL	815	61068	Ogle	9	2-20
Rochelle Park	NJ	201	07662	Bergen	6	2-52
Rochester*	IN	219	46975	Fulton	5	2-22

Bold = Over 15,000......ALL CAPS = STATE CAPITAL......* = County Seat......# = Changes to 510 in 9/91..... ## = Changes to 410 in 11/91......(+) = City located in addional counties......NAV= Population not available......C.H.= Court House......(IC) = Independent City

CITY	STATE	AREA CODE	ZIP CODE	COUNTY	POPULATION (in thousands)	MAP PAGE
Rochester	MA	508	02770	Plymouth	4	2-36&37
Rochester	MI	313	48063-809	Oakland	7	2-39
Rochester*	MN	507	55901-04	Olmsted	58	2-41
Rochester	NH	603	03867	Strafford	21	2-49
Rochester*	NY	716	14601-99	Monroe	242	2-54
Rochester	PA	412	15074	Beaver	5	2-66
Rock Falls	IL	815	61071	Whiteside	11	2-20
Rock Hill	MO	314	63124	St. Louis	5	2-44&45
Rock Hill	SC	803	29730-33	York	40	2-70
Rock Island*	IL	309	61201-04	Rock Island	45	2-20
Rock Port*	MO	816	64482	Atchison	1	2-44
Rock Rapids*	IA	712	51246	Lyon	3	2-24
Rock Springs	WY	307	82901-02	Sweetwater	21	2-83
Rock Valley	IA	712	51247	Sioux	3	2-24
Rockaway	NJ	201	07866	Morris	7	2-52
Rockdale	MD	301##	21207	Baltimore	5	2-34&35
Rockdale	TX	512	76567	Milam	6	2-75
Rockford*	AL	205	35136	Coosa	1	2-2&3
Rockford*	IL	815	61101-99	Winnebago	138	2-20
Rockford	MI	616	49341	Kent	3	2-38&39
Rockingham*	NC	919	28379	Richmond	8	2-58&59
Rockingham	VT	802	05101	Windham	6	2-77
Rockland	MA	617	02370	Plymouth	16	2-36&37
Rockland*	ME	207	04841	Knox	8	2-32&33
Rockledge	FL	407	32955-56	Brevard	11	2-14&15
Rocklin	CA	916	95677	Placer	10	2-9
Rockmart	GA	404	30153	Polk	4	2-16&17
Rockport*	IN	812	47635	Spencer	3	2-23
Rockport	MA	508	01966	Essex	5	2-36&37
Rockport	ME	207	04856	Knox	3	2-32&33
Rockport*	TX	512	78382	Aransas	4	2-75
Rocksprings*	TX	512	78880	Edwards	1	2-75
Rockville*	CT	203	06066	Tolland	1	2-12&13
Rockville*	IN	317	47872	Parke	3	2-22&23
Rockville*	MD	301	20850-56	Montgomery	46	2-34
Rockville Centre	NY	516	11570-72	Nassau	26	2-56
Rockwall*	TX	214	75087	Rockwall	8	2-74
Rockwell City*	IA	712	50579	Calhoun	2	2-24
Rockwood	MI	313	48173	Wayne	3	2-39
Rockwood	TN	615	37854	Roane	6	2-72&73
Rocky Ford	CO	303	81067	Otero	5	2-10&11
Rocky Hill	CT	203	06067	Hartford	15	2-12&13
Rocky Mount	NC	919	27801-04	Edgecombe (+1)	48	2-58&59
Rocky Mount*	VA	703	24151	Franklin	4	2-78&79
Rocky River	OH	216	44116	Cuyahoga	21	2-62
Rogers	AR	501	72756-57	Benton	22	2-6
Rogers City*	MI	517	49779	Presque Isle	3	2-38&39
Rogersville*	TN	615	37857	Hawkins	4	2-72&73

Bold = Over 15,000.....ALL CAPS = STATE CAPITAL......* = County Seat......# = Changes to 510 in 9/91.....## = Changes to 410 in 11/91.....(+) = City located in additional counties......NAV = Population not available......C.H.= Court House......(IC)=Independent City

CITY	STATE	AREA CODE	ZIP CODE	COUNTY	POPULATION (in thousands)	MAP PAGE
Rohnert Park	CA	707	94927-28	Sonoma	30	2-8
Rolla*	MO	314	65401	Phelps	13	2-44&45
Rolla*	ND	701	58367	Rolette	1	2-57
Rolling Fork*	MS	601	39159	Sharkey	2	2-42&43
Rolling Hills	CA	213	90274	Los Angeles	2	2-7
Rolling Hills Ests.	CA	213	90274	Los Angeles	7	2-7
Rolling Meadows	IL	708	60008	Cook	20	2-19
Roma	TX	512	78584	Starr	3	2-75
Rome*	GA	404	30161-64	Floyd	32	2-16&17
Romeo	MI	313	48065	Macomb	4	2-39
Rome	NY	315	13440-41	Oneida	44	2-54&55
Romeoville	IL	815	60441	Will	15	2-20
Romney*	WV	304	26757	Hampshire	1	2-82
Romulus	MI	313	48174	Wayne	24	2-39
Ronkonkoma	NY	516	11779	Suffolk	20	2-56
Roosevelt	AL	205	35020	Jefferson	3	2-2&3
Roosevelt	NY	516	11575	Nassau	14	2-56
Roosevelt	UT	801	84066	Duchesne	4	2-76
Roosevelt Park	MI	616	49441	Muskegon	4	2-38&39
Rosamond	CA	805	93560	Kern	3	2-9
Roscommon*	MI	517	48653	Roscommon	1	2-38&39
Rose Hill	VA	703	22310	Fairfax	6	2-78&79
Rose Hill	WA	206	98033	King	4	2-80
Roseau*	MN	218	56751	Roseau	1	2-40
Roseburg*	OR	503	97470	Douglas	16	2-63
Rosedale*	MS	601	38769	Bolivar	3	2-42&43
Roseland	NJ	201	07068	Essex	6	2-52
Roselle	IL	708	60172-295	Du Page (+1)	20	2-19
Roselle	NJ	908	07203	Union	20	2-52
Roselle Park	NJ	908	07204	Union	13	2-52
Rosemead	CA	818	91770	Los Angeles	47	2-7
Rosemont	CA	916	95825-26	Sacramento	19	2-9
Rosemont	IL	708	60018	Cook	4	2-19
Rosemount	MN	612	55068	Dakota	5	2-41
Rosenberg	TX	713	77471	Fort Bend	21	2-74&75
Roseville	CA	916	95678	Placer	30	2-9
Roseville	MI	313	48066	Macomb	53	2-39
Roseville	MN	612	55113	Ramsey	35	2-41
Ross	CA	415	94957	Marin	2	2-7
Rossford	OH	419	43460	Wood	6	2-60
Rossville	GA	404	30741-42	Walker	4	2-16&17
Roswell	GA	404	30075-77	Fulton	35	2-16&17
Roswell*	NM	505	88201-02	Chaves	44	2-53
Rothschild	WI	715	54474	Marathon	3	2-84&85
Rotterdam	NY	518	12303	Schenectady	29	2-55
Round Lake	IL	708	60073	Lake	3	2-20
Round Lake Beach	IL	708	60073	Lake	14	2-20
Round Lake Park	IL	708	60073	Lake	4	2-20

Bold = Over 15,000......ALL CAPS = STATE CAPITAL......* = County Seat......# = Changes to 510 in 9/91..... ## = Changes to 410 in 11/91......(+) = City located in addional counties......NAV= Population not available......C.H.= Court House......(IC) = Independent City

CITY	STATE	AREA CODE	ZIP CODE	COUNTY	POPULATION (in thousands)	MAP PAGE
Round Rock	TX	512	78680-81	Williamson (+1)	13	2-75
Roundup*	MT	406	59072	Musselshell	1	2-46
Rowland Heights	CA	818	91748	Los Angeles	29	2-7
Rowlett	TX	214	75088	Dallas (+1)	7	2-74
Rowley	MA	508	01969	Essex	4	2-36&37
Roxboro*	NC	919	27573	Person	7	2-58&59
Roxbury	NJ	201	07876	Morris	19	2-52
Roy	UT	801	84067	Weber	20	2-76
Royal Oak	MI	313	48067-73	Oakland	71	2-39
Royal Palm Beach	FL	407	33411	Palm Beach	3	2-15
Royersford	PA	215	19468	Montgomery	4	2-68
Rubidoux	CA	714	92509	Riverside	13	2-9
Rugby*	ND	701	58368	Pierce	3	2-57
Ruidoso	NM	505	88345	Lincoln	5	2-53
Ruleville	MS	601	38771	Sunflower	3	2-42&43
Rumford	ME	207	04276	Oxford	8	2-32&33
Rumson	NJ	908	07760	Monmouth	8	2-50
Runnemede	NJ	609	08078	Camden	9	2-51
Rupert*	ID	208	83350	Minidoka	6	2-18
Rushville*	IL	217	62681	Schuyler	3	2-20&21
Rushville*	IN	317	46173	Rush	3	2-22&23
Rushville*	NE	308	69360	Sheridan	1	2-47
Rusk*	TX	903	75785	Cherokee	4	2-74
Ruskin	FL	813	33570-73	Hillsborough	5	2-14&15
Russell	KY	606	41169	Greenup	4	2-29
Russell*	KS	913	67665	Russell	6	2-26&27
Russellville*	AL	205	35653	Franklin	8	2-2&3
Russellville*	AR	501	72801	Pope	23	2-6
Russellville*	KY	502	42276	Logan	8	2-28&29
Rustburg*	VA	804	24588	Campbell	1	2-78&79
Ruston*	LA	318	71270-73	Lincoln	21	2-30
Rutherford	NJ	201	07070-75	Bergen	20	2-52
Rutherfordton*	NC	704	28139	Rutherford	3	2-58
Rutland	MA	508	01543	Worcester	4	2-36&37
Rutland*	VT	802	05701	Rutland	3	2-77
Rutledge*	TN	615	37861	Grainger	1	2-72&73
Rye	NH	603	03870	Rockingham	5	2-49
Rye	NY	914	10580-81	Westchester	15	2-56
Rye Brook	NY	914	10573	Westchester	8	2-56
Ryegate*	MT	406	59074	Golden Valley	1	2-46
Sabattus	ME	207	04280	Androscoggin	3	2-32&33
Sabina	OH	513	45169	Clinton	3	2-61
Sac City*	IA	712	50583	Sac	3	2-24
Saco	ME	207	04072	York	13	2-32&33
SACRAMENTO*	CA	916	94244-899	Sacramento	323	2-8
Saddle Brook	NJ	201	07662	Bergen	15	2-52
Saddle River	NJ	201	07458	Bergen	3	2-52
Safety Harbor	FL	813	34695	Pinellas	6	2-14&15

Bold = Over 15,000......ALL CAPS = STATE CAPITAL......* = County Seat......# = Changes to 510 in 9/91.....## = Changes to 410 in 11/91......(+) = City located in additional counties......NAV = Population not available......C.H.= Court House......(IC)=Independent City

CITY	STATE	AREA CODE	ZIP CODE	COUNTY	POPULATION (in thousands)	MAP PAGE
Safford*	AZ	602	85546	Graham	7	2-5
Sag Harbor	NY	516	11963	Suffolk	2	2-56
Saginaw	TX	817	76179	Tarrant	6	2-74
Saginaw*	MI	517	48601-08	Saginaw	73	2-38&39
Saguache*	CO	719	81149	Saguache	1	2-11
St. Albans	WV	304	25177	Kanawha	12	2-82
St. Albans*	VT	802	05478	Franklin	7	2-77
St. Ann	MO	314	63074	St. Louis	15	2-44&45
St. Anthony*	ID	208	83445	Fremont	3	2-18
St. Anthony	MN	612	55418	Hennepin (+1)	8	2-41
St. Augustine*	FL	904	32084-86	St. Johns	13	2-14
St. Bernard	OH	513	45217	Hamilton	5	2-62
St. Charles	IL	708	60174-75	Kane (+1)	20	2-19
St. Charles*	MO	314	63301-03	St. Charles	41	2-44&45
St. Clair	MI	313	48079	St. Clair	5	2-39
St. Clair	MO	314	63077	Franklin	3	2-44&45
St. Clair	PA	717	17970	Schuykill	4	2-67
St. Clair Shores	MI	313	48080-82	Macomb	3	2-39
St. Clairsville*	OH	614	43950	Belmont	5	2-61
St. Cloud	FL	305	34769-73	Osceola	7	2-15
St. Cloud*	MN	612	56301-04	Stearns (+2)	42	2-41
St. Francis*	KS	913	67756	Cheyenne	1	2-26&27
St. Francis	WI	414	53207	Milwaukee	10	2-85
St. Francisville*	LA	504	70775	W. Feliciana	1	2-31
St. George*	NY	718	10301	Richmond	1	2-56
St. George*	SC	803	29477	Dorchester	1	2-70
St. George*	UT	801	84770-71	Washington	19	2-76
St. Helena	CA	707	94574	Napa	5	2-8
St. Helens*	OR	503	97051	Columbia	7	2-63
St. Ignace*	MI	906	49781	Mackinac	3	2-38
St. James	MO	314	65559	Phelps	3	2-44&45
St. James*	MN	507	56081	Watonwan	4	2-41
St. James	NY	516	11780	Suffolk	12	2-56
St. John	IN	219	46373	Lake	4	2-22
St. John*	KS	316	67576	Stafford	2	2-26&27
St. Johns	MO	314	63114	St. Louis	8	2-44&45
St. Johns*	AZ	602	85936	Apache	3	2-5
St. Johns*	MI	517	48879	Clinton	8	2-38&39
St. Johnsbury*	VT	802	05819	Caledonia	7	2-77
St. Joseph*	LA	318	71366	Tensas	2	2-30
St. Joseph*	MI	616	49085	Berrien	9	2-38&39
St. Joseph	MN	612	56374	Stearns	3	2-41
St. Joseph*	MO	816	64501-99	Buchanan	74	2-44
St. Louis	MO	314	63101-99	St. Louis (I)	429	2-44&45
St. Louis Park	MN	612	55426	Hennepin	44	2-41
St. Maries*	ID	208	83861	Benewah	3	2-18
St. Martinville*	LA	318	70582	St. Martin	8	2-30
St. Marys	GA	912	31558	Camden	4	2-16&17

Bold = Over 15,000......ALL CAPS = STATE CAPITAL......* = County Seat......# = Changes to 510 in 9/91......## = Changes to 410 in 11/91......(+) = City located in addional counties......NAV= Population not available......C.H.= Court House......(IC) = Independent City

CITY	STATE	AREA CODE	ZIP CODE	COUNTY	POPULATION (in thousands)	MAP PAGE
St. Marys	OH	419	45885	Auglaize	8	2-60
St. Marys	PA	814	15857	Elk	6	2-66
St. Marys*	WV	304	26170	Pleasants	2	2-82
St. Matthews	KY	502	40206	Jefferson	14	2-28
St. Matthews*	SC	803	29135	Calhoun	1	2-70
St. PAUL*	MN	612	55101-99	Ramsey	276	2-41
St. Paul*	NE	308	68873	Howard	1	2-47
St. Paul Park	MN	612	55071	Washington	5	2-41
St. Peter*	MN	507	56082	Nicollet	8	2-41
St. Petersburg	FL	813	33701-99	Pinellas	246	2-14&15
St. Petersburg Bch	FL	813	33706	Pinellas	9	2-14
Saks	AL	205	36201	Calhoun	11	2-2&3
Salamanca	NY	716	14779	Cattaraugus	7	2-54
Salem*	AR	501	72576	Fulton	1	2-6
Salem	CT	203	06415	New London	2	2-12&13
Salem*	IL	618	62881	Marion	7	2-21
Salem*	IN	812	47167	Washington	5	2-23
Salem*	MA	508	01970-71	Essex	38	2-36&37
Salem*	MO	314	65560	Dent	4	2-44&45
Salem	NH	603	03079	Rockingham	27	2-49
Salem*	NJ	609	08079	Salem	6	2-51
Salem	OH	216	44460	Columbiana	13	2-60
SALEM*	OR	503	97301-09	Marion	93	2-63
Salem*	SD	605	57058	McCook	1	2-71
Salem*	VA	703	24153	Roanoke (IC)	24	2-78&79
Salem	WV	304	26426	Harrison	3	2-82
Salida*	CO	719	81201	Chaffee	5	2-11
Salina*	KS	913	67401-02	Saline	43	2-26&27
Salinas*	CA	408	93901-15	Monterey	96	2-9
Saline	MI	313	48176	Washtenaw	7	2-39
Salisbury	CT	203	06068	Litchfield	4	2-12&13
Salisbury	MA	508	01950-52	Essex	6	2-36&37
Salisbury*	MD	301##	21801	Wicomico	17	2-34&35
Salisbury*	NC	704	28144-45	Rowan	22	2-58
Salisbury	PA	215	18103	Lehigh	12	2-67
Sallisaw*	OK	918	74955	Sequoyah	7	2-65
Salmon*	ID	208	83467	Lemhi	3	2-18
SALT LAKE CITY*	UT	801	84101-99	Salt Lake	169	2-76
Saltwater	WA	206	98188	King	8	2-80
Saluda*	SC	803	29138	Saluda	1	2-70
Saluda*	VA	804	23149	Middlesex	1	2-78&79
Salyersville*	KY	606	41465	Magoffin	2	2-29
Samoset	FL	813	34208	Manatee	6	2-14&15
San Andreas*	CA	209	95249	Calaveras	1	2-8&9
San Angelo*	TX	915	76901-06	Tom Green	86	2-74&75
San Anselmo	CA	415	94960	Marin	11	2-7
San Antonio*	TX	512	78201-99	Bexar	842	2-75
San Augustine*	TX	409	75972	San Augustine	2	2-75

Bold = Over 15,000......ALL CAPS = STATE CAPITAL......* = County Seat......# = Changes to 510 in 9/91.....## = Changes to 410 in 11/91.....(+) = City located in additional counties......NAV = Population not available......C.H.= Court House......(IC)=Independent City

CITY	STATE	AREA CODE	ZIP CODE	COUNTY	POPULATION (in thousands)	MAP PAGE
San Benito	TX	512	78586	Cameron	18	2-75
San Bernardino*	CA	714	92401-99	San Bernardino	138	2-9
San Bruno	CA	415	94066	San Mateo	35	2-7
San Carlos	CA	415	94070	San Mateo	25	2-7
San Clemente	CA	714	92672	Orange	33	2-7
San Diego*	CA	619	92101-99	San Diego	1015	2-9
San Diego*	TX	512	78384	Duval	5	2-75
San Dimas	CA	714	91773	Los Angeles	28	2-7
San Fernando	CA	818	91340-46	Los Angeles	20	2-7
San Francisco*	CA	415	94101-99	San Francisco	749	2-8&9
San Gabriel	CA	818	91775-78	Los Angeles	33	2-7
San Jacinto	CA	714	92383	Riverside	8	2-9
San Jose*	CA	408	95101-99	Santa Clara	712	2-7
San Juan	TX	512	78589	Hidalgo	8	2-75
San Juan Capistrano	CA	714	92675	Orange	23	2-7
San Leandro	CA	415#	94577-79	Alameda	65	2-7
San Lorenzo	CA	415#	94580	Alameda	22	2-7
San Luis*	CO	719	81152	Costilla	1	2-11
San Luis Obispo*	CA	805	93401-12	S.L. Obispo	37	2-9
San Marcos	CA	619	92069	San Diego	21	2-9
San Marcos*	TX	512	78666-67	Hays	28	2-75
San Marino	CA	818	91118	Los Angeles	13	2-7
San Mateo	CA	415	94401-99	San Mateo	81	2-7
San Pablo	CA	415#	94806	Contra Costa	21	2-7
San Rafael*	CA	415	94901-15	Marin	44	2-7
San Ramon	CA	415#	94583	Contra Costa	26	2-7
San Remo	NY	516	11754	Suffolk	7	2-56
San Saba*	TX	915	76877	San Saba	1	2-74&75
Sand Springs	OK	918	74063	Osage (+1)	13	2-65
Sanderson*	TX	915	79848	Terrell	1	2-74&75
Sandersville*	GA	912	31082	Washington	6	2-16&17
Sandpoint*	ID	208	83862-65	Bonner	5	2-18
Sands Point	NY	516	11050	Nassau	3	2-56
Sandston	VA	703	23150	Fairfax	3	2-78&79
Sandusky*	MI	313	48471	Sanilac	2	2-39
Sandusky*	OH	419	44870-71	Erie	30	2-60
Sandwich	IL	815	60548	De Kalb (+1)	5	2-20
Sandwich	MA	508	02563	Barnstable	8	2-36&37
Sandy	OR	503	97055	Clackamas	3	2-63
Sandy	UT	801	84090-94	Salt Lake	65	2-76
Sandy Hook*	KY	606	41171	Elliott	1	2-29
Sandy Springs	GA	404	30328	Fulton	46	2-16&17
Sanford*	FL	407	32771-73	Seminole	31	2-14&15
Sanford*	NC	919	27330-31	Lee	17	2-58&59
Sanford	ME	207	04073	York	18	2-32&33
Sanger	CA	209	93657	Fresno	14	2-8&9
Sanger	TX	817	76266	Denton	3	2-74
Sanibel	FL	813	33957	Lee	3	2-14&15

Bold = Over 15,000......ALL CAPS = STATE CAPITAL......* = County Seat......# = Changes to 510 in 9/91.....## = Changes to 410 in 11/91......(+) = City located in addional counties......NAV= Population not available......C.H.= Court House......(IC) = Independent City

CITY	STATE	AREA CODE	ZIP CODE	COUNTY	POPULATION (in thousands)	MAP PAGE
Sansom Park	TX	817	76114	Tarrant	4	2-74
Santa Ana*	CA	714	92701-99	Orange	236	2-7
Santa Barbara*	CA	805	93101-90	Santa Barbara	79	2-9
Santa Clara	CA	408	95050-55	Santa Clara	88	2-7
Santa Cruz*	CA	408	95060-66	Santa Cruz	45	2-7
Santa Fe	TX	409	77517	Galveston	6	2-75
SANTA FE*	NM	505	87501-09	Santa Fe	52	2-53
Santa Fe Springs	CA	213	90670	Los Angeles	15	2-7
Santa Maria	CA	805	93454-56	Santa Barbara	51	2-9
Santa Monica	CA	213	90401-99	Los Angeles	93	2-7
Santa Paula	CA	805	93060	Ventura	22	2-9
Santa Rosa*	CA	707	95401-09	Sonoma	97	2-8
Santa Rosa*	NM	505	88435	Guadalupe	2	2-53
Santee	CA	619	92071	San Diego	51	2-9
Sapulpa*	OK	918	74066-67	Creek	17	2-65
Saraland	AL	205	36571	Mobile	10	2-2&3
Saranac Lake	NY	518	12982-83	Franklin (+1)	5	2-55
Saratoga	CA	408	95070-71	Santa Clara	29	2-7
Sarasota*	FL	813	34230-78	Sarasota	54	2-14&15
Saratoga Springs	NY	518	12866	Saratoga	25	2-55
Sardis*	MS	601	38666	Panola	2	2-42&43
Sarita*	TX	512	78385	Kenedy	1	2-75
Sartell	MN	612	56377	Benton (+1)	3	2-41
Satellite Beach	FL	407	32937	Brevard	9	2-14&15
Satsuma	AL	205	36572	Mobile	4	2-2&3
Saugerties	NY	914	12477	Ulster	4	2-56
Saugus	CA	818	91350	Los Angeles 16		2-7
Saugus	MA	617	01906	Essex	26	2-36&37
Sauk City	WI	608	53583	Sauk	3	2-85
Sauk Village	IL	708	60411	Cook (+1)	11	2-19
Saukville	WI	414	53080	Ozaukee	3	2-85
Saulk Centre	MN	612	56378	Stearns	4	2-41
Saulk Rapids	MN	612	56379	Benton	6	2-41
Sault Ste Marie*	MI	906	49783	Chippewa	14	2-38
Sausalito	CA	415	94965-66	Marin	7	2-7
Savage	MD	301##	20763	Howard	3	2-34&35
Savage	MN	612	55378	Scott	5	2-41
Savanna	IL	815	61074	Carroll	5	2-20
Savannah*	GA	912	31401-99	Chatham	150	2-16&17
Savannah*	MO	816	64485	Andrew	4	2-44
Savannah*	TN	901	38372	Hardin	7	2-72
Saylesville	RI	401	02865	Providence	4	2-69
Sayre	PA	717	18840	Bradford	7	2-67
Sayre Woods South	NJ	908	08857	Middlesex	10	2-50
Sayre*	OK	405	73662	Beckham	3	2-64&65
Sayreville	NJ	908	08872	Middlesex	31	2-50
Sayville	NY	516	11782	Suffolk	12	2-56
Scappoose	OR	503	97056	Columbia	3	2-63

Bold = Over 15,000......ALL CAPS = STATE CAPITAL......* = County Seat......# = Changes to 510 in 9/91.....## = Changes to 410 in 11/91.....(+) = City located in additional counties......NAV = Population not available......C.H.= Court House......(IC)=Independent City

CITY	STATE	AREA CODE	ZIP CODE	COUNTY	POPULATION (in thousands)	MAP PAGE
Scarborough	ME	207	04074	Cumberland	11	2-32&33
Scarsdale	NY	914	10583	Westchester	17	2-56
Schaumburg	IL	708	60194	Cook (+1)	58	2-19
Schenectady*	NY	518	12301-99	Schenectady	68	2-55
Schererville	IN	219	46375	Lake	13	2-22
Schertz	TX	512	78154	Guadalupe	7	2-75
Schiller Park	IL	708	60176	Cook	12	2-19
Schoharie*	NY	518	12157	Schoharie	1	2-55
Schuyler*	NE	402	68661	Colfax	4	2-47
Schuylkill Haven	PA	717	17972	Schuykill	6	2-67
Scituate	MA	617	02066	Plymouth	17	2-36&37
Scituate	RI	401	02857	Providence	8	2-69
Scobey*	MT	406	59263	Daniels	1	2-46
Scotch Plains	NJ	908	07076	Union	20	2-52
Scotia	NY	518	12302	Schenectady	7	2-55
Scotland Neck	NC	919	27874	Halifax	3	2-58&59
Scotlandville	LA	504	70807	East Baton Rouge	15	2-31
Scott City*	KS	316	67871	Scott	4	2-26&27
Scott City	MO	314	63780	Scott	4	2-44&45
Scottdale	GA	404	30079	De Kalb	9	2-16&17
Scottdale	PA	412	15683	Westmooreland	6	2-68
Scotts Valley	CA	408	95066	Santa Cruz	7	2-7
Scottsbluff	NE	308	69353 &61	Scotts Bluff	14	2-47
Scottsboro*	AL	205	35768	Jackson	15	2-2&3
Scottsburg*	IN	812	47170	Scott	5	2-23
Scottsdale	AZ	602	85250-71	Maricopa	113	2-5
Scottsville*	KY	502	42164	Allen	4	2-28&29
Scranton*	PA	717	18501-99	Lackawanna	82	2-67
Sea Cliff	NY	516	11579	Nassau	8	2-56
Seabrook	MD	301	20706	Prince Georges	7	2-34&35
Seabrook	NH	603	03874	Rockingham	6	2-49
Seabrook	TX	713	77586	Harris (+2)	5	2-74&75
Seaford	DE	302	19973	Sussex	5	2-35
Seaford	NY	516	11783	Nassau	16	2-56
Seagoville	TX	214	75159	Dallas (+1)	7	2-74
Seagraves	TX	806	79359	Gaines	3	2-74
Seal Beach	CA	213	90740	Orange	26	2-7
Sealy	TX	409	77474	Austin	4	2-75
Searcy*	AR	501	72143	White	14	2-6
Searsport	ME	207	04974	Waldo	2	2-32&33
Seaside	CA	408	93955	Monterey	37	2-9
Seaside	OR	503	97138	Clatsop	5	2-63
Seat Pleasant	MD	301	20743	Prince Georges	5	2-35
Seattle*	WA	206	98101-99	King	493	2-80
Sebastian	FL	407	32958	Indian River	3	2-14&15
Sebastopol	CA	707	95472-73	Sonoma	6	2-8
Sebring*	FL	813	33870-72	Highlands	60	2-14&15
Sebring	OH	216	44672	Mahoning	5	2-60

Bold = Over 15,000.......ALL CAPS = STATE CAPITAL.......* = County Seat.......# = Changes to 510 in 9/91..... ## = Changes to 410 in 11/91......(+) = City located in addional counties......NAV= Population not available......C.H.= Court House......(IC) = Independent City

CITY	STATE	AREA CODE	ZIP CODE	COUNTY	POPULATION (in thousands)	MAP PAGE
Secaucus	NJ	201	07094	Hudson	15	2-52
Security	CO	719	80911	El Paso	7	2-11
Sedalia*	MO	816	65301	Pettis	20	2-44
Sedan*	KS	316	67361	Chautauqua	2	2-26&27
Sedro Woolley	WA	206	98284	Skagit	6	2-80
Seekonk	MA	508	02771	Bristol	12	2-36&37
Seguin*	TX	512	78155-56	Guadalupe	18	2-75
Selah	WA	509	98942	Yakima	5	2-81
Selby*	SD	605	57472	Walworth	1	2-71
Selden	NY	516	11784	Suffolk	17	2-56
Selinsgrove	PA	717	17870	Snyder	5	2-67
Sellersburg	IN	812	47172	Clark	3	2-23
Sellersville	PA	215	18960	Bucks	3	2-68
Selma*	AL	205	36701-02	Dallas	27	2-2&3
Selma	CA	209	93662	Fresno	13	2-8&9
Selma	NC	919	27576	Johnston	5	2-58&59
Selmer*	TN	901	38375	McNairy	4	2-72
Seminole	OK	405	74868	Seminole	9	2-64&65
Seminole*	TX	915	79360	Gaines	7	2-74&75
Senatobia*	MS	601	38668	Tate	5	2-42&43
Seneca	SC	803	29678-79	Oconee	8	2-70
Seneca Falls	NY	315	13148	Seneca	7	2-54&55
Seneca*	KS	913	66538	Nemaha	2	2-26&27
Sequim	WA	206	98382	Clallam	3	2-80
Seven Harbors	MI	313	48031	Oakland	5	2-39
Seven Hills	OH	513	44131	Cuyahoga	3	2-61
Sevierville*	TN	615	37862-64	Sevier	5	2-72&73
Seward	AK	907	99664	Kenai Penisula	2	2-4
Seward*	NE	402	68434	Seward	6	2-47
Sewickley	PA	412	15143	Allegheny	5	2-68
Seymour	CT	203	06483	New Haven	13	2-12&13
Seymour	IN	812	47274	Jackson	15	2-23
Seymour*	TX	817	76380	Baylor	3	2-74
Seymour	WI	414	54165	Outagamie	2	2-85
Shadyside	OH	614	43947	Belmont	4	2-61
Shafter	CA	805	93263	Kern	7	2-9
Shaftsbury	VT	802	05262	Bennington	3	2-77
Shaker Heights	OH	216	44120	Cuyahoga	31	2-62
Shakopee*	MN	612	55379	Scott	10	2-41
Shaler Twp.	PA	412	15116	Allegheny	32	2-68
Shamokin	PA	717	17876	Northumberland	10	2-67
Shamrock	TX	806	79079	Wheeler	3	2-74
Sharon	CT	203	06069	Litchfield	3	2-12&13
Sharon	MA	617	02067	Norfolk	13	2-36&37
Sharon	PA	412	16148	Mercer	17	2-66
Sharon Hill	PA	215	19079	Delaware	6	2-68
Sharon Springs*	KS	913	67758	Wallace	32	2-26&27
Sharonville	OH	513	45241	Hamilton	10	2-62

Bold = Over 15,000......ALL CAPS = STATE CAPITAL......* = County Seat......# = Changes to 510 in 9/91.....## = Changes to 410 in 11/91.....(+) = City located in additional counties......NAV = Population not available......C.H.= Court House......(IC)=Independent City

CITY	STATE	AREA CODE	ZIP CODE	COUNTY	POPULATION (in thousands)	MAP PAGE
Sharpsburg	PA	412	15215	Allegheny	4	2-68
Sharpsville	PA	412	16150	Mercer	5	2-66
Shawano*	WI	715	54166	Shawano	7	2-84&85
Shawnee*	OK	405	74801-02	Pottawatomie	27	2-64&65
Shawnee Mission	KS	913	66201-99	Johnson	32	2-26&27
Shawneetown*	IL	618	62984	Gallatin	2	2-21
Sheboygan*	WI	414	53081-83	Sheboygan	27	2-85
Sheboygan Falls	WI	414	53085	Sheboygan	5	2-85
Sheffield	AL	205	35660-62	Colbert	12	2-2&3
Sheffield	MA	413	01257	Berkshire	3	2-36
Sheffield Lake	OH	216	44054	Lorain	10	2-60
Shelburne	VT	802	05482	Chittenden	5	2-77
Shelby	MS	601	38774	Bolivar	3	2-42&43
Shelby*	MT	406	59474	Toole	3	2-46
Shelby	OH	419	44875	Richland	10	2-60
Shelby*	NC	704	28150-51	Cleveland	14	2-58
Shelbyville*	IL	217	62565	Shelby	5	2-20&21
Shelbyville*	IN	317	46176	Shelby	14	2-22&23
Shelbyville*	KY	502	40065-66	Shelby	5	2-28&29
Shelbyville*	MO	314	63469	Shelby	1	2-44&45
Shelbyville*	TN	615	37160	Bedford	13	2-72&73
Sheldon	IA	712	51201	O'Brien (+1)	5	2-24
Shell Lake*	WI	715	54871	Washburn	1	2-84&85
Shelley	ID	208	83274	Bingham	3	2-18
Shelton	CT	203	06484	Fairfield	31	2-12&13
Shelton*	WA	206	98584	Mason	8	2-80
Shenandoah	IA	712	51601	Fremont (+1)	6	2-24
Shenandoah	PA	717	17976	Schuykill	7	2-67
Shepherdsville*	KY	502	40165	Bullitt	5	2-28
Sherborn	MA	508	01770	Middlesex	4	2-36&37
Sherburne	NY	607	13460	Chenango	3	2-54&55
Sheridan*	AR	501	72150	Grant	3	2-6
Sheridan	CO	303	80110	Arapahoe	5	2-10&11
Sheridan*	WY	307	82801	Sheridan	16	2-83
Sherman*	TX	903	75090-93	Grayson	31	2-74
Sherrill	NY	315	13461	Oneida	3	2-54&55
Sherwood	AR	501	72116	Pulaski	12	2-6
Sherwood	OR	503	97140	Washington	3	2-63
Sherwood Hall	VA	703	22306	Fairfax	3	2-78&79
Shields	MI	517	48603	Saginaw	4	2-38&39
Shillington	PA	215	19607	Berks	6	2-67
Shinnston	WV	304	26431	Harrison	3	2-82
Shippensburg	PA	717	17257	Cumberland (+1)	6	2-67
Shirley	MA	508	01464	Middlesex	5	2-36&37
Shively	KY	502	40216	Jefferson	16	2-28
Shoals*	IN	812	47581	Martin	1	2-23
Shoreview	MN	612	55126	Ramsey	17	2-41
Shorewood	WI	414	53211	Milwaukee	14	2-85

Bold = Over 15,000......ALL CAPS = STATE CAPITAL......* = County Seat......# = Changes to 510 in 9/91..... ## = Changes to 410 in 11/91......(+) = City located in addional counties......NAV= Population not available......C.H.= Court House......(IC) = Independent City

CITY	STATE	AREA CODE	ZIP CODE	COUNTY	POPULATION (in thousands)	MAP PAGE
Shoshone*	ID	208	83352	Lincoln	1	2-18
Show Low	AZ	602	85901	Navajo	5	2-5
Shreveport*	LA	318	71101-66	Caddo	220	2-30
Shrewsbury	MA	508	01545	Worcester	23	2-36&37
Shrewsbury	MO	314	63119	St. Louis	5	2-44&45
Shrewsbury	PA	717	17361	York	3	2-67
Sibley*	IA	712	51249	Osceola	3	2-24
Sidney	NY	607	13838	Delaware	5	2-54&55
Sidney*	IA	712	51652	Fremont	1	2-24
Sidney*	MT	406	59270	Richland	6	2-46
Sidney*	NE	308	69162	Cheyenne	6	2-47
Sidney*	OH	513	45365	Shelby	18	2-61
Sierra Blanca*	TX	915	79851	Hudspeth	1	2-74&75
Sierra Madre	CA	818	91024	Los Angeles	10	2-7
Sierra Vista	AZ	602	85613	Cochise	32	2-5
Signal Hill	CA	213	90806	Los Angeles	7	2-7
Signal Mountain	TN	615	37377	Hamilton	6	2-72&73
Sigourney*	IA	515	52591	Keokuk	2	2-24&25
Sikeston	MO	314	63801	New Madrid (+1)	17	2-44&45
Siler City	NC	919	27344	Chatham	5	2-58&59
Siloam Springs	AR	501	72761	Benton	8	2-6
Silsbee	TX	409	77656	Hardin	8	2-75
Silver Bay	MN	218	55614	Lake	3	2-40
Silver City*	NM	505	88061-62	Grant	11	2-53
Silver Creek	NY	716	14136	Chautauqua	3	2-54
Silver Lake	OH	216	44221	Summit	3	2-62
Silver Lake	WA	206	98201	Snohomish	4	2-80
Silver Spring	MD	301	20901-99	Montgomery	70	2-34&35
Silver Spring	PA	717	17055	Cumberland	7	2-67
Silverton*	CO	303	81433	San Juan	1	2-10&11
Silverton	NJ	908	08753	Ocean	6	2-50&51
Silverton	OH	513	45236	Hamilton	6	2-62
Silverton	OR	503	97381	Marion	5	2-63
Silverton*	TX	806	79257	Briscoe	1	2-74
Silvis	IL	309	61282	Rock Island	7	2-20
Simi Valley	CA	805	93062-65	Ventura	84	2-9
Simpsonville	SC	803	29681	Greenville	9	2-70
Simsbury	CT	203	06070	Hartford	21	2-12&13
Sinking Spring	PA	215	19608	Berks	3	2-67
Sinton*	TX	512	78387	San Patricio	1	2-75
Sioux Center	IA	712	51250	Sioux	5	2-24
Sioux City*	IA	712	51101-99	Woodbury	80	2-24
Sioux Falls*	SD	605	57101-99	Minnehaha	97	2-71
Sisseton*	SD	605	57262	Roberts	2	2-71
Sitka	AK	907	99835	Sitka	8	2-4
Skagway	AK	907	99840	Skag. Yak. Angoon	3	2-4
Skiatook	OK	918	74070	Osage (+1)	4	2-65
Skokie	IL	708	60076-77	Cook	60	2-19

Bold = Over 15,000......ALL CAPS = STATE CAPITAL......* = County Seat......# = Changes to 510 in 9/91.....## = Changes to 410 in 11/91.....(+) = City located in additional counties......NAV = Population not available......C.H.= Court House......(IC)=Independent City

CITY	STATE	AREA CODE	ZIP CODE	COUNTY	POPULATION (in thousands)	MAP PAGE
Skowhegan*	ME	207	04976	Somerset	8	2-32&33
Skyway	WA	206	98178	King	9	2-80
Slackwoods	NJ	609	08638	Mercer	8	2-50
Slatington	PA	215	18080	Lehigh	4	2-67
Slaton	TX	806	79364	Lubbock	7	2-74
Slayton*	MN	507	56172	Murray	1	2-41
Sleepy Eye	MN	507	56085	Brown	4	2-41
Slidell	LA	504	70458-61	St. Tammany	36	2-30&31
Slippery Rock	PA	412	16057	Butler	3	2-66
Sloan	NY	716	14225	Erie	5	2-54
Sloatsburg	NY	914	10974	Rockland	3	2-56
Smethport*	PA	814	16749	McKean	1	2-66
Smith Center*	KS	913	66967	Smith	2	2-26&27
Smithfield*	NC	919	27577	Johnston	7	2-58&59
Smithfield	RI	401	02917	Providence	17	2-69
Smithfield	UT	801	84335	Cache	5	2-76
Smithfield	VA	804	23430	Isle of Wight	4	2-78&79
Smithland*	KY	502	42081	Livingston	1	2-28&29
Smithtown	NY	516	11787	Suffolk	30	2-56
Smithville*	TN	615	37166	De Kalb	4	2-72&73
Smithville	TX	512	78957	Bastrop	4	2-75
Smyrna	DE	302	19977	Kent (+1)	5	2-35
Smyrna	GA	404	30080	Cobb	24	2-16&17
Smyrna	TN	615	37167	Rutherford	11	2-72&73
Sneedville*	TN	615	37869	Hancock	1	2-72&73
Snellville	GA	404	30278	Gwinnett	9	2-16&17
Snohomish	WA	206	98290	Snohomish	5	2-80
Snow Hill*	MD	301##	21863	Worcester	2	2-34&35
Snow Hill*	NC	919	28580	Greene	1	2-58&59
Snowflake	AZ	602	85937	Navajo	4	2-5
Snyder*	TX	915	79549	Scurry	1	2-74&75
Social Circle	GA	404	30279	Walton	3	2-16&17
Socorro*	NM	505	87801	Socorro	8	2-53
Soda Springs*	ID	208	83276	Caribou	4	2-18
Soddy-Daisy	TN	615	37379	Hamilton	8	2-72&73
Solana Beach	CA	619	92075	San Diego	14	2-9
Soledad	CA	408	93960	Monterey	6	2-9
Solon	OH	216	44139	Cuyahoga	14	2-62
Solvay	NY	315	13209	Onondaga	7	2-54&55
Somerdale	NJ	609	08083	Camden	6	2-51
Somers	CT	203	06071	Tolland	8	2-12&13
Somers Point	NJ	609	08244	Atlantic	10	2-51
Somerset*	KY	606	42501-02	Pulaski	12	2-29
Somerset	MA	508	02725	Bristol	18	2-36&37
Somerset*	PA	814	15501	Somerset	6	2-66
Somersworth	NH	603	03878	Strafford	10	2-49
Somerton	AZ	602	85350	Yuma	4	2-5
Somerville	MA	617	02143-45	Middlesex	76	2-36&37

Bold = Over 15,000......ALL CAPS = STATE CAPITAL......* = County Seat......# = Changes to 510 in 9/91..... ## = Changes to 410 in 11/91......(+) = City located in addional counties......NAV= Population not available......C.H.= Court House......(IC) = Independent City

CITY	STATE	AREA CODE	ZIP CODE	COUNTY	POPULATION (in thousands)	MAP PAGE
Somerville*	NJ	908	08873-77	Somerset	11	2-50
Somerville*	TN	901	38068	Fayette	1	2-72
Sonoma	CA	707	95476	Sonoma	7	2-8
Sonora*	CA	209	95370	Tuolumne	4	2-8&9
Sonora*	TX	915	76950	Sutton	3	2-74&75
Soperton*	GA	912	30457	Treutlen	3	2-16&17
Souderton	PA	215	18964	Montgomery	7	2-68
South Amboy	NJ	908	08879	Middlesex	8	2-50
South Bay	FL	407	33493	Palm Beach	4	2-14&15
South Beloit	IL	815	61080	Winnebago	4	2-20
South Bend*	IN	219	46601-99	St. Joseph	109	2-22
South Bend*	WA	509	98586	Pacific	2	2-81
South Berwick	ME	207	03908	York	4	2-32&33
South Boston	VA	804	24592	(IC)	8	2-78&79
South Bound Brook	NJ	908	08880	Somerset	4	2-50
South Brunswick	NJ	908	08540	Middlesex	18	2-50
South Burlington	VT	802	05403	Chittenden	12	2-77
South Charleston	WV	304	25303	Kanawha	17	2-82
South Chicago Heights	IL	708	60411	Cook	4	2-19
South Daytona	FL	904	32121	Volusia	12	2-14
South El Monte	CA	818	91733	Los Angeles	17	2-7
South Elgin	IL	708	60177	Kane	6	2-19
South Euclid	OH	216	44121	Cuyahoga	25	2-62
South Fayette	PA	412	15064	Allegheny	10	2-68
South Fulton	TN	901	38257	Obion	3	2-72
South Gate	CA	213	90280	Los Angeles	80	2-7
South Gate	MD	301##	21061	A. Arundel	7	2-34&35
South Glens Falls	NY	518	12803	Saratoga	4	2-55
South Greensburg	PA	412	15601	Westmooreland	3	2-68
South Hadley	MA	413	01075	Hampshire	16	2-36
South Hanover	PA	717	17033	Dauphin	3	2-67
South Haven	MI	616	49090	Van Buren	6	2-38&39
South Hempstead	NY	516	11550	Nassau	3	2-56
South Hill	VA	804	23970	Mecklenburg	4	2-78&79
South Hill	WA	206	98373	Pierce	4	2-80
South Holland	IL	708	60473	Cook	24	2-19
South Houston	TX	713	77587	Harris	13	2-74&75
South Int'l Falls	MN	218	56679	Koochiching	3	2-40
South Jordan	UT	801	84065	Salt Lake	7	2-76
South Kingstown	RI	401	02879-80	Washington	20	2-69
South Lake Tahoe	CA	916	95705-08	El Dorado	21	2-8
South Laurel	MD	301	20707	Prince Georges	9	2-34&35
South Lawn	MD	301	20745	Prince Georges	3	2-35
South Lebanon	OH	513	45065	Warren	3	2-61
South Lebanon	PA	717	17042	Lebanon	7	2-67
South Miami	FL	305	33143	Dade	10	2-15
South Milwaukee	WI	414	53172	Milwaukee	21	2-85
South Nyack	NY	914	10960	Rockland	4	2-56

Bold = Over 15,000......ALL CAPS = STATE CAPITAL......* = County Seat......# = Changes to 510 in 9/91.....## = Changes to 410 in 11/91......(+) = City located in additional counties......NAV = Population not available......C.H.= Court House......(IC)=Independent City

CITY	STATE	AREA CODE	ZIP CODE	COUNTY	POPULATION (in thousands)	MAP PAGE
South Ogden	UT	801	84403	Weber	11	2-76
South Orange	NJ	201	07079	Essex	16	2-52
South Paris*	ME	207	04281	Oxford	2	2-32&33
South Park	PA	412	15129	Allegheny	14	2-68
South Pasadena	CA	818	91030	Los Angeles	23	2-7
South Pasadena	FL	813	33707	Pinellas	4	2-14&15
South Pittsburg	TN	615	37380	Marion	4	2-72&73
South Plainfield	NJ	908	07080	Middlesex	20	2-50
South Point	OH	614	45680	Lawrence	4	2-61
South Portland	ME	207	04106	Cumberland	3	2-32&33
South River	NJ	908	08882	Middlesex	14	2-50
South Russell	OH	216	44022	Geauga	3	2-60
South St. Paul	MN	612	55075-77	Dakota	21	2-41
South Salt Lake	UT	801	84115	Salt Lake	10	2-76
South San Francisco ..	CA	415	94080	San Mateo	51	2-7
South San Jose Hills ..	CA	818	91744	Los Angeles	17	2-7
South Setauket	NY	516	11733	Suffolk	6	2-56
South Sioux City	NE	402	68776	Dakota	9	2-47
South Strabane	PA	412	15301	Washington	7	2-66
South Toms River	NJ	908	08757	Ocean	4	2-50&51
South Tucson	AZ	602	85713	Pima	7	2-5
South Whitehall	PA	215	18104	Lehigh	15	2-67
South Whittier	CA	213	90605	Los Angeles	46	2-7
South Williamsport	PA	717	17701	Lycoming	7	2-67
South Windsor	CT	203	06074	Hartford	17	2-12&13
Southampton	MA	413	01073	Hampshire	4	2-36
Southampton	NY	516	11968	Suffolk	4	2-56
Southaven	MS	601	38671	De Soto	17	2-42&43
Southborough	MA	508	01772	Worcester	6	2-36&37
Southbridge	MA	508	01550	Worcester	16	2-36&37
Southbury	CT	203	06488	New Haven	14	2-12&13
Southern Pines	NC	919	28387	Moore	5	2-58&59
Southfield	MI	313	48075-76	Oakland	74	2-39
Southgate	KY	606	41071	Campbell	3	2-29
Southgate	MI	313	48195	Wayne	30	2-39
Southington	CT	203	06489	Hartford	39	2-12&13
Southlake	TX	817	76092	Denton (+1)	3	2-74
Southmont	PA	814	15905	Cambria	6	2-66
Southport*	NC	919	28461	Brunswick	3	2-58&59
Southside	AL	205	35901	Etowah (+1)	5	2-2&3
S.W. Greensburg	PA	412	15601	Westmooreland	3	2-68
Southwick	MA	413	01077	Hampden	7	2-36
Spanish Fork	UT	801	84660	Utah	10	2-76
Sparks	NV	702	89431-36	Washoe	51	2-48
Sparta*	GA	404	31087	Hancock	1	2-16&17
Sparta	IL	618	62286	Randolph	5	2-21
Sparta	MI	616	49345	Kent	3	2-38&39
Sparta*	NC	919	28675	Alleghany	1	2-58&59

Bold = Over 15,000......ALL CAPS = STATE CAPITAL......* = County Seat......# = Changes to 510 in 9/91..... ## = Changes to 410 in 11/91......(+) = City located in addional counties......NAV= Population not available......C.H.= Court House......(IC) = Independent City

CITY	STATE	AREA CODE	ZIP CODE	COUNTY	POPULATION (in thousands)	MAP PAGE
Sparta	NJ	201	07871	Sussex	8	2-50
Sparta*	TN	615	38583	White	5	2-72&73
Sparta*	WI	608	54656	Monroe	7	2-85
Spartanburg*	SC	803	29301-18	Spartanburg	43	2-70
Spearfish	SD	605	57783	Lawrence	5	2-71
Spearman*	TX	806	79081	Hansford	3	2-74
Speedway	IN	317	46224	Marion	13	2-22&23
Spencer*	IA	712	51301	Clay	11	2-24
Spencer*	IN	812	47460	Owen	3	2-23
Spencer	MA	508	01562	Worcester	10	2-36&37
Spencer	NC	704	28159	Rowan	3	2-58
Spencer	OK	405	73084	Oklahoma	4	2-64&65
Spencer*	TN	615	38585	Van Buren	1	2-72&73
Spencer*	WV	304	25276	Roane	2	2-82
Spencerport	NY	716	14559	Monroe	3	2-54
Spindale	NC	704	28160	Rutherford	4	2-58
Spirit Lake*	IA	712	51360	Dickenson	4	2-24
Spokane*	WA	509	99201-99	Spokane	176	2-81
Spotswood	NJ	908	08884	Middlesex	8	2-50
Spotsylvania*	VA	703	22553	Spotsylvania	1	2-79
Spring	TX	713	77386-91	Harris	3	2-74&75
Spring City	PA	215	19475	Chester	3	2-67
Spring Garden	PA	717	17403	York	11	2-67
Spring Lake	MI	616	49456	Ottawa	3	2-38&39
Spring Lake	NC	919	28390	Cumberland	6	2-58&59
Spring Lake	NJ	908	07762	Monmouth	4	2-50
Spring Lake Heights	NJ	908	07762	Monmouth	5	2-50
Spring Lake Pk.	MN	612	55432	Anoka (+1)	6	2-41
Spring Valley	CA	619	92077-78	San Diego	46	2-9
Spring Valley	IL	815	61362	Bureau	6	2-20
Spring Valley	MN	507	55975	Fillmore	2	2-41
Spring Valley	NY	914	10977	Rockland	22	2-56
Spring Valley	TX	713	77055	Harris	3	2-74&75
Springboro	OH	513	45066	Warren	5	2-61
Springbrook Forest	VA	703	22030	Fairfax	4	2-78&79
Springdale	AR	501	72764-65	Washington (+1)	26	2-6
Springdale	OH	513	45246	Hamilton	10	2-62
Springdale	PA	412	15144	Allegheny	4	2-68
Springerville	AZ	602	85938	Apache	2	2-5
Springettsbury	PA	717	17402	York	19	2-67
Springfield*	CO	719	81073	Baca	1	2-11
Springfield	FL	904	32401	Bay	7	2-14
Springfield*	GA	912	31329	Effingham	1	2-16&17
SPRINGFIELD*	IL	217	62701-99	Sangamon	178	2-20&21
Springfield*	KY	606	40069	Washington	3	2-29
Springfield*	MA	413	01101-99	Hampden	149	2-36
Springfield	MI	616	49015	Calhoun	6	2-38&39
Springfield*	MO	417	65801-99	Greene	136	2-44

Bold = Over 15,000......ALL CAPS = STATE CAPITAL......* = County Seat......# = Changes to 510 in 9/91.....## = Changes to 410 in 11/91.....(+) = City located in additional counties......NAV = Population not available......C.H.= Court House......(IC)=Independent City

CITY	STATE	AREA CODE	ZIP CODE	COUNTY	POPULATION (in thousands)	MAP PAGE
Springfield	NJ	908	07081	Union	14	2-52
Springfield*	OH	513	45501-99	Clark	70	2-61
Springfield	OR	503	97477-78	Lane	40	2-63
Springfield	PA	215	19064	Delaware	25	2-68
Springfield*	TN	615	37172	Robertson	10	2-72&73
Springfield	VA	703	22150-61	Fairfax	13	2-78&79
Springfield	VT	802	05156	Windsor	10	2-77
Springfield Twp.	PA	215	19118	Montgomery	20	2-68
Springhill	LA	318	71075	Webster	6	2-30
Springview*	NE	402	68778	Keya Paha	1	2-47
Springville	UT	801	84663-64	Utah	12	2-76
Stafford	TX	713	77477	Fort Bend (+1)	5	2-74&75
Stafford*	VA	703	22554	Stafford	1	2-78&79
Stamford	CT	203	06901-99	Fairfield	103	2-12&13
Stamford	TX	915	79548-53	Haskell (+1)	5	2-74&75
Stamps	AR	501	71860	Lafayette	3	2-6
Stanardsville*	VA	804	22973	Greene	1	2-78&79
Standish	ME	207	04084	Cumberland	6	2-32&33
Standish*	MI	517	48658	Arenac	2	2-38&39
Stanford*	KY	606	40484	Lincoln	3	2-29
Stanford*	MT	406	59479	Judith Basin	1	2-46
Stanhope	NJ	201	07874	Sussex	4	2-50
Stanley*	ND	701	58784	Mountrail	1	2-57
Stanton	CA	714	90680	Orange	27	2-7
Stanton*	KY	606	40380	Powell	3	2-29
Stanton*	MI	517	48888	Montcalm	2	2-38&39
Stanton*	ND	701	58571	Mercer	1	2-57
Stanton*	NE	402	68779	Stanton	1	2-47
Stanton*	TX	915	79782	Martin	1	2-74&75
Staples	MN	218	56479	Todd (+1)	3	2-40
Stapleton*	NE	308	69163	Logan	1	2-47
Star City*	AR	501	71667	Lincoln	1	2-6
Starke*	FL	904	32091	Bradford	5	2-14
Starkville*	MS	601	39759	Oktibbeha	16	2-42&43
State College	PA	814	16801-05	Centre	35	2-66
Staten Island	NY	718	10301-99	Richmond	NAV	2-56
Statenville*	GA	912	31648	Echols	1	2-16&17
Statesboro*	GA	912	30458	Bulloch	15	2-16&17
Statesville*	NC	704	28677	Iredell	18	2-58
Staunton	IL	618	62088	Macoupin	5	2-21
Staunton*	VA	703	24401	Augusta (IC)	21	2-78&79
Stayton	OR	503	97383	Marion	4	2-63
Ste Genevieve*	MO	314	63670	Ste Genevieve	4	2-44&45
Steamboat Springs*	CO	303	80477-88	Routt	5	2-10&11
Steele*	ND	701	58482	Kidder	1	2-57
Steelton	PA	717	17113	Dauphin	6	2-67
Steelville*	MO	314	65565	Crawford	1	2-44&45
Steger	IL	708	60475	Will (+1)	9	2-20

Bold = Over 15,000......ALL CAPS = STATE CAPITAL......* = County Seat......# = Changes to 510 in 9/91..... ## = Changes to 410 in 11/91......(+) = City located in additional counties......NAV= Population not available......C.H. = Court House......(IC) = Independent City

CITY	STATE	AREA CODE	ZIP CODE	COUNTY	POPULATION (in thousands)	MAP PAGE
Steilacoom	WA	206	98388	Pierce	5	2-80
Stephenville*	TX	817	76401	Erath	12	2-74
Sterling*	CO	303	80751	Logan	12	2-10&11
Sterling	IL	815	61081	Whiteside	16	2-20
Sterling	MA	508	01564	Worcester	5	2-36&37
Sterling City*	TX	915	76951	Sterling	1	2-74&75
Sterling Heights	MI	313	48310	Macomb	112	2-39
Steubenville*	OH	614	43952	Jefferson	24	2-61
Stevens Point*	WI	715	54481	Portage	21	2-84&85
Stevenson	AL	205	35772	Jackson	3	2-2&3
Stevenson*	WA	509	98648	Skamania	1	2-81
Stewartville	MN	507	55976	Olmsted	4	2-41
Stickney	IL	708	60402	Cook	6	2-19
Stickney Lake	WA	206	98036	Snohomish	2	2-80
Stigler*	OK	918	74462	Haskell	2	2-65
Stillwater*	MN	612	55082-83	Washington	12	2-41
Stillwater*	OK	405	74074-76	Payne	38	2-64&65
Stilwell*	OK	918	74960	Adair	1	2-65
Stinnett*	TX	806	79083	Hutchinson	1	2-74
Stockton*	CA	209	95201-13	San Joaquin	183	2-8&9
Stockton*	KS	913	67669	Rooks	1	2-26&27
Stockton*	MO	417	65785	Cedar	1	2-44
Stockville*	NE	308	69042	Frontier	1	2-47
Stone Mountain	GA	404	30086-88	De Kalb	5	2-16&17
Stone Park	IL	708	60165	Cook	5	2-19
Stoneham	MA	617	02180	Middlesex	23	2-36&37
Stony Brook	NY	516	11790	Suffolk	6	2-56
Storm Lake*	IA	712	50588	Buena Vista	8	2-24
Story City	IA	515	50248	Story	3	2-24&25
Stoughton	MA	617	02072	Norfolk	27	2-36&37
Stoughton	WI	608	53589	Dane	8	2-85
Stow	MA	508	01775	Middlesex	6	2-36&37
Stow	OH	216	44224	Summit	26	2-62
Stowe	VT	802	05672	Lamoille	3	2-77
Stowe Twp.	PA	412	15136	Allegheny	10	2-68
Strafford	PA	215	19087	Chester	5	2-67
Stratford	CT	203	06497	Fairfield	51	2-12&13
Stratford	NJ	609	08084	Camden	8	2-51
Stratford*	TX	806	79084	Sherman	1	2-74
Stratford Landing	VA	703	22308	Fairfax	3	2-78&79
Stratham	NH	603	03885	Rockingham	3	2-49
Streamwood	IL	708	60103	Cook	27	2-19
Streator	IL	815	61364	La Salle (+1)	15	2-20
Streetsboro	OH	216	44240	Portage	9	2-60
Strongsville	OH	216	44136	Cuyahoga	31	2-62
Stroud	OK	918	74079	Creek (+1)	3	2-65
Stroudsburg*	PA	717	18360	Monroe	5	2-67
Struthers	OH	216	44471	Mahoning	14	2-60

Bold = Over 15,000......ALL CAPS = STATE CAPITAL......* = County Seat......# = Changes to 510 in 9/91.....## = Changes to 410 in 11/91.....(+) = City located in additional counties......NAV = Population not available......C.H.= Court House......(IC)=Independent City

CITY	STATE	AREA CODE	ZIP CODE	COUNTY	POPULATION (in thousands)	MAP PAGE
Stuart*	FL	407	34994-97	Martin	11	2-14&15
Stuart*	VA	703	24171	Patrick	1	2-78&79
Sturbridge	MA	508	01566	Worcester	6	2-36&37
Sturgeon Bay*	WI	414	54235	Door	9	2-85
Sturgis	MI	616	49091	St. Joseph	10	2-38&39
Sturgis*	SD	605	57785	Meade	5	2-71
Sturtevant	WI	414	53177	Racine	4	2-85
Stuttgart*	AR	501	72160	Arkansas	11	2-6
Sublette*	KS	316	67877	Haskell	1	2-26&27
Sudbury	MA	508	01776	Middlesex	14	2-36&37
Suffern	NY	914	10901	Rockland	11	2-56
Suffield	CT	203	06078	Hartford	9	2-12&13
Suffolk	VA	804	23432-38	(IC)	52	2-78&79
Sugar Land	TX	713	77478-79	Fort Bend	12	2-74&75
Sugar Loaf	VA	703	24018	Roanoke	6	2-78&79
Sugarcreek	PA	814	16323	Venango	6	2-66
Suisun City	CA	707	94585	Solano	16	2-8
Suitland	MD	301	20746	Prince Georges	33	2-35
Sullivan*	IL	217	61951	Moultrie	5	2-20&21
Sullivan*	IN	812	47882	Sullivan	5	2-23
Sullivan	MO	314	63080	Crawford (+1)	5	2-44&45
Sulphur	LA	318	70663-64	Calcasieu	20	2-30
Sulphur*	OK	405	73086	Murray	5	2-64&65
Sulphur Springs*	TX	903	75482	Hopkins	14	2-74
Sumiton	AL	205	35148	Walker (+1)	3	2-2&3
Summersville*	WV	304	26651	Nicholas	3	2-82
Summerville*	GA	404	30747	Chattooga	5	2-16&17
Summerville	SC	803	29483-85	Dorchester (+1)	12	2-70
Summit	IL	708	60501	Cook	10	2-19
Summit	NJ	908	07901-02	Union	21	2-52
Summit Hill	PA	717	18250	Carbon	3	2-67
Sumner*	MS	601	38957	Tallahatchie	1	2-42&43
Sumter*	SC	803	29150-54	Sumter	28	2-70
Sumner	WA	206	98390	Pierce	5	2-80
Sun City	AZ	602	85372-75	Maricopa	52	2-5
Sun Prairie	WI	608	53590	Dane	13	2-85
Sunbury*	PA	717	17801	Northumberland	11	2-67
Sundance*	WY	307	82729	Crook	1	2-83
Sunderland	MA	413	01375	Franklin	3	2-36
Sunland Park	NM	505	88063	Dona Ana	4	2-53
Sunnydale	WA	206	98155	King	3	2-80
Sunnymead	CA	714	92388	Riverside	12	2-9
Sunnyside	WA	509	98944	Yakima	9	2-81
Sunnyvale	CA	408	94086-89	Santa Clara	112	2-7
Sunset	UT	801	84015	Davis	6	2-76
Sunset Hills	MO	314	63127	St. Louis	4	2-44&45
Superior	AZ	602	85273	Pinal	5	2-5
Superior	NE	402	68978	Nuckolls	3	2-47

Bold = Over 15,000......ALL CAPS = STATE CAPITAL......* = County Seat......# = Changes to 510 in 9/91..... ## = Changes to 410 in 11/91......(+) = City located in addional counties......NAV= Population not available......C.H.= Court House......(IC) = Independent City

CITY	STATE	AREA CODE	ZIP CODE	COUNTY	POPULATION (in thousands)	MAP PAGE
Superior*	MT	406	59872	Mineral	1	2-46
Superior*	WI	715	54880	Douglas	26	2-84&85
Surfside	FL	305	33154	Dade	4	2-5
Surfside Beach	SC	803	29577	Horry	3	2-70
Surprise	AZ	602	85345	Maricopa	4	2-5
Surry*	VA	804	23883	Surry	1	2-78&79
Susanville*	CA	916	96130	Lassen	6	2-8
Sussex*	VA	804	23884	Sussex	1	2-78&79
Sussex	WI	414	53089	Waukesha	4	2-85
Sutherlin	OR	503	97479	Douglas	5	2-63
Sutton	MA	508	01527	Worcester	5	2-36&37
Sutton*	WV	304	26601	Braxton	1	2-82
Swainsboro*	GA	912	30401	Emanuel	8	2-16&17
Swampscott	MA	617	01907	Essex	14	2-36&37
Swannanoa	NC	704	28778	Buncombe	6	2-58
Swanquarter*	NC	919	27885	Hyde	1	2-58&59
Swansea	IL	618	62221	St. Clair	6	2-21
Swansea	MA	508	02777	Bristol	16	2-36&37
Swanton	OH	419	43558	Fulton (+1)	4	2-60
Swanton	VT	802	05488	Franklin	3	2-77
Swanzey	NH	603	03431	Cheshire	5	2-49
Swarthmore	PA	215	19081	Delaware	6	2-68
Swartz Creek	MI	313	48473	Genesee	5	2-39
Swatara	PA	717	17111	Dauphin	19	2-67
Sweeny	TX	409	77480	Brazoria	4	2-75
Sweet Home	OR	503	97386	Linn	7	2-63
Sweetwater	TN	615	37874	Monroe	5	2-72&73
Sweetwater*	TX	915	79556	Nolan	12	2-74&75
Sweetwater Crk	FL	813	33614	Hillsborough	18	2-14
Swissvale	PA	412	15218	Allegheny	11	2-68
Swoyerville	PA	717	18704	Luzerne	6	2-67
Sycamore*	IL	815	60178	De Kalb	9	2-20
Sylacauga	AL	205	35150	Talladega	13	2-2&3
Sylva*	NC	704	28779	Jackson	1	2-58
Sylvania*	GA	912	30467	Screven	3	2-16&17
Sylvania	OH	419	43560	Lucas	16	2-60
Sylvester*	GA	912	31791	Worth	6	2-16&17
Syosset	NY	516	11791	Nassau	9	2-56
Syracuse	IN	219	46567	Kosciusko	3	2-22
Syracuse*	KS	316	67878	Hamilton	1	2-26&27
Syracuse*	NY	315	13201-99	Onondaga	165	2-54&55
Syracuse	UT	801	84041	Davis	4	2-76
Tabor City	NC	919	28463	Columbus	3	2-58&59
Tacoma*	WA	206	98397-499	Pierce	164	2-80
Taft	CA	805	93268	Kern	6	2-9
Taft	TX	512	78390	San Patricio	4	2-75
Tahlequah*	OK	918	74464-65	Cherokee	12	2-65
Tahoka*	TX	806	79373	Lynn	3	2-74

Bold = Over 15,000......ALL CAPS = STATE CAPITAL......* = County Seat......# = Changes to 510 in 9/91.....## = Changes to 410 in 11/91.....(+) = City located in additional counties......NAV = Population not available......C.H. = Court House......(IC)=Independent City

CITY	STATE	AREA CODE	ZIP CODE	COUNTY	POPULATION (in thousands)	MAP PAGE
Takoma Pk	MD	301	20912	Montgomery (+1)	17	2-34
Talbotton*	GA	404	31827	Talbot	1	2-16&17
Talent	OR	503	97540	Jackson	3	2-63
Talladega*	AL	205	35160	Talladega	20	2-2&3
TALLAHASSEE*	FL	904	32301-17	Leon	121	2-14
Tallapoosa	GA	404	30176	Haralson	3	2-16&17
Tallassee	AL	205	36078	Elmore (+1)	5	2-2&3
Tallmadge	OH	216	44278	Summit	14	2-62
Tallulah*	LA	318	71282-84	Madison	11	2-30
Taloga*	OK	405	73667	Dewey	1	2-64&65
Tama	IA	515	52339	Tama	3	2-24&25
Tamaqua	PA	717	18252	Schuykill	9	2-67
Tamarac	FL	305	33321	Broward	34	2-15
Tampa*	FL	813	33601-99	Hillsborough	290	2-14&15
Taneytown	MD	301##	21787	Carroll	3	2-34&35
Tanglewilde	WA	206	98501	Thurston	4	2-80
Taos*	NM	505	87571	Taos	3	2-53
Tappahannock*	VA	804	22560	Essex	1	2-78&79
Tappan	NY	914	10983	Rockland	7	2-56
Tarboro*	NC	919	27886	Edgecombe	10	2-58&59
Tarentum	PA	412	15084	Allegheny	6	2-68
Tarpon Springs	FL	813	34688-91	Pinellas	13	2-14&15
Tarrant	AL	205	35217	Jefferson	8	2-2&3
Tarrytown	NY	914	10591	Westchester	10	2-56
Taunton*	MA	508	02780	Bristol	47	2-36&37
Tavares*	FL	904	32778	Lake	4	2-14
Tawas City*	MI	517	48763	Iosco	3	2-38&39
Taylor	MI	313	48180	Wayne	73	2-39
Taylor*	NE	308	68879	Loup	1	2-47
Taylor	PA	717	18517	Lackawanna	7	2-67
Taylor	TX	512	76574	Williamson	11	2-75
Taylor Lake Vlg.	TX	713	77586	Harris	4	2-74&75
Taylor Mill	KY	606	41015	Kenton	5	2-29
Taylorsville*	KY	502	40071	Spencer	1	2-28&29
Taylorsville*	NC	704	28681	Alexander	1	2-58
Taylorville*	IL	217	62568	Christian	11	2-20&21
Tazewell*	TN	615	37879	Claiborne	1	2-72&73
Tazewell*	VA	703	24651	Tazewell	4	2-78&79
Teague	TX	817	75860	Freestone	3	2-74
Teaneck	NJ	201	07666	Bergen	39	2-52
Tecumseh	MI	517	49286	Lenawee	7	2-38&39
Tecumseh	OK	405	74873	Pottawatomie	5	2-64&65
Tecumseh*	NE	402	68450	Johnson	1	2-47
Tehachapi	CA	805	93561	Kern	4	2-9
Tekamah*	NE	402	68061	Burt	1	2-47
Telford	PA	215	18969	Bucks (+1)	3	2-68
Tell City	IN	812	47586	Perry	9	2-23
Telluride*	CO	303	81435	San Miguel	1	2-10&11

Bold = Over 15,000......ALL CAPS = STATE CAPITAL......* = County Seat......# = Changes to 510 in 9/91..... ## = Changes to 410 in 11/91......(+) = City located in additional counties......NAV= Population not available......C.H.= Court House......(IC) = Independent City

CITY	STATE	AREA CODE	ZIP CODE	COUNTY	POPULATION (in thousands)	MAP PAGE
Tempe	AZ	602	85281-89	Maricopa	135	2-5
Temperance	MI	313	48182	Monroe	4	2-39
Temple	TX	817	76501-05	Bell	47	2-74
Temple City	CA	818	91780	Los Angeles	31	2-7
Temple Hills Pk	MD	301	20748	Prince Georges	3	2-35
Temple Terrace	FL	813	33617	Hillsborough	11	2-14&15
Templeton	MA	508	01468	Worcester	6	2-36&37
Tenafly	NJ	201	07670	Bergen	13	2-52
Tequesta	FL	407	33469	Palm Beach	26	2-14&15
Terre Haute*	IN	812	47801-08	Vigo	58	2-23
Terrell	TX	214	75160	Kaufman	13	2-74
Terrell Hills	TX	512	77024	Bexar	5	2-75
Terry*	MT	406	59349	Prairie	1	2-46
Terryville	CT	203	06786	Litchfield	5	2-12&13
Terryville	NY	516	11776	Suffolk	7	2-56
Tewksbury	MA	508	01876	Middlesex	11	2-36&37
Texarkana*	AR	501	75502-04	Miller	22	2-6
Texarkana	TX	903	75501-05	Bowie	34	2-74
Texas City	TX	409	77590-92	Galveston	44	2-75
Thatcher	AZ	602	85552	Graham	3	2-5
The Colony	TX	214	75056	Denton	12	2-74
The Dalles*	OR	503	97058	Wasco	10	2-63
Thedford*	NE	308	69166	Thomas	1	2-47
Thermopolis*	WY	307	82443	Hot Springs	4	2-83
Thibodaux*	LA	504	70301-02	Lafourche	16	2-30&31
Thief River Falls*	MN	218	56701	Pennington	7	2-40
Thiells	NY	516	10984	Nassau	3	2-56
Thiensville	WI	414	53092	Ozaukee	3	2-85
Thomaston	CT	203	06787	Litchfield	5	2-12&13
Thomaston*	GA	404	30286	Upson	10	2-16&17
Thomaston	ME	207	04861	Knox	2	2-32&33
Thomaston	NY	516	11021	Nassau	3	2-56
Thomasville	AL	205	36784	Clarke	4	2-2&3
Thomasville*	GA	912	31792	Thomas	18	2-16&17
Thomasville	NC	919	27360-61	Davidson	16	2-58&59
Thompson	CT	203	06277	Windham	8	2-12&13
Thomson*	GA	404	30824	McDuffie	7	2-16&17
Thompson Falls*	MT	406	59873	Sanders	1	2-46
Thompson Place	WA	206	98501	Thurston	3	2-80
Thornton	CO	303	80229	Adams	49	2-10&11
Thornton	IL	708	60476	Cook	3	2-19
Thousand Oaks	CA	805	91359-67	Ventura	93	2-9
Three Rivers	MI	616	49093	St. Joseph	7	2-39
Throckmorton*	TX	817	76083	Throckmorton	1	2-74
Throop	PA	717	18512	Lackawanna	5	2-67
Thunderbolt	GA	912	31404	Chatham	2	2-16&17
Thurmount	MD	301	21788	Frederick	3	2-34&35
Tiburon	CA	415	94920	Marin	7	2-7

Bold = Over 15,000......ALL CAPS = STATE CAPITAL......* = County Seat......# = Changes to 510 in 9/91.....## = Changes to 410 in 11/91.....(+) = City located in additional counties......NAV = Population not available......C.H.= Court House......(IC)=Independent City

CITY	STATE	AREA CODE	ZIP CODE	COUNTY	POPULATION (in thousands)	MAP PAGE
Tice	FL	813	33905	Lee	6	2-14&15
Ticonderoga	NY	518	12883	Essex	3	2-55
Tierra Amarilla*	NM	505	87575	Rio Arriba	1	2-53
Tiffin*	OH	419	44883	Seneca	19	2-60
Tifton*	GA	912	31792-94	Tift	14	2-16&17
Tigard	OR	503	97223	Washington	18	2-63
Tilden*	TX	512	78072	McMullen	1	2-75
Tillamook*	OR	503	97141	Tillamook	3	2-63
Tillmans Corner	AL	205	36619	Mobile	5	2-2&3
Tilton	NH	603	03276	Belknap	3	2-49
Timber Lake*	SD	605	57656	Dewey	1	2-71
Timberlake	VA	804	24502	Campbell	9	2-78&79
Timberlane	WA	206	98031	King	3	2-80
Tinley Park	IL	708	60477-78	Cook (+1)	29	2-19
Tinton Falls	NJ	908	07724	Monmouth	8	2-50
Tionesta*	PA	814	16353	Forest	1	2-66
Tipp City	OH	513	45371	Miami	6	2-61
Tipton*	IA	319	52772	Cedar	3	2-25
Tipton*	IN	317	46072	Tipton	5	2-22&23
Tiptonville*	TN	901	38079	Lake	1	2-72
Tisbury	MA	508	02568	Dukes	3	2-36&37
Tishomingo*	OK	405	73460	Johnston	3	2-64&65
Titusville*	FL	407	32780-83	Brevard	42	2-14&15
Titusville	PA	814	16354	Crawford	7	2-66
Tiverton	RI	401	02878	Newport	8	2-69
Toccoa*	GA	404	30577	Stephens	9	2-16&17
Toledo*	IA	515	52341-42	Tama	3	2-24&25
Toledo*	IL	217	62468	Cumberland	1	2-20&21
Toledo*	OH	419	43601-99	Lucas	343	2-60
Toledo	OR	503	97391	Lincoln	3	2-63
Tolland	CT	203	06084	Tolland	10	2-12&13
Tolleson	AZ	602	85353	Maricopa	5	2-5
Tomah	WI	608	54660	Monroe	7	2-85
Tomahawk	WI	715	54487	Lincoln	4	2-84&85
Tomball	TX	713	77375	Harris	4	2-74&75
Tombstone	AZ	602	85638	Cochise	2	2-5
Tompkinsville*	KY	502	42167	Monroe	4	2-28&29
Toms River*	NJ	908	08753-57	Ocean	7	2-50
Tonawanda	NY	716	14150&223	Erie	19	2-54
Tonkawa	OK	405	74653	Kay	4	2-64&65
Tonopah*	NV	702	89049	Nye	1	2-48
Tooele*	UT	801	84074	Tooele	4	2-76
TOPEKA*	KS	913	66601-99	Shawnee	119	2-26&27
Toppenish	WA	509	98948	Yakima	6	2-81
Topsfield	MA	508	01983	Essex	6	2-36&37
Topsham	ME	207	04086	Sagadahoc	6	2-32&33
Toronto	OH	614	43964	Jefferson	7	2-61
Torrance	CA	213	90501-99	Los Angeles	135	2-7

Bold = Over 15,000......**ALL CAPS** = STATE CAPITAL......* = County Seat......# = Changes to 510 in 9/91..... ## = Changes to 410 in 11/91......(+) = City located in addional counties......NAV= Population not available......C.H.= Court House......(IC) = Independent City

CITY	STATE	AREA CODE	ZIP CODE	COUNTY	POPULATION (in thousands)	MAP PAGE
Torrington	CT	203	06790	Litchfield	32	2-12&13
Torrington*	WY	307	82240	Goshen	5	2-83
Totowa	NJ	201	07512	Passaic	11	2-52
Toulon*	IL	309	61483	Stark	1	2-20
Towamencin	PA	215	19443	Montgomery	12	2-68
Towanda*	PA	717	18848	Bradford	3	2-67
Town & Country	MO	314	63131	St. Louis	3	2-44&45
Towner*	ND	701	58788	McHenry	1	2-57
Townsend	MA	508	01469	Middlesex	7	2-36&37
Townsend*	MT	406	59644	Broadwater	1	2-46
Towson*	MD	301##	21204	Baltimore	1	2-34&35
Tracy	CA	209	95376 &85	San Joaquin	26	2-8&9
Trafford	PA	412	15085	Allegheny (+1)	4	2-66
Trail Creek	IN	219	46360	La Porte	3	2-22
Travelers Rest	SC	803	29690	Greenville	3	2-70
Traverse City*	MI	616	49684	Grand Traverse	15	2-38&39
Treasure Island	FL	813	33706	Pinellas	6	2-14&15
Tredyffrin	PA	215	19312	Chester	23	2-67
Tremonton	UT	801	84337	Box Elder	3	2-76
Trenton*	FL	904	32693	Gilchrist	1	2-14
Trenton*	GA	404	30752	Dade	1	2-16&17
Trenton	IL	618	62293	Clinton	2	2-21
Trenton	MI	313	48183	Wayne	22	2-39
Trenton*	MO	816	64683	Grundy	6	2-44
Trenton*	NC	919	28585	Jones	1	2-58&59
Trenton*	NE	308	69044	Hitchcock	1	2-47
TRENTON*	NJ	609	08601-99	Mercer	94	2-50
Trenton*	TN	901	38382	Gibson	1	2-72
Tribune*	KS	316	67879	Greeley	1	2-26&27
Trinidad*	CO	303	81082	Las Animas	10	2-10&11
Trotwood	OH	513	45426	Montgomery	8	2-61
Troutdale	OR	503	97060	Multnomah	6	2-63
Troy*	AL	205	36081	Pike	13	2-2&3
Troy*	KS	913	66087	Doniphan	1	2-26&27
Troy	IL	618	62294	Madison	5	2-21
Troy	MI	313	48098-99	Oakland	67	2-39
Troy*	MO	314	63379	Lincoln	1	2-44&45
Troy*	NC	919	27371	Montgomery	3	2-58&59
Troy*	NY	518	12180-83	Rensselaer	55	2-55
Troy*	OH	513	45373	Miami	19	2-61
Trumann	AR	501	72472	Poinsett	6	2-6
Trumbull	CT	203	06611-12	Fairfield	33	2-12&13
Trussville	AL	205	35173	Jefferson	4	2-2&3
Truth or Consequences*	NM	505	87901	Sierra	5	2-53
Tryon*	NE	308	69167	McPherson	1	2-47
Tualatin	OR	503	97062	Washington (+1)	12	2-63
Tuba City	AZ	602	86045	Coconino	4	2-5
Tuckahoe	NY	914	10707	Westchester	6	2-56

Bold = Over 15,000......ALL CAPS = STATE CAPITAL......* = County Seat......# = Changes to 510 in 9/91.....## = Changes to 410 in 11/91.....(+) = City located in additional counties......NAV = Population not available......C.H.= Court House......(IC)=Independent City

CITY	STATE	AREA CODE	ZIP CODE	COUNTY	POPULATION (in thousands)	MAP PAGE
Tucson*	AZ	602	85701-99	Pima	378	2-5
Tucumcari*	NM	505	88401	Quay	7	2-53
Tukwila	WA	206	98188	King	5	2-80
Tulare	CA	209	93274-75	Tulare	26	2-8&9
Tularosa	NM	505	88352	Otero	3	2-53
Tulia*	TX	806	79088	Swisher	4	2-74
Tullahoma	TN	615	37388	Coffee (+1)	16	2-72&73
Tulsa*	OK	918	74101-99	Tulsa	373	2-65
Tumwater	WA	206	98502	Thurston	7	2-80
Tunica*	MS	601	38676	Tunica	1	2-42&43
Tunkhannock*	PA	717	18657	Wyoming	1	2-67
Tupelo*	MS	601	38801-03	Lee	25	2-42&43
Tupper Lake	NY	518	12986	Franklin	5	2-55
Turlock	CA	209	95380-81	Stanislaus	33	2-8&9
Turners Falls	MA	413	01376	Franklin	5	2-36
Turtle Creek	PA	412	15145	Allegheny	7	2-68
Tuscaloosa*	AL	205	35401-87	Tuscaloosa	155	2-2&3
Tuscola*	IL	217	61953	Douglas	4	2-20&21
Tuscumbia*	AL	205	35674	Colbert	9	2-2&3
Tuscumbia*	MO	314	65082	Miller	1	2-44&45
Tuskegee*	AL	205	36083	Macon	13	2-2&3
Tustin	CA	714	92680-81	Orange	41	2-7
Tustin Foothills	CA	714	92680	Orange	30	2-7
Tuttle	OK	405	73089	Grady	3	2-64&65
Twentynine Palms	CA	619	92277-78	San Bernardino	8	9
Twin Falls*	ID	208	83301-03	Twin Falls	28	2-18
Twin Lakes	WI	414	53181	Kenosha	3	2-85
Twinsburg	OH	216	44087	Summit	7	2-62
Two Harbors*	MN	218	55616	Lake	4	2-40
Two Rivers	WI	414	54241	Manitowoc	13	2-85
Tyler*	TX	903	75701-13	Smith	73	2-74
Tylertown*	MS	601	39667	Walthall	1	2-42&43
Tyndall*	SD	605	57066	Bon Homme	1	2-71
Tyngsborough	MA	508	01879	Middlesex	6	2-36&37
Tyrone	PA	814	16686	Blair	6	2-66
Tysons Corner	VA	703	22101 &03	Fairfax	8	2-78&79
Uhrichsville	OH	614	44683	Tuscarawas	6	2-61
Ukiah*	CA	707	95482	Mendocino	13	2-8
Ulysses*	KS	316	67880	Grant	5	2-26&27
Umatilla	OR	503	97882	Umatilla	3	2-63
Union*	MO	314	63084	Franklin	5	2-44&45
Union	NJ	908	07083	Union	50	2-52
Union	NY	607	13760	Broome	61	2-54&55
Union	OH	513	45322	Montgomery	5	2-61
Union*	SC	803	29379	Union	10	2-70
Union	UT	801	84047	Salt Lake	3	2-76
Union*	WV	304	24983	Monroe	1	2-82
Union Beach	NJ	908	07735	Monmouth	6	2-50

Bold = Over 15,000......ALL CAPS = STATE CAPITAL......* = County Seat......# = Changes to 510 in 9/91..... ## = Changes to 410 in 11/91......(+)
= City located in addional counties......NAV= Population not available......C.H.= Court House......(IC) = Independent City

CITY	STATE	AREA CODE	ZIP CODE	COUNTY	POPULATION (in thousands)	MAP PAGE
Union City	CA	415#	94587	Alameda	50	2-7
Union City	GA	404	30291	Fulton	6	2-16&17
Union City	IN	317	47390	Randolph	4	2-22&23
Union City	NJ	201	07087	Hudson	57	2-52
Union City	PA	814	16438	Erie	4	2-66
Union City*	TN	901	38261	Obion	10	2-72
Union Gap	WA	509	98903	Yakima	3	2-81
Union Grove	WI	414	53182	Racine	4	2-85
Union Lake	MI	313	48085	Oakland	12	2-39
Union Springs*	AL	205	36089	Bullock	4	2-2&3
Uniontown*	PA	412	15401	Fayette	13	2-66
Unionville*	MO	816	63565	Putnam	1	2-44
Universal City	TX	512	78148	Bexar	11	2-75
University City	MO	314	63130	St. Louis	42	2-44&45
University Gardens	NY	516	11020	Nassau	5	2-56
University Heights	OH	216	44118	Cuyahoga	15	2-62
University Park	IL	708	60466	Cook (+1)	6	2-20
University Park	MD	301	20784	Prince Georges	3	2-35
University Park	TX	214	75205	Dallas	24	2-74
Upland	CA	714	91785-86	San Bernardino	57	2-9
Upland	IN	317	46989	Grant	3	2-22&23
Upland	PA	215	19015	Delaware	3	2-68
Upper Allen	PA	717	17055	Cumberland	10	2-67
Upper Arlington	OH	614	43221	Franklin	37	2-61
Upper Darby	PA	215	19082-83	Delaware	85	2-68
Upper Dublin Twp.	PA	215	19002&34	Montgomery	23	2-68
Upper Gwynedd	PA	215	19454	Montgomery	10	2-68
Upper Marlboro*	MD	301	20772-75	Prince Georges	1	2-35
Upper Merion Twp.	PA	215	19406	Montgomery	26	2-68
Upper Moreland Twp.	PA	215	19090	Montgomery	25	2-68
Upper Providence	PA	215	19063	Montgomery	10	2-68
Upper Saddle River	NJ	201	07458	Bergen	8	2-52
Upper St. Clair	PA	412	15241	Allegheny	19	2-68
Upper Sandusky*	OH	419	43351	Wyandot	6	2-60
Upper Saucon	PA	215	18034	Lehigh	10	2-67
Upper Southampton T.	PA	215	19006	Bucks	16	2-68
Upper Yoder	PA	814#	15905	Cambria	6	2-66
Upton	MA	508	01568	Worcester	4	2-36&37
Urbana*	IL	217	61801	Champaign	34	2-20&21
Urbana*	OH	513	43078	Champaign	11	2-61
Urbandale	IA	515	50322	Polk	19	2-24&25
Utica	MI	313	48087-311	Genesee	5	2-39
Utica*	NY	315	13501-99	Oneida	73	2-54&55
Uvalde*	TX	512	78801-02	Uvalde	16	2-75
Uwchlan	PA	215	19480	Chester	8	2-67
Uxbridge	MA	508	01569	Worcester	4	2-36&37
Vacaville	CA	707	95687-88	Solono	54	2-8
Vadnais Heights	MN	612	55127	Ramsey	5	2-41

Bold = Over 15,000......ALL CAPS = STATE CAPITAL......* = County Seat......# = Changes to 510 in 9/91.....## = Changes to 410 in 11/91......(+) = City located in additional counties......NAV = Population not available......C.H.= Court House......(IC)=Independent City

CITY	STATE	AREA CODE	ZIP CODE	COUNTY	POPULATION (in thousands)	MAP PAGE
Vaiden*	MS	601	39176	Carroll	1	2-42&43
Vail	CO	303	81657	Eagle	4	2-10&11
Valdese	NC	704	28690	Burke	3	2-58
Valdez	AK	907	99686	Valdez-Cordova	3	2-4
Valdosta*	GA	912	31601-899	Lowndes	40	2-16&17
Vale*	OR	503	97918	Malheur	1	2-63
Valentine*	NE	402	69201	Cherry	3	2-47
Valhalla	NY	914	10595	Westchester	6	2-56
Valinda	CA	818	91744	Los Angeles	19	2-7
Vallejo	CA	707	94589-92	Solano	93	2-8
Valley	AL	205	36854	Chambers	9	2-2&3
Valley Center	KS	316	67147	Sedgwick	3	2-26&27
Valley City*	ND	701	58072	Barnes	7	2-57
Valley Falls	KS	913	66088	Jefferson	1	2-26&27
Valley Park	MO	314	63088	St. Louis	3	2-44&45
Valley Ridge	WA	206	98118	King	7	2-80
Valley Station	KY	502	40272	Jefferson	24	2-28
Valley Stream	NY	516	11580-82	Nassau	35	2-56
Valparaiso	FL	904	32580	Okaloosa	6	2-14
Valparaiso*	IN	219	46383-84	Porter	23	2-22
Van Buren*	AR	501	72956	Crawford	12	2-6
Van Buren	ME	207	04785	Aroostook	4	2-32&33
Van Buren*	MO	314	63965	Carter	1	2-44&45
Van Horn*	TX	915	79855	Culberson	2	2-74&75
Van Wert*	OH	419	45891	Van Wert	10	2-60
Vanceburg*	KY	606	41179	Lewis	2	2-29
Vancouver*	WA	206	98660-86	Clark	44	2-80
Vandalia*	IL	618	62471	Fayette	6	2-21
Vandalia	MO	314	63382	Audrain (+1)	2	2-44&45
Vandalia	OH	513	45377	Montgomery	13	2-61
Vandergrift	PA	412	15690	Westmooreland	6	2-68
Vassalborough	ME	207	04989	Kennebec	3	2-32&33
Vassar	MI	517	48768	Tuscola	3	2-38&39
Vega*	TX	806	79092	Oldham	1	2-74
Venice	FL	813	34284-93	Sarasota	14	2-14&15
Venice	IL	618	62090	Madison	3	2-21
Ventnor City	NJ	609	08406	Atlantic	12	2-51
Ventura*	CA	805	93001-07	Ventura	85	2-9
Vermilion	OH	216	44089	Lorain	11	2-62
Vermillion*	SD	605	57069	Clay	10	2-71
Vernal*	UT	801	84078-79	Uintah	7	2-76
Vernon*	AL	205	35592	Lamar	3	2-2&3
Vernon	CT	203	06066	Tolland	30	2-12&13
Vernon*	IN	812	47282	Jennings	1	2-23
Vernon*	TX	817	76384	Wilbarger	13	2-74
Vernon Hills	IL	708	60061	Lake	12	2-20
Vero Beach*	FL	407	32960-67	Indian River	18	2-14&15
Verona	NJ	201	07044	Essex	14	2-52

Bold = Over 15,000......ALL CAPS = STATE CAPITAL......* = County Seat......# = Changes to 510 in 9/91..... ## = Changes to 410 in 11/91......(+) = City located in addional counties......NAV= Population not available......C.H.= Court House......(IC) = Independent City

CITY	STATE	AREA CODE	ZIP CODE	COUNTY	POPULATION (in thousands)	MAP PAGE
Verona	PA	412	15147	Allegheny	3	2-68
Verona	WI	608	53592	Dane	3	2-85
Versailles*	IN	812	47042	Ripley	2	2-23
Versailles*	KY	606	40383	Woodford	6	2-29
Versailles*	MO	314	65084	Morgan	1	2-44&45
Vestal	NY	607	13850-51	Broome	6	2-54&55
Vestavia Hills	AL	205	35216	Jefferson	17	2-2&3
Vevay*	IN	812	47043	Switzerland	2	2-23
Vicksburg*	MS	601	39180-82	Warren	26	2-42&43
Victoria*	TX	512	77901-05	Victoria	56	2-75
Victorville	CA	619	92392-94	San Bernardino	22	2-9
Vidalia	GA	912	30474	Toombs (+1)	10	2-16&17
Vidalia*	LA	318	71373	Concordia	6	2-30
Vidor	TX	409	77662	Orange	13	2-75
Vienna*	GA	912	31092	Dooley	3	2-16&17
Vienna*	IL	618	62995	Johnson	1	2-21
Vienna*	MO	314	65582	Maries	1	2-44&45
Vienna	VA	703	22180-83	Fairfax	16	2-78&79
Vienna	WV	304	26105	Wood	12	2-82
Villa Grove	IL	217	61956	Douglas	2	2-20&21
Villa Hills	KY	606	41016	Kenton	5	2-29
Villa Park	CA	714	92667	Orange	6	2-7
Villa Park	IL	708	60181	Du Page	24	2-19
Villa Rica	GA	404	30180	Carroll (+1)	3	2-17
Village (The)	OK	405	73120	Oklahoma	11	2-64&65
Ville Platte*	LA	318	70586	Evangeline	9	2-30
Vincennes*	IN	812	47591	Knox	21	2-23
Vine Grove	KY	502	40175	Hardin	4	2-28&29
Vineland	NJ	609	08360	Cumberland	55	2-51
Vinita*	OK	918	74301	Craig	6	2-65
Vinton*	IA	319	52349	Benton	5	2-25
Vinton	LA	318	70668	Calcasieu	4	2-30
Vinton	VA	703	24179	Roanoke	8	2-78&79
Violet	LA	504	70092	St. Bernard	6	2-30&31
Virden	IL	217	62690	Macoupin (+1)	2	2-20&21
Virginia*	IL	217	62691	Cass	2	2-20&21
Virginia	MN	218	55792	St. Louis	10	2-40
Virginia Beach	VA	804	23450-64	(I)	329	2-78&79
Virginia City*	MT	406	59755	Madison	1	2-46
Virginia City*	NV	702	89440	Storey	1	2-48
Viroqua*	WI	608	54665	Vernon	3	2-85
Visalia*	CA	209	93277-79	Tulare	61	2-8&9
Vista	CA	619	92083-84	San Diego	48	2-9
Vivian	LA	318	71082	Caddo	4	2-30
Voorheesville	NY	518	12186	Albany	3	2-55
Wabash*	IN	219	46992	Wabash	13	2-22
Wabasha*	MN	612	55981	Wabasha	1	2-41
Waco*	TX	817	76701-99	McLennan	104	2-74

Bold = Over 15,000......ALL CAPS = STATE CAPITAL......* = County Seat......# = Changes to 510 in 9/91.....## = Changes to 410 in 11/91.....(+) = City located in additional counties......NAV = Population not available......C.H.= Court House......(IC)=Independent City

CITY	STATE	AREA CODE	ZIP CODE	COUNTY	POPULATION (in thousands)	MAP PAGE
Waconia	MN	612	55387	Carver	3	2-41
Wadena*	MN	218	56482	Wadena	4	2-40
Wadesboro*	NC	704	28170	Anson	4	2-58
Wadsworth	OH	216	44281	Medina	15	2-60
Wagoner*	OK	918	74467	Wagoner	6	2-65
Wahoo*	NE	402	68066	Saunders	4	2-47
Wahpeton*	ND	701	58074-7	Richland	10	2-57
Wailuku*	HI	808	96786	Maui	10	2-19
Waite Park	MN	612	56387	Stearns	4	2-41
Wake Forest	NC	919	27587	Wake	4	2-58&59
Wake Village	TX	903	75501	Bowie	4	2-74
WaKeeney*	KS	913	67672	Trego	2	2-26&27
Wakefield	MA	617	01880	Middlesex	25	2-36&37
Wakefield	MI	906	49968	Gogebic	2	2-38
Wakefield	RI	401	02879-83	Washington	4	2-69
Walden*	CO	303	80480	Jackson	1	2-10&11
Walden	NY	914	12586	Orange	5	2-56
Waldoboro	ME	207	04572	Lincoln	4	2-32&33
Waldorf	MD	301	20601-04	Charles	8	2-34&35
Waldron*	AR	501	72958	Scott	3	2-6
Waldwick	NJ	201	07463	Bergen	11	2-52
Walhalla*	SC	803	29691	Oconee	4	2-70
Walker	LA	504	70785	Livingston	3	2-30&31
Walker*	MN	218	56484	Cass	1	2-40
Wall	NJ	908	07719	Monmouth	19	2-50
Walla Walla*	WA	509	99362	Walla Walla	26	2-81
Wallace	NC	919	28466	Duplin (+1)	3	2-58&59
Wallace*	ID	208	83873-74	Shoeshone	1	2-18
Walled Lake	MI	313	48088	Oakland	5	2-39
Wallingford	CT	203	06492	New Haven	38	2-12&13
Wallington	NJ	201	07057	Bergen	11	2-52
Walnut	CA	714	9178-89	Los Angeles	20	2-7
Walnut Creek	CA	415#	94593-98	Contra Costa	58	2-7
Walnut Park	CA	213	90255	Los Angeles	11	2-7
Walnut Ridge*	AR	501	72476	Lawrence	4	2-6
Walpole	MA	508	02081	Norfolk	18	2-36&37
Walpole	NH	603	03608	Cheshire	3	2-49
Walsenburg*	CO	719	81089	Huerfano	4	2-11
Walterboro*	SC	803	29488	Colleton	7	2-70
Walters*	OK	405	73572	Cotton	2	2-64&65
Walthall*	MS	601	39771	Webster	1	2-42&43
Waltham	MA	617	02154	Middlesex	58	2-36&37
Walton	NY	607	13856	Delaware	3	2-54&55
Wamego	KS	913	66547	Pottawatomie	3	2-26&27
Wampsville*	NY	315	13163	Madison	1	2-54&55
Wanaque	NJ	201	07465	Passaic	10	2-52
Wantagh	NY	516	11793	Nassau	20	2-56
Wapakoneta*	OH	419	45895	Auglaize	8	2-60

Bold = Over 15,000......ALL CAPS = STATE CAPITAL......* = County Seat......# = Changes to 510 in 9/91..... ## = Changes to 410 in 11/91......(+) = City located in addional counties......NAV= Population not available......C.H.= Court House......(IC) = Independent City

CITY	STATE	AREA CODE	ZIP CODE	COUNTY	POPULATION (in thousands)	MAP PAGE
Wapato	WA	509	98951	Yakima	3	2-81
Wapello*	IA	319	52653	Louisa	2	2-25
Wappingers Falls	NY	914	12950	Dutchess	5	2-56
Ware	MA	413	01082	Hampshire	7	2-36
Wareham	MA	508	02571	Plymouth	18	2-36&37
Warm Springs*	VA	703	24484	Bath	1	2-78&79
Warminster	PA	215	18974&91	Bucks	37	2-68
Warner Robins	GA	912	31098-99	Houston	45	2-16&17
Warr Acres	OK	405	73132	Oklahoma	10	2-64&65
Warren*	AR	501	71671	Bradley	7	2-6
Warren	MA	413	01083	Worcester	4	2-36
Warren	ME	207	04864	Knox	3	2-32&33
Warren	MI	313	48089-93	Macomb	155	2-39
Warren*	MN	218	56762	Marshall	1	2-40
Warren	NJ	908	07060	Somerset	9	2-50
Warren*	OH	216	44481-85	Trumbull	52	2-60
Warren*	PA	814	16365	Warren	11	2-66
Warren	RI	401	02885	Bristol	11	2-69
Warrensburg*	MO	816	64093	Johnson	12	2-44
Warrensville Hts	OH	216	44122	Cuyahoga	17	2-62
Warrenton*	GA	404	30828	Warren	1	2-16&17
Warrenton*	MO	314	63383	Warren	4	2-44&45
Warrenton*	NC	919	27589	Warren	1	2-58&59
Warrenton*	VA	703	22186	Fauquier	5	2-78&79
Warrenville	IL	708	60555	Du Page	9	2-19
Warrington	FL	904	32507	Escambia	15	2-14
Warrington	PA	215	18976	Bucks	7	2-68
Warrior	AL	205	35180	Jefferson	3	2-2&3
Warsaw*	IN	219	46580	Kosciusko	12	2-22
Warsaw*	KY	606	41095	Gallatin	1	2-29
Warsaw*	MO	816	65355	Benton	1	2-44
Warsaw*	NY	716	14569	Wyoming	3	2-54
Warsaw*	VA	804	22572	Richmond	1	2-78&79
Wartburg*	TN	615	37887	Morgan	1	2-72&73
Warwick	NY	914	10990	Orange	4	2-56
Warwick*	RI	401	02886-89	Kent	86	2-69
Wasco	CA	805	93280	Kern	11	2-9
Waseca*	MN	507	56093	Waseca	8	2-41
Washburn	ME	207	04786	Aroostook	2	2-32&33
Washburn*	ND	701	58577	McLean	1	2-57
Washburn*	WI	715	54891	Bayfield	1	2-84&85
Washington	CT	203	06793	Litchfield	4	2-12&13
Washington*	GA	404	30673	Wilkes	5	2-16&17
Washington*	IA	319	52353	Washington	6	2-25
Washington*	IL	309	61571	Tazewell	10	2-20
Washington*	IN	812	47501	Daviess	12	2-23
Washington*	KS	913	66968	Washington	22	2-26&27
Washington	MO	314	63090	Franklin	9	2-44&45

Bold = Over 15,000......ALL CAPS = STATE CAPITAL......* = County Seat......# = Changes to 510 in 9/91......## = Changes to 410 in 11/91......(+) = City located in additional counties......NAV = Population not available......C.H.= Court House......(IC)=Independent City

CITY	STATE	AREA CODE	ZIP CODE	COUNTY	POPULATION (in thousands)	MAP PAGE
Washington*	NC	919	27889	Beaufort	9	2-58&59
Washington	NJ	908	07882	Warren	6	2-50
Washington*	PA	412	15301	Washington	18	2-66
Washington	UT	801	84780	Washington	3	2-76
Washington*	VA	703	22747	Rappahannock	1	2-78&79
Washington C.H.*	OH	513	43160	Fayette	12	2-61
Washington Park	IL	618	62204	St. Clair	8	2-21
Washington Terrace	UT	801	84403	Weber	8	2-76
Washougal	WA	206	98671	Clark	4	2-80
Watauga	TX	817	76137	Tarrant	10	2-74
Watchung	NJ	908	07060	Somerset	6	2-50
Water Valley*	MS	601	38965	Yalobusha	4	2-42&43
Waterboro	ME	207	04087	York	3	2-32&33
Waterbury	CT	203	06701-26	New Haven	103	2-12&13
Waterbury	VT	802	05676	Washington	4	2-77
Waterford	CA	209	95386	Stanislaus	3	2-8&9
Waterford	CT	203	06385	New London	18	2-12&13
Waterloo*	IA	319	50701-99	Black Hawk	70	2-25
Waterloo*	IL	618	62298	Monroe	4	2-21
Waterloo*	NY	315	13165	Seneca	5	2-54&55
Watertown	CT	203	06795	Litchfield	6	2-12&13
Watertown	MA	617	02172	Middlesex	33	2-36&37
Watertown*	NY	315	13601	Jefferson	28	2-54&55
Watertown*	SD	605	57201-02	Codington	16	2-71
Watertown	WI	414	53094	Dodge (+1)	19	2-85
Waterville	ME	207	04901	Kennebec	18	2-32&33
Waterville*	WA	509	98858	Douglas	1	2-81
Watervliet	NY	518	12189	Albany	12	2-55
Watford City*	ND	701	58854	McKenzie	1	2-57
Watkins Glen*	NY	607	14891	Schuyler	2	2-54&55
Watkinsville*	GA	404	30677	Oconee	1	2-16&17
Watonga*	OK	405	73772	Blaine	4	2-64&65
Watseka*	IL	815	60970	Iroquois	2	2-20
Watsontown	PA	717	17777	Northumberland	2	2-67
Watsonville	CA	408	95076-77	Santa Cruz	28	2-7
Wauchula*	FL	813	33873	Hardee	3	2-14&15
Wauconda	IL	708	60084	Lake	78	2-20
Waukegan*	IL	708	60085-87	Lake	72	2-20
Waukesha*	WI	414	53186-88	Waukesha	52	2-85
Waukon*	IA	319	52172	Allamakee	4	2-25
Waunakee	WI	608	53597	Dane	4	2-85
Waupaca*	WI	715	54981	Waupaca	4	2-84&85
Waupun	WI	414	53963	Dodge (+1)	8	2-85
Waurika*	OK	405	73573	Jefferson	2	2-64&65
Wausau*	WI	715	54401	Marathon	31	2-84&85
Wauseon*	OH	419	43567	Fulton	6	2-60
Wautoma*	WI	414	54982	Waushara	1	2-85
Wauwatosa	WI	414	53226	Milwaukee	50	2-85

Bold = Over 15,000......ALL CAPS = STATE CAPITAL......* = County Seat......# = Changes to 510 in 9/91..... ## = Changes to 410 in 11/91......(+) = City located in addional counties......NAV= Population not available......C.H.= Court House......(IC) = Independent City

CITY	STATE	AREA CODE	ZIP CODE	COUNTY	POPULATION (in thousands)	MAP PAGE
Waveland	MS	601	39576	Hancock	4	2-42&43
Waverly*	IA	319	50677	Bremer	9	2-25
Waverly	MI	517	48917	Eaton	7	2-38&39
Waverly	NY	607	14892	Tioga	5	2-54&55
Waverly*	OH	614	45690	Pike	4	2-61
Waverly*	TN	615	37185	Humphreys	4	2-72&73
Waxahachie*	TX	214	75165	Ellis	15	2-74
Waycross*	GA	912	31501-02	Ware	19	2-16&17
Wayland	MA	508	01778	Middlesex	3	2-36&37
Wayne	MI	313	48184-88	Wayne	21	2-39
Wayne*	NE	402	68787	Wayne	5	2-47
Wayne	NJ	201	07470-74	Passaic	49	2-52
Wayne*	WV	304	25570	Wayne	1	2-82
Waynesboro*	GA	404	30830	Burke	6	2-16&17
Waynesboro*	MS	601	39367	Wayne	5	2-42&43
Waynesboro*	TN	615	38485	Wayne	1	2-72&73
Waynesboro	PA	717	17268	Franklin	10	2-67
Waynesboro	VA	703	22980	(IC)	18	2-78&79
Waynesburg*	PA	412	15370	Greene	4	2-66
Waynesville*	MO	314	65583	Pulaski	3	2-44&45
Waynesville*	NC	704	28786	Haywood	7	2-58
Wayzata	MN	612	55391	Hennepin	4	2-41
Weare	NH	603	03281	Hillsborough	3	2-49
Weatherford	OK	405	73096	Custer	10	2-64&65
Weatherford*	TX	817	76086-87	Parker	14	2-74
Weatherly	PA	717	18255	Carbon	3	2-67
Weathersfield	VT	802	05151	Windsor	3	2-77
Weaver	AL	205	36277	Calhoun	3	2-2&3
Weaverville*	CA	916	96093	Trinity	3	2-8
Webb City	MO	417	64870	Jasper	7	2-44
Webster	MA	508	01570	Worcester	15	2-36&37
Webster	NY	716	14580	Monroe	5	2-54
Webster*	SD	605	57274	Day	1	2-71
Webster City*	IA	515	50595	Hamilton	9	2-24&25
Webster Groves	MO	314	63119	St. Louis	23	2-44&45
Webster Springs*	WV	304	26288	Webster	1	2-82
Wedowee*	AL	205	36278	Randolph	1	2-2&3
Weed	CA	916	96094	Siskiyou	2	2-8
Weehawken	NJ	201	07087	Hudson	13	2-52
Weirton	WV	304	26062	Brooke (+1)	24	2-82
Weiser*	ID	208	83672	Washington	5	2-18
Welch*	WV	304	24801	McDowell	3	2-82
Wellesley	MA	617	02181	Norfolk	27	2-36&37
Wellfleet	MA	508	02667	Barnstable	2	2-36&37
Wellington*	KS	316	67152	Sumner	8	2-26&27
Wellington	OH	216	44090	Lorain	4	2-60
Wellington*	TX	806	79095	Collingsworth	2	2-74
Wells	ME	207	04090	York	8	2-32&33

Bold = Over 15,000......ALL CAPS = STATE CAPITAL......* = County Seat......# = Changes to 510 in 9/91.....## = Changes to 410 in 11/91.....(+) = City located in additional counties......NAV = Population not available......C.H.= Court House......(IC)=Independent City

CITY	STATE	AREA CODE	ZIP CODE	COUNTY	POPULATION (in thousands)	MAP PAGE
Wellsboro*	PA	717	16901	Tioga	3	2-67
Wellsburg*	WV	304	26070	Brooke	3	2-82
Wellston	MO	314	63112	St. Louis	5	2-44&45
Wellston	OH	614	45692	Jackson	6	2-61
Wellsville	NY	716	14895	Allegany	6	2-54&55
Wellsville	OH	216	43968	Columbiana	5	2-60
Welsh	LA	318	70591	Jefferson Davis	4	2-30
Wenatchee*	WA	509	98801-07	Chelan	18	2-81
Wenham	MA	508	01984	Essex	4	2-36&37
Wentworth*	NC	919	27375	Rockingham	1	2-58&59
Wentzville	MO	314	63385	St. Charles	4	2-44&45
Weslaco	TX	512	78596	Hidalgo	24	2-75
Wesleyville	PA	814	16510	Erie	4	2-66
Wessington Springs*	SD	605	57382	Jerauld	1	2-71
West Allis	WI	414	53214	Milwaukee	65	2-85
West Bellport	NY	516	11772	Suffolk	14	2-56
West Bend*	WI	414	53095	Washington	21	2-85
West Bountiful	UT	801	84087	Davis	4	2-76
West Boylston	MA	508	01583	Worcester	3	2-36&37
West Bradford	PA	215	19335	Chester	7	2-67
West Branch*	MI	517	48661	Ogemaw	1	2-38&39
West Bridgewater	MA	508	02379	Plymouth	6	2-36&37
West Brookfield	MA	508	01585	Worcester	3	2-36&37
West Burlington	IA	319	52655	Des Moines	3	2-25
West Caldwell	NJ	201	07006	Essex	11	2-52
West Carrollton	OH	513	45449	Montgomery	13	2-61
West Carson	CA	213	90502	Los Angeles	18	2-7
West Chester*	PA	215	19380-83	Chester	18	2-67
West Chicago	IL	708	60185	Du Page	12	2-19
West Columbia	SC	803	29169-71	Lexington	11	2-70
West Covina	CA	818	91790-93	Los Angeles	96	2-7
West Deptford	NJ	609	08086	Gloucester	18	2-51
West Des Moines	IA	515	50265	Polk	23	2-24&25
West Fargo	ND	701	58078	Cass	10	2-57
West Fort Salonga	NY	516	11768	Suffolk	4	2-56
West Frankfort	IL	618	62896	Franklin	10	2-21
West Goshen	PA	215	19380	Chester	8	2-67
West Greenwich	RI	401	02816	Kent	3	2-69
West Hartford	CT	203	06090	Hartford	61	2-12&13
West Haven	CT	203	06516	New Haven	53	2-12&13
West Haven	OR	503	97225	Washington	3	2-63
West Haverstraw	NY	914	10993	Rockland	9	2-56
West Hazleton	PA	717	18201	Luzerne	5	2-67
West Helena	AR	501	72390	Phillips	11	2-6
West Hollywood	CA	213	90069	Los Angeles	38	2-7
West Jordan	UT	801	84084	Salt Lake	41	2-76
West Kingston*	RI	401	02892	Washington	1	2-69
West Lafayette	IN	317	47906	Tippecanoe	21	2-22&23

Bold = Over 15,000......ALL CAPS = STATE CAPITAL......* = County Seat......# = Changes to 510 in 9/91..... ## = Changes to 410 in 11/91......(+) = City located in addional counties......NAV= Population not available......C.H.= Court House......(IC) = Independent City

CITY	STATE	AREA CODE	ZIP CODE	COUNTY	POPULATION (in thousands)	MAP PAGE
West Lanham Hills	MD	301	20784	P. Georges	4	2-35
West Laurel	MD	301	20707	Prince Georges	5	2-34&35
West Liberty	IA	319	52776	Muscatine	3	2-25
West Liberty*	KY	606	41472	Morgan	1	2-29
West Linn	OR	503	97068	Clackamas	12	2-63
West Long Branch	NJ	908	07764	Monmouth	8	2-50
West Los Angeles	CA	213	90025	Los Angeles	37	2-7
West Melbourne	FL	407	32901	Brevard	5	2-14&15
West Memphis	AR	501	72301	Crittenden	28	2-6
West Miami	FL	305	33144	Dade	6	2-15
West Mifflin	PA	412	15122-23	Allegheny	25	2-68
West Milford	NJ	201	07480	Passaic	22	2-52
West Milton	OH	513	45383	Miami	4	2-61
West Milwaukee	WI	414	53214	Milwaukee	4	2-85
West Monroe	LA	318	71291-94	Ouachita	15	2-30
West New York	NJ	201	07093	Hudson	41	2-52
West Newbury	MA	508	01985	Essex	1	2-36&37
West Newton	MA	617	02165	Middlesex	12	2-36&37
West Newton	PA	412	15089	Westmooreland	3	2-68
West Norriton	PA	215	19401	Montgomery	15	2-68
West Orange	NJ	201	07052	Essex	41	2-52
West Palm Beach*	FL	407	33401-20	Palm Beach	71	2-15
West Paterson	NJ	201	07424	Passaic	12	2-52
West Pensacola	FL	904	32505	Escambia	29	2-14
West Pittston	PA	717	18643	Luzerne	6	2-67
West Plains*	MO	417	65775	Howell	8	2-44
West Point	GA	404	31833	Troup (+1)	4	2-16&17
West Point*	MS	601	39773	Clay	9	2-42&43
West Point*	NE	402	68788	Cuming	3	2-47
West Pottsgrove	PA	215	19464	Montgomery	4	2-68
West Puente Valley	CA	714	91744	Los Angeles	20	2-7
West Reading	PA	215	19611	Berks	5	2-67
West Richland	WA	509	99352	Benton	3	2-81
West Sacramento	CA	916	95691	Yolo	25	2-8
West St. Paul	MN	612	55118	Dakota	19	2-41
West Salem	WI	608	54669	La Crosse	3	2-85
West Seneca	NY	716	14224	Erie	49	2-54
West Springfield	MA	413	01089-90	Hampden	27	2-36
West Union*	IA	319	52175	Fayette	2	2-25
West Union*	OH	513	45693	Adams	2	2-61
West Union*	WV	304	26456	Doddridge	1	2-82
West Valley City	UT	801	84119-20	Salt Lake	92	2-76
West View	PA	412	15229	Allegheny	8	2-68
West Warwick	RI	401	02893	Kent	29	2-69
West Whiteland	PA	215	19341	Chester	9	2-67
West Willow	MI	313	48198	Washtenaw	6	2-39
West Windsor	NJ	609	08550	Mercer	8	2-50
West Wyoming	PA	717	18644	Luzerne	3	2-67

Bold = Over 15,000......ALL CAPS = STATE CAPITAL......* = County Seat......# = Changes to 510 in 9/91.....## = Changes to 410 in 11/91.....(+)
= City located in additional counties......NAV = Population not available......C.H.= Court House......(IC)=Independent City

CITY	STATE	AREA CODE	ZIP CODE	COUNTY	POPULATION (in thousands)	MAP PAGE
West York	PA	717	17404	York	5	2-67
Westborough	MA	508	01581	Worcester	13	2-36&37
Westbrook	ME	207	04092	Cumberland	15	2-32&33
Westbury	NY	516	11590	Nassau	14	2-56
Westchester	IL	708	60153	Cook	17	2-19
Westcliffe*	CO	303	81252	Custer	1	2-10&11
Westerly	RI	401	02891	Washington	16	2-69
Western Springs	IL	708	60558	Cook	13	2-19
Westernport	MD	301	21562	Allegany	3	2-34&35
Westerville	OH	614	43081	Franklin (+1)	23	2-61
Westfield	IN	317	46074	Hamilton	3	2-22&23
Westfield	MA	413	01085-86	Hampden	37	2-36
Westfield	NJ	908	07090-92	Union	30	2-52
Westfield	NY	716	14787	Chautauqua	3	2-54
Westford	MA	508	01886	Middlesex	13	2-36&37
Westlake	LA	318	70669	Calcasieu	5	2-30
Westlake	OH	216	44145	Cuyahoga	19	2-62
Westlake Vlg	CA	818	91361	Los Angeles	6	2-7
Westland	MI	313	48185	Wayne	80	2-39
Westminster	CA	714	92683-84	Orange	73	2-7
Westminster	CO	303	80030-36	Jefferson (+1)	63	2-10&11
Westminster	MA	508	01473	Worcester	6	2-36&37
Westminster*	MD	301##	21157	Carroll	9	2-34&35
Westminster	SC	803	29693	Oconee	3	2-70
Westmont	CA	213	90044	Los Angeles	28	2-7
Westmont	IL	708	60559	Du Page	20	2-19
Westmont	PA	814	15905	Cambria	6	2-66
Westmoreland*	KS	913	66549	Pottawatomie	1	2-26&27
Weston	MA	617	02193	Middlesex	12	2-36&37
Weston*	WV	304	26452	Lewis	5	2-82
Westover	WV	304	26505	Monongalia	5	2-82
Westport	CT	203	06880-83	Fairfield	25	2-12&13
Westport	MA	508	02790	Bristol	14	2-36&37
Westview Park	MD	301##	21228	Baltimore	3	2-34&35
Westville	IL	217	61883	Vermilion	3	2-20&21
Westville	NJ	609	08093	Gloucester	5	2-51
Westwego	LA	504	70094-96	Jefferson	12	2-30&31
Westwood	MA	617	02090	Norfolk	6	2-36&37
Westwood	NJ	201	07675	Bergen	11	2-52
Westwood Lakes	FL	305	33165	Dade	12	2-15
Wethersfield	CT	203	06109	Hartford	26	2-12&13
Wetumpka*	AL	205	36092	Elmore	4	2-2&3
Wewoka*	OK	405	74884	Seminole	4	2-64&65
Weymouth	MA	617	02188	Norfolk	55	2-36&37
Wharton	NJ	201	07885	Morris	5	2-52
Wharton*	TX	409	77488	Wharton	9	2-75
Wheat Ridge	CO	303	80033-34	Jefferson	32	2-10&11
Wheatland*	WY	307	82201	Platte	4	2-83

Bold = Over 15,000......ALL CAPS = STATE CAPITAL......* = County Seat......# = Changes to 510 in 9/91..... ## = Changes to 410 in 11/91......(+) = City located in addional counties......NAV= Population not available......C.H.= Court House......(IC) = Independent City

CITY	STATE	AREA CODE	ZIP CODE	COUNTY	POPULATION (in thousands)	MAP PAGE
Wheaton*	IL	708	60187-89	Du Page	51	2-19
Wheaton	MD	301	20902	Montgomery	54	2-34&35
Wheaton*	MN	612	56296	Traverse	1	2-41
Wheeler*	TX	806	79096	Wheeler	1	2-74
Wheeling	IL	708	60090	Cook (+1)	26	2-19
Wheeling*	WV	304	26003	Ohio (& Marshall)	39	2-82
White Bear Lake	MN	612	56381	Ramsey (+1)	24	2-41
White Center	WA	206	98126	King	18	2-80
White Cloud*	MI	616	49349	Newaygo	1	2-38&39
White Hall	AR	501	71602	Jefferson	3	2-6
White Hall	IL	217	62092	Greene	3	2-20&21
White Lake	MI	313	48019	Oakland	3	2-39
White Oak	MD	301	20904	Montgomery (+1)	4	2-34&35
White Oak	PA	412	15131	Allegheny	9	2-68
White Plains*	NY	914	10601-99	Westchester	45	2-56
White River*	SD	605	57579	Mellette	1	2-71
White Settlement	TX	817	76108	Tarrant	13	2-74
White Sulphur Springs	WV	304	24986	Greenbrier	3	2-82
White Sulphur Springs*	MT	406	59645	Meagher	1	2-46
Whitefish	MT	406	59937	Flathead	4	2-46
Whitefish Bay	WI	414	53217	Milwaukee	15	2-85
Whitehall	MI	616	49461	Muskegon	3	2-38&39
Whitehall	NY	518	12887	Washington	3	2-55
Whitehall	OH	614	43213	Franklin	23	2-61
Whitehall	PA	412	18052	Lehigh	15	2-66
Whitehall*	WI	715	54773	Trempealeau	1	2-84&85
Whitemarsh Twp.	PA	215	19428	Montgomery	14	2-68
Whitesboro	NY	315	13492	Oneida	5	2-54&55
Whitesburg*	KY	606	41858	Letcher	2	2-29
Whiteville*	NC	919	28472	Columbus	4	2-58&59
Whitewater	WI	414	53190	Walworth (+1)	12	2-85
Whiting	IN	219	46394	Lake	5	2-22
Whitinsville	MA	508	01588	Worcester	6	2-36&37
Whitley City*	KY	606	42653	McCreary	2	2-29
Whitman	MA	617	02382	Plymouth	14	2-36&37
Whitpain	PA	215	19422	Montgomery	11	2-68
Whittier	CA	213	90601-10	Los Angeles	72	2-7
Wibaux*	MT	406	59353	Wibaux	1	2-46
Wichita Falls*	TX	817	76301-11	Wichita	99	2-74
Wichita*	KS	316	67201-99	Sedgwick	290	2-26&27
Wickenburg	AZ	602	85358	Maricopa	4	2-5
Wickliffe	OH	216	44092	Lake	7	2-62
Wickliffe*	KY	502	42087	Ballard	6	2-28&29
Wiggins*	MS	601	39577	Stone	3	2-42&43
Wilber*	NE	402	68465	Saline	1	2-47
Wilbraham	MA	413	01095	Hampden	4	2-36
Wilburton*	OK	918	74578	Latimer	3	2-65
Wilcox	AZ	602	85643-44	Cochise	3	2-5

**Bold = Over 15,000......ALL CAPS = STATE CAPITAL......* = County Seat......# = Changes to 510 in 9/91.....## = Changes to 410 in 11/91.....(+)
= City located in additional counties......NAV = Population not available......C.H.= Court House......(IC)=Independent City**

CITY	STATE	AREA CODE	ZIP CODE	COUNTY	POPULATION (in thousands)	MAP PAGE
Wildwood	FL	904	34785	Sumter	3	2-14
Wildwood	NJ	609	08260	Cape May	5	2-51
Wildwood Crest	NJ	609	08260	Cape May	4	2-51
Wilkes-Barre*	PA	717	18701-99	Luzerne	47	2-67
Wilkesboro*	NC	919	28697	Wilkes	2	2-58&59
Wilkins Twp.	PA	412	15145	Allegheny	8	2-68
Wilkinsburg	PA	412	15221	Allegheny	22	2-68
Willard	OH	419	44890	Huron	6	2-60
Williamsburg*	KY	606	40769	Whitley	6	2-29
Williamsburg*	VA	804	23185-87	James City (IC)	10	2-79
Williamson*	WV	304	25661	Mingo	4	2-82
Williamsport*	IN	317	47993	Warren	2	2-22&23
Williamsport*	PA	717	17701	Lycoming	31	2-67
Williamston	MI	517	48895	Ingham	3	2-38&39
Williamston*	NC	919	27892	Martin	6	2-58&59
Williamston	SC	803	29697	Anderson	4	2-70
Williamstown*	KY	606	41097	Grant	3	2-29
Williamstown	MA	413	01267	Berkshire	4	2-36
Williamstown	WV	304	26187	Wood	3	2-82
Williamsville	NY	716	14221	Erie	6	2-54
Willimantic	CT	203	06226	Windham	5	2-12&13
Willingboro	NJ	609	08046	Burlington	40	2-51
Willington	CT	203	06279	Tolland	5	2-12&13
Williston Park	NY	516	11596	Nassau	8	2-56
Williston*	ND	701	58801-02	Williams	15	2-57
Willistown	PA	215	19355	Chester	8	2-67
Willits	CA	707	95490	Mendocino	4	2-8
Willmar*	MN	612	56201	Kandiyohi	15	2-41
Willoughby	OH	216	44094-95	Lake	20	2-62
Willoughby Hills	OH	216	44092	Lake	9	2-62
Willow Brook	CA	213	90222	Los Angeles	32	2-7
Willow Ridge Estates	NY	716	14150	Erie	5	2-54
Willow Run	MI	313	48198	Washtenaw	6	2-39
Willow Springs	IL	708	60480	Cook (+1)	4	2-19
Willowick	OH	216	44094	Lake	18	2-62
Willows*	CA	916	95988	Glenn	5	2-8
Willston	SC	803	29853	Barnwell	3	2-70
Wilmette	IL	708	60091	Cook	27	2-19
Wilmington	IL	815	60481	Will	4	2-20
Wilmington*	DE	302	19801-99	New Castle	70	2-35
Wilmington	MA	508	01887	Middlesex	17	2-36&37
Wilmington*	NC	919	28401-12	New Hanover	54	2-58&59
Wilmington*	OH	513	45177	Clinton	10	2-61
Wilmore	KY	606	40390	Jessamine	4	2-29
Wilson*	NC	919	27893-95	Wilson	35	2-58&59
Wilson	NY	716	14172	Niagara	6	2-54
Wilson	PA	215	18042	Northampton	8	2-67
Wilsonville	OR	503	97070	Clackamas (+1)	3	2-63

Bold = Over 15,000......ALL CAPS = STATE CAPITAL......* = County Seat......# = Changes to 510 in 9/91..... ## = Changes to 410 in 11/91......(+) = City located in addional counties......NAV= Population not available......C.H.= Court House......(IC) = Independent City

CITY	STATE	AREA CODE	ZIP CODE	COUNTY	POPULATION (in thousands)	MAP PAGE
Wilton	CT	203	06897	Fairfield	15	2-12&13
Wilton	IA	319	52778	Cedar (+1)	2	2-25
Wilton	ME	207	04294	Franklin	4	2-32&33
Wilton	NH	603	03086	Hillsborough	3	2-49
Wilton Manors	FL	305	33334	Broward	13	2-15
Winamac*	IN	219	46996	Pulaski	3	2-22
Winchendon	MA	508	01475	Worcester	7	2-36&37
Winchester	CT	203	06094	Litchfield	11	2-12&13
Winchester*	IL	217	62694	Scott	1	2-20&21
Winchester*	IN	317	47394	Randolph	5	2-22&23
Winchester*	KY	606	40391	Clark	15	2-29
Winchester	MA	617	01890	Middlesex	20	2-36&37
Winchester	NH	603	03470	Cheshire	4	2-49
Winchester*	TN	615	37398	Franklin	6	2-72&73
Winchester*	VA	703	22601	Frederick (IC)	20	2-78&79
Windber	PA	814	15963	Somerset	5	2-66
Windemere	MI	517	48917	Ingham	3	2-38&39
Winder*	GA	404	30680	Barrow	7	2-16&17
Windgap	PA	215	18091	Northampton	3	2-67
Windham	ME	207	04062	Cumberland	11	2-32&33
Windham	NH	603	03087	Rockingham	6	2-49
Windham	OH	216	44288	Portage	4	2-60
Windom*	MN	507	56101	Cottonwood	4	2-41
Windsor	CO	303	80550	Weld	4	2-10&11
Windsor	CT	203	06095	Hartford	25	2-12&13
Windsor	MO	816	65360	Henry (+1)	2	2-44
Windsor*	NC	919	27983	Bertie	1	2-58&59
Windsor	VT	802	05089	Windsor	4	2-77
Windsor Heights	IA	515	50311	Polk	5	2-24&25
Windsor Locks	CT	203	06096	Hartford	12	2-12&13
Winfield	AL	205	35594	Marion (+1)	4	2-2&3
Winfield	IL	708	60185	Du Page	5	2-19
Winfield*	KS	316	67156	Cowley	11	2-26&27
Winfield*	WV	304	25213	Putnam	1	2-82
Winkelman	AZ	602	85292	Gila	1	2-5
Winnemucca*	NV	702	89445	Humboldt	4	2-48
Winner*	SD	605	57580	Tripp-Todd	3	2-71
Winnetka	IL	708	60093	Cook	13	2-19
Winnett*	MT	406	59087	Petroleum	1	2-46
Winnfield*	LA	318	71483	Winn	7	2-30
Winnsboro*	LA	318	71295	Franklin	5	2-30
Winnsboro*	SC	803	29180	Fairfield	2	2-70
Winona*	MN	507	55987	Winona	24	2-41
Winona*	MS	601	38967	Montgomery	5	2-42&43
Winona Lake	IN	219	46590	Kosciusko	12	2-22
Winooski	VT	802	05404	Chittenden	3	2-77
Winslow	AZ	602	86047	Navajo	8	2-5
Winslow	ME	207	04901	Kennebec	8	2-32&33

Bold = Over 15,000......ALL CAPS = STATE CAPITAL......* = County Seat......# = Changes to 510 in 9/91.....## = Changes to 410 in 11/91......(+) = City located in additional counties......NAV = Population not available......C.H.= Court House......(IC)=Independent City

CITY	STATE	AREA CODE	ZIP CODE	COUNTY	POPULATION (in thousands)	MAP PAGE
Winsted	CT	203	06098	Litchfield	9	2-12&13
Winston	OR	503	97496	Douglas	3	2-63
Winston-Salem*	NC	919	27101-27	Forsyth	148	2-58&59
Winter Garden	FL	407	34787	Orange	7	2-14&15
Winter Haven	FL	813	33880-84	Polk	23	2-14&15
Winter Park	FL	407	32789-93	Orange	24	2-14&15
Winter Springs	FL	407	32708	Seminole	10	2-14&15
Winterport	ME	207	04496	Waldo	3	2-32&33
Winters	CA	916	95694	Yolo	3	2-8
Winterset*	IA	515	50273	Madison	4	2-24&25
Wintersville	OH	614	43952	Jefferson	5	2-61
Winthrop	MA	617	02152	Suffolk	19	2-36&37
Winthrop	ME	207	04364	Kennebec	6	2-32&33
Winthrop Harbor	IL	708	60096	Lake	5	2-20
Winton*	NC	919	27986	Hertford	1	2-58&59
Wiscasset*	ME	207	04578	Lincoln	3	2-32&33
Wisconsin Dells	WI	608	53965	Columbia (+1)	3	2-85
Wisconsin Rapids*	WI	715	54493	Wood	18	2-84&85
Wise*	VA	703	24293	Wise	4	2-78&79
Wixom	MI	313	48096	Oakland	6	2-39
Woburn	MA	617	01801	Middlesex	37	2-36&37
Wolcott	CT	203	06716	New Haven	13	2-12&13
Wolf Point*	MT	406	59201	Roosevelt	3	2-46
Wolfeboro	NH	603	03894	Carroll	4	2-49
Wolverine Lake	MI	313	48088	Oakland	5	2-39
Wonder Lake	IL	815	60097	McHenry	6	2-20
Wood Dale	IL	708	60191	Du Page	11	2-19
Wood River	IL	618	62095	Madison	12	2-21
Wood-Ridge	NJ	201	07074-75	Bergen	8	2-52
Woodbine*	GA	912	31569	Camden	1	2-16&17
Woodbridge	CT	203	06525	New Haven	7	2-12&13
Woodbridge	NJ	908	07095	Middlesex	95	2-50
Woodbridge	VA	703	22191-99	Prince William	28	2-78&79
Woodburn	OR	503	97071	Marion	11	2-63
Woodbury	MN	612	55125	Washington	15	2-41
Woodbury*	NJ	609	08096	Gloucester	10	2-51
Woodbury*	TN	615	37190	Cannon	1	2-72&73
Woodcliff Lake	NJ	201	07675	Bergen	6	2-52
Woodfin	NC	704	28804	Buncombe	3	2-58
Woodhaven	MI	313	48183	Wayne	11	2-39
Woodlake	CA	209	93286	Tulare	5	2-8&9
Woodland*	CA	916	95695	Yolo	34	2-8
Woodland Park	CO	303	80863	Teller	3	2-10&11
Woodlawn	MD	301##	21207	Baltimore	8	2-34&35
Woodlawn	OH	513	45215	Hamilton	3	2-62
Woodlynne	NJ	609	08107	Camden	3	2-51
Woodmere	NY	516	11598	Nassau	17	2-56
Woodridge	IL	708	60517	Du Page	25	2-19

Bold = Over 15,000......ALL CAPS = STATE CAPITAL......* = County Seat......# = Changes to 510 in 9/91..... ## = Changes to 410 in 11/91......(+) = City located in addional counties......NAV= Population not available......C.H.= Court House......(IC) = Independent City

CITY	STATE	AREA CODE	ZIP CODE	COUNTY	POPULATION (in thousands)	MAP PAGE
Woodruff	SC	803	29388	Spartanburg	5	2-70
Woods Cross	UT	801	84087	Davis	4	2-76
Woods Hole	MA	508	02543	Barnstable	1	2-36&37
Woodsfield*	OH	614	43793	Monroe	2	2-61
Woodside	CA	415	94061	San Mateo	5	2-7
Woodson Terrace	MO	314	63134	St. Louis	5	2-44&45
Woodstock	GA	404	30188	Cherokee	2	2-16&17
Woodstock*	IL	815	60098	McHenry	13	2-20
Woodstock*	VA	703	22664	Shenandoah	1	2-78&79
Woodstock*	VT	802	05091	Windsor	3	2-77
Woodstown	NJ	609	08098	Salem	3	2-51
Woodsville*	NH	603	03785	Grafton	1	2-49
Woodville*	MS	601	39669	Wilkinson	1	2-42&43
Woodville*	TX	409	75979	Tyler	3	2-75
Woodward*	OK	405	73801-02	Woodward	14	2-64&65
Woonsocket	RI	401	02895	Providence	45	2-69
Woonsocket*	SD	605	57385	Sanborn	1	2-71
Wooster*	OH	216	44691	Wayne	19	2-60
Worcester*	MA	508	01601-99	Worcester	162	2-36&37
Worland*	WY	307	82401	Washakie	6	2-83
Wormleysburg	PA	717	17043	Cumberland	3	2-67
Worth	IL	708	60482	Cook	11	2-19
Worthington*	MN	507	56187	Nobles	9	2-41
Worthington	OH	614	43085	Franklin	15	2-61
Wrangell	AK	907	99929	Wrangell P'burg	2	2-4
Wray*	CO	303	80758	Yuma	1	2-10&11
Wrentham	MA	508	02093	Norfolk	7	2-36&37
Wrightstown	NJ	609	08562	Burlington	3	2-51
Wrightsville*	GA	912	31096	Johnson	3	2-16&17
Wrightsville Beach	NC	919	28480	New Hanover	3	2-59
Wyandotte	MI	313	48192	Wayne	32	2-39
Wyckoff	NJ	201	07481	Bergen	16	2-52
Wynantskill	NY	518	12198	Rensselaer	3	2-55
Wynne*	AR	501	72396-97	Cross	8	2-6
Wynnewood	OK	405	73098	Garvin	3	2-64&65
Wyoming	MI	616	49509	Kent	63	2-38&39
Wyoming	OH	513	45215	Hamilton	8	2-62
Wyoming	PA	717	18644	Luzerne	4	2-67
Wyomissing	PA	215	19610	Berks	7	2-67
Wytheville*	VA	703	24382	Wythe	7	2-78&79
Xenia*	OH	513	45385	Greene	24	2-61
Yadkinville*	NC	919	27055	Yadkin	1	2-58&59
Yakima*	WA	509	98901-99	Yakima	50	2-81
Yanceyville*	NC	919	27379	Caswell	2	2-58&59
Yankton*	SD	605	57078	Yankton	12	2-71
Yardley	PA	215	19067	Bucks	3	2-68
Yarmouth	MA	508	02675	Barnstable	18	2-36&37
Yarmouth	ME	207	04096	Cumberland	7	2-32&33

Bold = Over 15,000......ALL CAPS = STATE CAPITAL......* = County Seat......# = Changes to 510 in 9/91.....## = Changes to 410 in 11/91.....(+) = City located in additional counties......NAV = Population not available......C.H. = Court House......(IC)=Independent City

CITY	STATE	AREA CODE	ZIP CODE	COUNTY	POPULATION (in thousands)	MAP PAGE
Yates Center*	KS	316	66783	Woodson	2	2-26&27
Yazoo City*	MS	601	39194	Yazoo	12	2-42&43
Yeadon	PA	215	19050	Delaware	12	2-68
Yellow Springs	OH	513	45387	Greene	4	2-61
Yellville*	AR	501	72687	Marion	1	2-6
Yerington*	NV	702	89447	Lyon	1	2-48
Yoakum	TX	512	77995	De Witt (+1)	6	2-75
Yonkers	NY	914	10701-99	Westchester	191	2-56
Yorba Linda	CA	714	92686	Orange	39	2-7
York	AL	205	36925	Sumter	3	2-2&3
York	ME	207	03909	York	10	2-32&33
York*	NE	402	68467	York	7	2-47
York*	PA	717	17401-99	York	16	2-67
York*	SC	803	29745	York	8	2-70
Yorktown	IN	317	47396	Delaware	3	2-22&23
Yorktown	NY	914	10598	Westchester	5	2-56
Yorktown*	VA	804	23690	York	1	2-78&79
Yorktown Heights	NY	914	10598	Westchester	6	2-56
Yorkville*	IL	708	60560	Kendall	3	2-20
Yorkville	NY	315	13495	Oneida	3	2-54&55
Youngstown	NY	716	14174	Niagara	2	2-54
Youngstown*	OH	216	44501-99	Mahoning	104	2-60
Youngtown	AZ	602	85363	Maricopa	2	2-5
Youngwood	PA	412	15697	Westmooreland	4	2-68
Ypsilanti	MI	313	48197-98	Washtenaw	24	2-39
Yreka*	CA	916	96097	Siskiyou	5	2-8
Yuba City*	CA	916	95991-93	Sutter	21	2-8
Yucaipa	CA	714	92399	San Bernardino	20	2-9
Yukon	OK	405	73099	Canadian	17	2-64&65
Yuma*	AZ	602	85364-69	Yuma	47	2-5
Yuma	CO	303	80759	Yuma	3	2-10&11
Zachary	LA	504	70791	East Baton Rouge	5	2-30&31
Zanesville*	OH	614	43701-02	Muskingum	28	2-61
Zapata*	TX	512	78076	Zapata	1	2-75
Zebulon*	GA	404	30295	Pike	1	2-16&17
Zeeland	MI	616	49464	Ottawa	5	2-38&39
Zelienople	PA	412	16063	Butler	4	2-66
Zephyrhills	FL	813	33539-44	Pasco	6	2-14&15
Zion	IL	708	60099	Lake	17	2-20
Zionsville	IN	317	46077	Boone	4	2-22&23

Bold = Over 15,000......ALL CAPS = STATE CAPITAL......* = County Seat......# = Changes to 510 in 9/91..... ## = Changes to 410 in 11/91......(+) = City located in addional counties......NAV= Population not available......C.H.= Court House......(IC) = Independent City

section 2

Use the first three digits of the Zip Code to find Cities & Towns. Bold lines indicate Area Code changes.

State Maps

Alabama

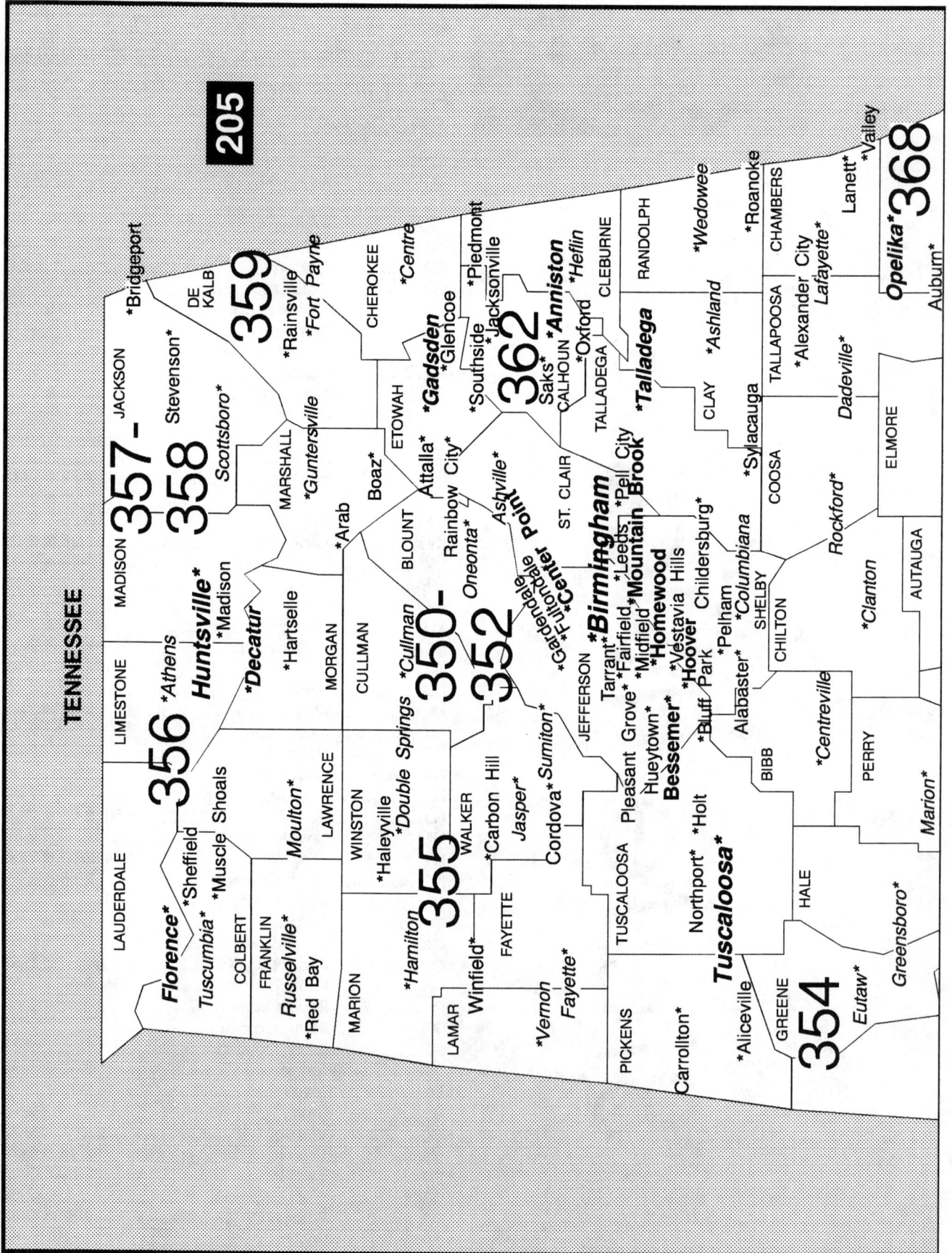

205

TENNESSEE

350-352 · 354 · 355 · 356 · 357-358 · 359 · 362 · *368

Counties and cities:

LAUDERDALE · LIMESTONE · MADISON · JACKSON · DE KALB · CHEROKEE · RANDOLPH · CHAMBERS

Bridgeport* · *Stevenson · Scottsboro* · *Rainsville · *Fort Payne · *Centre · *Piedmont · *Jacksonville · Heflin · CLEBURNE · *Wedowee · *Roanoke · Lanett* · *Valley

*Athens · *Huntsville · *Madison · MARSHALL · *Guntersville · ETOWAH · Boaz · Attalla · *Gadsden · Glencoe · Southside · Saks* · *Anniston · *Oxford · CALHOUN · TALLADEGA · *Talladega · CLAY · *Ashland · TALLAPOOSA · Alexander City* · Lafayette* · *Opelika · Auburn*

COLBERT · *Sheffield · *Tuscumbia · *Muscle Shoals · FRANKLIN · Russellville* · *Red Bay · LAWRENCE · Moulton* · MORGAN · *Decatur · *Hartselle · BLOUNT · Rainbow City · Oneonta* · Ashville* · Gardendale · *Fultondale · *Center Point · *Birmingham · Tarrant* · Pell City* · *Leeds · Mountain Brook* · *Homewood · Vestavia Hills · Childersburg* · *Columbiana · Pelham* · SHELBY · COOSA · Rockford* · *Clanton · ELMORE · *Clanton

*Florence · MARION · WINSTON · *Haleyville · *Double Springs · *Cullman · CULLMAN · *Arab · JEFFERSON · Pleasant Grove · *Fairfield · *Midfield · Hueytown* · *Hoover · Bessemer · Bluff Park · *Holt · *Alabaster · CHILTON · BIBB · *Centreville · PERRY · AUTAUGA

LAMAR · Winfield* · *Vernon · FAYETTE · Fayette* · WALKER · *Carbon Hill · Jasper* · Cordova* · Sumiton* · TUSCALOOSA · Northport* · *Tuscaloosa · HALE · Greensboro* · Marion*

PICKENS · Carrollton* · *Aliceville · GREENE · Eutaw* · Hamilton*

section 2 / page 2

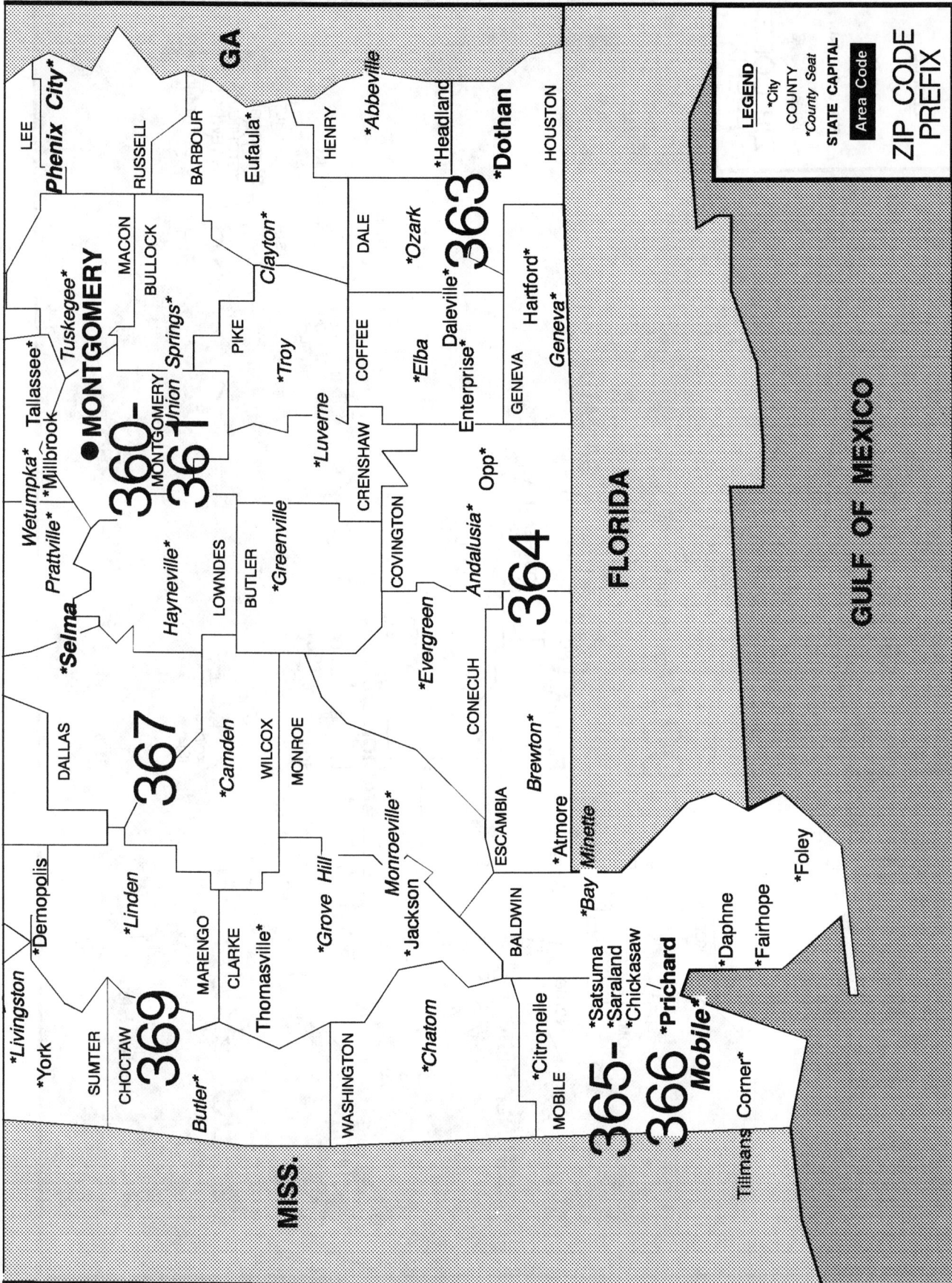

LEGEND
*City
COUNTY
*County Seat
STATE CAPITAL
Area Code
ZIP CODE PREFIX

GA

LEE
Phenix City*
RUSSELL
MACON
BARBOUR
Eufaula*
HENRY
*Abbeville
*Headland
*Dothan
HOUSTON

BULLOCK
Tuskegee*
Tallassee*
Wetumpka*
*Millbrook
MONTGOMERY
Union Springs*
PIKE
Clayton*
*Troy
DALE
*Ozark
Daleville*
Enterprise*
Hartford*
Geneva*
GENEVA

363

Prattville*
●MONTGOMERY
MONTGOMERY

360-
361

*Luverne
COFFEE
*Elba
CRENSHAW

Selma*
Hayneville*
LOWNDES
BUTLER
*Greenville
COVINGTON
Andalusia*
Opp*

364

FLORIDA

GULF OF MEXICO

DALLAS

367

*Camden
WILCOX
MONROE
*Evergreen
CONECUH
Brewton*
ESCAMBIA
*Atmore
Bay Minette*

Demopolis
*Linden
MARENGO
CLARKE
Thomasville*
*Grove Hill
Monroeville*
*Jackson
BALDWIN
*Daphne
*Fairhope
*Foley

*Livingston
*York
SUMTER
CHOCTAW
Butler*

369

WASHINGTON
*Chatom
*Citronelle
MOBILE
*Satsuma
*Saraland
*Chickasaw
*Prichard
Mobile*

365-
366

Tillmans Corner*

MISS.

Alaska

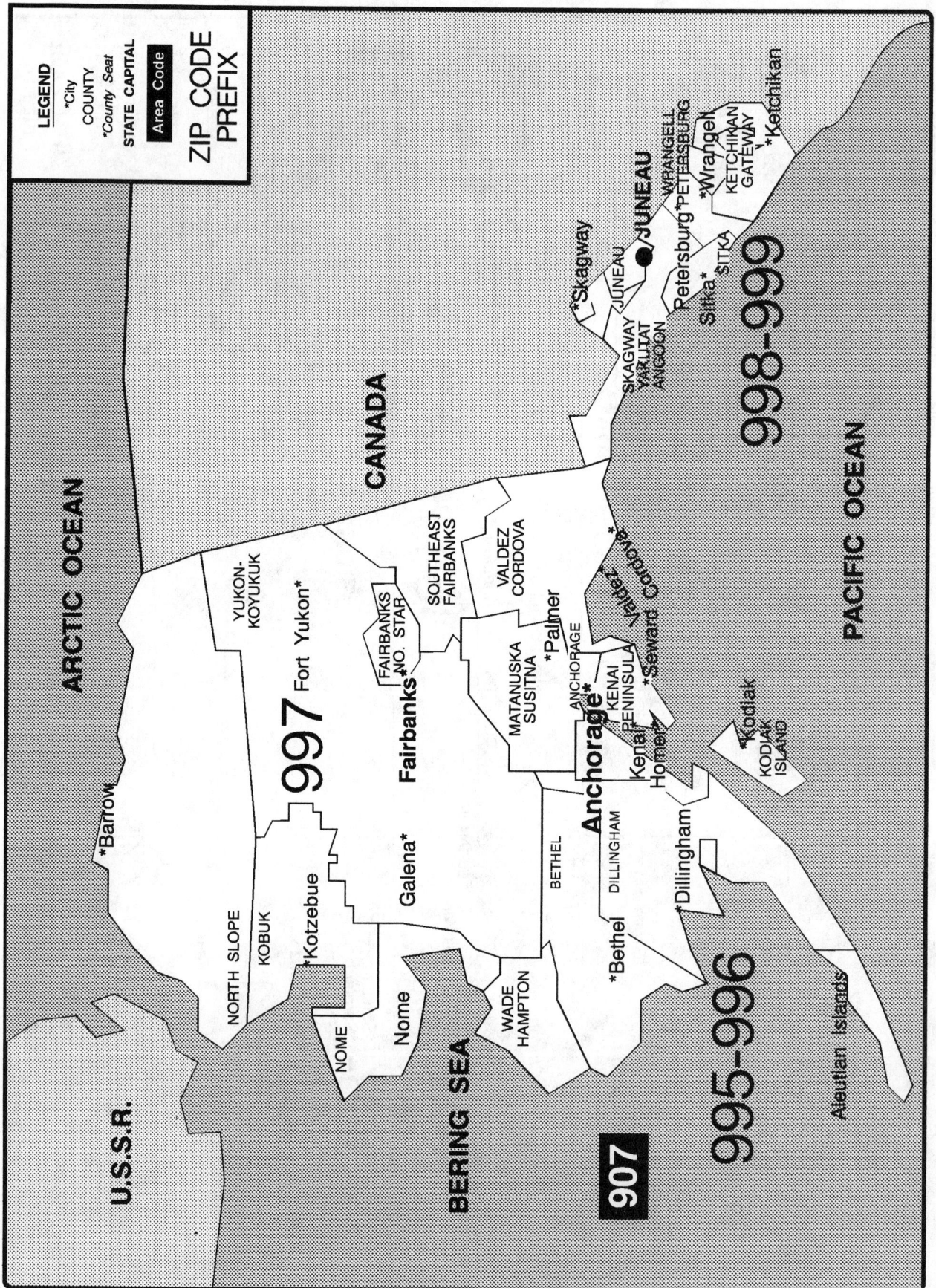

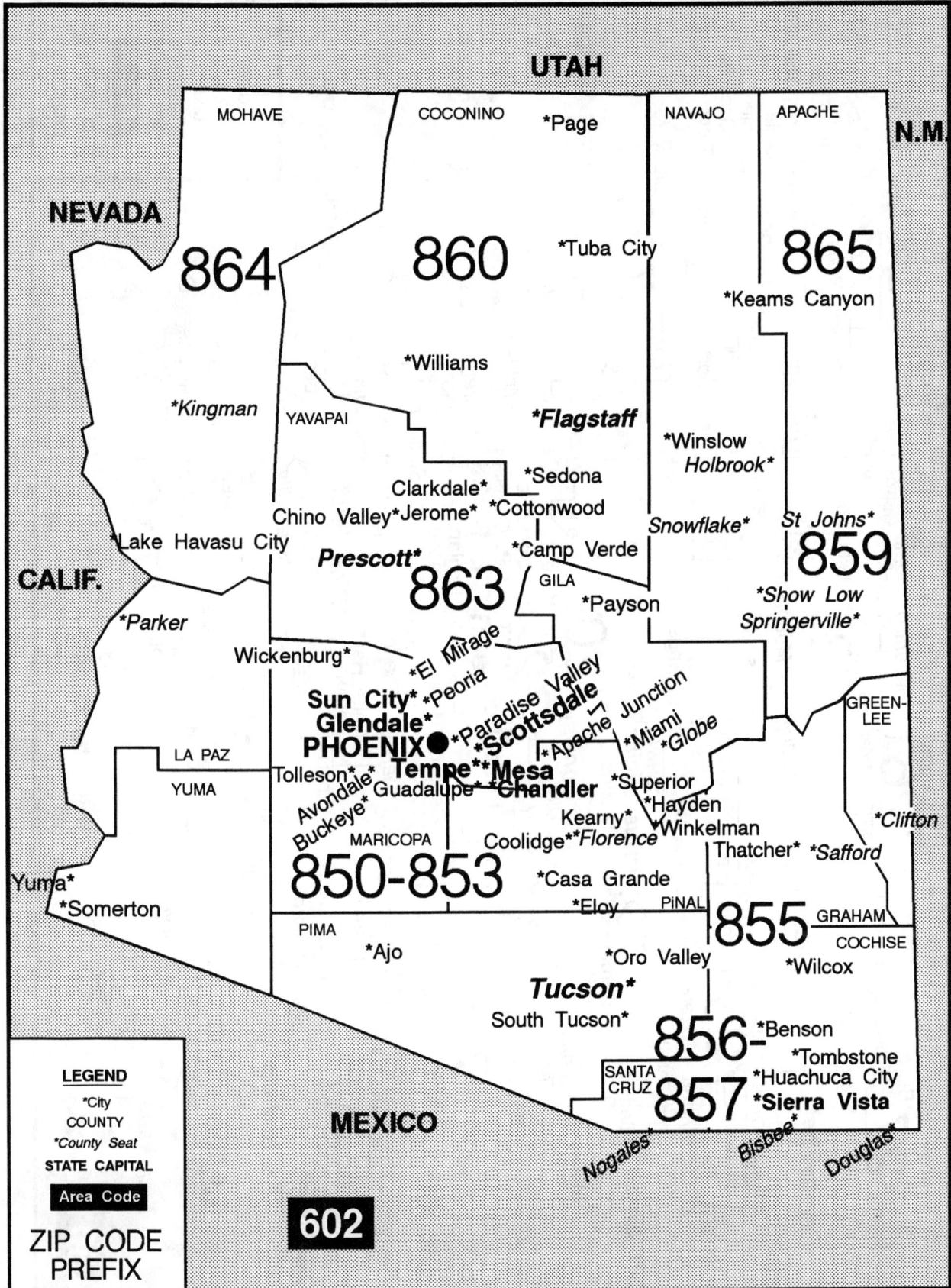

UTAH

MOHAVE   COCONINO   *Page   NAVAJO   APACHE   N.M.

NEVADA

864

860

*Tuba City

865

*Keams Canyon

*Williams

*Kingman

YAVAPAI

*Flagstaff

*Winslow
Holbrook*

*Sedona

Clarkdale*
Chino Valley *Jerome*   *Cottonwood

Snowflake*

St Johns*

859

CALIF.

Prescott*

*Camp Verde

863

GILA

*Payson

*Show Low
Springerville*

*Parker

Wickenburg*

*El Mirage

GREEN-
LEE

Lake Havasu City

*Peoria

Sun City*   Paradise Valley
Glendale*   *Scottsdale

Apache Junction

*Miami
*Globe

PHOENIX●

LA PAZ

YUMA

Tolleson*
Avondale*
Buckeye*

Tempe **Mesa
Guadalupe* *Chandler

*Apache

*Superior
*Hayden

*Clifton

MARICOPA

Kearny*
Coolidge* *Florence

Winkelman

Thatcher*   *Safford

Yuma*
*Somerton

850-853

*Casa Grande
*Eloy   PiNAL

855   GRAHAM

PIMA

*Ajo

*Oro Valley

*Wilcox

COCHISE

Tucson*

South Tucson*

856- *Benson

*Tombstone

SANTA
CRUZ

857

*Huachuca City
*Sierra Vista

MEXICO

Nogales*   Bisbee*   Douglas*

LEGEND
*City
COUNTY
*County Seat
STATE CAPITAL
Area Code

602

ZIP CODE
PREFIX

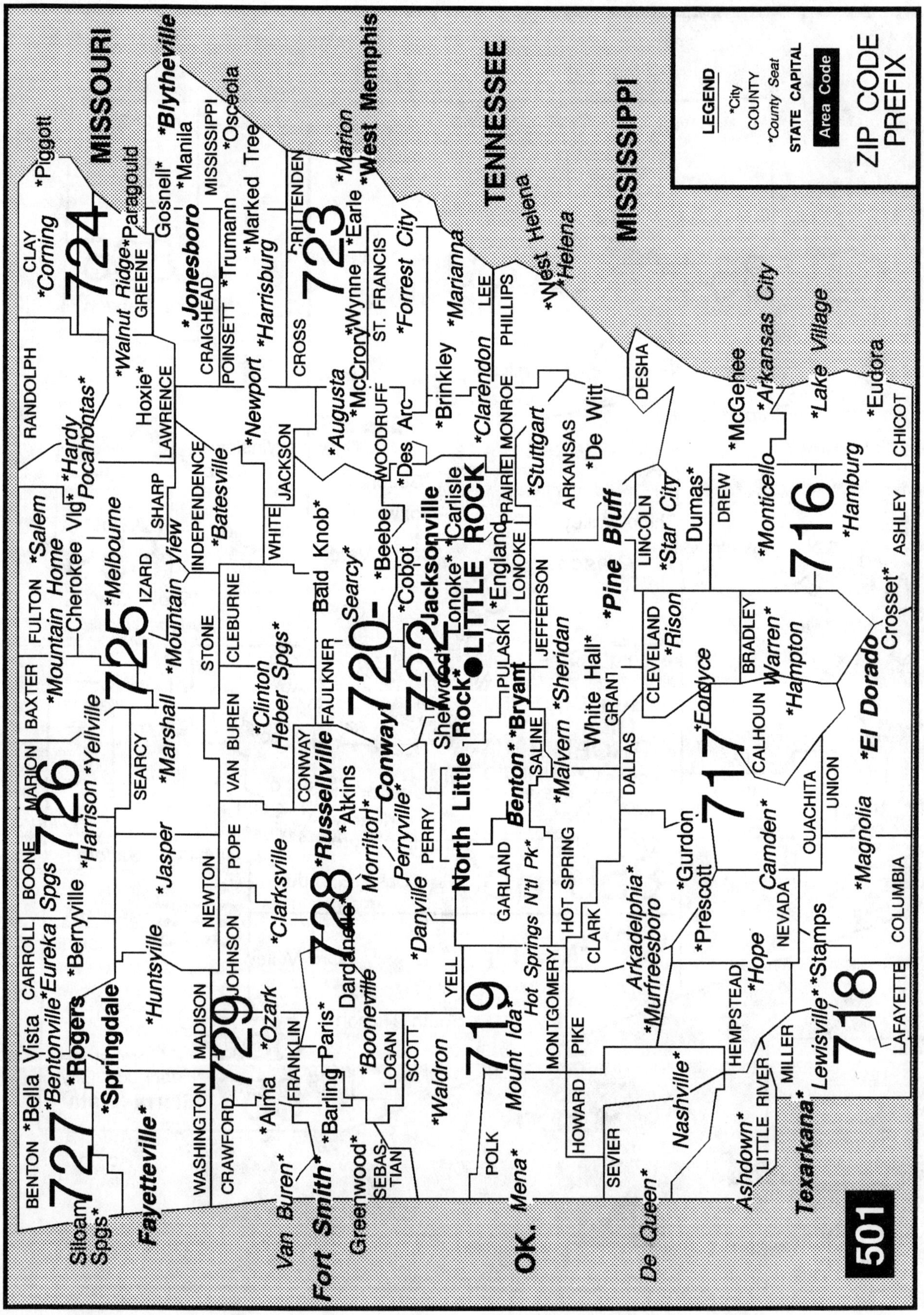
LEGEND
*City
COUNTY
*County Seat
STATE CAPITAL
Area Code
ZIP CODE PREFIX
501
MISSOURI
TENNESSEE
MISSISSIPPI
OK.
727
724
725
726
729
728
720-
722
723
719
717
716
718
●LITTLE ROCK
North Little Rock
*Jacksonville
Sherwood*
*Bryant
Benton*
*Pine Bluff
*Jonesboro
*Blytheville
*West Memphis
Fort Smith*
Fayetteville*
*Springdale
*Rogers
*El Dorado
Texarkana*
*Conway
*Russellville
Hot Springs N'tl Pk*
*Searcy
*Batesville
*Paragould
*Forrest City
*Helena
*West Helena
*Arkadelphia
*Camden
*Magnolia
*Hope
*Mountain Home
*Harrison
BENTON
CARROLL
BOONE
MARION
BAXTER
FULTON
RANDOLPH
CLAY
GREENE
LAWRENCE
SHARP
IZARD
STONE
SEARCY
NEWTON
MADISON
WASHINGTON
CRAWFORD
FRANKLIN
JOHNSON
POPE
VAN BUREN
CLEBURNE
INDEPENDENCE
JACKSON
WHITE
CRAIGHEAD
POINSETT
MISSISSIPPI
CRITTENDEN
CROSS
ST. FRANCIS
WOODRUFF
LEE
PHILLIPS
MONROE
PRAIRIE
LONOKE
PULASKI
FAULKNER
CONWAY
PERRY
YELL
LOGAN
SEBASTIAN
SCOTT
POLK
MONTGOMERY
GARLAND
SALINE
HOT SPRING
GRANT
JEFFERSON
ARKANSAS
DESHA
LINCOLN
CLEVELAND
DALLAS
CLARK
PIKE
HOWARD
SEVIER
LITTLE RIVER
HEMPSTEAD
NEVADA
OUACHITA
CALHOUN
BRADLEY
DREW
ASHLEY
CHICOT
UNION
COLUMBIA
LAFAYETTE
MILLER

SAN FRANCISCO BAY AREA

MARIN

*Novato

949

Fairfax*
San Anselmo*
*San Rafael
*Larkspur
Corte Madera*
Tiburon*
Belvedere*
Mill Valley*
Sausalito*

415

Pinole*
*Hercules
*Martinez
*San Pablo
*El Cerrito

CONTRA COSTA

945-948

Pittsburg* *Antioch
*Concord
*Pleasant Hill
*Walnut Creek
Lafayette*
*Orinda

Alameda & Contra Costa
Co's Change to Area
Code 510 on 9/2/1991.

Oakland
921
*Albany
*Alameda

SAN FRANCISCO

San Francisco
South San Francisco*
*Daly City
Pacifica*
San Bruno Hayward
Hillsborough* *Millbrae
Burlingame* *San Mateo
Belmont* *Foster City
San Carlos*
Half Moon Bay*
Atherton*
Menlo Park*
Palo Alto*
Portola Valley*
Los Altos*

San Lorenzo

953

*San Leandro
*Castro Valley
*Union City
*Fremont
*Newark
*Redwood City

*East Palo Altos
*Mountain View
*Sunnyvale

*Danville
*San Ramon
*Dublin
*Livermore
*Pleasanton

ALAMEDA

415
950-951

*Milpitas

408

SAN MATEO

940-944

Cupertino*
Saratoga*
*Santa Clara
*Campbell
*Los Gatos

*San Jose

SANTA CRUZ

*Boulder Creek
Felton*
Capitola*
*Scotts Valley
*Aptos

*Morgan Hill
*Gilroy
SANTA CLARA

PACIFIC OCEAN

Santa Cruz*

*Watsonville

LOS ANGELES & ORANGE COUNTIES

LOS ANGELES
San Fernando*

818
913-916

Glendale*
910-912
Burbank*
San Gabriel*
Alhambra*
Rosemead*

La Canada*
*Altadena
*Pasadena
*Sierra Madre
South Pasadena
San Marino
*Arcadia
*Temple City
*El Monte
Monterey Park*

*Monrovia
Azusa*
917-918
*Glendora
*Covina
*West Covina
*Baldwin Park
*La Puente

*Claremont
*San Dimas
*La Verne
*Walnut *Pomona

714

Bevery Hills*
*West Hollywood
*E Los Angeles

Los Angeles*
900-901
*Malibu
Culver City*
*Santa Monica
Hawthorne*
El Segundo*

Maywood*
Huntington Park*
*Bell
Walnut Park*
Cudahy*
Inglewood*

*Pico Rivera
*Bell Gardens
*Downey

*Whittier
*Willow Brook
*Santa Fe Sprs

*Diamond Bar

917-918

*La Mirada
*La Habra
*Brea
*Yorba Linda
*Placentia
*Fullerton

902-905

Lynnwood*
Gardena* Compton*
Manhattan Beach*
Torrance* Lakewood*
Hermosa Beach*
Redondo Beach*
Rolling Hills Estates*
*Lomita
Long Beach
*Signal Hill
Seal Beach*
Rancho Palos Verdes*

*Bellflower
*Norwalk
Paramount*
*Artesia
Cerritos*
*Hawaiian Gardens
*Los Alamitos
Westminster*
Fountain Valley*

906

*Buena Park
*Anaheim
*Garden Grove

*Orange

926-928

*Tustin
Irvine*

Santa Ana

213
907-908

*Cypress *Stanton

Huntington Beach* *Costa Mesa
Newport Beach*

*Laguna Hills
*Mission Viejo

Laguna Beach*
San Clemente*
*San Juan Capistrano
ORANGE

California

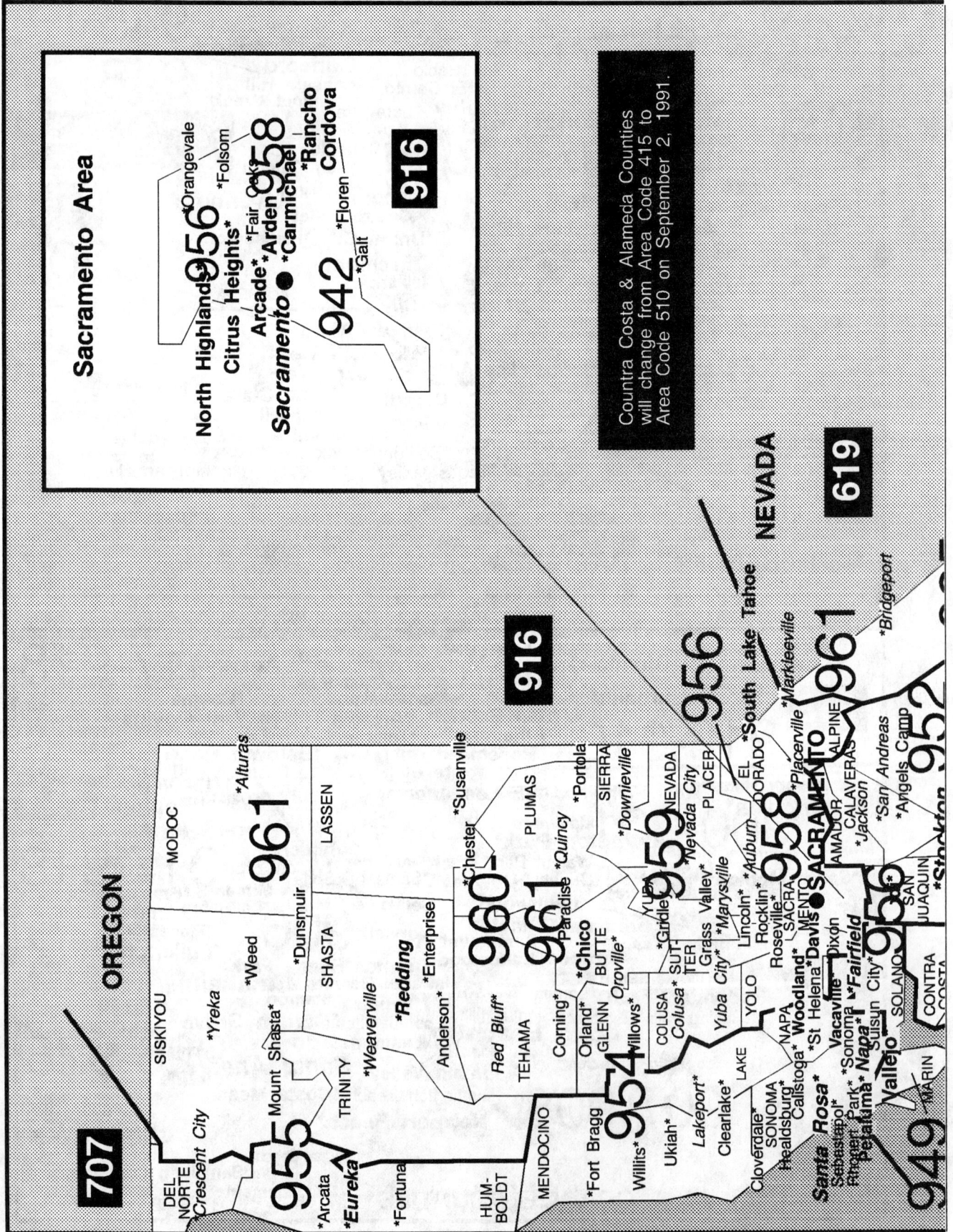

Sacramento Area

North Highlands 956 *Orangevale
Citrus Heights *Folsom
Arcade* *Fair
*Arden 958
Sacramento ● *Carmichael
942 *Galt
*Floren
*Rancho Cordova

916

Countra Costa & Alameda Counties will change from Area Code 415 to Area Code 510 on September 2, 1991.

OREGON

707

955
DEL NORTE
*Crescent City
*Arcata
*Eureka
*Fortuna

SISKIYOU
*Yreka
Mount Shasta*
*Weed
*Dunsmuir

961
MODOC
*Alturas

LASSEN
*Susanville

SHASTA
*Enterprise
*Redding
Anderson*
*Weaverville
TRINITY

HUM-BOLDT

MENDOCINO
*Fort Bragg
Willits*
Ukiah*
*Lakeport
Clearlake
LAKE

960
Red Bluff*
TEHAMA
Corning*
Orland*
GLENN
Willows*
Colusa*
COLUSA

961
*Paradise
*Chico
BUTTE
Oroville*
YUBA
Gridley*
SUTTER
Yuba City*
YOLO

PLUMAS
*Quincy
*Chester

960

SIERRA
*Downieville
NEVADA
Nevada City*
Grass Valley*
PLACER
*Marysville
Lincoln*
Rocklin*
Roseville*
Auburn

959

916

956
*South Lake Tahoe
EL DORADO
*Placerville
958 SACRAMENTO
Davis
Dixon
Woodland
SACRA-MENTO
NEVADA
*Markleeville
ALPINE
619

*Portola

SANTA ROSA*
Sebastopol*
*Sonoma
Petaluma*
*Napa
Vallejo
MARIN

954
NAPA
Calistoga*
*St Helena
Vacaville*
*Fairfield
Suisun City*
SOLANO
CONTRA COSTA

949

952
CALAVERAS
*San Andreas
*Angels Camp
AMADOR
*Jackson
*Stockton
SAN JOAQUIN
955

961

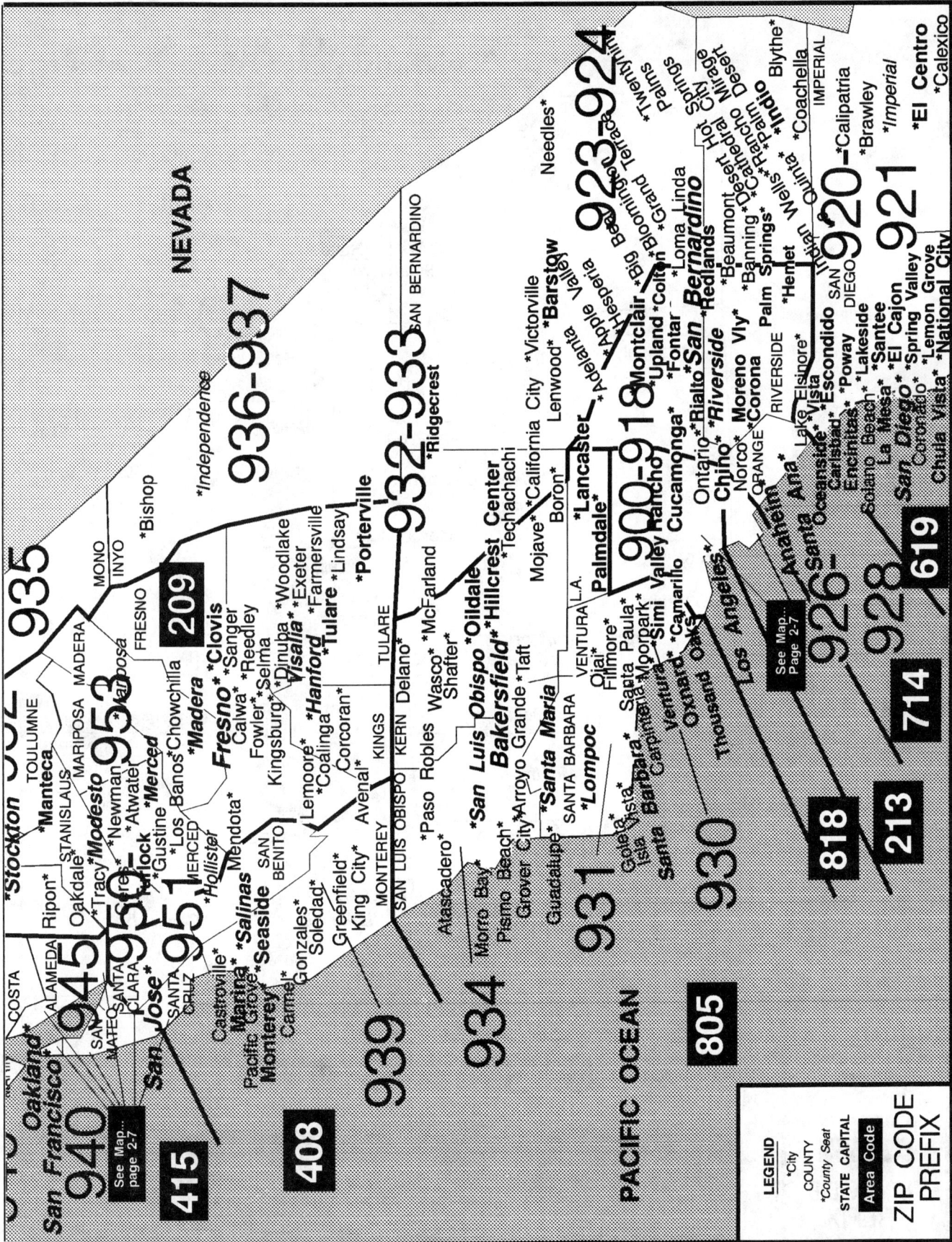

NEVADA

PACIFIC OCEAN

Oakland*
San Francisco*
940
See Map... page 2-7
415

COSTA
ALAMEDA
Ripon*
Stockton*
932
935
San Jose*
945
950-
951
951
SANTA CLARA
SAN MATEO
SANTA CRUZ
*Tracy
Oakdale*
STANISLAUS
TOULUMNE
Manteca
*Turlock-
Modesto
953
*Newman
MARIPOSA
MADERA
MADERA
Mariposa*
MONO
INYO
FRESNO
209
408

Castroville*
Marina*
Salinas
Seaside*
Monterey
Pacific Grove*
Carmel*
Gonzales*
Soledad*
Greenfield*
King City*
MONTEREY
SAN BENITO
BENITO
Mendota
Hollister*
MERCED
*Los Banos
*Gustine
*Atwater
Merced
Chowchilla*
*Madera
Fresno*Clovis
*Sanger
Calwa*
Fowler*
*Reedley
*Selma
Kingsburg*
Lemoore
*Coalinga
Corcoran*
Avenal*
KINGS
Hanford
*Dinuba *Woodlake
Visalia *Exeter
*Farmersville
*Lindsay
Tulare
TULARE
*Porterville
*Bishop
*Independence

939
934
931
930

Atascadero*
Paso Robles*
SAN LUIS OBISPO
Morro Bay*
Pismo Beach*
*Arroyo Grande
Grover City*
Guadalupe*
Santa Maria
San Luis Obispo *Oildale
Bakersfield *Hillcrest Center
KERN
Delano*
McFarland*
Wasco*
Shafter*
*Taft
*Ridgecrest
932-933
936-937

Goleta*
Isla Vista*
Santa Barbara
Carpinteria*
SANTA BARBARA
Lompoc
VENTURA
Ojai*
Fillmore*
Santa Paula*
Moorpark*
Ventura
Oxnard*
*Camarillo
*Simi Valley
Thousand Oaks
L.A.
Techachachi*
Mojave*
*California City
Boron*
Lancaster*
Palmdale
900-918

Los Angeles
See Map...
Page 2-7
805
818
213
714
619

Victorville*
Lenwood* **Barstow**
Adelanto Valley
Apple Valley
*Hesperia
*Rancho Cucamonga
Montclair*
*Upland *Colton
Fontar-
*Rialto **San Bernardino**
Ontario* **Redlands**
Chino* **Riverside**
Norco* Moreno Vly*
*Corona
ORANGE
RIVERSIDE
Anaheim
Santa Ana
926-
Lake Elsinore*
*Oceanside
Carlsbad*
*Encinitas
Solano Beach*
Escondido
*Poway
*Lakeside
*Santee
La Mesa*
*El Cajon
*Spring Valley
*Lemon Grove
*National City
San Diego
Coronado*
Chula Vista
928
920
921

Needles*
SAN BERNARDINO
923-924
Twentynine Palms
*Grand Terrace
*Big Bear
*Bloomington
*Beaumont
*Banning
Palm Springs*
*Desert Hot Springs
Desert Hot
Springs
Cathedral*
*Rancho Mirage
Palm*
Indio
*Coachella
*La Quinta
Hemet*
Indian Wells*
SAN DIEGO
*Calipatria
*Brawley
*Imperial
IMPERIAL
*Blythe
*Coachella
El Centro
*Calexico

LEGEND
*City
COUNTY
*County Seat
STATE CAPITAL
Area Code
ZIP CODE PREFIX

Colorado

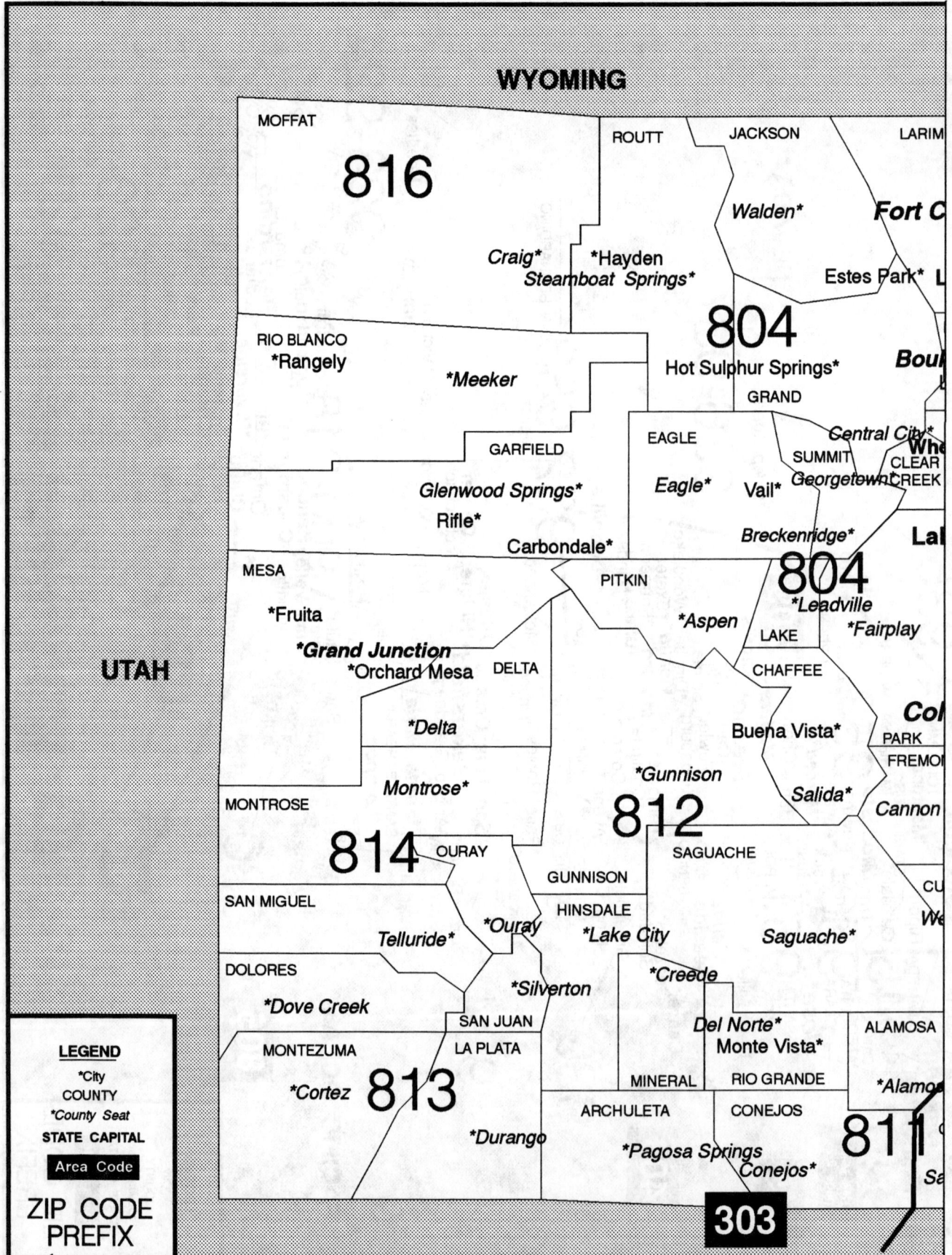

WYOMING

MOFFAT

816

ROUTT JACKSON LARIM

Walden* **Fort C**

Craig* *Hayden
Steamboat Springs* Estes Park* L

804 **Bou**

RIO BLANCO
Rangely Hot Sulphur Springs

*Meeker GRAND

GARFIELD EAGLE Central City* **Wh**
SUMMIT CLEAR
Glenwood Springs* Eagle* Vail* Georgetown CREEK
Rifle* Breckenridge* **Lal**
Carbondale*

MESA PITKIN **804**
*Fruita *Leadville
*Aspen *Fairplay
*Grand Junction LAKE
*Orchard Mesa DELTA
CHAFFEE **Co**

UTAH *Delta Buena Vista* PARK
FREMO

Gunnison Salida
MONTROSE Montrose* **812** Cannon
SAGUACHE

814 OURAY
GUNNISON CU
SAN MIGUEL HINSDALE We
Telluride* *Ouray *Lake City Saguache*

DOLORES *Creede
*Dove Creek *Silverton
SAN JUAN Del Norte* ALAMOSA

MONTEZUMA LA PLATA Monte Vista*
*Cortez **813** MINERAL RIO GRANDE *Alamo
ARCHULETA CONEJOS
*Durango **811**
*Pagosa Springs
Conejos* Sa

303

NEBRASKA

WELD

805

ollins

*Windsor   *Eaton

*Greeley

LOGAN

806

LA SALLE *Evans

Loveland*   La Salle *Evans

Berthoud*

BOULDER

der*

Longmont

*Louisville *Platteville

*Lafayette *Fort Lupton

*Broomfield *Brighton

Westminster

MORGAN

*Fort Morgan

*Brush

*Julesburg

SEDGWICK

PHILLIPS

*Sterling

807 *Holyoke

YUMA

WASHINGTON

*Akron

*Yuma

Wray

Arvada*   *Northglenn

at Ridge* *Thornton

Golden* DENVER

DENVER ●

GILPIN

ADAMS

*Commerce City

*Aurora

ARAPAHOE

*Englewood

kewood* *Littleton

JEFFER-
SON

*Castle
Rock

*Kiowa

DOUGLAS   ELBERT

TELLER

*Woodland Park

*Manitou Springs

olorado Springs*

*Cripple Creek

NT

City*

STER

stcliffe*

LINCOLN

*Limon

*Hugo

**800-
803**

KIT CARSON

*Burlington

719

CHEYENNE

Cheyenne Wells*

**808-
809**

*Security

*Fountain

PEUBLO

*Florence

*Peublo

CROWLEY

*Ordway

KIOWA

*Eads

BENT

ROCKY FORD

Rocky Ford*

*La Junta

PROWERS

*Lamar

*Las Animas

OTERO

KANSAS

HUERFANO

*Walsenburg   LAS ANIMAS

810

BACA

*Springfield

COSTILLA

an Luis*   *Trinidad

NEW MEXICO   **OKLAHOMA**

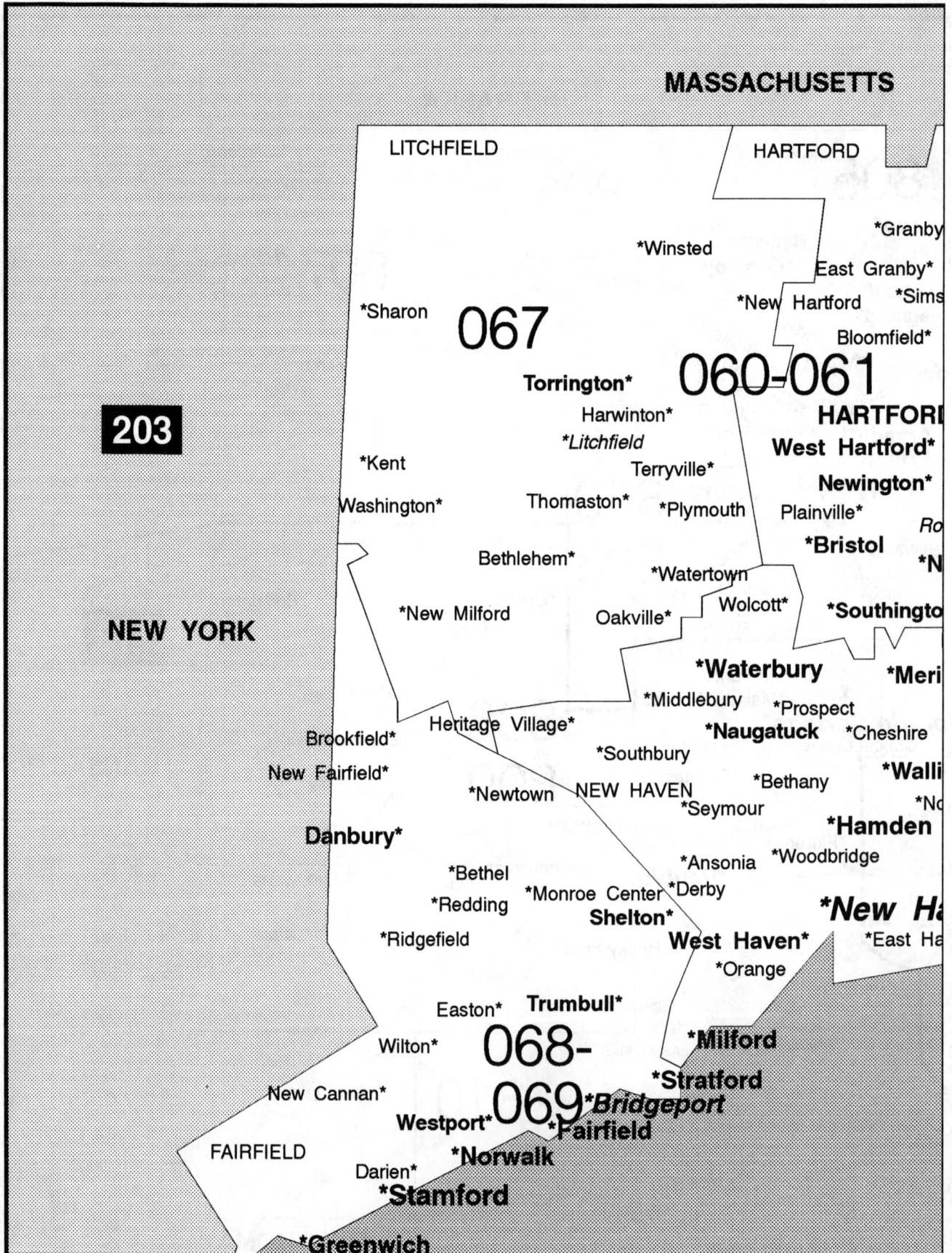

Connecticut

MASSACHUSETTS

LITCHFIELD

HARTFORD

*Granby

*Winsted

East Granby*

*New Hartford

*Sims

Bloomfield*

*Sharon

067

060-061

HARTFORD

Torrington*

Harwinton*

West Hartford*

203

*Litchfield

Terryville*

Newington*

*Kent

Thomaston*

*Plymouth

Plainville*

Washington*

Bristol

*N

Ro

Bethlehem*

*Watertown

*Southingto

NEW YORK

*New Milford

Oakville*

Wolcott*

Waterbury

*Meri

*Middlebury

*Prospect

Naugatuck

*Cheshire

Heritage Village*

*Southbury

*Walli

Brookfield*

*Bethany

*N

New Fairfield*

*Newtown

NEW HAVEN

*Seymour

Hamden

Danbury*

*Ansonia

*Woodbridge

*Bethel

*Derby

*New Ha

*Redding

*Monroe Center

Shelton*

*Ridgefield

West Haven*

*East Ha

*Orange

Easton*

Trumbull*

068-

Milford

Wilton*

Stratford

069

Bridgeport

New Cannan*

Fairfield

Westport*

Norwalk

FAIRFIELD

Darien*

Stamford

Greenwich

TOLLAND   WINDHAM

Suffield*   *Enfield   *Somers   Thompson*

*Windsor Locks   *Putnam

                    *Ellington   *Willington   *Pomfret
bury *Windsor   *East Windsor   *Tolland   062

*South Windsor

        *Vernon   *Coventry   *Danielson

● *Manchester   *Brooklyn
  *East Hartford   *Bolton   RHODE
Wethersfield   Columbia *Willimatic *Windham   ISLAND

    *Glastonbury   *Hebron   Canterbury*   *Plainfield
cky Hill*
    *Marlborough
ew Britain   NEW LONDON
                                              *Jewett City
  *Cromwell   *Lebanon   *Griswold
Portland* *East Hampton *Colchester *Lisbon   *Preston
*Middletown
                                              *Norwich
den   MIDDLESEX
  *Middlefield   *Salem   063
  *Durham   *East Haddam
ngford   *Ledyard
   064-066   *North Stonington
rth Haven
*Northford   *Deep River   *Pawcatuck
North Branford   Essex   *East Lyme
aven *Killingworth   *Waterford *New London
ven   *Groton
  *Branford *Guilford *Madison *Clinton *Old Saybrook *Old Lyme

LONG ISLAND SOUND

LEGEND
*City
COUNTY
*County Seat
STATE CAPITAL
Area Code

ZIP CODE
PREFIX

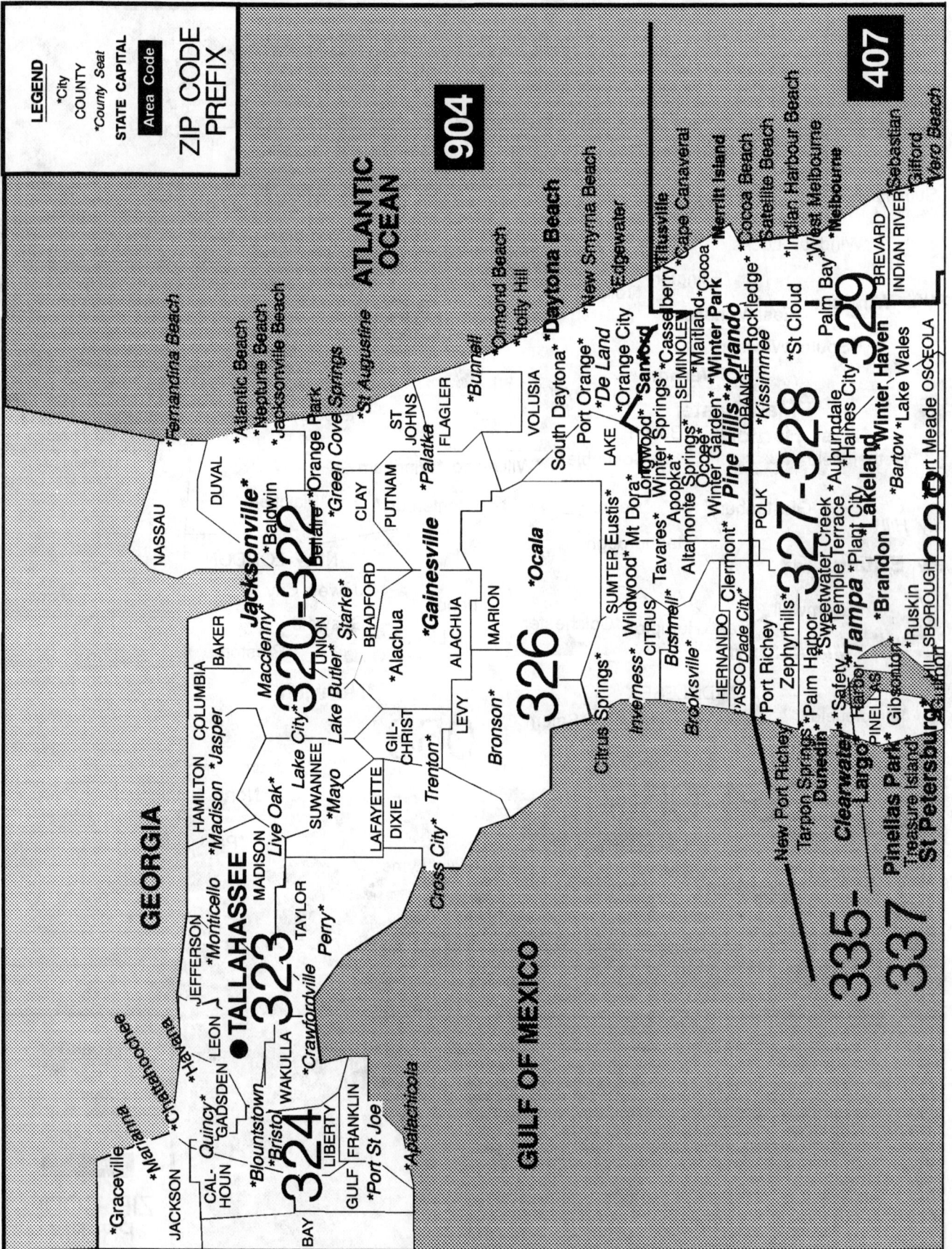

Florida

LEGEND
*City
COUNTY
*County Seat
STATE CAPITAL
Area Code
ZIP CODE PREFIX

904

407

ATLANTIC OCEAN

GEORGIA

GULF OF MEXICO

*Graceville
*Marianna
*Chattahoochee
*Havana
JACKSON
CALHOUN
*Quincy
GADSDEN
LEON
*Monticello
JEFFERSON
*Bristol
*Blountstown
LIBERTY
WAKULLA
*Crawfordville
GULF
*Port St Joe
FRANKLIN
*Apalachicola
BAY

TALLAHASSEE
323

324

HAMILTON
COLUMBIA
*Madison *Jasper
MADISON
Live Oak
TAYLOR
*Perry
Lake City*
SUWANNEE
*Mayo *Lake Butler*
LAFAYETTE
DIXIE
Cross City
GIL-CHRIST
Trenton

NASSAU
*Fernandina Beach
DUVAL
*Atlantic Beach
*Neptune Beach
*Jacksonville Beach
BAKER
*Macclenny
UNION
*Starke
BRADFORD
*Alachua
*Baldwin
Jacksonville*
*Orange Park
*Green Cove Springs

320-322

LEVY
Bronson
ALACHUA
Gainesville
MARION

326

*Ocala

CLAY
PUTNAM
*Palatka
ST JOHNS
*St Augustine
FLAGLER
*Bunnell

VOLUSIA
*Ormond Beach
*Holly Hill
Daytona Beach
*New Smyrna Beach
*Edgewater

SUMTER
Eustis*
Wildwood*
Mt Dora*
*Tavares
LAKE
*De Land
*Orange City
Port Orange*
South Daytona*

CITRUS
Inverness
Bushnell
HERNANDO
Brooksville

PASCO
Dade City
New Port Richey
*Tarpon Springs
*Dunedin
*Palm Harbor
Zephyrhills*
Safety Harbor
*Clearwater
*Largo
PINELLAS
*Treasure Island
Pinellas Park*
St Petersburg*

335-337

Citrus Springs*
Port Richey

Clermont*
POLK
Plant City*
*Auburndale
*Haines City
*Winter Haven
Lakeland
*Bartow *Lake Wales
*Port Meade
*Brandon
*Ruskin
*Gibsonton
HILLSBOROUGH
Tampa*
*Temple Terrace
*Sweetwater Creek

327-328

329

OSCEOLA
*Kissimmee
*St Cloud
Orlando
ORANGE
Pine Hills
*Ocoee
Apopka*
Altamonte Springs
SEMINOLE
*Winter Park
*Winter Garden
*Maitland
*Casselberry
*Longwood
Winter Springs*
*Sanford
*Rockledge
*Cocoa

BREVARD
INDIAN RIVER
*Titusville
*Cape Canaveral
*Merritt Island
*Cocoa Beach
*Satellite Beach
*Indian Harbour Beach
*West Melbourne
*Melbourne
Palm Bay*
*Sebastian
*Gifford
*Vero Beach

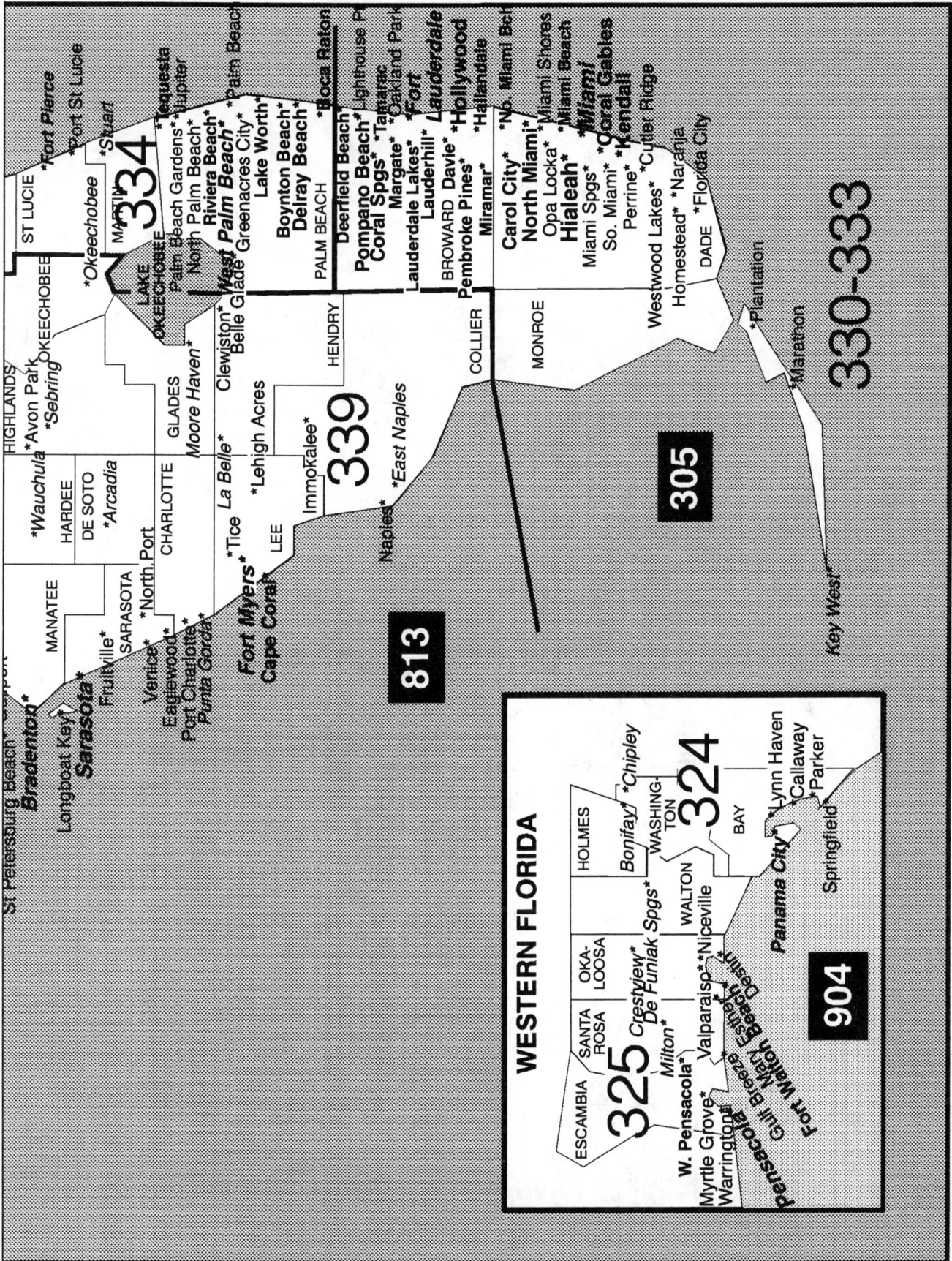

334

330-333

339

305

813

WESTERN FLORIDA

324

325

904

ST LUCIE

MARTIN

*Fort Pierce
*Port St Lucie
*Stuart

*Tequesta
*Jupiter
Palm Beach Gardens*
North Palm Beach*
Riviera Beach*
West Palm Beach
Lake Worth*
Greenacres City*
Boynton Beach*
Delray Beach*

Palm Beach
*Boca Raton
Deerfield Beach*
*Lighthouse Pt
Pompano Beach*
Coral Spgs*
Tamarac*
Margate*
*Oakland Park
Lauderdale Lakes*
Lauderhill*
Fort
Lauderdale
*Davie
*Hollywood
*Hallandale

*Okeechobee

LAKE
OKEECHOBEE

OKEECHOBEE
*Sebring
*Avon Park
HIGHLANDS

*Wauchula
HARDEE
DE SOTO
*Arcadia

*Okeechobee

Clewiston*
Belle Glade
Moore Haven*
GLADES

HENDRY

La Belle
*Lehigh Acres
ImmoKalee*
*East Naples

*Tice
CHARLOTTE
*North Port
SARASOTA
Fruitville*
*Venice
Eagiewood*
Port Charlotte*
*Punta Gorda

Naples*

COLLIER

MONROE

BROWARD
Pembroke Pines*
Miramar*

Carol City*
North Miami*
Opa Locka*
Hialeah*
Miami Spgs*
So. Miami*
Perrine*

*No. Miami Bch
Miami Shores*
Miami Beach
Miami
Coral Gables*
Kendall*
*Cutler Ridge

Westwood Lakes*
Homestead*
*Naranja
*Florida City
DADE

*Plantation

*Marathon

Key West

St Petersburg Beach*
Longboat Key*
Sarasota
Bradenton*
MANATEE

Fort Myers
Cape Coral*
LEE

PALM BEACH

HOLMES
Bonifay*
*Chipley
WASHING-
TON
BAY
*Lynn Haven
Callaway*
Parker*

ESCAMBIA
SANTA
ROSA
OKA-
LOOSA
Crestview*
De Funiak Spgs*
Milton*
Valparaiso*
*Niceville
WALTON

Panama City*
Springfield

W. Pensacola*
Myrtle Grove*
Warrington*
Pensacola
Gulf Breeze*
Fort Walton Beach
Destin*

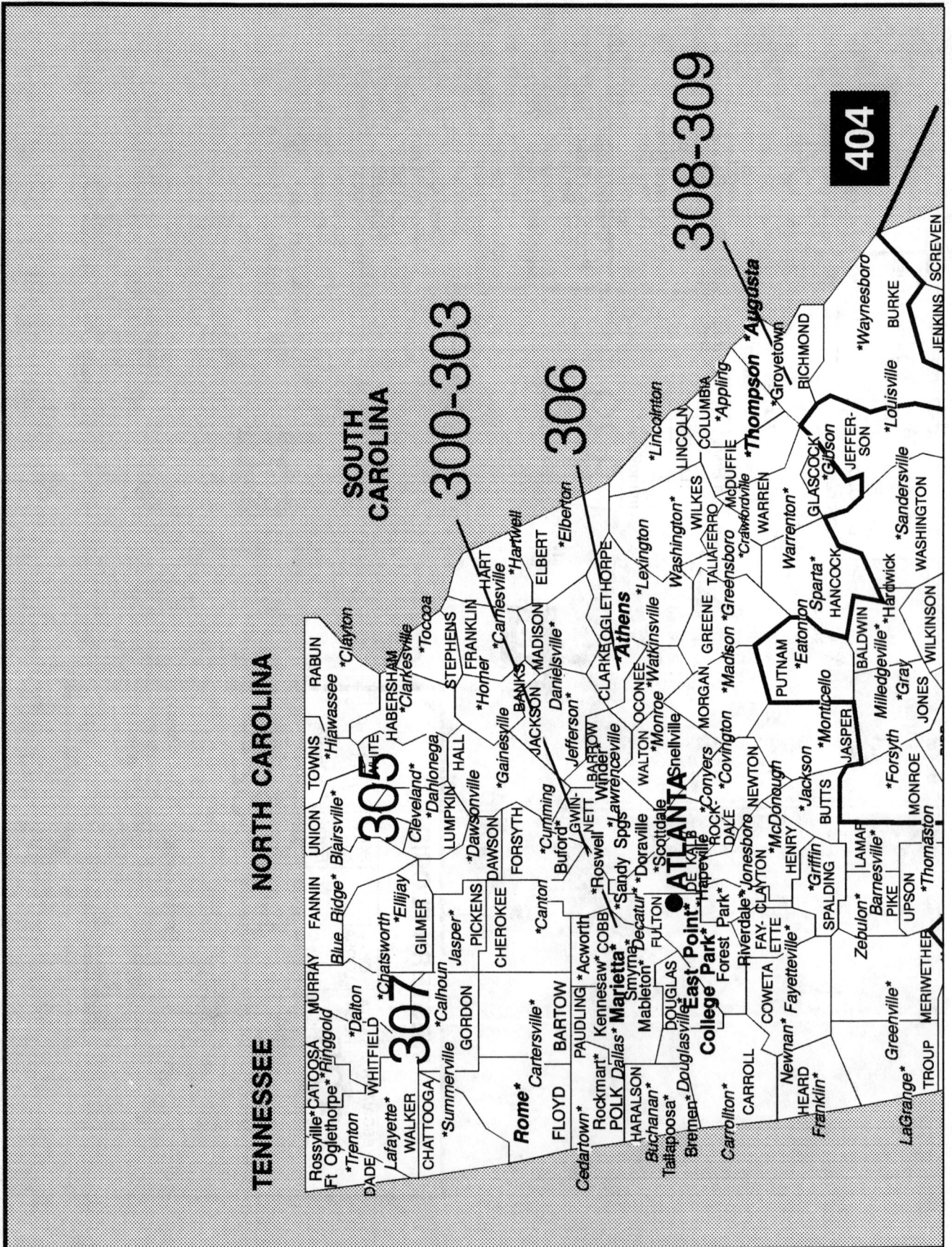

Georgia

TENNESSEE

NORTH CAROLINA

SOUTH CAROLINA

300-303

306

305

307

308-309

404

RABUN
TOWNS
UNION
FANNIN
MURRAY
CATOOSA
WHITFIELD
DADE
WALKER
CHATTOOGA
GORDON
GILMER
PICKENS
CHEROKEE
BARTOW
FLOYD
POLK
HARALSON
PAULDING
COBB
FULTON
DE KALB
DOUGLAS
CARROLL
COWETA
HEARD
TROUP
MERIWETHER
PIKE
UPSON
SPALDING
LAMAR
BUTTS
HENRY
CLAYTON
FAY-ETTE
NEWTON
MORGAN
GREENE
TALIAFERRO
WILKES
LINCOLN
COLUMBIA
RICHMOND
McDUFFIE
WARREN
GLASCOCK
HANCOCK
BALDWIN
JONES
MONROE
JASPER
PUTNAM
JACKSON
WALTON
OCONEE
CLARKE
OGLETHORPE
MADISON
BANKS
FRANKLIN
HART
ELBERT
STEPHENS
HABERSHAM
HALL
LUMPKIN
DAWSON
FORSYTH
GWIN-NETT
BARROW
JEFFER-SON
BURKE
JENKINS
SCREVEN
WILKINSON
WASHINGTON
JACKSON
MONROE
CRAWFORD

Rossville*
Ft Oglethorpe*
*Ringgold
*Trenton
Lafayette*
*Dalton
*Chatsworth
*Summerville
*Calhoun
*Ellijay
*Jasper
*Canton
Cartersville*
Rome*
Cedartown*
Rockmart*
Dallas*
Buchanan*
Tallapoosa*
Bremen*
Douglasville*
Carrollton*
Franklin*
Greenville*
LaGrange*
Newnan*
Fayetteville*
Riverdale*
Jonesboro*
McDonough*
Griffin*
Zebulon*
Barnesville*
*Thomaston
*Forsyth
*Gray
Milledgeville*
Hardwick*
Sandersville*
*Louisville
*Waynesboro
Sparta*
*Eatonton
*Monticello
*Jackson
*Covington
*Conyers
Snellville*
*Lawrenceville
Winder*
*Jefferson
*Watkinsville
Athens
*Monroe
*Madison
Greensboro*
*Crawfordville
Washington*
*Lexington
*Lincolnton
*Appling
Columbia
RICHMOND
*Groveton
*Thomson
*Augusta
*Gibson
*Warrenton
*Danielsville
*Carnesville
*Horner
*Hartwell
*Elberton
*Toccoa
*Clarkesville
*Cleveland
*Dahlonega
*Dawsonville
*Gainesville
*Cumming
*Buford
Roswell*
Sandy Spgs*
Marietta*
Kennesaw*
Acworth*
Smyrna*
Mableton*
*Decatur
*Doraville
*Scottdale
ATLANTA
East Point*
College Park*
Forest Park*
Hapeville*
*Blairsville
*Hiawassee
*Clayton
*Blue Ridge
Chatsworth
Ellijay

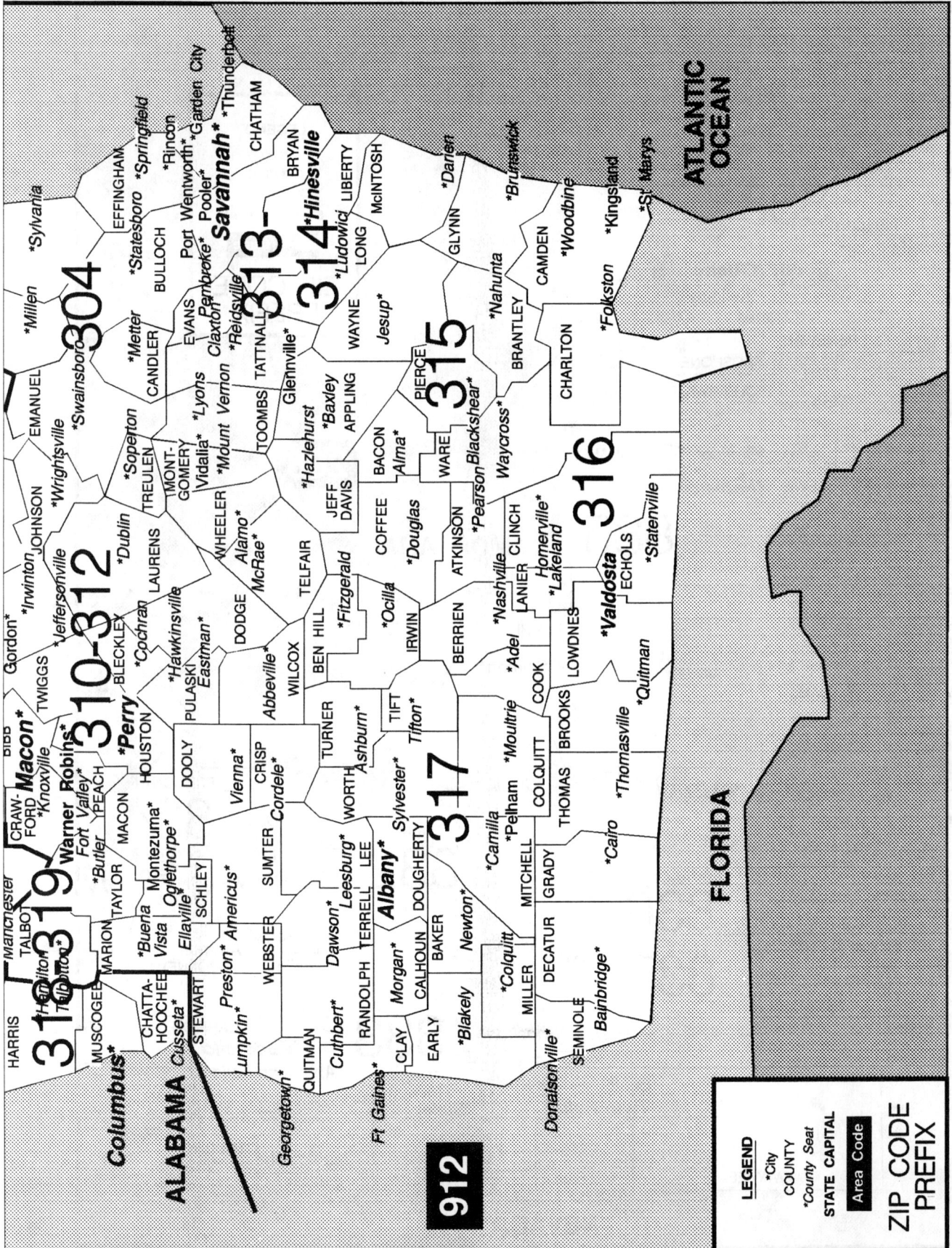

ATLANTIC OCEAN

FLORIDA

ALABAMA

304

310-312

313-

314

315

316

317

318

319

912

LEGEND
*City
COUNTY
*County Seat
STATE CAPITAL
Area Code
ZIP CODE PREFIX

*Sylvania
*Millen
EFFINGHAM
*Springfield
*Statesboro
*Rincon
Port Wentworth
*Garden City
*Pooler
*Thunderbolt
CHATHAM
Savannah
BRYAN
*Hinesville
LIBERTY
LONG
*Ludowici
McINTOSH
*Darien
*Brunswick
GLYNN
*Woodbine
CAMDEN
*Kingsland
*St. Marys
*Folkston
CHARLTON
BULLOCH
EVANS
CANDLER
*Metter
Pembroke*
Claxton*
*Reidsville
TATTNALL
TOOMBS
*Glennville
WAYNE
Jesup*
BRANTLEY
*Nahunta
EMANUEL
*Swainsboro
*Wrightsville
JOHNSON
*Lyons
*Mount Vernon
Vidalia*
MONT-GOMERY
TREUTLEN
WHEELER
Alamo*
McRae*
TELFAIR
*Hazlehurst
*Baxley
APPLING
BACON
Alma*
PIERCE
*Blackshear
WARE
Pearson*
*Waycross
CLINCH
*Homerville
ECHOLS
*Statenville
*Gordon
*Irwinton
TWIGGS
*Jeffersonville
*Dublin
LAURENS
*Cochran
BLECKLEY
*Hawkinsville
Eastman*
PULASKI
DODGE
WILCOX
Abbeville*
BEN HILL
*Fitzgerald
JEFF DAVIS
COFFEE
*Douglas
ATKINSON
*Nashville
LANIER
*Lakeland
LOWNDES
*Valdosta
*Quitman
BERRIEN
Macon*
*Knoxville
CRAW-FORD
BIBB
Warner Robins*
Fort Valley*
*Butler
PEACH
MACON
Montezuma*
Oglethorpe*
HOUSTON
*Perry
DOOLY
Vienna*
CRISP
Cordele*
TURNER
Ashburn*
WORTH
TIFT
Tifton*
IRWIN
*Ocilla
*Adel
COOK
COLQUITT
*Moultrie
BROOKS
*Quitman
Manchester
TALBOT
*Hamilton
HARRIS
Columbus*
MUSCOGEE
*Cusseta
CHATTA-HOOCHEE
STEWART
*Buena Vista
Ellaville*
SCHLEY
Americus*
SUMTER
*Leesburg
LEE
Albany*
DOUGHERTY
Newton*
BAKER
MITCHELL
*Camilla
*Pelham
THOMAS
*Thomasville
GRADY
*Cairo
*Thompson
*Thomaston
MARION
TAYLOR
Lumpkin*
Preston*
WEBSTER
Cuthbert*
RANDOLPH
Dawson*
TERRELL
Morgan*
CALHOUN
Newton*
Colquitt*
MILLER
DECATUR
Bainbridge*
SEMINOLE
Donalsonville*
QUITMAN
Georgetown*
CLAY
Ft. Gaines*
EARLY
*Blakely

Idaho

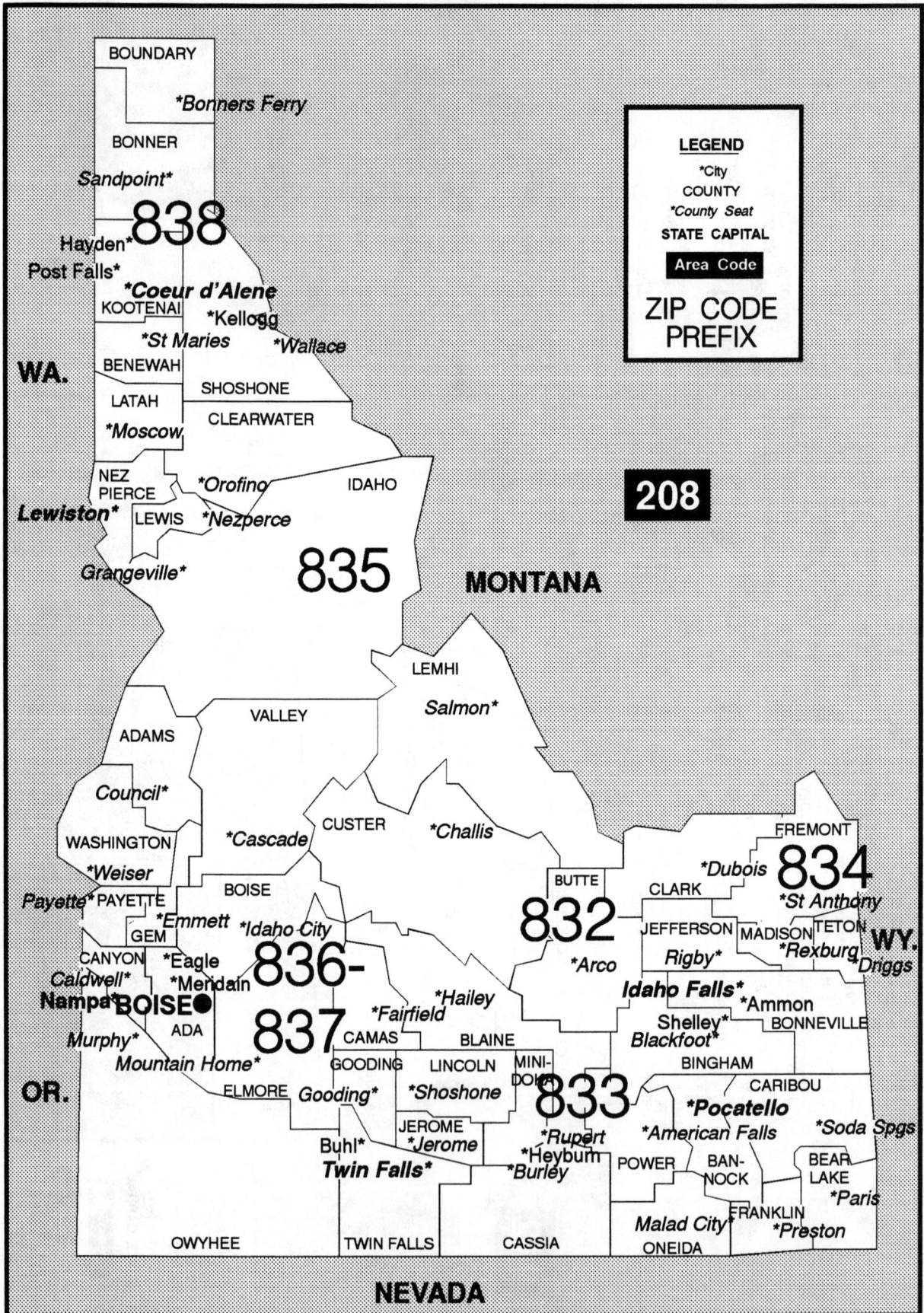

BOUNDARY

Bonners Ferry

BONNER

*Sandpoint**

838

Hayden**
Post Falls**

Coeur d'Alene
KOOTENAI
Kellogg

St Maries *Wallace*

BENEWAH

WA.

SHOSHONE

LATAH

CLEARWATER

Moscow

NEZ PIERCE *Orofino* **IDAHO**

Lewiston **LEWIS** *Nezperce*

Grangeville**

835 **MONTANA**

208

LEMHI

VALLEY *Salmon**

ADAMS

*Council**

CUSTER *Challis*

WASHINGTON

Weiser

BUTTE

832

FREMONT

Dubois **834**

CLARK *St Anthony*

JEFFERSON **MADISON** **TETON**

Rigby *Rexburg* **WY.**
Driggs

Arco

Payette* **PAYETTE**

Emmett

BOISE

Idaho City

GEM

Eagle

836-

Meridian

CANYON

Caldwell**

Nampa **BOISE**●

Murphy** **ADA**

Mountain Home**

837

CAMAS

Fairfield

Hailey

Idaho Falls

Shelley** *Ammon*
BONNEVILLE
Blackfoot

BINGHAM

CARIBOU

Pocatello

BLAINE

LINCOLN

Shoshone

MINIDOKA

833

OR.

ELMORE *Gooding*

GOODING

JEROME

Jerome

Buhl**

Twin Falls

Rupert
*Heyburn
Burley

American Falls

Soda Spgs

POWER **BANNOCK**

BEAR LAKE

Paris

FRANKLIN
Malad City* *Preston*

ONEIDA

OWYHEE

TWIN FALLS

CASSIA

NEVADA

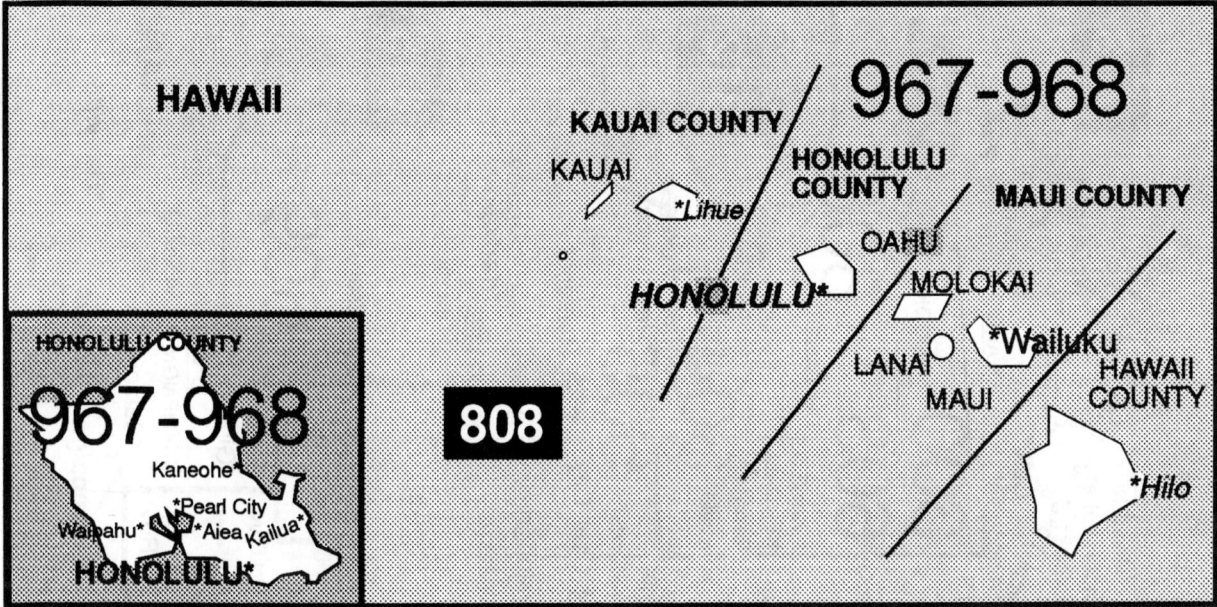

HAWAII

KAUAI COUNTY

967-968

KAUAI

*Lihue

HONOLULU COUNTY

MAUI COUNTY

OAHU

HONOLULU*

MOLOKAI

*Wailuku

LANAI

MAUI

HAWAII COUNTY

*Hilo

808

HONOLULU COUNTY

967-968

Kaneohe*

*Pearl City

Waipahu*   *Aiea Kailua*

HONOLULU*

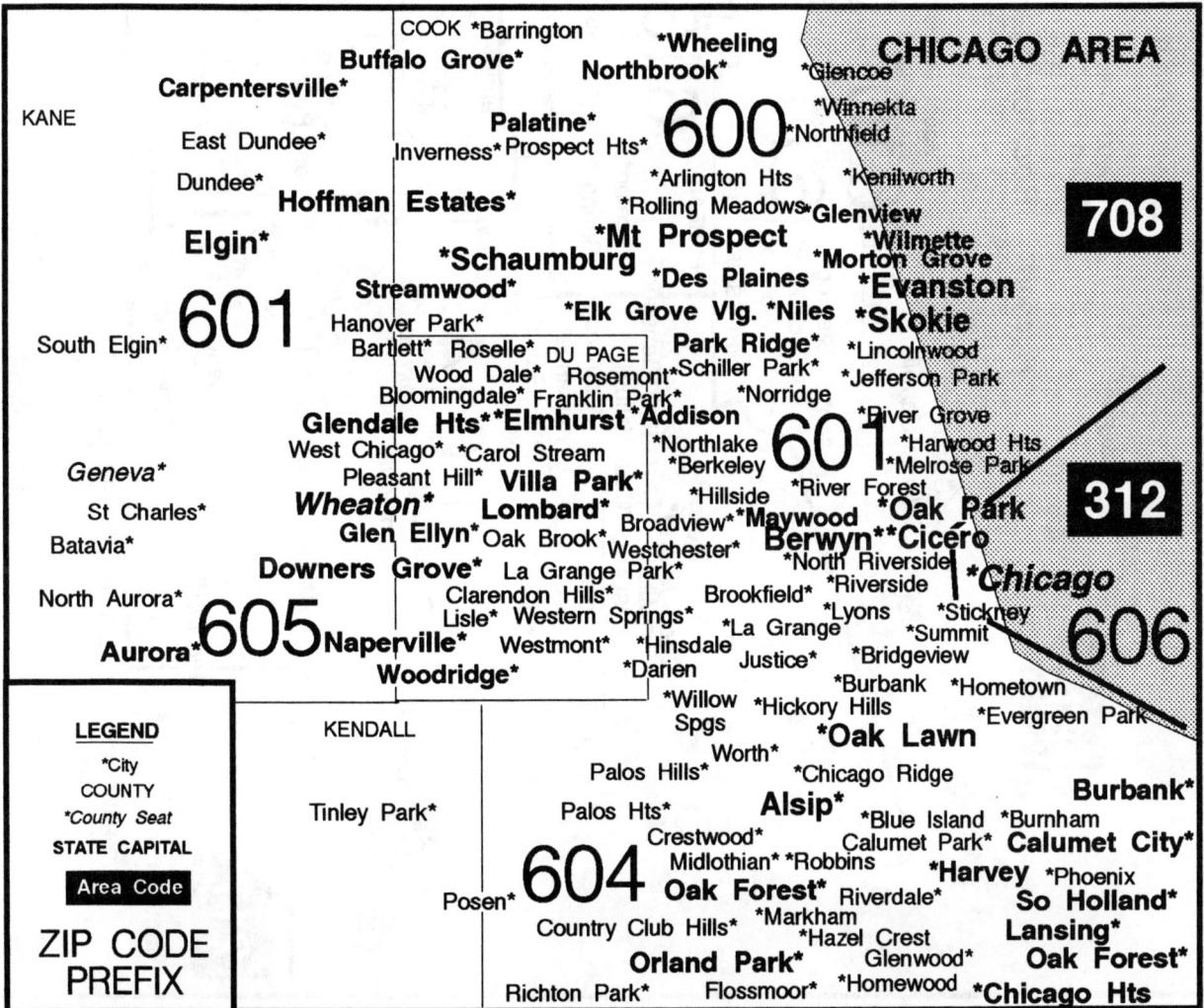

CHICAGO AREA

COOK *Barrington

Buffalo Grove*   *Wheeling

Carpentersville*   Northbrook*   *Glencoe

KANE   *Winnekta

East Dundee*   Palatine*   600 *Northfield

Inverness* Prospect Hts*

Dundee*   *Kenilworth

Hoffman Estates*   *Arlington Hts   *Glenview

*Rolling Meadows

Elgin*   *Mt Prospect   *Wilmette

*Schaumburg   *Morton Grove

Streamwood   *Des Plaines   *Evanston

601   Hanover Park*   *Elk Grove Vlg. *Niles   *Skokie

South Elgin*   Bartlett* Roselle* DU PAGE   Park Ridge*   *Lincolnwood

Wood Dale* Rosemont *Schiller Park* *Jefferson Park

Bloomingdale* Franklin Park*   *Norridge

Glendale Hts**Elmhurst*Addison   *River Grove

West Chicago* *Carol Stream   *Northlake   601 *Harwood Hts

Geneva*   Pleasant Hill* Villa Park*   *Berkeley   *Melrose Park

St Charles*   Wheaton*   Lombard*   *Hillside   *River Forest

Batavia*   Glen Ellyn* Oak Brook* Broadview* *Maywood *Oak Park

Westchester*   Berwyn**Cicero

North Aurora*   Downers Grove* La Grange Park*   *North Riverside *Chicago

605   Clarendon Hills*   Brookfield* *Riverside

Aurora*   Naperville* Lisle* Western Springs*   *Lyons   *Stickney   606

Woodridge*   Westmont* *Hinsdale Justice* *Summit

*Darien   *Bridgeview

312

*Willow   *Burbank *Hometown

Spgs *Hickory Hills   *Evergreen Park

Worth*   *Oak Lawn

KENDALL   Palos Hills*   *Chicago Ridge   Burbank*

Tinley Park*   Palos Hts*   Alsip*   *Blue Island *Burnham

Crestwood*   Calumet Park* Calumet City*

Midlothian* *Robbins   *Harvey *Phoenix

604 Oak Forest* Riverdale*   So Holland*

Posen*   *Markham   Lansing*

Country Club Hills* *Hazel Crest   Oak Forest*

Orland Park*   Glenwood*

Richton Park* Flossmoor* *Homewood *Chicago Hts

LEGEND

*City

COUNTY

*County Seat

STATE CAPITAL

Area Code

ZIP CODE PREFIX

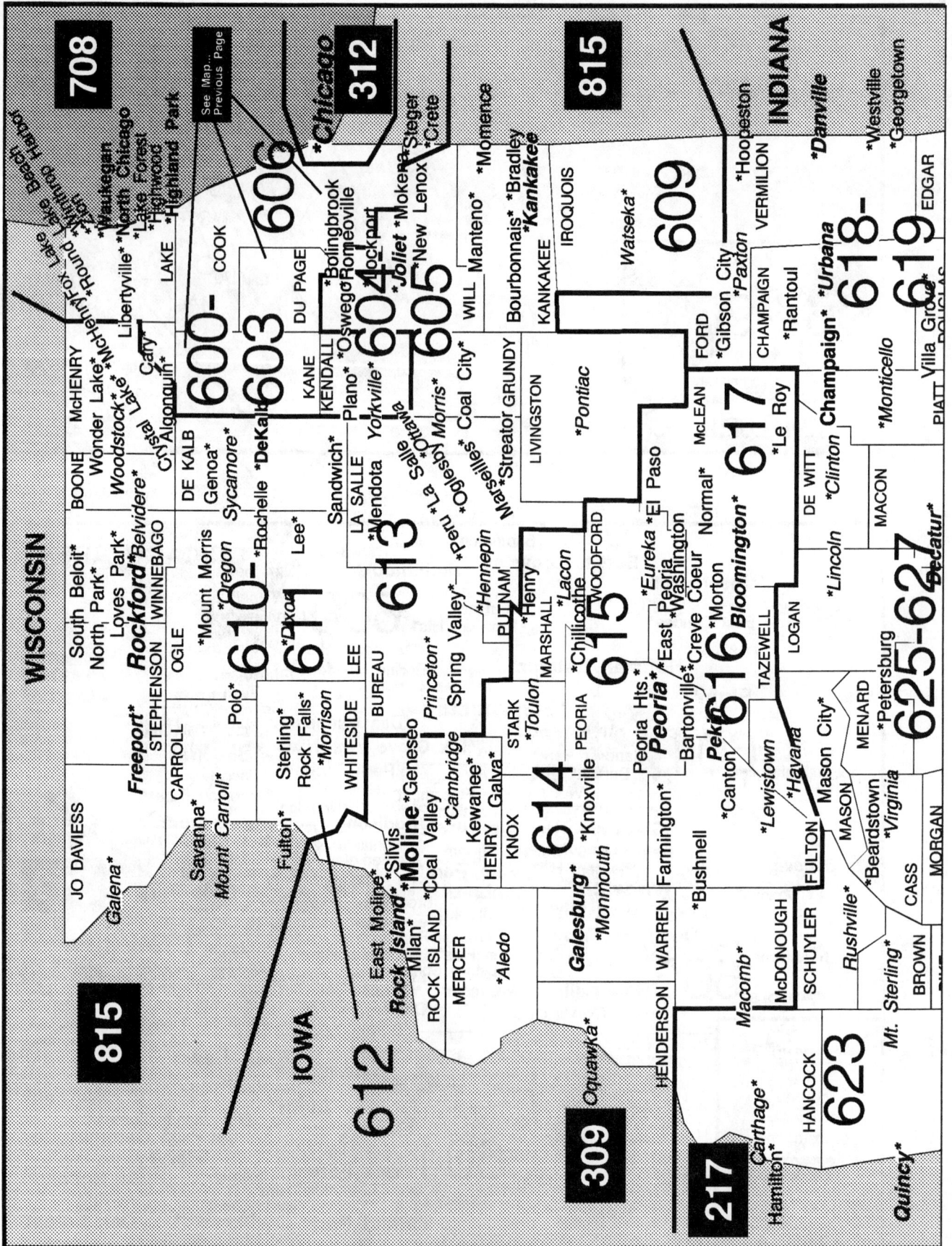

WISCONSIN

INDIANA

IOWA

708

312
*Chicago

815

815

309

217

600-
603
606
604-
605
609
618-
619
610-
611
612
613
614
615
616
617
623
625-627

See Map...
Previous Page

JO DAVIESS
Galena*
STEPHENSON
Freeport*
CARROLL
Savanna*
Mount Carroll*
Fulton*

BOONE
South Beloit*
North Park*
Loves Park*
Rockford*
Belvidere*
WINNEBAGO
OGLE
*Mount Morris
*Oregon
Polo*

McHENRY
Wonder Lake*
Woodstock*
Crystal Lake*
*McHenry
*Algonquin
Cary*
Genoa*
Sycamore*
*Rochelle *DeKalb
DE KALB
Lee*
LEE
*Dixon

LAKE
Libertyville
*Round
Lake
*Fox Lake
Waukegan*
*North Chicago
*Lake Forest
*Highwood
*Highland Park

COOK

DU PAGE
*Bolingbrook
*Oswego*Romeoville
KANE
KENDALL
Plano* *Lockport
Yorkville* *Joliet *Mokena
*New Lenox *Crete
*Steger

Sandwich*
LA SALLE
*Mendota
Peru* *La Salle
Oglesby Morris
Coal City*
*Marseilles
*Streator GRUNDY

Sterling*
Rock Falls*
*Morrison
WHITESIDE
BUREAU
Princeton*
Spring Valley*
*Hennepin
PUTNAM
Henry*
MARSHALL
*Lacon

Milan*
East Moline*
*Silvis
Rock Island*
*Moline *Geneseo
*Coal Valley
*Cambridge
Kewanee*
HENRY Galva*
STARK
*Toulon
ROCK ISLAND
MERCER
*Aledo

HENDERSON
*Oquawka
WARREN
Monmouth*
Galesburg*
KNOX
*Knoxville
PEORIA
Farmington*
*Bushnell
McDONOUGH
Macomb*

HANCOCK
Carthage*
Hamilton*
Quincy*
SCHUYLER
Rushville*
Mt.
Sterling*
BROWN
CASS
Beardstown*
*Virginia
MASON
MENARD
Petersburg*

WILL Manteno*
*Momence
Bourbonnais* *Bradley
*Kankakee
KANKAKEE
IROQUOIS
Watseka *
FORD
Gibson City*
*Paxton
VERMILION
*Hoopeston
*Rantoul
CHAMPAIGN
*Urbana
Champaign*
*Monticello
PIATT Villa Grove*
DOUGLAS
EDGAR
INDIANA
*Danville
*Westville
*Georgetown

WOODFORD
*Eureka *El Paso
Peoria Hts.*
Peoria*
*East Peoria
Bartonville*Creve Coeur
*Washington
Pekin*
*Morton
TAZEWELL
*Canton
FULTON
*Lewistown
*Havana
Mason City*

McLEAN
Normal*
Bloomington*
*Le Roy
DE WITT
*Clinton
LOGAN
*Lincoln
MACON
Decatur*

LIVINGSTON
*Pontiac

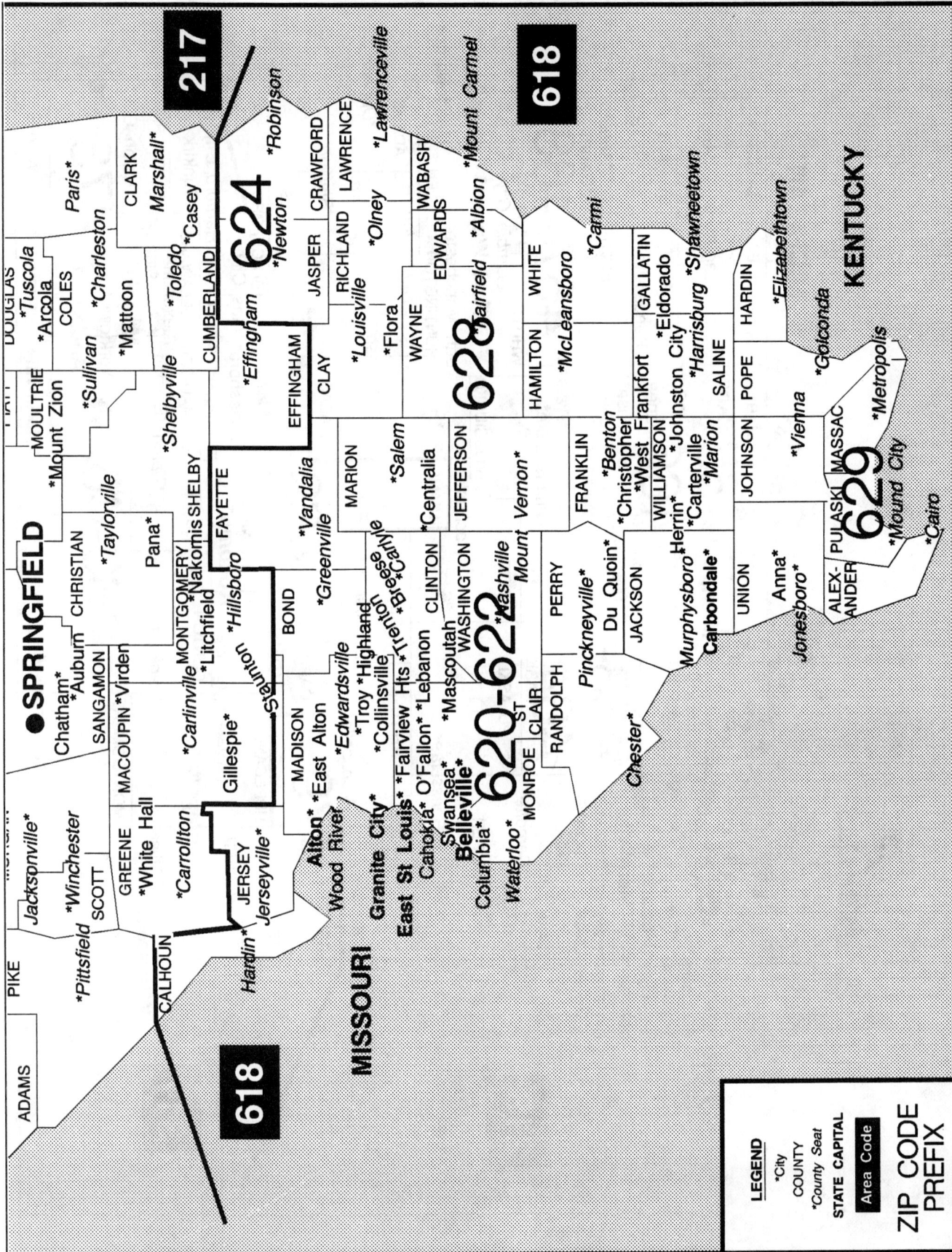

217

618

624
Robinson
Newton

628

618

629

KENTUCKY

MISSOURI

●SPRINGFIELD

DOUGLAS
*Tuscola
COLES
*Arcola
*Paris
CLARK
*Charleston
Marshall*
*Mattoon
*Toledo *Casey
*Sullivan
CUMBERLAND
MOULTRIE
*Mount Zion
*Shelbyville
*Effingham
EFFINGHAM
JASPER CRAWFORD
LAWRENCE
*Olney
*Lawrenceville
RICHLAND
*Louisville
WABASH
*Mount Carmel
EDWARDS
*Albion
WHITE
*Carmi
GALLATIN
*Shawneetown
*Eldorado
*Elizabethtown
HARDIN
*Golconda
MASSAC
*Metropolis
PULASKI
*Mound City
*Cairo

*Taylorville
CHRISTIAN
*Auburn
SANGAMON
Chatham*
*Carlinville
MACOUPIN *Virden
Pana*
*Nokomis SHELBY
MONTGOMERY
*Litchfield
*Hillsboro
FAYETTE
*Vandalia
BOND
*Greenville
MARION
*Salem
*Centralia
CLAY
*Flora
WAYNE
*Fairfield
HAMILTON
*McLeansboro
FRANKLIN
*Benton
*West Frankfort
*Christopher
WILLIAMSON
Herrin*
*Carterville
*Marion
JOHNSON
*Vienna
POPE
SALINE
*Harrisburg
*Johnston City

JERSEY
Jerseyville*
Gillespie*
Staunton*
MADISON
*East Alton
Alton*
Wood River
*Edwardsville
*Troy Highland
*Collinsville
Granite City*
East St Louis*
Cahokia*
Swansea*
Belleville*
Fairview Hts
O'Fallon* *Lebanon
*Mascoutah
WASHINGTON
*Nashville
Mount Vernon*
JEFFERSON
CLINTON
*Breese
*Carlyle
*Trenton
Columbia*
Waterloo*
MONROE
ST CLAIR
RANDOLPH
Chester*
PERRY
Pinckneyville*
Du Quoin*
JACKSON
Murphysboro*
Carbondale*
UNION
Anna*
Jonesboro*
ALEX-ANDER

PIKE
ADAMS
Jacksonville*
*Winchester
*White Hall
SCOTT
GREENE
*Carrollton
*Pittsfield
*Hardin
CALHOUN

620-622

LEGEND
*City
COUNTY
*County Seat
STATE CAPITAL
Area Code
ZIP CODE PREFIX

Indiana

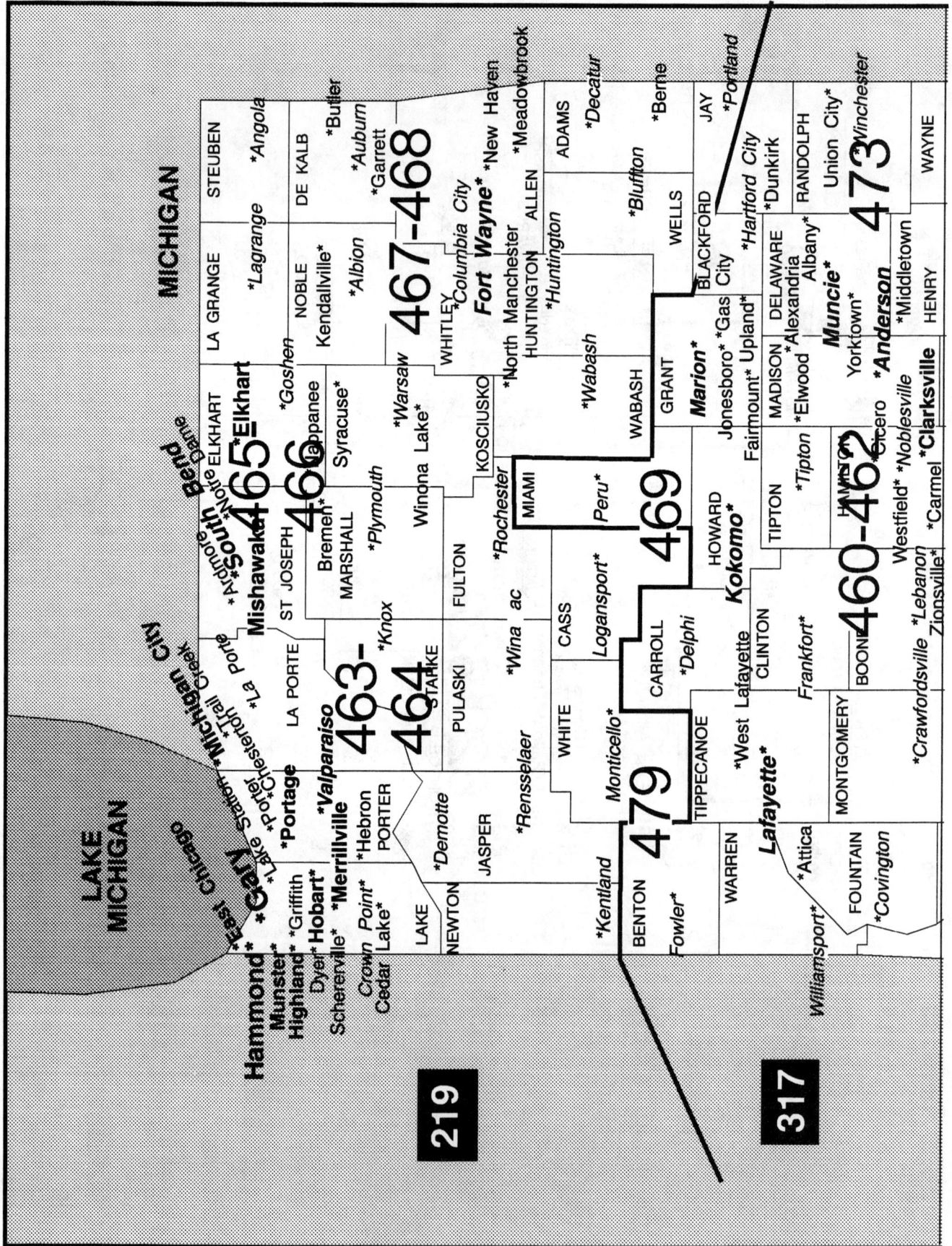

OHIO

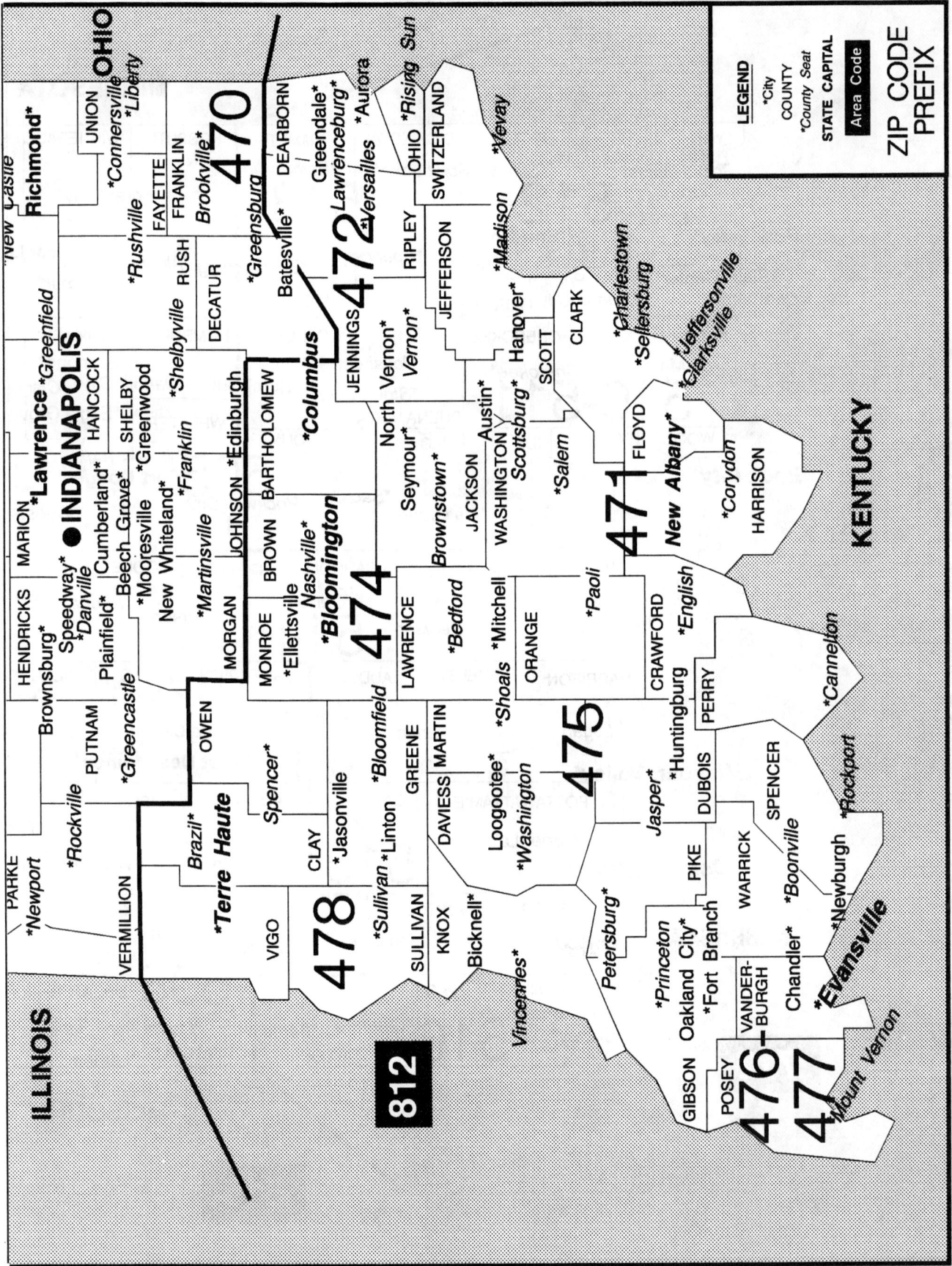

LEGEND
*City
COUNTY
*County Seat
STATE CAPITAL
Area Code
ZIP CODE PREFIX

*New Castle

Richmond*

UNION OHIO
*Connersville *Liberty

470

FAYETTE
FRANKLIN
*Rushville
RUSH
*Brookville
DEARBORN
*Greensburg
*Batesville
Greendale*
*Lawrenceburg
*Aurora
*Versailles
472
*Rising Sun
SWITZERLAND
*Vevay

Lawrence *Greenfield
INDIANAPOLIS
HANCOCK
SHELBY
*Shelbyville
DECATUR
RIPLEY
JEFFERSON
*Madison
*Vernon
North Vernon*
*Hanover

MARION
Speedway*
*Danville
Plainfield*
*Greenwood
*Franklin
*Edinburgh
*Columbus
BARTHOLOMEW
JENNINGS
SCOTT
*Scottsburg
Austin*
CLARK
*Charlestown
*Sellersburg
*Jeffersonville
*Clarksville

HENDRICKS
Brownsburg*
Beech Grove*
*Mooresville
New Whiteland*
*Martinsville
JOHNSON
BROWN
Nashville*
*Bloomington
474
Seymour*
JACKSON
WASHINGTON
*Salem
FLOYD
New Albany*
*Corydon
HARRISON

PUTNAM
*Greencastle
OWEN
*Ellettsville
MONROE
Brownstown*
LAWRENCE
*Bedford
*Mitchell
ORANGE
*Paoli
CRAWFORD
*English
*Cannelton

PARKE
*Newport
*Rockville
Brazil*
Terre Haute
Spencer*
CLAY
*Jasonville
478
GREENE
*Bloomfield
MARTIN
*Shoals
DAVIESS
Loogootee*
*Washington
475
*Huntingburg
DUBOIS
PERRY
*Rockport

VERMILLION
VIGO
*Sullivan
SULLIVAN
*Linton
KNOX
Bicknell*
Vincennes*
Petersburg*
*Princeton
Oakland City*
*Fort Branch
Jasper*
PIKE
SPENCER
*Boonville
*Newburgh
WARRICK
Chandler*
*Evansville

ILLINOIS

812

GIBSON
POSEY
VANDER-BURGH
476-477
*Mount Vernon

KENTUCKY

Iowa

MINNESOTA

| LYON | OSCEOLA | DICKINSON | EMMET | KOSSUTH | WINNEBAGO |
| Rock Rapids* | *Sibley | Spirit Lake* | *Estherville | | |

512

513

Forest City*

SIOUX

Rock Valley*

CLAY

HANCOCK

*Sheldon

*Spencer

Clear L

Sioux Center*

*Emmetsburg *Algona

Garner*

Howarden*

Primghar*

*Orange City O'BRIEN

PALO ALTO

PLYMOUTH

CHEROKEE

POCAHONTAS HUMBOLDT

WRIGHT

Le Mars*

Pocahontas*

Belmond*

Cherokee*

Humboldt* *Dakota City *Clario

510-511

*Storm Lake

*Eagle Grove

WOODBURY

BUENA VISTA

WEBSTER

IDA SAC CALHOUN

HAMILTON

Sioux City*

505 *Fort Dodge

*Sac City *Rockwell City *Webste

*Ida Grove

| MONONA | CRAWFORD | CARROLL | GREENE | BOONE | *Stor |
| | | *Carroll | *Jefferson | *Boone | STORY |

Onawa*

514

HARRISON SHELBY AUDUBON GUTHRIE DALLAS POLK

*Perry *Urbanda

Logan* *Harlan *Audubon

*Guthrie Center *Clive

West Des Moines* ●DE

Missouri Valley* *Adel

POTTAWATTAMIE CASS ADAIR MADISON WARREN

*Atlantic *Norw

*Carter Lake

515

Council Bluffs* *Greenfield *Winterset *India

MILLS MONTGOMERY ADAMS UNION CLARKE

NEBRASKA Glenwood* *Red Oak *Creston *Osceola

*Corning

508

FREMONT PAGE DECATUR V

Shenandoah*

516 *Clarinda *Bedford *Mount Ayr *Leon

Sidney*

TAYLOR RINGGOLD *Lamoni

712

MISSOURI

515

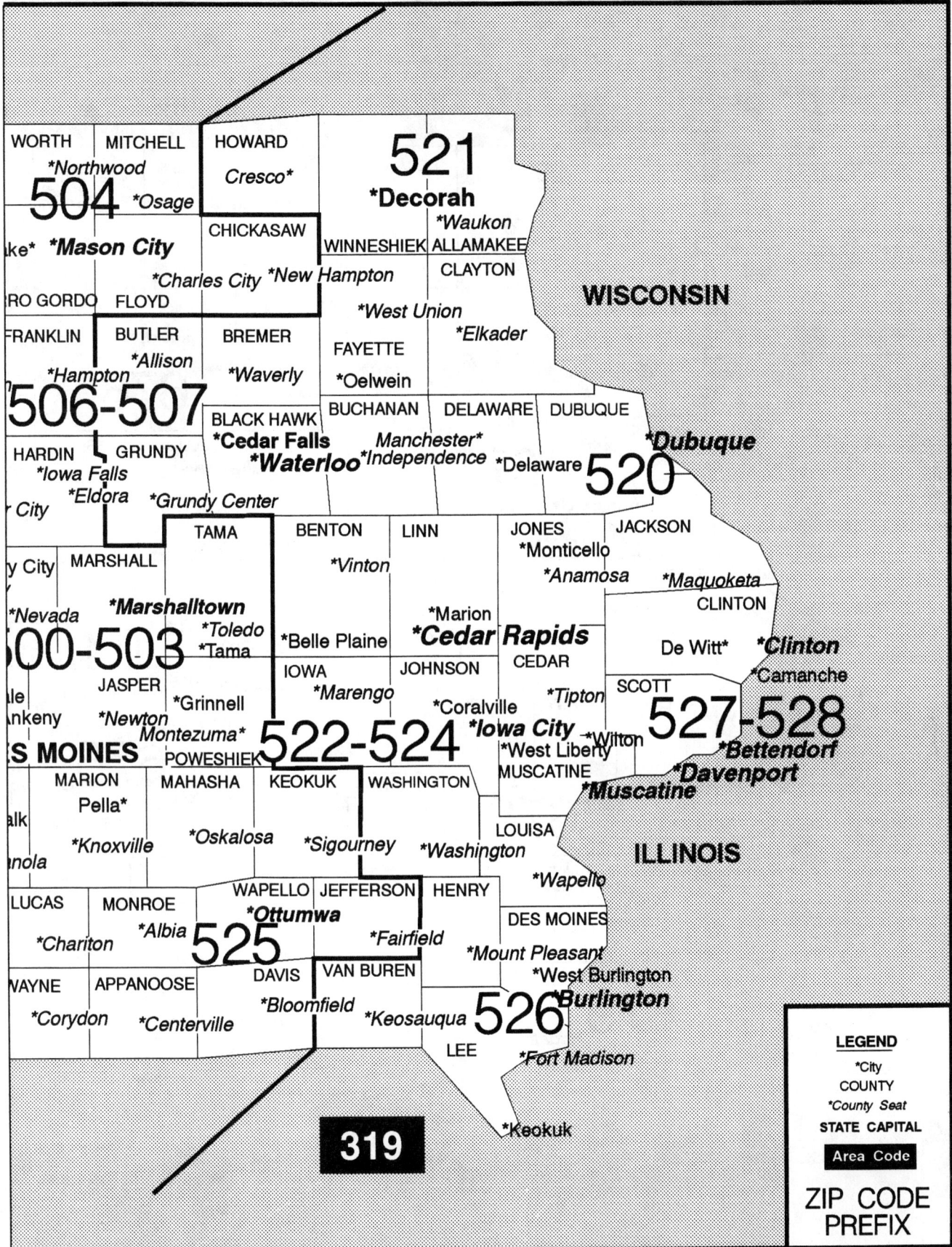

WORTH MITCHELL HOWARD
Northwood Cresco
504 *Osage

521
*Decorah

CHICKASAW
ke* **Mason City**
*Charles City *New Hampton

*Waukon
WINNESHIEK ALLAMAKEE
CLAYTON

WISCONSIN

RO GORDO FLOYD
*West Union
*Elkader

FRANKLIN BUTLER BREMER
*Allison FAYETTE
*Hampton *Waverly *Oelwein

506-507

BLACK HAWK BUCHANAN DELAWARE DUBUQUE
HARDIN GRUNDY **Cedar Falls** Manchester* *Dubuque
*Iowa Falls **Waterloo** *Independence *Delaware **520**
*Eldora *Grundy Center
City

TAMA BENTON LINN JONES JACKSON
*Monticello
*Vinton *Anamosa *Maquoketa
y City MARSHALL CLINTON
*Marion

Marshalltown *Cedar Rapids De Witt* *Clinton
*Nevada *Toledo *Belle Plaine CEDAR *Camanche
500-503 *Tama SCOTT
IOWA JOHNSON *Tipton **527-528**
JASPER *Marengo
le *Grinnell *Coralville *Wilton
nkeny *Newton Montezuma* **522-524** **Iowa City** **Bettendorf**
S MOINES POWESHIEK *West Liberty **Davenport**
MUSCATINE
MARION MAHASHA KEOKUK WASHINGTON **Muscatine**
alk Pella*
LOUISA ILLINOIS
*Knoxville *Oskalosa *Sigourney *Washington
nola *Wapello

LUCAS MONROE WAPELLO JEFFERSON HENRY
Ottumwa DES MOINES
*Chariton *Albia **525** *Fairfield *Mount Pleasant
DAVIS VAN BUREN *West Burlington
WAYNE APPANOOSE **526** **Burlington**
*Corydon *Centerville *Bloomfield *Keosauqua
LEE *Fort Madison

319

*Keokuk

LEGEND
*City
COUNTY
*County Seat
STATE CAPITAL
Area Code

ZIP CODE
PREFIX

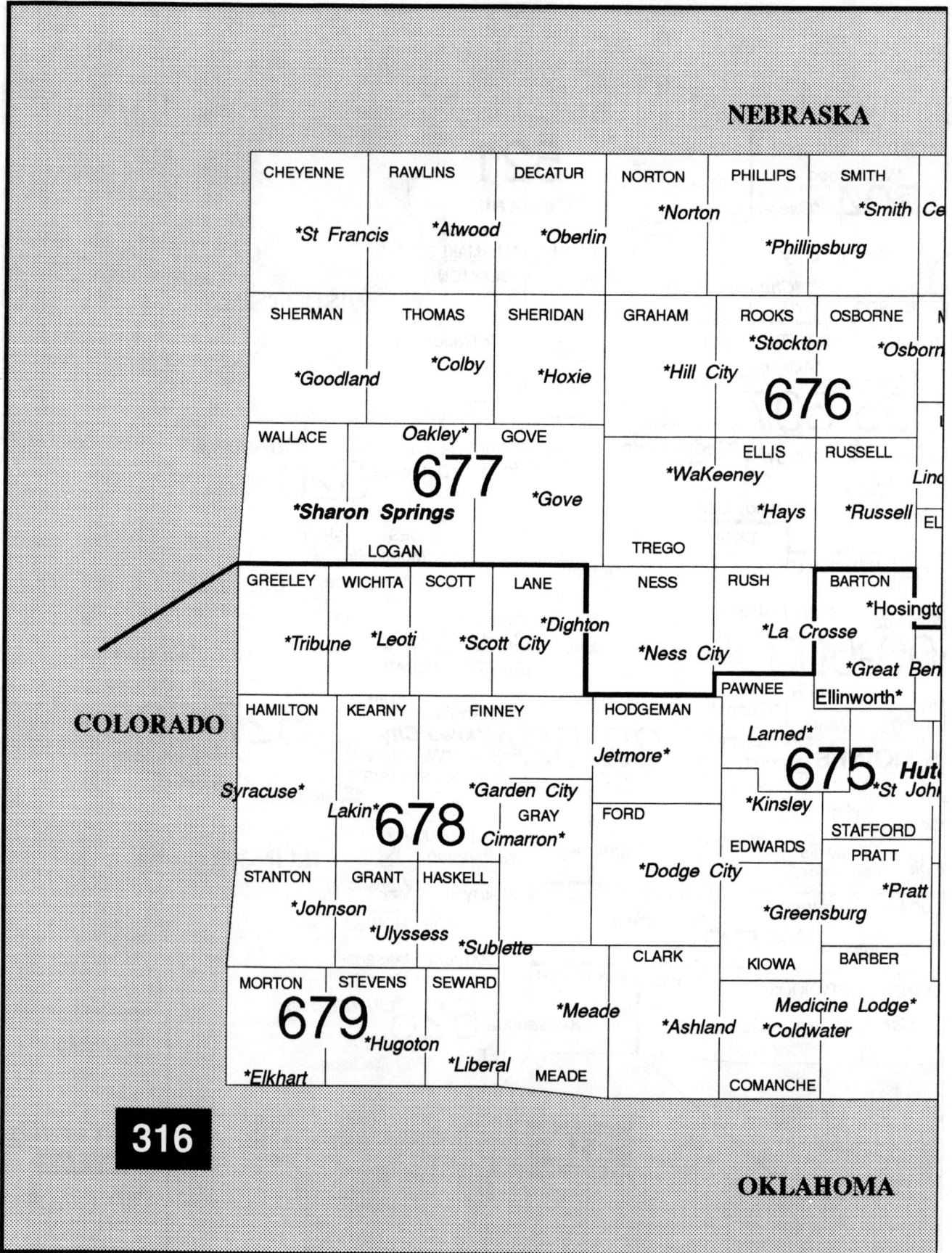

Kansas

NEBRASKA

| CHEYENNE | RAWLINS | DECATUR | NORTON | PHILLIPS | SMITH |
| *St Francis | *Atwood | *Oberlin | *Norton | *Phillipsburg | *Smith Ce |

SHERMAN THOMAS SHERIDAN GRAHAM ROOKS OSBORNE

*Goodland *Colby *Hoxie *Hill City *Stockton *Osborn

676

WALLACE Oakley* GOVE ELLIS RUSSELL

677 *WaKeeney Lind

*Sharon Springs *Gove *Hays *Russell EL

LOGAN TREGO

GREELEY WICHITA SCOTT LANE NESS RUSH BARTON

*Hosingto

*Tribune *Leoti *Scott City *Dighton *La Crosse

*Ness City *Great Ben

PAWNEE Ellinworth*

HAMILTON KEARNY FINNEY HODGEMAN Larned*

Jetmore* **675** *Hut*

*St Joh

Syracuse* *Garden City

Lakin* **678** GRAY FORD *Kinsley

Cimarron* STAFFORD

*Dodge City EDWARDS PRATT

STANTON GRANT HASKELL *Pratt

*Johnson *Greensburg

*Ulyssess *Sublette CLARK KIOWA BARBER

MORTON STEVENS SEWARD Medicine Lodge*

679 *Meade *Coldwater

*Hugoton *Ashland

*Elkhart *Liberal MEADE COMANCHE

COLORADO

316

OKLAHOMA

913

JEWELL | REPUBLIC | WASHINGTON | MARSHALL | NEMAHA | BROWN

nter Belleville*
*Mankato
*Marysville *Seneca *Hiawatha *Troy
DONIPHAN
669 *Washington
664-666
ATCHISON
*Atchison

CLOUD
*Concordia
RILEY
POTTA-
WATOMIE
JACKSON
Holton*
*Westmoreland

ITCHELL
*Beliot
CLAY
Clay Center*
JEFFER-
SON
LEAVENWORTH
*Leavenworth

OTTAWA
Manhatten
Oskaloosa* Lansing*
Kansas City

INCOLN
Minneapolis*
DICKINSON
*Wamego
TOPEKA●
WYANDOTTE
*Shawnee Mission

oln*
674 Junction City*
Alma*
Lawrence*
SHAWNEE Endora*
*Merriam
*Overland Park

LSWORTH
Abilene*
*Salina
GEARY
*Olathe

Ellsworth
SALINE
Herrington*
MORRIS
Council Grove*
WABAUNSEE
OSAGE DOUGLAS
JOHNSON
660-662
MIAMI
MISSOURI

*Lindsborg
LYON
Osage City*
*Lyndon *Ottawa *Paola

RICE
*McPherson
CHASE
*Cottonwood Falls
FRANKLIN
*Osawatomie

*Lyons
Hillsboro*
*Marion
Emporia*
COFFEY
LINN
*Garnett

McPHERSON MARION
*Burlington
*Mound City

RENO
*Hesston
ANDERSON
668

chinson*
Newton*
BUTLER
WOODSON
BOURBON

HARVEY
Yates Center*
*Iola
667 *Fort Scott

SEDGWICK
*El Dorado
*Eureka
ALLEN

KINGMAN
*Andover
WILSON
NEOSHO CRAWFORD

Wichita*
*Augusta
GREENWOOD
*Chanute
*Girard

*Kingman
*Haysville
ELK
*Fredonia *Erie
*Pittsburg

Derby*
*Howard
*Neodesha

670-672
MONTGOMERY
LABETTE CHEROKEE

HARPER
*Wellington *Winfield
Cherryvale*
*Parsons
*Columbus

*Anthony
SUMNER
COWLEY
Sedan* **673**
Oswego*
Independence Galena

Arkansas City*
CHAUTAUQUA
*Coffeyville
*Baxter Springs

LEGEND
*City
COUNTY
*County Seat
STATE CAPITAL
Area Code

ZIP CODE PREFIX

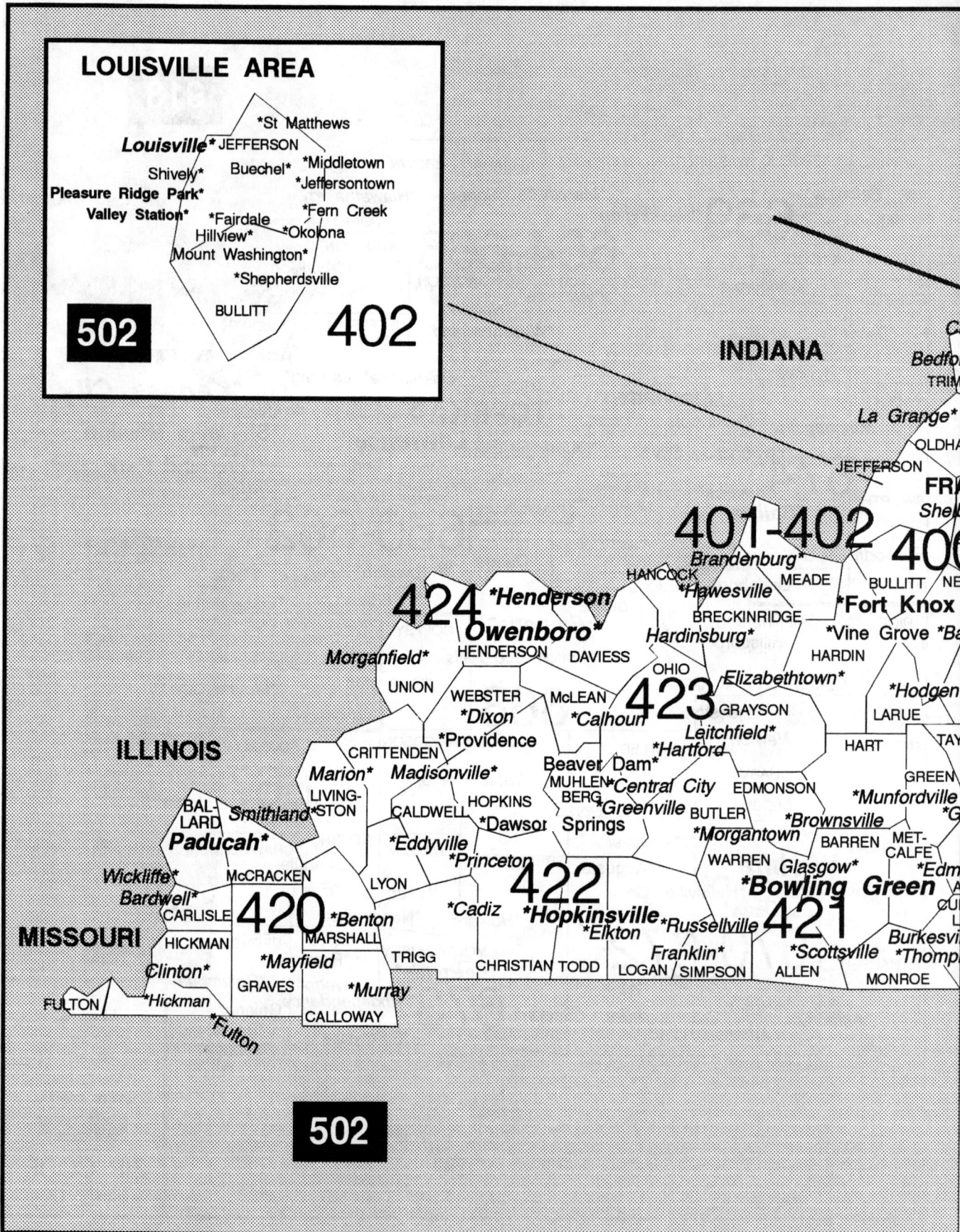

LOUISVILLE AREA

*St Matthews
Louisville* *JEFFERSON
Shively* Buechel* *Middletown
*Jeffersontown
Pleasure Ridge Park*
Valley Station* *Fern Creek
*Fairdale
Hillview* *Okolona
Mount Washington*
*Shepherdsville
BULLITT

502 **402**

INDIANA

Bedfo
TRIM

La Grange*

OLDHA

JEFFERSON

FR
Shel

401-402 **40**

Brandenburg*
HANCOCK MEADE BULLITT NE
*Hawesville *Fort Knox
424 *Henderson BRECKINRIDGE
Owenboro* Hardinsburg* *Vine Grove *Ba
HENDERSON DAVIESS HARDIN
Morganfield* OHIO *Elizabethtown*
UNION *Hodgen
423 GRAYSON LARUE
WEBSTER McLEAN
ILLINOIS *Dixon *Calhoun Leitchfield* HART TAY
*Providence *Hartford GREEN
CRITTENDEN Beaver Dam* *Munfordville
Marion* Madisonville* MUHLEN-*Central City EDMONSON *G
LIVING- BERG Greenville BUTLER *Brownsville
BAL- Smithland *STON HOPKINS *Morgantown BARREN MET-
LARD CALDWELL *Dawso Springs WARREN Glasgow* CALFE *Edm
Paducah* *Eddyville *Bowling Green A
Wickliffe* McCRACKEN *Princeton LYON **422**
Bardwell* **420** *Cadiz *Hopkinsville*Russellville **421** Burkesvi
CARLISLE *Benton *Elkton *Scottsville *Thomp
MISSOURI HICKMAN MARSHALL Franklin*
Clinton* TRIGG CHRISTIAN TODD LOGAN/SIMPSON ALLEN MONROE
*Mayfield
FULTON *Hickman GRAVES *Murray
*Fulton CALLOWAY

502

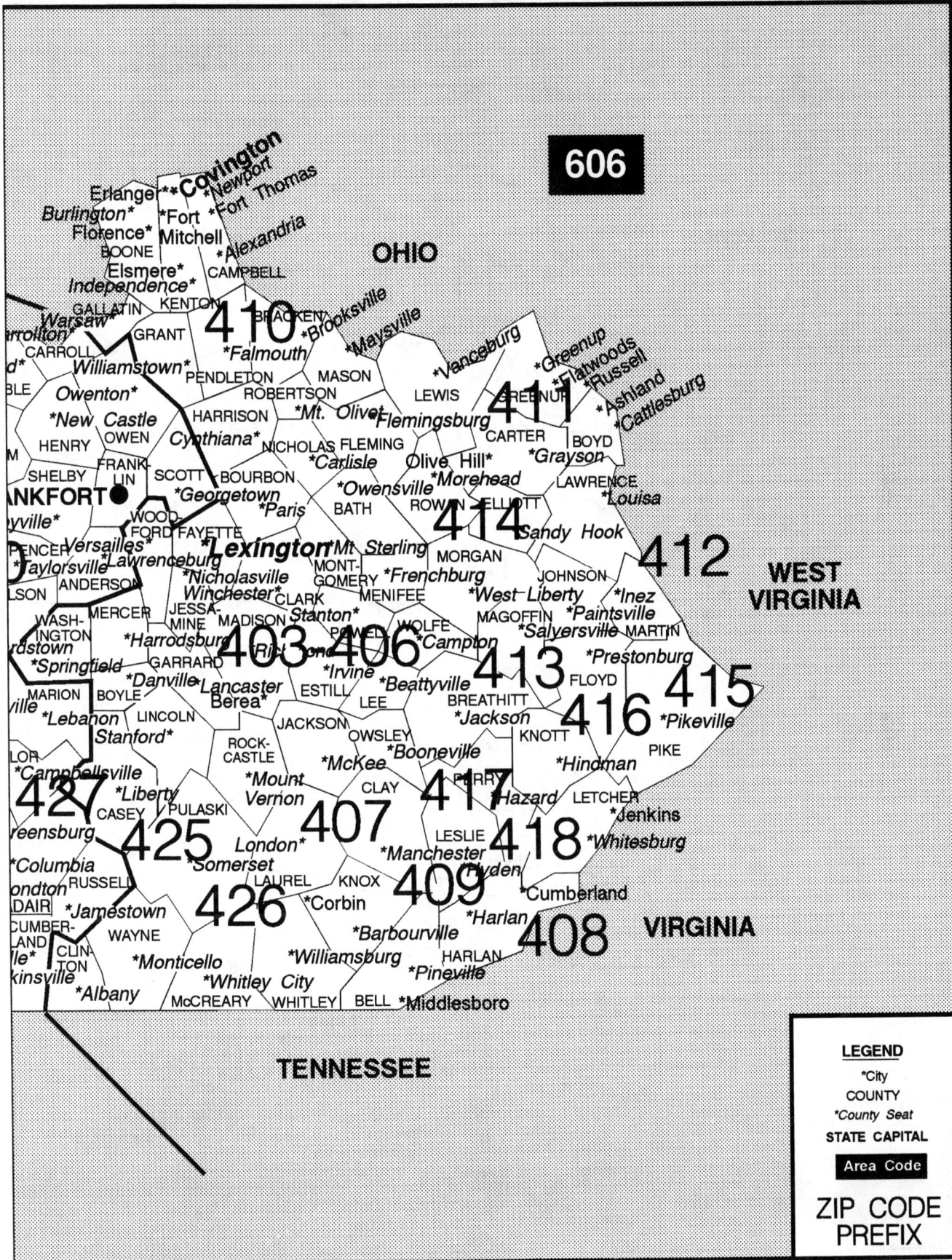

606

OHIO

Covington**
*Newport
Erlange** *Fort Thomas
Burlington* *Fort Alexandria
Florence* Mitchell
BOONE CAMPBELL
Elsmere*
Independence*
GALLATIN KENTON
Warsaw* GRANT BRACKEN *Brooksville
Carrollton* *Falmouth *Maysville
CARROLL Williamstown* PENDLETON
Owenton* ROBERTSON LEWIS *Vanceburg *Greenup *Flatwoods
*New Castle HARRISON *Mt. Olivet Flemingsburg GREENUP *Russell
HENRY OWEN Cynthiana* NICHOLAS FLEMING CARTER *Ashland
SHELBY Carlisle* Olive Hill* *Cattlesburg
FRANK-LIN SCOTT BOURBON BATH Grayson* BOYD
FRANKFORT *Georgetown *Owensville *Morehead LAWRENCE
*Paris ROWAN ELLIOTT *Louisa
Versailles* Lexington Mt. Sterling *Sandy Hook
Taylorsville* *Lawrenceburg MONT- MORGAN

410

411

414

412

WEST VIRGINIA

WOOD-FORD FAYETTE
SPENCER ANDERSON *Nicholasville GOMERY *Frenchburg JOHNSON
NELSON Winchester* CLARK MENIFEE *West Liberty *Inez
WASH-INGTON MERCER JESSA-MINE MADISON Stanton* MAGOFFIN *Paintsville
Harrodsburg* PADWE WOLFE *Salyersville MARTIN
Bardstown *Springfield GARRARD Richmond *Campton
*Danville *Irvine *Prestonburg
MARION BOYLE Lancaster *Beattyville FLOYD
Lebanon* Berea* ESTILL LEE BREATHITT *Pikeville
Stanford* LINCOLN JACKSON OWSLEY *Jackson KNOTT PIKE
*Campbellsville ROCK-CASTLE *Booneville *Hindman
CASEY *Mount *McKee CLAY PERRY LETCHER
*Liberty Vernon Hazard *Jenkins
Greensburg PULASKI London* LESLIE *Whitesburg
*Columbia RUSSELL *Somerset *Manchester Hyden
Londton DAIR LAUREL KNOX *Cumberland
*Jamestown *Corbin
CUMBER-LAND WAYNE *Harlan VIRGINIA
*Monticello *Barbourville
*Albany *Williamsburg HARLAN
CLIN-TON *Whitley City *Pineville
Hawkinsville McCREARY WHITLEY BELL *Middlesboro

403-406
413
416
415
427
425
407
417
418
426
409
408

TENNESSEE

LEGEND
*City
COUNTY
*County Seat
STATE CAPITAL
Area Code

ZIP CODE PREFIX

Louisiana

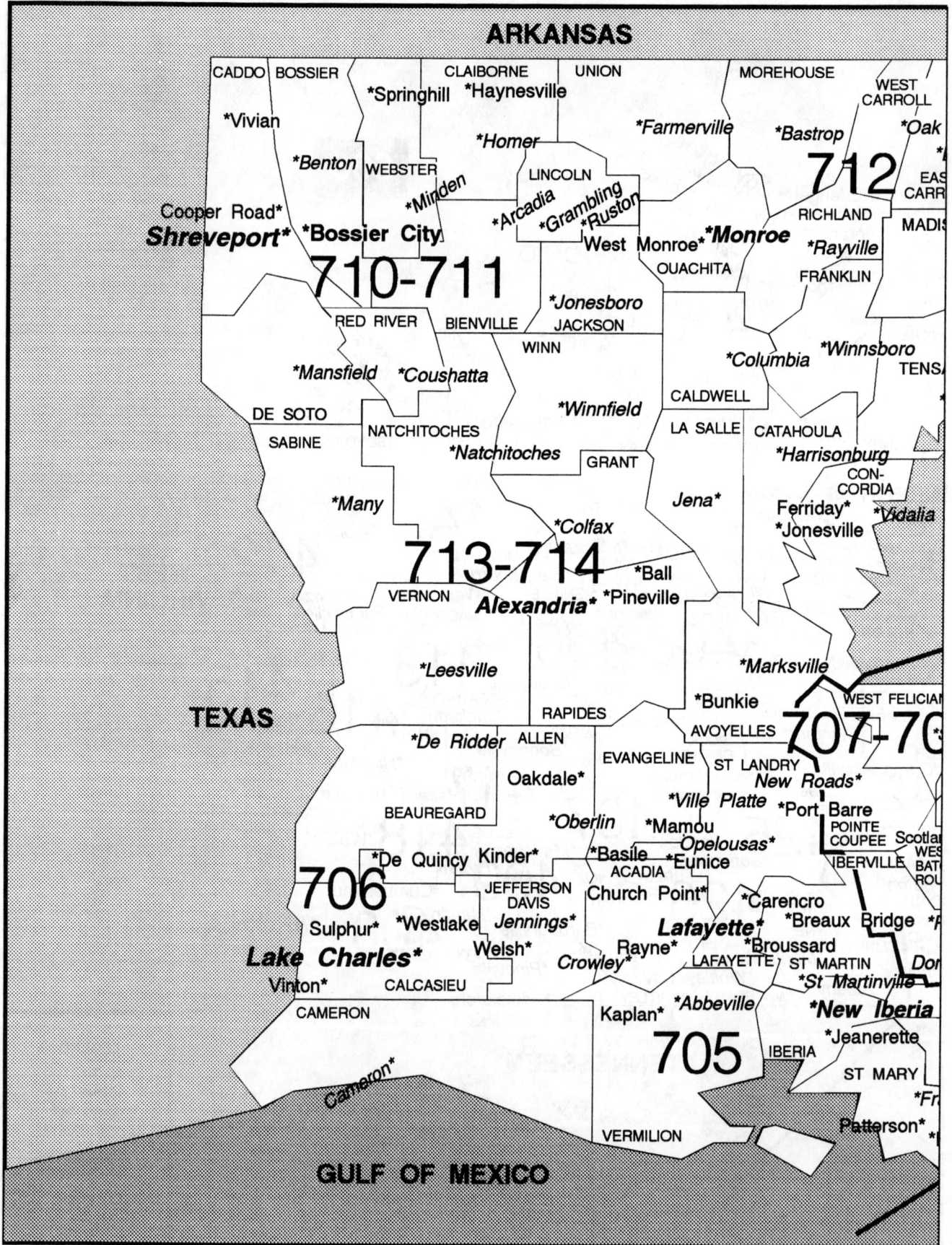

ARKANSAS

CADDO BOSSIER   CLAIBORNE   UNION   MOREHOUSE   WEST CARROLL

*Springhill   *Haynesville

*Vivian   *Farmerville   *Bastrop   *Oak

*Benton   WEBSTER   *Homer   LINCOLN   712   EAST CARR

*Minden   *Arcadia   *Grambling   *Ruston   RICHLAND   MADIS

Cooper Road*   *Bossier City   West Monroe   *Monroe   *Rayville

Shreveport*   **710-711**   OUACHITA   FRANKLIN

RED RIVER   BIENVILLE   *Jonesboro   JACKSON   *Columbia   *Winnsboro   TENSA

WINN   CALDWELL

*Mansfield   *Coushatta   *Winnfield   LA SALLE   CATAHOULA

DE SOTO   NATCHITOCHES   *Harrisonburg   CON-CORDIA

SABINE   *Natchitoches   GRANT   Jena*   Ferriday*   *Vidalia

*Many   *Colfax   *Jonesville

713-714   *Ball

VERNON   *Pineville   *Alexandria***

TEXAS   *Leesville   *Marksville

RAPIDES   *Bunkie   WEST FELICIA

AVOYELLES   **707-70**

De Ridder   ALLEN   EVANGELINE   ST LANDRY   New Roads

Oakdale*   *Ville Platte   *Port Barre   POINTE COUPEE   Scotla

BEAUREGARD   *Oberlin   *Mamou   *Opelousas*   WES BAT ROU

De Quincy   Kinder   *Basile   *Eunice   IBERVILLE

706   JEFFERSON DAVIS   Church Point*   *Carencro   *Breaux Bridge

Sulphur*   *Westlake   Jennings*   Rayne*   *Broussard   Dor

Lake Charles*   Welsh*   Crowley*   LAFAYETTE   ST MARTIN   *St Martinville

Vinton*   CALCASIEU   *Abbeville   **New Iberia**

CAMERON   Kaplan*   *Jeanerette

705   IBERIA   ST MARY

Cameron*   *Fr

VERMILION   Patterson*

GULF OF MEXICO

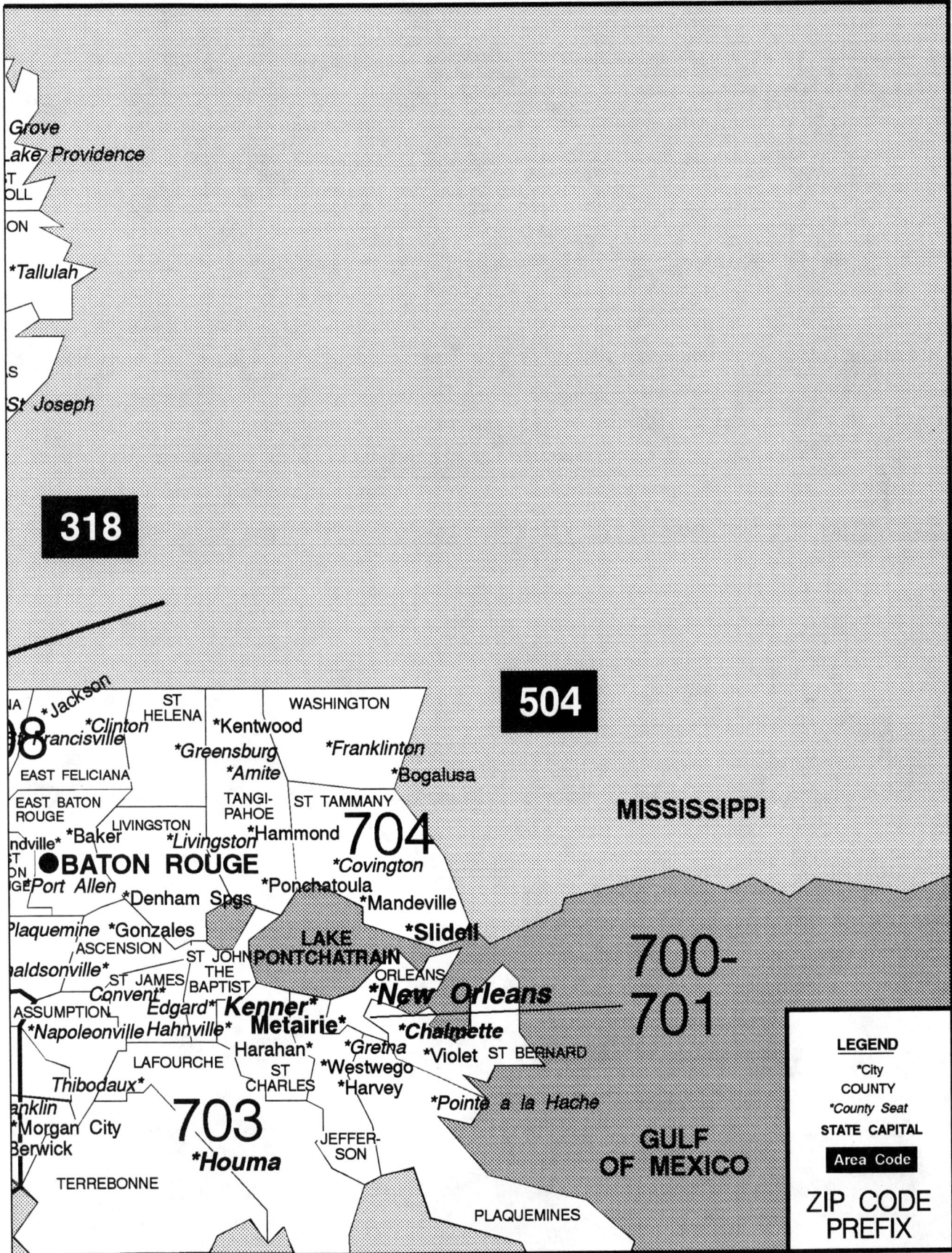

318

504

Grove

Lake Providence

ST
OLL

ON

*Tallulah

S

St Joseph

8 *Jackson   ST
*Clinton   HELENA   WASHINGTON
ancisville   *Kentwood
              *Greensburg   *Franklinton
EAST FELICIANA   *Amite   *Bogalusa

EAST BATON   TANGI-   ST TAMMANY   MISSISSIPPI
ROUGE   PAHOE
        LIVINGSTON   *Hammond   704
ndville* *Baker   *Livingston
●BATON ROUGE   *Covington
Port Allen   *Ponchatoula
ge   *Denham Spgs   *Mandeville

Plaquemine *Gonzales   *Slidell
    ASCENSION   LAKE   700-
aldsonville*   ST JOHN PONTCHATRAIN   701
        ST JAMES THE   ORLEANS
    Convent* BAPTIST *New Orleans
ASSUMPTION   Edgard* *Kenner*
    Napoleonville Hahnville Metairie*   *Chalmette   LEGEND
            Harahan *Gretha *Violet ST BERNARD   *City
    LAFOURCHE   ST *Westwego   COUNTY
    Thibodaux*   CHARLES *Harvey   *County Seat
anklin   *Pointe a la Hache   STATE CAPITAL
*Morgan City   703   Area Code
Berwick   *Houma   JEFFER-   GULF
            SON   OF MEXICO   ZIP CODE
    TERREBONNE   PREFIX
                PLAQUEMINES

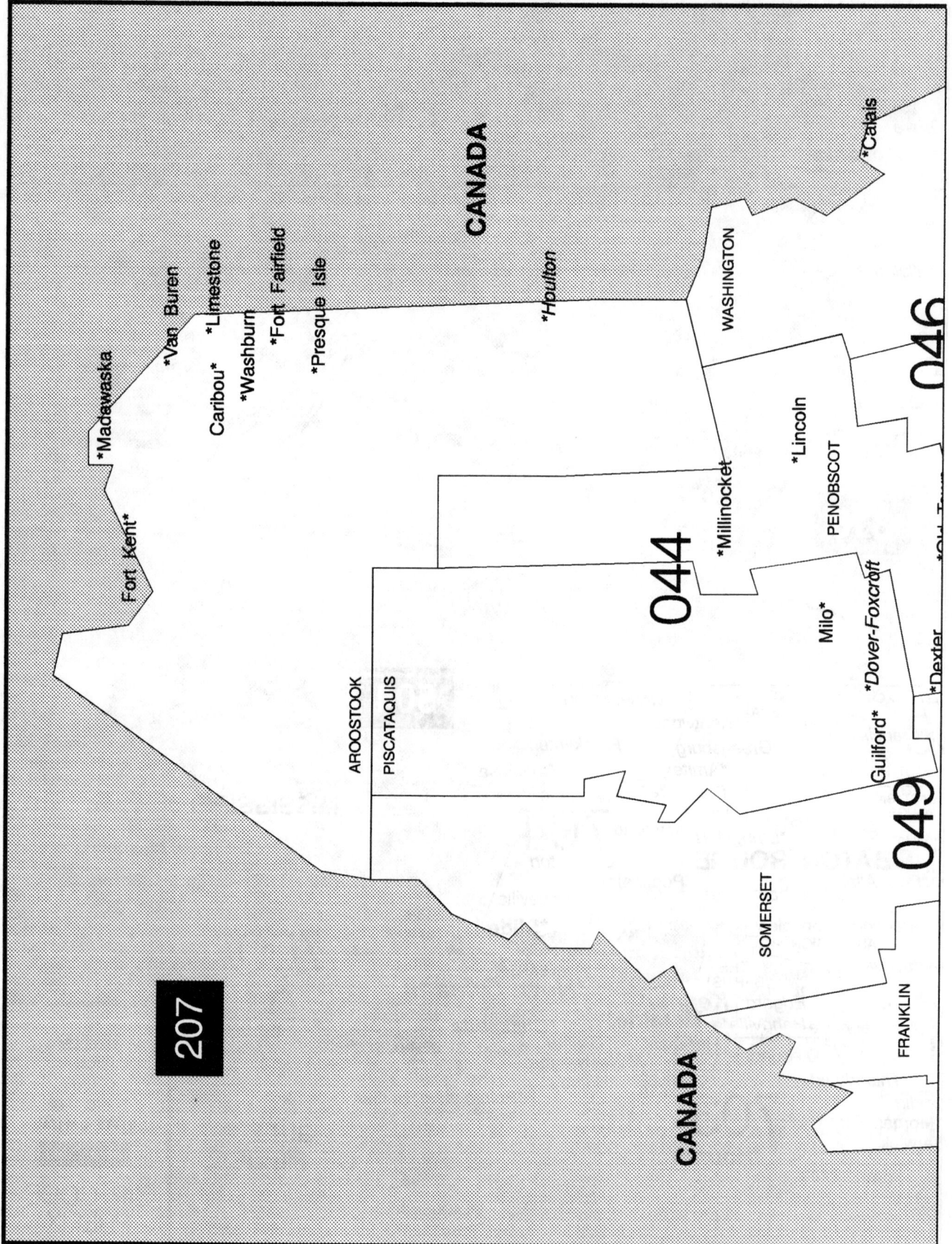

207

CANADA

CANADA

CANADA

*Calais

WASHINGTON

*Houlton

*Madawaska

*Van Buren

Caribou*

*Limestone

*Washburn

*Fort Fairfield

*Presque Isle

Fort Kent*

*Lincoln

PENOBSCOT

046

*Millinocket

044

Milo*

*Dover-Foxcroft

*Dexter

*Old Town

AROOSTOOK

PISCATAQUIS

Guilford*

049

SOMERSET

FRANKLIN

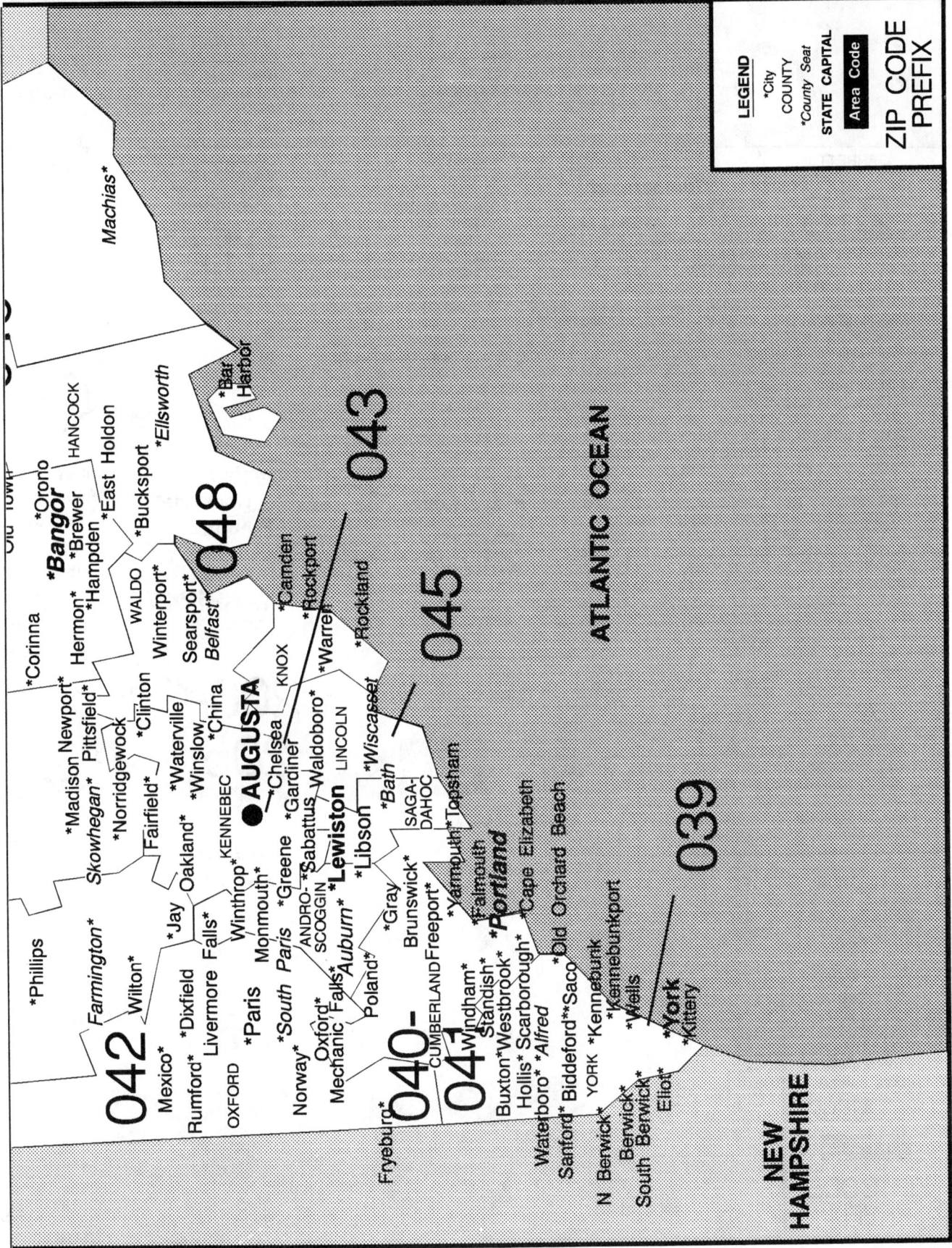

Maine Map

LEGEND

*City
COUNTY
*County Seat
STATE CAPITAL
Area Code

ZIP CODE PREFIX

ATLANTIC OCEAN

NEW HAMPSHIRE

Machias*

*Orono
*Bangor
*Brewer
*Hampden
HANCOCK
*East Holden
*Ellsworth
*Bucksport
Bar Harbor

048

043

*Corinna
*Hermon
Newport*
Pittsfield*
WALDO
Winterport*
Searsport*
Belfast*
*Camden
Rockport*
*Rockland
*Warren

045

*Madison
Skowhegan*
*Norridgewock
Fairfield*
*Clinton
*Waterville
*Winslow
*China
KENNEBEC
KNOX
LINCOLN

*Phillips

Farmington*
Wilton*

*Mexico
Rumford*
*Dixfield
Livermore Falls*
Jay*
Oakland*
*Paris
*South Paris
Winthrop*
Monmouth*
Greene*
*Sabattus
Gardiner*
Chelsea*
● AUGUSTA
*Lewiston
*Lisbon
*Bath
*Wiscasset
SAGA-DAHOC
Topsham*

042

Norway*
Oxford*
Mechanic Falls*
ANDRO-SCOGGIN
Auburn*
Poland*
*Gray
Brunswick*
Freeport*
*Yarmouth
Falmouth*
*Portland
Cape Elizabeth*
Old Orchard Beach*

Fryeburg*

040-

041

CUMBERLAND
Windham*
Standish*
Buxton*Westbrook*
Hollis*
Scarborough*
*Alfred
Waterboro*
Biddeford**Saco
Sanford*
YORK
*Kennebunk
*Kennebunkport
*Wells

039

N Berwick*
Berwick*
South Berwick*
Eliot*
*York
Kittery

OXFORD

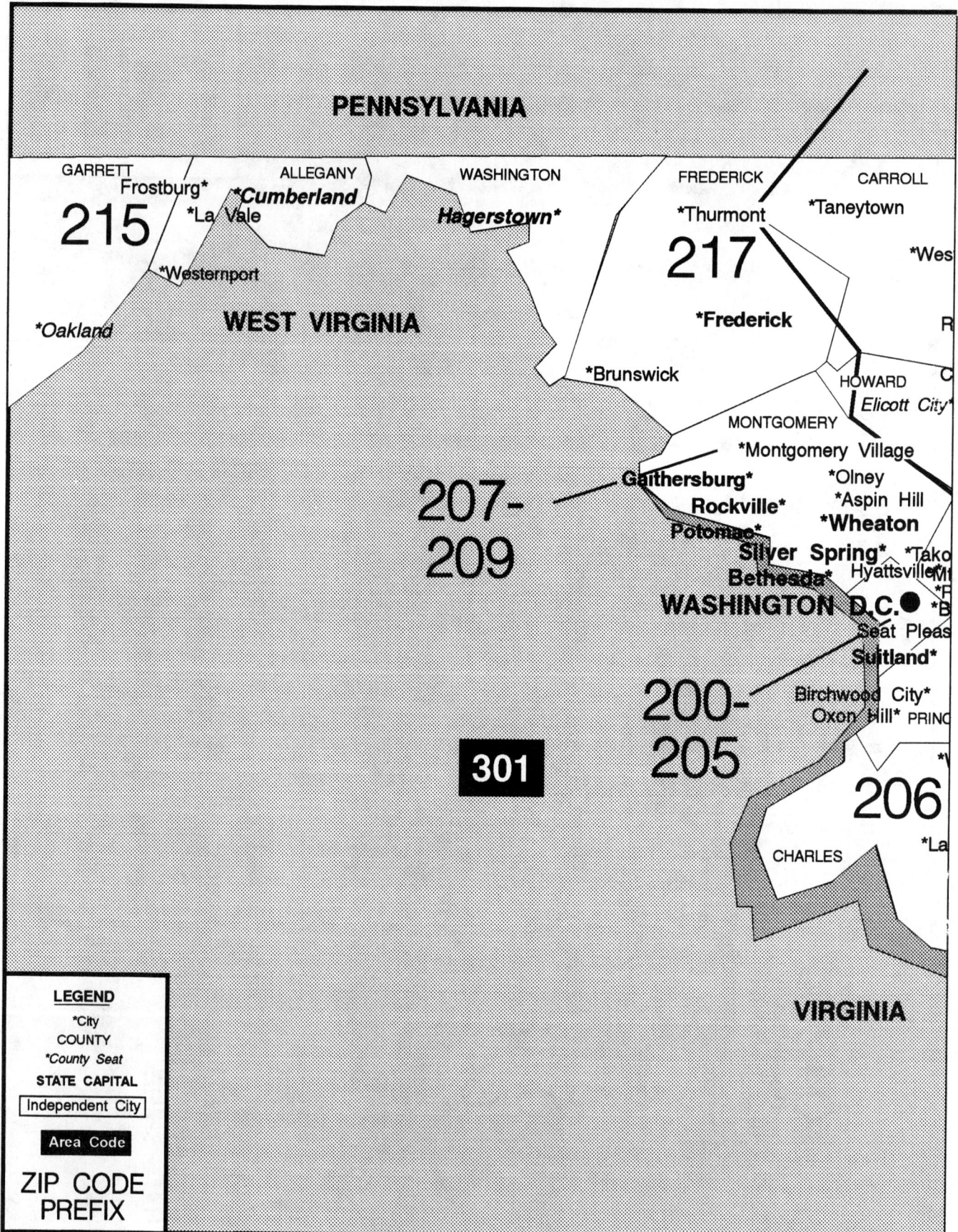

Maryland

GARRETT
Frostburg*
215
*La Vale   *Cumberland

ALLEGANY

WASHINGTON
Hagerstown*

FREDERICK
*Thurmont
217
*Frederick

CARROLL
*Taneytown

*Wes

*Westernport

*Oakland

*Brunswick

HOWARD
Elicott City

MONTGOMERY
*Montgomery Village

**207-
209**

Gaithersburg*
Rockville*
Potomac*
Bethesda

*Olney
*Aspin Hill
*Wheaton
Silver Spring*   *Tako
Hyattsville

WASHINGTON D.C.●

**200-
205**

Seat Pleas
Suitland*
Birchwood City*
Oxon Hill*   PRINC

301

206
*La

CHARLES

LEGEND
*City
COUNTY
*County Seat
STATE CAPITAL
| Independent City |
| Area Code |

**ZIP CODE
PREFIX**

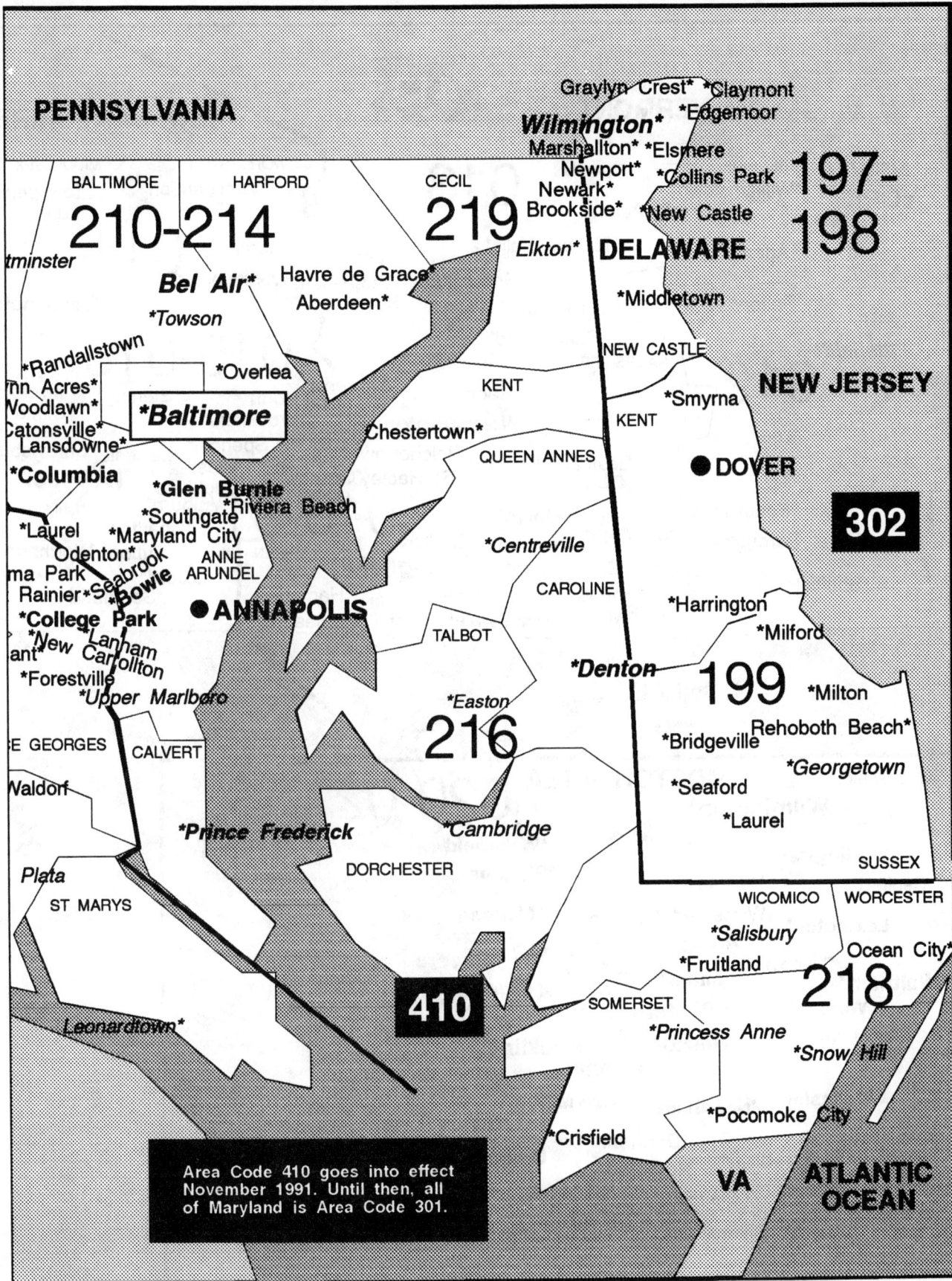

PENNSYLVANIA

BALTIMORE

210-214

HARFORD

CECIL

219

Graylyn Crest* *Claymont

Wilmington *Edgemoor

Marshallton* *Elsmere

Newport* *Collins Park

Newark*

Brookside* *New Castle

197-198

*tminster

Bel Air Havre de Grace*

Aberdeen*

Elkton* **DELAWARE**

*Towson

*Randallstown

nn Acres*

Woodlawn*

Catonsville*

Lansdowne*

*Columbia

*Baltimore

*Overlea

*Middletown

NEW CASTLE

*Smyrna

NEW JERSEY

KENT

KENT

*Glen Burnie

*Southgate *Riviera Beach

*Maryland City

Odenton*

*Laurel

ma Park

Rainier* Seabrook

*Bowie

ANNE
ARUNDEL

Chestertown*

QUEEN ANNES

*Centreville

●DOVER

302

*College Park

*New Lanham

ant* Carrollton

*Forestville

*Upper Marlboro

●ANNAPOLIS

TALBOT

CAROLINE

*Harrington

*Milford

*Denton

199

*Milton

Rehoboth Beach*

*Bridgeville

*Georgetown

*Easton

216

*Seaford

*Laurel

E GEORGES

CALVERT

*Prince Frederick

*Cambridge

SUSSEX

Plata

ST MARYS

DORCHESTER

Waldorf

WICOMICO WORCESTER

*Salisbury

Ocean City*

*Fruitland

218

410

Leonardtown*

SOMERSET

*Princess Anne

*Snow Hill

*Pocomoke City

*Crisfield

VA **ATLANTIC OCEAN**

Area Code 410 goes into effect
November 1991. Until then, all
of Maryland is Area Code 301.

413

VERMONT

NEW HAMPSHIRE

NEW YORK

BERKSHIRE

FRANKLIN

WORCESTER

MIDDLESEX

013

*Williamstown

*North Adams

Turners Falls*

*Greenfield

Adams*

Dalton*

Deerfield*

Sunderland*

HAMPSHIRE

*Winchendon

Townsend*

*Lunenburg

Gardner*

Orange*

Templeton*

*Montague

Westminster*

014

*Harv

Fitchburg

*Leominster

Lancaster*

Pittsfield*

012

*Lee

Hadley*

*Amherst

*Northampton

North Brookfield*

Belchertown*

Easthampton*

*S. Hadley*Granby*

*Ware

Holyoke*

Southampton*

Westfield*Chicopee* *Ludlow

West Springfield* *Springfield

*Great Barrington

*Sheffield

Feeding Hills* *Agawam

Southwick*Longmeadow* *East Longmeadow

Spencer*

*West Brookfield

015-016

*Sterling

Marlbor

*Clinton F

Southb

*Leicester*Shrewsbury

*Worcester

Auburn*

*Millbury *(

*Charlton

Sutton* *Northbridge

Oxford*

*Southbridge

*Whiti

Blac

010-011

HAMPDEN

*Hampden

CONNECTICUT

BOSTON AREA 020-022

617

MIDDLESEX

Wilmington*

Burlington*

Bedford*

Lexington*

Waltham*

Weston*

West Newton*

Wellesley*

Westwood*

Reading*

***Woburn**

Wincester* **Malden***

Arlington*

*Lincoln

Belmont*

Somerville*

Cambridge

Watertown*

Newton*

*Brookline

NORFOLK

*Wakefield

*Stoneham

*Melrose

SUFFOLK

Everett

*Revere

*Chelsea

*Winthrop

BOSTON

Milton*

Hull

Needham*

Quincy*

Weymouth

*Hingham

*Cohasset

NORFOLK

Scituate*

Braintree

Randolph*

Norwell*

Marshfield*

Dedham

*Dedham

Norwood*

Canton*

Holbrook*

Rockland*

Hanover*

Duxbury*

Abington*

Hanson*

*Whitman

*Pembroke

*Stoughton

Sharon*

*Hailifax

NORFOLK

PLYMOUTH

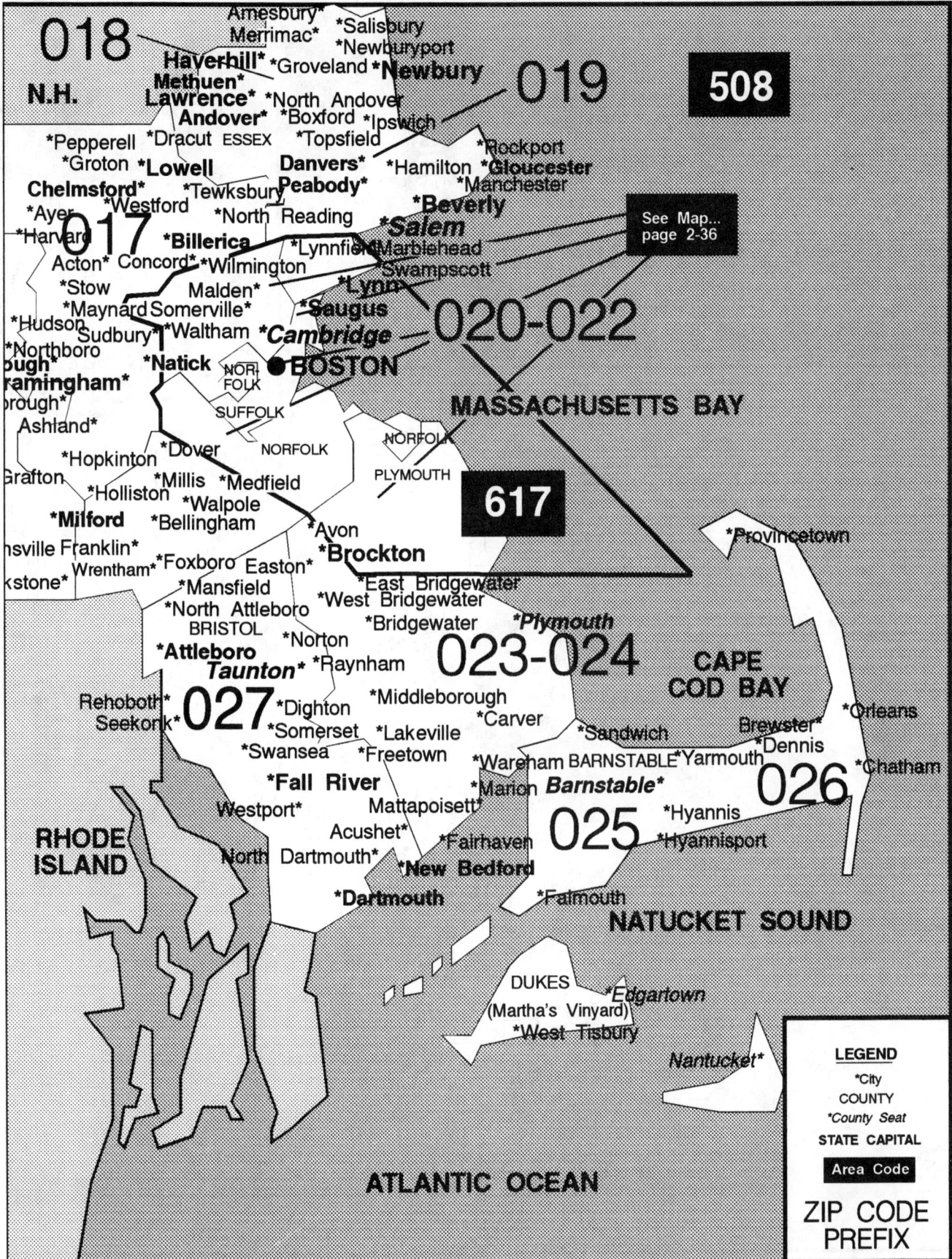

018

Amesbury*
Merrimac* *Salisbury
*Newburyport
Haverhill* *Groveland *Newbury

N.H.
Methuen*
Lawrence* *North Andover 019 508
Andover* *Boxford Ipswich
*Pepperell *Dracut ESSEX *Topsfield *Rockport
*Groton Lowell *Hamilton *Gloucester
Chelmsford* Danvers* *Manchester
*Ayer *Westford Tewksbury Peabody*
*Harvard 017 *North Reading *Beverly See Map...
page 2-36
*Billerica *Salem
Acton* Concord* *Wilmington *Lynnfield Marblehead
Stow Malden Swampscott
Maynard Somerville *Lynn 020-022
*Hudson Sudbury *Waltham *Saugus
*Northboro *Natick Cambridge
ough* NORFOLK BOSTON MASSACHUSETTS BAY
ramingham* SUFFOLK
rough* NORFOLK
Ashland* NORFOLK
*Hopkinton *Dover NORFOLK
Grafton* *Millis *Medfield PLYMOUTH 617
*Holliston *Walpole
*Milford *Bellingham *Avon *Provincetown
nsville Franklin* *Brockton
Wrentham* *Foxboro Easton* *East Bridgewater
kstone* *Mansfield West Bridgewater CAPE
*North Attleboro *Bridgewater *Plymouth COD BAY
BRISTOL *Norton 023-024
*Attleboro *Raynham *Orleans
Taunton* *Middleborough Brewster*
Rehoboth* 027 *Dighton *Carver *Dennis
Seekonk* *Somerset *Lakeville *Sandwich 026
*Swansea *Freetown *Wareham BARNSTABLE *Yarmouth *Chatham
*Fall River *Marion Barnstable*
Westport* Mattapoisett* 025 *Hyannis
Acushet* *Fairhaven *Hyannisport
RHODE North Dartmouth*
ISLAND *New Bedford
*Dartmouth *Falmouth
NATUCKET SOUND

DUKES *Edgartown
(Martha's Vinyard)
*West Tisbury

Nantucket* LEGEND
*City
COUNTY
*County Seat
STATE CAPITAL
Area Code

ATLANTIC OCEAN

ZIP CODE
PREFIX

Michigan

CANADA

CANADA

LAKE SUPERIOR

LAKE HURON

906

517

616

497

498-499

497

CHIPPEWA
*Sault Ste Marie
*Newberry

LUCE

ALGER
*Munising

SCHOOLCRAFT

MACKINAC

Manistique

DELTA

Gladstone
Escanaba

MENOMINEE

Menominee

St Ignace*

MARQUETTE
Marquette
Negaunee
Ishpeming

DICKIN-
SON

Iron Mountain
Kingsford
Norway

Crystal Falls

IRON

BARAGA

L'Anse

KEWEENAW
Eagle River
Laurium
Hancock
Houghton

HOUGH-
TON

Ontonagon

ONTONAGON

Wakefield
Bessemer
Ironwood

GOGEBIC

WISCONSIN

Cheboygan

EMMET

CHEBOYGAN

PRESQUE ISLE
Rogers City

MONT-
MORENCY

ALPENA
Alpena

Petoskey
CHARLEVOIX

ANTRIM
Bellaire

OTSEGO
Gaylord

Atlanta

CRAWFORD
Grayling

ALCONA

Mio

Kalkaska

Harrisville

Leland
LEE-
LANAU

BENZIE
Beulah

GRAND
TRAVERSE

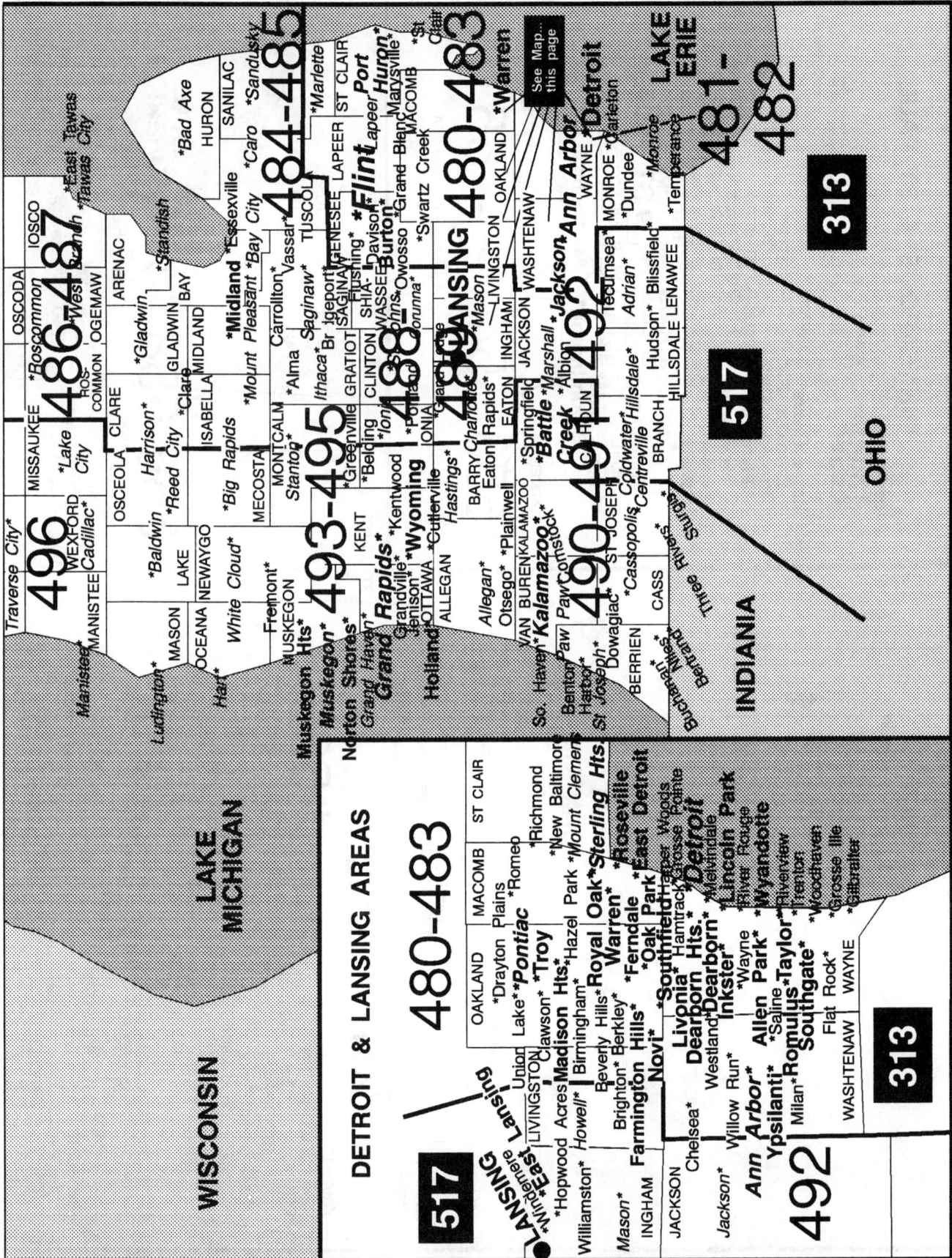

LAKE ERIE

481-482

313

517

OHIO

INDIANA

WISCONSIN

LAKE MICHIGAN

480-483

484-485

486-487

496

493-495

488-489

490-491

492

*Bad Axe
HURON
SANILAC
*Sandusky
*Caro
*Essexville
*Bay City
ST CLAIR
*Port Huron
*Marysville
*Lapeer Peer
*Flint
*Burton
MACOMB
*Warren
*Detroit
*Carleton
MONROE
*Dundee
*Monroe
*Temperance

*East Tawas
*Tawas City
IOSCO
OSCODA
*Boscommon
IOSGO
OGEMAW
ARENAC
*Standish
BAY
*West Branch
GLADWIN
*Gladwin
MIDLAND
*Midland
*Mount Pleasant
ISABELLA
*Carrollton
*Saginaw
SAGINAW
*Ithaca
GRATIOT
*Alma
*Owosso
*Corunna
GENESEE
*Flushing
*Davison
SHIA-WASSEE
LAPEER
*Marlette
TUSCOL

Traverse City*
WEXFORD
*Cadillac
*Lake City
MISSAUKEE
*Ros-COMMON
CLARE
*Harrison
*Clare
*Reed City
OSCEOLA
*Big Rapids
MECOSTA
MONTCALM
*Stantop
MANISTEE
*Baldwin
LAKE
NEWAYGO
*White Cloud
*Fremont
MUSKEGON
*Greenville
*Belding
IONIA
*Ionia
CLINTON
LANSING
INGHAM
*Mason
LIVINGSTON
OAKLAND
WASHTENAW
*Ann Arbor
WAYNE
Detroit
TECUMSEH
*Adrian
LENAWEE
*Blissfield
HILLSDALE
*Hudson

Manistee*
Ludington*
MASON
OCEANA
*Hart
Muskegon Hts*
Muskegon*
Norton Shores*
Grand Haven*
Grand Rapids
*Kentwood
*Wyoming
*Grandville
*Jenison
Holland*
KENT
OTTAWA
ALLEGAN
*Allegan
*Otsego
*Plainwell
*Hastings
BARRY
*Charlotte
EATON
*Eaton Rapids
*Springfield
Battle Creek
*Marshall
*Albion
CALHOUN
*Jackson
JACKSON
*Guiterville

VAN BUREN
*So. Haven
*Paw Paw
Kalamazoo
KALAMAZOO
*Comstock
*Hartford
*Benton Harbor
St. Joseph*
*Dowagiac
BERRIEN
*Cassopolis
*Centreville
CASS
ST JOSEPH
*Coldwater
*Hillsdale
BRANCH
*Buchanan
*Niles
Three Rivers*
*Sturgis

DETROIT & LANSING AREAS

480-483

517

LANSING
*East Lansing
Windemere*
*Hopwood Acres
Howell*
LIVINGSTON
Union Lake*
*Drayton Plains
*Romeo
OAKLAND
Clawson
*Troy
Madison Hts*
*Birmingham
*Hazel Park
*Pontiac
MACOMB
ST CLAIR
*Richmond
*New Baltimore
*Mount Clemens
Sterling Hts*
Roseville*
East Detroit*
Harper Woods
Grosse Pointe
Detroit*
*Beverly Hills
*Berkley
Royal Oak*
*Ferndale
Warren*
*Oak Park
*Hamtramck
*Melvindale
*River Rouge
Lincoln Park*
*Wyandotte
*Riverview
*Trenton
*Woodhaven
*Grosse Ile
Gibraltar*
*Southfield
*Novi
Farmington Hills*
*Brighton
*Livonia
Dearborn Hts*
*Dearborn
*Westland
*Inkster
*Wayne
Allen Park*
*Taylor
Southgate*
*Romulus
Flat Rock*
WAYNE
*Chelsea
*Willow Run
Ann Arbor*
*Saline
*Ypsilanti
*Milan
WASHTENAW
INGHAM
Mason*
Williamston*
Jackson*
JACKSON

492

313

Minnesota

MINNEAPOLIS & ST PAUL

612

550

551

553-554

556-558

WASHINGTON
*Forest Lake
*Ham Lake
Andover*
*Anoka
*Circle Pines
ANOKA
*Blaine
*Coon Rapids
Maple Grove*
Brooklyn Pk*
Brooklyn Ctr*
Plymouth* *Crystal
New Hope*
Robbinsdale*
Hopkins*
Columbia Hts*
Fridley*
White Bear Lake*
*Mounds View *Stillwater*
*Lake Elmo
Shoreview* *No St Paul
*New Brighton *Oakdale
Roseville* *Maplewood
*St Louis Pk
Minneapolis*
Minnetonka*
HENNEPIN
*Edina
Richfield*
Eden Prairie*
Bloomington*
CARVER

●ST PAUL
W St Paul RAMSEY
So St Paul
*Mendota Hts*St Paul Park
Eagan* Cottage Grove*
Inver Grove Hts*
*Woodbury
*Burnsville
*Lakeview
Northfield*
DAKOTA
Hastings*
SCOTT

218

CANADA

*Roseau
ROSEAU
KITTSON
*Hallock
MARSHALL
567
*Warren
PENNINGTON
*Thief River Falls
RED LAKE
*East Grand Forks
*Red Lake Falls
POLK
*Crookston
NORMAN
*Ada
CLAY

*Baudette
LAKE OF THE WOODS
BELTRAMI
So. International Falls
International Falls*
International Falls

566
KOOCHICHING
ITASCA
Grand Rapids*
CASS
*Walker
*Bemidji
HUBBARD
*Park Rapids
*Bagley
CLEAR-WATER
MAHNOMEN
*Mahnomen
MAHNOMEN
BECKER
565

ST LOUIS
*Ely
Mountain Iron* *Virginia
*Chisholm *Aurora
Hibbing* *Gilbert* Hoyt Lakes*
Eveleth*
AITKIN

LAKE SUPERIOR
COOK
Grand Marais
LAKE
*Silver Bay
*Two Harbors

WISCONSIN

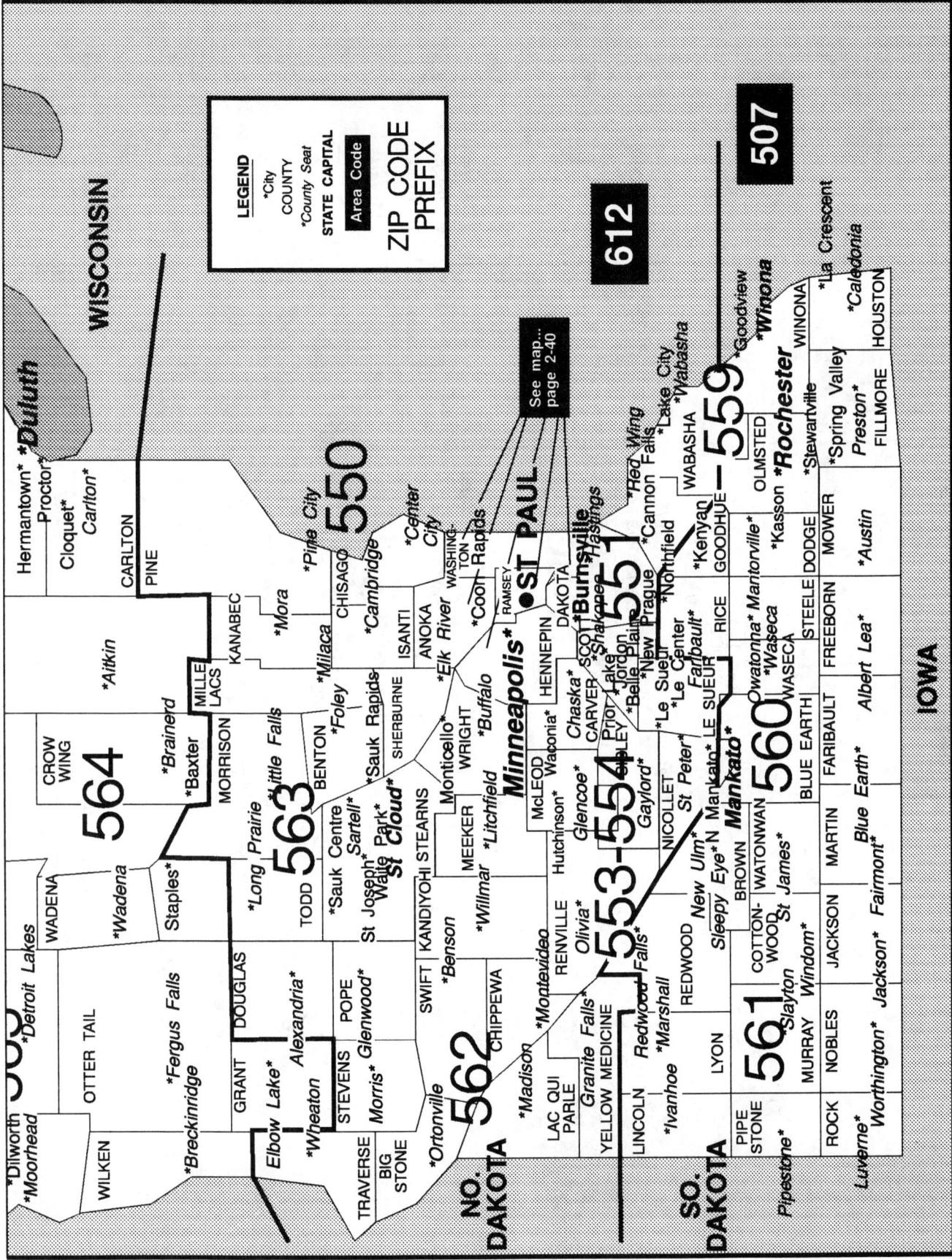

LEGEND
*City
COUNTY
*County Seat
STATE CAPITAL
Area Code
ZIP CODE PREFIX

See map...
page 2-40

507

612

*Duluth
Hermantown*
Proctor*
Cloquet*
Carlton*
CARLTON
PINE

550

559

Goodview
*Winona
WINONA
*La Crescent
*Caledonia
HOUSTON

*Pine City
*Mora
KANABEC
*Milaca
CHISAGO
*Cambridge
*Center City
ISANTI
ANOKA
*Elk River
WASHING-TON
*Coon Rapids
RAMSEY
•ST PAUL
DAKOTA
*Hastings
Red Wing
Lake City
*Wabasha
WABASHA
GOODHUE
*Red Wing
Cannon Falls
*Northfield
*Kenyon
OLMSTED
*Rochester
*Kasson
Mantorville
Stewartville*
*Spring Valley
*Preston
FILLMORE

*Aitkin

564
*Brainerd
*Baxter
CROW WING
MILLE LACS
MORRISON
*Little Falls
BENTON
*Foley
Sauk Rapids*
SHERBURNE
*Buffalo
WRIGHT
Monticello*
*Litchfield
MEEKER
HENNEPIN
Minneapolis*
Chaska*
CARVER
SCOTT
*Shakopee
Prior Lake*
Jordan*
Belle Plaine*
*New Prague
*Le Center
*Faribault
RICE
STEELE
Owatonna
*Waseca
WASECA
FREEBORN
Albert Lea
MOWER
*Austin

WADENA
*Wadena
*Staples
TODD
563
*Long Prairie
*Sauk Centre
Sartell*
St Joseph*
*St Cloud
Waite Park*
STEARNS
KANDIYOHI
*Willmar
McLEOD
Hutchinson*
Glencoe*
Gaylord*
NICOLLET
*St Peter
LE SUEUR
*Le Sueur
BLUE EARTH
*Mankato
Mankato*
N Mankato*
560
BROWN
WATONWAN
*St James
FARIBAULT
*Faribault
Blue Earth*
MARTIN
Fairmont*

505
*Dilworth
*Moorhead
OTTER TAIL
*Fergus Falls
*Breckinridge
WILKEN
GRANT
DOUGLAS
Alexandria*
Elbow Lake*
*Wheaton
STEVENS
POPE
Morris*
Glenwood
TRAVERSE
BIG STONE
*Ortonville
562
SWIFT
*Benson
CHIPPEWA
*Madison
LAC QUI PARLE
*Montevideo
RENVILLE
Olivia*
YELLOW MEDICINE
*Granite Falls
LINCOLN
*Ivanhoe
Redwood Falls*
REDWOOD
*Marshall
LYON
561
*Slayton
MURRAY
Windom*
JACKSON
Jackson*
*Worthington
NOBLES
Luverne*
ROCK

Detroit Lakes*

WADENA

*Wheaton

Sleepy Eye*
New Ulm*
COTTON-WOOD
Windom*
PIPE STONE
Pipestone*

WATONWAN

DETROIT Lakes

NO. DAKOTA
SO. DAKOTA
IOWA

553-554

551

State & City Maps

section 2 / page 41

Mississippi

ALABAMA

GULF OF MEXICO

LAUDERDALE

Meridian

393

NEWTON

*Decatur

*Newton

SCOTT

Forest

*Morton

*Brandon

JASPER

SMITH

Raleigh*

*Bay Springs

CLARKE

*Quitman

WAYNE

GREENE

*Laurel

*Ellisville

*Waynesboro

JONES

COVINGTON

*Collins

*Prentiss

*New Augusta

*Leakesville

GEORGE

*Lucedale

JACKSON

*Ocean Springs

*Moss Point

*Pascagoula

*Gautier

PERRY

394

*Wiggins

STONE

HARRISON

395

Biloxi

Gulfport

*Long Beach

*Pass Christian

*Canton

MADISON

*Ridgeland

*Clinton

HINDS

●

JACKSON

390-392

WARREN

Vicksburg

Port Gibson*

CLAIBORNE

*Pearl

*Richland

RANKIN

SIMPSON

Mendenhall*

*Magee

LAWRENCE

*Monticello

JEFFERSON DAVIS

MARION

*Columbia

FORREST

Hattiesburg*Petal

*Purvis

LAMAR

*Tylertown

WALTHALL

PEARL RIVER

*Poplarville

HAN-COCK

*Picayune

*Bay St Louis

*Waveland

Crystal Springs*

Hazlehurst

COPIAH

*Fayette

JEFFERSON

FRANKLIN

Brookhaven

Meadville*

LINCOLN

PIKE

*McComb

*Magnolia

396

*Liberty

AMITE

ADAMS

*Natchez

WILKINSON

*Woodville

LOUISIANA

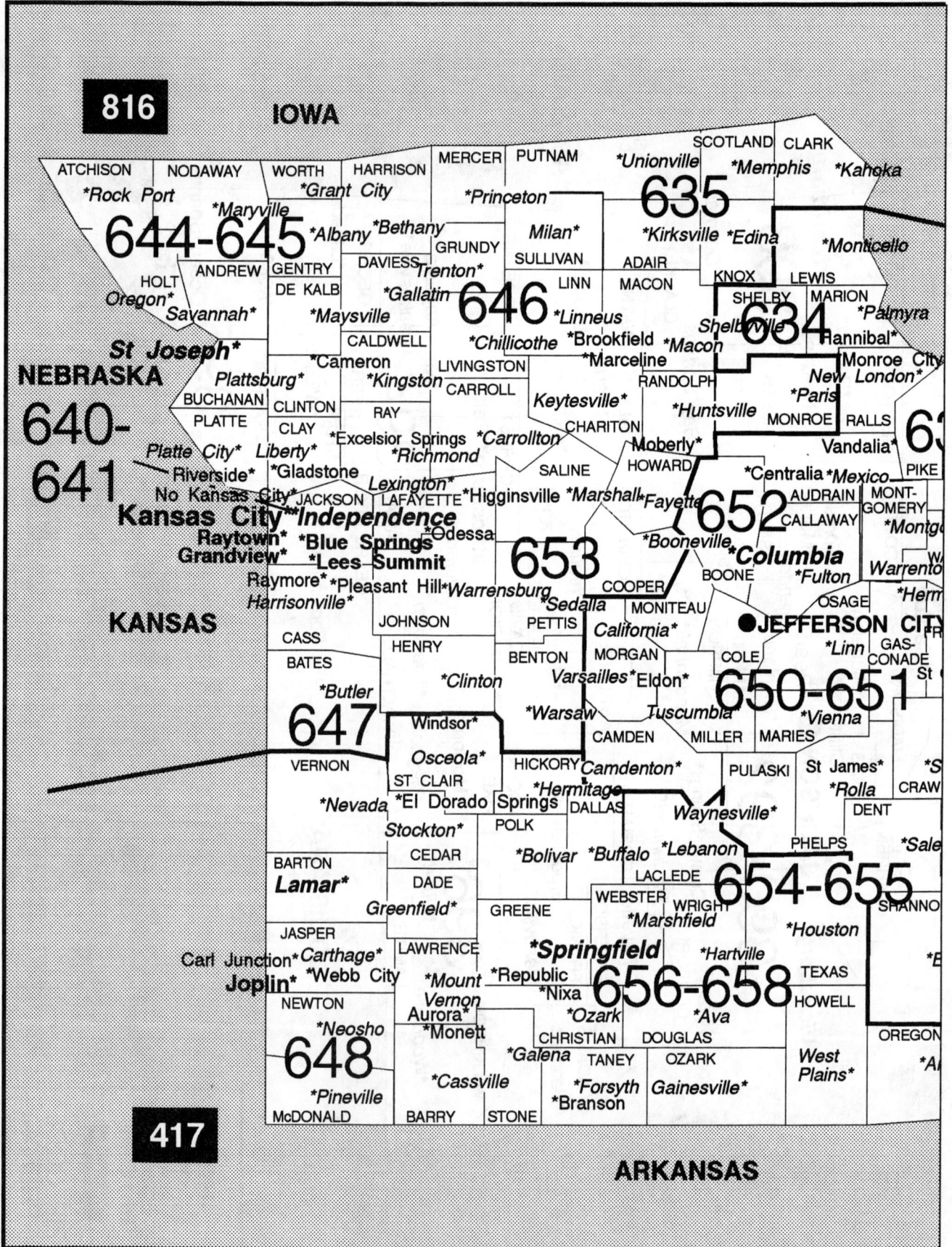

Missouri

816

IOWA

SCOTLAND CLARK

ATCHISON NODAWAY WORTH HARRISON MERCER PUTNAM *Unionville *Memphis *Kahoka

*Rock Port *Grant City *Princeton **635** *Kirksville *Edina *Monticello

*Maryville **644-645** *Albany *Bethany GRUNDY Milan* ADAIR KNOX LEWIS

ANDREW GENTRY DAVIESS *Trenton SULLIVAN *Kirksville SHELBY MARION

HOLT *Gallatin **646** LINN MACON **634** *Palmyra

Oregon DE KALB *Maysville *Linneus Shelbyville Hannibal*

Savannah CALDWELL *Chillicothe *Brookfield *Macon Monroe City

St Joseph* *Cameron LIVINGSTON *Marceline New London*

NEBRASKA *Kingston CARROLL RANDOLPH *Paris

Plattsburg* RAY Keytesville* MONROE RALLS 63

640- BUCHANAN CLINTON CHARITON *Huntsville PIKE

PLATTE CLAY *Excelsior Springs *Carrollton Moberly* Vandalia*

641 Platte City* Liberty* *Richmond SALINE HOWARD *Centralia *Mexico

Riverside* *Gladstone Lexington* *Higginsville *Marshall *Fayette **652** AUDRAIN MONT-GOMERY

No Kansas City JACKSON LAFAYETTE *Booneville CALLAWAY *Montg

Kansas City **Independence *Odessa **653** *Columbia Warrento

Raytown* *Blue Springs COOPER BOONE *Fulton *Herm

Grandview* *Lees Summit MONITEAU OSAGE

Raymore* *Pleasant Hill *Warrensburg *Sedalia ●JEFFERSON CITY

Harrisonville* JOHNSON PETTIS California* COLE *Linn GAS-CONADE

KANSAS CASS HENRY BENTON MORGAN **650-651** St G

BATES *Clinton Varsailles*Eldon *Vienna

*Butler *Warsaw Tuscumbia MILLER MARIES

647 Windsor* CAMDEN PULASKI St James* *S

VERNON Osceola* HICKORY Camdenton* *Rolla CRAW

ST CLAIR *Hermitage Waynesville* DENT

*Nevada *El Dorado Springs DALLAS *Lebanon PHELPS *Sale

Stockton* POLK LACLEDE **654-655**

BARTON CEDAR *Bolivar *Buffalo WEBSTER WRIGHT SHANNO

Lamar* DADE GREENE *Marshfield *Houston

Greenfield* GREENE *Springfield *Hartville TEXAS

JASPER LAWRENCE *Republic **656-658** HOWELL

Carl Junction*Carthage* *Nixa *Ava

Joplin* *Webb City *Mount Vernon *Ozark OREGON

NEWTON Aurora* CHRISTIAN DOUGLAS West Plains* *A

*Neosho *Monett *Galena TANEY OZARK

648 *Cassville *Forsyth Gainesville*

*Pineville *Branson

McDONALD BARRY STONE

417

ARKANSAS

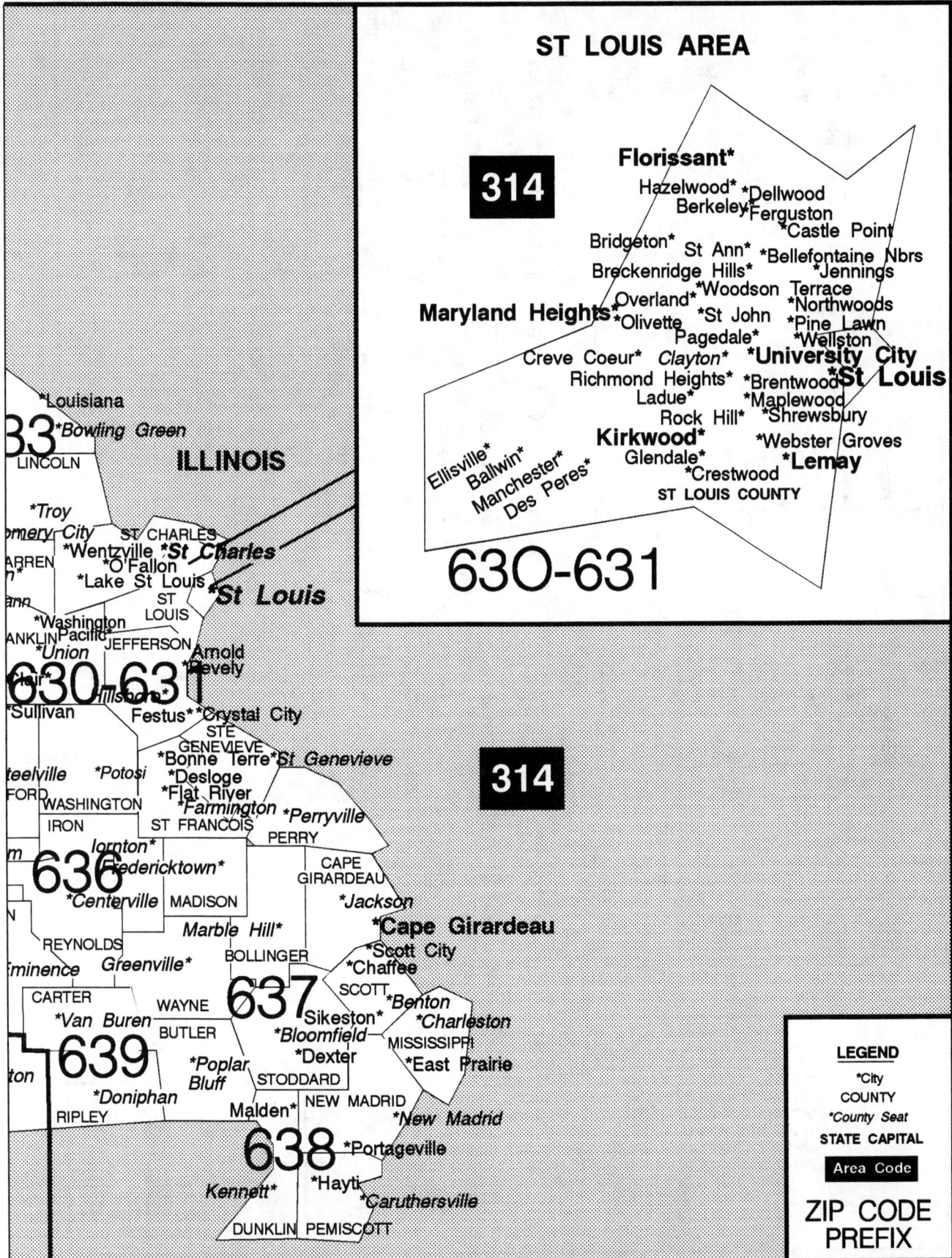

ST LOUIS AREA

314

Florissant*

Hazelwood* *Dellwood
Berkeley*Ferguston
*Castle Point
Bridgeton* St Ann* *Bellefontaine Nbrs
Breckenridge Hills* *Jennings
*Woodson Terrace
Overland* *Northwoods
Maryland Heights*Olivette *St John *Pine Lawn
Pagedale* *Wellston
Creve Coeur* *Clayton* *University City
Richmond Heights* *Brentwood *St Louis
Ladue* *Maplewood
Rock Hill* *Shrewsbury
Kirkwood* *Webster Groves
Ellisville* Glendale* *Lemay
Ballwin* *Crestwood
Manchester* ST LOUIS COUNTY
Des Peres*

630-631

*Louisiana
33 *Bowling Green
LINCOLN **ILLINOIS**
*Troy
omery City ST CHARLES
*Wentzville *St Charles
*O'Fallon
*Lake St Louis *St Louis
ARREN *Washington ST
n *Pacific LOUIS
ann JEFFERSON
ANKLIN *Union Arnold
lair *Hillsboro *Pevely
630-631
Sullivan Festus *Crystal City
STE
GENEVIEVE
teelville *Potosi *Bonne Terre* *St Genevieve
FORD *Desloge
WASHINGTON *Flat River
IRON *Farmington *Perryville
ST FRANCOIS
PERRY
m lornton* **314**
636 Fredericktown* CAPE
GIRARDEAU
*Centerville MADISON *Jackson
Marble Hill* *Cape Girardeau
REYNOLDS BOLLINGER *Scott City
minence Greenville* *Chaffee
SCOTT
CARTER WAYNE **637** *Benton
Van Buren BUTLER Sikeston *Charleston
639 *Bloomfield MISSISSIPPI
*Poplar *Dexter *East Prairie
ton Bluff STODDARD
*Doniphan NEW MADRID
RIPLEY Malden* *New Madrid
638 *Portageville
Kennett* *Hayti
*Caruthersville
DUNKLIN PEMISCOTT

Montana — Area Code 406

ZIP CODE PREFIXES:
- 590-591 Billings* (Hardin*)
- 592 Roosevelt (Scobey*, West Point*, Plentywood*)
- 593 Fallon (Miles City*, Baker*, Ekalaka*, Broadus*)
- 594 Great Falls (Chouteau, Fort Benton*)
- 595 Chinook* (Havre*, Malta*)
- 596 Helena (Lewis & Clark)
- 597 Dillon* (Beaverhead, Bozeman*, Virginia City*)
- 598 Missoula* (Superior*)
- 599 Libby* (Lincoln, Whitefish*, Kalispell*)

LEGEND
- *City
- COUNTY
- *County Seat
- STATE CAPITAL
- Area Code
- ZIP CODE PREFIX

Counties and cities shown: CANADA, IDAHO, WYOMING, LINCOLN, GLACIER, TOOLE, LIBERTY, HILL, BLAINE, PHILLIPS, VALLEY, DANIELS, SHERIDAN, ROOSEVELT, RICHLAND, DAWSON, WIBAUX, FALLON, CARTER, POWDER RIVER, CUSTER, PRAIRIE, GARFIELD, McCONE, ROSEBUD, TREASURE, BIG HORN, YELLOWSTONE, MUSSELSHELL, GOLDEN VALLEY, WHEATLAND, STILLWATER, SWEET GRASS, PARK, GALLATIN, MADISON, BEAVERHEAD, SILVER BOW, DEER LODGE, GRANITE, RAVALLI, MINERAL, SANDERS, FLATHEAD, LAKE, MISSOULA, POWELL, LEWIS & CLARK, MEAGHER, CASCADE, BROADWATER, JEFFERSON, JUDITH BASIN, FERGUS, PETROLEUM, TETON, PONDERA, CARBON

Cities (*): Plentywood, Scobey, West Point, Sidney, Glendive, Wibaux, Terry, Baker, Ekalaka, Broadus, Glasgow, Circle, Jordon, Miles City, Forsyth, Malta, Chinook, Havre, Winnett, Lewistown, Roundup, Hysham, Hardin, Billings, Laurel, Columbus, Red Lodge, Livingston, Big Timber, Ryegate, Stanford, White Sulphur Spgs, Harlowton, Townsend, Bozeman, Virginia City, Shelby, Chester, Conrad, Fort Benton, Great Falls, Choteau, Cut Bank, Columbia Falls, Kalispell, Polson, Thompson Falls, Whitefish, Libby, Superior, Missoula, Hamilton, Philipsburg, Anaconda, Deer Lodge, Boulder, Butte, Dillon, HELENA

SOUTH DAKOTA

IOWA

680

681

402

680

681

687

686

688

691

692

693

689

690

308

683-685

MO

KANSAS

COLORADO

South Sioux City
*Hartington
*Ponca
DAKOTA City
Dakota City
THURSTON
*Tekamah
WASHINGTON
*Blair
*West Point
BURT
*Pender
CUMING
*Wayne
Wayne*
PIERCE
*Pierce
Neligh*
ANTELOPE
Center*
*Butte
KNOX
CEDAR DIXON
Mai son*
MADISON
Norfolk*
STANTON
*Stanton
PLATTE
*Albion
BOONE
Columbus*
COL-FAX
DODGE
*Fremont
Omaha
DOUGLAS
SARPY
Papillion*
Bellevue
*Plattsmouth
CASS
SAUNDERS
*Wahoo
BUTLER
David City*
*Schuyler
NANCE
*Fullerton
MERRICK
*Central City
POLK
*Osceola
York*
YORK
*Aurora
HAMILTON
LINCOLN
LAN-CASTER
SEWARD
*Seward
SALINE
*Wilber
*Crete
Nebraska City
OTOE
*Auburn
*Tecumseh
NEMAHA
JOHNSON
*Beatrice
GAGE
*Fairbury
JEFFERSON
*Pawnee City
Falls City*
PAWNEE RICHARDSON
FILLMORE
Geneva*
*Clay Ctr
CLAY
*Hebron
THAYER
*Nelson
NUCKOLLS
*Superior
WEBSTER
Red Cloud*
*Franklin
FRANKLIN
*Alma
HARLAN
*Beaver City
FURNAS
*McCook
RED WILLOW
*Trenton
HITCHCOCK
DUNDY
*Benkelman
CHASE
*Imperial
PERKINS
*Grant
KEITH
*Ogallala
DEUEL
*Chappell
CHEYENNE
*Sidney
KIMBALL
Kimball*
BANNER
*Harrisburg
MORRILL
*Bridgeport
GARDEN
*Oshkosh
ARTHUR
*Arthur
McPHERSON
*Tryon
LINCOLN
North Platte*
LOGAN
*Stapleton
THOMAS
*Thedford
HOOKER
*Mullen
GRANT
*Hyannis
SCOTTS BLUFF
*Gering
*Scottsbluff
BOX BUTTE
*Alliance
DAWES
*Chadron
SHERIDAN
*Rushville
SIOUX
*Harrison
CHERRY
Valentine*
*Springview
KEYA PAHA
*Ainsworth
BROWN ROCK HOLT
BOYD
*Bassett
*O'Neill
GARFIELD
*Burwell
WHEELER
*Bartlett
LOUP
BLAINE
*Brewster
CUSTER
Taylor*
VALLEY
*Ord
GREELEY
*Greeley
SHERMAN
*Loup City
HOWARD
*St Paul
HALL
Grand Island*
BUFFALO
Kearney*
Hastings*
ADAMS
PHELPS
*Holdrege
KEARNEY
*Minden
GOSPER
*Elwood
FRONTIER
*Stockville
HAYES
*Hayes Ctr
Broken Bow*
DAWSON
*Lexington
*Cozad
*Gothenburg

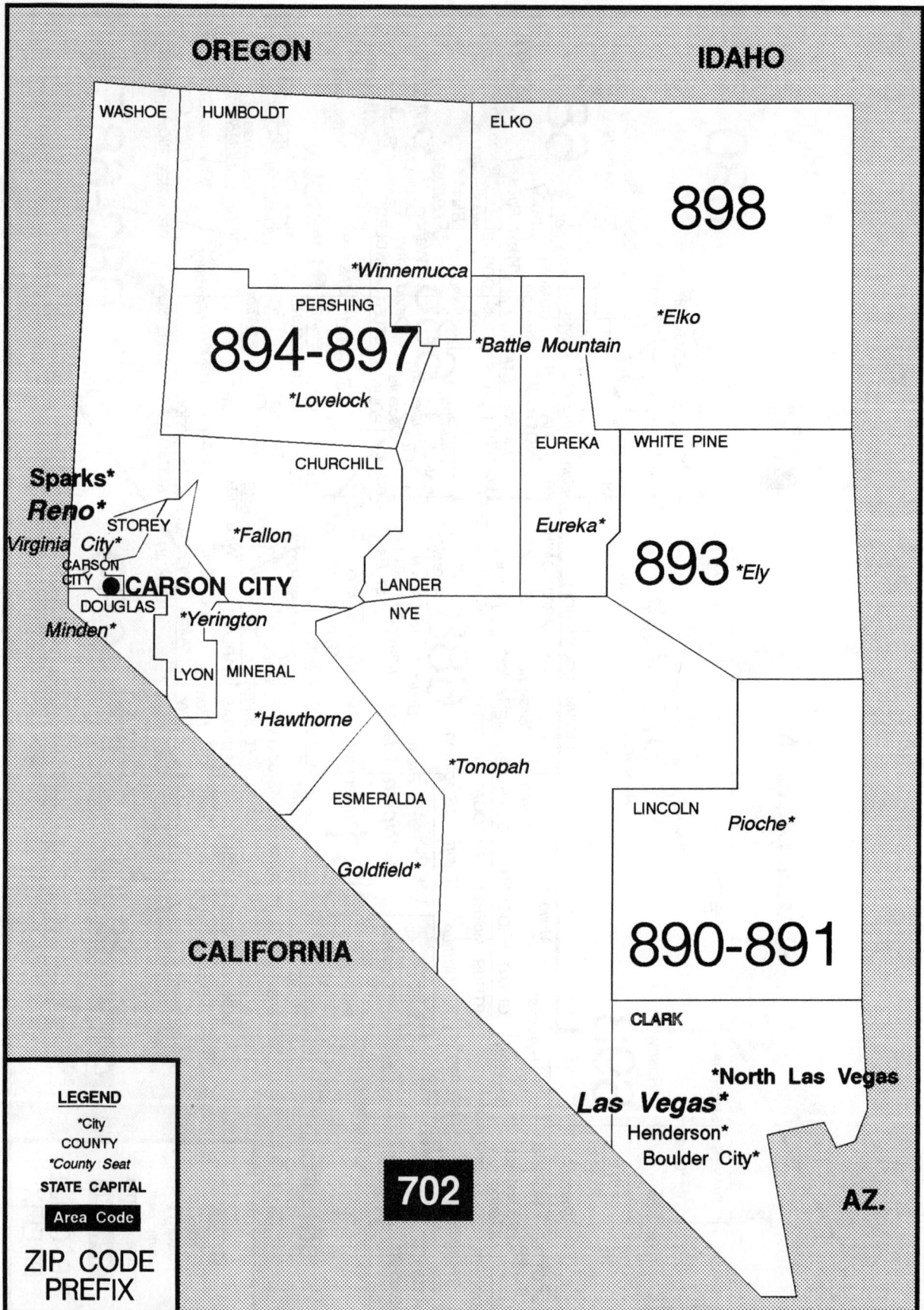

Nevada

OREGON   IDAHO

WASHOE   HUMBOLDT   ELKO

898

*Winnemucca

PERSHING   *Elko

894-897

*Battle Mountain

*Lovelock

CHURCHILL   EUREKA   WHITE PINE

Sparks*
*Reno**   Eureka*
STOREY   *Fallon
Virginia City*   **893** *Ely
CARSON
CITY ●**CARSON CITY**   LANDER
DOUGLAS   NYE
*Minden**   *Yerington

LYON   MINERAL

*Hawthorne

*Tonopah

ESMERALDA   LINCOLN   Pioche*

Goldfield*

890-891

CALIFORNIA

CLARK

North Las Vegas

*Las Vegas**
Henderson*
Boulder City*

LEGEND
*City
COUNTY
*County Seat
STATE CAPITAL
Area Code

**ZIP CODE
PREFIX**

702   AZ.

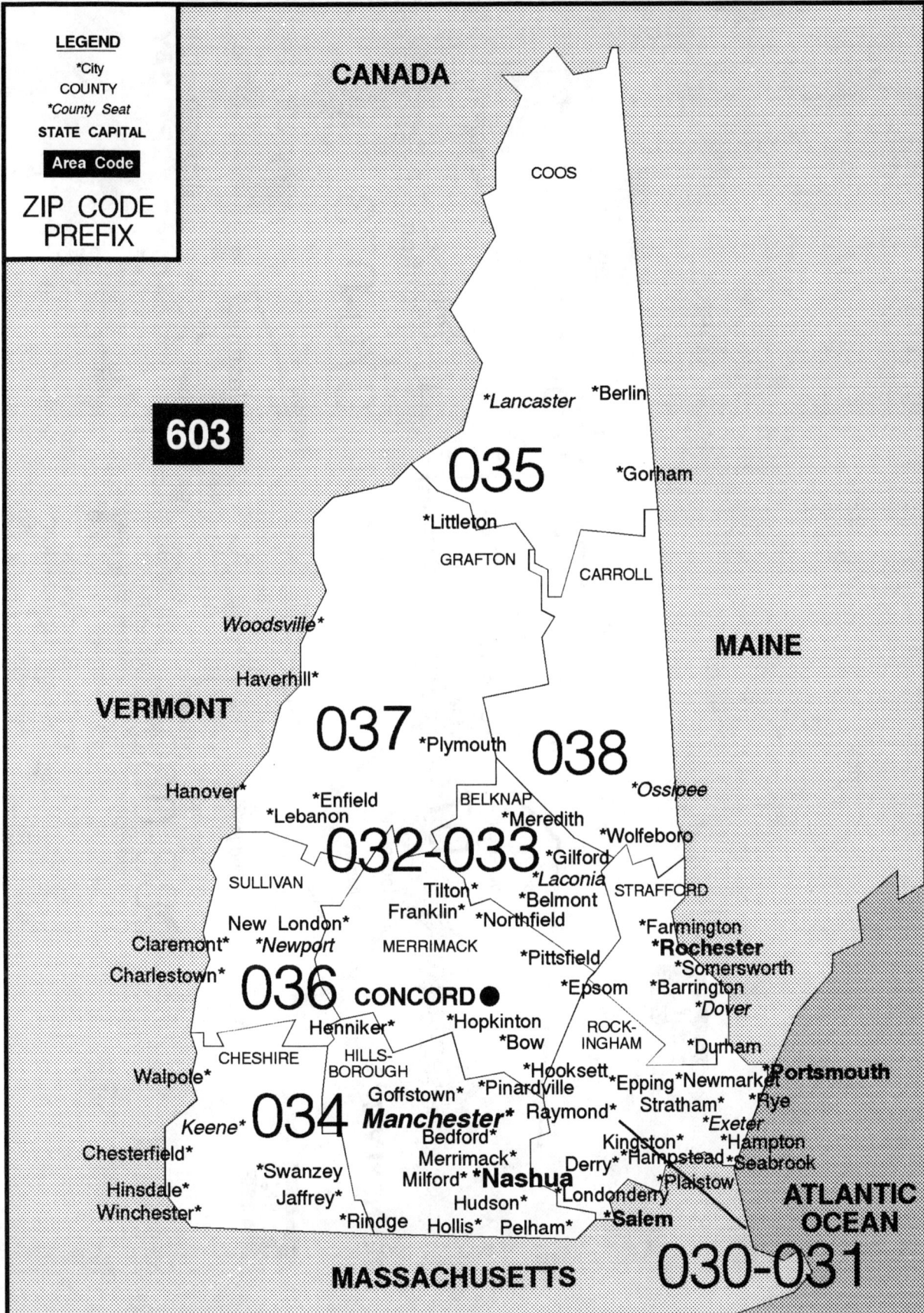

LEGEND
*City
COUNTY
*County Seat
STATE CAPITAL
Area Code

ZIP CODE PREFIX

603

CANADA

COOS

MAINE

VERMONT

*Lancaster   *Berlin

035

*Gorham

*Littleton

GRAFTON   CARROLL

Woodsville*

Haverhill*

037 *Plymouth   **038**

*Ossipee

Hanover*   *Enfield   BELKNAP
            *Lebanon   *Meredith
                                    *Wolfeboro
032-033   *Gilford   STRAFFORD

SULLIVAN   *Laconia
            Tilton   *Belmont
New London* Franklin* *Northfield   *Farmington

Claremont* *Newport   **Rochester**
                MERRIMACK   *Somersworth
Charlestown*   *Pittsfield *Barrington
        036 CONCORD●   *Dover
                            *Epsom
            Henniker* *Hopkinton   ROCK-   *Durham
CHESHIRE   *Bow   INGHAM
        HILLS-   **Portsmouth**
Walpole* BOROUGH   *Hooksett
                *Pinardville *Epping*Newmarket *Rye
        034 Goffstown* Raymond* Stratham*
Keene*   **Manchester***   *Exeter
                Bedford*   Kingston* *Hampton
Chesterfield*   Merrimack*   Derry* *Hampstead Seabrook
        Swanzey Milford **Nashua**   *Plaistow
Hinsdale*   Jaffrey*   Hudson* *Londonderry   ATLANTIC
Winchester*   *Rindge Hollis* Pelham* **Salem**   OCEAN

030-031

MASSACHUSETTS

NEW YORK

LOWER NEW YORK BAY

NEW YORK CITY

Jersey City

*Hackensack

BERGEN

076

*Paterson

*Clifton

070-073

HUDSON

ESSEX

Newark

UNION

*Westfield

PASSAIC

074-075

*Dover

MORRIS

079

Franklin*

Newton*

Andover*

*Sparta

Hopatcong*

Stanhope*

SUSSEX

SOMERSET

*Bernardsville

North Plainfield*

Warren*

*Watchung

*So Plainfield

Dunellen*

Middlesex*

Bound Brook*

*Piscataway

*Edison

Metuchen*

Carteret

Woodbridge

*Perth Amboy

South Amboy

Sayreville

Keyport*

Keansburg*

*Middletown

*Red B.

*Rumson

*Long Branch

*W Long Branch

Asbury Park

*Neptune

*Holmdel

Hazlet*

Aberdeen*

Matawan

MIDDLESEX

Spotswood*

*So River

Milltown*

Highland Park*

New Brunswick

Manville*

Bridgewater*

Somerville*

Raritan*

Lebanon*

High Bridge*

HUNTERDON

088-089

Flemington*

Hopewell*

No Brunswick*

East Brunswick*

*So Brunswick

Princeton*

East Windsor*

*Slackwood

*Mercerville

085-086

Lambertville*

Lawrenceville*

Freehold*

Eatontown*

Tinton Falls*

WARREN

078

Hackettstown*

*Belvidere

Washington*

*Phillipsburg

Alpha*

201

PENNSYLVANIA

908

See Map...
page 2-52

LEGEND
*City
COUNTY
*County Seat
STATE CAPITAL
Area Code
ZIP CODE PREFIX

077

*Manasquan

MONMOUTH

OCEAN

*Brookwood
*Lakewood
*Point Pleasant
*Silverton
*Holiday City

Jackson *Brick
*Lakehurst

087

Toms River*
*Gifford Park
*Beachwood

So Toms River*

*Manahawkin

*Hamilton Square

MERCER

*Bordentown

BURLINGTON

*Mount Holly
*Lumberton
*Marlton *Mt Laurel
*Maple Shade
*Medford Lakes

TRENTON●
CODE 609

Florence*
Beverly*
*Burlington
Delanco*
*Riverside *Willingboro
Riverton* *Palmyra *Delran
*Cinnaminson
*Cherry Hill *Moorestown
*Audubon *Haddonfield
Hadden *Barrington *Evesham
Hts* *Somerdale
Bellmawr* *Stratford
Runnemede* *Lindenwold
*Clementon
*Berlin

CAMDEN

080-084

*Hammonton

Egg Harbor*

**Brigantine*
*Atlantic City**
*Ventnor City
*Margate City

Absecon*

Pleasantville*
Northfield*
Linwood* *Somers Point

*Ocean City

ATLANTIC OCEAN

Pennsauken*
Camden
Collingswood*
Gloucester City*

*Woodbury
Oak Valley*

Pine Hill

*Clayton

GLOUCESTER

Buena*

Mays Landing*

Vineland

Millville

ATLANTIC

CAPE MAY

*Cape May Court House
*North Wildwood
*Wildwood
*Wildwood Crest
*Cape May

Gibbstown*
Glassboro*
*Woodstown

SALEM

Bridgeton*

CUMBERLAND

DELAWARE BAY

*Penns Grove
Carneys Point*

Pennsville*
Salem*

609

DEL.

PENNSYLVANIA

NEW YORK

NEW YORK

ATLANTIC OCEAN

201

070-073

076

908

PASSAIC

BERGEN

MORRIS

HUDSON

ESSEX

UNION

*West Milford
*Ringwood
Mahwah*
*Park Ridge
Hillsdale*
*Westwood
*New Milford
*River Edge *Closter
*Dumont *Cresskill
Maywood* Tenafly*
Bergenfield
Englewood Cliffs
Palisades Park
NEW York
North Bergen
Guttenberg
West New York

*Allendale
*Franklin Lakes
*Waldwick
*Wyckoff
*Paramus
*Elmwood Park
Teaneck
Hackensack Englewood
Fort Lee*
Leonia*
Ridgefield Park*
Ridgefield*
Cliffside Park*
Fairview*

*Wanaque
Oakland*
*Pompton Lakes
Hawthorne*
Glen Rock*
Ridgewood
Fair Lawn
Paterson
Saddle Brook*
Clifton
*Lodi
Garfield*
Wood-Ridge*
Passaic
Carlstadt*
Rutherford* *E Rutherford
Lyndhurst*
Secaucus*
Hoboken
Jersey City

Bloomingdale*
Butler*
Haledon*
Wayne* *Totowa
*West Paterson
Verona*
Belleville
No Arlington*
Kearney
Union City
Newark
*Elizabeth
*Bayonne

*Kinnelon
Lincoln Park*
Little Falls*
Cedar Grove*
North Caldwell* *Fairfield
*Caldwell
Montclair
Glen Ridge*
Nutley
Bloomfield
East Orange
Harrison*
*Irvington
Rahway

*Rockaway
Boonton*
Hanover W Caldwell
Roseland*
West Orange
Orange
*Maplewood
*Millburn
Hillside*
Roselle Park *Roselle
*Clark

*Mt Arlington
East Hanover*
Florham Park*
Madison*
Livingston
*So Orange
Union
*Summit *Mountainside
Cranford*
Garwood*

Morristown*
Parsippany*
*Netcong **Dover***
Chatham*
Springfield*
New Providence*
*Kenilworth
UNION

Berkeley Hts*
Scotch Plains*
Westfield
Fanwood*
Plainfield*

LEGEND
*City
COUNTY
*County Seat
STATE CAPITAL
Area Code

ZIP CODE PREFIX

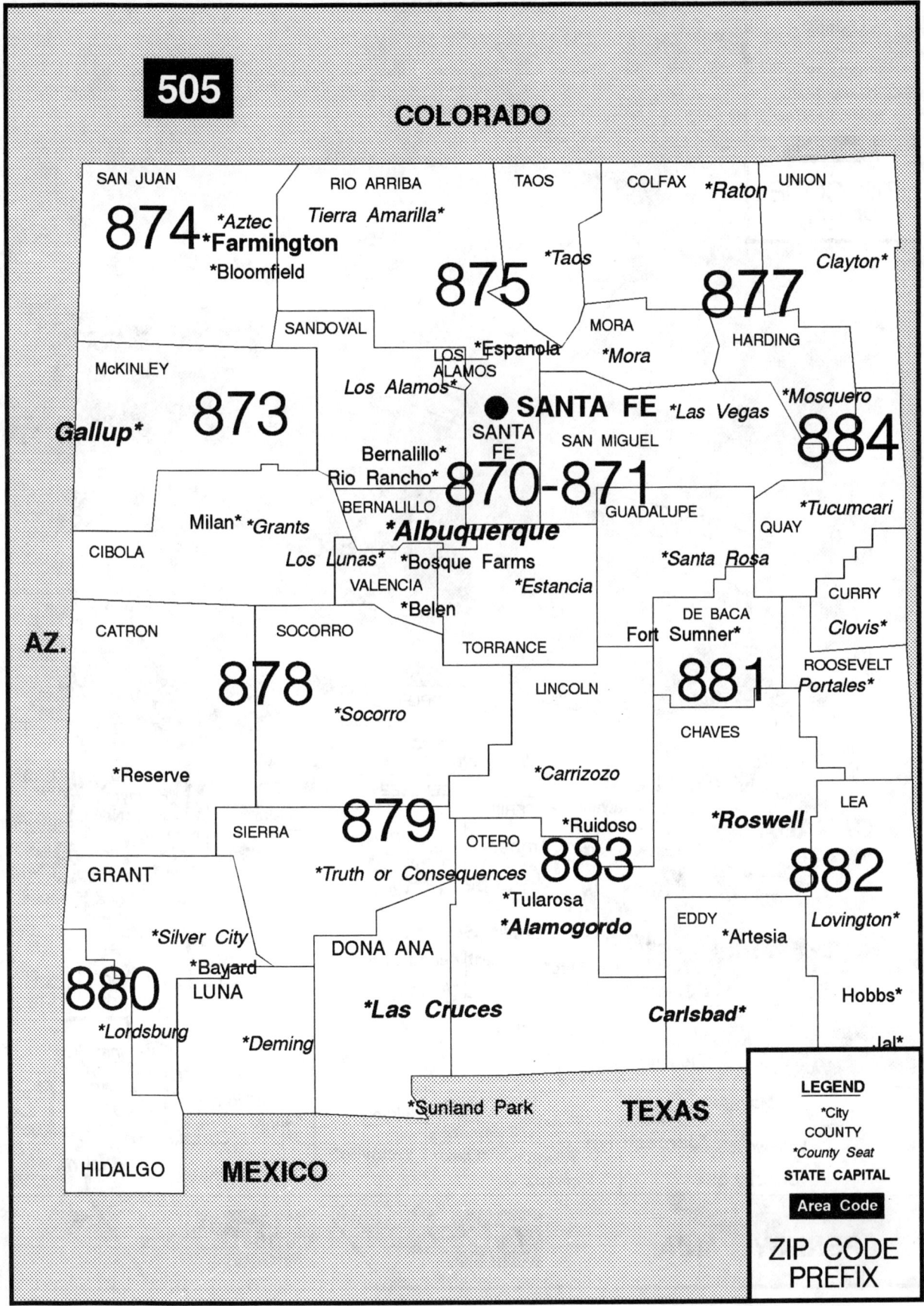

505

COLORADO

SAN JUAN

RIO ARRIBA

TAOS

COLFAX

UNION

*Raton

874 *Aztec

Tierra Amarilla*

*Farmington

Clayton*

*Bloomfield

877

SANDOVAL

*Taos

MORA

HARDING

McKINLEY

*Espanola

LOS ALAMOS

*Mora

Los Alamos*

873

Gallup*

*Las Vegas

*Mosquero

884

Bernalillo*

SANTA FE

● **SANTA FE**

Rio Rancho*

SAN MIGUEL

BERNALILLO

870-871

GUADALUPE

*Tucumcari

QUAY

Milan* *Grants

*Albuquerque

CIBOLA

Los Lunas*

*Bosque Farms

*Santa Rosa

VALENCIA

*Estancia

CURRY

*Belen

DE BACA

Clovis*

CATRON

SOCORRO

Fort Sumner*

TORRANCE

878

LINCOLN

ROOSEVELT

*Socorro

881

Portales*

CHAVES

*Reserve

*Carrizozo

LEA

SIERRA

879

*Ruidoso

*Roswell

OTERO

883

882

GRANT

*Truth or Consequences

*Tularosa

EDDY

Lovington*

*Silver City

*Alamogordo

*Artesia

*Bayard

DONA ANA

Hobbs*

880

LUNA

*Las Cruces

Carlsbad*

*Lordsburg

Jal*

*Deming

*Sunland Park

TEXAS

HIDALGO

MEXICO

AZ.

LEGEND

*City

COUNTY

*County Seat

STATE CAPITAL

Area Code

ZIP CODE PREFIX

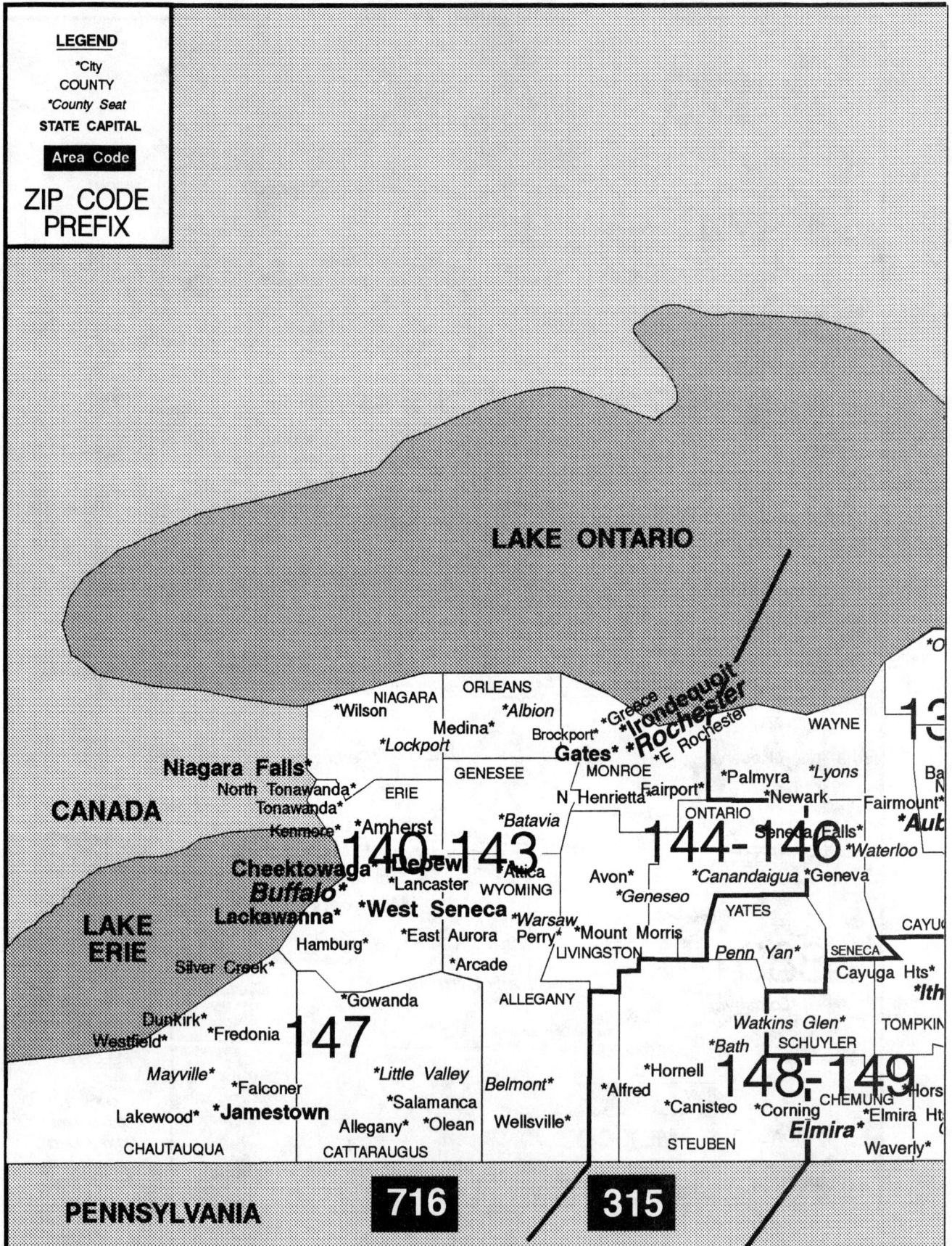

LEGEND
*City
COUNTY
*County Seat
STATE CAPITAL
Area Code

ZIP CODE PREFIX

LAKE ONTARIO

NIAGARA
*Wilson

ORLEANS
*Albion

Medina*
*Lockport

Brockport*

*Greece *Irondequoit
*Rochester
*E Rochester

WAYNE

13

Niagara Falls*

GENESEE

Gates*

MONROE

Fairport*

*Palmyra *Lyons
*Newark

Ba

North Tonawanda*
Tonawanda*

ERIE

N Henrietta

ONTARIO

Fairmount*

*Aub

Kenmore* *Amherst

*Batavia

140-143

*Depew

WYOMING

Avon*

144-146

Seneca Falls*

*Waterloo

CANADA

Cheektowaga *Attica

Buffalo*

*Lancaster

*Geneseo

*Canandaigua *Geneva

LAKE ERIE

Lackawanna*

West Seneca*

*Warsaw
Perry*

YATES

CAYU

*Mount Morris

Hamburg*

*East Aurora

LIVINGSTON

Penn Yan*

SENECA

Cayuga Hts*

Silver Creek*

*Arcade

ALLEGANY

*Ith

*Gowanda

Watkins Glen*

TOMPKIN

Dunkirk*
Westfield* *Fredonia

147

*Bath

SCHUYLER

148-149

Mayville*

*Little Valley

Belmont*

*Hornell

*Falconer

*Alfred

*Canisteo

CHEMURG

*Hors

Lakewood* **Jamestown**

*Salamanca

*Corning

*Elmira Ht

Allegany* *Olean

Wellsville*

STEUBEN

Elmira

CHAUTAUQUA

CATTARAUGUS

Waverly*

PENNSYLVANIA

716

315

CANADA

*Massena

Champlain*

518

*Ogdensburg

*Malone

*Dannemora

*Plattsburgh

*Potsdam

129

*Canton

CLINTON

136

*Gouverneur

ESSEX

Saranac Lake*
*Tupper Lake

JEFFERSON

VERMONT

ST LAWRENCE

FRANKLIN

Elizabethtown*

LEWIS

HERKIMER

*Carthage

HAMILTON

Watertown

Ticonderoga*

WARREN

Lowville*

128

Whitehall*

OSWEGO

WASHING-
TON

swego

133-135

Lake George*

ONEIDA

Lake Pleasant*

Granville*

Glens Falls*
Corinth*
S Glenns Falls*

*Hudson Falls

30-132 Rome*

*Fort Edward

ulton

Dolgeville*

Saratoga Springs

MASS.

Sherrill*

*Frankfort *Little Falls

*Greenwich

*Bayberry

Yorkville* **Utica**

*Herkimer FULTON *Gloversville

dwinsville*
N Syracuse*
Solvay* **Syracuse**

New York Mills*
*Ilion *Mohawk

*Ballston Spa

**120-
123**

*Oneida
*Wampsville

*Johnsontown

urn

Fonda*

SARATOGA RENSSELAER

Fayetteville*

*Chittenango

Fort Plain*Amsterdam*

SCHENEC-
TADY

Clifton Park

ONONDAGA

MADISON

*Cazenovia

MONTGOMERY

Schenectady

OTSEGO

Rotterdam*

*Cohoes

CORTLAND

CHENANGO

Cooperstown*

*Niskayuna
Colonie*
Menands*

*Watervliet
Troy
*Loudonville

GA

*Homer

*Sherburne

Schoharie*

ALBANY

*Cortland

Norwich*

Oneonta*

SCHOHARIE

ALBANY

*Renssaelaer

aca

137-139

DELAWARE

*Coxsackie

**ZIP CODES:
100 - 118 &
125 - 127...
See next page**

S

Bainbridge*

*Sidney

124

*Cairo

*Hudson

TIOGA

*Delhi

Catskill*

eheads

BROOME

GREENE

Union Ctr

Endwell* **Binghamton**

*Walton

COLUMBIA

wego*

*Johnson City

Endicott* *Vestal

East Vestal

607

Bronx, Dutchess, Kings, Nassau,
Orange, Putnam, Queens, Richmond,
Rockland, Suffolk, Sullivan, Westchester, Ulster Counties...
see map next page

CONNECTICUT

State & City Maps

section 2 / page 55

LEGEND
*City
COUNTY
*County Seat
STATE CAPITAL
Area Code
ZIP CODE PREFIX

914

516

212

716

127

124-126

105

109

105-108

115-116

117-118

110-114

100-104

103

112

LONG ISLAND SOUND

ATLANTIC OCEAN

CONNECTICUT

NEW JERSEY

NEW YORK

ULSTER
SULLIVAN
DUTCHESS
ORANGE
PUTNAM
WESTCHESTER
ROCKLAND
BRONX
QUEENS
NASSAU
SUFFOLK
RICHMOND

*Liberty
Fallsburg*
Monticello
Saugerties*
*Rhinebeck
Kingston
New Paltz*
*Poughkeepsie
Arlington
*Wappingers Falls
Pawling*
*Carmel
*Ellenville
*Walden
*Beacon
Newburgh
Cornwall*
Monroe*
Goshen*
Middletown
Warwick*
Greenwood Lake*
Highland Falls*
Port Jervis*
Peekskill*
*Jefferson Valley
*Yorktown Hts
*Croton-on-Hudson *Chappaqua
*Ossining
*Pleasantville
*Briarcliff Manor
*No Terrytown
*Tarrytown *Valhalla
*Irvington *White Plains
Dobbs Ferry* *Hartsdale *Port Chester
Hastings-on-Hudson* *Scarsdale *Rye
Tappan* *Pearl River* *Blauvelt
W Haverstraw*
Haverstraw*
New City
Suffern
Nyack*
*Spring Valley
Bronxville*
Mount Vernon*
*Pelham *Pelham Manor
*New Rochelle
*Larchmont
*Mamaroneck
Tuckahoe*
Yonkers
Bronx
Flushing
Jamaica
Brooklyn
KINGS
Staten Island
Sag Harbor*
Riverhead*
*Centereach
St James*
Smithtown*
Hauppauge*
Kings Park*
East Northport*
Huntington*
*Huntington Station
*Commack
Selden*
*Ronkonkoma
*Deer Park
*Oyster Bay
Westbury*
*Syosset
*Plainview *Melville
*Bethpage
Mineola*
*New Hyde Park
Garden City
*Glen Cove
Manhasset*
*Brentwood
*Central Islip
Patchogue*
*East Islip
Bayport*
Sayville*
*East Islip
Bay Shore*
Babylon*
*Lindenhurst
Copiague*
Amityville*
Massapequa*
Wantagh*
Merrick*
*Freeport
*Oceanside
Lynbrook*
Rockaway
*Hicksville
Floral Park*
*E Meadow
*Elmont *Rockville Ctre
Levittown
Valley Stream* *East Rockaway
*Long Beach

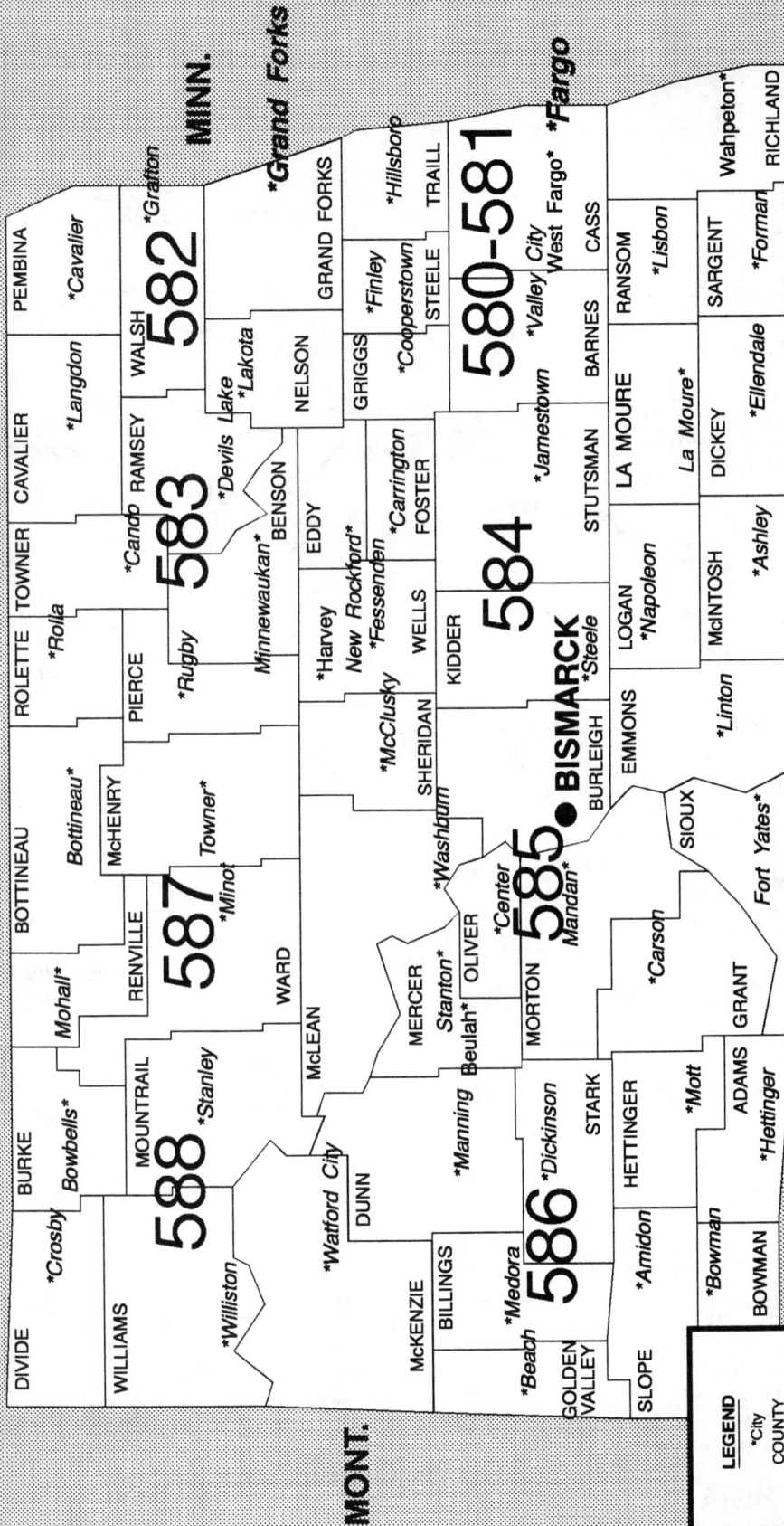

701

MINN.

*Gratton

*Grand Forks

*Fargo

RICHLAND

PEMBINA

*Cavalier

582

*Langdon

WALSH

GRAND FORKS

*Hillsboro

TRAILL

580-581

*Wahpeton

CAVALIER

*Canod

RAMSEY

*Lakota

NELSON

GRIGGS

*Finley

*Cooperstown

STEELE

*Valley City

West Fargo*

CASS

RANSOM

*Lisbon

SARGENT

*Forman

TOWNER

ROLETTE

*Rolla

*Cando

583

*Devils Lake

BENSON

EDDY

*Carrington

FOSTER

*Jamestown

BARNES

LA MOURE

La Moure*

DICKEY

*Ellendale

Minnewaukan

584

STUTSMAN

CANADA

PIERCE

*Rugby

*Harvey

New Rockford*

*Fessenden

WELLS

LOGAN

*Napoleon

McINTOSH

*Ashley

BOTTINEAU

Bottineau

McHENRY

Towner*

*Minot

WARD

*McClusky

SHERIDAN

KIDDER

BISMARCK

*Steele

585

*Linton

RENVILLE

Mohall

587

McLEAN

*Washburn

BURLEIGH

EMMONS

*Center

Mandan*

SIOUX

Fort Yates*

BURKE

Bowbells*

MOUNTRAIL

*Stanley

MERCER

Stanton*

Beulah*

OLIVER

MORTON

*Carson

GRANT

DIVIDE

*Crosby

588

WILLIAMS

*Williston

*Watford City

DUNN

*Manning

STARK

*Dickinson

HETTINGER

*Mott

ADAMS

*Hettinger

McKENZIE

BILLINGS

*Medora

586

*Beach

GOLDEN VALLEY

SLOPE

*Amidon

*Bowman

BOWMAN

MONT.

SOUTH DAKOTA

LEGEND
*City
COUNTY
*County Seat
STATE CAPITAL
Area Code
ZIP CODE PREFIX

919

ASHE ALLEGHANY SURRY STOKES ROCKINGHAM CASWELL PERSON GRA

Jefferson

*Sparta

*Mt Airy

*Danbury *Eden *Yanceyville *Roxboro

*Dobson

WILKES

270-274

*Reidsville Oxfor

WATAUGA

Boone

King

YADKIN FORSYTH GUILFORD ORANGE

N Wilkesboro Kernersville *Burlington

Newland* AVERY *Wilkesboro *Yadkinville *Winston-Salem *Graham *Hillsborou

MITCHELL CALDWELL IREDELL DAVIE *Greensboro DURHAM

YANCEY *Bakersville *Lenoir ALEXANDER High Point* *Archdale ALAMANCE *Du

rnsville* *Taylorsville *Mocksville Carrboro*

286 DAVID-SON *Thomasville Chapel Hill* WA

Mc BURKE CHATHAM Cary*

DOWELL *Hickory *Statesville *Lexington

Marion* Morganton* *Newton Spencer* Siler City* *Pittsboro *Apex

asheville CATAWBA *Salisbury *Asheboro Fuquay-Varin

ville LINCOLN *Mooresville ROWAN

DERSON RUTHERFORD Lincolnton* **280-282** RANDOLPH LEE

*Rutherfordton *Kannapolis MOORE *Sanford

rd *Hendersonville *Forest City GASTON CABARRUS Lillington*

Columbus Shelby* *Cherryville *Concord *Troy *Carthage

POLK Kings Mountain* Mount Holly* Albemarie* HARNETT

CLEVELAND *Charlotte STANLY MONTGOMERY CUMBERLAN

Bessemer City Gastonia Belmont MECKLENBURG RICHMOND *Spring L

704 Mint Hill* UNION HOKE *Fay

SOUTH CAROLINA Monroe* Wadesboro* *Rockingham *Raeford *Hop

ANSON *Hamlet

SCOTLAND *Red Springs B

Laurinburg* *Maxton

Pembroke*

Fairmont* Lumberton*

ROBESON

COLUMBE

WESTERN NORTH CAROLINA MITCHELL **704**

YANCEY *Bakersville

287-289 MADISON Burnsville*

Marshall*

TENN HAYWOOD McDOWELL

Canton* BUNCOMBE *Marion

SWAIN *Asheville

Bryson City* *Waynesville

GRAHAM JACKSON RUTHERFORD

Robbinsville* *Silva HENDERSON POLK *Rutherfordton

MACON *Hendersonville *Forest City

CHEROKEE *Brevard *Columbus

Murphy* CLAY *Franklin

*Hayesville TRANSYLVANIA SOUTH CAROLINA

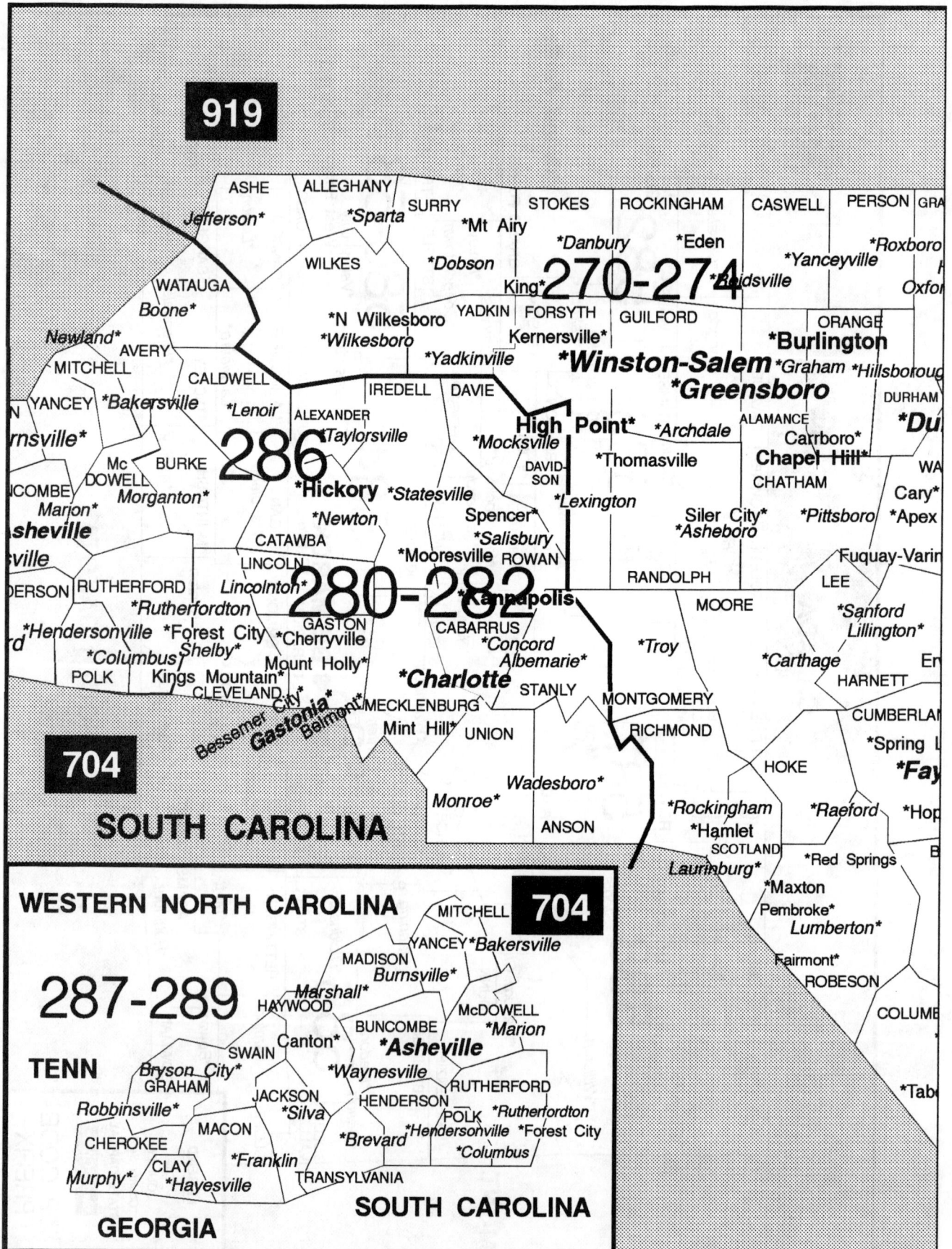

GEORGIA

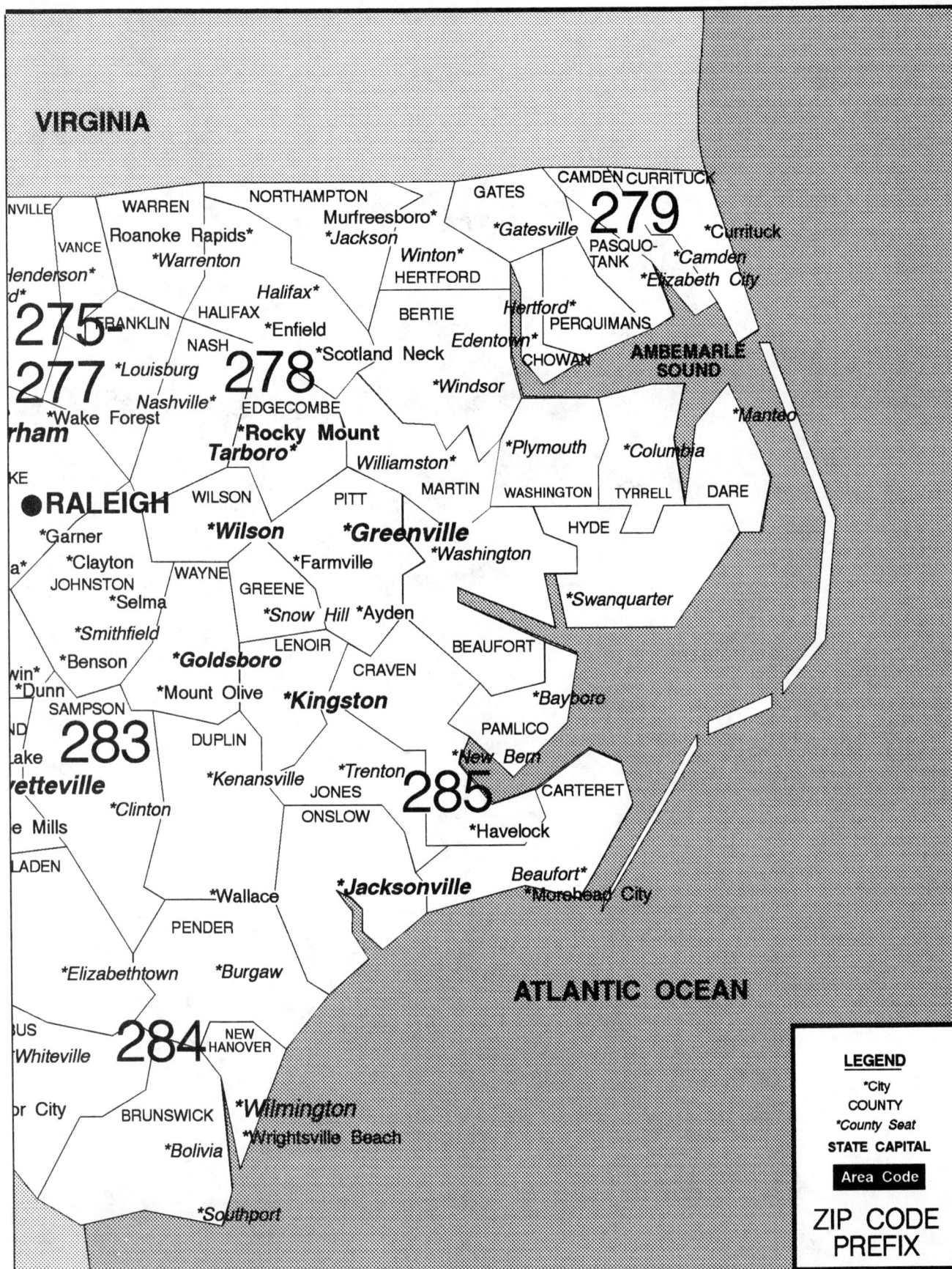

VIRGINIA

NVILLE

WARREN

NORTHAMPTON

GATES

CAMDEN CURRITUCK

Murfreesboro*

*Jackson

*Gatesville

279

*Currituck

VANCE

Roanoke Rapids*

*Warrenton

Winton*

PASQUO-
TANK

*Camden

Henderson*

HERTFORD

*Elizabeth City

d*

Halifax*

BERTIE

Hertford*

PERQUIMANS

275

FRANKLIN

HALIFAX

*Enfield

Edenton*

CHOWAN

**AMBEMARLE
SOUND**

277

*Louisburg

NASH

278

*Scotland Neck

*Windsor

*Manteo

Nashville*

EDGECOMBE

*Wake Forest

rham

Rocky Mount

Williamston*

*Plymouth

*Columbia

KE

RALEIGH

Tarboro*

WILSON

PITT

MARTIN

WASHINGTON

TYRRELL

DARE

*Garner

***Wilson**

***Greenville**

HYDE

a*

*Clayton

*Farmville

*Washington

JOHNSTON

WAYNE

GREENE

*Swanquarter

*Selma

*Snow Hill

*Ayden

*Smithfield

LENOIR

BEAUFORT

win*

*Benson

***Goldsboro**

CRAVEN

*Dunn

*Mount Olive

***Kingston**

*Bayboro

SAMPSON

DUPLIN

PAMLICO

ND

283

*New Bern

Lake

*Kenansville

*Trenton

285

CARTERET

etteville

JONES

ONSLOW

e Mills

*Clinton

*Havelock

LADEN

*Wallace

***Jacksonville**

Beaufort*

*Morehead City

PENDER

*Elizabethtown

*Burgaw

ATLANTIC OCEAN

BUS

284

NEW
HANOVER

Whiteville

BRUNSWICK

***Wilmington**

or City

*Wrightsville Beach

*Bolivia

*Southport

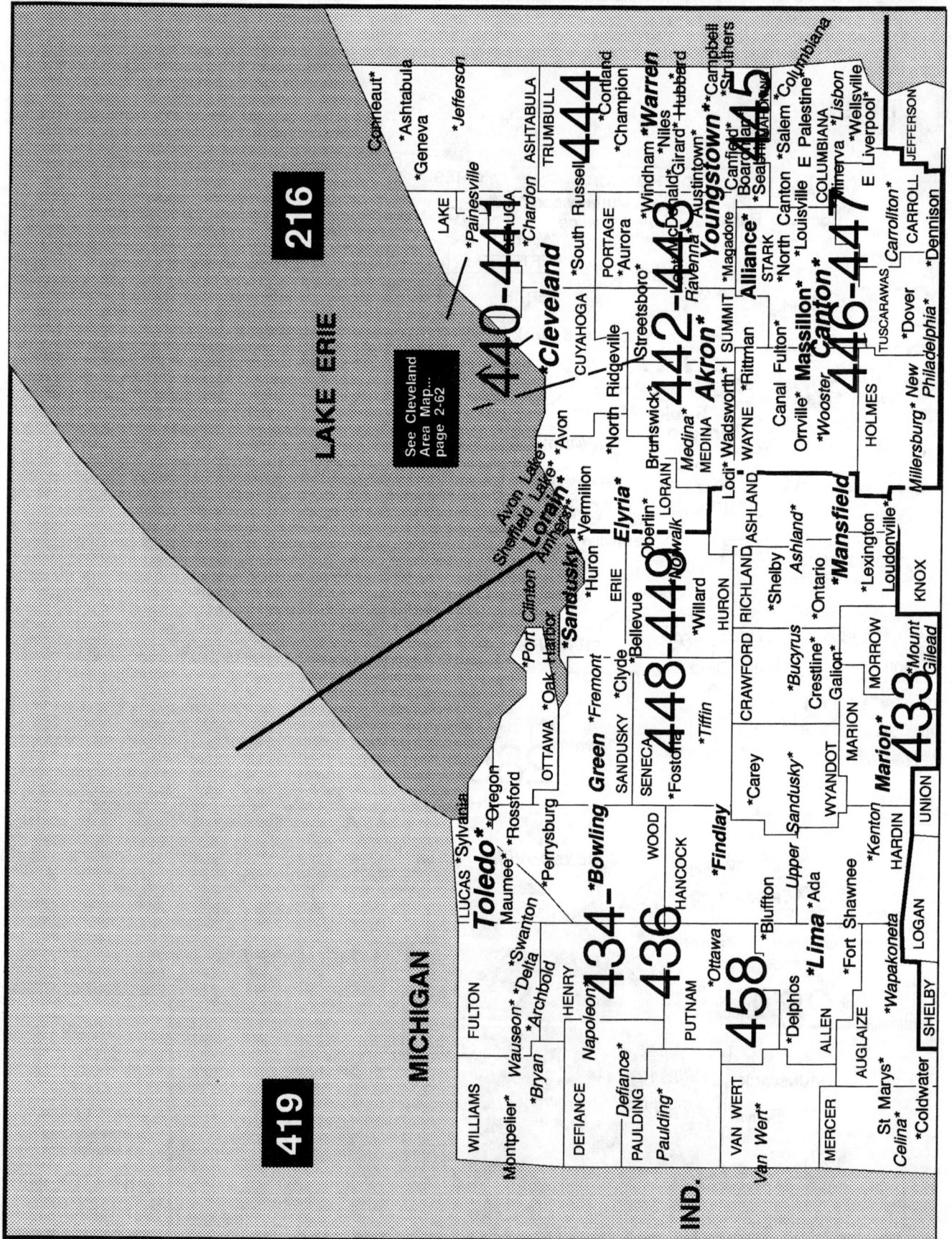

LAKE ERIE

216

419

See Cleveland Area Map... page 2-62

440-441

442-443

445

446-447

448-449

434-

436

458

433

Cleveland
Lorain
Sandusky
Elyria
Akron
Youngstown
Warren
Canton
Massillon
Alliance
Mansfield
Toledo
Bowling Green
Findlay
Lima
Marion

MICHIGAN

IND.

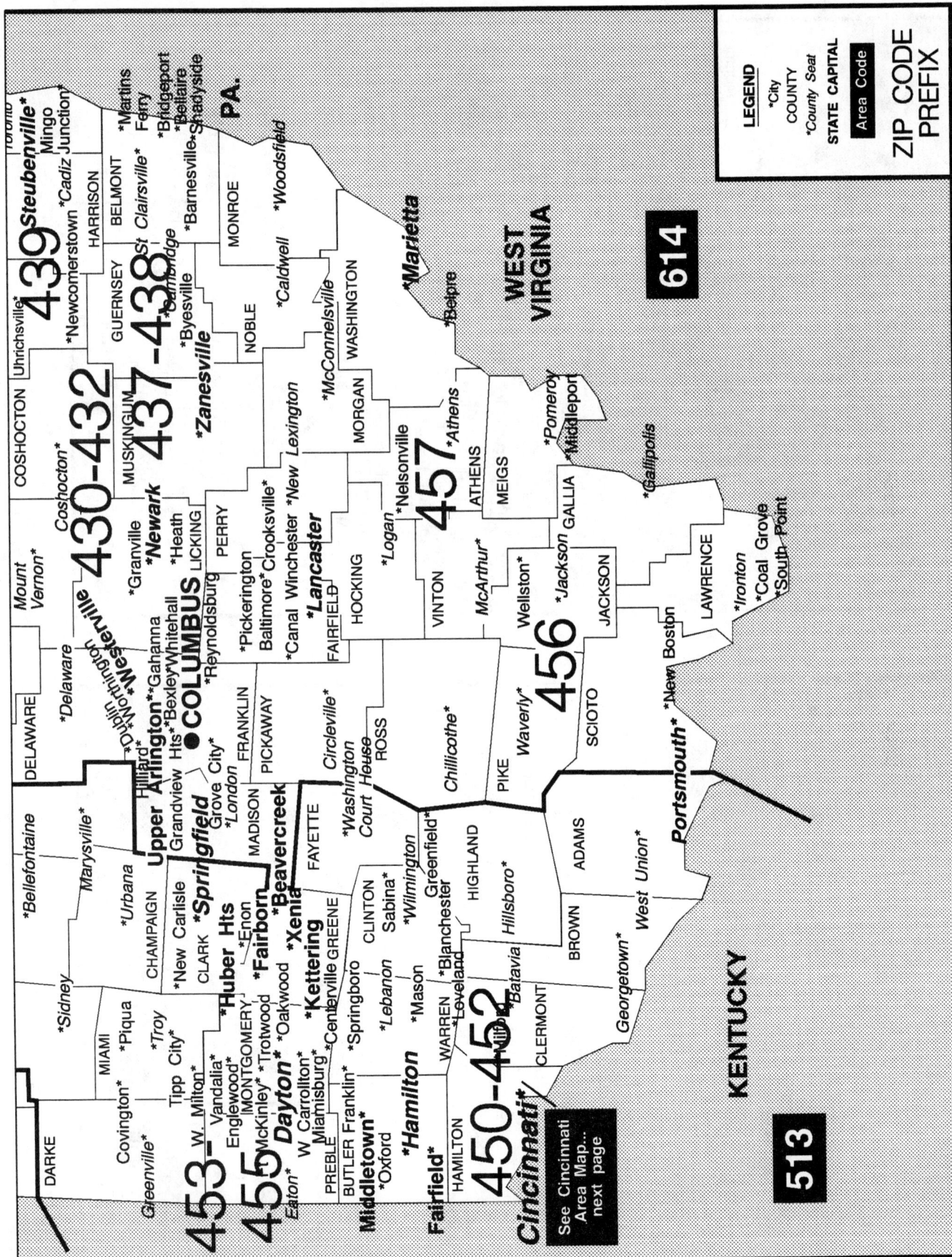

LEGEND
*City
COUNTY
*County Seat
STATE CAPITAL
Area Code
ZIP CODE PREFIX

439 *Steubenville*
Mingo
*Cadiz Junction
*Newcomerstown
*Toronto
Martins Ferry*
*Bridgeport
*Bellaire
*Shadyside
PA.

COSHOCTON
HARRISON
BELMONT
St Clairsville*
*Cambridge
*Barnesville
Byesville*
437-438
MONROE
*Woodsfield

430-432
Uhrichsville*
Coshocton*
GUERNSEY
MUSKINGUM
*Zanesville
*Caldwell
NOBLE
*Marietta
*Belpre
WEST VIRGINIA

614

Mount Vernon*
*Delaware
*Granville
*Newark
*Heath
*McConnelsville
WASHINGTON
MORGAN

*Westerville
*Dublin
*Worthington
Gahanna
*New Lexington
LICKING
PERRY
Crooksville*
*Crooksville

457 *Athens
ATHENS
MEIGS
*Pomeroy
*Middleport
*Gallipolis

DELAWARE
*Bellefontaine
*Marysville
*Urbana
CHAMPAIGN
New Carlisle*
CLARK
Upper Arlington
Grandview Hts*
Bexley
Whitehall
●COLUMBUS
FRANKLIN
Hilliard*
Grove City*
*London
MADISON
*Reynoldsburg
*Pickerington
Baltimore*
*Canal Winchester
FAIRFIELD
*Lancaster
HOCKING
*Logan
VINTON
McArthur
*Nelsonville
Wellston*
*Jackson
GALLIA
JACKSON
LAWRENCE
*Coal Grove
*South Point
*Ironton

456
SCIOTO
*Waverly
PIKE
ROSS
*Chillicothe
Circleville*
PICKAWAY
*Washington Court House
FAYETTE
*Wilmington
Greenfield*
HIGHLAND
ADAMS
West Union
*New Boston
Portsmouth*

*Springfield
*Huber Hts
*Fairborn
*Beavercreek
*Xenia
*Kettering
Enon*
Oakwood*
GREENE
Centerville*
Springboro*
CLINTON
Sabina*
*Blanchester
*Loveland
WARREN
Mason*
*Lebanon
*Milford
*Batavia
CLERMONT
BROWN
*Georgetown
KENTUCKY

513

453
W. Milton*
*Sidney
*Piqua
*Troy
Tipp City*
MIAMI
*Vandalia
Englewood*
*Trotwood
*McKinley
MONTGOMERY
Dayton*
W Carrollton*
Miamisburg*
PREBLE
Eaton*
BUTLER
Franklin*
*Oxford
455
Middletown*
Fairfield*
*Hamilton
HAMILTON
450-452
Cincinnati*

*Covington
*Greenville
DARKE

See Cincinnati Area Map... next page

WEST VIRGINIA

Cincinnati & Cleveland Areas

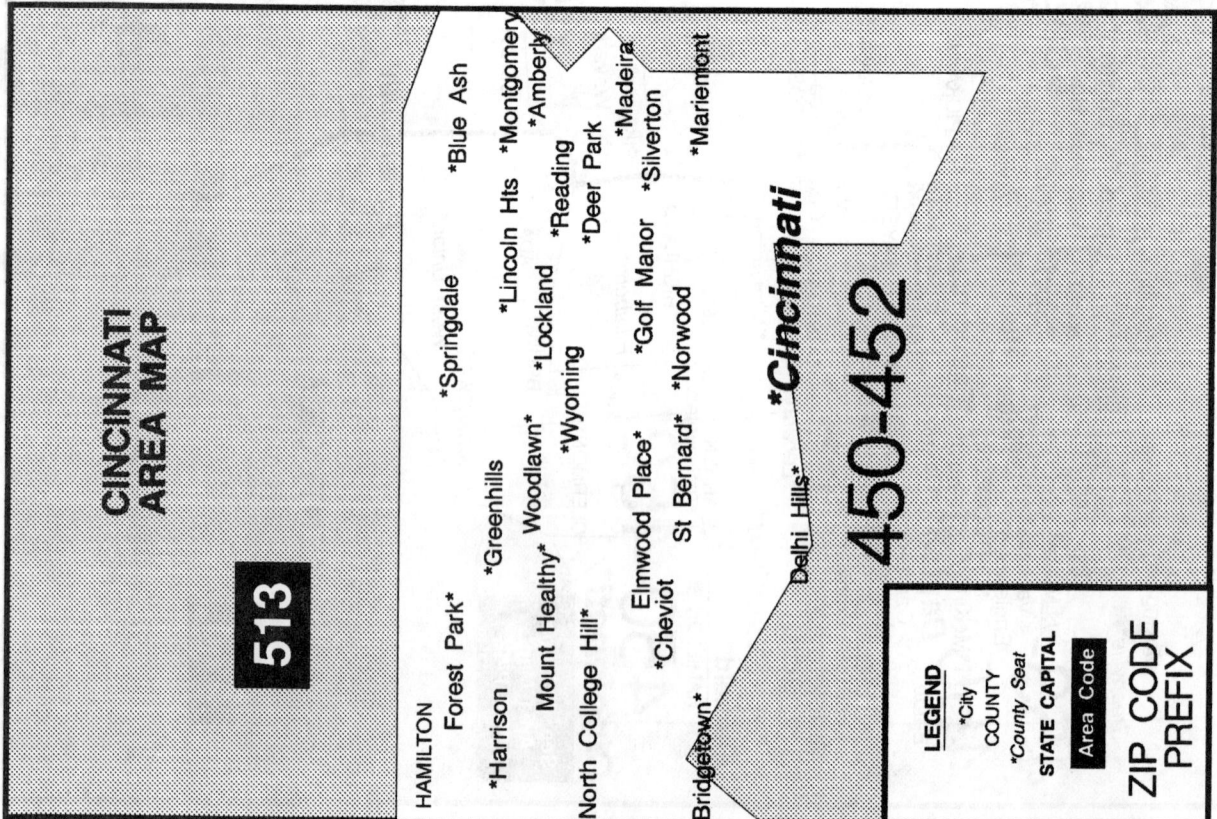

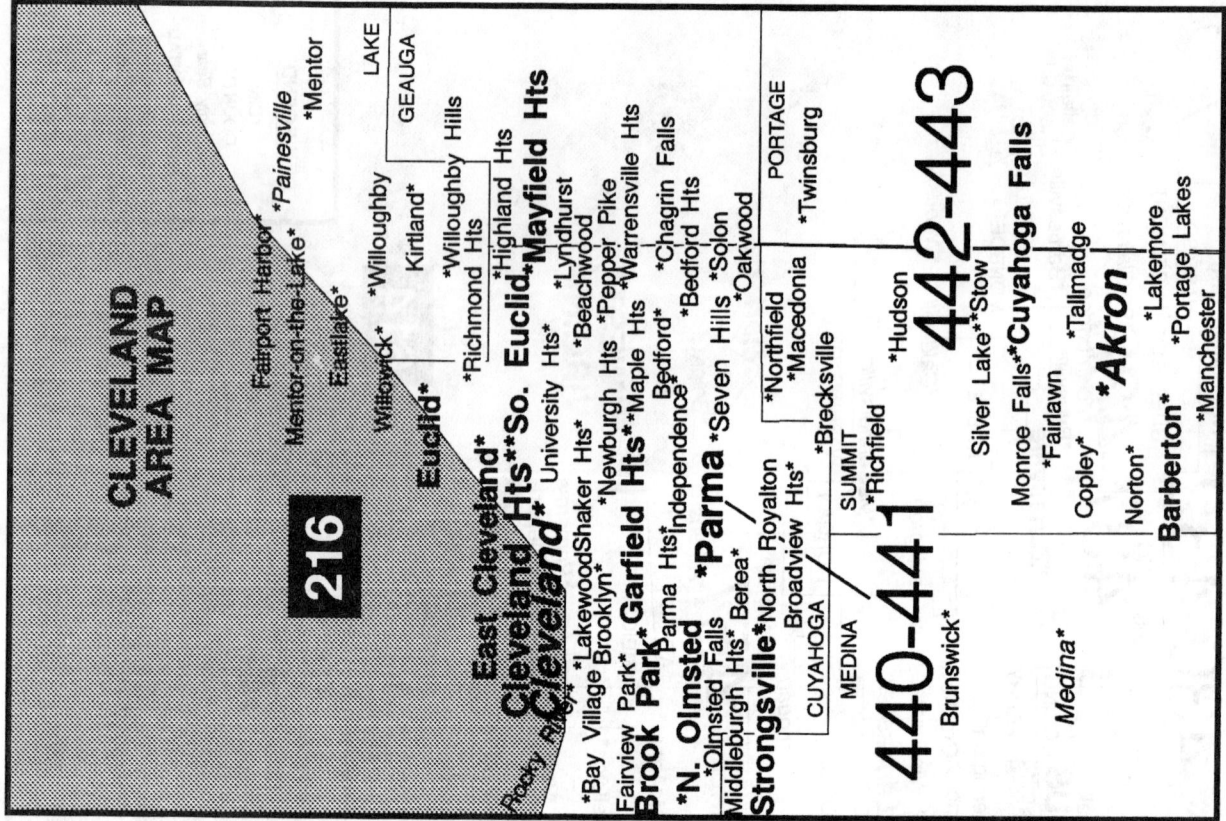

CLEVELAND AREA MAP

216

LAKE
GEAUGA
*Painesville
*Mentor
Fairport Harbor*
*Mentor-on-the-Lake
Eastlake*
*Willoughby Hills
*Willoughby
*Kirtland
*Willowick
Willoughby Hts
*Highland Hts
Richmond Hts*
*Lyndhurst
**So. Euclid
University Hts*
*Beachwood
**Mayfield Hts
*Pepper Pike
*Warrensville Hts
*Chagrin Falls
*Bedford Hts
**Cleveland Hts
Euclid*
East Cleveland*
*Cleveland
*Lakewood
Shaker Hts*
*Newburgh Hts
*Maple Hts
Bedford*
*Solon
*Oakwood
*Seven Hills
*Independence
*Parma
Parma Hts*
*Garfield Hts
Brook Park*
*Brooklyn
Fairview Park*
*Bay Village
*N. Olmsted
*Olmsted Falls
Middleburgh Hts*
*Berea
*North Royalton
Broadview Hts*
Strongsville*
Rocky River*
CUYAHOGA
MEDINA
*Northfield
*Macedonia
*Brecksville
SUMMIT
*Richfield
*Hudson
*Twinsburg
PORTAGE
**Cuyahoga Falls
Silver Lake*
*Stow
Monroe Falls*
*Tallmadge
*Fairlawn
Copley*
*Akron
*Lakemore
Norton*
*Portage Lakes
Barberton*
*Manchester
440-441
442-443
Brunswick*
Medina*

CINCINNATI AREA MAP

513

HAMILTON
Forest Park*
*Greenhills
*Springdale
*Blue Ash
*Montgomery
*Amberly
*Harrison
*Lincoln Hts
*Reading
Madeira*
*Mariemont
Mount Healthy*
Woodlawn*
*Lockland
*Deer Park
*Silverton
*Wyoming
North College Hill*
Elmwood Place*
*Golf Manor
St Bernard*
*Norwood
*Cheviot
Delhi Hills*
*Cincinnati
450-452
Bridgetown*

LEGEND
*City
COUNTY
*County Seat
STATE CAPITAL
Area Code
ZIP CODE PREFIX

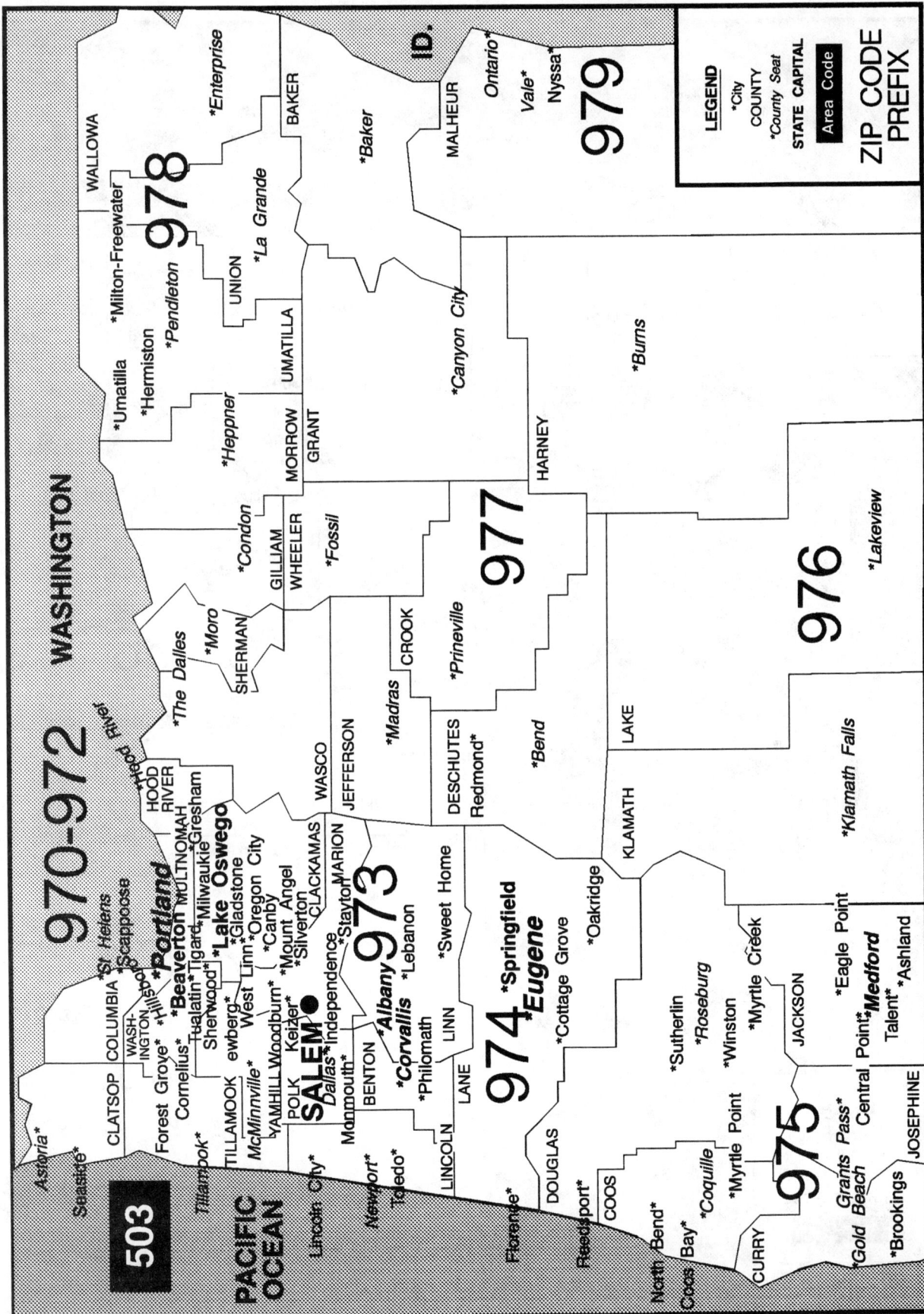

LEGEND
*City
COUNTY
*County Seat
*STATE CAPITAL
Area Code
ZIP CODE PREFIX

WASHINGTON

ID.

WALLOWA
*Enterprise
978
*Milton-Freewater
*Umatilla
*Hermiston
*Pendleton
*Heppner
UMATILLA
UNION
*La Grande
BAKER
*Baker

MALHEUR
*Ontario
*Vale
*Nyssa
979

*Canyon City

MORROW
GRANT

HARNEY

*Burns

GILLIAM
WHEELER
*Fossil
*Condon

SHERMAN
*Moro
*The Dalles

HOOD RIVER

CROOK
*Prineville
977
*Madras

DESCHUTES
Redmond*
*Bend

LAKE
976
*Lakeview

970-972

Hood River

Portland
St Helens
Scappoose
Hillsboro
Beaverton
Forest Grove*
Cornelius*
WASH-INGTON
CLATSOP
COLUMBIA
MULTNOMAH
Gresham
Milwaukie
Tigard
Tualatin*
Sherwood*
Lake Oswego
ewberg*
West Linn*
Oregon City
*Gladstone
*Canby
CLACKAMAS
*Mount Angel
Silverton
*Woodburn
MARION
*Stayton
973
*Lebanon
*Sweet Home

JEFFERSON
WASCO

Astoria*
Seaside*
*Tillamook
TILLAMOOK
McMinnville
YAMHILL
POLK
Keizer
SALEM
Dallas*
Monmouth*
Independence
BENTON
*Albany
*Corvallis
*Philomath
LINN

Lincoln City*
Newport*
Toledo*
LINCOLN

974
*Springfield
Eugene
*Cottage Grove
LANE
*Oakridge

KLAMATH
*Klamath Falls

PACIFIC OCEAN
503

Florence*
Reedsport*
North Bend*
Coos Bay*
COOS
*Coquille
*Myrtle Point
DOUGLAS
Gold Beach*
CURRY
975
*Grants Pass
Central Point*
JOSEPHINE
*Brookings

*Sutherlin
*Roseburg
*Winston
*Myrtle Creek
JACKSON
*Eagle Point
Medford
Talent*
*Ashland

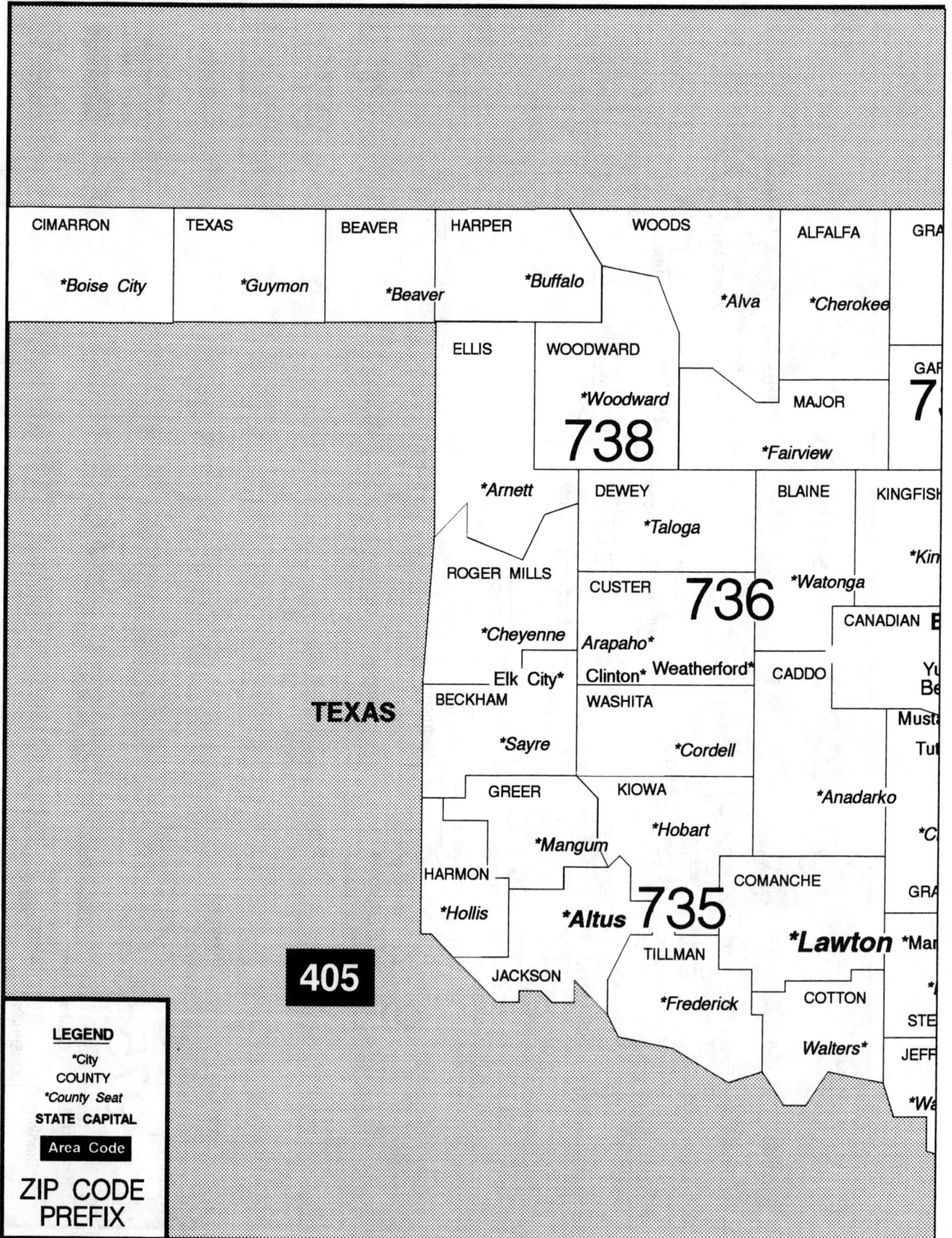

Oklahoma

CIMARRON

*Boise City

TEXAS

*Guymon

BEAVER

*Beaver

HARPER

*Buffalo

WOODS

*Alva

ALFALFA

*Cherokee

GR

ELLIS

WOODWARD

*Woodward

738

MAJOR

*Fairview

GA

7

*Arnett

DEWEY

*Taloga

BLAINE

KINGFISH

*Kir

ROGER MILLS

CUSTER

736

*Watonga

CANADIAN

*Cheyenne

Arapaho*

Clinton* Weatherford*

CADDO

Yu
Be

Must

Tu

Elk City*

BECKHAM

WASHITA

TEXAS

*Sayre

*Cordell

*Anadarko

GREER

KIOWA

*C

*Mangum

*Hobart

COMANCHE

GR

HARMON

*Hollis

*Altus ## 735

*Lawton *Mar

TILLMAN

*Frederick

COTTON

STE

JACKSON

Walters*

JEFF

*W

405

LEGEND
*City
COUNTY
*County Seat
STATE CAPITAL
Area Code

ZIP CODE
PREFIX

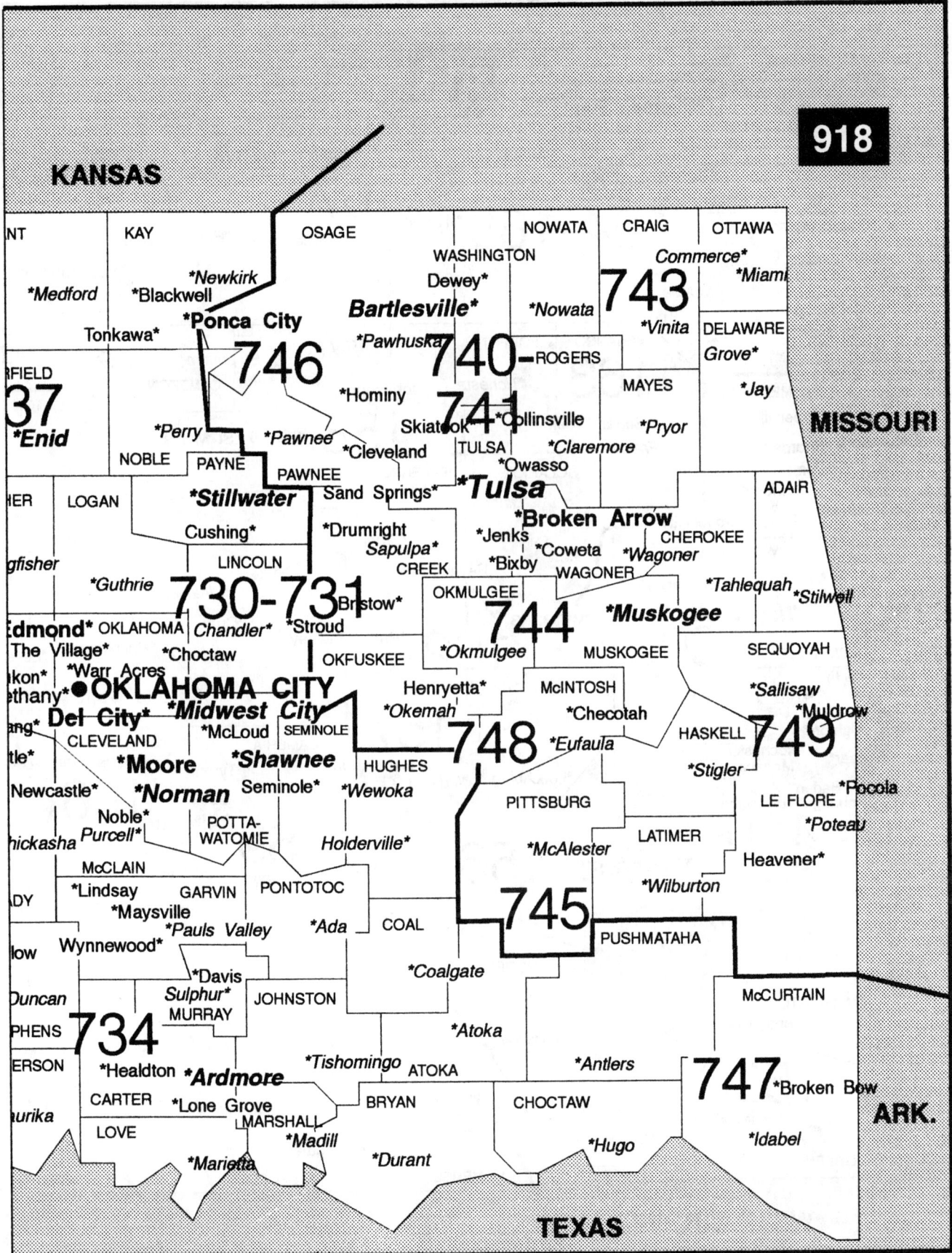

918

KANSAS

MISSOURI

County	City

NT

KAY

OSAGE

NOWATA

CRAIG

OTTAWA

WASHINGTON

*Newkirk

Dewey*

Commerce

*Miami

*Medford

*Blackwell

Bartlesville*

*Nowata

743

Tonkawa*

*Ponca City

*Pawhuska

740

*Vinita

DELAWARE

746

ROGERS

Grove*

RFIELD

37

*Hominy

MAYES

*Jay

*Enid

Skiatook

*Collinsville

*Pryor

*Perry

*Pawnee

741

*Claremore

NOBLE

*Cleveland

TULSA

*Owasso

ADAIR

PAYNE

PAWNEE

Sand Springs*

*Tulsa

HER

LOGAN

*Stillwater

*Broken Arrow

CHEROKEE

gfisher

Cushing*

*Drumright

*Jenks

*Coweta

*Wagoner

*Tahlequah

*Stilwell

*Guthrie

Sapulpa*

*Bixby

WAGONER

LINCOLN

CREEK

730-731

Bristow*

OKMULGEE

Edmond*

OKLAHOMA

Chandler*

*Stroud

744

*Muskogee

SEQUOYAH

The Village*

*Choctaw

OKFUSKEE

*Okmulgee

MUSKOGEE

kon*

*Warr Acres

Henryetta*

McINTOSH

*Sallisaw

ethany*

OKLAHOMA CITY

*Checotah

*Muldrow

Del City*

*Midwest City

*Okemah

749

ang*

*McLoud

SEMINOLE

*Eufaula

HASKELL

tle*

CLEVELAND

748

*Stigler

*Pocola

*Moore

*Shawnee

HUGHES

LE FLORE

Newcastle*

Seminole*

*Wewoka

PITTSBURG

*Poteau

*Norman

Noble*

*McAlester

LATIMER

Heavener*

hickasha

Purcell*

POTTA-WATOMIE

*Holderville

*Wilburton

McCLAIN

PONTOTOC

DY

*Lindsay

GARVIN

745

PUSHMATAHA

*Maysville

*Pauls Valley

*Ada

COAL

low

Wynnewood*

*Coalgate

McCURTAIN

*Davis

JOHNSTON

Duncan

Sulphur*

MURRAY

PHENS

734

*Atoka

ERSON

*Healdton

*Ardmore

*Tishomingo

ATOKA

*Antlers

747

*Broken Bow

CARTER

*Lone Grove

BRYAN

CHOCTAW

aurika

LOVE

MARSHALL

*Madill

*Hugo

*Idabel

ARK.

*Marietta

*Durant

TEXAS

Pennsylvania

LAKE ERIE

814

412

OHIO

North East

*Erie** *Wesleyville*
Millcreek Twp.
Glrard*

ERIE
Edinboro
CRAWFORD

Corry*
Union City
WARREN

164-165 *Warren*

McKEAN *Bradford*

POTTER

Smethport* *Port Allegany*

Kane

Coudersport

Meadville

Titusville*

VENANGO
163

FOREST
Tionesta

ELK
Johnsonburg*

Emporium*
CAMERON
CLINTON

MERCER
Greenville
Sharpsville
Sharon
Farrell* *Mercer*
Hermitage*

Sugar Creek
Franklin

CLARION
Clarion

158 *Ridgway* *St Marys*

JEFFERSON

CLEARFIELD
Clearfield
Curwensville

Philpsburg
CENTRE

Brookville

Du Bois

Grove City

New Wilmington

161
New Castle

160 *Butler*

Slippery Rock

ARMSTRONG

Reynoldsville*

162

Kittanning

Ford City

Punxsutawney
INDIANA

157

Belle

State College*

LAWRENCE
Ellwood City*
BEAVER
Beaver Falls*
New Brighton*
Beaver* *Rochester
*Monaca
Baden*
Ambridge* *Economy

Zelienople

BUTLER
ALLEGHENY

Leechburg

Barnesboro*
Indiana

CAMBRIA

Tyrone*
BLAIR
Altoona
Hollidaysburg

HUNTINGDON Lew

166
Huntingdon*

150-152

Pittsburgh

156

Ebensburg*

Nanty Glo*

159
Portage

Roaring Spring

172

See Pittsburg
Area Map...
next page

Johnstown* *Geistown
*Westmont
Southmont*

Windber

Canonsburg
Strabane
Monongahela
Washington* Charleroi
WASHINGTON
Centerville*
Bentleyville
California
Brownsville

*Donora
Connellsville

WESTMORELAND

155

FULTON

FRANK

153
Waynesburg

Uniontown

Masontown

GREENE

154

Somerset

Bedford
McConnellsburg* *Chambersburg*

Meyersdale

FAYETTE

SOMERSET

BEDFORD

*Gre
Waynes

WEST VIRGINIA

Pennsylvania

717

NEW YORK

TIOGA
69
Mansfield*
*Wellsboro

*Sayre
*Athens
*Towanda

SUSQUEHANNA

WAYNE

Montrose*
188

Honesdale*

BRADFORD
WYOMING

Carbondale*
Clarks Summit* Blakely*
*Archbald
*Olyphant
*Dickson City
*Dunmore
*Scranton

184-185

*Milford

SULLIVAN
LYCOMING
177
Tunkhannock*
Laporte*
186
187
West Pittston*
Old Forge*
Taylor*
Moosic*
Exeter*
Swoyerville*
Forty Fort*
*Pittston
*Duryea
LACKA-WANNA

MONROE
PIKE

Williamsport* *Montoursville
South Williamsport*
*Jersey Shore
*Muncy

Dallas*
Edwardsville* *Luzerne
Plymouth*
Nanticoke*
LUZERNE
*Wilkes Barre
183
*E. Stroudsburg
*Stroudsburg

ck aven*

178

*Berwick
182
CARBON
*Freeland
W. Hazleton* *Hazleton

UNION
68
Lewisburg*
MON-TOUR
COLUMBIA
*Danville *Bloomsburg
McAdoo
*Jim Thorpe
*Lansford
*Bangor
NORTHAMPTON
*Lehighton
*Nazareth
180-181

fonte
*Mifflinburg
Sunbury*
NORTH UNBERLAND
*Northumberland
Shenandoah*
Shamokin Milton
*Tamaqua
*Mahanoy City
*Frackville
*Palmerton
*Northampton
*Catasauqua
*Easton

Middleburg* Selinsgrove*
Kulpmont*
*Mount Carmel
LEHIGH
*Bethlehem
NEW JERSEY

MIFFLIN
SNYDER
istown*
JUNIATA
Minersville* SCHUYLKILL
Pottsville*
*Schuylkill Haven
Allentown
*Fountain Hill
*Hellertown
Emmaus
195

*Mifflintown
PERRY
DAUPHIN
*Millersburg
179
*Hamburg
BUCKS
See Philadelphia Area Map...next page

ew Bloomfield*
170-171
BERKS
Fleetwood*
*Laureldale
196
189

HARRISBURG ●
LEBANON
Wyomissing*

*Steelton *Palmyra
So. Lebanon*
*Lebanon
Shillington*
Kenhorst*
*Reading
*West Reading
*Birdsboro
Spring City*
Phoenixville*
MONTGOMERY
194
190-191

Carlisle Middletown
Manchester*
Mount Joy* *E Petersburg
Manheim**Lititz
*Elizabethtown
*Ephrata
Akron
*New Holland
Malvern*
*Uwchland
*Downingtown
PHILA-DELPHIA
*Haverford Twp.

CUMBERLAND
Dover*
Marietta
Columbia*
173-174
*York
Millersville*
175-176
*Lancaster
Coatesville
West Chester*
DELAWARE
*Philadelphia

LIN
ADAMS
Gettysburg*
McSherrystown*
*Hanover
*West York
*Red Lion
*Dallastown
*Spring Garden Twp.
Parkesburg*
193
*Ridley Twp.
*Springfield

encastle
oro*
Littlestown*
YORK
LANCASTER
Oxford*
*Kennett Square
CHESTER

215

MARYLAND
DELAWARE

PITTSBURGH AREA

150-152

156

412

WESTMORELAND

ALLEGHENY

McCandless

Franklin Park*
West View*
Sewickley*
Allison Park*
Fox Chapel*
O'Hara*
Etna*
Coraopolis*
Avalon*
Bellevue*
Oakmont*
Verona*
Sharpsburg*
Moon*
McKees Rocks*
Stowe Twp*
Ingram*
Pittsburgh*
Crafton*
Carnegie*
Swissvale*
Green Tree*
Forest Hills*
Dormont*
McDonald*
Brentwood*
Munhall*
Castle Shannon*
Bridgeville*
Mt Lebanon*
Upper St Clair*
South Fayette*
Bethel Park*
Jefferson*

Blackridge
Lower Burrell
Tarentum*
Vandergrift
New Kensington*
Arnold*
Plum*
Penn Hills*
Monroeville*
Wilkinsburg*
Murrysville*
Wilkins Twp
Turtle Creek
N Braddock*
Baldwin*
West Mifflin*
N Versailles*
McKeesport*
Pleasant Hills*
Port Vue*
Clairton*
South Park
SW Greensburg*
New Stanton*
Monessen*

Labrobe*
Derry*
Greensburg*
Jeannette*
*Greensburg
So Greensburg*
Youngwood*
Mount Pleasant*
Scottdale*

LEGEND
*City
COUNTY
*County Seat
STATE CAPITAL
Area Code
ZIP CODE PREFIX

PHILADELPHIA AREA MAP

189

190-191

215

BUCKS
MONTGOMERY
DELAWARE

*Quakertown
*Doylestown
*Perkasie
*Buckingham
*Doylestown
*Sellersville
*Telford
*New Britain
*Lansdale
Pottstown*
*West Pottsgrove
Souderton*
*Lower Pottsgrove
*Limerick
Lower Providence*
*East Norriton
Norristown*
Ambler*
*Hatboro
Morrisville*
*Lower Makefield
Warringtondown*
Warminster*
Middletown*
*Penndel
Yardley*
Levittown*
*Fetis Twp
Bristol
Middletown Twp
Upper Southampton Twp*
*Lower Moreland
Abington Twp*
Springfield Twp*
Cheltenham*
Upper Dublin Twp*
Upper Moreland*
Plymouth Twp*
Whitemarsh Twp*
Audubon*
*Jenkintown
*Conshohocken
*Lower Merion Twp
Philadelphia*
PHILADELPHIA
Upper Merion Twp*
Haverford Twp.*
Clifton Hts*
Upper Darby*
*Lansdowne
Yeadon*
Darby*
Colwyn*
Sharon Hill*
Glenolden*
Folcroft*
Norwood*
Prospect Park*
Ridley Park*
Brookhaven*
Chester*
Aston*
Springfield*
Media*
Ridley Twp.*
Swarthmore*
Collingdale*

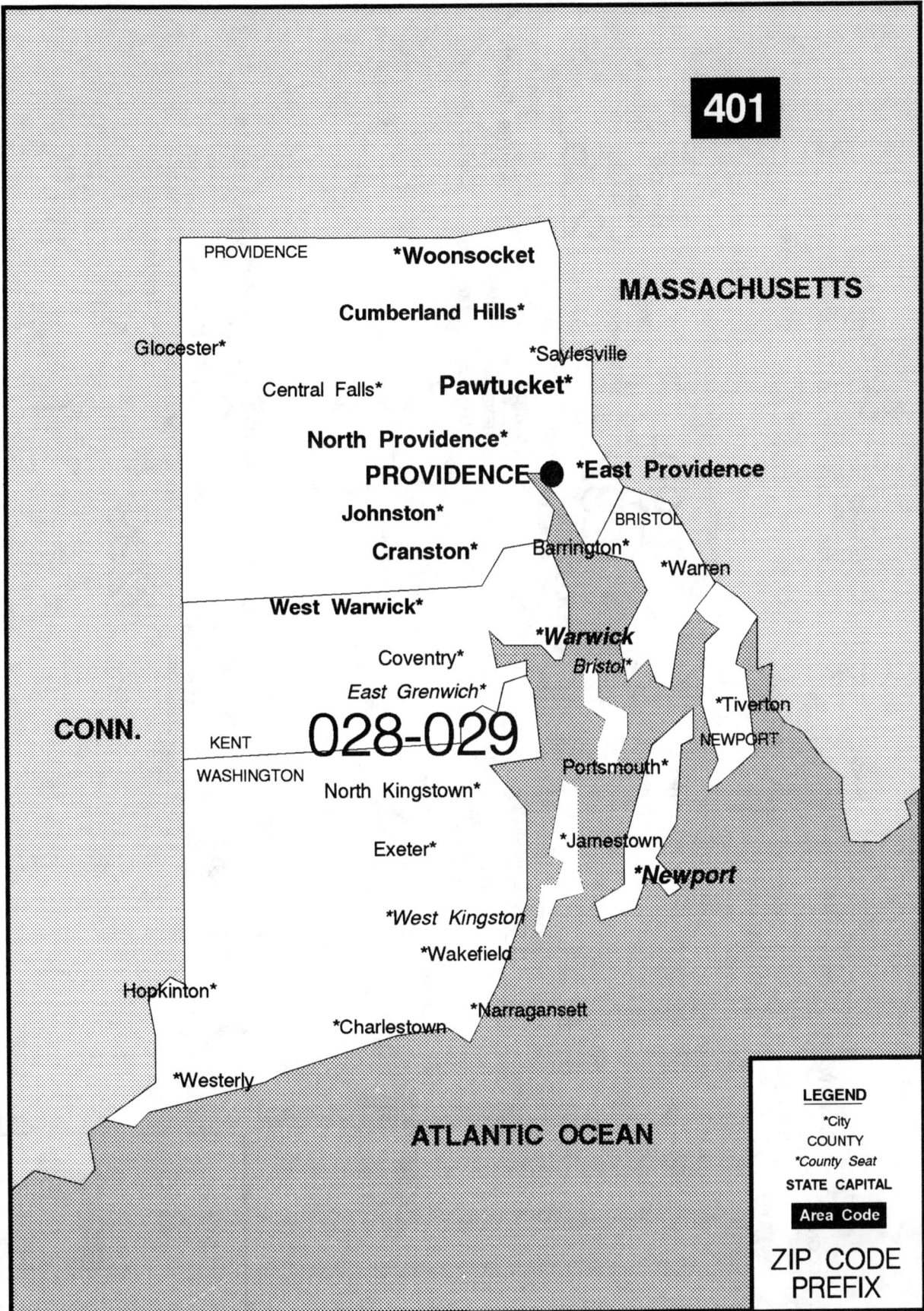

401

PROVIDENCE

*Woonsocket

MASSACHUSETTS

Cumberland Hills*

Glocester*

*Saylesville

Central Falls*   Pawtucket*

North Providence*

PROVIDENCE ● *East Providence

Johnston*   BRISTOL

Cranston*   Barrington*   *Warren

West Warwick*   *Warwick

Coventry*   Bristol*

East Grenwich*

028-029   *Tiverton

CONN.   KENT   NEWPORT

WASHINGTON   Portsmouth*

North Kingstown*

Exeter*   *Jamestown

*Newport

*West Kingston

*Wakefield

Hopkinton*

*Narragansett

*Charlestown

*Westerly

ATLANTIC OCEAN

<u>LEGEND</u>
*City
COUNTY
*County Seat
STATE CAPITAL
Area Code

ZIP CODE
PREFIX

South Carolina

ATLANTIC OCEAN

NORTH CAROLINA

GEORGIA

803 Area Code

290-292

293

294

295

296

297

298

299

HORRY

*Conway

No Myrtle Beach*

Myrtle Beach*

Surfside Beach*

*Georgetown

DILLON

*Dillon

MARION

MARION

Mullins*

*Marion

*McColl

*Bennettsville

MARLBORO

CHESTERFIELD

*Pageland

*Chesterfield

CHESTERFIELD

*Cheraw

DARLINGTON

*Hartsville

*Darlington

FLORENCE

FLORENCE

*Florence

*Lake City

*Andrews

GEORGETOWN

GEORGETOWN

WILLIAMSBURG

*Kingstree

BERKELEY

*Moncks Corner

Goose Creek*

*Hanahan

Mt. Pleasant*

*Isle of Palms

*Charleston

*Charleston

No Charleston*

CHARLESTON

LANCASTER

*Lancaster

KERSHAW

Camden*

*Bishopville

LEE

SUMTER

*Sumter

CLARENDON

*Manning

*St Matthews

CALHOUN

DORCHESTER

*St George

COLLETON

*Walterboro

Summerville*

*Denmark

BAMBERG

*Bamberg

ALLENDALE

*Allendale

HAMPTON

Hampton*

BEAUFORT

*Beaufort

*Port Royal

Hilton Head Island

JASPER

Ridgeland*

CHEROKEE

*Gaffney

YORK

Clover*

*York

Fort Mill*

Rock Hill*

SPARTAN-BURG

Spartanburg*

Greer*

Travelers Rest*

GREENVILLE

PICKENS

Pickens*

Greenville*

Easley*

*Liberty

Simpsonville*

*Pendleton

Williamston*

*Belton

ANDERSON

Anderson

OCONEE

Walhalla*

*Westminster

Clemson*

Seneca*

UNION

Union*

*Woodruff

Mauldin*

Fountain Inn*

LAURENS

*Laurens

Honea Path*

Clinton*

ABBEVILLE

Abbeville*

NEWBERRY

*Newberry

*Winnsboro

FAIRFIELD

Chester*

CHESTER

Great Falls*

RICHLAND

●COLUMBIA

*Forest Acres

*Cayce

Lexington*

West Columbia*

LEXINGTON

SALUDA

*Saluda

Batesburg*

AIKEN

Aiken*

*Edgefield

EDGEFIELD

Johnston*

No Augusta*

Williston*

Blackville*

Barnwell*

BARNWELL

GREEN-WOOD

*Greenwood

McCORMICK

*McCormick

ORANGEBURG

*Orangeburg

*Moncks

LEGEND
*City
COUNTY
*County Seat
STATE CAPITAL
Area Code
ZIP CODE PREFIX

605

NORTH DAKOTA

MINN.

IOWA

NEBRASKA

ROBERTS
*Milbank
GRANT
DEUEL
Clear Lake

MARSHALL
*Britton
DAY
*Webster
Sisseton*
CODINGTON
Watertown*
HAMLIN
*Hayti
Clear Lake*
BROOKINGS
Brookings*

BROWN
Aberdeen
572
CLARK
Clark*
KINGSBURY
*De Smet
LAKE
MOODY
Flandreau*
MINNEHAHA
*Brandon

SPINK
*Redfield
BEADLE
Huron*
573
MINER
Howard*
MADISON
McCOOK
*Salem
Alexandria*
HANSON
Sioux Falls
LINCOLN
*Canton
UNION
*Vermillion
Elk Point*

McPHERSON
*Leola
574
EDMUNDS
Ipswich*
FAULK
Faulkton*
HAND
*Miller
JERAULD
Wessington Spgs*
SANBORN
*Woonsocket
AURORA
DAVISON
Mitchell*
DOUGLAS
*Armour
HUTCHINSON
TURNER
*Parker
Olive*
YANKTON
Yankton*
571
CLAY
BON HOMME
Tyndall*

CAMPBELL
Mound City*
WALWORTH
*Selby
POTTER
Gettysburg*
SULLY
*Onida
HYDE
*Highmore
BUFFALO
Gann Valley*
BRULE
Chamberlain*
CHARLES MIX
*Burke
GREGORY
Lake Andes*

*McIntosh
Mobridge*
ZIEBACH
Timber Lake*
576
DEWEY
*Dupree
STANLEY
HUGHES
PIERRE
Fort Pierre*
LYMAN
575
Kennebec*
TRIPP
Winner*
(co seat for both counties)

CORSON
CAMPBELL
MEADE
HAAKON
*Philip
JACKSON
Kadoka*
JONES
Murdo*
*White River
MELLETTE
TODD
577

PERKINS
*Bison
*Buffalo
HARDING
BUTTE
*Belle Fourche
MEADE
*Sturgis
Deadwood*
Lead*
*Spearfish
LAWRENCE
PENNINGTON
Rapid City*
*Box Elder
CUSTER
*Custer
SHANNON
(co seat for both counties)
*Hot Springs
FALL RIVER
BENNETT
*Wounded Knee
*Martin
*Pine Ridge

LEGEND
*City
COUNTY
*County Seat
STATE CAPITAL
Area Code

ZIP CODE PREFIX

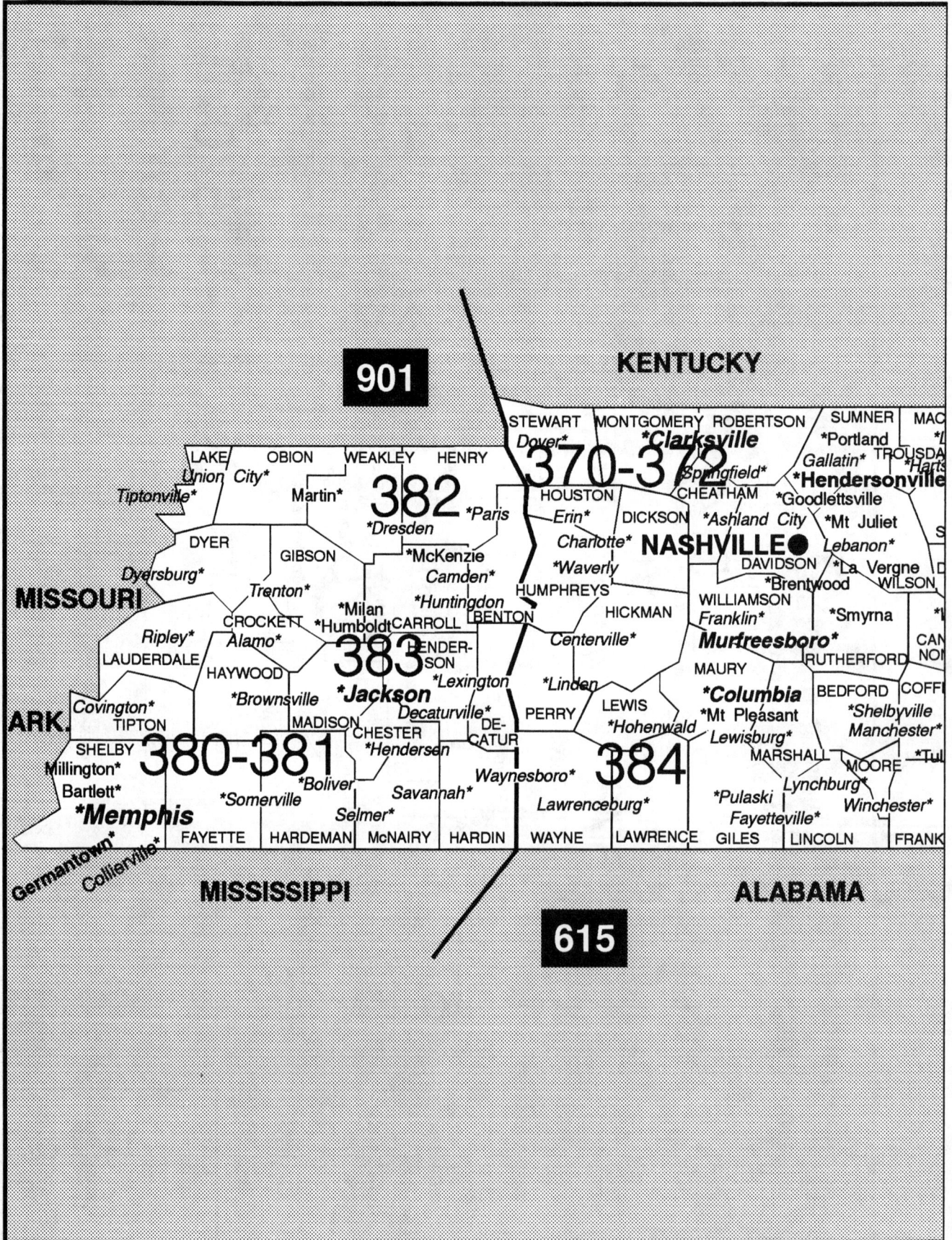

Tennessee

901

KENTUCKY

370-372

STEWART MONTGOMERY ROBERTSON SUMNER MAC

Dover *Clarksville* *Portland* TROUSDA

HOUSTON *Springfield* Gallatin* *Harts

CHEATHAM *Hendersonville

Erin* DICKSON *Ashland City *Goodlettsville

LAKE OBION WEAKLEY HENRY Charlotte* *Mt Juliet

Union City* *Paris *Waverly NASHVILLE Lebanon*

Tiptonville* Martin* DAVIDSON *La Vergne D

382 *Brentwood WILSON

*Dresden HUMPHREYS *Brentwood

DYER *McKenzie HICKMAN WILLIAMSON *Smyrna *

Dyersburg* GIBSON Camden* Franklin*

Trenton* *Huntingdon Centerville* Murfreesboro* CAN

MISSOURI CROCKETT *Milan CARROLL MAURY RUTHERFORD NON

Ripley* Alamo* *Humboldt HENDER-SON *Linden *Columbia BEDFORD COFFI

LAUDERDALE HAYWOOD 383 *Lexington LEWIS *Mt Pleasant *Shelbyville

ARK. *Brownsville *Jackson PERRY *Hohenwald Lewisburg* Manchester*

Covington* Decaturville* DE- MARSHALL *Tul

TIPTON MADISON CHESTER CATUR Waynesboro* 384 Lynchburg* MOORE

SHELBY 380-381 *Hendersen LAWRENCE *Pulaski Winchester*

Millington* *Boliver Savannah* Lawrenceburg* Fayetteville*

Bartlett* *Somerville Selmer* GILES LINCOLN FRANK

*Memphis FAYETTE HARDEMAN McNAIRY HARDIN WAYNE LAWRENCE

Germantown* Collierville*

MISSISSIPPI ALABAMA

615

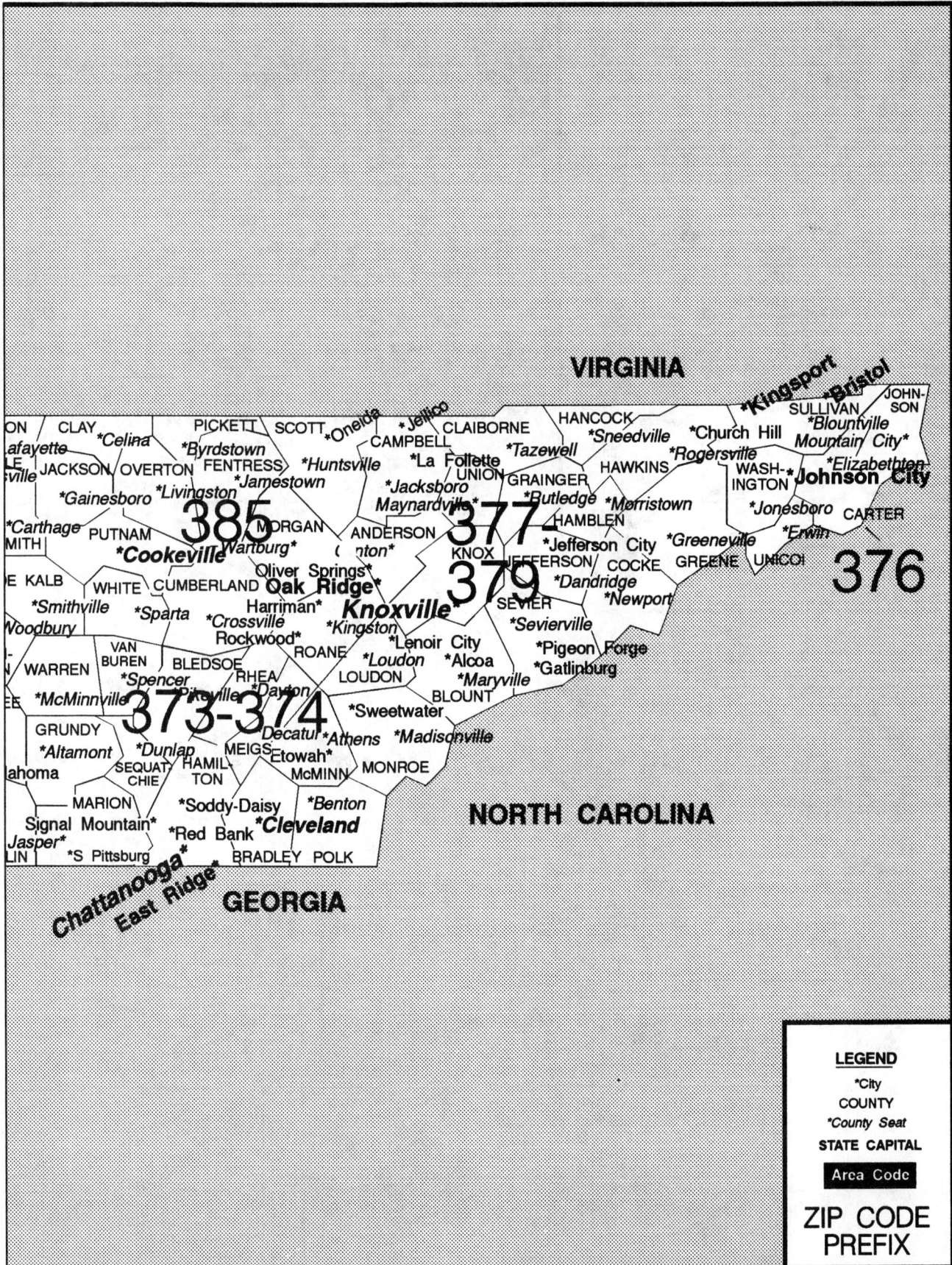

VIRGINIA

*Kingsport *Bristol

JOHN-SON

SULLIVAN

HANCOCK

*Sneedville *Church Hill *Blountville

Mountain City*

ON CLAY PICKETT SCOTT *Oneida *Jellico CLAIBORNE

*Celina *Byrdstown CAMPBELL *Tazewell HAWKINS *Rogersville WASH-INGTON *Elizabethton

Lafayette *Huntsville *La Follette GRAINGER Johnson City

JACKSON OVERTON FENTRESS UNION

ville *Jamestown *Jacksboro *Butledge *Morristown *Jonesboro CARTER

*Gainesboro *Livingston Maynardville HAMBLEN *Greeneville *Erwin

*Carthage PUTNAM 385 MORGAN ANDERSON *Jefferson City COCKE GREENE UNICOI 376

SMITH Wartburg* nton* KNOX JEFFERSON

*Cookeville 377 *Dandridge

E KALB WHITE CUMBERLAND Oak Ridge 379 SEVIER *Newport

*Smithville *Sparta Harriman* Knoxville *Sevierville

Woodbury *Crossville *Kingston

Rockwood* *Lenoir City *Pigeon Forge

ROANE *Loudon *Alcoa *Gatlinburg

VAN BUREN BLEDSOE LOUDON *Maryville

WARREN RHEA *Dayton BLOUNT

*Spencer *Pikeville* 373-374 *Sweetwater

EE *McMinnville Decatur* *Athens *Madisonville

GRUNDY *Dunlap MEIGS Etowah* MONROE

*Altamont HAMIL TON McMINN

ahoma SEQUAT CHIE NORTH CAROLINA

MARION *Soddy-Daisy *Benton

Signal Mountain* *Red Bank *Cleveland

Jasper* *S Pittsburg BRADLEY POLK

LIN Chattanooga* GEORGIA

East Ridge*

LEGEND
*City
COUNTY
*County Seat
STATE CAPITAL
Area Code
ZIP CODE PREFIX

Fort Worth/Dallas Area

214

TARRANT

Carrollton* *Addison *Richardson
*Coppell
DALLAS
Grapevine* Farmers Branch *Garland *Rowlett
Colleyville* *University Park
Bedford* *Euless *N Richland Hills *Highland Park
Saginaw* Watauga* *Hurst* *Irving* *Dallas *Seagoville
River Oaks* *Haltom City *Mesquite
White Settlement* Richland Hills* *Grand Prairie
Fort Worth *Arlington *Cockrell Hill *Balch Spgs
Benbrook* Duncanville* *Hutchins
Everman* De Soto* *Lancaster
Crowley* *Cedar Hill

760-
76
753
752

817
214

806

817

OKLAHOMA

DALLAM Stratford* SHERMAN HANS-FORD
Dalhart Spearman
HARTLEY Dumas* HUTCH-INSON
Channing* MOORE *Stinnett *Canadian
*Borger *Miami
OLDHAM POTTER CARSON WHEELER
*Vega Amarillo *Panhandle *Pampa *Wheeler
*Shamrock
DEAF SMITH RANDALL *Claude ARM-STRONG GRAY DONLEY COLLINGS-WORTH
Hereford* Canyon* *Clarendon *Wellington

790-791
792

PARMER CASTRO SWISHER BRISCOE HALL *Memphis
*Friona *Dimmitt *Tulia *Silverton *Childress
*Farwell HARDE-MAN

BAILEY LAMB HALE MOTLEY COTTLE
*Muleshoe *Plainview FLOYD *Matador
Littlefield* Abernathy* *Floydada Paducah* FOARD
COCHRAN HOCKLEY CROSBY DICKENS KING
*Morton *Levelland Lubbock *Crosbyton *Dickens *Guthrie
YOAKUM TERRY LYNN GARZA KENT STONE-WALL
Plains* *Brownfield *Post *Jayton *Aspermont
*Denver City *Tahoka
Seagraves BORDEN SCURRY Hamlin SHACKEL-FORD
DAWSON Gail* *Snyder FISHER JONES Albany*
Seminole* Lamesa* Sweetwater* Anson* CALLAHAN
ANDREWS MARTIN HOWARD NOLAN Abilene* Baird*
Andrews* *Stanton Big Spring* *Colorado City TAYLOR
MITCHELL Clyde*
*Midland STERLING COKE RUNNELS
WINK-LER ECTOR GLASS-COCK Sterling City* *Robert Lee *Ballinger
*Kermit MIDLAND UPTON REAGAN TOM GREEN CONCHO
Odessa* *Mohanas CRANE Rankin* Big Lake* IRION San Angelo*
WARD Crane* *Eldorado
PECOS *Fort

793-794
795
796
797
769

903
ARKANSAS
Tex-arkana
754
Paris* Clarksville* RED RIVER Boston* BOWIE
75
53
52
Longview* *Tyler
75
756
Nacogdoches*
75
58
Lufkin*
75
L.A.
*Center
75

Denison* *Sherman
762
Denton* Dallas* Fort Worth*
760-
214
Waco*
76
765
Killeen* Temple*
768
San Angelo*
769

Wichita Falls*
817
Witchita Falls
763

section 2 / page 74

Texas

WESTERN TEXAS

915

798-799

713

409

512

770-772

775 Galveston

713 Houston

786-787

780-782-779

783-784

788 San Antonio

LEGEND

*City

COUNTY

*County Seat

STATE CAPITAL

Area Code

ZIP CODE PREFIX

915

512

MEXICO

GULF OF MEXICO

Corpus Christi

785

HOUSTON & GALVESTON AREA

409

713

770-772

775

AUSTIN●

*Bryan

*College Station

*Silsbee Beaumont

Pasadena Missouri City

Houston

San Marcos* New Braunfels

*Victoria

*Kingsville

*Harlingen

McAllen Mission

Brownsville

Laredo*

Del Rio*

*Ozona

*Sanderson

Stockton

*El Paso *Alpine *Fort Davis PRESIDIO BREWSTER

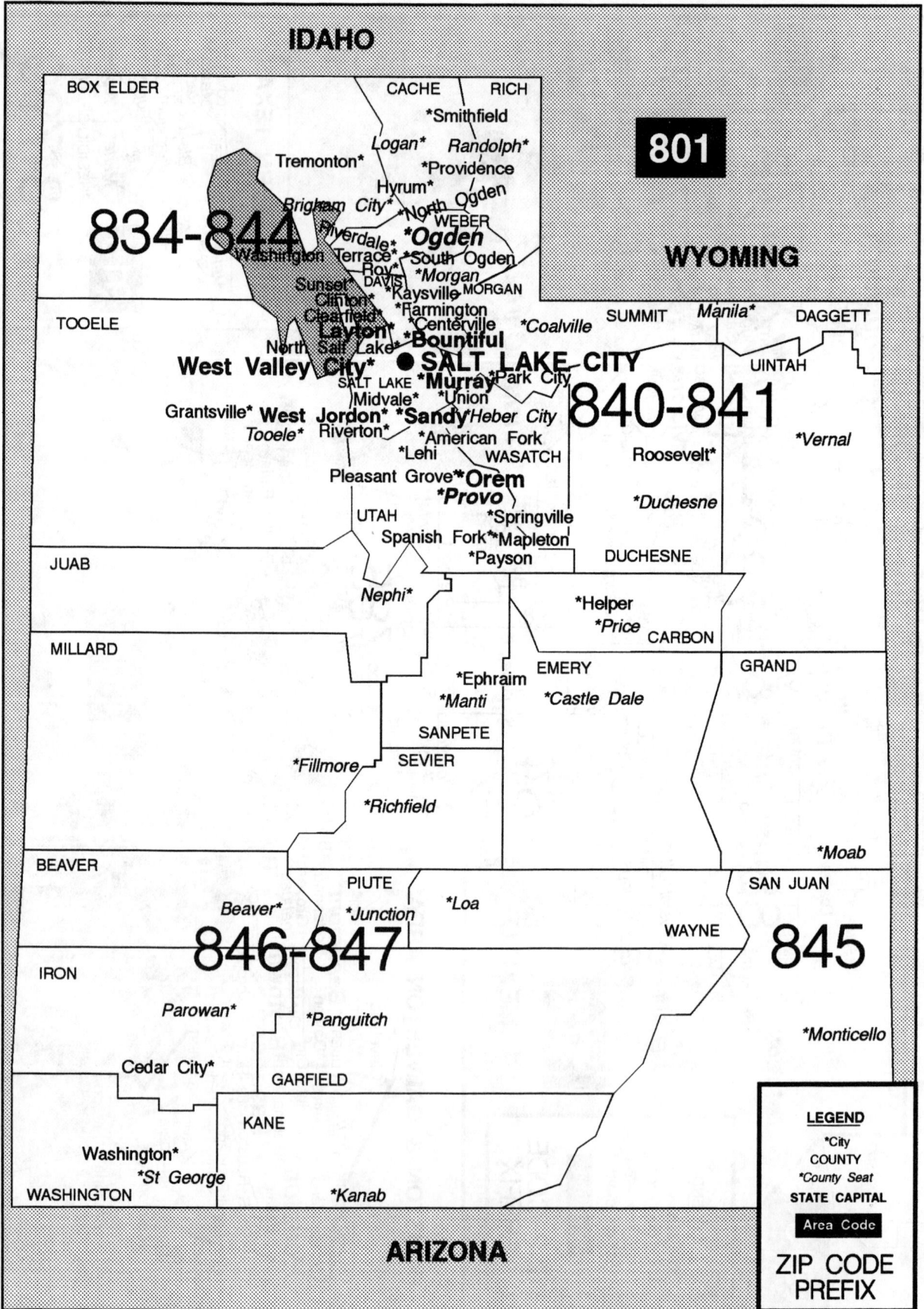

Utah

IDAHO

BOX ELDER

CACHE   RICH

*Smithfield

Logan   *Randolph*

Tremonton*

*Providence

Hyrum*

*North Ogden

Brigham City*

WEBER

834-844

Riverdale*

*Ogden

Washington Terrace*

*South Ogden

Roy*

DAVIS

*Morgan

Sunset*

MORGAN

Clinton*

*Kaysville

Clearfield*

*Farmington

Layton*

*Centerville

North Salt Lake*

Coalville   SUMMIT   Manila   DAGGETT

*Bountiful

TOOELE

UINTAH

West Valley City*

●SALT LAKE CITY

SALT LAKE   *Murray   *Park City

Midvale*   *Union

840-841

Grantsville* West *Jordon* *Sandy *Heber City

Tooele*   Riverton*   WASATCH

*American Fork

*Lehi   *Vernal

Pleasant Grove* *Orem

Roosevelt*

UTAH   *Provo

*Springville

*Duchesne

Spanish Fork* *Mapleton

*Payson   DUCHESNE

JUAB

Nephi*

*Helper

*Price

CARBON

MILLARD

EMERY   GRAND

*Ephraim

*Manti   *Castle Dale

SANPETE

*Fillmore   SEVIER

*Richfield

*Moab

BEAVER   PIUTE   SAN JUAN

Beaver*   *Junction   *Loa

WAYNE

846-847   **845**

IRON

Parowan*   *Panguitch

*Monticello

Cedar City*   GARFIELD

KANE

Washington*

*St George

WASHINGTON   *Kanab

ARIZONA

WYOMING

801

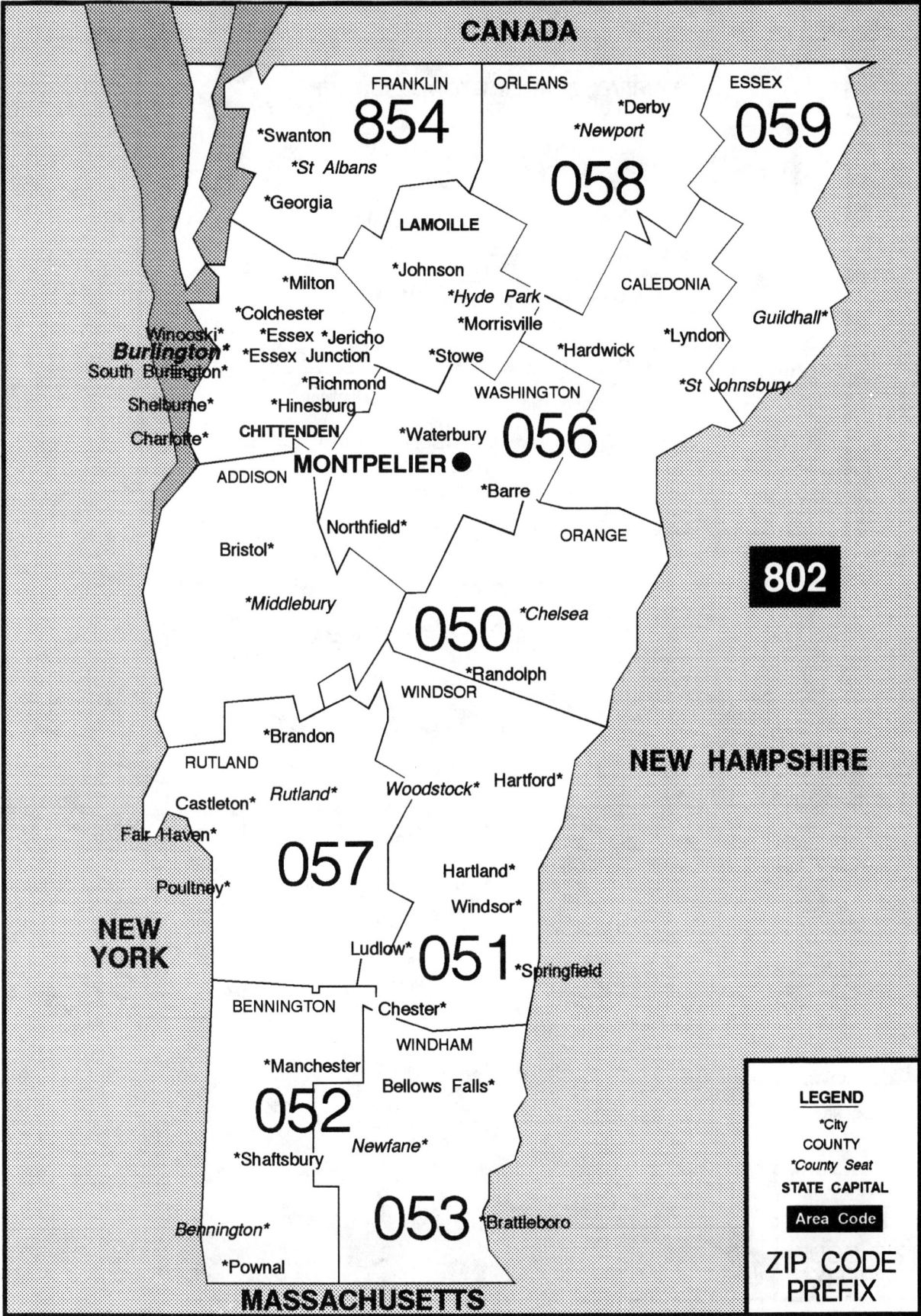

CANADA

FRANKLIN
854

ORLEANS
*Derby
*Newport
058

ESSEX
059

*Swanton

*St Albans

*Georgia

LAMOILLE

*Johnson

CALEDONIA

*Milton

*Hyde Park

*Colchester
*Essex *Jericho
*Essex Junction
*Morrisville
*Stowe

*Lyndon

Guildhall*

Winooski*
*Hardwick

*Richmond

*St Johnsbury

Burlington*
South Burlington*

WASHINGTON

Shelburne*
*Hinesburg

056

Charlotte*

CHITTENDEN

*Waterbury

ADDISON

MONTPELIER ●

*Barre

Northfield*

ORANGE

Bristol*

802

*Middlebury

*Chelsea

050

*Randolph

WINDSOR

*Brandon

RUTLAND

NEW HAMPSHIRE

Castleton*

Rutland*

Woodstock*   Hartford*

Fair Haven*

057

Hartland*

Poultney*

Windsor*

NEW
YORK

Ludlow*

051

*Springfield

BENNINGTON   Chester*

WINDHAM

*Manchester

Bellows Falls*

052

*Shaftsbury

Newfane*

053   *Brattleboro

Bennington*

*Pownal

MASSACHUSETTS

Virginia

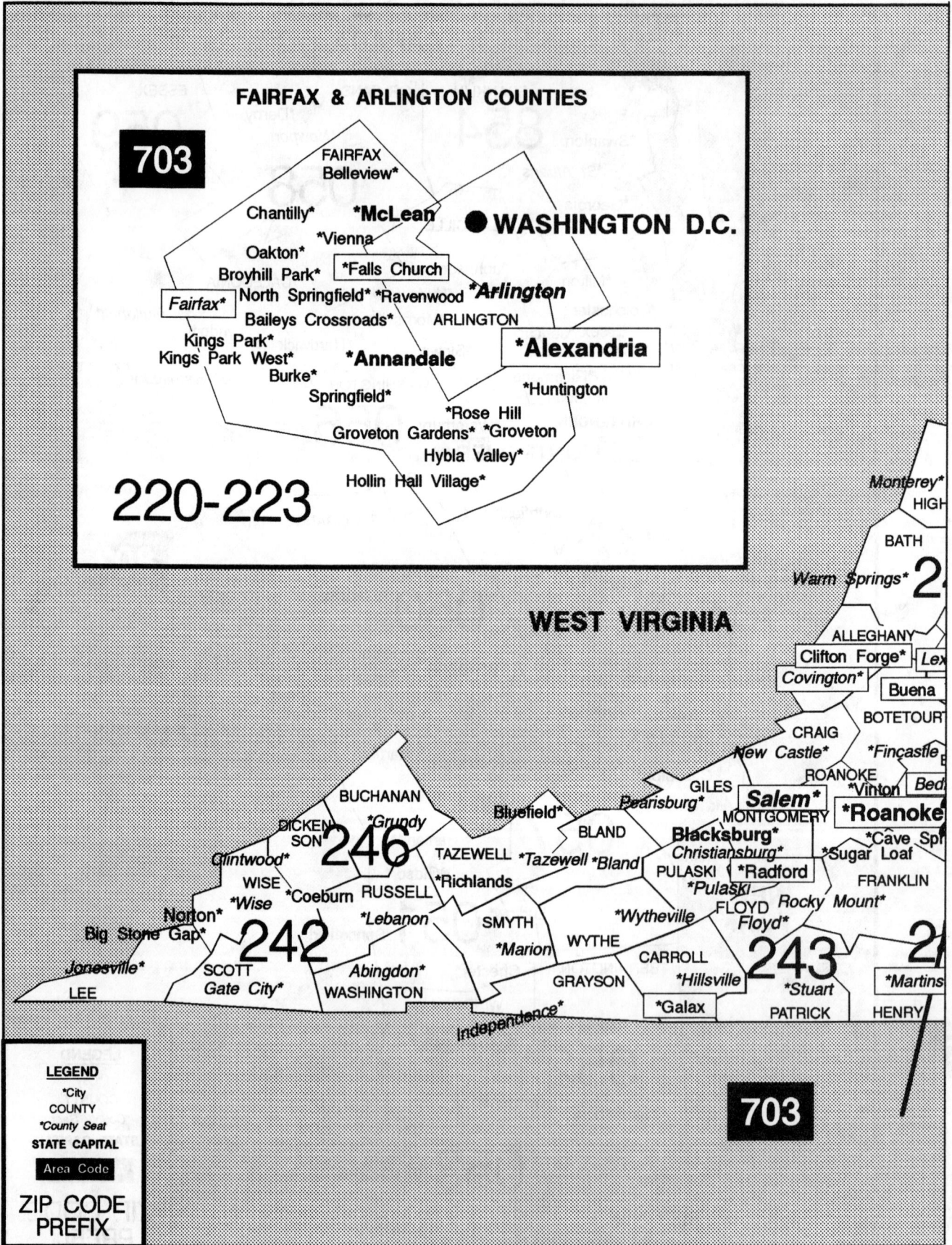

FAIRFAX & ARLINGTON COUNTIES

703

FAIRFAX
Belleview*

Chantilly*   ***McLean**   ● **WASHINGTON D.C.**
*Vienna
Oakton*
Broyhill Park*   ***Falls Church**
Fairfax*   North Springfield* *Ravenwood   ***Arlington**
Baileys Crossroads*   ARLINGTON
Kings Park*
Kings Park West*   ***Annandale**   ***Alexandria**
Burke*
Springfield*   *Huntington
*Rose Hill
Groveton Gardens* *Groveton
Hybla Valley*
Hollin Hall Village*

220-223

WEST VIRGINIA

Monterey*
HIGH

BATH
Warm Springs*   2

ALLEGHANY
Clifton Forge* Lex
Covington*   Buena

BOTETOUR
CRAIG
New Castle*   *Fincastle
ROANOKE   Bed
GILES   Salem*   *Vinton
BUCHANAN   Pearisburg* MONTGOMERY   *Roanoke
Grundy   Bluefield   BLAND   Blacksburg*   *Cave Spr
DICKEN   246   BLAND   Christiansburg*   *Sugar Loaf
Clintwood*   SON   TAZEWELL *Tazewell *Bland   PULASKI   *Radford   FRANKLIN
WISE   RUSSELL   *Richlands   *Pulaski   FLOYD   Rocky Mount
*Wise *Coeburn   SMYTH   *Wytheville   Floyd*
Norton*   *Lebanon   WYTHE   243   2
Big Stone Gap*   242   *Marion   CARROLL   *Martins
Jonesville*   Abingdon*   GRAYSON   *Hillsville *Stuart
SCOTT   WASHINGTON   *Galax   PATRICK   HENRY
LEE   Gate City*   Independence*

703

LEGEND
*City
COUNTY
*County Seat
STATE CAPITAL
Area Code

ZIP CODE
PREFIX

LEGEND
*City
COUNTY
*County Seat
STATE CAPITAL
Independent City
Area Code
ZIP CODE PREFIX

FREDERICK

LOUDOUN

Winchester*

226

*Leesburg

Berryville*

CLARKE

WARREN

220-223

FAIRFAX

● WASHINGTON D.C.

*Arlington

*Alexandria

CHESAPEAKE BAY

SHENANDOAH

Front Royal*

FAUQUIER

Manassas Park*

*Fairfax

228

*Woodstock

RAPPA-HANNOCK

Manassas*

*Warrenton

PRINCE WILLIAM

*Woodbridge

227

Washington*

Dumfries*

STAFFORD

See Map... this page

Luray*

ROCKINGAM

PAGE

CULPEPER

*Culpeper

*Stafford

MARYLAND

Harrisonburg*

MADISON

*Madison

224

KING GEORGE

King George

804

GREENE

*Stanardsville

Fredericksburg*

WEST MORELAND

Bridgewater*

AUGUSTA

Orange*

ORANGE

SPOTSYLVANIA

*Montross

LAND

AMBEMARLE

229

Spotsylvania*

225

ESSEX

Staunton*

LOUISA

*Louisa

*Bowling Green

RICH-MOND

NORTHUMBERLAND

44

Waynesboro*

*Warsaw

*Heathsville

Charlottesville*

230-232

CAROLINE

*Tappahannock

*Lancaster

ROCKBRIDGE

NELSON

Palmyra*

Ashland*

HANOVER

KING & QUEEN

*King & Queen CH

LANCASTER

ington*

FLUVANNA

GOOCH-LAND

Hanover*

KING WILLIAM

MIDDLE SEX

*Saluda

Vista*

*Lovingston

Goochland*

Laurel*

*King William

GLOU-CESTER

NORTHAMPTON

Amherst*

AMHERST

BUCKINGHAM

CUMBER-LAND

Highland Springs

*Lakeside

NEW KENT

*Mathews

MATHEWS

Buckingham*

RICHMOND

HENRICO

*New Kent

JAMES CITY

*Gloucester

233-

BEDFORD

APPOMA

Cumberland*

Bon Air

Bensley

CHARLES CITY

*Charles City

*Williamsburg

Danville

*Lynchburg

*Powhatan

CHESTERFIELD

ford*

Appomattox*

Farmville*

AMELIA

Chesterfield*

Chester*

SURRY

*Prince George

YORK

Yorktown*

237

240-

*Timberlake

*Rustburg

Amelia CH*

Colonial Hts*

*Hopewell

*Poquoson

CAMPBELL

PRINCE EDWARD

NOTTOWAY

238

Surry

ISLE

*Smithfield

*Hampton

241

*Altavista

Nottoway*

Petersburg*

PRINCE GEORGE

OF WIGHT

PITTSYLVANIA

CHARLOTTE

LUNENBURG

*Blackstone

*Dinwiddie

SUSSEX

*Newport News

45

HALIFAX

239

*Charlotte CH

DINWIDDIE

Sussex*

Isle of Wight

Norfolk*

Virginia Bch

*Chatham

*Lunenburg

BRUNSWICK

GREENS-VILLE

SOUTHAMPTON

Portsmouth*

NORFOLK

Halifax*

hase City

Lawrenceville*

Courtland*

*Suffolk

*Chesapeake

ville

South Hill*

Boydton*

Emporia*

Franklin*

*Danville

*South Boston

MECKLENBURG

NORTH CAROLINA

804

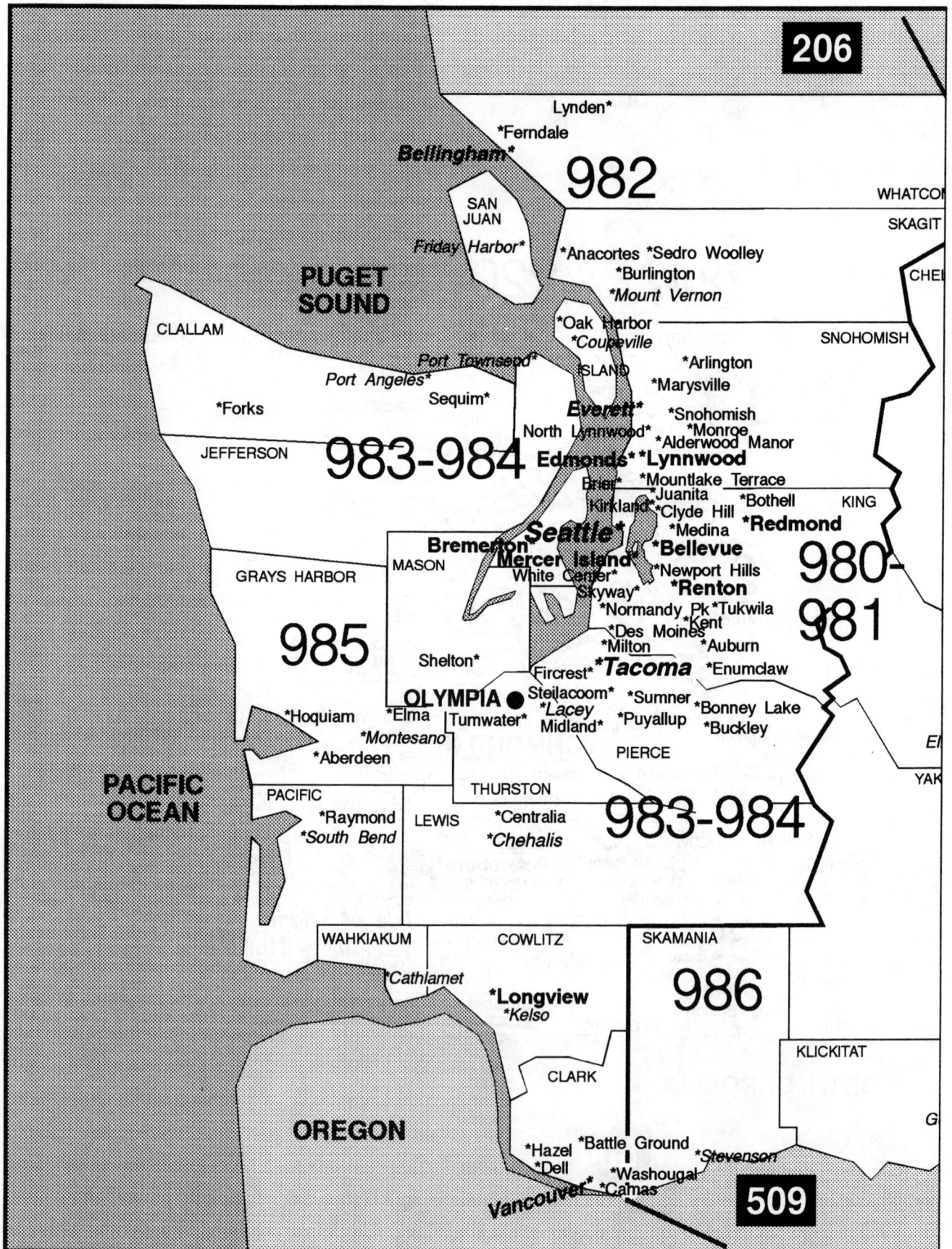

Washington

206

Lynden*
*Ferndale
Bellingham
982
WHATCO

SAN
JUAN

Friday Harbor*

PUGET
SOUND

*Anacortes *Sedro Woolley
SKAGIT
*Burlington
*Mount Vernon
CHEL

CLALLAM

*Oak Harbor
*Coupeville
ISLAND
SNOHOMISH

Port Townsend*
Port Angeles*
Sequim*
*Forks

JEFFERSON

983-984

*Arlington
*Marysville

Everett*
North Lynnwood*
Edmonds**Lynnwood
Brier*
Kirkland*

*Snohomish
*Monroe
*Alderwood Manor

*Mountlake Terrace
*Juanita
*Clyde Hill
*Medina
*Bothell   KING
*Redmond

Seattle*
Bremerton*
MASON
Mercer Island*
White Center*
Skyway*

*Bellevue
*Newport Hills
*Renton

980-
981

GRAYS HARBOR

985

Shelton*

*Normandy Pk *Tukwila
Kent
*Des Moines
*Milton
*Auburn
*Enumclaw

Fircrest* *Tacoma

OLYMPIA ●
*Elma
Tumwater*

Steilacoom*
*Sumner
*Lacey
Midland* *Puyallup
*Bonney Lake
*Buckley

PIERCE

*Hoquiam
*Montesano
*Aberdeen

PACIFIC
OCEAN

PACIFIC

THURSTON

E

YAK

*Raymond
*South Bend

LEWIS

*Centralia
*Chehalis

983-984

WAHKIAKUM
COWLITZ
SKAMANIA

986

*Cathlamet

*Longview
*Kelso

KLICKITAT

CLARK

OREGON

*Hazel
*Dell
*Battle Ground
*Stevenson
*Washougal
Vancouver* *Camas

G

509

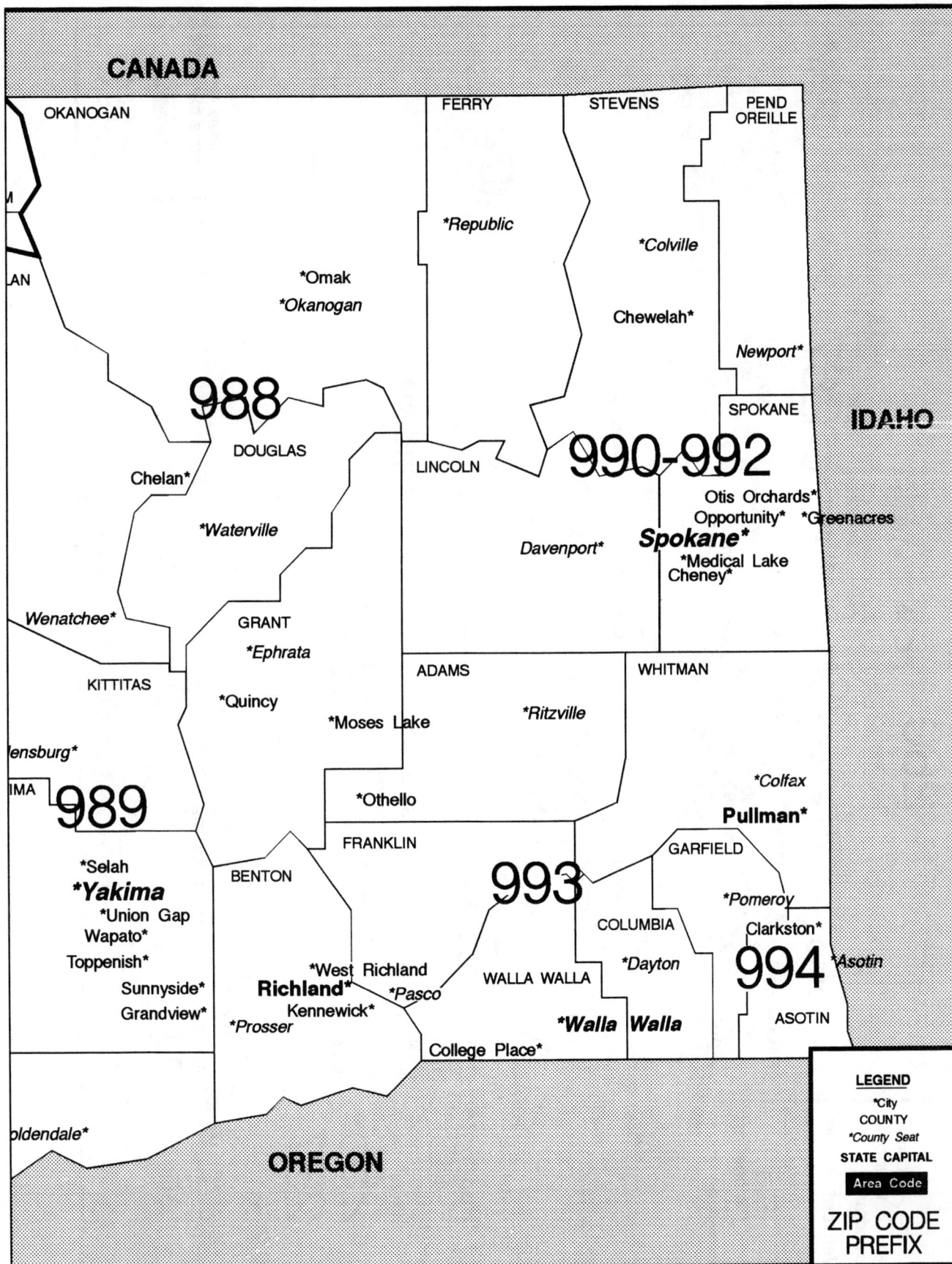

CANADA

OKANOGAN

FERRY

STEVENS

PEND
OREILLE

*Republic

*Colville

*Omak

*Okanogan

Chewelah*

Newport*

988

SPOKANE

IDAHO

DOUGLAS

LINCOLN

990-992

Chelan*

Otis Orchards*

Opportunity* *Greenacres

*Waterville

Davenport*

Spokane*

*Medical Lake

Cheney*

Wenatchee*

GRANT

*Ephrata

ADAMS

WHITMAN

KITTITAS

*Quincy

*Moses Lake

*Ritzville

lensburg*

*Colfax

IMA

989

*Othello

Pullman*

FRANKLIN

GARFIELD

*Selah

BENTON

993

*Pomeroy

Yakima

COLUMBIA

Clarkston*

*Union Gap

*Dayton

994 *Asotin

Wapato*

*West Richland

WALLA WALLA

Toppenish*

Richland* *Pasco

ASOTIN

Sunnyside*

Walla Walla

Kennewick*

Grandview*

*Prosser

College Place*

oldendale*

OREGON

LEGEND

*City

COUNTY

*County Seat

STATE CAPITAL

Area Code

**ZIP CODE
PREFIX**

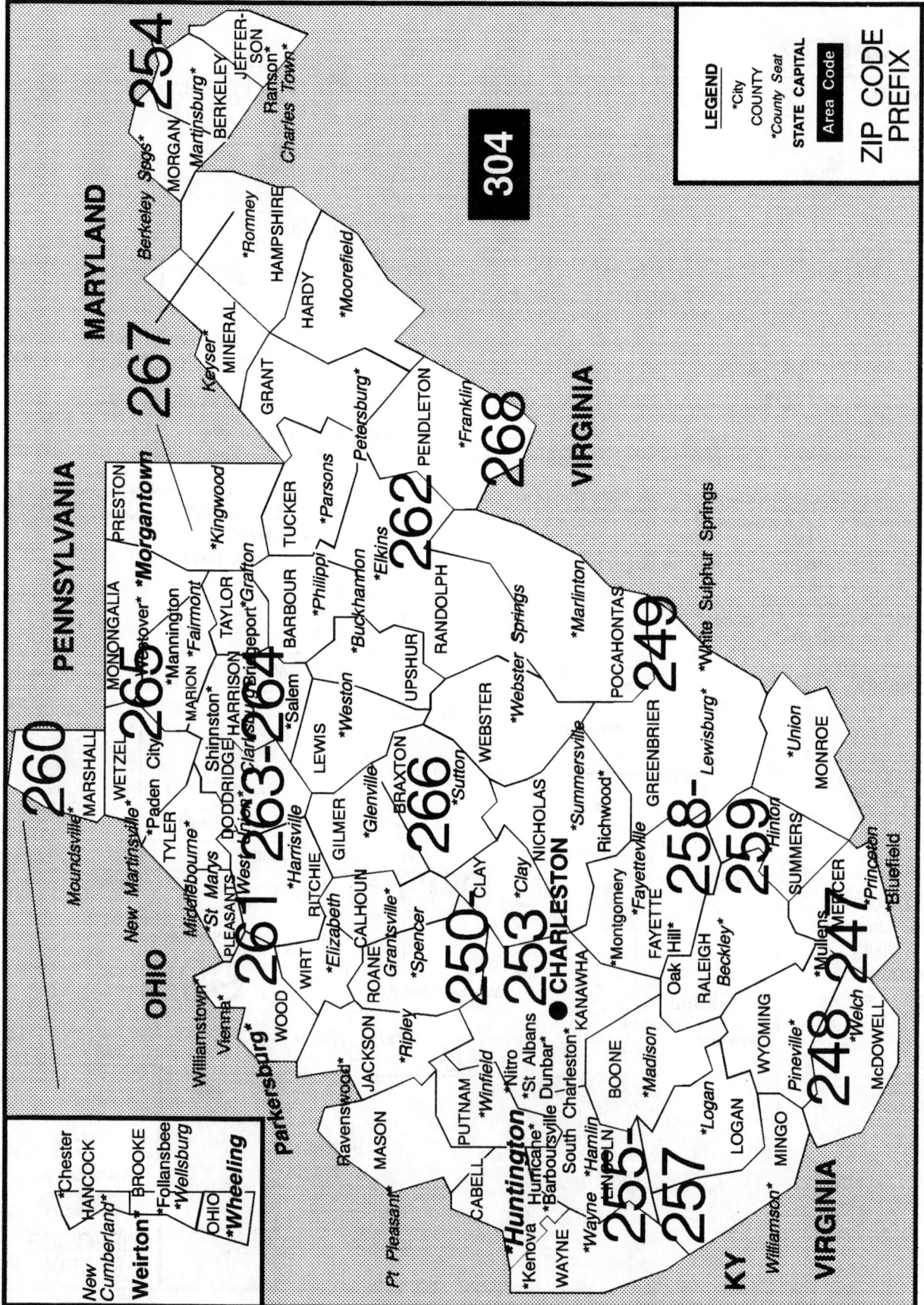

West Virginia

MARYLAND

PENNSYLVANIA

OHIO

VIRGINIA

KY

VIRGINIA

LEGEND
*City
COUNTY
*County Seat
STATE CAPITAL
Area Code

ZIP CODE PREFIX

304

254

267

268

262

260

265

261

263-264

266

249

250

253

258-

259

247

248-

255-

257

Area Codes / Zip Prefixes

HANCOCK
*Chester
*New Cumberland
BROOKE
*Follansbee
**Weirton*
*Wellsburg
OHIO
*Wheeling

MARSHALL
*Moundsville
WETZEL
*New Martinsville
MONONGALIA
PRESTON
*Morgantown
Westover
*Paden City
TYLER
*Middlebourne
MARION
*Mannington
*Fairmont
TAYLOR
*Grafton
HARRISON
*Shinnston
*Clarksburg
*Bridgeport
DODDRIDGE
*West Union
BARBOUR
Philippi
TUCKER
*Parsons
*Kingwood

PLEASANTS
*St Marys
Williamstown
*Vienna
RITCHIE
*Harrisville
*Salem
LEWIS
*Weston
UPSHUR
*Buckhannon
RANDOLPH
*Elkins

WOOD
Parkersburg
WIRT
*Elizabeth
GILMER
*Glenville
BRAXTON
*Sutton
WEBSTER
*Webster Springs
POCAHONTAS
*Marlinton

CALHOUN
*Grantsville
ROANE
*Spencer
CLAY
*Clay
NICHOLAS
*Summersville
*Richwood
GREENBRIER
Lewisburg
*White Sulphur Springs

JACKSON
*Ripley
Ravenswood
MASON
*Pt Pleasant
PUTNAM
*Winfield
Hurricane
*Nitro
*St Albans
*South Charleston
Dunbar
KANAWHA
CHARLESTON
*Montgomery
FAYETTE
*Fayetteville
*Oak Hill
RALEIGH
Beckley
SUMMERS
*Hinton
MONROE
*Union

CABELL
Huntington
Barboursville
LINCOLN
*Hamlin
BOONE
*Madison
*Montgomery
WYOMING
*Pineville
MERCER
*Princeton
*Bluefield

WAYNE
*Kenova
*Wayne
MINGO
*Williamson
LOGAN
*Logan
*Mullens
MCDOWELL
*Welch

HAMPSHIRE
*Romney
MINERAL
*Keyser
GRANT
HARDY
*Moorefield
PENDLETON
*Franklin
GRANT
Petersburg

MORGAN
Berkeley Spgs
BERKELEY
Martinsburg
JEFFERSON
Charles Town
Ranson

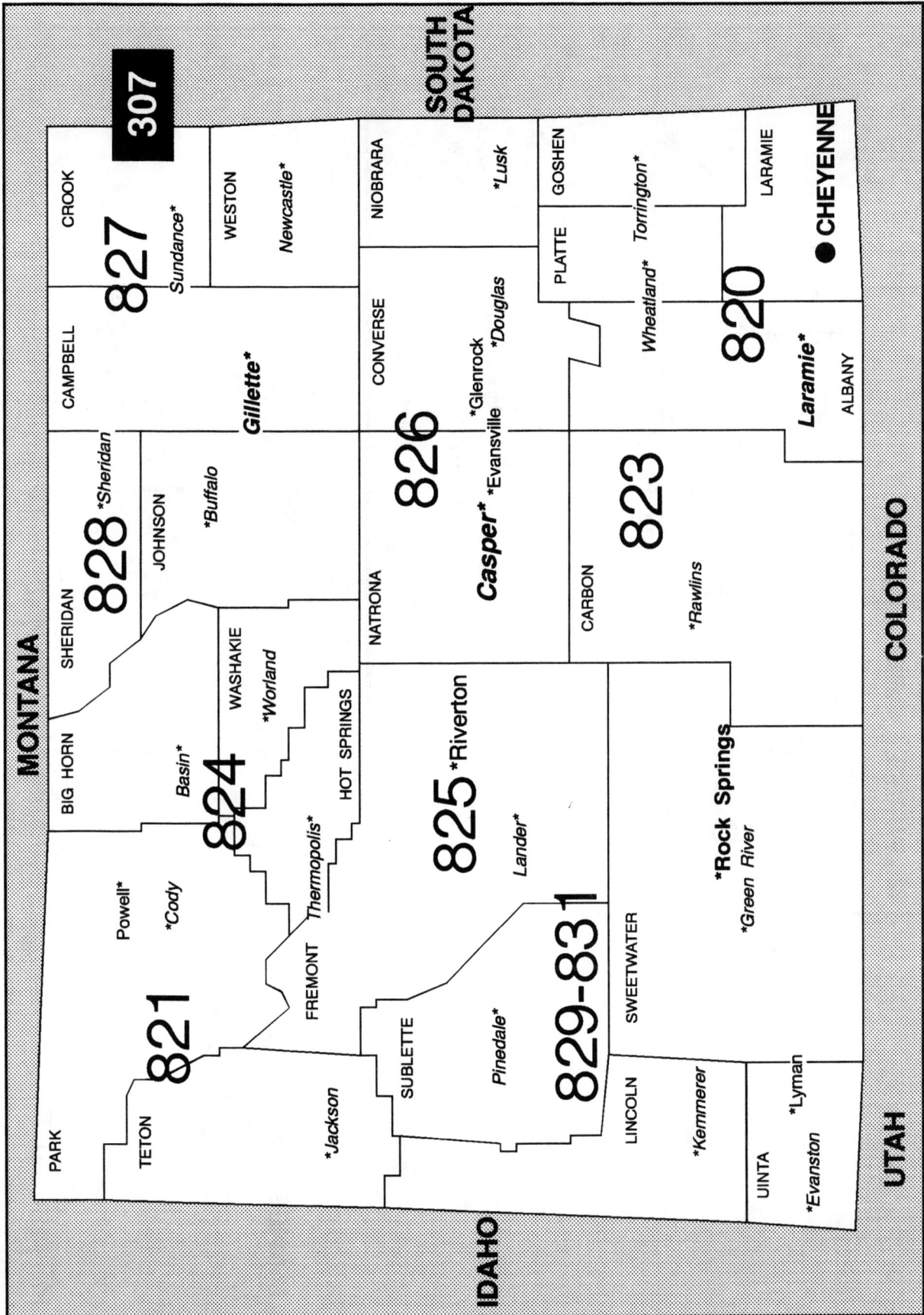

MONTANA

SOUTH DAKOTA

IDAHO

UTAH

COLORADO

307

CROOK
827
Sundance*

WESTON
Newcastle*

NIOBRARA
*Lusk

GOSHEN
Torrington*

LARAMIE
●CHEYENNE

PLATTE
Wheatland*

820

CAMPBELL
Gillette*

CONVERSE
826
*Glenrock
*Douglas
Casper* *Evansville

CARBON
823
*Rawlins

Laramie*
ALBANY

SHERIDAN
828 *Sheridan

JOHNSON
*Buffalo

NATRONA

BIG HORN

WASHAKIE
*Worland

HOT SPRINGS

Basin*
824
Thermopolis*

825 *Riverton
Lander*

*Rock Springs
*Green River

Powell*
*Cody

FREMONT

SUBLETTE
Pinedale*

829-831

SWEETWATER

PARK
TETON
821
*Jackson

LINCOLN
*Kemmerer

UINTA
*Lyman
*Evanston

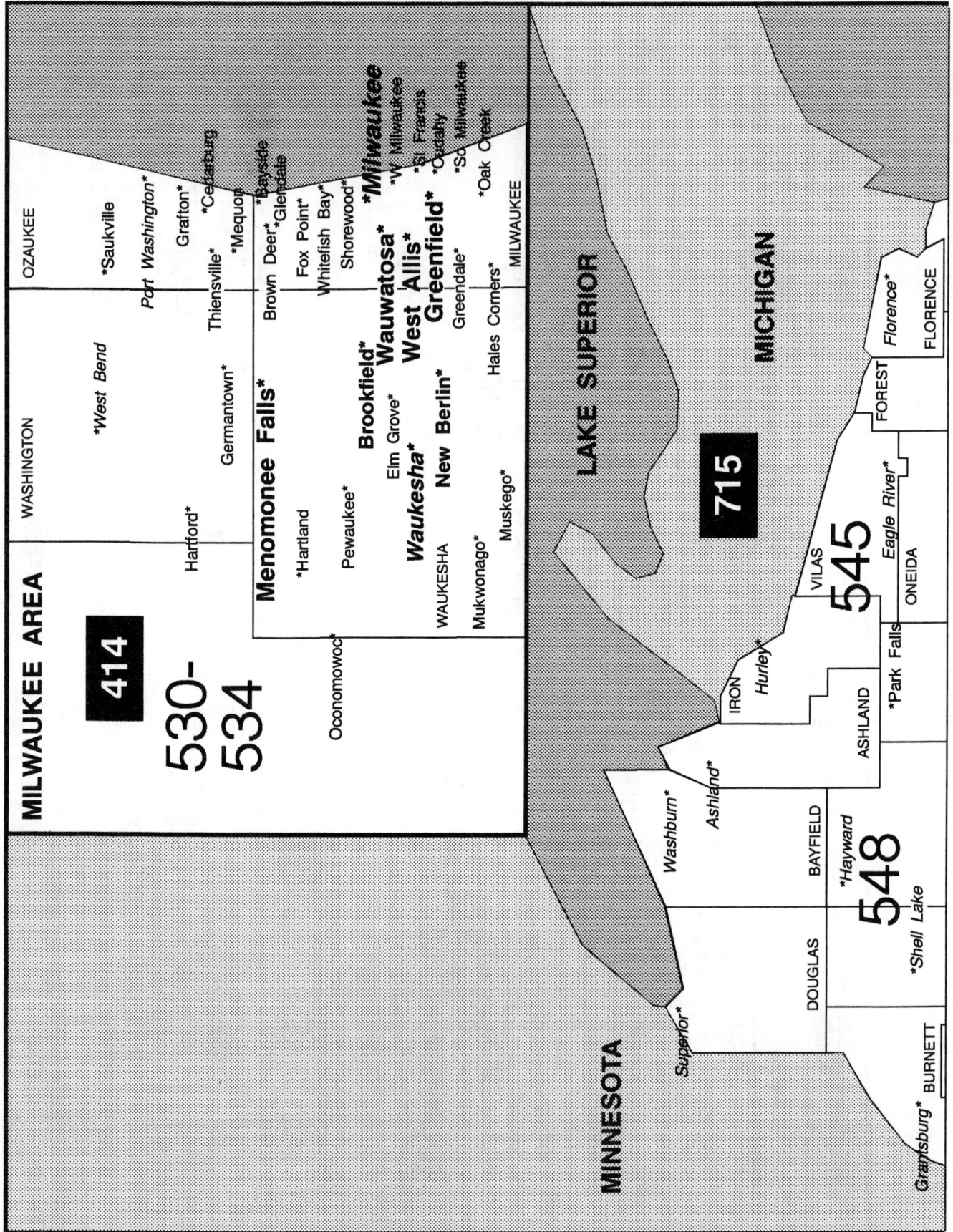

MILWAUKEE AREA
414
530–534

WASHINGTON

*West Bend

Hartford*

Oconomowoc*

OZAUKEE

*Saukville

Port Washington*

Grafton*

Thiensville*

*Cedarburg

*Mequon

Germantown*

Menomonee Falls*

*Hartland

Pewaukee*

Brookfield*

Elm Grove*

Wauwatosa*

Waukesha*

WAUKESHA

New Berlin*

West Allis*

Greenfield*

Mukwonago*

Muskego*

Brown Deer*

Fox Point*

Whitefish Bay*

Shorewood*

*Bayside

*Glendale

*Milwaukee

*W. Milwaukee

*St. Francis

*Cudahy

*So. Milwaukee

*Oak Creek

Greendale*

Hales Corners*

MILWAUKEE

MINNESOTA

Superior*

Grantsburg*

BURNETT

DOUGLAS

*Shell Lake

*Hayward
548

BAYFIELD

Washburn*

Ashland*

ASHLAND

IRON

Hurley*

*Park Falls

LAKE SUPERIOR

715

MICHIGAN

VILAS
545

Eagle River*

ONEIDA

FOREST

Florence*

FLORENCE

LAKE MICHIGAN

414

530-534

541-543

542

549

544

539

546

535-538

547

540

608

MINNESOTA

IOWA

ILLINOIS

MARINETTE

*Crandon

*Rhinelander

*Phillips

LANGLADE

LINCOLN

Antigo*

Merrill*

Tomahawk*

PRICE

*Medford

TAYLOR

CLARK

MARATHON

Wausau*

Rothschild*

*Mosinee

*Marshfield

WOOD

PORTAGE

Stevens Point*

Plover*

Wisconsin Rapids*

Nekoosa*

JUNEAU

ADAMS

*Friendship

*Tomah

*Sparta

West Salem*

MONROE

JACKSON

*Whitehall

Black River Falls*

TREMP-EALEAU

BUFFALO

*Alma

PEPIN

PIERCE

*Mondovi

Durand*

Altoona*

Menomonie*

Chippewa Falls*

*Eau Claire

EAU CLAIRE

Neillsville*

CHIPPEWA

*Bloomer

DUNN

RUSK

BARRON

*Barron

Ladysmith*

SAWYER

WASHBURN

Rice Lake*

*New Richmond

*Hudson

ST CROIX

POLK

Balsam Lake*

*River Falls

*Prescott

Ellsworth*

*Menominee

KESHENA

*Keshena

SHAWANO

Shawano*

OCONTO

MENOMINEE

Marinette*

Peshtigo*

*Oconto

Sturgeon Bay*

DOOR

KEWAUNEE

Algoma*

*Kewaunee

BROWN

Green Bay

Howard*

*De Pere

OUTAGAMIE

Clintonville*

*Appleton

Little Chute*

*Kaukauna

Seymour*

*Kimberly

Menasha*

Neenah*

WINNEBAGO

*Oshkosh

CALUMET

Chilton*

*Brillion

MANITOWOC

Two Rivers

*Manitowoc

New Holstein*

Kiel*

WAUPACA

New London

Waupaca*

Ashwaubenon*

WAUSHARA

*Wautoma

Omro*

Berlin*

GREEN LAKE

Ripon*

Green Lake*

MARQUETTE

Montello*

Mauston*

SAUK

Baraboo*

*Wisconsin Dells

Richland Center*

RICHLAND

*Richland Center

CRAWFORD

*Prairie du Chien

Viroqua*

VERNON

Onalaska*

La Crosse*

LA CROSSE

GRANT

Boscobel*

Lancaster*

Platteville*

Dodgeville*

IOWA

N. Fond du Lac*

*Fond du Lac

FOND DU LAC

Waupun*

DODGE

Horicon*

Beaver Dam*

Mayville*

Juneau*

COLUMBIA

*Portage

*De Forest

Columbus*

Sun Prairie*

DANE

Waunakee*

Middleton*

MADISON

Mt Horeb*

Verona*

Monona*

McFarland*

*Oregon

Stoughton*

Mt Horeb*

JEFFERSON

*Lake Mills

*Jefferson

Fort Atkinson*

*Watertown

Whitewater*

WASHINGTON

WAUKESHA

WAUKESHA

See Map... page 2-84

OZAUKEE

*Port Washington

*Mayville

Plymouth*

*Sheboygan

Sheboygan Falls*

SHEBOYGAN

MIL-WAUKEE

*Milwaukee

RACINE

*Racine

Sturtevant*

*Kenosha

KENOSHA

Union Grove*

Burlington*

ROCK

*Milton

Edgerton*

Evansville*

*Janesville

Beloit*

Brodhead*

GREEN

Monroe*

LAFAYETTE

Darlington*

WALWORTH

Elkhorn*

*Lake Geneva

Delavan*

Twin Lakes*

*Beloit

LEGEND
*City
COUNTY
*County Seat
STATE CAPITAL
Area Code
ZIP CODE PREFIX

Use to find State Capitals, Counties & County Seats.

County Seats

COUNTY	COUNTY SEAT	COUNTY	COUNTY SEAT
ALABAMA.....MONTGOMERY			
Autauga	Prattville	Marshall	Guntersville
Baldwin	Bay Minette	Mobile	Mobile
Barbour	Clayton	Monroe	Monroeville
Bibb	Centreville	Montgomery	Montgomery
Blount	Oneonta	Morgan	Decatur
Bullock	Union Springs	Perry	Marion
Butler	Greenville	Pickens	Carrollton
Calhoun	Anniston	Pike	Troy
Chambers	Lafayette	Randolph	Wedowee
Cherokee	Centre	Russell	Phenix City
Chilton	Clanton	St Clair	Ashville & Pell City
Choctaw	Butler	Shelby	Columbiana
Clarke	Grove Hill	Sumter	Livingston
Clay	Ashland	Talladega	Talladega
Cleburne	Heflin	Tallapoosa	Dadeville
Coffee	Elba	Tuscaloosa	Tuscaloosa
Colbert	Tuscumbia	Walker	Jasper
Conecuh	Evergreen	Washington	Chatom
Coosa	Rockford	Wilcox	Camden
Covington	Andalusia	Winston	Double Springs
Crenshaw	Luverne		
Cullman	Cullman	**ALASKA**	**JUNEAU**
Dale	Ozark		
Dallas	Selma	**ARIZONA**	**PHOENIX**
De Kalb	Fort Payne	Apache	St Johns
Elmore	Wetumpka	Cochise	Bisbee
Escambia	Brewton	Coconino	Flagstaff
Etowah	Gadsden	Gila	Globe
Fayette	Fayette	Graham	Safford
Franklin	Russellville	Greenlee	Clifton
Geneva	Geneva	La Paz	Parker
Greene	Eutaw	Maricopa	Phoenix
Hale	Greensboro	Mohave	Kingman
Henry	Abbeville	Navajo	Holbrook
Houston	Dothan	Pima	Tucson
Jackson	Scottsboro	Pinal	Florence
Jefferson	Birmingham	Santa Cruz	Nogales
Lamar	Vernon	Yavapai	Prescott
Lauderdale	Florence	Yuma	Yuma
Lawrence	Moulton		
Lee	Opelika	**ARKANSAS..LITTLE ROCK**	
Limestone	Athens	Arkansa	Stuttgart/De Witt
Lowndes	Hayneville	Ashley	Hamburg
Macon	Tuskegee	Baxter	Mountain Home
Madison	Huntsville	Benton	Bentonville
Marengo	Linden	Boone	Harrison
Marion	Hamilton	Bradley	Warren

COUNTY	COUNTY SEAT
Calhoun	Hampton
Carroll	Berryville/Eureka Spgs
Chicot	Lake Village
Clark	Arkadelphia
Clay	Corning/Piggott
Cleburne	Heber Springs
Cleveland	Rison
Columbia	Magnolia
Conway	Morrilton
Craighead	Jonesboro/Lake City
Crawford	Van Buren
Crittenden	Marion
Cross	Wynne
Dallas	Fordyce
Desha	Arkansas City
Drew	Monticello
Faulkner	Conway
Franklin	Ozark & Charleston
Fulton	Salem
Garland	Hot Springs Nat'l Pk
Grant	Sheridan
Greene	Paragould
Hemstead	Hope
Hot Spring	Malvern
Howard	Nashville
Independence	Batesville
Izard	Melbourne
Jackson	Newport
Jefferson	Pine Bluff
Johnson	Clarksville
Lafayette	Lewisville
Lawrence	Walnut Ridge
Lee	Marianna
Lincoln	Star City
Little River	Ashdown
Logan	Paris & Booneville
Lonoke	Lonoke
Madison	Huntsville
Marion	Yellville
Miller	Texarkana
Mississippi	Blytheville/Osceola
Monroe	Clarendon
Montgomery	Mount Ida
Nevada	Prescott
Newton	Jasper
Ouachita	Camden
Perry	Perryville
Phillips	Helena
Pike	Murfreesboro
Poinsett	Harrisburg
Polk	Mena
Pope	Russellville
Prairie	Des Arc/De Valls Bluff
Pulaski	Little Rock
Randolph	Pocahontas
St Francis	Forrest City
Saline	Benton
Scott	Waldron
Searcy	Marshall
Sebastian	Fort Smith & Greenwood
Sevier	De Queen
Sharp	Ash Flat
Stone	Mountain View
Union	El Dorado
Van Buren	Clinton
Washington	Fayetteville
White	Searcy
Woodruff	Augusta
Yell	Danville/Dardanelle

CALIFORNIA......SACRAMENTO

COUNTY	COUNTY SEAT
Alameda	Oakland
Alpine	Markleeville
Amador	Jackson
Butte	Oroville
Calaveras	San Andreas
Colusa	Colusa
Contra Costa	Martinez
Del Norte	Crescent City
El Dorado	Placerville
Fresno	Fresno
Glenn	Willows
Humboldt	Eureka
Imperial	El Centro
Inyo	Independence
Kern	Bakersfield
Kings	Hanford
Lake	Lakeport
Lassen	Susanville
Los Angeles	Los Angeles
Madera	Madera
Marin	San Rafael
Mariposa	Mariposa
Mendocino	Ukiah
Merced	Merced
Modoc	Alturas
Mono	Bridgeport
Monterey	Salinas
Napa	Napa
Nevada	Nevada City
Orange	Santa Ana
Placer	Auburn
Plumas	Quincy
Riverside	Riverside
Sacramento	Sacramento
San Benito	Hollister
San Bernardino	San Bernardino
San Diego	San Diego
San Francisco	San Francisco
San Joaquin	Stockton
San Luis Obispo	San Luis Obispo
San Mateo	Redwood City
Santa Barbara	Santa Barbara
Santa Clara	San Jose
Santa Cruz	Santa Cruz
Shasta	Redding
Sierra	Downieville
Siskiyou	Yreka
Solano	Fairfield
Sonoma	Santa Rosa
Stanislaus	Modesto
Sutter	Yuba City
Tehama	Red Bluff
Trinity	Weaverville
Tulare	Visalia
Tuolumne	Sonora
Ventura	Ventura
Yolo	Woodland
Yuba	Marysville

COLORADO.................DENVER

COUNTY	COUNTY SEAT
Adams	Brighton
Alamosa	Alamosa
Arapahoe	Littleton
Archuleta	Pagosa Springs
Baca	Springfield
Bent	Las Animas
Boulder	Boulder
Chaffee	Salida
Cheyenne	Cheyenne Wells
Clear Creek	Georgetown
Conejos	Conejos
Costilla	San Luis
Crowley	Ordway
Custer	Westcliffe
Delta	Delta
Denver	Denver
Dolores	Dove Creek
Douglas	Castle Rock
Eagle	Eagle
El Paso	Colorado Springs
Elbert	Kiowa
Fremont	Canon City
Garfield	Glenwood Springs
Gilpin	Central City
Grand	Hot Sulphur Springs
Gunnison	Gunnison
Hinsdale	Lake City
Huerfano	Walsenburg
Jackson	Walden
Jefferson	Golden

COUNTY	COUNTY SEAT	COUNTY	COUNTY SEAT	COUNTY	COUNTY SEAT
Kiowa	Eads	Broward	Fort Lauderdale	Union	Lake Butler
Kit Carson	Burlington	Calhoun	Blountstown	Volusia	De Land
La Plata	Durango	Charlotte	Punta Gorda	Wakulla	Crawfordville
Lake	Leadville	Citrus	Inverness	Walton	De Funiak Springs
Larimer	Fort Collins	Clay	Green Cove Springs	Washington	Chipley
Las Animas	Trinidad	Collier	Naples		
Lincoln	Hugo	Columbia	Lake City	**GEORGIA**	**ATLANTA**
Logan	Sterling	Dade	Miami	Appling	Baxley
Mesa	Grand Junction	De Soto	Arcadia	Atkinson	Pearson
Mineral	Creede	Dixie	Cross City	Bacon	Alma
Moffat	Craig	Duval	Jacksonville	Baker	Newton
Montezuma	Cortez	Escambia	Pensacola	Baldwin	Milledgeville
Montrose	Montrose	Flagler	Bunnell	Banks	Homer
Morgan	Fort Morgan	Franklin	Apalachicola	Barrow	Winder
Otero	La Junta	Gadsden	Quincy	Bartow	Cartersville
Ouray	Ouray	Gilchrist	Trenton	Ben Hill	Fitzgerald
Park	Fairplay	Glades	Moore Haven	Berrien	Nashville
Phillips	Holyoke	Gulf	Port St Joe	Bibb	Macon
Pitkin	Aspen	Hamilton	Jasper	Bleckley	Cochran
Prowers	Lamar	Hardee	Wauchula	Brantley	Nahunta
Pueblo	Pueblo	Hendry	La Belle	Brooks	Quitman
Rio Grande	Del Norte	Hernando	Brooksville	Bryan	Pembroke
Rio Blanco	Meeker	Highlands	Sebring	Bulloch	Statesboro
Routt	Steamboat Spgs	Hillsborough	Tampa	Burke	Waynesboro
Saguache	Saguache	Holmes	Bonifay	Butts	Jackson
San Juan	Silverton	Indian River	Vero Beach	Calhoun	Morgan
San Miguel	Telluride	Jackson	Marianna	Camden	Woodbine
Sedgwick	Julesburg	Jefferson	Monticello	Candler	Metter
Summit	Breckenridge	Lafayette	Mayo	Carroll	Carrollton
Teller	Cripple Creek	Lake	Tavares	Catoosa	Ringgold
Washington	Akron	Lee	Fort Myers	Charlton	Folkston
Weld	Greeley	Leon	Tallahassee	Chatham	Savannah
Yuma	Wray	Levy	Bronson	Chattahoochee	Cusseta
		Liberty	Bristol	Chattooga	Summerville
CONNECTICUT	**HARTFORD**	Madison	Madison	Cherokee	Canton
Fairfield	Bridgeport	Manatee	Bradenton	Clarke	Athens
Hartford	Hartford	Marion	Ocala	Clay	Fort Gaines
Litchfield	Litchfield	Martin	Stuart	Clayton	Jonesboro
Middlesex	Middletown	Monroe	Key West	Clinch	Homerville
New Haven	New Haven	Nassau	Fernandina Beach	Cobb	Marietta
New London	Norwich	Okaloosa	Crestview	Coffee	Douglas
Tolland	Rockville	Okeechobee	Okeechobee	Colquitt	Moultrie
Windham	Putnam	Orange	Orlando	Columbia	Appling
		Osceola	Kissimmee	Cook	Adel
DELEWARE	**DOVER**	Palm Beach	W. Palm Beach	Coweta	Newnan
Kent	Dover	Pasco	Dade City	Crawford	Knoxville
New Castle	Wilmington	Pinellas	Clearwater	Crisp	Cordele
Sussex	Georgetown	Polk	Bartow	Dade	Trenton
		Putnam	Palatka	Dawson	Dawsonville
D.C.	**WASHINGTON**	St Johns	St Augustine	De Kalb	Decatur
		St Lucie	Fort Pierce	Decatur	Bainbridge
FLORIDA	**TALLAHASSEE**	Santa Rosa	Milton	Dodge	Eastman
Alachua	Gainesville	Sarasota	Sarasota	Dooley	Vienna
Baker	Macclenny	Seminole	Sanford	Dougherty	Albany
Bay	Panama City	Sumter	Bushnell	Douglas	Douglasville
Bradford	Starke	Suwannee	Live Oak	Early	Blakely
Brevard	Titusville	Taylor	Perry	Echols	Statenville

COUNTY	COUNTY SEAT	COUNTY	COUNTY SEAT	COUNTY	COUNTY SEAT
Effingham	Springfield	Newton	Covington	Honolulu	Honolulu
Elbert	Elberton	Oconee	Watkinsville	Kauai	Lihue
Emanuel	Swainsboro	Oglethorpe	Lexington	Maui	Wailuku
Evans	Claxton	Paudling	Dallas		
Fannin	Blue Ridge	Peach	Fort Valley	**IDAHO**	**BOISE**
Fayette	Fayetteville	Pickens	Jasper	Ada	Boise
Floyd	Rome	Pierce	Blackshear	Adams	Council
Forsyth	Cumming	Pike	Zebulon	Bannock	Pocatello
Franklin	Carnesville	Polk	Cedartown	Bear Lake	Paris
Fulton	Atlanta	Pulaski	Hawkinsville	Benewah	St Maries
Gilmer	Ellijay	Putnam	Eatonton	Bingham	Blackfoot
Glascock	Gibson	Quitman	Georgetown	Blaine	Hailey
Glynn	Brunswick	Rabun	Clayton	Boise	Idaho City
Gordon	Calhoun	Randolph	Cuthbert	Bonner	Sandpoint
Grady	Cairo	Richmond	Augusta	Bonneville	Idaho Falls
Greene	Greensboro	Rockdale	Conyers	Boundary	Bonners Ferry
Gwinnett	Lawrenceville	Schley	Ellaville	Butte	Arco
Habersham	Clarkesville	Screven	Sylvania	Camas	Fairfield
Hall	Gainesville	Seminole	Donalsonville	Canyon	Caldwell
Hancock	Sparta	Spalding	Griffin	Caribou	Soda Springs
Haralson	Buchanan	Stephens	Toccoa	Cassia	Burley
Harris	Hamilton	Stewart	Lumpkin	Clark	Dubois
Hart	Hartwell	Sumter	Americus	Clearwater	Orofino
Heard	Franklin	Talbot	Talbotton	Custer	Challis
Henry	McDonough	Taliaferro	Crawfordville	Elmore	Mountain Home
Houston	Perry	Tattnall	Reidsville	Franklin	Preston
Irwin	Ocilla	Taylor	Butler	Fremont	St Anthony
Jackson	Jefferson	Telfair	McRae	Gem	Emmett
Jasper	Monticello	Terrell	Dawson	Gooding	Gooding
Jeff Davis	Hazlehurst	Thomas	Thomasville	Idaho	Grangeville
Jefferson	Louisville	Tift	Tifton	Jefferson	Rigby
Jenkins	Millen	Toombs	Lyons	Jerome	Jerome
Johnson	Wrightsville	Towns	Hiawassee	Kootenai	Coeur d'Alene
Jones	Gray	Treutlen	Soperton	Latah	Moscow
Lamar	Barnesville	Troup	La Grange	Lemhi	Salmon
Lanier	Lakeland	Turner	Ashburn	Lewis	Nezperce
Laurens	Dublin	Twiggs	Jeffersonville	Lincoln	Shoshone
Lee	Leesburg	Union	Blairsville	Madison	Rexburg
Liberty	Hinesville	Upson	Thomaston	Minidoka	Rupert
Lincoln	Lincolnton	Walker	La Fayette	Nez Perce	Lewiston
Long	Ludowici	Walton	Monroe	Oneida	Malad City
Lowndes	Valdosta	Ware	Waycross	Owyhee	Murphy
Lumpkin	Dahlonega	Warren	Warrenton	Payette	Payette
Macon	Oglethorpe	Washington	Sandersville	Power	American Falls
Madison	Danielsville	Wayne	Jesup	Shoshone	Wallace
Marion	Buena Vista	Webster	Preston	Teton	Driggs
McDuffie	Thomson	Wheeler	Alamo	Twin Falls	Twin Falls
McIntosh	Darien	White	Cleveland	Valley	Cascade
Meriwether	Greenville	Whitfield	Dalton	Washington	Weiser
Miller	Colquitt	Wilcox	Abbeville		
Mitchell	Camilla	Wilkes	Washington	**ILLINOIS**	**SPRINGFIELD**
Monroe	Forsyth	Wilkinson	Irwinton	Adams	Quincy
Montgomery	Mount Vernon	Worth	Sylvester	Alexander	Cairo
Morgan	Madison			Bond	Greenville
Murray	Chatsworth	**HAWAII**	**HONOLULU**	Boone	Belvidere
Muscogee	Columbus	Hawaii	Hilo	Brown	Mount Sterling

COUNTY	COUNTY SEAT	COUNTY	COUNTY SEAT	COUNTY	COUNTY SEAT
Bureau	Princeton	McDonough	Macomb	Daviess	Washington
Calhoun	Hardin	McHenry	Woodstock	De Kalb	Auburn
Carroll	Mount Carroll	McLean	Bloomington	Dearborn	Lawrenceburg
Cass	Virginia	Menard	Petersburg	Decatur	Greensburg
Champaign	Urbana	Mercer	Aledo	Delaware	Muncie
Christian	Taylorville	Monroe	Waterloo	Dubois	Jasper
Clark	Marshall	Montgomery	Hillsboro	Elkhart	Goshen
Clay	Louisville	Morgan	Jacksonville	Fayette	Connersville
Clinton	Carlyle	Moultrie	Sullivan	Floyd	New Albany
Coles	Charleston	Ogle	Oregon	Fountain	Covington
Cook	Chicago	Peoria	Peoria	Franklin	Brookville
Crawford	Robinson	Perry	Pinckneyville	Fulton	Rochester
Cumberland	Toledo	Piatt	Monticello	Gibson	Princeton
De Kalb	Sycamore	Pike	Pittsfield	Grant	Marion
De Witt	Clinton	Pope	Golconda	Greene	Bloomfield
Douglas	Tuscola	Pulaski	Mound City	Hamilton	Noblesville
Du Page	Wheaton	Putnam	Hennepin	Hancock	Greenfield
Edgar	Paris	Randolph	Chester	Harrison	Corydon
Edwards	Albion	Richland	Olney	Hendricks	Danville
Effingham	Effingham	Rock Island	Rock Island	Henry	New Castle
Fayette	Vandalia	St Clair	Belleville	Howard	Kokomo
Ford	Paxton	Saline	Harrisburg	Huntington	Huntington
Franklin	Benton	Sangamon	Springfield	Jackson	Brownstown
Fulton	Lewistown	Schuyler	Rushville	Jasper	Rensselaer
Gallatin	Shawneetown	Scott	Winchester	Jay	Portland
Greene	Carrollton	Shelby	Shelbyville	Jefferson	Madison
Grundy	Morris	Stark	Toulon	Jennings	Vernon
Hamilton	McLeansboro	Stephenson	Freeport	Johnson	Franklin
Hancock	Carthage	Tazewell	Pekin	Knox	Vincennes
Hardin	Elizabethtown	Union	Jonesboro	Kosciusko	Warsaw
Henderson	Oquawka	Vermilion	Danville	La Porte	La Porte
Henry	Cambridge	Wabash	Mount Carmel	Lagrange	Lagrange
Iroquois	Watseka	Warren	Monmouth	Lake	Crown Point
Jackson	Murphysboro	Washington	Nashville	Lawrence	Bedford
Jasper	Newton	Wayne	Fairfield	Madison	Anderson
Jefferson	Mount Vernon	White	Carmi	Marion	Indianapolis
Jersey	Jerseyville	Whiteside	Morrison	Marshall	Plymouth
Jo Daviess	Galena	Will	Joliet	Martin	Shoals
Johnson	Vienna	Williamson	Marion	Miami	Peru
Kane	Geneva	Winnebago	Rockford	Monroe	Bloomington
Kankakee	Kankakee	Woodford	Eureka	Montgomery	Crawfordsville
Kendall	Yorkville			Morgan	Martinsville
Knox	Galesburg	**INDIANA.....INDIANAPOLIS**		Newton	Kentland
La Salle	Ottawa	Adams	Decatur	Noble	Albion
Lake	Waukegan	Allen	Fort Wayne	Ohio	Rising Sun
Lawrence	Lawrenceville	Bartholomew	Columbus	Orange	Paoli
Lee	Dixon	Benton	Fowler	Owen	Spencer
Livingston	Pontiac	Blackford	Hartford City	Parke	Rockville
Logan	Lincoln	Boone	Lebanon	Perry	Cannelton
Macon	Decatur	Brown	Nashville	Pike	Petersburg
Macoupin	Carlinville	Carroll	Delphi	Porter	Valparaiso
Madison	Edwardsville	Cass	Logansport	Posey	Mount Vernon
Marion	Salem	Clark	Jeffersonville	Pulaski	Winamac
Marshall	Lacon	Clay	Brazil	Putnam	Greencastle
Mason	Havana	Clinton	Frankfort	Randolph	Winchester
Massac	Metropolis	Crawford	English	Ripley	Versailles

Indiana - Kansas

County	County Seat
Rush	Rushville
St Joseph	South Bend
Scott	Scottsburg
Shelby	Shelbyville
Spencer	Rockport
Starke	Knox
Steuben	Angola
Sullivan	Sullivan
Switzerland	Vevay
Tippecanoe	Lafayette
Tipton	Tipton
Union	Liberty
Vanderburgh	Evansville
Vermillion	Newport
Vigo	Terre Haute
Wabash	Wabash
Warren	Williamsport
Warrick	Boonville
Washington	Salem
Wayne	Richmond
Wells	Bluffton
White	Monticello
Whitley	Columbia City

IOWA .... DES MOINES

County	County Seat
Adair	Greenfield
Adams	Corning
Allamakee	Waukon
Appanoose	Centerville
Audubon	Audubon
Benton	Vinton
Black Hawk	Waterloo
Boone	Boone
Bremer	Waverly
Buchanan	Independence
Buena Vista	Storm Lake
Butler	Allison
Calhoun	Rockwell City
Carroll	Carroll
Cass	Atlantic
Cedar	Tipton
Cerro Gordo	Mason City
Cherokee	Cherokee
Chickasaw	New Hampton
Clarke	Osceola
Clay	Spencer
Clayton	Elkader
Clinton	Clinton
Crawford	Denison
Dallas	Adel
Davis	Bloomfield
Decatur	Leon
Delaware	Manchester
Des Moines	Burlington
Dickenson	Spirit Lake
Dubuque	Dubuque

County	County Seat
Emmet	Estherville
Fayette	West Union
Floyd	Charles City
Franklin	Hampton
Fremont	Sidney
Greene	Jefferson
Grundy	Grundy Center
Guthrie	Guthrie Center
Hamilton	Webster City
Hancock	Garner
Hardin	Eldora
Harrison	Logan
Henry	Mount Pleasant
Howard	Cresco
Humboldt	Dakota City
Ida	Ida Grove
Iowa	Marengo
Jackson	Maquoketa
Jasper	Newton
Jefferson	Fairfield
Johnson	Iowa City
Jones	Anamosa
Keokuk	Sigourney
Kossuth	Algona
Lee	Fort Madison/Keokuk
Linn	Cedar Rapids
Louisa	Wapello
Lucus	Chariton
Lyon	Rock Rapids
Madison	Winterset
Mahaska	Oskaloosa
Marion	Knoxville
Marshall	Marshalltown
Mills	Glenwood
Mitchell	Osage
Monona	Onawa
Monroe	Albia
Montgomery	Red Oak
Muscatine	Muscatine
O'Brien	Primghar
Osceola	Sibley
Page	Clarinda
Palo Alto	Emmetsburg
Plymouth	Le Mars
Pocahontas	Pocahontas
Polk	Des Moines
Pottawattamie	Council Bluffs
Poweshiek	Montezuma
Ringgold	Mount Ayr
Sac	Sac City
Scott	Davenport
Shelby	Harlan
Sioux	Orange City
Story	Nevada
Tama	Toledo

County	County Seat
Taylor	Bedford
Union	Creston
Van Buren	Keosauqua
Wapello	Ottumwa
Warren	Indianola
Washington	Washington
Wayne	Corydon
Webster	Fort Dodge
Winnebago	Forest City
Winneshiek	Decorah
Woodbury	Sioux City
Worth	Northwood
Wright	Clarion

KANSAS .... TOPEKA

County	County Seat
Allen	Iola
Anderson	Garnett
Atchison	Atchison
Barber	Medicine Lodge
Barton	Great Bend
Bourbon	Fort Scott
Brown	Hiawatha
Butler	El Dorado
Chase	Cottonwood Falls
Chautauqua	Sedan
Cherokee	Columbus
Cheyenne	St Francis
Clark	Ashland
Clay	Clay Center
Cloud	Concordia
Coffey	Burlington
Comanche	Coldwater
Cowley	Winfield
Crawford	Girard
Decatur	Oberlin
Dickinson	Abilene
Doniphan	Troy
Douglas	Lawrence
Edwards	Kinsley
Elk	Howard
Ellis	Hays
Ellsworth	Ellsworth
Finney	Garden City
Ford	Dodge City
Franklin	Ottawa
Geary	Junction City
Gove	Gove
Graham	Hill City
Grant	Ulysses
Gray	Cimarron
Greeley	Tribune
Greenwood	Eureka
Hamilton	Syracuse
Harper	Anthony
Harvey	Newton
Haskell	Sublette

COUNTY	COUNTY SEAT	COUNTY	COUNTY SEAT	COUNTY	COUNTY SEAT
Hodgeman	Jetmore	Trego	WaKeeney	Hardin	Elizabethtown
Jackson	Holton	Wabaunsee	Alma	Harlan	Harlan
Jefferson	Oskaloosa	Wallace	Sharon Springs	Harrison	Cynthiana
Jewell	Mankato	Washington	Washington	Hart	Munfordville
Johnson	Olathe	Wichita	Leoti	Henderson	Henderson
Kearny	Lakin	Wilson	Fredonia	Henry	New Castle
Kingman	Kingman	Woodson	Yates Center	Hickman	Clinton
Kiowa	Greensburg	Wyandotte	Kansas City	Hopkins	Madisonville
Labette	Oswego			Jackson	McKee
Lane	Dighton	KENTUCKY	FRANKFORT	Jefferson	Louisville
Leavenworth	Leavenworth	Adair	Columbia	Jessamine	Nicholasville
Lincoln	Lincoln	Allen	Scottsville	Johnson	Paintsville
Linn	Mound City	Anderson	Lawrenceburg	Kenton	Independence
Logan	Oakley	Ballard	Wickliffe	Knott	Hindman
Lyon	Emporia	Barren	Glasgow	Knox	Barbourville
Marion	Marion	Bath	Owingsville	Larue	Hodgenville
Marshall	Marysville	Bell	Pineville	Laurel	London
McPherson	McPherson	Boone	Burlington	Lawrence	Louisa
Meade	Meade	Bourbon	Paris	Lee	Beattyville
Miami	Paola	Boyd	Catlettsburg	Leslie	Hyden
Mitchell	Beloit	Boyle	Danville	Letcher	Whitesburg
Montgomery	Independence	Bracken	Brooksville	Lewis	Vanceburg
Morris	Council Grove	Breathitt	Jackson	Lincoln	Stanford
Morton	Elkhart	Breckinridge	Hardinsburg	Livingston	Smithland
Nemaha	Seneca	Bullitt	Shepherdsville	Logan	Russellville
Neosho	Erie	Butler	Morgantown	Lyon	Eddyville
Ness	Ness City	Caldwell	Princeton	Madison	Richmond
Norton	Norton	Calloway	Murray	Magoffin	Salyersville
Osage	Lyndon	Campbell	Alexandria	Marion	Lebanon
Osborne	Osborne	Carlisle	Bardwell	Marshall	Benton
Ottawa	Minneapolis	Carroll	Carrollton	Martin	Inez
Pawnee	Larned	Carter	Grayson	Mason	Maysville
Phillips	Phillipsburg	Casey	Liberty	McCracken	Paducah
Pottawatomie	Westmoreland	Christian	Hopkinsville	McCreary	Whitley City
Pratt	Pratt	Clark	Winchester	McLean	Calhoun
Rawlins	Atwood	Clay	Manchester	Meade	Brandenburg
Reno	Hutchinson	Clinton	Albany	Menifee	Frenchburg
Republic	Belleville	Crittenden	Marion	Mercer	Harrodsburg
Rice	Lyons	Cumberland	Burkesville	Metcalfe	Edmonton
Riley	Manhattan	Daviess	Owensboro	Monroe	Tompkinsville
Rooks	Stockton	Edmonson	Brownsville	Montgomery	Mount Sterling
Rush	La Crosse	Elliott	Sandy Hook	Morgan	West Liberty
Russell	Russell	Estill	Irvine	Muhlenberg	Greenville
Saline	Salina	Fayette	Lexington	Nelson	Bardstown
Scott	Scott City	Fleming	Flemingsburg	Nicholas	Carlisle
Sedgwick	Wichita	Floyd	Prestonsburg	Ohio	Hartford
Seward	Liberal	Franklin	Frankfort	Oldham	La Grange
Shawnee	Topeka	Fulton	Hickman	Owen	Owenton
Sheridan	Hoxie	Gallatin	Warsaw	Owsley	Booneville
Sherman	Goodland	Garrard	Lancaster	Pendleton	Falmouth
Smith	Smith Center	Grant	Williamstown	Perry	Hazard
Stafford	St John	Graves	Mayfield	Pike	Pikeville
Stanton	Johnson	Grayson	Leitchfield	Powell	Stanton
Stevens	Hugoton	Green	Greensburg	Pulaski	Somerset
Sumner	Wellington	Greenup	Greenup	Robertson	Mount Olivet
Thomas	Colby	Hancock	Hawesville	Rockcastle	Mount Vernon

COUNTY	COUNTY SEAT	COUNTY	COUNTY SEAT	COUNTY	COUNTY SEAT
Rowan	Morehead	Morehouse	Bastrop	Calvert	Prince Frederick
Russell	Jamestown	Natchitoches	Natchitoches	Caroline	Denton
Scott	Georgetown	Orleans	New Orleans	Carroll	Westminster
Shelby	Shelbyville	Ouachita	Monroe	Cecil	Elkton
Simpson	Franklin	Plaquemines		Charles	La Plata
Spencer	Taylorsville		Pointe a la Hache	Dorchester	Cambridge
Taylor	Campbellsville	Pointe Coupee	New Roads	Frederick	Frederick
Todd	Elkton	Rapides	Alexandria	Garrett	Oakland
Trigg	Cadiz	Red River	Coushatta	Harford	Bel Air
Trimble	Bedford	Richland	Rayville	Howard	Ellicott City
Union	Morganfield	Sabine	Many	Kent	Chestertown
Warren	Bowling Green	St Bernard	Chalmette	Montgomery	Rockville
Washington	Springfield	St Charles	Hahnville	Prince Georges	
Wayne	Monticello	St Helena	Greensburg		Upper Marlboro
Webster	Dixon	St James	Convent	Queen Anne's	Centreville
Whitley	Williamsburg	St John the Baptist	Edgard	St Mary's	Leonardtown
Wolfe	Campton	St Landry	Opelousas	Somerset	Princess Anne
Woodford	Versailles	St Martin	St Martinville	Talbot	Easton
		St Mary	Franklin	Washington	Hagerstown

LOUISIANA .... BATON ROUGE

COUNTY	COUNTY SEAT	COUNTY	COUNTY SEAT	COUNTY	COUNTY SEAT
Acadia	Crowley	St Tammany	Covington	Wicomico	Salisbury
Allen	Oberlin	Tangipahoa	Amite	Worcester	Snow Hill
Ascension	Donaldsonville	Tensas	St Joseph		
Assumption	Napoleonville	Terrebonne	Houma	Baltimore	Independent City
Avoyelles	Marksville	Union	Farmerville		
Beauregard	De Ridder	Vermilion	Abbeville	**MASSACHUSETTS**	**BOSTON**
Bienville	Arcadia	Vernon	Leesville	Barnstable	Barnstable
Bossier	Benton	Washington	Franklinton	Berkshire	Pittsfield
Caddo	Shreveport	Webster	Minden	Bristol	Taunton
Calcasieu	Lake Charles	West Baton Rouge	Port Allen	Dukes	Edgartown
Caldwell	Columbia	West Carroll	Oak Grove	Essex	Salem
Cameron	Cameron	West Feliciana	St Francisville	Franklin	Greenfield
Catahoula	Harrisonburg	Winn	Winnfield	Hampden	Springfield
Claiborne	Homer			Hampshire	Northampton
Concordia	Vidalia	**MAINE**	**AUGUSTA**	Middlesex	Cambridge
De Soto	Mansfield	Androscoggin	Auburn	Nantucket	Nantucket
East Baton Rouge		Aroostook	Houlton	Norfolk	Dedham
	Baton Rouge	Cumberland	Portland	Plymouth	Plymouth
East Carroll		Franklin	Farmington	Suffolk	Boston
	Lake Providence	Hancock	Ellsworth	Worcester	Worcester
East Feliciana	Clinton	Kennebec	Augusta		
Evangeline	Ville Platte	Knox	Rockland	**MICHIGAN**	**LANSING**
Franklin	Winnsboro	Lincoln	Wiscasset	Alcona	Harrisville
Grant	Colfax	Oxford	South Paris	Alger	Munising
Iberia	New Iberia	Penobscot	Bangor	Allegan	Allegan
Iberville	Plaquemine	Piscataquis	Dover-Foxcroft	Alpena	Alpena
Jackson	Jonesboro	Sagadahoc	Bath	Antrim	Bellaire
Jefferson	Gretna	Somerset	Skowhegan	Arenac	Standish
Jefferson Davis	Jennings	Waldo	Belfast	Baraga	L'Anse
La Salle	Jena	Washington	Machias	Barry	Hastings
Lafayette	Lafayette	York	Alfred	Bay	Bay City
Lafourche	Thibodaux			Benzie	Beulah
Lincoln	Ruston	**MARYLAND**	**ANNAPOLIS**	Berrien	St Joseph
Livingston	Livingston	Allegany	Cumberland	Branch	Coldwater
Madison	Tallulah	Anne Arundel	Annapolis	Calhoun	Marshall
		Baltimore	Baltimore	Cass	Cassopolis
		Baltimore	Towson	Charlevoix	Charlevoix

COUNTY	COUNTY SEAT	COUNTY	COUNTY SEAT	COUNTY	COUNTY SEAT
Cheboygan	Cheboygan	Presque Isle	Rogers City	Le Sueur	Le Center
Chippewa	Sault Ste Marie	Roscommon	Roscommon	Lincoln	Ivanhoe
Clare	Harrison	St Clair	Port Huron	Lyon	Marshall
Clinton	St Johns	St Joseph	Centreville	Mahnomen	Mahnomen
Crawford	Grayling	Saginaw	Saginaw	Marshall	Warren
Delta	Escanaba	Sanilac	Sandusky	Martin	Fairmont
Dickinson	Iorn Mountain	Schoolcraft	Manistique	McLeod	Glencoe
Eaton	Charlotte	Shiawassee	Corunna	Meeker	Litchfield
Emmet	Petoskey	Tuscola	Caro	Mille Lacs	Milaca
Genesee	Flint	Van Buren	Paw Paw	Morrison	Little Falls
Gladwin	Gladwin	Washtenaw	Ann Arbor	Mower	Austin
Gogebic	Bessemer	Wayne	Detroit	Murray	Slayton
Grand Traverse	Traverse City	Wexford	Cadillac	Nicollet	St Peter
Gratiot	Ithaca			Nobles	Worthington
Hillsdale	Hillsdale	**MINNESOTA**	**ST. PAUL**	Norman	Ada
Houghton	Houghton	Aitkin	Aitkin	Olmsted	Rochester
Huron	Bad Axe	Anoka	Anoka	Otter Tail	Fergus Falls
Ingham	Lansing	Becker	Detroit Lakes	Pennington	Thief River Falls
Ionia	Ionia	Beltrami	Bemidji	Pine	Pine City
Iosco	Tawas City	Benton	Foley	Pipeston	Pipestone
Iron	Crystal Falls	Big Stone	Ortonville	Polk	Crookston
Isabella	Mount Pleasant	Blue Earth	Mankato	Pope	Glenwood
Jackson	Jackson	Brown	New Ulm	Ramsey	St Paul
Kalamazoo	Kalamazoo	Carlton	Carlton	Red Lake	Red Lake Falls
Kalkaska	Kalkaska	Carver	Chaska	Redwoo	Redwood Falls
Kent	Grand Rapids	Cass	Walker	Renville	Olivia
Keweenaw	Eagle River	Chippewa	Montevideo	Rice	Faribault
Lake	Baldwin	Chisago	Center City	Rock	Luverne
Lapeer	Lapeer	Clay	Moorhead	Roseau	Roseau
Leelanau	Leland	Clearwater	Bagley	St Louis	Duluth
Lenawee	Adrian	Cook	Grand Marais	Scott	Shakopee
Livingston	Howell	Cottonwood	Windom	Sherburne	Elk River
Luce	Newberry	Crow Wing	Brainerd	Sibley	Gaylord
Mackinac	St Ignace	Dakota	Hastings	Stearns	St Cloud
Macomb	Mount Clemens	Dodge	Mantorville	Steele	Owatonna
Manistee	Manistee	Douglas	Alexandria	Stevens	Morris
Marquette	Marquette	Faribault	Blue Earth	Swift	Benson
Mason	Ludington	Fillmore	Preston	Todd	Long Prairie
Mecosta	Big Rapids	Freeborn	Albert Lea	Traverse	Wheaton
Menominee	Menominee	Goodhue	Red Wing	Wabasha	Wabasha
Midland	Midland	Grant	Elbow Lake	Wadena	Wadena
Missaukee	Lake City	Hennepin	Minneapolis	Waseca	Waseca
Monroe	Monroe	Houston	Caledonia	Washington	Stillwater
Montcalm	Stanton	Hubbard	Park Rapids	Watonwan	St James
Montmorency	Atlanta	Isanti	Cambridge	Wilkin	Breckenridge
Muskegon	Muskegon	Itasca	Grand Rapids	Winona	Winona
Newaygo	White Cloud	Jackson	Jackson	Wright	Buffalo
Oakland	Pontiac	Kanabec	Mora	Yellow Medicine	Granite Falls
Oceana	Hart	Kandiyohi	Willmar		
Ogemaw	West Branch	Kittson	Hallock	**MISSISSIPPI**	**JACKSON**
Ontonagon	Ontonagon	Koochiching	International Falls	Adams	Natchez
Osceola	Reed City	Lac Qui Parle	Madison	Alcorn	Corinth
Oscoda	Mio	Lake of the Woods	Baudette	Amite	Liberty
Otsego	Gaylord			Attala	Kosciusko
Ottawa	Grand Haven	Lake	Two Harbors	Benton	Ashland

COUNTY	COUNTY SEAT	COUNTY	COUNTY SEAT	COUNTY	COUNTY SEAT
Bolivar	Cleveland/Rosedale	Pontotoc	Pontotoc	Cooper	Boonville
Calhoun	Pittsboro	Prentiss	Booneville	Crawford	Steelville
Carroll	Carrollton	Quitman	Marks	Dade	Greenfield
Carroll	Vaiden	Rankin	Brandon	Dallas	Buffalo
Chickasaw	Houston/Okolona	Scott	Forest	Daviess	Gallatin
Choctaw	Ackerman	Sharkey	Rolling Fork	De Kalb	Maysville
Claiborne	Port Gibson	Simpson	Mendenhall	Dent	Salem
Clarke	Quitman	Smith	Raleigh	Douglas	Ava
Clay	West Point	Stone	Wiggins	Dunklin	Kennett
Coahoma	Clarksdale	Sunflower	Indianola	Franklin	Union
Copiah	Hazlehurst	Tallahatchie	Charleston/Sumner	Gasconade	Hermann
Covington	Collins	Tate	Senatobia	Gentry	Albany
De Soto	Hernando	Tippah	Ripley	Greene	Springfield
Forrest	Hattiesburg	Tishomingo	Iuka	Grundy	Trenton
Franklin	Meadville	Tunica	Tunica	Harrison	Bethany
George	Lucedale	Union	New Albany	Henry	Clinton
Greene	Leakesville	Walthall	Tylertown	Hickory	Hermitage
Grenada	Grenada	Warren	Vicksburg	Holt	Oregon
Hancock	Bay St Louis	Washington	Greenville	Howard	Fayette
Harrison	Gulfport	Wayne	Waynesboro	Howell	West Plains
Hinds	Jackson	Webster	Walthall	Iron	Ironton
Hinds	Raymond	Wilkinson	Woodville	Jackson	Independence
Holmes	Lexington	Winston	Louisville	Jasper	Carthage
Humphreys	Belzoni	Yalobusha	Coffeeville/Water Valley	Jefferson	Hillsboro
Issaquena	Mayersville	Yazoo	Yazoo City	Johnson	Warrensburg
Itawamba	Fulton			Knox	Edina
Jackson	Pascagoula	**MISSOURI.**	**JEFFERSON CITY**	Laclede	Lebanon
Jasper	Bay Sprgs/Paulding	Adair	Kirksville	Lafayette	Lexington
Jefferson	Fayette	Andrew	Savannah	Lawrence	Mount Vernon
Jefferson Davis	Prentiss	Atchison	Rock Port	Lewis	Monticello
Jones	Laurel/Ellisville	Audrain	Mexico	Lincoln	Troy
Kemper	De Kalb	Barry	Cassville	Linn	Linneus
Lafayette	Oxford	Barton	Lamar	Livingston	Chillicothe
Lamar	Purvis	Bates	Butler	Macon	Macon
Lauderdale	Meridian	Benton	Warsaw	Madison	Fredericktown
Lawrence	Monticello	Bollinger	Marble Hill	Maries	Vienna
Leake	Carthage	Boone	Columbia	Marion	Palmyra
Lee	Tupelo	Buchanan	St Joseph	McDonald	Pineville
Leflore	Greenwood	Butler	Poplar Bluff	Mercer	Princeton
Lincoln	Brookhaven	Caldwell	Kingston	Miller	Tuscumbia
Lowndes	Columbus	Callaway	Fulton	Mississippi	Charleston
Madison	Canton	Camden	Camdenton	Moniteau	California
Marion	Columbia	Cape Girardeau	Jackson	Monroe	Paris
Marshall	Holly Springs	Carroll	Carrollton	Montgomery	Montgomery City
Monroe	Aberdeen	Carter	Van Buren	Morgan	Versailles
Montgomery	Winona	Cass	Harrisonville	New Madrid	New Madrid
Neshoba	Philadelphia	Cedar	Stockton	Newton	Neosho
Newton	Decatur	Chariton	Keytesville	Nodaway	Maryville
Noxubee	Macon	Christian	Ozark	Oregon	Alton
Oktibbeha	Starkville	Clark	Kahoka	Osage	Linn
Panola	Batesville	Clay	Liberty	Ozark	Gainesville
Panola	Sardis	Clinton	Plattsburg	Pemiscot	Caruthersville
Pearl River	Poplarville	Cole	Jefferson City	Perry	Perryville
Perry	New Augusta			Pettis	Sedalia
Pike	Magnolia			Phelps	Rolla

COUNTY	COUNTY SEAT	COUNTY	COUNTY SEAT	COUNTY	COUNTY SEAT
Pike	Bowling Green	Hill	Havre	Colfax	Schuyler
Platte	Platte City	Jefferson	Boulder	Cuming	West Point
Polk	Bolivar	Judith Basin	Stanford	Custer	Broken Bow
Pulaski	Waynesville	Lake	Polson	Dakota	Dakota City
Putnam	Unionville	Lewis & Clark	Helena	Dawes	Chadron
Ralls	New London	Liberty	Chester	Dawson	Lexington
Randolph	Huntsville	Lincoln	Libby	Deuel	Chappell
Ray	Richmond	Madison	Virginia City	Dixon	Ponca
Reynolds	Centerville	McCone	Circle	Dodge	Fremont
Ripley	Doniphan	Meagher	White Sulphur Spgs	Douglas	Omaha
St Charles	St Charles	Mineral	Superior	Dundy	Benkelman
St Clair	Osceola	Missoula	Missoula	Fillmore	Geneva
St Francois	Farmington	Musselshell	Roundup	Franklin	Franklin
St Louis	Clayton	Park	Livingston	Frontier	Stockville
Ste Genevieve		Petroleum	Winnett	Furnas	Beaver City
	SteGenevieve	Phillips	Malta	Gage	Beatrice
Saline	Marshall	Pondera	Conrad	Garden	Oshkosh
Schuyler	Lancaster	Powder River	Broadus	Garfield	Burwell
Scotland	Memphis	Powell	Deer Lodge	Gosper	Elwood
Scott	Benton	Prairie	Terry	Grant	Hyannis
Shannon	Eminence	Ravalli	Hamilton	Greeley	Greeley
Shelby	Shelbyville	Richland	Sidney	Hall	Grand Island
Stoddard	Bloomfield	Roosevelt	Wolf Point	Hamilton	Aurora
Stone	Galena	Rosebud	Forsyth	Harlan	Alma
Sullivan	Milan	Sanders	Thompson Falls	Hayes	Hayes Center
Taney	Forsyth	Sheridan	Plentywood	Hitchcock	Trenton
Texas	Houston	Silver Bow	Butte	Holt	O'Neill
Vernon	Nevada	Stillwater	Columbus	Hooker	Mullen
Warren	Warrenton	Sweet Grass	Big Timber	Howard	St Paul
Washington	Potosi	Teton	Choteau	Jefferson	Fairbury
Wayne	Greenville	Toole	Shelby	Johnson	Tecumseh
Webster	Marshfield	Treasure	Hysham	Kearney	Minden
Worth	Grant City	Valley	Glasgow	Keith	Ogallala
Wright	Hartville	Wheatland	Harlowton	Keya Paha	Springview
		Wibaux	Wibaux	Kimball	Kimball
MONTANA	**HELENA**	Yellowstone	Billings	Knox	Center
Beaverhead	Dillon			Lancaster	Lincoln
Big Horn	Hardin	**NEBRASKA**	**LINCOLN**	Lincoln	North Platte
Blaine	Chinook	Adams	Hastings	Logan	Stapleton
Broadwater	Townsend	Antelope	Neligh	Loup	Taylor
Carbon	Red Lodge	Arthur	Arthur	Madison	Madison
Carter	Ekalaka	Banner	Harrisburg	McPherson	Tryon
Cascade	Great Falls	Blaine	Brewster	Merrick	Central City
Chouteau	Fort Benton	Boone	Albion	Morrill	Bridgeport
Custer	Miles City	Box Butte	Alliance	Nance	Fullerton
Daniels	Scobey	Boyd	Butte	Nemaha	Auburn
Dawson	Glendive	Brown	Ainsworth	Nuckolls	Nelson
Deer Lodge	Anaconda	Buffalo	Kearney	Otoe	Nebraska City
Fallon	Baker	Burt	Tekamah	Pawnee	Pawnee City
Fergus	Lewistown	Butler	David City	Perkins	Grant
Flathead	Kalispell	Cass	Plattsmouth	Phelps	Holdrege
Gallatin	Bozeman	Cedar	Hartington	Pierce	Pierce
Garfield	Jordan	Chase	Imperial	Platte	Columbus
Glacier	Cut Bank	Cherry	Valentine	Polk	Osceola
Golden Valley	Ryegate	Cheyenne	Sidney	Red Willow	McCook
Granite	Philipsburg	Clay	Clay Center	Richardson	Falls City

COUNTY	COUNTY SEAT	COUNTY	COUNTY SEAT	COUNTY	COUNTY SEAT
Rock	Bassett	Camden	Camden	**NEW YORK**	**ALBANY**
Saline	Wilber	Cape May	Cape May C.H.	Albany	Albany
Sarpy	Papillion	Cumberland	Bridgeton	Allegany	Belmont
Saunders	Wahoo	Essex	Newark	Bronx	Bronx
Scotts Bluff	Gering	Gloucester	Woodbury	Broome	Binghamton
Seward	Seward	Hudson	Jersey City	Cattaraugus	Little Valley
Sheridan	Rushville	Hunterdon	Flemington	Cayuga	Auburn
Sherman	Loup City	Mercer	Trenton	Chautauqua	Mayville
Sioux	Harrison	Middlesex	New Brunswick	Chemung	Elmira
Stanton	Stanton	Monmouth	Freehold	Chenango	Norwich
Thayer	Hebron	Morris	Morristown	Clinton	Plattsburgh
Thomas	Thedford	Ocean	Toms River	Columbia	Hudson
Thurston	Pender	Passaic	Paterson	Cortland	Cortland
Valley	Ord	Salem	Salem	Delaware	Delhi
Washington	Blair	Somerset	Somerville	Dutchess	Poughkeepsie
Wayne	Wayne	Sussex	Newton	Erie	Buffalo
Webster	Red Cloud	Union	Elizabeth	Essex	Elizabethtown
Wheeler	Bartlett	Warren	Belvidere	Franklin	Malone
York	York			Fulton	Johnstown
		NEW MEXICO	**SANTA FE**	Genesee	Batavia
NEVADA	**CARSON CITY**	Bernalillo	Albuquerque	Greene	Catskill
Carson City	Carson City	Catron	Reserve	Hamilton	Lake Pleasant
Churchill	Fallon	Chaves	Roswell	Herkimer	Herkimer
Clark	Las Vegas	Cibola	Grants	Jefferson	Watertown
Douglas	Minden	Colfax	Raton	Kings	Brooklyn
Elko	Elko	Curry	Clovis	Lewis	Lowville
Esmeralda	Goldfield	De Baca	Fort Sumner	Livingston	Geneseo
Eureka	Eureka	Dona Ana	Las Cruces	Madison	Wampsville
Humboldt	Winnemucca	Eddy	Carlsbad	Monroe	Rochester
Lander	Austin	Grant	Silver City	Montgomery	Fonda
Lincoln	Pioche	Guadalupe	Santa Rosa	Nassau	Mineola
Lyon	Yerington	Harding	Mosquero	New York	New York
Mineral	Hawthorne	Hidalgo	Lordsburg	Niagara	Lockport
Nye	Tonopah	Lea	Lovington	Oneida	Utica
Pershing	Lovelock	Lincoln	Carrizozo	Onondaga	Syracuse
Storey	Virginia City	Los Alamos	Los Alamos	Ontario	Canandaigua
Washoe	Reno	Luna	Deming	Orange	Goshen
White Pine	Ely	McKinley	Gallup	Orleans	Albion
		Mora	Mora	Oswego	Oswego
NEW HAMPSHIRE	**CONCORD**	Otero	Alamogordo	Otsego	Cooperstown
Belknap	Laconia	Quay	Tucumcari	Putnam	Carmel
Carroll	Ossipee	Rio Arriba	Tierra Amarilla	Queens	Jamaica
Cheshire	Keene	Roosevelt	Portales	Rensselaer	Troy
Coos	Lancaster	San Juan	Aztec	Richmond	St George
Grafton	Woodsville	San Miguel	Las Vegas	Rockland	New City
Hillsborough	Nashua	Sandoval	Bernalillo	St Lawrence	Canton
Merrimack.	Concord	Santa Fe	Santa Fe	Saratoga	Ballston Spa
Rockingham	Exeter	Sierra	Truth or Consequences	Schenectady	Schenectady
Strafford	Dover	Socorro	Socorro	Schoharie	Schoharie
Sullivan	Newport	Taos	Taos	Schuyler	Watkins Glen
		Torrance	Estancia	Seneca	Waterloo & Ovid
NEW JERSEY	**TRENTON**	Union	Clayton	Steuben	Bath
Atlantic	Mays Landing	Valencia	Los Lunas	Suffolk	Riverhead
Bergen	Hackensack			Sullivan	Monticello
Burlington	Mount Holly			Tioga	Owego
				Tompkins	Ithica

COUNTY	COUNTY SEAT	COUNTY	COUNTY SEAT	COUNTY	COUNTY SEAT
Ulster	Kingston	Hyde	Swanquarter	**NORTH DAKOTA**	
Warren	Lake George	Iredell	Statesville		**BISMARCK**
Washington	Hudson Falls	Jackson	Sylva	Adams	Hettinger
Wayne	Lyons	Johnston	Smithfield	Barnes	Valley City
Westchester	White Plains	Jones	Trenton	Benson	Minnewaukan
Wyoming	Warsaw	Lee	Sanford	Billings	Medora
Yates	Penn Yan	Lenoir	Kinston	Bottineau	Bottineau
		Lincoln	Lincolnton	Bowman	Bowman
NORTH CAROLINA		Macon	Franklin	Burke	Bowbells
	RALEIGH	Madison	Marshall	Burleigh	Bismarck
Alamance	Graham	Martin	Williamston	Cass	Fargo
Alexander	Taylorsville	McDowell	Marion	Cavalier	Langdon
Alleghany	Sparta	Mecklenburg	Charlotte	Dickey	Ellendale
Anson	Wadesboro	Mitchell	Bakersville	Divide	Crosby
Ashe	Jefferson	Montgomery	Troy	Dunn	Manning
Avery	Newland	Moore	Carthage	Eddy	New Rockford
Beaufort	Washington	Nash	Nashville	Emmons	Linton
Bertie	Windsor	New Hanover	Wilmington	Foster	Carrington
Bladen	Elizabethtown	Northampton	Jackson	Golden Valley	Beach
Brunswick	Southport	Onslow	Jacksonville	Grand Forks	Grand Forks
Buncombe	Asheville	Orange	Hillsboro	Grant	Carson
Burke	Morganton	Pamlico	Bayboro	Griggs	Cooperstown
Cabarrus	Concord	Pasquotank	Elizabeth City	Hettinger	Mott
Caldwell	Lenoir	Pender	Burgaw	Kidder	Steele
Camden	Camden	Perquimans	Hertford	La Moure	La Moure
Carteret	Beaufort	Person	Roxboro	Logan	Napoleon
Caswell	Yanceyville	Pitt	Greenville	McHenry	Towner
Catawba	Newton	Polk	Columbus	McIntosh	Ashley
Chatham	Pittsboro	Randolph	Asheboro	McKenzie	Watford City
Cherokee	Murphy	Richmond	Rockingham	McLean	Washburn
Chowan	Edenton	Robeson	Lumberton	Mercer	Stanton
Clay	Hayesville	Rockingham	Wentworth	Morton	Mandan
Cleveland	Shelby	Rowan	Salisbury	Mountrail	Stanley
Columbus	Whiteville	Rutherford	Rutherfordton	Nelson	Lakota
Craven	New Bern	Sampson	Clinton	Oliver	Center
Cumberland	Fayetteville	Scotland	Laurinburg	Pembina	Cavalier
Currituck	Currituck	Stanly	Albemarle	Pierce	Rugby
Dare	Manteo	Stokes	Danbury	Ramsey	Devils Lake
Davidson	Lexington	Surry	Dobson	Ransom	Lisbon
Davie	Mocksville	Swain	Bryson City	Renville	Mohall
Duplin	Kenansville	Transylvania	Brevard	Richland	Wahpeton
Durham	Durham	Tyrrell	Columbia	Rolette	Rolla
Edgecombe	Tarboro	Union	Monroe	Sargent	Forman
Forsyth	Winston-Salem	Vance	Henderson	Sheridan	McClusky
Franklin	Louisburg	Wake	Raleigh	Sioux	Fort Yates
Gaston	Gastonia	Warren	Warrenton	Slope	Amidon
Gates	Gatesville	Washington	Plymouth	Stark	Dickinson
Graham	Robbinsville	Watauga	Boone	Steele	Finley
Granville	Oxford	Wayne	Goldsboro	Stutsman	Jamestown
Greene	Snow Hill	Wilkes	Wilkesboro	Towner	Cando
Guilford	Greensboro	Wilson	Wilson	Traill	Hillsboro
Halifax	Halifax	Yadkin	Yadkinville	Walsh	Grafton
Harnett	Lillington	Yancey	Burnsville	Ward	Minot
Haywood	Waynesville			Wells	Fessenden
Henderson	Hendersonville			Williams	Williston
Hertford	Winton				
Hoke	Raeford				

Ohio - Oklahoma

COUNTY	COUNTY SEAT	COUNTY	COUNTY SEAT	COUNTY	COUNTY SEAT
Woods	Alva	Chester	West Chester	**RHODE ISLAND**	**PROVIDENCE**
Woodward	Woodward	Clarion	Clarion	Bristol	Bristol
		Clearfield	Clearfield	Kent	East Greenwich
OREGON	**SALEM**	Clinton	Lock Haven	Newport	Newport
Baker	Baker	Columbia	Bloomsburg	Providence	Providence
Benton	Corvallis	Crawford	Meadville	Washington	West Kingston
Clackamas	Oregon City	Cumberland	Carlisle		
Clatsop	Astoria	Dauphin	Harrisburg	**SOUTH CAROLINA**	**COLUMBIA**
Columbia	St Helens	Delaware	Media	Abbeville	Abbeville
Coos	Coquille	Elk	Ridgway	Aiken	Aiken
Crook	Prineville	Erie	Erie	Allendale	Allendale
Curry	Gold Beach	Fayette	Uniontown	Anderson	Anderson
Deschutes	Bend	Forest	Tionesta	Bamberg	Bamberg
Douglas	Roseburg	Franklin	Chambersburg	Barnwell	Barnwell
Gilliam	Condon	Fulton	McConnellsburg	Beaufort	Beaufort
Grant	Canyon City	Greene	Waynesburg	Berkeley	Moncks Corner
Harney	Burns	Huntingdon	Huntingdon	Calhoun	St Matthews
Hood River	Hood River	Indiana	Indiana	Charleston	Charleston
Jackson	Medford	Jefferson	Brookville	Cherokee	Gaffney
Jefferson	Madras	Juniata	Mifflintown	Chester	Chester
Josephine	Grants Pass	Lackawanna	Scranton	Chesterfield	Chesterfield
Klamath	Klamath Falls	Lancaster	Lancaster	Clarendon	Manning
Lake	Lakeview	Lawrence	New Castle	Colleton	Walterboro
Lane	Eugene	Lebanon	Lebanon	Darlington	Darlington
Lincoln	Newport	Lehigh	Allentown	Dillon	Dillon
Linn	Albany	Luzerne	Wilkes-Barre	Dorchester	St George
Malheur	Vale	Lycoming	Williamsport	Edgefield	Edgefield
Marion	Salem	McKean	Smethport	Fairfield	Winnsboro
Morrow	Heppner	Mercer	Mercer	Florence	Florence
Multnomah	Portland	Mifflin	Lewistown	Georgetown	Georgetown
Polk	Dallas	Monroe	Stroudsburg	Greenville	Greenville
Sherman	Moro	Montgomery	Norristown	Greenwood	Greenwood
Tillamook	Tillamook	Montour	Danville	Hampton	Hampton
Umatilla	Pendleton	Northampton	Easton	Horry	Conway
Union	La Grande	Northumberland	Sunbury	Jasper	Ridgeland
Wallowa	Enterprise	Perry	New Bloomfield	Kershaw	Camden
Wasco	The Dalles	Philadelphia	Philadelphia	Lancaster	Lancaster
Washington	Hillsboro	Pike	Milford	Laurens	Laurens
Wheeler	Fossil	Potter	Coudersport	Lee	Bishopville
Yamhill	McMinnville	Schuylkill	Pottsville	Lexington	Lexington
		Snyder	Middleburg	Marion	Marion
PENNSLYVANIA	**HARRISBURG**	Somerset	Somerset	Marlboro	Bennettsville
Adams	Gettysburg	Sullivan	Laporte	McCormick	McCormick
Allegheny	Pittsburgh	Susquehanna	Montrose	Newberry	Newberry
Armstrong	Kittanning	Tioga	Wellsboro	Oconee	Walhalla
Beaver	Beaver	Union	Lewisburg	Orangeburg	Orangeburg
Bedford	Bedford	Venango	Franklin	Pickens	Pickens
Berks	Reading	Warren	Warren	Richland	Columbia
Blair	Hollidaysburg	Washington	Washington	Saluda	Saluda
Bradford	Towanda	Wayne	Honesdale	Spartanburg	Spartanburg
Bucks	Doylestown	Westmoreland	Greensburg	Sumter	Sumter
Butler	Butler	Wyoming	Tunkhannock	Union	Union
Cambria	Ebensburg	York	York	Williamsburg	Kingstree
Cameron	Emporium			York	York
Carbon	Jim Thorpe				
Centre	Bellefonte				

COUNTY	COUNTY SEAT	COUNTY	COUNTY SEAT	COUNTY	COUNTY SEAT
SOUTH DAKOTA	**PIERRE**	Shannon	Hot Springs	Jackson	Gainesboro
Aurora	Plankinton	Spink	Redfield	Jefferson	Dandridge
Beadle	Huron	Stanley	Fort Pierre	Johnson	Mountain City
Bennett	Martin	Sully	Onida	Knox	Knoxville
Bon Homme	Tyndall	Tripp	Winner	Lake	Tiptonville
Brookings	Brookings	Todd	Winner	Lauderdale	Ripley
Brown	Aberdeen	Turner	Parker	Lawrence	Lawrenceburg
Brule	Chamberlain	Union	Elk Point	Lewis	Hohenwald
Buffalo	Gann Valley	Walworth	Selby	Lincoln	Fayetteville
Butte	Belle Fourche	Yankton	Yankton	Loudon	Loudon
Campbell	Mound City	Ziebach	Dupree	Macon	Lafayette
Charles Mix	Lake Andes			Madison	Jackson
Clark	Clark	**TENNESSEE**	**NASHVILLE**	Marion	Jasper
Clay	Vermillion	Anderson	Clinton	Marshall	Lewisburg
Codington	Watertown	Bedford	Shelbyville	Maury	Columbia
Corson	McIntosh	Benton	Camden	McMinn	Athens
Custer	Custer	Bledsoe	Pikeville	McNairy	Selmer
Davison	Mitchell	Blount	Maryville	Meigs	Decatur
Day	Webster	Bradley	Cleveland	Monroe	Madisonville
Deuel	Clear Lake	Campbell	Jacksboro	Montgomery	Clarksville
Dewey	Timber Lake	Cannon	Woodbury	Moore	Lynchburg
Douglas	Armour	Carroll	Huntingdon	Morgan	Wartburg
Edmunds	Ipswich	Carter	Elizabethton	Obion	Union City
Fall River	Hot Springs	Cheatham	Ashland City	Overton	Livingston
Faulk	Faulkton	Chester	Henderson	Perry	Linden
Grant	Milbank	Claiborne	Tazewell	Pickett	Byrdstown
Gregory	Burke	Clay	Celina	Polk	Benton
Haakon	Philip	Cocke	Newport	Putman	Cookeville
Hamlin	Hayti	Coffee	Manchester	Rhea	Dayton
Hand	Miller	Crockett	Alamo	Roane	Kingston
Hanson	Alexandria	Cumberland	Crossville	Robertson	Springfield
Harding	Buffalo	Davidson	Nashville	Rutherford	Murfreesboro
Hughes	Pierre	De Kalb	Smithville	Scott	Huntsville
Hutchinson	Olivet	Decatur	Decaturville	Sequatchie	Dunlap
Hyde	Highmore	Dickson	Charlotte	Sevier	Sevierville
Jackson	Kadoka	Dyer	Dyersburg	Shelby	Memphis
Jerauld	Wessington Springs	Fayette	Somerville	Smith	Carthage
Jones	Murdo	Fentress	Jamestown	Stewart	Dover
Kingsbury	De Smet	Franklin	Winchester	Sullivan	Blountville
Lake	Madison	Gibson	Trenton	Sumner	Gallatin
Lawrence	Deadwood	Giles	Pulaski	Tipton	Covington
Lincoln	Canton	Grainger	Rutledge	Trousdale	Hartsville
Lyman	Kennebec	Greene	Greeneville	Unicoi	Erwin
Marshall	Britton	Grundy	Altamont	Union	Maynardville
McCook	Salem	Hamblen	Morristown	Van Buren	Spencer
McPherson	Leola	Hamilton	Chattanooga	Warren	McMinnville
Meade	Sturgis	Hancock	Sneedville	Washington	Jonesboro
Mellette	White River	Hardeman	Bolivar	Wayne	Waynesboro
Miner	Howard	Hardin	Savannah	Weakley	Dresden
Minnehaha	Sioux Falls	Hawkins	Rogersville	White	Sparta
Moody	Flandreau	Haywood	Brownsville	Williamson	Franklin
Pennington	Rapid City	Henderson	Lexington	Wilson	Lebanon
Perkins	Bison	Henry	Paris		
Potter	Gettysburg	Hickman	Centerville	**TEXAS**	**AUSTIN**
Roberts	Sisseton	Houston	Erin	Anderson	Palestine
Sanborn	Woonsocket	Humphreys	Waverly	Andrews	Andrews

COUNTY	COUNTY SEAT	COUNTY	COUNTY SEAT	COUNTY	COUNTY SEAT
Angelina	Lufkin	Deaf Smith	Hereford	Hutchinson	Stinnett
Aransas	Rockport	Delta	Cooper	Irion	Mertzon
Archer	Archer City	Denton	Denton	Jack	Jacksboro
Armstrong	Claude	Dickens	Dickens	Jackson	Edna
Atascosa	Jourdanton	Dimmit	Carrizo Springs	Jasper	Jasper
Austin	Bellville	Donley	Clarendon	Jeff Davis	Fort Davis
Bailey	Muleshoe	Duval	San Diego	Jefferson	Beaumont
Bandera	Bandera	Eastland	Eastland	Jim Hogg	Hebbronville
Bastrop	Bastrop	Ector	Odessa	Jim Wells	Alice
Baylor	Seymour	Edwards	Rocksprings	Johnson	Cleburne
Bee	Beeville	El Paso	El Paso	Jones	Anson
Bell	Belton	Ellis	Waxahachie	Karnes	Karnes City
Bexar	San Antonio	Erath	Stephenville	Kaufman	Kaufman
Blanco	Johnson City	Falls	Marlin	Kendall	Boerne
Bordon	Gail	Fannin	Bonham	Kenedy	Sarita
Bosque	Meridian	Fayette	La Grange	Kent	Jayton
Bowie	Boston	Fisher	Roby	Kerr	Kerrville
Brazoria	Angleton	Floyd	Floydada	Kimble	Junction
Brazos	Bryan	Foard	Crowell	King	Guthrie
Brewster	Alpine	Fort Bend	Richmond	Kinney	Brackettville
Briscoe	Silverton	Franklin	Mount Vernon	Kleberg	Kingsville
Brooks	Falfurrias	Freestone	Fairfield	Knox	Benjamin
Brown	Brownwood	Frio	Pearsall	La Salle	Cotulla
Burleson	Caldwell	Gaines	Seminole	Lamar	Paris
Burnet	Burnet	Galveston	Galveston	Lamb	Littlefield
Caldwell	Lockhart	Garza	Post	Lampasas	Lampasas
Calhoun	Port Lavaca	Gillespie	Fredericksburg	Lavaca	Hallettsville
Callahan	Baird	Glasscock	Garden City	Lee	Giddings
Cameron	Brownsville	Goliad	Goliad	Leon	Centerville
Camp	Pittsburg	Gonzales	Gonzales	Liberty	Liberty
Carson	Panhandle	Gray	Pampa	Limestone	Groesbeck
Cass	Linden	Grayson	Sherman	Lipscomb	Lipscomb
Castro	Dimmitt	Gregg	Longview	Live	George West
Chambers	Anahuac	Grimes	Anderson	Llano	Llano
Cherokee	Rusk	Guadalupe	Seguin	Loving	Mentrone
Childress	Childress	Hale	Plainview	Lubbock	Lubbock
Clay	Henrietta	Hall	Memphis	Lynn	Tahoka
Cochran	Morton	Hamilton	Hamilton	Madison	Madisonville
Coke	Robert Lee	Hansford	Spearman	Marion	Jefferson
Coleman	Coleman	Hardeman	Quanah	Martin	Stanton
Collin	McKinney	Hardin	Kountze	Mason	Mason
Collingsworth	Wellington	Harris	Houston	Matagorda	Bay City
Colorado	Columbus	Harrison	Marshall	Maverick	Eagle Pass
Comal	New Braunfels	Hartley	Channing	McCulloch	Brady
Comanche	Comanche	Haskell	Haskell	McLennan	Waco
Concho	Paint Rock	Hays	San Marcos	McMullen	Tilden
Cooke	Gainesville	Hemphill	Canadian	Medina	Hondo
Coryell	Gatesville	Henderson	Athens	Menard	Menard
Cottle	Paducah	Hidalgo	Edinburg	Midland	Midland
Crane	Crane	Hill	Hillsboro	Milam	Cameron
Crockett	Ozona	Hockley	Levelland	Mills	Goldthwaite
Crosby	Crosbyton	Hood	Granbury	Mitchell	Colorado City
Culberson	Van Horn	Hopkins	Sulphur Springs	Montague	Montague
Dallam	Dalhart	Houston	Crockett	Montgomery	Conroe
Dallas	Dallas	Howard	Big Spring	Moore	Dumas
Dawson	Lamesa	Hudspeth	Sierra Blanca	Morris	Daingerfield
De Witt	Cuero	Hunt	Greenville	Motley	Matador

Counties & County Seats

Texas - Virginia

COUNTY	COUNTY SEAT
Grayson	Independence
Greene	Stanardsville
Greensville	Emporia
Halifax	Halifax
Hanover	Hanover
Henrico	Richmond
Henry	Martinsville
Highland	Monterey
Isle of Wight	Isle of Wight
James City	Williamsburg
King & Queen	King & Queen C.H.
King George	King George
King William	King William
Lancaster	Lancaster
Lee	Jonesville
Loudoun	Leesburg
Louisa	Louisa
Lunenburg	Lunenburg
Madison	Madison
Mathews	Mathews
Mecklenburg	Boydton
Middlesex	Saluda
Montgomery	Christiansburg
Nelson	Lovingston
New Kent	New Kent
Northampton	Eastville
Northumberland	Heathsville
Nottoway	Nottoway
Orange	Orange
Page	Luray
Patrick	Stuart
Pittsylvania	Chatham
Powhatan	Powhatan
Prince Edward	Farmville
Prince George	Prince George
Prince William	Manassas
Pulaski	Pulaski
Rappahannock	Washington
Richmond	Warsaw
Roanoke	Salem
Rockbridge	Lexington
Rockingham	Harrisonburg
Russell	Lebanon
Scott	Gate City
Shenandoah	Woodstock
Smyth	Marion
Southampton	Courtland
Spotsylvania	Spotsylvania
Stafford	Stafford
Surry	Surry
Sussex	Sussex
Tazewell	Tazewell
Warren	Front Royal
Washington	Abingdon

COUNTY	COUNTY SEAT
Westmoreland	Montross
Wise	Wise
Wythe	Wytheville
York	Yorktown

VA....INDEPENDENT CITIES

Alexandria
Bedford
Bristol
Buena Vista
Charlottesville
Chesapeake
Clifton Forge
Colonial Heights
Covington
Danville
Emporia
Fairfax
Falls Church
Franklin
Fredericksburg
Galax
Hampton
Harrisonburg
Hopewell
Lexington
Lynchburg
Manassas
Manassas Park
Martinsville
Newport News
Norfolk
Norton
Petersburg
Poquoson
Portsmouth
Radford
Richmond
Roanoke
Salem
South Boston
Staunton
Suffolk
Virginia Beach
Waynesboro
Williamsburg
Winchester

WASHINGTON.........OLYMPIA

COUNTY	COUNTY SEAT
Adams	Ritzville
Asotin	Asotin
Benton	Prosser
Chelan	Wenatchee
Clallam	Port Angeles
Clark	Vancouver
Columbia	Dayton
Cowlitz	Kelso

COUNTY	COUNTY SEAT
Douglas	Waterville
Ferry	Republic
Franklin	Pasco
Garfield	Pomeroy
Grant	Ephrata
Grays Harbor	Montesano
Island	Coupeville
Jefferson	Port Townsend
King	Seattle
Kitsap	Port Orchard
Kittitas	Ellensburg
Klickitat	Goldendale
Lewis	Chehalis
Lincoln	Davenport
Mason	Shelton
Okanogan	Okanogan
Pacific	South Bend
Pend Oreille	Newport
Pierce	Tacoma
San Juan	Friday Harbor
Skagit	Mount Vernon
Skamania	Stevenson
Snohomish	Everett
Spokane	Spokane
Stevens	Colville
Thurston	Olympia
Wahkiakum	Cathlamet
Walla Walla	Walla Walla
Whatcom	Bellingham
Whitman	Colfax
Yakima	Yakima

WEST VIRGINIA.....................CHARLESTON

COUNTY	COUNTY SEAT
Barbour	Philippi
Berkeley	Martinsburg
Boone	Madison
Braxton	Sutton
Brooke	Wellsburg
Cabell	Huntington
Calhoun	Grantsville
Clay	Clay
Doddridge	West Union
Fayette	Fayetteville
Gilmer	Glenville
Grant	Petersburg
Greenbrier	Lewisburg
Hampshire	Romney
Hancock	New Cumberland
Hardy	Moorefield
Harrison	Clarksburg
Jackson	Ripley
Jefferson	Charles Town
Kanawha	Charleston
Lewis	Weston
Lincoln	Hamlin

West Virginia - Wyoming

COUNTY	COUNTY SEAT	COUNTY	COUNTY SEAT	COUNTY	COUNTY SEAT
Logan	Logan	Clark	Neillsville	Rock	Janesville
Marion	Fairmont	Columbia	Portage	Rusk	Ladysmith
Marshall	Moundsville	Crawford	Prairie du Chien	Sauk	Baraboo
Mason	Point Pleasant	Dane	Madison	Sawyer	Hayward
McDowell	Welch	Dodge	Juneau	Shawano	Shawano
Mercer	Princeton	Door	Sturgeon Bay	Sheboygan	Sheboygan
Mineral	Keyser	Douglas	Superior	St Croix	Hudson
Mingo	Williamson	Dunn	Menomonie	Taylor	Medford
Monongalia	Morgantown	Eau Claire	Eau Claire	Trempealeau	Whitehall
Monroe	Union	Florence	Florence	Vernon	Viroqua
Morgan	Berkeley Springs	Fond du Lac	Fond du Lac	Vilas	Eagle River
Nicholas	Summersville	Forest	Crandon	Walworth	Elkhorn
Ohio	Wheeling	Grant	Lancaster	Washburn	Shell Lake
Pendleton	Franklin	Green	Monroe	Washington	West Bend
Pleasants	St Marys	Green Lake	Green Lake	Waukesha	Waukesha
Pocahontas	Marlinton	Iowa	Dodgeville	Waupaca	Waupaca
Preston	Kingwood	Iron	Hurley	Waushara	Wautoma
Putnam	Winfield	Jackson	Black River Falls	Winnebago	Oshkosh
Raleigh	Beckley	Jefferson	Jefferson	Wood	Wisconsin Rapids
Randolph	Elkins	Juneau	Mauston		
Ritchie	Harrisville	Kenosha	Kenosha	**WYOMING**	**CHEYENNE**
Roane	Spencer	Kewaunee	Kewaunee	Albany	Laramie
Summers	Hinton	La Crosse	La Crosse	Big Horn	Basin
Taylor	Grafton	Lafayette	Darlington	Campbell	Gillette
Tucker	Parsons	Langlade	Antigo	Carbon	Rawlins
Tyler	Middlebourne	Lincoln	Merrill	Converse	Douglas
Upshur	Buckhannon	Manitowoc	Manitowoc	Crook	Sundance
Wayne	Wayne	Marathon	Wausau	Fremont	Lander
Webster	Webster Springs	Marinette	Marinette	Goshen	Torrington
Wetzel	New Martinsville	Marquette	Montello	Hot Springs	Thermopolis
Wirt	Elizabeth	Menominee	Keshena	Johnson	Buffalo
Wood	Parkersburg	Milwaukee	Milwaukee	Laramie	Cheyenne
Wyoming	Pineville	Monroe	Sparta	Lincoln	Kemmerer
		Oconto	Oconto	Natrona	Casper
WISCONSIN	**MADISON**	Oneida	Rhinelander	Niobrara	Lusk
Adams	Friendship	Outagamie	Appleton	Park	Cody
Ashland	Ashland	Ozaukee	Port Washington	Platte	Wheatland
Barron	Barron	Pepin	Durand	Sheridan	Sheridan
Bayfield	Washburn	Pierce	Ellsworth	Sublette	Pinedale
Brown	Green Bay	Polk	Balsam Lake	Sweetwater	Green River
Buffalo	Alma	Portage	Stevens Point	Teton	Jackson
Burnett	Grantsburg	Price	Phillips	Uinta	Evanston
Calumet	Chilton	Racine	Racine	Washakie	Worland
Chippewa	Chippewa Falls	Richland	Richland Center	Weston	Newcastle

Zip Codes

ZIP	CITY	ZIP	CITY
01001	Agawam MA	01475	Winchendon MA
01002-04	Amherst MA	01501	Auburn MA
01007	Belchertown MA	01504	Blackstone MA
01013-22	Chicopee MA	01505	Boylston MA
01027	Easthampton MA	01507	Charlton MA
01028	E Longmeadow MA	01510	Clinton MA
01030	Feeding Hills MA	01516	Douglas MA
01033	Granby MA	01519	Grafton MA
01035	Hadley MA	01520	Holden MA
01036	Hampden MA	01523	Lancaster MA
01038	Hatfield MA	01524	Leicester MA
01040-41	Holyoke MA	01527	Millbury MA
01056	Ludlow MA	01527	Sutton MA
01057	Monson MA	01532	Northborough MA
01060-63	Northampton MA	01534	Northbridge MA
01069	Palmer MA	01535	N Brookfield MA
01073	Southampton MA	01540	Oxford MA
01075	S Hadley MA	01543	Rutland MA
01077	Southwick MA	01545	Shrewsbury MA
01082	Ware MA	01550	Southbridge MA
01083	Warren MA	01562	Spencer MA
01085-86	Westfield MA	01564	Sterling MA
01089-90	W Springfield MA	01566	Sturbridge MA
01095	Wilbraham MA	01568	Upton MA
01101-99	Springfield MA	01569	Uxbridge MA
01106	Longmeadow MA	01570	Dudley MA
01201-03	Pittsfield MA	01570	Webster MA
01220	Adams MA	01581	Westborough MA
01225	Cheshire MA	01583	W Boylston MA
01226-27	Dalton MA	01585	W Brookfield MA
01230	Great Barrington MA	01588	Whitinsville MA
01237	Lanesboro MA	01601-99	Worcester MA
01238	Lee MA	01612	Paxton MA
01240	Lenox MA	01701	Framingham MA
01247	N Adams MA	01719	Boxborough MA
01257	Sheffield MA	01720	Acton MA
01267	Williamstown MA	01721	Ashland MA
01301-02	Greenfield MA	01730	Bedford MA
01342	Deerfield MA	01740	Bolton MA
01351	Montague MA	01741	Carlisle MA
01364	Orange MA	01742	Concord MA
01375	Sunderland MA	01746	Holliston MA
01376	Turners Falls MA	01747	Hopedale MA
01420	Fitchburg MA	01748	Hopkinton MA
01430	Ashburnham MA	01749	Hudson MA
01432-33	Ayer MA	01752	Marlborough MA
01440	Gardner MA	01754	Maynard MA
01450	Groton MA	01756	Mendon MA
01451	Harvard MA	01757	Milford MA
01453	Leominster MA	01760	Natick MA
01460	Littleton MA	01770	Sherborn MA
01462	Lunenburg MA	01772	Southborough MA
01463	Pepperell MA	01773	Lincoln MA
01464	Shirley MA	01775	Stow MA
01468	Templeton MA	01776	Sudbury MA
01469	Townsend MA	01778	Wayland MA
01473	Westminster MA	01801	Woburn MA

ZIP	CITY	ZIP	CITY	ZIP	CITY	ZIP	CITY
01803	Burlington MA	02072	Stoughton MA	02645	Harwich MA	02910	Cranston RI
01810	Andover MA	02081	Walpole MA	02647	Hyannisport MA	02911	N Providence RI
01821-22	Billerica MA	02090	Westwood MA	02653	Orleans MA	02914	E Providence RI
01824	Chelmsford MA	02093	Wrentham MA	02657	Provincetown MA	02917	Smithfield RI
01826	Dracut MA	02101-99	BOSTON MA	02667	Wellfleet MA	02919	Johnston RI
01830-35	Haverhill MA	02126	Mattapan MA	02675	Yarmouth MA	03032	Auburn NH
01833	Georgetown MA	02138-42	Cambridge MA	02702	Freetown MA	03034	Candia NH
01834	Groveland MA	02143-45	Somerville MA	02703	Attleboro MA	03038	Derry NH
01840-45	Lawrence MA	02146	Brookline MA	02714	Dartmouth MA	03042	Epping NH
01844	Methuen MA	02148	Malden MA	02715	Dighton MA	03045	Goffstown NH
01845	N Andover MA	02149	Everett MA	02719	Fairhaven MA	03045	Pinardville NH
01850-54	Lowell MA	02150	Chelsea MA	02720-26	Fall River MA	03049	Hollis NH
01860	Merrimac MA	02151	Revere MA	02725	Somerset MA	03051	Hudson NH
01864	N Reading MA	02152	Winthrop MA	02738	Marion MA	03051	Litchfield NH
01867	Reading MA	02154	Waltham MA	02739	Mattapoisett MA	03053	Londonderry NH
01876	Tewksbury MA	02155	Medford MA	02740-48	New Bedford MA	03054	Merrimack NH
01879	Tyngsborough MA	02158	Newton MA	02743	Acushnet MA	03055	Milford NH
01880	Wakefield MA	02165	W Newton MA	02747	N Dartmouth MA	03060-63	Nashua NH
01886	Westford MA	02169	Quincy MA	02760-63	N Attleboro MA	03076	Pelham NH
01887	Wilmington MA	02172	Watertown MA	02762	Plainville MA	03077	Raymond NH
01890	Winchester MA	02173	Lexington MA	02766	Norton MA	03079	Salem NH
01901-08	Lynn MA	02174	Arlington MA	02767	Raynham MA	03086	Wilton NH
01906	Saugus MA	02176-77	Melrose MA	02769	Rehoboth MA	03087	Windham NH
01907	Swampscott MA	02178	Belmont MA	02770	Rochester MA	03101-99	Manchester NH
01908	Nahant MA	02180	Stoneham MA	02771	Seekonk MA	03102	Bedford NH
01913	Amesbury MA	02181	Wellesley MA	02777	Swansea MA	03106	Hooksett NH
01915	Beverly MA	02184	Braintree MA	02780	Berkley MA	03220	Belmont NH
01921	Boxford MA	02186	Milton MA	02780	Taunton MA	03234	Epsom NH
01923	Danvers MA	02188	Weymouth MA	02790	Westport MA	03235	Franklin NH
01929	Essex MA	02192	Needham MA	02806	Barrington RI	03242	Henniker NH
01930-31	Gloucester MA	02193	Weston MA	02809	Bristol RI	03244	Hillsborough NH
01936	Hamilton MA	02322	Avon MA	02812	Richmond RI	03246	Gilford NH
01938	Ipswich MA	02324	Bridgewater MA	02813	Charlestown RI	03246-47	Laconia NH
01940	Lynnfield MA	02330	Carver MA	02814	Glocester RI	03253	Meredith NH
01944	Manchester MA	02331-32	Duxbury MA	02816	Coventry RI	03257	New London NH
01945	Marblehead MA	02333	E Bridgewater MA	02816	W Greenwich RI	03263	Pittsfield NH
01949	Middleton MA	02334	Easton MA	02818	E Greenwich RI	03264	Plymouth NH
01950	Newbury MA	02338	Halifax MA	02822	Exeter RI	03275	Pembroke NH
01950-52	Newburyport MA	02339	Hanover MA	02825	Foster RI	03276	Northfield NH
01950-52	Salisbury MA	02341	Hanson MA	02830	Burrilville RI	03276	Tilton NH
01960-61	Peabody MA	02343	Holbrook MA	02833	Hopkinton RI	03281	Weare NH
01966	Rockport MA	02346	Lakeville MA	02835	Jamestown RI	03301	Boscawen NH
01969	Rowley MA	02346	Middleborough MA	02837	Little Compton RI	03301	Bow NH
01970-71	Salem MA	02351	Abington MA	02840	Middletown RI	03301	Hopkinton NH
01983	Topsfield MA	02359	Pembroke MA	02840	Newport RI	03301-04	CONCORD NH
01984	Wenham MA	02360	Plymouth MA	02852-54	N Kingstown RI	03431	Keene NH
01985	W Newbury MA	02364	Kingston MA	02857	Scituate RI	03431	Swanzey NH
02019	Bellingham MA	02368	Randolph MA	02860	Lincoln RI	03443	Chesterfield NH
02021	Canton MA	02370	Rockland MA	02860-65	Pawtucket RI	03451	Hinsdale NH
02025	Cohasset MA	02379	W Bridgewater MA	02863	Central Falls RI	03452	Jaffrey NH
02026	Dedham MA	02382	Whitman MA	02864	Cumberland RI	03458	Peterborough NH
02030	Dover MA	02401-99	Brockton MA	02865	Saylesville RI	03461	Rindge NH
02035	Foxborough MA	02532	Bourne MA	02871	Portsmouth RI	03470	Winchester NH
02038	Franklin MA	02539	Edgartown MA	02876	N Smithfield RI	03561	Littleton NH
02043	Hingham MA	02540-41	Falmouth MA	02878	Tiverton RI	03570	Berlin NH
02045	Hull MA	02543	Woods Hole MA	02879-80	S Kingstown RI	03581	Gorham NH
02048	Mansfield MA	02554	Nantucket MA	02879-83	Wakefield RI	03584	Lancaster NH
02050	Marshfield MA	02563	Sandwich MA	02881	Kingston RI	03603	Charlestown NH
02052	Medfield MA	02568	Tisbury MA	02882	Narragansett RI	03608	Walpole NH
02053	Medway MA	02571	Wareham MA	02885	Warren RI	03743	Claremont NH
02054	Millis MA	02601	Hyannis MA	02886-89	Warwick RI	03748	Enfield NH
02056	Norfolk MA	02630	Barnstable MA	02891	Westerly RI	03755	Hanover NH
02061	Norwell MA	02631	Brewster MA	02892	W Kingston RI	03765	Haverhill NH
02062	Norwood MA	02633	Chatham MA	02893	W Warwick RI	03766	Lebanon NH
02066	Scituate MA	02638	Dennis MA	02895	Woonsocket RI	03773	Newport NH
02067	Sharon MA	02642	Eastham MA	02901-40	PROVIDENCE RI	03785	Woodsville NH

ZIP	CITY	ZIP	CITY	ZIP	CITY	ZIP	CITY
03801	Portsmouth NH	04256	Mechanic Falls ME	04937	Fairfield ME	06002	Bloomfield CT
03811	Atkinson NH	04257	Mexico ME	04938	Farmington ME	06010	Bristol CT
03820	Dover NH	04259	Monmouth ME	04950	Madison ME	06019	Canton CT
03824	Durham NH	04260	New Gloucester ME	04953	Newport ME	06026	E Granby CT
03825	Barrington NH	04268	Norway ME	04957	Norridgewock ME	06029	Ellington CT
03833	Exeter NH	04270	Oxford ME	04963	Oakland ME	06032	Farmington CT
03835	Farmington NH	04271	Paris ME	04966	Phillips ME	06033	Glastonbury CT
03841	Hampstead NH	04273	Poland ME	04967	Pittsfield ME	06035	Granby CT
03842	Hampton NH	04276	Rumford ME	04974	Searsport ME	06037	Berlin CT
03848	Kingston NH	04280	Sabattus ME	04976	Skowhegan ME	06040-43	Manchester CT
03857	Newmarket NH	04281	S Paris ME	04989	Vassalborough ME	06043	Bolton CT
03858	Newton NH	04294	Wilton ME	05038	Chelsea VT	06050-53	New Britain CT
03862	N Hampton NH	04330	AUGUSTA ME	05047	Hartford VT	06057	New Hartford CT
03864	Ossipee NH	04345	Chelsea ME	05048	Hartland VT	06062	Plainville CT
03865	Plaistow NH	04345	Farmingdale ME	05060	Randolph VT	06066	Rockville CT
03867	Rochester NH	04345	Gardiner ME	05089	Windsor VT	06066	Vernon CT
03870	Rye NH	04347	Hallowell ME	05091	Woodstock VT	06067	Rocky Hill CT
03874	Seabrook NH	04350	Litchfield ME	05101	Bellows Falls VT	06068	Salisbury CT
03878	Somersworth NH	04357	Richmond ME	05101	Rockingham VT	06069	Sharon CT
03885	Stratham NH	04364	Winthrop ME	05143	Chester VT	06070	Simsbury CT
03894	Wolfeboro NH	04401	Bangor ME	05149	Ludlow VT	06071	Somers CT
03901	Berwick ME	04401	Hermon ME	05151	Weathersfield VT	06074	S Windsor CT
03903	Eliot ME	04412	Brewer ME	05156	Springfield VT	06078	Suffield CT
03904	Kittery ME	04416	Bucksport ME	05201	Bennington VT	06082	Enfield CT
03906	N Berwick ME	04426	Dover-Foxcroft ME	05255	Manchester VT	06084	Tolland CT
03908	S Berwick ME	04427	Clinton ME	05261	Pownal VT	06085	Burlington CT
03909	York ME	04429	Holden ME	05262	Shaftsbury VT	06088	E Windsor CT
04002	Alfred ME	04443	Guilford ME	05301	Brattleboro VT	06090	W Hartford CT
04005	Lyman ME	04444	Hampden ME	05345	Newfane VT	06094	Winchester CT
04005-07	Biddeford ME	04457	Lincoln ME	05401-07	Burlington VT	06095	Windsor CT
04008	Bowdoinham ME	04462	Millinocket ME	05403	S Burlington VT	06096	Windsor Locks CT
04009	Bridgton ME	04463	Milo ME	05404	Winooski VT	06098	Winsted CT
04011	Brunswick ME	04468	Old Town ME	05443	Bristol VT	06101-99	HARTFORD CT
04021	Cumberland Ctr. ME	04473	Orono ME	05445	Charlotte VT	06108	E Hartford CT
04027	Lebanon ME	04474	Orrington ME	05446	Colchester VT	06109	Wethersfield CT
04032	Freeport ME	04496	Winterport ME	05452	Essex Junction VT	06111	Newington CT
04037	Fryeburg ME	04530	Bath ME	05452	Essex VT	06226	Willimantic CT
04038	Gorham ME	04537	Boothbay ME	05461	Hinesburg VT	06234	Brooklyn CT
04039	Gray ME	04538	Boothbay Harbor ME	05465	Jericho VT	06237	Columbia CT
04042	Hollis Ctr. ME	04572	Waldoboro ME	05468	Milton VT	06238	Coventry CT
04043	Kennebunk ME	04578	Wiscasset ME	05474	N Hero VT	06239	Danielson CT
04046	Kennebunkport ME	04605	Ellsworth ME	05477	Richmond VT	06248	Hebron CT
04062	Windham ME	04609	Bar Harbor ME	05478	Georgia VT	06249	Lebanon CT
04064	Old Orchard Bch ME	04619	Calais ME	05478	St Albans VT	06258	Pomfret CT
04072	Saco ME	04654	Machias ME	05482	Shelburne VT	06260	Putnam CT
04073	Sanford ME	04660	Mount Desert ME	05488	Swanton VT	06277	Thompson CT
04074	Scarborough ME	04730	Houlton ME	05602	MONTPELIER VT	06279	Willington CT
04079	Harpswell ME	04736	Caribou ME	05641	Barre VT	06320	New London CT
04084	Standish ME	04742	Fort Fairfield ME	05655	Hyde Park VT	06331	Canterbury CT
04086	Topsham ME	04743	Fort Kent ME	05656	Johnson VT	06333	E Lyme CT
04087	Waterboro ME	04750-51	Limestone ME	05661	Morrisville VT	06339	Ledyard CT
04090	Wells ME	04756	Madawaska ME	05663	Northfield VT	06340-49	Groton CT
04092	Westbrook ME	04769	Presque Isle ME	05672	Stowe VT	06351	Griswold CT
04093	Buxton ME	04785	Van Buren ME	05676	Waterbury VT	06351	Jewett City CT
04096	Yarmouth ME	04786	Washburn ME	05701	Rutland VT	06351	Lisbon CT
04101-99	Portland ME	04841	Rockland ME	05733	Brandon VT	06353	Montville CT
04105	Falmouth ME	04843	Camden ME	05735	Castleton VT	06359	N Stonington CT
04106	S Portland ME	04856	Rockport ME	05743	Fair Haven VT	06360	Norwich CT
04107	Cape Elizabeth ME	04861	Thomaston ME	05753	Middlebury VT	06360	Preston CT
04210-12	Auburn ME	04864	Warren ME	05764	Poultney VT	06371	Old Lyme CT
04224	Dixfield ME	04901	Waterville ME	05819	St Johnsbury VT	06374	Plainfield CT
04236	Greene ME	04901	Winslow ME	05829	Derby VT	06379	Pawcatuck CT
04239	Jay ME	04915	Belfast ME	05843	Hardwick VT	06385	Waterford CT
04240-43	Lewiston ME	04926	China ME	05849	Lyndon VT	06401	Ansonia CT
04250	Lisbon ME	04928	Corinna ME	05855	Newport VT	06405	Branford CT
04254	Livermore Falls ME	04930	Dexter ME	05905	Guildhall VT	06410	Cheshire CT

ZIP .... CITY	ZIP .... CITY	ZIP .... CITY	ZIP .... CITY
06413 .... Clinton CT	06840 .... New Cannan CT	07087 .... Weehawken NJ	07643 .... Little Ferry NJ
06415 .... Colchester CT	06850-56 .... Norwalk CT	07090-92 .... Westfield NJ	07644 .... Lodi NJ
06415 .... Salem CT	06875 .... Redding CT	07092 .... Mountainside NJ	07645 .... Montvale NJ
06416 .... Cromwell CT	06877 .... Ridgefield CT	07093 .... Guttenberg NJ	07646 ...... New Milford NJ
06417 .... Deep River CT	06880-83 .... Westport CT	07093 .... W New York NJ	07647 .... Northvale NJ
06417 .... Killingworth CT	06897 .... Wilton CT	07094 .... Secaucus NJ	07648 .... Norwood NJ
06418 .... Derby CT	06901-99 .... Stamford CT	07095 .... Woodbridge NJ	07649 .... Oradell NJ
06422 .... Durham CT	07002 .... Bayonne NJ	07101-99 .... Newark NJ	07650 .... Palisades Park NJ
06423 .... E Haddam CT	07003 .... Bloomfield NJ	07109 .... Belleville NJ	07652-53 .... Paramus NJ
06424 .... E Hampton CT	07005 .... Boonton NJ	07110 .... Nutley NJ	07656 .... Park Ridge NJ
06426 .... Essex CT	07006 .... Fairfield NJ	07111 .... Irvington NJ	07657 .... Ridgefield NJ
06430-32 .... Fairfield CT	07006 .... N Caldwell NJ	07201-99 .... Elizabeth NJ	07660 ...... Ridgefield Park NJ
06437 .... Guilford CT	07006 .... W Caldwell NJ	07203 .... Roselle NJ	07661 .... River Edge NJ
06443 .... Madison CT	07006-07 .... Caldwell NJ	07204 .... Roselle Park NJ	07662 .... Rochelle Park NJ
06447 .... Marlborough CT	07008 .... Carteret NJ	07205 .... Hillside NJ	07662 .... Saddle Brook NJ
06450 .... Meriden CT	07009 .... Cedar Grove NJ	07301-99 .... Jersey City NJ	07666 .... Teaneck NJ
06455 .... Middlefield CT	07010 .... Cliffside Park NJ	07401 .... Allendale NJ	07670 .... Tenafly NJ
06457 .... Middletown CT	07011-15 .... Clifton NJ	07403 .... Bloomingdale NJ	07675 .... Old Tappan NJ
06460 .... Milford CT	07016 .... Cranford NJ	07405 .... Butler NJ	07675 .... River Vale NJ
06468 .... Monroe CT	07017-19 .... E Orange NJ	07405 .... Kinnelon NJ	07675 .... Westwood NJ
06470 .... Newtown CT	07020 .... Edgewater NJ	07407 .... Elmwood Park NJ	07675 .... Woodcliff Lake NJ
06471 .... N Branford CT	07022 .... Fairview NJ	07410 .... Fair Lawn NJ	07701 .... Fairview NJ
06472 .... Northford CT	07023 .... Fanwood NJ	07416 .... Franklin NJ	07701-04 .... Fair Haven NJ
06473 .... N Haven CT	07024 .... Fort Lee NJ	07417 .... Franklin Lakes NJ	07701-04 .... Red Bank NJ
06475 .... Old Saybrook CT	07026 .... Garfield NJ	07423 .... Ho Ho Kus NJ	07712 .... Asbury Park NJ
06477 .... Orange CT	07027 .... Garwood NJ	07424 .... Little Falls NJ	07716 .. Atlantic Highlands NJ
06480 .... Portland CT	07028 .... Glen Ridge NJ	07424 .... W Paterson NJ	07718 .... Belford NJ
06483 .... Seymour CT	07029 .... Harrison NJ	07430 .... Mahwah NJ	07719 .... Belmar NJ
06484 .... Shelton CT	07030 .... Hoboken NJ	07432 .... Midland Park NJ	07719 .... Wall NJ
06488 ...... Heritage Village CT	07032 .... Kearny NJ	07436 .... Oakland NJ	07720 .... Bradley Beach NJ
06488 .... Southbury NJ	07032 .... N Arlington NJ	07442 .... Pompton Lakes NJ	07724 .... Eatontown NJ
06489 .... Southington CT	07033 .... Kenilworth NJ	07446 .... Ramsey NJ	07724 .... Tinton Falls NJ
06492 .... Wallingford CT	07035 .... Lincoln Park NJ	07450-52 .... Ridgewood NJ	07728 .... Freehold NJ
06497 .... Stratford CT	07036 .... Linden NJ	07452 .... Glen Rock NJ	07728 .... Manalapan NJ
06501-99 ...... New Haven CT	07039 .... Livingston NJ	07456 .... Ringwood NJ	07730 .... Hazlet NJ
06512 .... E Haven CT	07040 .... Maplewood NJ	07457 .... Riverdale NJ	07732 .... Highlands NJ
06514 .... Hamden CT	07041 .... Millburn NJ	07458 .... Saddle River NJ	07733 .... Holmdel NJ
06516 .... West Haven CT	07042-44 .... Montclair NJ	07458 . Upper Saddle River NJ	07734 .... Keansburg NJ
06525 .... Bethany CT	07044 .... Verona NJ	07460 .... Hardyston NJ	07735 .... Keyport NJ
06525 .... Woodbridge CT	07045 .... Montville NJ	07463 .... Waldwick NJ	07735 .... Union Beach NJ
06601-99 .... Bridgeport CT	07046 ...... Mountain Lakes NJ	07465 .... Wanaque NJ	07739 .... Little Silver NJ
06611-12 .... Trumbull CT	07047 .... N Bergen NJ	07470-74 .... Wayne NJ	07740 .... Long Branch NJ
06612 .... Easton CT	07050-52 .... Orange NJ	07480 .... W Milford NJ	07747 .... Aberdeen NJ
06701-26 .... Waterbury CT	07052 .... W Orange NJ	07481 .... Wyckoff NJ	07747 .... Matawan NJ
06712 .... Prospect CT	07054 .... Parsippany NJ	07501-99 .... Paterson NJ	07748 .... Middletown NJ
06716 .... Wolcott CT	07055 .... Passaic NJ	07506 .... Hawthorne NJ	07753 .... Neptune City NJ
06751 .... Bethlehem CT	07057 .... Wallington NJ	07508 .... Haledon NJ	07753-54 .... Neptune NJ
06757 .... Kent CT	07060 .... N Plainfield NJ	07508 .... N Haledon NJ	07757 .... Oceanport NJ
06759 .... Litchfield CT	07060 .... Warren NJ	07508 .... Prospect Park NJ	07758 ...... Port Monmouth NJ
06762 .... Middlebury CT	07060 .... Watchung NJ	07512 .... Totowa NJ	07760 .... Rumson NJ
06770 .... Naugatuck CT	07060-63 .... Plainfield NJ	07601-08 .... Hackensack NJ	07762 .... Spring Lake NJ
06776 .... New Milford CT	07065-67 .... Rahway NJ	07603 .... Bogota NJ	07762 .... Spring Lake Hts NJ
06779 .... Oakville CT	07066 .... Clark NJ	07604 .... Hasbrouck Hts NJ	07764 ...... W Long Branch NJ
06782 .... Plymouth CT	07068 .... Roseland NJ	07605 .... Leonia NJ	07801-02 .... Dover NJ
06786 .... Terryville CT	07070-75 .... Rutherford NJ	07607 .... Maywood NJ	07821 .... Andover NJ
06787 .... Thomaston CT	07071 .... Lyndhurst NJ	07621 .... Bergenfield NJ	07821 .... Byram NJ
06790 .... Torrington CT	07072 .... Carlstadt NJ	07624 .... Closter NJ	07823 .... Belvidere NJ
06790-91 .... Harwinton CT	07073 .... E Rutherford NJ	07626 .... Cresskill NJ	07828 .... Mount Olive NJ
06793 .... Washington CT	07074 .... Moonachie NJ	07627 .... Demarest NJ	07830 .... Lebanon NJ
06795 .... Watertown CT	07074-75 .... Wood-Ridge NJ	07628 .... Dumont NJ	07834 .... Denville NJ
06801 .... Bethel CT	07076 .... Scotch Plains NJ	07630 .... Emerson NJ	07840 .... Hackettstown NJ
06804 .... Brookfield CT	07079 .... S Orange NJ	07631-32 .... Englewood NJ	07843 .... Hopatcong NJ
06810-12 .. New Fairfield CT	07080 .... S Plainfield NJ	07632 .... Englewood Cliffs NJ	07849 .... Jefferson NJ
06810-13 .... Danbury CT	07081 .... Springfield NJ	07640 ...... Harrington Park NJ	07856 .... Mount Arlington NJ
06820 .... Darien CT	07083 .... Union NJ	07641 .... Haworth NJ	07857 .... Netcong NJ
06830-36 .... Greenwich CT	07087 .... Union City NJ	07642 .... Hillsdale NJ	07860 .... Newton NJ

ZIP	CITY	ZIP	CITY	ZIP	CITY	ZIP	CITY
07866	Rockaway NJ	08079	Salem NJ	08730	Brielle NJ	10570-72	Pleasantville NY
07871	Sparta NJ	08081	New Brooklyn NJ	08733	Lakehurst NJ	10573	Port Chester NY
07874	Stanhope NJ	08083	Somerdale NJ	08736	Manasquan NJ	10573	Rye Brook NY
07876	Roxbury NJ	08084	Stratford NJ	08742	Point Pleasant NJ	10580-81	Rye NY
07882	Washington NJ	08086	W Deptford NJ	08753	Gilford Park NJ	10583	Scarsdale NY
07885	Wharton NJ	08090	Oak Valley NJ	08753	Holiday City/Berk NJ	10591	N Tarrytown NY
07901-02	Summit NJ	08093	Westville NJ	08753	Silverton NJ	10591	Tarrytown NY
07920	Bernards NJ	08096	Deptford NJ	08753-57	Toms River NJ	10595	Valhalla NY
07922	Berkeley Hts NJ	08096	Woodbury NJ	08757	S Toms River NJ	10598	Yorktown Hts NY
07924	Bernardsville NJ	08098	Woodstown NJ	08805	Bound Brook NJ	10598	Yorktown NY
07928	Chatham NJ	08101-99	Camden NJ	08807	Bridgewater NJ	10601-99	White Plains NY
07930	Chester NJ	08106	Audubon NJ	08807	Finderne NJ	10701-99	Yonkers NY
07932	Florham Park NJ	08107	Oaklyn NJ	08812	Dunellen NJ	10706	Hastings-on-Hudson NY
07936	E Hanover NJ	08107	Woodlynne NJ	08816	E Brunswick NJ	10707	Tuckahoe NY
07940	Madison NJ	08108	Collingswood NJ	08817-20	Edison NJ	10708	Bronxville NY
07945	Mendham NJ	08108	Haddon NJ	08822	Flemington NJ	10801-99	New Rochelle NY
07950	Morris Plains NJ	08109	Merchantville NJ	08829	High Bridge NJ	10803	Pelham Manor NY
07960-63	Morristown NJ	08110	Delair NJ	08831	Jamesburg NJ	10803	Pelham NY
07974	New Providence NJ	08110	Pennsauken NJ	08835	Manville NJ	10901	Montebello NY
07981	Hanover NJ	08201	Absecon NJ	08840	Metuchen NJ	10901	Suffern NY
08002-03	Cherry Hill NJ	08203	Brigantine NJ	08846	Middlesex NJ	10913	Blauvelt NY
08007	Barrington NJ	08204	Cape May NJ	08850	Milltown NJ	10924	Goshen NY
08009	Berlin NJ	08204	Lower NJ	08852	Monmouth Junct NJ	10925	Greenwood Lake NY
08010	Beverly NJ	08210	Cape May C.H. NJ	08854-55	Piscataway NJ	10927	Haverstraw NY
08012	Blackwood NJ	08213	Galloway NJ	08857	Browntown NJ	10928	Highland Falls NY
08012	Gloucester NJ	08215	Egg Harbor City NJ	08857	Old Bridge NJ	10940	Middletown NY
08016	Burlington NJ	08221	Linwood NJ	08857	Sayre Woods So NJ	10950	Monroe NY
08021	Clementon NJ	08225	Northfield NJ	08861-63	Perth Amboy NJ	10952	Chestnut Ridge NY
08021	Lindenwold NJ	08226	Ocean City NJ	08865	Alpha NJ	10956	New City NY
08021	Pine Hill NJ	08232	Pleasantville NJ	08865	Phillipsburg NJ	10960	Nyack NY
08026	Gibbsboro NJ	08244	Somers Point NJ	08869	Raritan NJ	10960	S Nyack NY
08027	Gibbstown NJ	08260	N Wildwood NJ	08872	Sayreville NJ	10962	Orangeburg NY
08028	Glassboro NJ	08260	Wildwood Crest NJ	08873-77	Somerville NJ	10965	Pearl River NY
08029	Glendora NJ	08260	Wildwood NJ	08876	Green Knoll NJ	10974	Sloatsburg NY
08031	Bellmawr NJ	08302	Bridgeton NJ	08879	S Amboy NJ	10977	New Hempstead NY
08033	Haddonfield NJ	08302	Hopewell NJ	08880	S Bound Brook NJ	10977	Spring Valley NY
08035	Haddon Hts NJ	08310	Buena NJ	08882	South River NJ	10983	Tappan NY
08037	Hammonton NJ	08312	Clayton NJ	08884	Spotswood NJ	10984	Thiells NY
08046	Willingboro NJ	08330	Mays Landing NJ	08901-99	New Brunswick NJ	10990	Warwick NY
08048	Lumberton NJ	08332	Millville NJ	08902	N Brunswick NJ	10993	W Haverstraw NY
08049	Magnolia NJ	08360	Vineland NJ	08904	Highland Park NJ	11001-05	Floral Park NY
08050	Manahawkin NJ	08401-99	Atlantic City NJ	10001-299	NEW YORK NY	11003	Elmont NY
08052	Maple Shade NJ	08402	Margate City NJ	10027	Manhattan NY	11020	University Gardens NY
08053	Evesham NJ	08406	Ventnor City NJ	10301	St George NY	11020-27	Great Neck NY
08053	Marlton NJ	08505	Bordentown NJ	10301-99	Staten Island NY	11021	Great Neck Ests NY
08054	Lawnside NJ	08511	New Hanover NJ	10401-99	Bronx NY	11021	Thomaston NY
08054	Mount Laurel NJ	08518	Florence NJ	10502	Ardsley NY	11024	Kings Point NY
08055	Medford Lakes NJ	08520	E Windsor NJ	10510	Briarcliff Manor NY	11030	Manhasset NY
08057	Fellowship NJ	08520	Hightstown NJ	10512	Carmel NY	11030	Munsey Park NY
08057	Moorestown NJ	08527	Brookwood NJ	10514	Chappaqua NY	11040	Herricks NY
08059	Mount Ephraim NJ	08527	Jackson NJ	10520-21	Croton-on-Hudson NY	11040	Hillside Manor NY
08060	Eastampton NJ	08530	Lambertville NJ	10522	Dobbs Ferry NY	11040-43	New Hyde Park NY
08060	Mount Holly NJ	08540	S Brunswick NJ	10523	Elmsford NY	11050	Flower Hill NY
08063	National Park NJ	08540-44	Princeton NJ	10528	Harrison NY	11050	Manorhaven NY
08065	Palmyra NJ	08550	W Windsor NJ	10530	Hartsdale NY	11050	Port Washington NY
08066	Paulsboro NJ	08560	Hopewell NJ	10532	Hawthorne NY	11050	Sands Point NY
08069	Carneys Point NJ	08562	Wrightstown NJ	10533	Irvington NY	11201-99	Brooklyn NY
08069	Penns Grove NJ	08601-99	TRENTON NJ	10535	Jefferson Vly NY	11301-99	Flushing NY
08070	Pennsville NJ	08618	Ewing NJ	10538	Larchmont NY	11401	Queens NY
08071	Pitman NJ	08619	Mercerville NJ	10543	Mamaroneck NY	11401-99	Jamaica NY
08075	Delanco NJ	08638	Lawrence NJ	10547	Mohegan Lake NY	11501	Mineola NY
08075	Delran NJ	08638	Slackwoods NJ	10549	Mount Kisco NY	11514	Carle Place NY
08075	Riverside NJ	08690	Hamilton Sq NJ	10550-59	Mount Vernon NY	11516	Cedarhurst NY
08077	Cinnaminson NJ	08701	Lakewood NJ	10562	Ossining NY	11518	E Rockaway NY
08077	Riverton NJ	08722	Beachwood NJ	10566	Peekskill NY		
08078	Runnemede NJ	08723-24	Brick NJ				

ZIP	CITY	ZIP	CITY	ZIP	CITY	ZIP	CITY
11520	Freeport NY	11754	Kings Park NY	12301-99	Schenectady NY	13214	De Witt NY
11530	Garden City NY	11754	San Remo NY	12302	Scotia NY	13316	Camden NY
11542	Glen Cove NY	11755	Lake Grove NY	12303	Rotterdam NY	13326	Cooperstown NY
11545	Brookville NY	11756	Levittown NY	12309	Niskayuna NY	13329	Dolgeville NY
11545	Glen Head NY	11757	Lindenhurst NY	12401	Kingston NY	13339	Fort Plain NY
11548	Greenvale NY	11758	Arlyn Oaks NY	12413	Cairo NY	13340	Frankfort NY
11550	S Hempstead NY	11758	E Massapequa NY	12414	Catskill NY	13346	Hamilton NY
11550-54	Hempstead NY	11758	Massapequa NY	12428	Ellenville NY	13350	Herkimer NY
11554	E Meadow NY	11762	Massapequa Pk NY	12477	Saugerties NY	13357	Ilion NY
11558	Barnum Island NY	11768	Northport NY	12508	Beacon NY	13365	Little Falls NY
11558	Island Park NY	11768	W Fort Salonga NY	12518	Cornwall NY	13367	Lowville NY
11559	Lawrence NY	11771	Oyster Bay NY	12534	Hudson NY	13407	Mohawk NY
11560	Locust Valley NY	11772	E Patchogue NY	12550	Newburgh NY	13417	New York Mills NY
11561	Lido Beach NY	11772	Patchogue NY	12561	New Paltz NY	13421	Oneida NY
11561	Long Beach NY	11772	W Bellport NY	12564	Pawling NY	13440-41	Rome NY
11563	Lynbrook NY	11776	Terryville NY	12572	Rhinebeck NY	13460	Sherburne NY
11565	Malverne NY	11779	Ronkonkoma NY	12586	Walden NY	13461	Sherrill NY
11566	Merrick NY	11780	St James NY	12601-99	Poughkeepsie NY	13492	Whitesboro NY
11568	Old Westbury NY	11782	Sayville NY	12603	Arlington NY	13495	Yorkville NY
11570-72	Rockville Ctr NY	11783	Seaford NY	12701	Monticello NY	13501-99	Utica NY
11572	Oceanside NY	11784	Selden NY	12733	Fallsburg NY	13601	Watertown NY
11575	Roosevelt NY	11787	Smithtown NY	12754	Liberty NY	13617	Canton NY
11576	E Hills NY	11787-88	Hauppauge NY	12771	Port Jervis NY	13619	Carthage NY
11579	Sea Cliff NY	11790	Stony Brook NY	12801	Glens Falls NY	13642	Gouverneur NY
11580-82	Valley Stream NY	11791	Muttontown NY	12803	S Glens Falls NY	13662	Massena NY
11590	Westbury NY	11791	Syosset NY	12822	Corinth NY	13669	Ogdensburg NY
11596	E Williston NY	11793	Wantagh NY	12828	Fort Edward NY	13676	Potsdam NY
11596	Williston Park NY	11801-99	Hicksville NY	12832	Granville NY	13733	Bainbridge NY
11598	Woodmere NY	11803	Plainview NY	12834	Greenwich NY	13753	Delhi NY
11601-99	Far Rockaway NY	11901	Riverhead NY	12839	Hudson Falls NY	13760	Endicott NY
11701	Amityville NY	11933	Calverton NY	12845	Lake George NY	13760	Endwell NY
11702-04	Babylon NY	11942	E Quogue NY	12866	Saratoga Sprgs NY	13760	Union NY
11705	Bayport NY	11946	Hampton Bays NY	12883	Ticonderoga NY	13790	Johnson City NY
11706	Bay Shore NY	11950	Mastic NY	12887	Whitehall NY	13815	Norwich NY
11709	Bayville NY	11961	Ridge NY	12901	Plattsburgh NY	13820	Oneonta NY
11710	Bellmore NY	11963	Sag Harbor NY	12919	Champlain NY	13827	Owego NY
11713	Bellport NY	11968	Southampton NY	12929	Dannemora NY	13838	Sidney NY
11714	Bethpage NY	12010	Amsterdam NY	12932	Elizabethtown NY	13850-51	Vestal NY
11715	Blue Point NY	12020	Ballston Spa NY	12950	Wappingers Falls NY	13856	Walton NY
11716	Bohemia NY	12043	Cobleskill NY	12953	Malone NY	13901-99	Binghamton NY
11717	Brentwood NY	12047	Cohoes NY	12982-83	Saranac Lake NY	13902	E Vestal NY
11719	Brookhaven NY	12051	Coxsackie NY	12986	Tupper Lake NY	14001	Akron NY
11720	Centereach NY	12054	Delmar NY	13021	Auburn NY	14004	Alden NY
11721	Centerport NY	12054	Elsmere NY	13027	Baldwinsville NY	14009	Arcade NY
11721	Huntington Beach NY	12061	E Greenbush NY	13031	Fairmount NY	14011	Attica NY
11722	Central Islip NY	12065	Clifton Park NY	13032	Canastota NY	14020-21	Batavia NY
11722	Islandia NY	12068	Fonda NY	13035	Cazenovia NY	14043	Depew NY
11724	Cold Spring Hbr NY	12078	Gloversville NY	13037	Chittenango NY	14048	Dunkirk NY
11725	Commack NY	12090	Hoosick Falls NY	13045	Cortland NY	14052	E Aurora NY
11726	Copiague NY	12095	Johnstown NY	13057	E Syracuse NY	14063	Fredonia NY
11729	Deer Park NY	12108	Lake Pleasant NY	13057	Franklin Park NY	14070	Gowanda NY
11730	E Islip NY	12110	Latham NY	13066	Fayetteville NY	14072	Grand Island NY
11731	E Northport NY	12118	Mechanicville NY	13069	Fulton NY	14075	Hamburg NY
11733	S Setauket NY	12143	Ravena NY	13077	Homer NY	14086	Lancaster NY
11735	Farmingdale NY	12144	Rensselaer NY	13088	Bayberry NY	14092	Lewiston NY
11740	Greenlawn NY	12157	Schoharie NY	13088-90	Liverpool NY	14094	Lockport NY
11743	E Huntington NY	12180-83	Troy NY	13104	Manlius NY	14103	Medina NY
11743	Halsite NY	12183	Green Island NY	13116	Minoa NY	14108	Newfane NY
11743	Huntington NY	12186	Voorheesville NY	13126	Oswego NY	14120	N Tonawanda NY
11743	Lloyd Harbor NY	12189	Watervliet NY	13148	Seneca Falls NY	14123	Tonawanda NY
11746	E Half Hollow Hills NY	12198	Wynantskill NY	13163	Wampsville NY	14127	Orchard Park NY
11746	Half Hollow Hills NY	12201-99	ALBANY NY	13165	Waterloo NY	14136	Silver Creek NY
11746	Huntington Sta NY	12204	Menands NY	13201-99	Syracuse NY	14150	Tonawanda NY
11747	Melville NY	12205	Maywood NY	13209	Lakeland NY	14150	Willow Ridge Ests NY
11751	Islip NY	12211	Loudonville NY	13209	Solvay NY	14172	Wilson NY
		12212	Colonie NY	13212	N Syracuse NY	14174	Youngstown NY

ZIP	CITY	ZIP	CITY	ZIP	CITY	ZIP	CITY
14201-99	Buffalo NY	15010	Big Beaver PA	15218	Edgewood PA	15904	Geistown PA
14217	Kenmore NY	15010	Chippewa PA	15218	Swissvale PA	15905	Southmont PA
14218	Lackawanna NY	15014	Brackenridge PA	15220	Green Tree PA	15905	Upper Yoder PA
14219	Blasdell NY	15017	Bridgeville PA	15221	Braddock Hills PA	15905	Westmont PA
14221	Williamsville NY	15022	Charleroi PA	15221	Forest Hills PA	15931	Ebensburg PA
14224	W Seneca NY	15025	Clairton PA	15221	Wilkinsburg PA	15943	Nanty Glo PA
14225	Cheektowaga NY	15027	Conway PA	15223	Etna PA	15946	Portage PA
14225	Sloan NY	15033	Donora PA	15227	Brentwood PA	15963	Windber PA
14226	Amherst NY	15034	Dravosburg PA	15228	Mount Lebanon PA	16001-03	Butler PA
14301-99	Niagara Falls NY	15035	E McKeesport PA	15229	West View PA	16057	Slippery Rock PA
14411	Albion NY	15045	Glassport PA	15234	Baldwin PA	16063	Zelienople PA
14414	Avon NY	15057	McDonald PA	15234	Castle Shannon PA	16101-08	New Castle PA
14420	Brockport NY	15059	Midland PA	15235	Churchill PA	16117	Ellwood City PA
14424-25	Canandaigua NY	15059	Ohioville PA	15235	Penn Hills PA	16121	Farrell PA
14445	E Rochester NY	15061	Monaca PA	15236	Broughton PA	16125	Greenville PA
14450	Fairport NY	15062	Monessen PA	15236	Pleasant Hills PA	16127	Grove City PA
14454	Geneseo NY	15063	Monongahela PA	15237	McCandless PA	16137	Mercer PA
14456	Geneva NY	15064	S Fayette PA	15238	Fox Chapel PA	16142	New Wilmington PA
14468	Hilton NY	15065	Harrison PA	15238	O'Hara PA	16148	Hermitage PA
14489	Lyons NY	15066	New Brighton PA	15239	Plum PA	16148	Sharon PA
14510	Mount Morris NY	15067	New Eagle PA	15241	Upper St Clair PA	16150	Sharpsville PA
14513	Newark NY	15068	Lower Burrell PA	15301	S Strabane PA	16172	New Wilmington PA
14522	Palmyra NY	15068	New Kensington PA	15301	Washington PA	16201	Kittanning PA
14527	Penn Yan NY	15074	Rochester PA	15314	Bentleyville PA	16214	Clarion PA
14530	Perry NY	15084	Tarentum PA	15317	Canonsburg PA	16226	Ford City PA
14559	Spencerport NY	15085	Trafford PA	15317	N Strabane PA	16323	Franklin PA
14569	Warsaw NY	15089	W Newton PA	15344	Jefferson PA	16323	Sugarcreek PA
14580	Webster NY	15101	Allison Park PA	15370	Waynesburg PA	16335	Meadville PA
14601-99	Rochester NY	15102	Bethel Park PA	15401	Uniontown PA	16353	Tionesta PA
14616	Greece NY	15104	Braddock PA	15417	Brownsville PA	16354	Titusville PA
14617	Irondequoit NY	15104	N Braddock PA	15417	Centerville PA	16365	Warren PA
14624	Chili Corner NY	15104	Rankin PA	15419	California PA	16407	Corry PA
14624	Gates NY	15106	Carnegie PA	15425	Connellsville PA	16412	Edinboro PA
14701-02	Jamestown NY	15108	Coraopolis PA	15461	Masontown PA	16417	Girard PA
14706	Allegany NY	15108	Moon PA	15501	Somerset PA	16428	N East PA
14722	Chautauqua NY	15110	Duquesne PA	15522	Bedford PA	16438	Union City PA
14733	Falconer NY	15116	Shaler Twp. PA	15552	Meyersdale PA	16501-99	Erie PA
14750	Lakewood NY	15120	Homestead PA	15601	Greensburg PA	16506	Millcreek Twp. PA
14755	Little Valley NY	15120	Munhall PA	15601	S Greensburg PA	16510	Wesleyville PA
14757	Mayville NY	15122-23	W Mifflin PA	15601	SW Greensburg PA	16601-03	Altoona PA
14760	Olean NY	15122-299	Pittsburgh PA	15627	Derry PA	16648	Hollidaysburg PA
14779	Salamanca NY	15129	South Park PA	15642	Irwin PA	16652	Huntingdon PA
14787	Westfield NY	15130-35	McKeesport PA	15642	N Huntingdon PA	16673	Roaring Spring PA
14802	Alfred NY	15131	White Oak PA	15644	Jeannette PA	16686	Tyrone PA
14810	Bath NY	15133	Port Vue PA	15650	Latrobe PA	16701	Bradford PA
14813	Belmont NY	15136	McKees Rocks PA	15656	Leechburg PA	16735	Kane PA
14817	Caroline NY	15136	Stowe Twp. PA	15666	Mount Pleasant PA	16743	Port Allegany PA
14823	Canisteo NY	15137	N Versailles PA	15668	Murrysville PA	16749	Smethport PA
14830	Corning NY	15139	Oakmont PA	15672	New Stanton PA	16801	Patton PA
14843	Hornell NY	15140	Pitcairn PA	15683	Scottdale PA	16801-05	State College PA
14844-45	Horseheads NY	15143	Franklin Park PA	15690	Vandergrift PA	16823	Bellefonte PA
14850	Cayuga Hts NY	15143	Sewickley PA	15697	Youngwood PA	16827	Harris PA
14850-53	Ithica NY	15144	Springdale PA	15701	Indiana PA	16830	Clearfield PA
14882	Lansing NY	15145	Turtle Creek PA	15714	Barnesboro PA	16833	Curwensville PA
14891	Watkins Glen NY	15145	Wilkins Twp. PA	15717	Blairsville PA	16866	Philipsburg PA
14892	Waverly NY	15146	Monroeville PA	15767	Punxsutawney PA	16880	Bellefonte PA
14895	Wellsville NY	15147	Verona PA	15801	Du Bois PA	16901	Wellsboro PA
14901-99	Elmira NY	15202	Avalon PA	15806	Arnold PA	16915	Coudersport PA
14903	Elmira Hts NY	15202	Bellevue PA	15825	Brookville PA	16930	Liberty PA
15001	Aliquippa PA	15205	Crafton PA	15834	Emporium PA	16933	Mansfield PA
15003	Ambridge PA	15205	Ingram PA	15845	Johnsonburg PA	17011	Camp Hill PA
15003-05	Economy PA	15209	Millvale PA	15851	Reynoldsville PA	17011	Lower Allen PA
15005	Baden PA	15210	Mount Oliver PA	15853	Ridgway PA	17013	Carlisle PA
15009	Beaver PA	15215	Aspinwall PA	15857	Benzinger PA	17013	N Middleton PA
15009	Brighton PA	15215	Sharpsburg PA	15857	St Marys PA	17016	Cornwall PA
15010	Beaver Falls PA	15216	Dormont PA	15901-09	Johnstown PA	17022	Elizabethtown PA

ZIP	CITY	ZIP	CITY	ZIP	CITY	ZIP	CITY
17025	E Pennsboro PA	17801	Sunbury PA	18431	Honesdale PA	19014	Aston PA
17033	S Hanover PA	17815	Bloomsburg PA	18434	Jessup PA	19015	Brookhaven PA
17034	Highspire PA	17821	Danville PA	18447	Blakely PA	19015	Upland PA
17036	Hummelstown PA	17834	Kulpmont PA	18447	Olyphant PA	19018	Aldan PA
17042	Lebanon PA	17837	Lewisburg PA	18501-99	Scranton PA	19018	Clifton Hts PA
17042	S Lebanon PA	17842	Middleburg PA	18512	Dunmore PA	19020	Bensalem PA
17043	Lemoyne PA	17844	Mifflinburg PA	18512	Throop PA	19023	Collingdale PA
17043	Wormleysburg PA	17847	Milton PA	18517	Moosic PA	19023	Colwyn PA
17044	Lewistown PA	17851	Mount Carmel PA	18517	Taylor PA	19023	Darby PA
17055	Hampden PA	17857	Northumberland PA	18518	Old Forge PA	19032	Folcroft PA
17055	Mechanicsburg PA	17870	Selinsgrove PA	18519	Dickson City PA	19033	Ridley PA
17055	Silver Spring PA	17876	Shamokin PA	18603	Berwick PA	19034	
17055	Upper Allen PA	17901	Pottsville PA	18612	Dallas PA		Upper Dublin Twp. PA
17057	Lower Swatara PA	17921	Ashland PA	18626	Laporte PA	19036	Glenolden PA
17057	Middletown PA	17931	Frackville PA	18634	Nanticoke PA	19037	Middletown Twp. PA
17059	Mifflintown PA	17948	Mahanoy City PA	18640-44	Pittston PA	19040	Hatboro PA
17061	Millersburg PA	17954	Minersville PA	18641	Avoca PA	19044	Horsham PA
17067	Myerstown PA	17961	Orwigsburg PA	18641	Dupont PA	19046	Jenkintown PA
17068	New Bloomfield PA	17965	Port Carbon PA	18642	Duryea PA	19047	
17070	New Cumberland PA	17970	St Clair PA	18643	Exeter PA		Lower Southampton PA
17078	N Londonderry PA	17972	Schuylkill Haven PA	18643	W Pittston PA	19047	Penndel PA
17078	Palmyra PA	17976	Shenandoah PA	18644	W Wyoming PA	19050	E Lansdowne PA
17083	Cornwall PA	18013-50	Bangor PA	18644	Wyoming PA	19050	Lansdowne PA
17101-99	HARRISBURG PA	18015	Fountain Hill PA	18651	Plymouth PA	19050	Yeadon PA
17103	Penbrook PA	18015	Lower Saucon PA	18657	Tunkhannock PA	19053-59	Levittown PA
17109	Glenwood PA	18015-18	Bethlehem PA	18690	Dallas PA	19056	Middletown PA
17109	Lower Paxton PA	18017	Middletown PA	18701-99	Wilkes-Barre PA	19061	Marcus Hook PA
17111	Swatara PA	18032	Catasauqua PA	18704	Edwardsville PA	19063	Upper Providence PA
17113	Steelton PA	18032	N Catasauqua PA	18704	Forty Fort PA	19063-65	Media PA
17201	Chambersburg PA	18034	Upper Saucon PA	18704	Kingston PA	19064	Springfield PA
17225	Greencastle PA	18036	Coopersburg PA	18704	Larksville PA	19067	Lower Makefield PA
17233	McConnellsburg PA	18037	Coplay PA	18704	Swoyerville PA	19067	Morrisville PA
17257	Shippensburg PA	18042	Wilson PA	18706	Ashley PA	19067	Yardley PA
17268	Waynesboro PA	18042-44	Easton PA	18708	Kingston PA	19072	Narberth PA
17313	Dallastown PA	18049	Emmaus PA	18709	Luzerne PA	19074	Norwood PA
17315	Dover PA	18052	Hokendauqua PA	18801	Montrose PA	19076	Prospect Park PA
17325	Gettysburg PA	18052	Whitehall PA	18810	Athens PA	19078	Ridley Park PA
17331	Hanover PA	18055	Hellertown PA	18840	Sayre PA	19079	Sharon Hill PA
17340	Littlestown PA	18064	Nazareth PA	18848	Towanda PA	19081	Swarthmore PA
17344	McSherrystown PA	18067	Northampton PA	18901	Doylestown PA	19082-83	Upper Darby PA
17345	Manchester PA	18071	Palmerton PA	18912	Buckingham PA	19083	Haverford PA
17356	Red Lion PA	18072	Pen Argyl PA	18914	New Britain PA	19086	
17361	Shrewsbury PA	18080	Slatington PA	18940	Newtown PA		Nether Providence PA
17401-99	York PA	18091	Warminster PA	18943	Penns Park PA	19087	Radnor PA
17402	Springettsbury PA	18091	Windgap PA	18944	Perkasie PA	19087	Strafford PA
17403	Spring Garden PA	18100-99	Allentown PA	18951	Quakertown PA	19090	Upper Moreland PA
17404	W York PA	18103	Salisbury PA	18960	Sellersville PA	19101-99	Philadelphia PA
17501	Akron PA	18104	S Whitehall PA	18964	Souderton PA	19118	Springfield Twp. PA
17512	Columbia PA	18201	Hazleton PA	18966	Holland PA	19312	Tredyffrin PA
17520	E Petersburg PA	18201	W Hazleton PA	18969	Telford PA	19320	Coatesville PA
17522	Ephrata PA	18218	Coaldale PA	18974	Warminster PA	19333	Devon PA
17543	Lititz PA	18224	Freeland PA	18976	Warrington PA	19335	Downingtown PA
17545	Manheim PA	18229	Jim Thorpe PA	19001	Abington Twp. PA	19335	W Bradford PA
17547	Marietta PA	18232	Lansford PA	19002	Ambler PA	19341	W Whiteland PA
17551	Millersville PA	18235	Lehighton PA	19002		19348	Kennett Square PA
17552	Mount Joy PA	18237	McAdoo PA		Upper Dublin Twp. PA	19355	E Whiteland PA
17557	New Holland PA	18240	Nesquehoning PA	19003	Lower Merion PA	19355	Malvern PA
17601-99	Lancaster PA	18250	Summit Hill PA	19006		19355	Willistown PA
17603	Hamilton Park PA	18252	Tamaqua PA		Lower Moreland PA	19363	Oxford PA
17701	S Williamsport PA	18255	Weatherly PA	19006		19365	Parkesburg PA
17701	Williamsport PA	18301	E Stroudsburg PA		Upper Southampton PA	19380	E Goshen PA
17740	Jersey Shore PA	18337	Milford PA	19007	Bristol PA	19380	W Goshen PA
17745	Lock Haven PA	18360	Stroudsburg PA	19008	Marple PA	19380-83	W Chester PA
17754	Montoursville PA	18403	Archbald PA	19012	Cheltenham PA	19401	E Norriton PA
17756	Muncy PA	18407	Carbondale PA	19013	Eddystone PA	19401	Lower Providence PA
17777	Watsontown PA	18411	Clarks Summit PA	19013-16	Chester PA		

ZIP	CITY	ZIP	CITY	ZIP	CITY	ZIP	CITY
19401	Plymouth Twp. PA	20678	Prince Frederick MD	21061	Glen Burnie Pk MD	22070-95	Herndon VA
19401	W Norriton PA	20706	Glenarden MD	21061	Marley MD	22075	Leesburg VA
19401-09	Norristown PA	20706	Lanham MD	21061	S Gate MD	22101	Tysons Corner VA
19405	Bridgeport PA	20706	Seabrook MD	21061-32	Glen Burnie MD	22101-06	McLean VA
19406	Upper Merion PA	20707	Maryland City MD	21078	Havre de Grace MD	22110-11	Manassas VA
19407	Audubon PA	20707	S Laurel MD	21113	Odenton MD	22111	Manassas Park VA
19422	Whitpain PA	20707	W Laurel MD	21122	Green Haven MD	22124	Oakton VA
19426	Collegeville PA	20707-08	Laurel MD	21122	Pasadena MD	22150-61	Springfield VA
19428	Conshohocken PA	20708	Montpelier MD	21122	Riviera Beach MD	22151	Kings Park VA
19428	Whitemarsh Twp. PA	20710	Bladensburg MD	21133	Randallstown MD	22151	N Springfield VA
19437	Lower Gwynedd PA	20712	Mount Rainier MD	21157	Hillside MD	22151	Ravensworth VA
19440	Hatfield PA	20715-16	Bowie MD	21157	Westminster MD	22180-83	Vienna VA
19443	Towamencin PA	20722	Brentwood MD	21201-99	Baltimore MD	22186	Warrenton VA
19446	Lansdale PA	20737	Riverdale Hts MD	21204	Towson MD	22191-99	Woodbridge VA
19454	N Wales PA	20737	Riverdale MD	21206	Overlea MD	22201-99	Arlington VA
19454	Upper Gwynedd PA	20740	Berwyn Hts MD	21207	Catonsville Manor MD	22301-99	Alexandria VA
19460	Phoenixville PA	20740	College Park MD	21207	Chadwick Manor MD	22303	Groveton Gardens VA
19464	Lower Pottsgrove PA	20743	Capitol Heights MD	21207	Lochearn MD	22303	Groveton VA
19464	Pottstown PA	20743	Coral Hills MD	21207	Lynne Acres MD	22303	Huntington VA
19464	W Pottsgrove PA	20743	Seat Pleasant MD	21207	Milford Ridge MD	22306	Hybla Valley VA
19468	Limerick PA	20745	Birchwood City MD	21207	Powhattan Mill MD	22306	Sherwood Hall VA
19468	Royersford PA	20745	Forest Heights MD	21207	Rockdale MD	22308	Stratford Landing VA
19475	Spring City PA	20745	Oxon Hill MD	21207	Woodlawn MD	22310	Rose Hill VA
19480	Uwchlan PA	20745	S Lawn MD	21227	Lansdowne MD	22401-05	Fredericksburg VA
19508	Birdsboro PA	20746	Suitland MD	21227	Pumphrey MD	22427	Bowling Green VA
19512	Boyertown PA	20747	Dist Ht-Forestville MD	21228	Westview Park MD	22473	Heathsville VA
19518	Amity Gardens PA	20748	Temple Hills Park MD	21237	Lutz Hill MD	22485	King George VA
19522	Fleetwood PA	20763	Savage MD	21401-99	ANNAPOLIS MD	22503	Lancaster VA
19525	New Hanover PA	20770	Greenbelt MD	21501-05	Cumberland MD	22520	Montross VA
19526	Hamburg PA	20772-75	Upper Marlboro MD	21502	La Vale MD	22553	Spotsylvania VA
19530	Kutztown PA	20780-88	Hyattsville MD	21532	Frostburg MD	22554	Stafford VA
19540	Cumru PA	20783	Chillum MD	21550	Oakland MD	22560	Tappahannock VA
19601-99	Reading PA	20783	Langley Park MD	21562	Westernport MD	22572	Warsaw VA
19605	Laureldale PA	20783	Lewisdale MD	21601	Easton MD	22601	Winchester VA
19606	Mount Penn PA	20784	New Carrollton MD	21613	Cambridge MD	22611	Berryville VA
19607	Kenhorst PA	20784	Quincy Manor MD	21617	Centreville MD	22630	Front Royal VA
19607	Shillington PA	20784	University Park MD	21620	Chestertown MD	22664	Woodstock VA
19608	Sinking Spring PA	20784	W Lanham Hills MD	21629	Denton MD	22701	Culpeper VA
19610	Wyomissing PA	20785	Cheverly MD	21701	Frederick MD	22727	Madison VA
19611	W Reading PA	20813-17	Bethesda MD	21716	Brunswick MD	22747	Washington VA
19703	Claymont DE	20814	Parkside MD	21740-42	Hagerstown MD	22801	Harrisonburg VA
19709	Middletown DE	20815	Chevy Chase MD	21787	Taneytown MD	22812	Bridgewater VA
19711-26	Newark DE	20832	Olney MD	21788	Thurmount MD	22835	Luray VA
19713	Brookside DE	20837	Poolesville MD	21801	Salisbury MD	22901-08	Charlottesville VA
19720	Collins Park DE	20850-56	Rockville MD	21817	Crisfield MD	22949	Lovingston VA
19720	New Castle DE	20851	Potomac MD	21826	Fruitland MD	22960	Orange VA
19801-99	Wilmington DE	20852	Old Farm MD	21842	Ocean City MD	22963	Palmyra VA
19802	Edgemoor DE	20852	Regency Ests MD	21851	Pocomoke City MD	22973	Stanardsville VA
19804	Newport DE	20853	Manor Woods MD	21853	Princess Anne MD	22980	Waynesboro VA
19805	Elsmere DE	20877-79	Gaithersburg MD	21863	Snow Hill MD	23002	Amelia C.H. VA
19808	Marshallton DE	20879	Montgomery Vlg MD	21921	Elkton MD	23005	Ashland VA
19810	Graylyn Crest DE	20901-99	Silver Spring MD	22003	Annandale VA	23030	Charles City VA
19901-03	DOVER DE	20902	Kemp Mill MD	22015	Burke VA	23040	Cumberland VA
19933	Bridgeville DE	20902	Wheaton MD	22020	Centreville VA	23060	Laurel VA
19947	Georgetown DE	20903	New Hampshire Est MD	22021	Chantilly VA	23061	Gloucester VA
19952	Harrington DE	20903	Oak View MD	22026	Dumfries VA	23063	Goochland VA
19956	Laurel DE	20904	White Oak MD	22030	Kings Park West VA	23069	Hanover VA
19963	Milford DE	20906	Aspin Hill MD	22030	Springbrook Forest VA	23075	Highland Sprgs VA
19968	Milton DE	20912	Takoma Park MD	22030-39	Fairfax VA	23085	King & Queen C.H. VA
19971	Rehoboth Beach DE	21001	Aberdeen MD	22040-48	Falls Church VA	23086	King William VA
19973	Seaford DE	21014	Bel Air MD	22041	Baileys Crossroads VA	23093	Louisa VA
19977	Smyrna DE	21043	Ellicott City MD	22041	Culmore VA	23109	Mathews VA
20001-599	Washington DC	21045-46	Columbia MD	22042	Broyhill Park VA	23124	New Kent VA
20601-04	Waldorf MD	21061	Ferndale MD	22044	Ravenwood VA	23139	Powhatan VA
20646	La Plata MD			22046	N Woodley VA	23149	Saluda VA
20650	Leonardtown MD						

ZIP	CITY	ZIP	CITY	ZIP	CITY	ZIP	CITY
23150	Sandston VA	24266	Lebanon VA	25840	Fayetteville WV	27284-85	Kernersville NC
23185-87	Williamsburg VA	24273	Norton VA	25882	Mullens WV	27288	Eden NC
23201-99	RICHMOND VA	24293	Wise VA	25901	Oak Hill WV	27292-93	Lexington NC
23227	Bellevue VA	24301	Pulaski VA	25951	Hinton WV	27302	Mebane NC
23228	Lakeside VA	24315	Bland VA	26003	Wheeling WV	27312	Pittsboro NC
23231	Montrose VA	24333	Galax VA	26034	Chester WV	27320-23	Reidsville NC
23234	Bensley VA	24343	Hillsville VA	26037	Follansbee WV	27330-31	Sanford NC
23235	Bon Air VA	24348	Independence VA	26041	Moundsville WV	27344	Siler City NC
23301	Accomac VA	24354	Marion VA	26047		27360-61	Thomasville NC
23320-25		24382	Wytheville VA		New Cumberland WV	27371	Troy NC
	Chesapeake City VA	24401	Staunton VA	26062	Weirton WV	27375	Wentworth NC
23347	Eastville VA	24416	Buena Vista VA	26070	Wellsburg WV	27379	Yanceyville NC
23397	Isle of Wight VA	24422	Clifton Forge VA	26101-06	Parkersburg WV	27401-99	Greensboro NC
23430	Smithfield VA	24426	Covington VA	26105	Vienna WV	27502	Apex NC
23432-38	Suffolk VA	24450	Lexington VA	26143	Elizabeth WV	27504	Benson NC
23450-64	Virginia Beach VA	24465	Monterey VA	26147	Grantsville WV	27510	Carrboro NC
23501-99	Norfolk VA	24484	Warm Springs VA	26149	Middlebourne WV	27511-13	Cary NC
23601-07	Newport News VA	24501-15	Lynchburg VA	26155	New Martinsville WV	27514-16	Chapel Hill NC
23661-70	Hampton VA	24502	Timberlake VA	26159	Paden City WV	27520	Clayton NC
23662	Poquoson VA	24517	Altavista VA	26164	Ravenswood WV	27526	Fuquay-Varina NC
23690	Yorktown VA	24521	Amherst VA	26170	St Marys WV	27529	Garner NC
23701-99	Portsmouth VA	24522	Appomattox VA	26187	Williamstown WV	27530-34	Goldsboro NC
23801-05	Petersburg VA	24523	Bedford VA	26201	Buckhannon WV	27536	Henderson NC
23824	Blackstone VA	24531	Chatham VA	26241	Elkins WV	27546	Lillington NC
23831	Chester VA	24540-43	Danville VA	26261	Richwood WV	27549	Louisburg NC
23832	Chesterfield VA	24558	Halifax VA	26287	Parsons WV	27565	Oxford NC
23834	Colonial Hts VA	24588	Rustburg VA	26288	Webster Spgs WV	27573	Roxboro NC
23837	Courtland VA	24592	S Boston VA	26301-02	Clarksburg WV	27576	Selma NC
23841	Dinwiddie VA	24605	Bluefield VA	26330	Bridgeport WV	27577	Smithfield NC
23847	Emporia VA	24614	Grundy VA	26351	Glenville WV	27587	Wake Forest NC
23851	Franklin VA	24641	Richlands VA	26354	Grafton WV	27589	Warrenton NC
23860	Hopewell VA	24651	Tazewell VA	26362	Harrisville WV	27601-99	RALEIGH NC
23868	Lawrenceville VA	24701	Bluefield WV	26416	Philippi WV	27701-99	Durham NC
23875	Prince George VA	24740	Princeton WV	26426	Salem WV	27801-04	Rocky Mount NC
23883	Surry VA	24801	Welch WV	26431	Shinnston WV	27823	Enfield NC
23884	Sussex VA	24874	Pineville WV	26452	Weston WV	27828	Farmville NC
23901	Farmville VA	24901-02	Lewisburg WV	26456	W Union WV	27834-36	Greenville NC
23917	Boydton VA	24954	Marlinton WV	26502-07	Morgantown WV	27839	Halifax NC
23921	Buckingham VA	24983	Union WV	26505	Westover WV	27845	Jackson NC
23923	Charlotte C.H. VA	24986		26537	Kingwood WV	27855	Murfreesboro NC
23924	Chase City VA		White Sulphur Sgs WV	26554-55	Fairmont WV	27856	Nashville NC
23952	Lunenburg VA	25043	Clay WV	26582	Mannington WV	27870	Roanoke Rapids NC
23955	Nottoway VA	25064	Dunbar WV	26601	Sutton WV	27874	Scotland Neck NC
23970	South Hill VA	25130	Madison WV	26651	Summersville WV	27885	Swanquarter NC
24001-38	Roanoke VA	25136	Montgomery WV	26726	Keyser WV	27886	Tarboro NC
24018	Cave Spring VA	25143	Nitro WV	26757	Romney WV	27889	Washington NC
24018	Sugar Loaf VA	25177	St Albans WV	26807	Franklin WV	27892	Williamston NC
24060-63	Blacksburg VA	25213	Winfield WV	26836	Moorefield WV	27893-95	Wilson NC
24073	Christiansburg VA	25271	Ripley WV	26847	Petersburg WV	27906-09	Elizabeth City NC
24090	Fincastle VA	25276	Spencer WV	27016	Danbury NC	27910	Ahoskie NC
24091	Floyd VA	25301-99	CHARLESTON WV	27017	Dobson NC	27921	Camden NC
24112-15	Martinsville VA	25303	S Charleston WV	27021	King NC	27925	Columbia NC
24127	New Castle VA	25401	Martinsburg WV	27025	Madison NC	27929	Currituck NC
24134	Pearisburg VA	25411	Berkeley Spgs WV	27027	Mayodan NC	27932	Edenton NC
24141-43	Radford VA	25414	Charles Town WV	27028	Mocksville NC	27938	Gatesville NC
24151	Rocky Mount VA	25438	Ranson WV	27030-31	Mount Airy NC	27944	Hertford NC
24153	Salem VA	25504	Barboursville WV	27055	Yadkinville NC	27954	Manteo NC
24171	Stuart VA	25523	Hamlin WV	27101-27	Winston-Salem NC	27962	Plymouth NC
24179	Vinton VA	25526	Hurricane WV	27203	Asheboro NC	27983	Windsor NC
24201-03	Bristol VA	25530	Kenova WV	27215-17	Burlington NC	27986	Winton NC
24210	Abingdon VA	25550	Point Pleasant WV	27244	Elon College NC	28001-02	Albemarle NC
24219	Big Stone Gap VA	25570	Wayne WV	27249	Gibsonville NC	28012	Belmont NC
24228	Clintwood VA	25601	Logan WV	27253	Graham NC	28016	Bessemer City NC
24230	Coeburn VA	25661	Williamson WV	27260-64	High Point NC	28021	Cherryville NC
24251	Gate City VA	25701-99	Huntington WV	27263	Archdale NC	28025-26	Concord NC
24263	Jonesville VA	25801-02	Beckley WV	27278	Hillsboro NC	28034	Dallas NC

ZIP	CITY	ZIP	CITY	ZIP	CITY	ZIP	CITY
28036	Davidson NC	28650	Maiden NC	29512	Bennettsville SC	30079	Scottdale GA
28043	Forest City NC	28655	Morganton NC	29520	Cheraw SC	30080	Smyrna GA
28052-55	Gastonia NC	28657	Newland NC	29526	Conway SC	30086-88	Stone Mountain GA
28081	Kannapolis NC	28658	Newton NC	29532	Darlington SC	30091-93	Norcross GA
28086	Kings Mountain NC	28659	N Wilkesboro NC	29536	Dillon SC	30101	Acworth GA
28092-93	Lincolnton NC	28675	Sparta NC	29550	Hartsville SC	30108	Bowdon GA
28098	Lowell NC	28677	Statesville NC	29556	Kingstree SC	30110	Bremen GA
28110	Monroe NC	28681	Taylorsville NC	29560	Lake City SC	30113	Buchanan GA
28115	Mooresville NC	28690	Valdese NC	29570	McColl SC	30114	Canton GA
28120	Mount Holly NC	28697	Wilkesboro NC	29571	Marion SC	30117	Carrollton GA
28139	Rutherfordton NC	28705	Bakersville NC	29572-87	Myrtle Beach SC	30120	Cartersville GA
28144-45	Salisbury NC	28711	Black Mountain NC	29574	Mullins SC	30125	Cedartown GA
28150-51	Shelby NC	28712	Brevard NC	29577	Surfside Beach SC	30130	Cumming GA
28159	Spencer NC	28713	Bryson City NC	29582	N Myrtle Beach SC	30132	Dallas GA
28160	Spindale NC	28714	Burnsville NC	29601-16	Greenville SC	30133-35	Douglasville GA
28170	Wadesboro NC	28716	Canton NC	29620	Abbeville SC	30136	Duluth GA
28201-99	Charlotte NC	28722	Columbus NC	29621	Anderson SC	30143	Jasper GA
28212	Mint Hill NC	28734	Franklin NC	29627	Belton SC	30144	Kennesaw GA
28301-14	Fayetteville NC	28739	Hendersonville NC	29631-33	Clemson SC	30153	Rockmart GA
28327	Carthage NC	28752	Marion NC	29640-41	Easley SC	30161-64	Rome GA
28328	Clinton NC	28753	Marshall NC	29644	Fountain Inn SC	30176	Tallapoosa GA
28334	Dunn NC	28771	Robbinsville NC	29646-49	Greenwood SC	30180	Villa Rica GA
28337	Elizabethtown NC	28778	Swannanoa NC	29650-52	Greer SC	30188	Woodstock GA
28339	Erwin NC	28779	Sylva NC	29654	Honea Path SC	30201	Alpharetta GA
28340	Fairmont NC	28786	Waynesville NC	29657	Liberty SC	30204	Barnesville GA
28345	Hamlet NC	28801-99	Asheville NC	29662	Mauldin SC	30207-08	Conyers GA
28348	Hope Mills NC	28804	Woodfin NC	29670	Pendleton SC	30209	Covington GA
28349	Kenansville NC	28904	Hayesville NC	29671	Pickens SC	30213	Fairburn GA
28352	Laurinburg NC	28906	Murphy NC	29678-79	Seneca SC	30214	Fayetteville GA
28358-59	Lumberton NC	29003	Bamberg SC	29681	Simpsonville SC	30217	Franklin GA
28364	Maxton NC	29006	Batesburg SC	29690	Travelers Rest SC	30222	Greenville GA
28365	Mount Olive NC	29010	Bishopville SC	29691	Walhalla SC	30223-24	Griffin GA
28372	Pembroke NC	29020	Camden SC	29693	Westminster SC	30230	Hogansville GA
28376	Raeford NC	29033	Cayce SC	29697	Williamston SC	30233	Jackson GA
28377	Red Springs NC	29042	Denmark SC	29706	Chester SC	30236-37	Jonesboro GA
28379	Rockingham NC	29055	Great Falls SC	29709	Chesterfield SC	30240-41	La Grange GA
28387	Southern Pines NC	29063	Irmo SC	29710	Clover SC	30243-46	Lawrenceville GA
28390	Spring Lake NC	29072	Lexington SC	29715	Fort Mill SC	30247	Lilburn GA
28401-12	Wilmington NC	29102	Manning SC	29720	Lancaster SC	30253	McDonough GA
28422	Bolivia NC	29108	Newberry SC	29728	Pageland SC	30260	Lake City GA
28425	Burgaw NC	29115-17	Orangeburg SC	29730-33	Rock Hill SC	30260	Morrow GA
28461	Southport NC	29135	St Matthews SC	29745	York SC	30263-65	Newnan GA
28463	Tabor City NC	29138	Saluda SC	29801-02	Aiken SC	30268	Palmetto GA
28466	Wallace NC	29150-54	Sumter SC	29810	Allendale SC	30269	Peachtree City GA
28472	Whiteville NC	29180	Winnsboro SC	29812	Barnwell SC	30274	Riverdale GA
28480	Wrightsville Bch NC	29201-99	COLUMBIA SC	29817	Blackville SC	30278	Snellville GA
28501-03	Kinston NC	29206	Forest Acres SC	29824	Edgefield SC	30279	Social Circle GA
28513	Ayden NC	29301-18	Spartanburg SC	29832	Johnston SC	30286	Thomaston GA
28515	Bayboro NC	29325	Clinton SC	29835	McCormick SC	30291	Union City GA
28516	Beaufort NC	29340-42	Gaffney SC	29841-42	N Augusta SC	30295	Zebulon GA
28532	Havelock NC	29360	Laurens SC	29853	Willston SC	30328	Sandy Springs GA
28540-46	Jacksonville NC	29379	Union SC	29901-03	Beaufort SC	30340	College Park GA
28557	Morehead City NC	29388	Woodruff SC	29924	Hampton SC	30340	Doraville GA
28560-62	New Bern NC	29401-23	Charleston SC	29925-28	Hilton Head SC	30341	Chamblee GA
28580	Snow Hill NC	29406	Hanahan SC	29935	Port Royal SC	30344	East Point GA
28585	Trenton NC	29406	N Charleston SC	29936	Ridgeland SC	30354	Hapeville GA
28601	Longview NC	29440	Georgetown SC	30001	Austell GA	30401	Swainsboro GA
28601-03	Hickory NC	29445	Goose Creek SC	30021	Clarkston GA	30411	Alamo GA
28607	Boone NC	29451	Isle of Palms SC	30030-38	Decatur GA	30417	Claxton GA
28613	Conover NC	29461	Moncks Corner SC	30042-199	ATLANTA GA	30427	Glennville GA
28621	Elkin NC	29464-65	Mount Pleasant SC	30050-51	Forest Park GA	30434	Louisville GA
28630	Granite Falls NC	29477	St George SC	30058	Lithonia GA	30436	Lyons GA
28638	Hudson NC	29483-85	Summerville SC	30059	Mableton GA	30439	Metter GA
28640	Jefferson NC	29488	Walterboro SC	30060-68	Marietta GA	30442	Millen GA
28645	Gamewell NC	29501-04	Florence SC	30073	Powder Spgs GA	30445	Mount Vernon GA
28645	Lenoir NC	29510	Andrews SC	30075-77	Roswell GA	30453	Reidsville GA

ZIP .... CITY	ZIP .... CITY	ZIP .... CITY	ZIP .... CITY
30457 .... Soperton GA	31050 .... Knoxville GA	31792 .... Thomasville GA	32569 .... Mary Esther FL
30458 .... Statesboro GA	31055 .... McRae GA	31792-94 .... Tifton GA	32570-71 .... Milton FL
30467 .... Sylvania GA	31061 .... Milledgeville GA	31803 .... Buena Vista GA	32578 .... Niceville FL
30474 .... Vidalia GA	31063 .... Montezuma GA	31805 .... Cusseta GA	32580 .... Valparaiso FL
30501-06 ...... Gainesville GA	31064 .... Monticello GA	31806 .... Ellaville GA	32601-13 .... Gainesville FL
30512 .... Blairsville GA	31068 .... Oglethorpe GA	31811 .... Hamilton GA	32606 .... Myrtle Grove FL
30513 .... Blue Ridge GA	31069 .... Perry GA	31815 .... Lumpkin GA	32615-16 .... Alachua FL
30518 .... Buford GA	31082 .... Sandersville GA	31816 .... Manchester GA	32620 .... Belleview FL
30521 .... Carnesville GA	31087 .... Sparta GA	31824 .... Preston GA	32621 .... Bronson FL
30523 .... Clarkesville GA	31092 .... Vienna GA	31827 .... Talbotton GA	32628 .... Cross City FL
30525 .... Clayton GA	31096 .... Wrightsville GA	31833 .... West Point GA	32629 .... Crystal River FL
30528 .... Cleveland GA	31098-99 Warner Robins GA	31901-95 .... Columbus GA	32650-52 .... Inverness FL
30529 .... Commerce GA	31201-99 .... Macon GA	32034 ..... Fernandina Bch FL	32670-78 .... Ocala FL
30531 .... Cornelia GA	31305 .... Darien GA	32043 .... Green Cove Spgs FL	32693 .... Trenton FL
30533 .... Dahlonega GA	31313 .... Hinesville GA	32052 .... Jasper FL	32703-4 .... Apopka FL
30534 .... Dawsonville GA	31316 .... Ludowici GA	32054 .... Lake Butler FL	32707-8 .... Casselberry FL
30540 .... Ellijay GA	31321 .... Pembroke GA	32055-56 .... Lake City FL	32708 .... Winter Springs FL
30546 .... Hiawassee GA	31322 .... Pooler GA	32060 .... Live Oak FL	32714-15 Altamonte Spgs FL
30547 .... Homer GA	31326 .... Rincon GA	32063 .... Macclenny FL	32720-24 .... De Land FL
30549 .... Jefferson GA	31329 .... Springfield GA	32066 .... Mayo FL	32726-27 .... Eustis FL
30577 .... Toccoa GA	31401-99 .... Savannah GA	32073 .... Orange Park FL	32746 .... Lake Mary FL
30601-13 .... Athens GA	31404 .... Thunderbolt GA	32084-86 ...... St Augustine FL	32750 .... Longwood FL
30631 .... Crawfordville GA	31407 .... Port Wentworth GA	32091 .... Starke FL	32751 .... Maitland FL
30633 .... Danielsville GA	31408 .... Garden City GA	32110 .... Bunnell FL	32757 .... Mount Dora FL
30635 .... Elberton GA	31501-02 .... Waycross GA	32114-24 .. Daytona Beach FL	32763 .... Orange City FL
30642 .... Greensboro GA	31510 .... Alma GA	32117 .... Holly Hill FL	32765-66 .... Oviedo FL
30643 .... Hartwell GA	31513 .... Baxley GA	32121 .... S Daytona FL	32771-73 .... Sanford FL
30648 .... Lexington GA	31516 .... Blackshear GA	32127 .... Port Orange FL	32778 .... Tavares FL
30650 .... Madison GA	31520-22 .... Brunswick GA	32132 .... Edgewater FL	32780-83 .... Titusville FL
30655 .... Monroe GA	31533 .... Douglas GA	32168-70 New Smyrna Bch FL	32789-93 .... Winter Park FL
30673 .... Washington GA	31537 .... Folkston GA	32174-76 .. Ormond Beach FL	32801-99 .... Orlando FL
30677 .... Watkinsville GA	31539 .... Hazlehurst GA	32177-78 .... Palatka FL	32808 .... Pine Hills FL
30680 .... Winder GA	31545 .... Jesup GA	32201-99 ..... Jacksonville FL	32809 .... Belle Isle FL
30701 .... Calhoun GA	31548 .... Kingsland GA	32233 .... Atantic Beach FL	32809 .... Pine Castle FL
30705 .... Chatsworth GA	31553 .... Nahunta GA	32233 .... Neptune Beach FL	32901 .... W Melbourne FL
30720-22 .... Dalton GA	31558 .... St Marys GA	32234 .... Baldwin FL	32901-40 .... Melbourne FL
30728 .... LaFayette GA	31569 .... Woodbine GA	32250 ..... Jacksonville Bch FL	32902 .... Indialantic FL
30736 .... Ringgold GA	31601-899 Valdosta GA	32301-17 TALLAHASSEE FL	32905 .... Palm Bay FL
30741-42 .... Rossville GA	31620 .... Adel GA	32320 .... Apalachicola FL	32920 .... Cape Canaveral FL
30742 .... Fort Oglethorpe GA	31634 .... Homerville GA	32321 .... Bristol FL	32922-27 .... Cocoa FL
30747 .... Summerville GA	31635 .... Lakeland GA	32324 .... Chattahoochee FL	32931-32 ...... Cocoa Beach FL
30752 .... Trenton GA	31639 .... Nashville GA	32327 .... Crawfordville FL	32937 ....
30802 .... Appling GA	31642 .... Pearson GA	32333 .... Havana FL	..........Indian Harbour Bch FL
30810 .... Gibson GA	31643 .... Quitman GA	32340 .... Madison FL	32937 .... Satellite Beach FL
30813 .... Grovetown GA	31648 .... Statenville GA	32344 .... Monticello FL	32951.....Melbourne Beach FL
30817 .... Lincolnton GA	31701-08 .... Albany GA	32347 .... Perry FL	32952-54 .... Merritt Island FL
30824 .... Thomson GA	31709 .... Americus GA	32351-52 .... Quincy FL	32955-56 .... Rockledge FL
30828 .... Warrenton GA	31714 .... Ashburn GA	32401 .... Parker FL	32958 .... Sebastian FL
30830 .... Waynesboro GA	31717 .... Bainbridge GA	32401 .... Springfield FL	32960 .... Gifford FL
30901-19 .... Augusta GA	31723 .... Blakely GA	32401-13 ...... Panama City FL	32960-67 .... Vero Beach FL
31001 .... Abbeville GA	31728 .... Cairo GA	32401-40 .... Callaway FL	33004 .... Dania FL
31006 .... Butler GA	31730 .... Camilla GA	32424 .... Blountstown FL	33009 .... Pembroke Park FL
31014 .... Cochran GA	31737 .... Colquitt GA	32425 .... Bonifay FL	33009-16 .... Hallandale FL
31015 .... Cordele GA	31740 .... Cuthbert GA	32428 .... Chipley FL	33010-16 .... Hialeah FL
31021 .... Dublin GA	31742 .... Dawson GA	32433 ...... De Funiak Spgs FL	33016 .... Hialeah Gardens FL
31021 .... E Dublin GA	31745 .... Donalsonville GA	32440 .... Graceville FL	33020-84 .... Hollywood FL
31023 .... Eastman GA	31750 .... Fitzgerald GA	32444 .... Lynn Haven FL	33023 .... Miramar FL
31024 .... Eatonton GA	31754 .... Georgetown GA	32446 .... Marianna FL	33030-35 .... Homestead FL
31029 .... Forsyth GA	31751 .... Fort Gaines GA	32456 ...... Port St Joe. FL	33034 .... Florida City FL
31030 .... Fort Valley GA	31763 .... Leesburg GA	32501-98 .... Pensacola FL	33034 ...... Pembroke Pines FL
31031 .... Gordon GA	31766 .... Morgan GA	32505 .... W Pensacola FL	33036 .... Plantation FL
31032 .... Gray GA	31768 .... Moultrie GA	32507 .... Warrington FL	33040-41 .... Key West FL
31034 .... Hardwick GA	31770 .... Newton GA	32536 .... Crestview FL	33050-52 .... Marathon FL
31036 .... Hawkinsville GA	31774 .... Ocilla GA	32541 .... Destin FL	33054-56 .... Opa Locka FL
31042 .... Irwinton GA	31779 .... Pelham GA	32548-49 Fort Walton Bch FL	33055 .... Carol City FL
31044 .... Jeffersonville GA	31791 .... Sylvester GA	32561-62 .... Gulf Breeze FL	33060-63 .. Coconut Creek FL

ZIP	CITY	ZIP	CITY	ZIP	CITY	ZIP	CITY
33060-75	Pompano Beach FL	33564-67	Plant City FL	34769-73	St Cloud FL	35592	Vernon AL
33063	Margate FL	33570-73	Ruskin FL	34785	Wildwood FL	35594	Winfield AL
33064	Lighthouse Point FL	33601-99	Tampa FL	34787	Winter Garden FL	35601-03	Decatur AL
33065	Coral Springs FL	33614	Sweetwater Creek FL	34945-88	Fort Pierce FL	35611	Athens AL
33068	N Lauderdale FL	33617	Temple Terrace FL	34952-92	Port St Lucie FL	35630-33	Florence AL
33092	Naranja FL	33698	Dunedin FL	34957-58	Jensen Beach FL	35640	Hartselle AL
33101-269	Miami FL	33701-99	St Petersburg FL	34972-74	Okeechobee FL	35650	Moulton AL
33134	Coral Gables FL	33706	St Petersburg Bch FL	34994-97	Stuart FL	35653	Russellville AL
33138	El Portal FL	33706	Treasure Island FL	35005	Adamsville AL	35660-61	Muscle Shoals AL
33138	Miami Shores FL	33707	Gulfport FL	35007-144	Alabaster AL	35660-62	Sheffield AL
33139	Miami Beach FL	33707	S Pasadena FL	35010	Alexander City AL	35674	Tuscumbia AL
33141	N Bay Village FL	33708	Madeira Beach FL	35016	Arab AL	35740	Bridgeport AL
33143	S Miami FL	33709	Kenneth City FL	35020	Brighton AL	35758	Madison AL
33144	W Miami FL	33801-13	Lakeland FL	35020	Lipscomb AL	35768	Scottsboro AL
33154	Bal Harbour FL	33821	Arcadia FL	35020	Roosevelt AL	35772	Stevenson AL
33154	Bay Harbor FL	33823	Auburndale FL	35020-23	Bessemer AL	35801-99	Huntsville AL
33154	Surfside FL	33825	Avon Park FL	35023	Hueytown AL	35901	Rainbow City AL
33156	Kendall FL	33830	Bartow FL	35042	Centreville AL	35901	Southside AL
33157	Cutler Ridge FL	33834	Bowling Green FL	35044	Childersburg AL	35901-05	Gadsden AL
33157	Perrine FL	33841	Fort Meade FL	35045	Clanton AL	35903	Hokes Bluff AL
33160-62	N Miami Beach FL	33843	Frostproof FL	35051	Columbiana AL	35905	Glencoe AL
33161	Biscayne Park FL	33844	Haines City FL	35055-56	Cullman AL	35953	Ashville AL
33161	N Miami FL	33850	Lake Alfred FL	35061	Dolomite AL	35954	Attalla AL
33165	Westwood Lakes FL	33853-59	Lake Wales FL	35064	Fairfield AL	35957	Boaz AL
33166	Miami Springs FL	33860	Mulberry FL	35068	Fultondale AL	35960	Centre AL
33180	Ojus FL	33870-72	Sebring FL	35071	Gardendale AL	35967	Fort Payne AL
33301-99	Fort Lauderdale FL	33873	Wauchula FL	35073	Graysville AL	35976	Guntersville AL
33304	Oakland Park FL	33880-84	Winter Haven FL	35094	Leeds AL	35986	Rainsville AL
33308	Lauderdale-by-the-Sea FL	33901-19	Fort Myers FL	35115	Montevallo AL	36016	Clayton AL
33313	Lauderdale Lakes FL	33904	Cape Coral FL	35121	Oneonta AL	36027	Eufaula AL
33313	Lauderhill FL	33905	Tice FL	35124	Pelham AL	36037	Greenville AL
33314	Davie FL	33934	Immokalee FL	35125	Pell City AL	36040	Hayneville AL
33321	Tamarac FL	33935	La Belle FL	35127	Pleasant Grove AL	36049	Luverne AL
33328	Cooper City FL	33939	E Naples FL	35136	Rockford AL	36054	Millbrook AL
33334	Wilton Manors FL	33939-64	Naples FL	35148	Sumiton AL	36067	Prattville AL
33401-20	W Palm Beach FL	33948-83	Punta Gorda FL	35150	Sylacauga AL	36078	Tallassee AL
33403	Lake Park FL	33952	Port Charlotte FL	35160	Talladega AL	36081	Troy AL
33404	Riviera Beach FL	33957	Sanibel FL	35173	Trussville AL	36083	Tuskegee AL
33406	Lake Clarke Shrs FL	33970-71	Lehigh Acres FL	35180	Warrior AL	36089	Union Springs AL
33408	N Palm Beach FL	34201-10	Bradenton FL	35200-59	Birmingham AL	36092	Wetumpka AL
33411	Royal Palm Bch FL	34208	Samoset FL	35209	Homewood AL	36101-99	MONTGOMERY AL
33420	Palm Beach Grdns FL	34218	Holmes Beach FL	35210	Irondale AL	36201	Saks AL
33424-37	Boynton Beach FL	34223-24	Englewood FL	35214	Forestdale AL	36201-06	Anniston AL
33427-99	Boca Raton FL	34228	Longboat Key FL	35215	Center Point AL	36203	Oxford AL
33430	Belle Glade FL	34230-78	Sarasota FL	35216	Hoover AL	36251	Ashland AL
33440	Clewiston FL	34232	Fruitville FL	35216	Vestavia Hills AL	36264	Heflin AL
33441-43	Deerfield Beach FL	34284-93	Venice FL	35217	Tarrant AL	36265	Jacksonville AL
33444-84	Delray Beach FL	34287	N Port FL	35223	Mountain Brook AL	36272	Piedmont AL
33460-67	Lake Worth FL	34601-14	Brooksville FL	35226	Bluff Park AL	36274	Roanoke AL
33462	Lantana FL	34615-30	Clearwater FL	35228	Midfield AL	36277	Weaver AL
33463	Greenacres City FL	34616	Bellair FL	35243	Cahaba Heights AL	36278	Wedowee AL
33468-79	Jupiter FL	34635	Belleair Bluffs FL	35401-87	Tuscaloosa AL	36301-04	Dothan AL
33469	Tequesta FL	34635	Indian Rocks Bch FL	35404	Holt AL	36310	Abbeville AL
33471	Moore Haven FL	34640-49	Largo FL	35442	Aliceville AL	36322	Daleville AL
33476	Pahokee FL	34652-56	New Port Richey FL	35447	Carrollton AL	36323	Elba AL
33480	Palm Beach FL	34664-66	Pinellas Park FL	35462	Eutaw AL	36330-31	Enterprise AL
33480	Palm Springs FL	34668-74	Port Richey FL	35470	Livingston AL	36340	Geneva AL
33493	South Bay FL	34677	Oldsmar FL	35476	Northport AL	36344	Hartford AL
33509-11	Brandon FL	34682-85	Palm Harbor FL	35501-02	Jasper AL	36345	Headland AL
33513	Bushnell FL	34688-91	Tarpon Springs FL	35549	Carbon Hill AL	36360-61	Ozark AL
33525-26	Dade City FL	34695	Safety Harbor FL	35550	Cordova AL	36401	Evergreen AL
33534	Gibsonton FL	34711-12	Clermont FL	35553	Double Springs AL	36420	Andalusia AL
33539-44	Zephyrhills FL	34731	Fruitland Park FL	35555	Fayette AL	36426	E Brewton AL
		34741-59	Kissimmee FL	35565	Haleyville AL	36426-27	Brewton AL
		34748-89	Leesburg FL	35570	Hamilton AL	36451	Grove Hill AL
		34761	Ocoee FL	35582	Red Bay AL		

ZIP	CITY	ZIP	CITY	ZIP	CITY	ZIP	CITY
36460-61	Monroeville AL	37311-12	Cleveland TN	38053-54	Millington TN	38829	Booneville MS
36467	Opp AL	37321	Dayton TN	38063	Ripley TN	38834	Corinth MS
36502&4	Atmore AL	37322	Decatur TN	38068	Somerville TN	38843	Fulton MS
36507	Bay Minette AL	37327	Dunlap TN	38079	Tiptonville TN	38851	Houston MS
36518	Chatom AL	37331	Etowah TN	38101-99	Memphis TN	38852	Iuka MS
36522	Citronelle AL	37334	Fayetteville TN	38134	Bartlett TN	38860	Okolona MS
36526	Daphne AL	37347	Jasper TN	38138	Germantown TN	38863	Pontotoc MS
36532-33	Fairhope AL	37352	Lynchburg TN	38201	McKenzie TN	38901	Grenada MS
36535-36	Foley AL	37354	Madisonville TN	38225	Dresden TN	38917	Carrollton MS
36541	Grand Bay AL	37355	Manchester TN	38237	Martin TN	38921	Charleston MS
36545	Jackson AL	37367	Pikeville TN	38242	Paris TN	38930	Greenwood MS
36571	Saraland AL	37377	Signal Mountain TN	38257	S Fulton TN	38941	Itta Bena MS
36572	Satsuma AL	37379	Soddy-Daisy TN	38261	Union City TN	38951	Pittsboro MS
36601-99	Mobile AL	37380	S Pittsburg TN	38301-08	Jackson TN	38957	Sumner MS
36610	Prichard AL	37388	Tullahoma TN	38320	Camden TN	38965	Water Vly MS
36611	Chickasaw AL	37398	Winchester TN	38329	Decaturville TN	38967	Winona MS
36619	Tillmans Corner AL	37401-99	Chattanooga TN	38340	Henderson TN	39038	Belzoni MS
36701-02	Selma AL	37412	E Ridge TN	38343	Humboldt TN	39042-43	Brandon MS
36726	Camden AL	37415	Red Bank TN	38344	Huntingdon TN	39046	Canton MS
36732	Demopolis AL	37601-15	Johnson City TN	38351	Lexington TN	39051	Carthage MS
36744	Greensboro AL	37617	Blountville TN	38358	Milan TN	39056-60	Clinton MS
36748	Linden AL	37620-25	Bristol TN	38372	Savannah TN	39059	Crystal Spgs MS
36756	Marion AL	37642	Church Hill TN	38375	Selmer TN	39063	Durant MS
36784	Thomasville AL	37643-44	Elizabethton TN	38382	Trenton TN	39069	Fayette MS
36801-03	Opelika AL	37650	Erwin TN	38401-02	Columbia TN	39074	Forest MS
36830-49	Auburn AL	37659	Jonesboro TN	38462	Hohenwald TN	39083	Hazlehurst MS
36853	Dadeville AL	37660-65	Kingsport TN	38464	Lawrenceburg TN	39090	Kosciusko MS
36854	Valley AL	37683	Mountain City TN	38474	Mount Pleasant TN	39095	Lexington MS
36862	Lafayette AL	37701	Alcoa TN	38478	Pulaski TN	39111-12	Magee MS
36863	Lanett AL	37716	Clinton TN	38485	Waynesboro TN	39113	Mayersville MS
36867-68	Phenix City AL	37725	Dandridge TN	38501-03	Cookeville TN	39114	Mendenhall MS
36904	Butler AL	37738	Gatlinburg TN	38549	Byrdstown TN	39117	Morton MS
36925	York AL	37743-44	Greeneville TN	38551	Celina TN	39120-22	Natchez MS
37015	Ashland City TN	37748	Harriman TN	38555	Crossville TN	39150	Port Gibson MS
37027	Brentwood TN	37756	Huntsville TN	38556	Jamestown TN	39153	Raleigh MS
37030	Carthage TN	37757	Jacksboro TN	38562	Gainesboro TN	39154	Raymond MS
37033	Centerville TN	37760	Jefferson City TN	38570	Livingston TN	39157-58	Ridgeland MS
37036	Charlotte TN	37762	Jellico TN	38583	Sparta TN	39159	Rolling Fork MS
37040-43	Clarksville TN	37763	Kingston TN	38585	Spencer TN	39176	Vaiden MS
37055	Dickson TN	37766	La Follette TN	38603	Ashland MS	39180-82	Vicksburg MS
37058	Dover TN	37771	Lenoir City TN	38606	Batesville MS	39194	Yazoo City MS
37061	Erin TN	37774	Loudon TN	38614	Clarksdale MS	39201-99	JACKSON MS
37064-65	Franklin TN	37801-04	Maryville TN	38632	Hernando MS	39208	Pearl MS
37066	Gallatin TN	37807	Maynardville TN	38635	Holly Springs MS	39218	Richland MS
37072	Goodlettsville TN	37813-16	Morristown TN	38637	Horn Lake MS	39301-09	Meridian MS
37074	Hartsville TN	37821	Newport TN	38646	Marks MS	39327	Decatur MS
37075	Hendersonville TN	37830-31	Oak Ridge TN	38652	New Albany MS	39328	De Kalb MS
37083	Lafayette TN	37840	Oliver Springs TN	38655	Oxford MS	39339	Louisville MS
37086	La Vergne TN	37841	Oneida TN	38663	Ripley MS	39341	Macon MS
37087-88	Lebanon TN	37854	Rockwood TN	38666	Sardis MS	39345	Newton MS
37091	Lewisburg TN	37857	Rogersville TN	38668	Senatobia MS	39348	Paulding MS
37096	Linden TN	37861	Rutledge TN	38671	Southaven MS	39350	Philadelphia MS
37110	McMinnville TN	37862-64	Sevierville TN	38676	Tunica MS	39355	Quitman MS
37122	Mount Juliet TN	37863	Pigeon Forge TN	38701-04	Greenville MS	39367	Waynesboro MS
37129-33	Murfreesboro TN	37869	Sneedville TN	38732-33	Cleveland MS	39401-07	Hattiesburg MS
37148	Portland TN	37874	Sweetwater TN	38737-38	Drew MS	39422	Bay Springs MS
37160	Shelbyville TN	37879	Tazewell TN	38748	Hollandale MS	39428	Collins MS
37166	Smithville TN	37887	Wartburg TN	38751	Indianola MS	39429	Columbia MS
37167	Smyrna TN	37901-99	Knoxville TN	38756	Leland MS	39437	Ellisville MS
37172	Springfield TN	37922	Farragut TN	38762	Mound Bayou MS	39440-42	Laurel MS
37185	Waverly TN	38001	Alamo TN	38769	Rosedale MS	39451	Leakesville MS
37190	Woodbury TN	38008	Bolivar TN	38771	Ruleville MS	39452	Lucedale MS
37201-99	NASHVILLE TN	38012	Brownsville TN	38774	Shelby MS	39462	New Augusta MS
37301	Altamont TN	38017	Collierville TN	38801-03	Tupelo MS	39465	Petal MS
37303	Athens TN	38019	Covington TN	38821	Amory MS	39466	Picayune MS
37307	Benton TN	38024-25	Dyersburg TN	38824	Baldwyn MS	39470	Poplarville MS

ZIP	CITY	ZIP	CITY	ZIP	CITY	ZIP	CITY
39474	Prentiss MS	40353	Mount Sterling KY	41224	Inez KY	42754-55	Leitchfield KY
39475	Purvis MS	40356	Nicholasville KY	41230	Louisa KY	42765	Munfordville KY
39501-07	Gulfport MS	40359	Owenton KY	41240	Paintsville KY	43008	Buckeye Lake OH
39520-29	Bay St Louis MS	40360	Owingsville KY	41301	Campton KY	43015	Delaware OH
39530-35	Biloxi MS	40361	Paris KY	41311	Beattyville KY	43017	Dublin OH
39553	Gautier MS	40380	Stanton KY	41314	Booneville KY	43023	Granville OH
39560	Long Beach MS	40383	Versailles KY	41339	Jackson KY	43026	Hilliard OH
39563	Moss Point MS	40390	Wilmore KY	41465	Salyersville KY	43040	Marysville OH
39563-68	Pascagoula MS	40391	Winchester KY	41472	W Liberty KY	43050	Mount Vernon OH
39564-65	Ocean Springs MS	40403	Berea KY	41501	Pikeville KY	43055-56	Newark OH
39571	Pass Christian MS	40422	Danville KY	41537	Jenkins KY	43056	Heath OH
39576	Waveland MS	40444	Lancaster KY	41653	Prestonsburg KY	43068	Reynoldsburg OH
39577	Wiggins MS	40447	McKee KY	41701	Hazard KY	43078	Urbana OH
39601	Brookhaven MS	40456	Mount Vernon KY	41749	Hyden KY	43081	Westerville OH
39645	Liberty MS	40475	Richmond KY	41822	Hindman KY	43085	Worthington OH
39648	McComb MS	40484	Stanford KY	41858	Whitesburg KY	43105	Baltimore OH
39652	Magnolia MS	40501-99	Lexington KY	42001-03	Paducah KY	43110	Canal Winchester OH
39653	Meadville MS	40601-22	FRANKFORT KY	42023	Bardwell KY	43113	Circleville OH
39654	Monticello MS	40701-02	Corbin KY	42025	Benton KY	43123	Grove City OH
39667	Tylertown MS	40741	London KY	42031	Clinton KY	43125	Groveport OH
39669	Woodville MS	40769	Williamsburg KY	42038	Eddyville KY	43130	Lancaster OH
39701-05	Columbus MS	40823	Cumberland KY	42041	Fulton KY	43138	Logan OH
39730	Aberdeen MS	40831	Harlan KY	42050	Hickman KY	43140	London OH
39735	Ackerman MS	40906	Barbourville KY	42064	Marion KY	43147	Pickerington OH
39759	Starkville MS	40962	Manchester KY	42066	Mayfield KY	43160	Washington C.H. OH
39771	Walthall MS	40965	Middlesboro KY	42071	Murray KY	43201-99	COLUMBUS OH
39773	West Point MS	40977	Pineville KY	42081	Smithland KY	43207	Obetz OH
39822	Coffeeville MS	41001	Alexandria KY	42087	Wickliffe KY	43209	Bexley OH
40004	Bardstown KY	41004	Brooksville KY	42101-04	Bowling Green KY	43212	Grandview Hts OH
40006	Bedford KY	41005	Burlington KY	42129	Edmonton KY	43213	Whitehall OH
40031	La Grange KY	41008	Carrollton KY	42134-35	Franklin KY	43221	Upper Arlington OH
40033	Lebanon KY	41011	Fort Wright KY	42141-42	Glasgow KY	43227	Amberley OH
40047	Mt Washington KY	41011-18	Covington KY	42164	Scottsville KY	43230	Gahanna OH
40050	New Castle KY	41015	Park Hills KY	42167	Tompkinsville KY	43301-02	Marion OH
40065-66	Shelbyville KY	41015	Taylor Mill KY	42210	Brownsville KY	43311	Bellefontaine OH
40069	Springfield KY	41016	Ludlow KY	42211	Cadiz KY	43316	Carey OH
40071	Taylorsville KY	41016	Villa Hills KY	42220	Elkton KY	43326	Kenton OH
40108	Brandenburg KY	41017	Edgewood KY	42240-41	Hopkinsville KY	43338	Mount Gilead OH
40118	Fairdale KY	41017	Fort Mitchell KY	42261	Morgantown KY	43351	Upper Sandusky OH
40121	Fort Knox KY	41017	Lakeside Park KY	42276	Russellville KY	43402	Bowling Green OH
40143	Hardinsburg KY	41018	Elsmere KY	42301-03	Owensboro KY	43410	Clyde OH
40165	Shepherdsville KY	41018	Erlanger KY	42320	Beaver Dam KY	43420	Fremont OH
40175	Vine Grove KY	41031	Cynthiana KY	42327	Calhoun KY	43449	Oak Harbor OH
40201-99	Louisville KY	41040	Falmouth KY	42330	Central City KY	43452	Port Clinton OH
40206	St Matthews KY	41041	Flemingsburg KY	42345	Greenville KY	43460	Rossford OH
40216	Hunters Trace KY	41042	Florence KY	42347	Hartford KY	43502	Archbold OH
40216	Shively KY	41051	Independence KY	42348	Hawesville KY	43506	Bryan OH
40218	Buechel KY	41056	Maysville KY	42408	Dawson Springs KY	43512	Defiance OH
40218	Newburg KY	41064	Mount Olivet KY	42409	Dixon KY	43515	Delta OH
40219	Okolona KY	41071	Southgate KY	42420	Henderson KY	43526	Hicksville OH
40222	Hurstbourne KY	41071-76	Newport KY	42431	Madisonville KY	43537	Maumee OH
40229	Charleswood KY	41073	Bellevue KY	42437	Morganfield KY	43543	Montpelier OH
40229	Hillview KY	41074	Dayton KY	42445	Princeton KY	43545	Napoleon OH
40243	Douglass Hills KY	41075	Fort Thomas KY	42450	Providence KY	43551	Perrysburg OH
40243	Middletown KY	41076	Highland Hts KY	42501-02	Somerset KY	43558	Swanton OH
40258	Pleasure Ridge Pk KY	41095	Warsaw KY	42539	Liberty KY	43560	Sylvania OH
40272	Valley Station KY	41097	Williamstown KY	42602	Albany KY	43567	Wauseon OH
40291	Fern Creek KY	41101-05	Ashland KY	42629	Jamestown KY	43601-99	Toledo OH
40299	Jeffersontown KY	41129	Catlettsburg KY	42633	Monticello KY	43606	Ottawa Hills OH
40311	Carlisle KY	41139	Flatwoods KY	42653	Whitley City KY	43616	Oregon OH
40322	Frenchburg KY	41143	Grayson KY	42701-02	Elizabethtown KY	43701-02	Zanesville OH
40324	Georgetown KY	41144	Greenup KY	42717	Burkesville KY	43713	Barnesville OH
40330	Harrodsburg KY	41164	Olive Hill KY	42718	Campbellsville KY	43723	Byesville OH
40336	Irvine KY	41169	Russell KY	42728	Columbia KY	43724	Caldwell OH
40342	Lawrenceburg KY	41171	Sandy Hook KY	42743	Greensburg KY	43725	Cambridge OH
40351	Morehead KY	41179	Vanceburg KY	42748	Hodgenville KY	43731	Crooksville OH

ZIP	CITY	ZIP	CITY	ZIP	CITY	ZIP	CITY
43756	McConnelsville OH	44125	Garfield Hts OH	44512	Boardman OH	45218	Greenhills OH
43764	New Lexington OH	44126	Fairview Park OH	44514	Poland OH	45224	Finneytown OH
43793	Woodsfield OH	44129	Parma OH	44601	Alliance OH	45227	Mariemont OH
43812	Coshocton OH	44130	Middleburgh Hts OH	44614	Canal Fulton OH	45231	Mount Healthy OH
43832	Newcomerstown OH	44130	Parma Hts OH	44615	Carrollton OH	45236	Deer Park OH
43906	Bellaire OH	44131	Independence OH	44621	Dennison OH	45236	Silverton OH
43907	Cadiz OH	44131	Seven Hills OH	44622	Dover OH	45237	Golf Manor OH
43912	Bridgeport OH	44133	N Royalton OH	44641	Louisville OH	45238	Delhi Hills OH
43920	E Liverpool OH	44136	Strongsville OH	44646-48	Massillon OH	45239	N College Hill OH
43935	Martins Ferry OH	44137	Maple Hts OH	44654	Millersburg OH	45240	Forest Park OH
43938	Mingo Junction OH	44138	Olmsted Falls OH	44657	Minerva OH	45241	Sharonville OH
43947	Shadyside OH	44139	Solon OH	44663	New Philadelphia OH	45242	Blue Ash OH
43950	St Clairsville OH	44140	Bay Village OH	44667	Orrville OH	45242	Montgomery OH
43952	Steubenville OH	44141	Brecksville OH	44672	Sebring OH	45243	Madeira OH
43952	Wintersville OH	44141	Broadview Hts OH	44683	Uhrichsville OH	45246	Springdale OH
43964	Toronto OH	44142	Brook Park OH	44691	Wooster OH	45305	Bellbrook OH
43968	Wellsville OH	44143	Richmond Hts OH	44701-99	Canton OH	45309	Brookville OH
44001	Amherst OH	44144	Brooklyn OH	44720	N Canton OH	45314	Cedarville OH
44004	Ashtabula OH	44145	Westlake OH	44805	Ashland OH	45318	Covington OH
44011	Avon OH	44146	Bedford Hts OH	44811	Bellevue OH	45320	Eaton OH
44012	Avon Lake OH	44146	Bedford OH	44820	Bucyrus OH	45322	Englewood OH
44017	Berea OH	44146	Oakwood OH	44827	Crestline OH	45322	Union OH
44022	Chagrin Falls OH	44202	Aurora OH	44830	Fostoria OH	45323	Enon OH
44022	Moreland Hills OH	44203	Barberton OH	44833	Galion OH	45324	Fairborn OH
44022	S Russell OH	44203	Norton OH	44839	Huron OH	45327	Germantown OH
44024	Chardon OH	44212	Brunswick OH	44842	Loudonville OH	45331	Greenville OH
44030	Conneaut OH	44216	Manchester OH	44857	Norwalk OH	45342-43	Miamisburg OH
44035-39	Elyria OH	44221	Silver Lake OH	44862	Ontario OH	45344	New Carlisle OH
44039	N Ridgeville OH	44221-24	Cuyahoga Falls OH	44870-71	Sandusky OH	45356	Piqua OH
44041	Geneva OH	44224	Stow OH	44875	Shelby OH	45365	Sidney OH
44047	Jefferson OH	44236	Hudson OH	44883	Tiffin OH	45371	Tipp City OH
44052-55	Lorain OH	44240	Kent OH	44890	Willard OH	45373	Troy OH
44054	Sheffield Lake OH	44240	Streetsboro OH	44901-99	Mansfield OH	45377	Vandalia OH
44056	Macedonia OH	44250	Lakemore OH	44904	Lexington OH	45383	W Milton OH
44060	Mentor-on-Lake OH	44254	Lodi OH	45005	Franklin OH	45385	Xenia OH
44060-61	Mentor OH	44256-59	Medina OH	45011	New Miami OH	45387	Yellow Spgs OH
44067	Northfield OH	44260	Mogadore OH	45011-15	Hamilton OH	45401	Beavercreek OH
44070	N Olmsted OH	44262	Monroe Falls OH	45014	Fairfield OH	45401-99	Dayton OH
44074	Oberlin OH	44266	Ravenna OH	45030	Harrison OH	45424	Huber Hts OH
44077	Fairport Harbor OH	44270	Rittman OH	45036	Lebanon OH	45426	Fort McKinley OH
44077	Painesville OH	44278	Tallmadge OH	45040	Mason OH	45426	Trotwood OH
44087	Twinsburg OH	44281	Wadsworth OH	45042-44	Middletown OH	45429	Kettering OH
44089	Vermilion OH	44286	Richfield OH	45050	Monroe OH	45439	Moraine OH
44090	Wellington OH	44288	Windham OH	45056	Oxford OH	45449	W Carrollton OH
44092	Wickliffe OH	44301-99	Akron OH	45065	S Lebanon OH	45459	Centerville OH
44092	Willoughby Hills OH	44313	Fairlawn OH	45066	Springboro OH	45501-99	Springfield OH
44094	Kirtland OH	44319	Portage Lakes OH	45103	Batavia OH	45601	Chillicothe OH
44094	Willowick OH	44321	Copley OH	45107	Blanchester OH	45631	Gallipolis OH
44094-95	Eastlake OH	44405	Campbell OH	45121	Georgetown OH	45638	Coal Grove OH
44094-95	Willoughby OH	44406	Canfield OH	45123	Greenfield OH	45638	Ironton OH
44101-99	Cleveland OH	44408	Columbiana OH	45133	Hillsboro OH	45640	Jackson OH
44105	Newburgh Hts OH	44410	Cortland OH	45140	Loveland OH	45651	McArthur OH
44107	Lakewood OH	44413	E Palestine OH	45150	Milford OH	45662	New Boston OH
44112	E Cleveland OH	44420	Girard OH	45169	Sabina OH	45662	Portsmouth OH
44116	Rocky River OH	44425	Hubbard OH	45177	Wilmington OH	45680	South Point OH
44117	Euclid OH	44432	Lisbon OH	45201-99	Cincinnati OH	45690	Waverly OH
44118	Cleveland Hts OH	44437	McDonald OH	45211	Bridgetown OH	45692	Wellston OH
44118	University Hts OH	44444	Newton Falls OH	45211	Cheviot OH	45693	W Union OH
44120	Shaker Hts OH	44446	Niles OH	45212	Norwood OH	45701	Athens OH
44121	S Euclid OH	44460	Salem OH	45215	Lincoln Hts OH	45714	Belpre OH
44122	Beachwood OH	44471	Struthers OH	45215	Lockland OH	45750	Marietta OH
44122	Warrensville Hts OH	44481	Champion OH	45215	Reading OH	45760	Middleport OH
44124	Highland Hts OH	44481	Lordstown OH	45215	Woodlawn OH	45764	Nelsonville OH
44124	Lyndhurst OH	44481-85	Warren OH	45215	Wyoming OH	45769	Pomeroy OH
44124	Mayfield Hts OH	44501-99	Youngstown OH	45216	Elmwood Place OH	45801-09	Lima OH
44124	Pepper Pike OH	44512	Austintown OH	45217	St Bernard OH	45806	Fort Shawnee OH

ZIP	CITY	ZIP	CITY	ZIP	CITY	ZIP	CITY
45810	Ada OH	46394	Whiting IN	47220	Brownstown IN	48008-12	Birmingham MI
45817	Bluffton OH	46401-99	Gary IN	47240	Greensburg IN	48009	Beverly Hills MI
45822	Celina OH	46405	Lake Station IN	47243	Hanover IN	48015	Center Line MI
45828	Coldwater OH	46406	Black Oak IN	47250	Madison IN	48017	Clawson MI
45833	Delphos OH	46410	Merrillville IN	47265	N Vernon IN	48018	Farmington Hills MI
45839-40	Findlay OH	46506	Bremen IN	47274	Seymour IN	48018	Farmington MI
45865	Minster OH	46514-17	Elkhart IN	47282	Vernon IN	48019	White Lake MI
45872	N Baltimore OH	46526	Goshen IN	47302-08	Muncie IN	48020	Drayton Plains MI
45873	Oakwood OH	46534	Knox IN	47320	Albany IN	48021	E Detroit MI
45875	Ottawa OH	46544-45	Mishawaka IN	47331	Connersville IN	48025	Franklin MI
45879	Paulding OH	46550	Nappanee IN	47336	Dunkirk IN	48030	Hazel Park MI
45885	St Marys OH	46556	Notre Dame IN	47348	Hartford City IN	48031	Seven Harbors MI
45891	Van Wert OH	46563	Plymouth IN	47353	Liberty IN	48035	Lake Orion MI
45895	Wapakoneta OH	46567	Syracuse IN	47356	Middletown IN	48039	Marine City MI
46001	Alexandria IN	46580	Warsaw IN	47362	New Castle IN	48040	Marysville MI
46011-18	Anderson IN	46590	Winona Lake IN	47371	Portland IN	48042	Milford MI
46032	Carmel IN	46601-99	South Bend IN	47374-75	Richmond IN	48043-46	Mount Clemens MI
46034	Cicero IN	46628	Ardmore IN	47390	Union City IN	48047	New Baltimore MI
46036	Elwood IN	46701	Albion IN	47394	Winchester IN	48050	Novi MI
46041	Frankfort IN	46703	Angola IN	47396	Yorktown IN	48053-59	Pontiac MI
46052	Lebanon IN	46706	Auburn IN	47401-08	Bloomington IN	48057	Auburn Hts MI
46060	Clarksville IN	46711	Berne IN	47421	Bedford IN	48060-61	Port Huron MI
46060	Noblesville IN	46714	Bluffton IN	47424	Bloomfield IN	48062	Richmond MI
46072	Tipton IN	46721	Butler IN	47429	Ellettsville IN	48063-809	Rochester MI
46074	Westfield IN	46725	Columbia City IN	47438	Jasonville IN	48065	Romeo MI
46077	Zionsville IN	46733	Decatur IN	47441	Linton IN	48066	Roseville MI
46107	Beech Grove IN	46738	Garrett IN	47446	Mitchell IN	48067-73	Royal Oak MI
46112	Brownsburg IN	46750	Huntington IN	47448	Nashville IN	48069	Pleasant Ridge MI
46122	Danville IN	46755	Kendallville IN	47454	Paoli IN	48070	Huntington Wds MI
46124	Edinburgh IN	46761	Lagrange IN	47460	Spencer IN	48071	Madison Hts MI
46131	Franklin IN	46767	Ligonier IN	47501	Washington IN	48072	Berkley MI
46135	Greencastle IN	46774	Meadowbrook IN	47512	Bicknell IN	48075-76	Southfield MI
46140	Greenfield IN	46774	New Haven IN	47520	Cannelton IN	48076	Lathrup Vlg MI
46142-43	Greenwood IN	46801-99	Fort Wayne IN	47542	Huntingburg IN	48079	St Clair MI
46151	Martinsville IN	46901-04	Kokomo IN	47546-47	Jasper IN	48085	Commerce MI
46158	Mooresville IN	46923	Delphi IN	47553	Loogootee IN	48085	Union Lake MI
46168	Plainfield IN	46928	Fairmount IN	47567	Petersburg IN	48087-311	Utica MI
46173	Rushville IN	46933	Gas City IN	47581	Shoals IN	48088	Walled Lake MI
46176	Shelbyville IN	46938	Jonesboro IN	47586	Tell City IN	48088	Wolverine Lake MI
46184	New Whiteland IN	46947	Logansport IN	47591	Vincennes IN	48089-93	Warren MI
46201-99	INDIANAPOLIS IN	46952-53	Marion IN	47601	Boonville IN	48096	Wixom MI
46224	Speedway IN	46962	N Manchester IN	47610	Chandler IN	48098-99	Troy MI
46226	Lawrence IN	46970-71	Peru IN	47620	Mount Vernon IN	48101	Allen Park MI
46229	Cumberland IN	46975	Rochester IN	47629-30	Newburgh IN	48103-08	Ann Arbor MI
46303	Cedar Lake IN	46989	Upland IN	47635	Rockport IN	48111	Belleville MI
46304	Chesterton IN	46992	Wabash IN	47648	Fort Branch IN	48116	Brighton MI
46304	Porter IN	46996	Winamac IN	47660	Oakland City IN	48117	Carleton MI
46307	Crown Point IN	47001	Aurora IN	47670	Princeton IN	48118	Chelsea MI
46310	Demotte IN	47006	Batesville IN	47701-99	Evansville IN	48120-28	Dearborn MI
46311	Dyer IN	47012	Brookville IN	47801-08	Terre Haute IN	48122	Melvindale MI
46312	E Chicago IN	47025	Greendale IN	47834	Brazil IN	48127	Dearborn Hts MI
46319	Griffith IN	47025	Lawrenceburg IN	47842	Clinton IN	48131	Dundee MI
46320-27	Hammond IN	47040	Rising Sun IN	47872	Rockville IN	48134	Flat Rock MI
46321	Munster IN	47042	Versailles IN	47882	Sullivan IN	48135	Garden City MI
46322	Highland IN	47043	Vevay IN	47901-06	Lafayette IN	48138	Grosse Ille MI
46341	Hebron IN	47102	Austin IN	47906	W Lafayette IN	48141	Inkster MI
46342	Hobart IN	47111	Charlestown IN	47918	Attica IN	48146	Lincoln Park MI
46342	New Chicago IN	47112	Corydon IN	47932	Covington IN	48150-54	Livonia MI
46350	La Porte IN	47118	English IN	47933	Crawfordsville IN	48160	Milan MI
46356	Lowell IN	47130	Clarksville IN	47944	Fowler IN	48161	Monroe MI
46360	Michigan City IN	47130-31	Jeffersonville IN	47951	Kentland IN	48167	Northville MI
46360	Trail Creek IN	47150	New Albany IN	47960	Monticello IN	48170	Plymouth MI
46368	Portage IN	47167	Salem IN	47966	Newport IN	48173	Gibraltar MI
46373	St John IN	47170	Scottsburg IN	47978	Rensselaer IN	48173	Rockwood MI
46375	Schererville IN	47172	Sellersburg IN	47993	Williamsport IN	48174	Romulus MI
46383-84	Valparaiso IN	47201-03	Columbus IN	48001	Algonac MI	48176	Saline MI

ZIP	CITY	ZIP	CITY	ZIP	CITY	ZIP	CITY
48180	Taylor MI	48817	Corunna MI	49426	Hudsonville MI	50047	Carlisle IA
48182	Temperance MI	48820	De Witt MI	49428-29	Jenison MI	50049	Chariton IA
48183	Trenton MI	48823	Meridian MI	49431	Ludington MI	50053	Clive IA
48183	Woodhaven MI	48823-26	E Lansing MI	49440-45	Muskegon MI	50060	Corydon IA
48184-88	Wayne MI	48827	Eaton Rapids MI	49441	Norton Shores MI	50112	Grinnell IA
48185	Westland MI	48837	Grand Ledge MI	49441	Roosevelt Park MI	50115	Guthrie Ctr IA
48187	Canton MI	48838	Greenville MI	49444	Muskegon Hts MI	50125	Indianola IA
48192	Riverview MI	48843	Howell MI	49445	N Muskegon MI	50126	Iowa Falls IA
48192	Wyandotte MI	48846	Ionia MI	49456	Spring Lake MI	50129	Jefferson IA
48195	Southgate MI	48847	Ithica MI	49461	Whitehall MI	50131	Johnston IA
48197-98	Ypsilanti MI	48854	Mason MI	49464	Zeeland MI	50138	Knoxville IA
48198	W Willow MI	48858-59	Mt Pleasant MI	49501-99	Grand Rapids MI	50140	Lamoni IA
48198	Willow Run MI	48867	Owosso MI	49505	Plainfield Hts MI	50144	Leon IA
48201-99	Detroit MI	48875	Portland MI	49506	E Grand Rapids MI	50158	Marshalltown IA
48203	Highland Park MI	48879	St Johns MI	49508	Cutlerville MI	50171	Montezuma IA
48212	Hamtramck MI	48888	Stanton MI	49508	Kentwood MI	50201	Nevada IA
48217	River Rouge MI	48895	Williamston MI	49509	Wyoming MI	50208	Newton IA
48220	Ferndale MI	48901-99	LANSING MI	49601	Cadillac MI	50211	Norwalk IA
48225	Grosse Pointe MI	48906	Delta MI	49615	Bellaire MI	50213	Osceola IA
48225	Harper Woods MI	48912	Hopwood Acres MI	49617	Beulah MI	50219	Pella IA
48229	Ecorse MI	48917	Waverly MI	49646	Kalkaska MI	50220	Perry IA
48237	Oak Park MI	48917	Windemere MI	49651	Lake City MI	50248	Story City IA
48302-04	Bloomfield Hills MI	49001-09	Kalamazoo MI	49654	Leland MI	50265	W Des Moines IA
48310	Sterling Hts MI	49010	Allegan MI	49660	Manistee MI	50273	Winterset IA
48320	Keego Harbor MI	49012	Augusta MI	49677	Reed City MI	50301	Pleasant Hill IA
48413	Bad Axe MI	49015	Springfield MI	49684	Traverse City MI	50301-99	DES MOINES IA
48420	Clio MI	49015-17	Battle Creek MI	49707	Alpena MI	50311	Windsor Hts IA
48423	Davison MI	49022	Benton Harbor MI	49709	Atlanta MI	50322	Urbandale IA
48429	Durand MI	49031	Cassopolis MI	49712	Boyne City MI	50401	Mason City IA
48430	Fenton MI	49032	Centreville MI	49720	Charlevoix MI	50421	Belmond IA
48433	Flushing MI	49036	Coldwater MI	49721	Cheboygan MI	50428	Clear Lake IA
48439	Grand Blanc MI	49041	Comstock MI	49735	Gaylord MI	50436	Forest City IA
48442	Holly MI	49047	Dowagiac MI	49738	Grayling MI	50438	Garner IA
48446	Lapeer MI	49058	Hastings MI	49770	Petoskey MI	50441	Hampton IA
48453	Marlette MI	49068	Marshall MI	49779	Rogers City MI	50459	Northwood IA
48458	Mount Morris MI	49078	Otsego MI	49781	St Ignace MI	50461	Osage IA
48471	Sandusky MI	49079	Paw Paw MI	49783	Sault Ste Marie MI	50501	Fort Dodge IA
48473	Swartz Creek MI	49080	Plainwell MI	4980-82	St Clair Shores MI	50511	Algona IA
48501-32	Flint MI	49085	St Joseph MI	49801	Iorn Mountain MI	50525	Clarion IA
48509	Burton MI	49090	South Haven MI	49801	Kingsford MI	50529	Dakota City IA
48601	Buena Vista MI	49091	Sturgis MI	49829	Escanaba MI	50533	Eagle Grove IA
48601-08	Saginaw MI	49093	Three Rivers MI	49837	Gladstone MI	50536	Emmetsburg IA
48603	Shields MI	49107	Buchanan MI	49849	Ishpeming MI	50548	Humboldt IA
48616	Chesaning MI	49117	New Buffalo MI	49854	Manistique MI	50574	Pocahontas IA
48617	Clare MI	49120	Bertrand MI	49855	Marquette MI	50579	Rockwell City IA
48624	Gladwin MI	49120	Niles MI	49858	Menominee MI	50583	Sac City IA
48625	Harrison MI	49201-04	Jackson MI	49862	Munising MI	50588	Storm Lake IA
48640-41	Midland MI	49221	Adrian MI	49866	Negaunee MI	50595	Webster City IA
48647	Mio MI	49224	Albion MI	49868	Newberry MI	50602	Allison IA
48653	Roscommon MI	49228	Blissfield MI	49870	Norway MI	50613	Cedar Falls IA
48658	Standish MI	49242	Hillsdale MI	49911	Bessemer MI	50616	Charles City IA
48661	West Branch MI	49247	Hudson MI	49913	Laurium MI	50627	Eldora IA
48706	Bangor MI	49286	Tecumseh MI	49920	Crystal Falls MI	50638	Grundy Center IA
48706-08	Bay City MI	49304	Baldwin MI	49924	Eagle River MI	50644	Independence IA
48722	Bridgeport MI	49307	Big Rapids MI	49930	Hancock MI	50659-61	New Hampton IA
48723	Caro MI	49319	Cedar Spgs MI	49931	Houghton MI	50662	Oelwein IA
48724	Carrollton MI	49331	Lowell MI	49938	Iornwood MI	50677	Waverly IA
48730	E Tawas MI	49341	Rockford MI	49946	L'Anse MI	50701-99	Waterloo IA
48732	Essexville MI	49345	Sparta MI	49953	Ontonagon MI	50707	Evansdale IA
48734	Frankenmuth MI	49349	White Cloud MI	49968	Wakefield MI	50801	Creston IA
48741	Harrisville MI	49404	Coopersville MI	50003	Adel IA	50833	Bedford IA
48763	Tawas City MI	49412	Fremont MI	50009	Altoona IA	50841	Corning IA
48768	Vassar MI	49417	Grand Haven MI	50021	Ankeny IA	50849	Greenfield IA
48801	Alma MI	49418	Grandville MI	50022	Atlantic IA	50854	Mount Ayr IA
48809	Belding MI	49420	Hart MI	50025	Audubon IA	51012	Cherokee IA
48813	Charlotte MI	49422-24	Holland MI	50036	Boone IA	51023	Hawarden IA

ZIP	CITY	ZIP	CITY	ZIP	CITY	ZIP	CITY
51031	Le Mars IA	52742	De Witt IA	53401-99	Racine WI	54303	Howard WI
51040	Onawa IA	52748	Eldridge IA	53511	Beloit WI	54304	Ashwaubenon WI
51041	Orange City IA	52753	Le Claire IA	53520	Brodhead WI	54401	Wausau WI
51101-99	Sioux City IA	52761	Muscatine IA	53530	Darlington WI	54409	Antigo WI
51201	Sheldon IA	52772	Tipton IA	53532	De Forest WI	54449	Marshfield WI
51245	Primghar IA	52776	W Liberty IA	53533	Dodgeville WI	54451	Medford WI
51246	Rock Rapids IA	52778	Wilton IA	53534	Edgerton WI	54452	Merrill WI
51247	Rock Valley IA	52801-99	Davenport IA	53536	Evansville WI	54455	Mosinee WI
51249	Sibley IA	53005	Brookfield WI	53538	Fort Atkinson WI	54456	Neillsville WI
51250	Sioux Center IA	53012	Cedarburg WI	53545-47	Janesville WI	54457	Nekoosa WI
51301	Spencer IA	53014	Chilton WI	53549	Jefferson WI	54467	Plover WI
51334	Estherville IA	53018	Delafield WI	53551	Lake Mills WI	54474	Rothschild WI
51360	Spirit Lake IA	53022	Germantown WI	53558	McFarland WI	54481	Stevens Point WI
51401	Carroll IA	53024	Grafton WI	53562	Middleton WI	54487	Tomahawk WI
51442	Denison IA	53027	Hartford WI	53563	Milton WI	54493	Wisconsin Rpds WI
51445	Ida Grove IA	53029	Hartland WI	53566	Monroe WI	54501	Rhinelander WI
51501-03	Council Bluffs IA	53032	Horicon WI	53572	Mount Horeb WI	54520	Crandon WI
51510	Carter Lake IA	53039	Juneau WI	53575	Fitchburg WI	54521	Eagle River WI
51534	Glenwood IA	53042	Kiel WI	53575	Oregon WI	54534	Hurley WI
51537	Harlan IA	53050	Mayville WI	53581	Richland Ctr WI	54552	Park Falls WI
51546	Logan IA	53051	Menomonee Falls WI	53583	Sauk City WI	54555	Phillips WI
51555	Missouri Vly IA	53061	New Holstein WI	53589	Stoughton WI	54601-03	La Crosse WI
51566	Red Oak IA	53066	Oconomowoc WI	53590	Sun Prairie WI	54610	Alma WI
51601	Shenandoah IA	53072	Pewaukee WI	53592	Verona WI	54615	Black River Falls WI
51632	Clarinda IA	53073	Plymouth WI	53597	Waunakee WI	54650	Onalaska WI
51652	Sidney IA	53074	Port Washington WI	53701-99	MADISON WI	54656	Sparta WI
52001-04	Dubuque IA	53080	Saukville WI	53716	Monona WI	54660	Tomah WI
52040	Dyersville IA	53081-83	Sheboygan WI	53805	Boscobel WI	54665	Viroqua WI
52043	Elkader IA	53085	Sheboygan Falls WI	53813	Lancaster WI	54669	W Salem WI
52057	Manchester IA	53089	Sussex WI	53818	Platteville WI	54701-03	Eau Claire WI
52060	Maquoketa IA	53092	Mequon WI	53821	Prairie du Chien WI	54720	Altoona WI
52101	Decorah IA	53092	Thiensville WI	53901	Portage WI	54724	Bloomer WI
52136	Cresco IA	53094	Watertown WI	53913	Baraboo WI	54729	Chippewa Falls WI
52172	Waukon IA	53095	West Bend WI	53916	Beaver Dam WI	54736	Durand WI
52175	W Union IA	53105	Burlington WI	53925	Columbus WI	54751	Menomonie WI
52205	Anamosa IA	53110	Cudahy WI	53934	Friendship WI	54755	Mondovi WI
52208	Belle Plaine IA	53115	Delavan WI	53948	Mauston WI	54773	Whitehall WI
52233	Hiawatha IA	53121	Elkhorn WI	53949	Montello WI	54806	Ashland WI
52240-46	Iowa City IA	53122	Elm Grove WI	53959	Reedsburg WI	54810	Balsam Lake WI
52241	Coralville IA	53129	Greendale WI	53963	Waupun WI	54812	Barron WI
52301	Marengo IA	53130	Hales Corners WI	53965	Wisconsin Dells WI	54840	Grantsburg WI
52302	Marion IA	53132	Franklin WI	54010-11	Ellsworth WI	54843	Hayward WI
52310	Monticello IA	53140-42	Kenosha WI	54016	Hudson WI	54848	Ladysmith WI
52314	Mount Vernon IA	53147	Lake Geneva WI	54017	New Richmond WI	54868	Rice Lake WI
52339	Tama IA	53149	Mukwonago WI	54021	Prescott WI	54871	Shell Lake WI
52341-42	Toledo IA	53150	Muskego WI	54022	River Falls WI	54880	Superior WI
52349	Vinton IA	53151	New Berlin WI	54110	Brillion WI	54891	Washburn WI
52353	Washington IA	53154	Oak Creek WI	54113	Combined Locks WI	54901-04	Oshkosh WI
52401-99	Cedar Rapids IA	53172	S Milwaukee WI	54115	De Pere WI	54911-15	Appleton WI
52501	Ottumwa IA	53177	Sturtevant WI	54121	Florence WI	54923	Berlin WI
52531	Albia IA	53181	Twin Lakes WI	54130	Kaukauna WI	54929	Clintonville WI
52537	Bloomfield IA	53182	Union Grove WI	54135	Keshena WI	54935	Fond du Lac WI
52544	Centerville IA	53186-88	Waukesha WI	54136	Kimberly WI	54935	N Fond du Lac WI
52556	Fairfield IA	53190	Whitewater WI	54140	Little Chute WI	54941	Green Lake WI
52565	Keosauqua IA	53201-99	Milwaukee WI	54143	Marinette WI	54952	Menasha WI
52577	Oskaloosa IA	53207	St Francis WI	54153	Oconto WI	54956	Neenah WI
52591	Sigourney IA	53209	Glendale WI	54157	Peshtigo WI	54961	New London WI
52601	Burlington IA	53211	Shorewood WI	54165	Seymour WI	54963	Omro WI
52627	Fort Madison IA	53214	W Allis WI	54166	Shawano WI	54971	Ripon WI
52632	Keokuk IA	53214	W Milwaukee WI	54201	Algoma WI	54981	Waupaca WI
52641-42	Mt Pleasant IA	53217	Bayside WI	54216	Kewaunee WI	54982	Wautoma WI
52653	Wapello IA	53217	Fox Point WI	54220	Manitowoc WI	55001	Afton MN
52655	W Burlington IA	53217	Whitefish Bay WI	54235	Sturgeon Bay WI	55003	Bayport MN
52722	Bettendorf IA	53220	Greenfield WI	54241	Two Rivers WI	55005	E Bethel MN
52730	Camanche IA	53223	Brown Deer WI	54301	Allouez WI	55008	Cambridge MN
52732	Clinton IA	53226	Wauwatosa WI	54301-99	Green Bay WI	55009	Cannon Falls MN

ZIP	CITY	ZIP	CITY	ZIP	CITY	ZIP	CITY
55012	Center City MN	55369	Maple Grove MN	56058	Le Sueur MN	57006	Brookings SD
55014	Circle Pines MN	55369	Osseo MN	56071	New Prague MN	57013	Canton SD
55014	Lino Lakes MN	55371	Princeton MN	56073	New Ulm MN	57025	Elk Point SD
55016	Cottage Grove MN	55372	Prior Lake MN	56081	St James MN	57028	Flandreau SD
55021	Faribault MN	55378	Savage MN	56082	St Peter MN	57042	Madison SD
55024	Farmington MN	55379	Shakopee MN	56085	Sleepy Eye MN	57052	Olivet SD
55025	Forest Lake MN	55387	Waconia MN	56093	Waseca MN	57053	Parker SD
55033	Hastings MN	55391	Deephaven MN	56101	Windom MN	57058	Salem SD
55038	Hugo MN	55391	Wayzata MN	56142	Ivanhoe MN	57066	Tyndall SD
55041	Lake City MN	55401-99	Minneapolis MN	56143	Jackson MN	57069	Vermillion SD
55042	Lake Elmo MN	55410	Edina MN	56156	Luverne MN	57078	Yankton SD
55044	Lakeville MN	55418	St Anthony MN	56164	Pipestone MN	57101-99	Sioux Falls SD
55051	Mora MN	55420	Bloomington MN	56172	Slayton MN	57201-02	Watertown SD
55055	Newport MN	55421	Columbia Hts MN	56187	Worthington MN	57225	Clark SD
55057	Northfield MN	55422	Robbinsdale MN	56201	Willmar MN	57226	Clear Lake SD
55060	Owatonna MN	55423	Richfield MN	56215	Benson MN	57231	De Smet SD
55063	Pine City MN	55426	St Louis Pk MN	56241	Granite Falls MN	57241	Hayti SD
55066	Red Wing MN	55427	Golden Vly MN	56256	Madison MN	57252	Milbank SD
55068	Rosemount MN	55428	Crystal MN	56258	Marshall MN	57262	Sisseton SD
55071	St Paul Park MN	55428	New Hope MN	56265	Montevideo MN	57274	Webster SD
55075	Inver Grove Hts MN	55429	Brooklyn Ctr MN	56267	Morris MN	57301	Mitchell SD
55075-77	S St Paul MN	55432	Fridley MN	56277	Olivia MN	57311	Alexandria SD
55082	Oak Park Hts MN	55432	Mounds View MN	56278	Ortonville MN	57313	Armour SD
55082-83	Stillwater MN	55432	Spring Lake Pk MN	56283	Redwood Falls MN	57325	Chamberlain SD
55101-99	St PAUL MN	55433	Coon Rapids MN	56296	Wheaton MN	57341	Gann Valley SD
55108	Falcon Hts MN	55434	Blaine MN	56301-04	St Cloud MN	57345	Highmore SD
55109	Maplewood MN	55441	Plymouth MN	56308	Alexandria MN	57349	Howard SD
55109	N St. Paul MN	55443	Brooklyn Pk MN	56329	Foley MN	57350	Huron SD
55112	Arden Hills MN	55604	Grand Marais MN	56334	Glenwood MN	57356	Lake Andes SD
55112	New Brighton MN	55614	Silver Bay MN	56345	Little Falls MN	57362	Miller SD
55113	Roseville MN	55616	Two Harbors MN	56347	Long Prairie MN	57368	Plankinton SD
55115	Mahtomedi MN	55705	Aurora MN	56353	Milaca MN	57382	Wessington Spgs SD
55117	Little Canada MN	55718	Carlton MN	56374	St Joseph MN	57385	Woonsocket SD
55118	Mendota Hts MN	55719	Chisholm MN	56377	Sartell MN	57401-02	Aberdeen SD
55118	W St Paul MN	55720	Cloquet MN	56378	Saulk Centre MN	57430	Britton SD
55120	Eagan MN	55731	Ely MN	56379	Saulk Rapids MN	57438	Faulkton SD
55124	Apple Valley MN	55734	Eveleth MN	56381	White Bear Lake MN	57442	Gettysburg SD
55125	Woodbury MN	55741	Gilbert MN	56387	Waite Park MN	57451	Ipswich SD
55126	Shoreview MN	55744	Grand Rapids MN	56401	Baxter MN	57456	Leola SD
55127	N Oaks MN	55746-47	Hibbing MN	56401	Brainerd MN	57469	Redfield SD
55127	Vadnais Hts MN	55750	Hoyt Lakes MN	56431	Aitkin MN	57472	Selby SD
55128	Oakdale MN	55768	Mountain Iron MN	56470	Park Rapids MN	57501	PIERRE SD
55303	Anoka MN	55792	Virginia MN	56479	Staples MN	57523	Burke SD
55303	Dayton MN	55801-99	Duluth MN	56482	Wadena MN	57532	Fort Pierre SD
55304	Andover MN	55810	Proctor MN	56484	Walker MN	57543	Kadoka SD
55304	Ham Lake MN	55811	Hermantown MN	56501-02	Detroit Lakes MN	57544	Kennebec SD
55313	Buffalo MN	55901-04	Rochester MN	56510	Ada MN	57551	Martin SD
55316	Champlin MN	55912	Austin MN	56520	Breckenridge MN	57559	Murdo SD
55317	Chanhassen MN	55921	Caledonia MN	56529	Dilworth MN	57564	Onida SD
55318	Chaska MN	55944	Kasson MN	56531	Elbow Lake MN	57567	Philip SD
55323	Orono MN	55946	Kenyon MN	56537	Fergus Falls MN	57579	White River SD
55330	Elk River MN	55947	La Crescent MN	56557	Mahnomen MN	57580	Winner SD
55331	Excelsior MN	55955	Mantorville MN	56560	Moorhead MN	57601	Mobridge SD
55334	Gaylord MN	55965	Preston MN	56601-19	Bemidji MN	57620	Bison SD
55336	Glencoe MN	55975	Spring Valley MN	56621	Bagley MN	57623	Dupree SD
55337	Burnsville MN	55976	Stewartville MN	56623	Baudette MN	57641	McIntosh SD
55340	Corcoran MN	55981	Wabasha MN	56649	Intern'l Falls MN	57646	Mound City SD
55343-47	Hopkins MN	55987	Goodview MN	56679	S Int'l Falls MN	57656	Timber Lake SD
55344	Eden Prairie MN	55987	Winona MN	56701	Thief River Falls MN	57701-09	Rapid City SD
55345	Minnetonka MN	56001	Mankato MN	56716	Crookston MN	57717	Belle Fourche SD
55350	Hutchinson MN	56001-02	N Mankato MN	56721	E Grand Forks MN	57719	Box Elder SD
55355	Litchfield MN	56007	Albert Lea MN	56728	Hallock MN	57720	Buffalo SD
55357	Jordon MN	56011	Belle Plaine MN	56750	Red Lake Falls MN	57730	Custer SD
55359	Independence MN	56013	Blue Earth MN	56751	Roseau MN	57732	Deadwood SD
55362	Monticello MN	56031	Fairmont MN	56762	Warren MN	57747	Hot Springs SD
55364	Mound MN	56057	Le Center MN	57005	Brandon SD	57754	Lead SD

ZIP	CITY	ZIP	CITY	ZIP	CITY	ZIP	CITY
57783	Spearfish SD	59072	Roundup MT	60025	Glenview IL	60162	Hillside IL
57785	Sturgis SD	59074	Ryegate MT	60030	Grayslake IL	60163	Berkeley IL
58032	Forman ND	59087	Winnett MT	60031	Gurnee IL	60164	Northlake IL
58045	Hillsboro ND	59101-99	Billings MT	60033	Harvard IL	60165	Stone Park IL
58054	Lisbon ND	59201	Wolf Point MT	60035	Highland Pk IL	60171	River Grove IL
58072	Valley City ND	59215	Circle MT	60040	Highwood IL	60172-295	Roselle IL
58074-7	Wahpeton ND	59230	Glasgow MT	60042	Island Lake IL	60174-75	St Charles IL
58078	W Fargo ND	59254	Plentywood MT	60043	Kenilworth IL	60176	Schiller Park IL
58102-99	Fargo ND	59263	Scobey MT	60044	Lake Bluff IL	60177	S Elgin IL
58201-07	Grand Forks ND	59270	Sidney MT	60045	Lake Forest IL	60178	Sycamore IL
58220	Cavalier ND	59301	Miles City MT	60046	Lindenhurst IL	60181	Villa Park IL
58230	Finley ND	59313	Baker MT	60047	Lake Zurich IL	60185	W Chicago IL
58237	Grafton ND	59317	Broadus MT	60048	Libertyville IL	60185	Winfield IL
58249	Langdon ND	59324	Ekalaka MT	60050	McHenry IL	60187	Pleasant Hill IL
58301	Devils Lake ND	59327	Forsyth MT	60053	Morton Grove IL	60187-89	Wheaton IL
58318	Bottineau ND	59330	Glendive MT	60056	Mt Prospect IL	60188	Carol Stream IL
58324	Cando ND	59337	Jordan MT	60060	Mundelein IL	60191	Wood Dale IL
58341	Harvey ND	59349	Terry MT	60061	Vernon Hills IL	60194	Schaumburg IL
58344	Lakota ND	59353	Wibaux MT	60062	Northbrook IL	60196	Hoffman Ests IL
58351	Minnewaukan ND	59401-06	Great Falls MT	60064	N Chicago IL	60201-99	Evanston IL
58356	New Rockford ND	59422	Choteau MT	60067	Inverness IL	60301-99	Oak Park IL
58367	Rolla ND	59425	Conrad MT	60067	Palatine IL	60305	River Forest IL
58368	Rugby ND	59427	Cut Bank MT	60068	Park Ridge IL	60402	Berwyn IL
58401-02	Jamestown ND	59442	Fort Benton MT	60069	Lincolnshire IL	60402	Stickney IL
58413	Ashley ND	59457	Lewistown MT	60070	Prospect Hts IL	60406	Blue Island IL
58421	Carrington ND	59474	Shelby MT	60073	Round Lake Pk IL	60406	Dixmoor IL
58425	Cooperstown ND	59479	Stanford MT	60073	Round Lake Bch IL	60408	Braidwood IL
58436	Ellendale ND	59501	Havre MT	60073	Round Lake IL	60409	Calumet City IL
58438	Fessenden ND	59522	Chester MT	60076-77	Skokie IL	60410	Channahon IL
58458	La Moure ND	59523	Chinook MT	60084	Wauconda IL	60411	Chicago Hts IL
58463	McClusky ND	59538	Malta MT	60085	Park City IL	60411	Sauk Village IL
58482	Steele ND	59601-26	Helena MT	60085-87	Waukegan IL	60411	S Chicago Hts IL
58501	BISMARCK ND	59632	Boulder MT	60090	Buffalo Grove IL	60415	Chicago Ridge IL
58523	Beulah ND	59644	Townsend MT	60090	Wheeling IL	60416	Coal City IL
58529	Carson ND	59645		60091	Wilmette IL	60417	Crete IL
58530	Center ND		White Sulphur Spgs MT	60093	Northfield IL	60419	Dolton IL
58538	Fort Yates ND	59701-03	Butte MT	60093	Winnetka IL	60420	Dwight IL
58552	Linton ND	59711	Anaconda MT	60096	Winthrop Harbor IL	60422	Flossmoor IL
58554	Mandan ND	59715-16	Bozeman MT	60097	Wonder Lake IL	60423	Frankfort IL
58561	Napoleon ND	59722	Deer Lodge MT	60098	Woodstock IL	60425	Glenwood IL
58571	Stanton ND	59725	Dillon MT	60099	Zion IL	60426	Harvey IL
58577	Washburn ND	59755	Virginia City MT	60101	Addison IL	60426	Markham IL
58601-02	Dickinson ND	59801-07	Missoula MT	60102	Algonquin IL	60429	Hazel Crest IL
58620	Amidon ND	59840	Hamilton MT	60103	Bartlett IL	60430	Homewood IL
58621	Beach ND	59858	Philipsburg MT	60103	Hanover Park IL	60431-36	Joliet IL
58623	Bowman ND	59860	Polson MT	60103	Streamwood IL	60435	Crest Hill IL
58639	Hettinger ND	59872	Superior MT	60108	Bloomingdale IL	60438	Lansing IL
58642	Manning ND	59873	Thompson Falls MT	60110	Carpentersville IL	60439	Bolingbrook IL
58645	Medora ND	59901-03	Kalispell MT	60115	De Kalb IL	60439	Lemont IL
58646	Mott ND	59912	Columbia Falls MT	60118	Dundee IL	60441	Lockport IL
58701-04	Minot ND	59923	Libby MT	60118	E Dundee IL	60441	Romeoville IL
58721	Bowbells ND	59937	Whitefish MT	60120-23	Elgin IL	60443	Matteson IL
58730	Crosby ND	60002	Antioch IL	60126	Elmhurst IL	60445	Crestwood IL
58761	Mohall ND	60004-09	Arlington Hts IL	60130	Forest Park IL	60445	Midlothian IL
58784	Stanley ND	60007	Elk Grove Vlg IL	60131	Franklin Park IL	60448	Mokena IL
58788	Towner ND	60008	Rolling Meadows IL	60134	Geneva IL	60450	Morris IL
58801-02	Williston ND	60010	Barrington IL	60135	Genoa IL	60451	New Lenox IL
58854	Watford City ND	60013	Cary IL	60137	Glen Ellyn IL	60452	Oak Forest IL
59011	Big Timber MT	60014	Crystal Lake IL	60137	Glendale Hts IL	60453-59	Oak Lawn IL
59019	Columbus MT	60015	Deerfield IL	60143	Itasca IL	60455	Bridge View IL
59034	Hardin MT	60016-17	Des Plaines IL	60148	Lombard IL	60456	Hometown IL
59036	Harlowton MT	60018	Rosemont IL	60152	Marengo IL	60457	Hickory Hills IL
59038	Hysham MT	60020	Fox Lake IL	60153	Broadview IL	60458	Justice IL
59044	Laurel MT	60021	Fox River Grove IL	60153	Westchester IL	60459	Burbank IL
59047	Livingston MT	60022	Glencoe IL	60153-54	Maywood IL	60461	Olympia Fields IL
59068	Red Lodge MT	60025	Bellwood IL	60160-65	Melrose Park IL	60462	Orland Park IL

ZIP	CITY	ZIP	CITY	ZIP	CITY	ZIP	CITY
60463	Palos Hts IL	60970	Watseka IL	61611	Creve Coeur IL	62286	Sparta IL
60464	Palos Park IL	61008	Belvidere IL	61611	E Peoria IL	62293	Trenton IL
60465	Palos Hills IL	61021	Dixon IL	61614	Peoria Hts IL	62294	Troy IL
60466	Park Forest IL	61032	Freeport IL	61701-04	Bloomington IL	62298	Waterloo IL
60466	University Pk IL	61036	Galena IL	61727	Clinton IL	62301-06	Quincy IL
60469	Posen IL	61053	Mount Carroll IL	61738	El Paso IL	62321	Carthage IL
60471	Richton Park IL	61054	Mount Morris IL	61739	Fairbury IL	62341	Hamilton IL
60472	Robbins IL	61061	Oregon IL	61752	Le Roy IL	62353	Mt Sterling IL
60473	S Holland IL	61064	Polo IL	61761	Normal IL	62363	Pittsfield IL
60475	Steger IL	61068	Rochelle IL	61764	Pontiac IL	62401	Effingham IL
60476	Thornton IL	61071	Rock Falls IL	61801	Urbana IL	62420	Casey IL
60477		61074	Savanna IL	61820-21	Champaign IL	62439	Lawrenceville IL
	Country Club Hills IL	61080	S Beloit IL	61832-34	Danville IL	62441	Marshall IL
60477-78	Tinley Park IL	61081	Sterling IL	61846	Georgetown IL	62448	Newton IL
60480	Willow Springs IL	61101-99	Rockford IL	61856	Monticello IL	62450	Olney IL
60481	Wilmington IL	61109	Ken Rock IL	61866	Rantoul IL	62454	Robinson IL
60482	Worth IL	61111	Loves Park IL	61883	Westville IL	62468	Toledo IL
60501	Summit IL	61111	N Park IL	61910	Arcola IL	62471	Vandalia IL
60504-07	Aurora IL	61201-04	Rock Island IL	61920	Charleston IL	62521-26	Decatur IL
60510	Batavia IL	61231	Aledo IL	61938	Mattoon IL	62549	Mount Zion IL
60513	Brookfield IL	61238	Cambridge IL	61944	Paris IL	62557	Pana IL
60514	Clarendon Hills IL	61240	Coal Valley IL	61951	Sullivan IL	62565	Shelbyville IL
60515-17	Downers Grove IL	61241	Green Rock IL	61953	Tuscola IL	62568	Taylorville IL
60515	Lake in Woods IL	61244	E Moline IL	61956	Villa Grove IL	62615	Auburn IL
60517	Woodridge IL	61252	Fulton IL	62002	Alton IL	62618	Beardstown IL
60521	Burr Ridge IL	61254	Geneseo IL	62023	Cahokia IL	62626	Carlinville IL
60521	Oak Brook IL	61254	Phoenix IL	62024	E Alton IL	62629	Chatham IL
60521-22	Hinsdale IL	61264	Milan IL	62025	Edwardsville IL	62644	Havana IL
60525	Countryside IL	61265	Moline IL	62033	Gillespie IL	62650-51	Jacksonville IL
60525	Indian Head Pk IL	61270	Morrison IL	62034	Glen Carbon IL	62656	Lincoln IL
60525	La Grange IL	61282	Silvis IL	62035	Godfrey IL	62664	Mason City IL
60532	Lisle IL	61301	La Salle IL	62040	Granite City IL	62675	Petersburg IL
60534	Lyons IL	61310	Amboy IL	62040	Pontoon Beach IL	62681	Rushville IL
60538	Montgomery IL	61327	Hennepin IL	62047	Hardin IL	62690	Virden IL
60542	N Aurora IL	61341	Marseilles IL	62049	Hillsboro IL	62691	Virginia IL
60543	Oswego IL	61342	Mendota IL	62052	Jerseyville IL	62694	Winchester IL
60544	Plainfield IL	61348	Oglesby IL	62056	Litchfield IL	62701-99	SPRINGFIELD IL
60545	Plano IL	61350	Ottawa IL	62060	Madison IL	62801	Centralia IL
60546	N Riverside IL	61354	Peru IL	62075	Nokomis IL	62806	Albion IL
60546	Riverside IL	61356	Princeton IL	62088	Staunton IL	62812	Benton IL
60548	Sandwich IL	61362	Spring Valley IL	62090	Venice IL	62821	Carmi IL
60555	Warrenville IL	61364	Streator IL	62092	White Hall IL	62822	Christopher IL
60558	Western Spgs IL	61401-02	Galesburg IL	62095	Wood River IL	62832	Du Quoin IL
60559	Darien IL	61410	Abingdon IL	62201-08	E St Louis IL	62837	Fairfield IL
60559	Westmont IL	61411	Eldorado IL	62204	Washington Pk IL	62839	Flora IL
60560	Yorkville IL	61422	Bushnell IL	62206	Carrollton IL	62858	Louisville IL
60563-67	Naperville IL	61434	Galva IL	62208	Fairview Hts IL	62859	McLeansboro IL
60601-99	Chicago IL	61443	Kewanee IL	62220-25	Belleville IL	62863	Mount Carmel IL
60627	Riverdale IL	61448	Knoxville IL	62221	Swansea IL	62864	Mount Vernon IL
60633	Burnham IL	61455	Macomb IL	62230	Breese IL	62881	Salem IL
60642	Evergreen Pk IL	61462	Monmouth IL	62231	Carlyle IL	62896	W Frankfort IL
60643	Calumet Park IL	61469	Oquawka IL	62232	Caseyville IL	62901-03	Carbondale IL
60645	Lincolnwood IL	61483	Toulon IL	62233	Chester IL	62906	Anna IL
60648	Niles IL	61520	Canton IL	62234	Collinsville IL	62914	Cairo IL
60650	Cicero IL	61523	Chillicothe IL	62236	Columbia IL	62918	Carterville IL
60656	Harwood Hts IL	61530	Eureka IL	62239	Dupo IL	62931	Elizabethtown IL
60656	Norridge IL	61531	Farmington IL	62243	Freeburg IL	62938	Golconda IL
60658	Alsip IL	61537	Henry IL	62246	Greenville IL	62946	Harrisburg IL
60901	Kankakee IL	61540	Lacon IL	62249	Highland IL	62948	Herrin IL
60914	Bourbonnais IL	61542	Lewistown IL	62254	Lebanon IL	62951	Johnston City IL
60915	Bradley IL	61550	Morton IL	62257	Marissa IL	62952	Jonesboro IL
60936	Gibson City IL	61554	Marquette Hts IL	62258	Mascoutah IL	62959	Marion IL
60942	Hoopeston IL	61554-55	Pekin IL	62260	Millstadt IL	62960	Metropolis IL
60950	Manteno IL	61571	Washington IL	62263	Nashville IL	62963	Mound City IL
60954	Momence IL	61601-99	Peoria IL	62269	O'Fallon IL	62966	Murphysboro IL
60957	Paxton IL	61607	Bartonville IL	62274	Pinckneyville IL	62984	Shawneetown IL

ZIP	CITY	ZIP	CITY	ZIP	CITY	ZIP	CITY
62995	Vienna IL	63334	Bowling Green MO	64076	Odessa MO	65360	Windsor MO
63010	Arnold MO	63353	Louisiana MO	64079	Platte City MO	65401	Rolla MO
63011	Ellisville MO	63361		64080	Pleasant Hill MO	65466	Eminence MO
63011	Manchester MO		Montgomery City MO	64083	Raymore MO	65483	Houston MO
63011-22	Ballwin MO	63366	O'Fallon MO	64085	Richmond MO	65536	Lebanon MO
63019	Crystal City MO	63367	Lake St Louis MO	64093	Warrensburg MO	65559	St James MO
63020	De Soto MO	63379	Troy MO	64101-99	Kansas City MO	65560	Salem MO
63025	Eureka MO	63382	Vandalia MO	64116	N Kansas City MO	65565	Steelville MO
63028	Festus MO	63383	Warrenton MO	64118	Gladstone MO	65582	Vienna MO
63031	Black Jack MO	63385	Wentzville MO	64133	Raytown MO	65583	Waynesville MO
63031-34	Florissant MO	63401	Hannibal MO	64150	Riverside MO	65605	Aurora MO
63042-45	Hazelwood MO	63445	Kahoka MO	64402	Albany MO	65606	Alton MO
63043	Maryland Hts MO	63456	Monroe City MO	64424	Bethany MO	65608	Ava MO
63044	Bridgeton MO	63457	Monticello MO	64429	Cameron MO	65613	Bolivar MO
63050	Hillsboro MO	63459	New London MO	64456	Grant City MO	65616	Branson MO
63069	Pacific MO	63461	Palmyra MO	64468	Maryville MO	65622	Buffalo MO
63070	Pevely MO	63469	Shelbyville MO	64469	Maysville MO	65625	Cassville MO
63074	St Ann MO	63501	Kirksville MO	64473	Oregon MO	65653	Forsyth MO
63077	St Clair MO	63537	Edina MO	64477	Plattsburg MO	65655	Gainesville MO
63080	Sullivan MO	63548	Lancaster MO	64482	Rock Port MO	65656	Galena MO
63084	Union MO	63552	Macon MO	64485	Savannah MO	65661	Greenfield MO
63088	Valley Park MO	63555	Memphis MO	64501-99	St Joseph MO	65667	Hartville MO
63090	Washington MO	63556	Milan MO	64601	Chillicothe MO	65668	Hermitage MO
63101-99	St Louis MO	63565	Unionville MO	64628	Brookfield MO	65706	Marshfield MO
63105	Clayton MO	63601	Desloge MO	64633	Carrollton MO	65708	Monett MO
63112	Wellston MO	63601	Flat River MO	64640	Gallatin MO	65712	Mount Vernon MO
63114		63628	Bonne Terre MO	64650	Kingston MO	65714	Nixa MO
	Breckenridge Hills MO	63633	Centerville MO	64653	Linneus MO	65721	Ozark MO
63114	Overland MO	63640	Farmington MO	64658	Marceline MO	65738	Republic MO
63114	St Johns MO	63645	Fredericktown MO	64673	Princeton MO	65775	W Plains MO
63117	Richmond Hts MO	63650	Ironton MO	64683	Trenton MO	65785	Stockton MO
63119	Shrewsbury MO	63664	Potosi MO	64701	Harrisonville MO	65801-99	Springfield MO
63119	Webster Groves MO	63670	Ste Genevieve MO	64730	Butler MO	66002	Atchison KS
63121	Normandy MO	63701-02	Cape Girardeau MO	64735	Clinton MO	66012	Bonner Spgs KS
63121	Northwoods MO	63736	Benton MO	64744	El Dorado Spgs MO	66025	Eudora KS
63121	Pine Lawn MO	63740	Chaffee MO	64759	Lamar MO	66032	Garnett KS
63122	Glendale MO	63755	Jackson MO	64772	Nevada MO	66043	Lansing KS
63122	Kirkwood MO	63764	Marble Hill MO	64776	Osceola MO	66044-46	Lawrence KS
63124	Ladue MO	63775	Perryville MO	64801-04	Joplin MO	66048	Leavenworth KS
63124	Rock Hill MO	63780	Scott City MO	64834	Carl Junction MO	66056	Mound City KS
63125	Lemay MO	63801	Sikeston MO	64836	Carthage MO	66061-62	Olathe KS
63126	Crestwood MO	63825	Bloomfield MO	64850	Neosho MO	66064	Osawatomie KS
63127	Sunset Hills MO	63830	Caruthersville MO	64856	Pineville MO	66066	Oskaloosa KS
63130	University City MO	63834	Charleston MO	64870	Webb City MO	66067	Ottawa KS
63131	Des Peres MO	63841	Dexter MO	65018	California MO	66071	Paola KS
63131	Frontenac MO	63845	E Prairie MO	65020	Camdenton MO	66087	Troy KS
63131		63851	Hayti MO	65026	Eldon MO	66088	Valley Falls KS
	Town & Country MO	63857	Kennett MO	65041	Hermann MO	66101-99	Kansas City KS
63132	Olivette MO	63863	Malden MO	65051	Linn MO	66113	Edwardsville KS
63133	Bel-Ridge MO	63869	New Madrid MO	65082	Tuscumbia MO	66201-99	
63133	Pagedale MO	63873	Portageville MO	65084	Versailles MO		Shawnee Mission KS
63134	Berkeley MO	63901	Poplar Bluff MO	65101-10		66203	Merriam KS
63134		63935	Doniphan MO		JEFFERSON CITY MO	66204	Overland Park KS
	Woodson Terrace MO	63944	Greenville MO	65201-05	Columbia MO	66205	Fairway KS
63135	Ferguson MO	63965	Van Buren MO	65233	Boonville MO	66205	Mission Hills KS
63136	Castle Point MO	64012	Belton MO	65240	Centralia MO	66205	Mission KS
63136	Dellwood MO	64013-15	Blue Springs MO	65248	Fayette MO	66206	Leawood KS
63136	Jennings MO	64016	Buckner MO	65251	Fulton MO	66208	Prairie Vlg KS
63137		64024	Excelsior Spgs MO	65259	Huntsville MO	66215	Lenexa KS
	Bellefontaine Nbrs MO	64030	Grandview MO	65261	Keytesville MO	66401	Alma KS
63137	Riverview MO	64037	Higginsville MO	65265	Mexico MO	66434	Hiawatha KS
63140	Kinloch MO	64050-58	Independence MO	65270	Moberly MO	66436	Holton KS
63141	Creve Coeur MO	64063-64	Lees Summit MO	65275	Paris MO	66441	Junction City KS
63143	Maplewood MO	64067	Lexington MO	65301	Sedalia MO	66502	Manhattan KS
63144	Brentwood MO	64068	Liberty MO	65340	Marshall MO	66508	Marysville KS
63301-03	St Charles MO	64075	Oak Grove MO	65355	Warsaw MO	66523	Osage City KS

ZIP	CITY	ZIP	CITY	ZIP	CITY	ZIP	CITY
66538	Seneca KS	67467	Minneapolis KS	68420	Pawnee City NE	69152	Mullen NE
66547	Wamego KS	67473	Osborne KS	68434	Seward NE	69153	Ogallala NE
66549	Westmoreland KS	67501-05	Hutchinson KS	68450	Tecumseh NE	69154	Oshkosh NE
66601-99	TOPEKA KS	67526	Ellinwood KS	68465	Wilber NE	69162	Sidney NE
66701	Fort Scott KS	67530	Great Bend KS	68467	York NE	69163	Stapleton NE
66713	Baxter Spgs KS	67544	Hoisington KS	68501-99	LINCOLN NE	69166	Thedford NE
66720	Chanute KS	67547	Kinsley KS	68601-02	Columbus NE	69167	Tryon NE
66725	Columbus KS	67548	La Crosse KS	68620	Albion NE	69201	Valentine NE
66733	Erie KS	67550	Larned KS	68622	Bartlett NE	69210	Ainsworth NE
66736	Fredonia KS	67554	Lyons KS	68632	David City NE	69301	Alliance NE
66739	Galena KS	67560	Ness City KS	68638	Fullerton NE	69336	Bridgeport NE
66743	Girard KS	67576	St John KS	68651	Osceola NE	69337	Chadron NE
66749	Iola KS	67601	Hays KS	68661	Schuyler NE	69341	Gering NE
66757	Neodesha KS	67642	Hill City KS	68701	Norfolk NE	69345	Harrisburg NE
66762	Pittsburg KS	67654	Norton KS	68714	Bassett NE	69346	Harrison NE
66783	Yates Center KS	67661	Phillipsburg KS	68722	Butte NE	69350	Hyannis NE
66801	Emporia KS	67665	Russell KS	68724	Center NE	69353	Scottsbluff NE
66839	Burlington KS	67669	Stockton KS	68731	Dakota City NE	69360	Rushville NE
66845	Cottonwood Falls KS	67672	WaKeeney KS	68739	Hartington NE	70001-11	Metairie LA
66846	Council Grove KS	67701	Colby KS	68748	Madison NE	70043-44	Chalmette LA
66861	Marion KS	67730	Atwood KS	68756	Neligh NE	70049	Edgard LA
66901	Concordia KS	67735	Goodland KS	68763	O'Neill NE	70052	Gramercy LA
66935	Belleville KS	67736	Gove KS	68767	Pierce NE	70053-54	Gretna LA
66956	Mankato KS	67740	Hoxie KS	68770	Ponca NE	70057	Hahnville LA
66967	Smith Center KS	67748	Oakley KS	68776	S Sioux City NE	70058	Harvey LA
66968	Washington KS	67749	Oberlin KS	68778	Springview NE	70062-65	Kenner LA
67002	Andover KS	67756	St Francis KS	68779	Stanton NE	70071	Lutcher LA
67003	Anthony KS	67758	Sharon Spgs KS	68787	Wayne NE	70082	Pte a la Hache LA
67005	Arkansas City KS	67801	Dodge City KS	68788	West Point NE	70092	Violet LA
67010	Augusta KS	67831	Ashland KS	68801-03	Grand Island NE	70094-96	Westwego LA
67029	Coldwater KS	67835	Cimarron KS	68818	Aurora NE	70101-99	New Orleans LA
67037	Derby KS	67839	Dighton KS	68821	Brewster NE	70123	Harahan LA
67042	El Dorado KS	67846	Garden City KS	68822	Broken Bow NE	70301-02	Thibodaux LA
67045	Eureka KS	67854	Jetmore KS	68823	Burwell NE	70342	Berwick LA
67054	Greensburg KS	67855	Johnson KS	68826	Central City NE	70346	Donaldsonville LA
67060	Haysville KS	67860	Lakin KS	68842	Greeley NE	70360-64	Houma LA
67062	Hesston KS	67861	Leoti KS	68847-48	Kearney NE	70380-81	Morgan City LA
67063	Hillsboro KS	67864	Meade KS	68850	Lexington NE	70390	Napoleonville LA
67068	Kingman KS	67871	Scott City KS	68853	Loup City NE	70392	Patterson LA
67104	Medicine Lodge KS	67877	Sublette KS	68862	Ord NE	70401-04	Hammond LA
67110	Mulvane KS	67878	Syracuse KS	68873	St Paul NE	70422	Amite LA
67114	Newton KS	67879	Tribune KS	68879	Taylor NE	70427	Bogalusa LA
67124	Pratt KS	67880	Ulysses KS	68901-02	Hastings NE	70433-34	Covington LA
67147	Valley Center KS	67901-05	Liberal KS	68920	Alma NE	70438	Franklinton LA
67152	Wellington KS	67950	Elkhart KS	68926	Beaver City NE	70441	Greensburg LA
67156	Winfield KS	67951	Hugoton KS	68933	Clay Center NE	70444	Kentwood LA
67201-99	Wichita KS	68005	Bellevue NE	68937	Elwood NE	70448	Mandeville LA
67216	Oaklawn KS	68008	Blair NE	68939	Franklin NE	70454	Ponchatoula LA
67219	Park City KS	68025	Fremont NE	68949	Holdrege NE	70458-61	Slidell LA
67301	Independence KS	68046	Papillion NE	68959	Minden NE	70501-09	Lafayette LA
67335	Cherryvale KS	68047	Pender NE	68961	Nelson NE	70510-11	Abbeville LA
67337	Coffeyville KS	68048	Plattsmouth NE	68970	Red Cloud NE	70514	Baldwin LA
67349	Howard KS	68061	Tekamah NE	68978	Superior NE	70515	Basile LA
67356	Oswego KS	68066	Wahoo NE	69001	McCook NE	70517	Breaux Bridge LA
67357	Parsons KS	68101-99	Omaha NE	69021	Benkelman NE	70518	Broussard LA
67361	Sedan KS	68127	Ralston NE	69032	Hayes Center NE	70520	Carencro LA
67401-02	Salina KS	68128	La Vista NE	69033	Imperial NE	70525	Church Point LA
67410	Abilene KS	68134	Lake Forest Ests NE	69042	Stockville NE	70526-27	Crowley LA
67420	Beloit KS	68305	Auburn NE	69044	Trenton NE	70535	Eunice LA
67432	Clay Center KS	68310	Beatrice NE	69101-03	N Platte NE	70538	Franklin LA
67439	Ellsworth KS	68333	Crete NE	69121	Arthur NE	70544	Jeanerette LA
67449	Herington KS	68352	Fairbury NE	69129	Chappell NE	70546	Jennings LA
67451	Lyndon KS	68355	Falls City NE	69130	Cozad NE	70548	Kaplan LA
67455	Lincoln KS	68361	Geneva NE	69138	Gothenburg NE	70549	Lake Arthur LA
67456	Lindsborg KS	68370	Hebron NE	69140	Grant NE	70554	Mamou LA
67460	McPherson KS	68410	Nebraska City NE	69145	Kimball NE	70560-62	New Iberia LA

ZIP	CITY	ZIP	CITY	ZIP	CITY	ZIP	CITY
70570-71	Opelousas LA	71405	Ball LA	72150	Sheridan AR	73034	Edmond OK
70577	Port Barre LA	71417	Colfax LA	72160	Stuttgart AR	73036	El Reno OK
70578	Rayne LA	71418	Columbia LA	72201-99	LITTLE ROCK AR	73044	Guthrie OK
70582	St Martinville LA	71446	Leesville LA	72301	W Memphis AR	73045	Harrah OK
70586	Ville Platte LA	71449	Many LA	72315-19	Blytheville AR	73052	Lindsay OK
70591	Welsh LA	71457-58	Natchitoches LA	72319	Gosnell AR	73055	Marlow OK
70601-29	Lake Charles LA	71463	Oakdale LA	72331	Earle AR	73057	Maysville OK
70631	Cameron LA	71483	Winnfield LA	72335	Forrest City AR	73064	Mustang OK
70633	De Quincy LA	71601-13	Pine Bluff AR	72342	Helena AR	73065	Newcastle OK
70634	De Ridder LA	71602	White Hall AR	72360	Marianna AR	73066	Nicoma Park OK
70648	Kinder LA	71630	Arkansas City AR	72364	Marion AR	73068	Noble OK
70655	Oberlin LA	71634	Dermott AR	72365	Marked Tree AR	73069-72	Norman OK
70663-64	Sulphur LA	71635	Crossett AR	72370	Osceola AR	73075	Pauls Valley OK
70668	Vinton LA	71639	Dumas AR	72390	W Helena AR	73077	Perry OK
70669	Westlake LA	71640	Eudora AR	72396-97	Wynne AR	73080	Purcell OK
70704	Baker LA	71646	Hamburg AR	72401-03	Jonesboro AR	73084	Spencer OK
70722	Clinton LA	71653	Lake Village AR	72422	Corning AR	73086	Sulphur OK
70723	Convent LA	71654	McGehee AR	72432	Harrisburg AR	73089	Tuttle OK
70726-27	Denham Spgs LA	71655	Monticello AR	72433	Hoxie AR	73096	Weatherford OK
70737	Gonzales LA	71665	Rison AR	72442	Manila AR	73098	Wynnewood OK
70748	Jackson LA	71667	Star City AR	72450-51	Paragould AR	73099	Yukon OK
70754	Livingston LA	71671	Warren AR	72454	Piggott AR	73101-99	
70760	New Roads LA	71701	Camden AR	72455	Pocahontas AR		OKLAHOMA CITY OK
70764-65	Plaquemine LA	71730-31	El Dorado AR	72472	Trumann AR	73110	Midwest City OK
70767	Port Allen LA	71742	Fordyce AR	72476	Walnut Ridge AR	73115	Del City OK
70775	St Francisville LA	71743	Gurdon AR	72501-03	Batesville AR	73116	Nichols Hills OK
70785	Walker LA	71744	Hampton AR	72513	Ash Flat AR	73120	Village (The) OK
70791	Zachary LA	71753	Magnolia AR	72525	Cherokee Vlg AR	73132	Warr Acres OK
70801-99	BATON ROUGE LA	71801	Hope AR	72542	Hardy AR	73160	Moore OK
70807	Scotlandville LA	71822	Ashdown AR	72543	Heber Spgs AR	73401-03	Ardmore OK
70811	Fountain Place LA	71832	De Queen AR	72560	Mountain View AR	73438	Healdton OK
71001	Arcadia LA	71845	Lewisville AR	72565	Melbourne AR	73443	Lone Grove OK
71006	Benton LA	71852	Nashville AR	72576	Salem AR	73446	Madill OK
71019	Coushatta LA	71857	Prescott AR	72601-02	Harrison AR	73448	Marietta OK
71038	Haynesville LA	71860	Stamps AR	72616	Berryville AR	73460	Tishomingo OK
71040	Homer LA	71901-14	Hot Spgs Ntl Pk AR	72632	Eureka Spgs AR	73501-07	Lawton OK
71052	Mansfield LA	71923	Arkadelphia AR	72641	Jasper AR	73521-23	Altus OK
71055	Minden LA	71953	Mena AR	72650	Marshall AR	73533-34	Duncan OK
71075	Springhill LA	71957	Mount Ida AR	72653	Mountain Home AR	73542	Frederick OK
71082	Vivian LA	71958	Murfreesboro AR	72687	Yellville AR	73550	Hollis OK
71101-66	Shreveport LA	72006	Augusta AR	72701-03	Fayetteville AR	73554	Mangum OK
71107	Cooper Road LA	72010	Bald Knob AR	72712	Bella Vista AR	73572	Walters OK
71171-72	Bossier City LA	72012	Beebe AR	72712-14	Bentonville AR	73573	Waurika OK
71201-12	Monroe LA	72015	Benton AR	72740	Huntsville AR	73601	Clinton OK
71220-21	Bastrop LA	72021	Brinkley AR	72756-57	Rogers AR	73620	Arapaho OK
71232	Delhi LA	72022	Bryant AR	72761	Siloam Spgs AR	73628	Cheyenne OK
71241	Farmerville LA	72023	Cabot AR	72764-65	Springdale AR	73632	Cordell OK
71245	Grambling LA	72024	Carlisle AR	72801	Russellville AR	73644	Elk City OK
71251	Jonesboro LA	72029	Clarendon AR	72823	Atkins AR	73651	Hobart OK
71254	Lake Providence LA	72031	Clinton AR	72830	Clarksville AR	73662	Sayre OK
71263	Oak Grove LA	72032	Conway AR	72833	Danville AR	73667	Taloga OK
71269	Rayville LA	72040	Des Arc AR	72834	Dardanelle AR	73701-06	Enid OK
71270-73	Ruston LA	72042	De Witt AR	72855	Paris AR	73717	Alva OK
71282-84	Tallulah LA	72046	England AR	72901-17	Fort Smith AR	73728	Cherokee OK
71291-94	W Monroe LA	72075	Gravel Ridge AR	72921	Alma AR	73737	Fairview OK
71295	Winnsboro LA	72076	Jacksonville AR	72923	Barling AR	73750	Kingfisher OK
71301-15	Alexandria LA	72086	Lonoke AR	72927	Booneville AR	73759	Medford OK
71322	Bunkie LA	72101	McCrory AR	72936+49	Greenwood AR	73772	Watonga OK
71334	Ferriday LA	72104-05	Malvern AR	72949	Ozark AR	73801-02	Woodward OK
71340	Harrisonburg LA	72110	Morrilton AR	72956	Van Buren AR	73832	Arnett OK
71342	Jena LA	72112	Newport AR	72958	Waldron AR	73834	Buffalo OK
71343	Jonesville LA	72114-19	N Little Rock AR	73005	Anadarko OK	73932	Beaver OK
71351	Marksville LA	72116	Sherwood AR	73008	Bethany OK	73933	Boise City OK
71360-61	Pineville LA	72118	Maumelle AR	73018	Chickasha OK	73942	Guymon OK
71366	St Joseph LA	72126	Perryville AR	73020	Choctaw OK	74003-06	Bartlesville OK
71373	Vidalia LA	72143	Searcy AR	73030	Davis OK	74008	Bixby OK

ZIP	CITY	ZIP	CITY	ZIP	CITY	ZIP	CITY
74010	Bristow OK	75006-11	Carrollton TX	75751	Athens TX	76266	Sanger TX
74012-14	Broken Arrow OK	75019	Coppell TX	75766	Jacksonville TX	76301-11	Wichita Falls TX
74017	Claremore OK	75020-21	Denison TX	75773	Mineola TX	76351	Archer City TX
74020	Cleveland OK	75023-75	Plano TX	75783	Quitman TX	76351	Palestine TX
74021	Collinsville OK	75034	Frisco TX	75785	Rusk TX	76354	Burkburnett TX
74023	Cushing OK	75040-48	Garland TX	75801-02	Palestine TX	76360	Electra TX
74029	Dewey OK	75050-53	Grand Prairie TX	75833	Centerville TX	76365	Henrietta TX
74030	Drumright OK	75056	The Colony TX	75835	Crockett TX	76367	Iowa Park TX
74033	Glenpool OK	75060-63	Irving TX	75840	Fairfield TX	76374	Olney TX
74035	Hominy OK	75065	Lake Dallas TX	75845	Groveton TX	76380	Seymour TX
74037	Jenks OK	75067	Flower Mound TX	75860	Teague TX	76384	Vernon TX
74048	Nowata OK	75067	Highland Vlg TX	75901-15	Lufkin TX	76401	Stephenville TX
74055	Owasso OK	75067	Lewisville TX	75935	Center TX	76430	Albany TX
74056	Pawhuska OK	75069-70	McKinney TX	75941	Diboll TX	76437	Cisco TX
74058	Pawnee OK	75077	Princeton TX	75948	Hemphill TX	76442	Comanche TX
74063	Sand Spgs OK	75080-83	Richardson TX	75951	Jasper TX	76446	Dublin TX
74066-67	Sapulpa OK	75087	Rockwall TX	75961-63	Nacogdoches TX	76448	Eastland TX
74070	Skiatook OK	75088	Rowlett TX	75966	Newton TX	76470	Ranger TX
74074-76	Stillwater OK	75090-93	Sherman TX	75972	San Augustine TX	76501-05	Temple TX
74079	Stroud OK	75103	Canton TX	75979	Woodville TX	76513	Belton TX
74101-99	Tulsa OK	75104	Cedar Hill TX	76003-18	Arlington TX	76520	Cameron TX
74301	Vinita OK	75110	Corsicana TX	76009	Alvarado TX	76522	Copperas Cove TX
74339	Commerce OK	75115	De Soto TX	76020	Azle TX	76528	Gatesville TX
74344	Grove OK	75119-20	Ennis TX	76021-22	Bedford TX	76531	Hamilton TX
74346	Jay OK	75137-38	Duncanville TX	76024	Breckenridge TX	76540-44	Killeen TX
74354-55	Miami OK	75140	Grand Saline TX	76026	Bridgeport TX	76543	Harker Hts TX
74361-62	Pryor OK	75141	Hutchins TX	76028	Burleson TX	76550	Lampasas TX
74401-03	Muskogee OK	75142	Kaufman TX	76031-33	Cleburne TX	76567	Rockdale TX
74426	Checotah OK	75146	Lancaster TX	76034	Colleyville TX	76574	Taylor TX
74429	Coweta OK	75149-82	Mesquite TX	76036	Crowley TX	76634	Clifton TX
74432	Eufaula OK	75159	Seagoville TX	76039-40	Euless TX	76642	Groesbeck TX
74437	Henryetta OK	75160	Terrell TX	76043	Glen Rose TX	76643	Hewitt TX
74447	Okmulgee OK	75165	Waxahachie TX	76046	Graham TX	76645	Hillsboro TX
74462	Stigler OK	75180	Balch Spgs TX	76048	Granbury TX	76661	Marlin TX
74464-65	Tahlequah OK	75201-399	Dallas TX	76051	Grapevine TX	76665	Meridian TX
74467	Wagoner OK	75205	Highland Pk TX	76053-54	Hurst TX	76667	Mexia TX
74501-02	McAlester OK	75205	University Pk TX	76056	Jacksboro TX	76701-99	Waco TX
74523	Antlers OK	75211	Cockrell Hill TX	76059	Keene TX	76705	Bellmead TX
74525	Atoka OK	75234	Farmers Branch TX	76060	Kennedale TX	76705	Lacy-Lakeview TX
74538	Coalgate OK	75401	Greenville TX	76063	Mansfield TX	76801-04	Brownwood TX
74578	Wilburton OK	75418	Bonham TX	76065	Midlothian TX	76821	Ballinger TX
74601-04	Ponca City OK	75426	Clarksville TX	76067	Mineral Wells TX	76825	Brady TX
74631	Blackwell OK	75428	Commerce TX	76072	Palo Pinto TX	76834	Coleman TX
74647	Newkirk OK	75432	Cooper TX	76083	Throckmorton TX	76844	Goldthwaite TX
74653	Tonkawa OK	75440	Emory TX	76086-87	Weatherford TX	76849	Junction TX
74701-02	Durant OK	75455	Mount Pleasant TX	76092	Southlake TX	76856	Mason TX
74728	Broken Bow OK	75457	Mount Vernon TX	76101-99	Fort Worth TX	76859	Menard TX
74743	Hugo OK	75460-61	Paris TX	76108	White Settlement TX	76866	Paint Rock TX
74745	Idabel OK	75482	Sulphur Spgs TX	76114	River Oaks TX	76877	San Saba TX
74801-02	Shawnee OK	75501	Wake Village TX	76114	Sansom Park TX	76901-06	San Angelo TX
74820-21	Ada OK	75501-05	Texarkana TX	76117	Haltom City TX	76932	Big Lake TX
74834	Chandler OK	75502-04	Texarkana AR	76118	N Richland Hills TX	76936	Eldorado TX
74848	Holdenville OK	75551	Atlanta TX	76118	Richland Hills TX	76941	Mertzon TX
74851	McLoud OK	75557	Boston TX	76126	Benbrook TX	76943	Ozona TX
74859	Okemah OK	75563	Linden TX	76134	Edgecliff TX	76945	Robert Lee TX
74868	Seminole OK	75601-15	Longview TX	76135	Lake Worth TX	76950	Sonora TX
74873	Tecumseh OK	75633	Carthage TX	76137	Watauga TX	76951	Sterling City TX
74884	Wewoka OK	75638	Daingerfield TX	76140	Everman TX	77001-299	Houston TX
74902	Pocola OK	75644	Gilmer TX	76179	Saginaw TX	77019	River Oaks TX
74937	Heavener OK	75647	Gladewater TX	76201-06	Denton TX	77024	Hedwig Village TX
74948	Muldrow OK	75652-55	Henderson TX	76230	Bowie TX	77024	
74953	Poteau OK	75657	Jefferson TX	76234	Decatur TX	77024	Hunters Creek Vlg TX
74955	Sallisaw OK	75662-63	Kilgore TX	76240	Gainesville TX	77024	Piney Point TX
74960	Stilwell OK	75670-71	Marshall TX	76248	Keller TX	77024	Terrell Hills TX
75001	Addison TX	75686	Pittsburg TX	76251	Montague TX	77029	Jacinto City TX
75002	Allen TX	75701-13	Tyler TX	76255	Nocona TX	77040	Jersey Village TX

ZIP	CITY	ZIP	CITY	ZIP	CITY	ZIP	CITY
77055	Spring Valley TX	77651	Port Neches TX	78382	Rockport TX	79068	Panhandle TX
77058	Nassau Bay TX	77656	Silsbee TX	78384	San Diego TX	79070	Perryton TX
77093	Greenwood Vlg TX	77662	Vidor TX	78385	Sarita TX	79072-73	Plainview TX
77301-85	Conroe TX	77701-99	Beaumont TX	78387	Sinton TX	79079	Shamrock TX
77302	Oak Ridge N TX	77801-06	Bryan TX	78390	Taft TX	79081	Spearman TX
77327-28	Cleveland TX	77830	Anderson TX	78401-99	Corpus Christi TX	79083	Stinnett TX
77331	Coldspring TX	77833	Brenham TX	78501-04	McAllen TX	79084	Stratford TX
77338-47	Humble TX	77836	Caldwell TX	78516	Alamo TX	79088	Tulia TX
77340-42	Huntsville TX	77840	College Station TX	78520-26	Brownsville TX	79092	Vega TX
77351	Livingston TX	77856	Franklin TX	78537	Donna TX	79095	Wellington TX
77362	Pinehurst TX	77859	Hearne TX	78538	Edcouch TX	79096	Wheeler TX
77375	Tomball TX	77864	Madisonville TX	78539-40	Edinburg TX	79101-99	Amarillo TX
77386-91	Spring TX	77868	Navasota TX	78543	Elsa TX	79201	Childress TX
77401-02	Bellair TX	77901-05	Victoria TX	78550-52	Harlingen TX	79226	Clarendon TX
77414	Bay City TX	77954	Cuero TX	78559	La Feria TX	79227	Crowell TX
77418	Bellville TX	77957	Edna TX	78570	Mercedes TX	79229	Dickens TX
77422	Brazoria TX	77963	Goliad TX	78572	Alton TX	79235	Floydada TX
77434	Eagle Lake TX	77964	Hallettsville TX	78572	Mission TX	79236	Guthrie TX
77437	El Campo TX	77979	Port Lavaca TX	78577	Pharr TX	79244	Matador TX
77445	Hempstead TX	77995	Yoakum TX	78578	Port Isabel TX	79245	Memphis TX
77446	Prairie View TX	78003	Bandera TX	78580	Raymondville TX	79248	Paducah TX
77449-94	Katy TX	78004-06	Boerne TX	78582	Rio Grande City TX	79252	Quanah TX
77459	Missouri City TX	78014	Cotulla TX	78584	Roma TX	79257	Silverton TX
77465	Palacios TX	78016	Devine TX	78586	San Benito TX	79311	Abernathy TX
77469	Richmond TX	78017	Dilley TX	78589	San Juan TX	79316	Brownfield TX
77471	Rosenberg TX	78022	George West TX	78596	Weslaco TX	79322	Crosbyton TX
77474	Sealy TX	78026	Jourdanton TX	78602	Bastrop TX	79323	Denver City TX
77477	Stafford TX	78028-29	Kerrville TX	78611	Burnet TX	79325	Farwell TX
77478-79	Sugar Land TX	78040-44	Laredo TX	78621	Elgin TX	79331	Lamesa TX
77480	Sweeny TX	78061	Pearsall TX	78624	Fredericksburg TX	79336-38	Levelland TX
77488	Wharton TX	78064	Pleasanton TX	78626-28	Georgetown TX	79339	Littlefield TX
77501-08	Pasadena TX	78065	Poteet TX	78629	Gonzales TX	79346	Morton TX
77511-12	Alvin TX	78072	Tilden TX	78636	Johnson City TX	79347	Muleshoe TX
77514	Anahuac TX	78076	Zapata TX	78643	Llano TX	79355	Plains TX
77515	Angleton TX	78102-04	Beeville TX	78644	Lockhart TX	79356	Post TX
77517	Santa Fe TX	78109	Converse TX	78648	Luling TX	79359	Seagraves TX
77520-22	Baytown TX	78114	Floresville TX	78654	Marble Falls TX	79360	Seminole TX
77530-31	Richwood TX	78118	Karnes City TX	78666-67	San Marcos TX	79364	Slaton TX
77531	Clute TX	78119	Kenedy TX	78680-81	Round Rock TX	79373	Tahoka TX
77535	Dayton TX	78125	Kenedy TX	78701-99	AUSTIN TX	79401-99	Lubbock TX
77536	Deer Park TX	78130-33	New Braunfels TX	78801-02	Uvalde TX	79501	Anson TX
77539	Dickinson TX	78148	Universal City TX	78832	Brackettville TX	79502	Aspermont TX
77541	Freeport TX	78154	Schertz TX	78834	Carrizo Spgs TX	79504	Baird TX
77541	Jones Creek TX	78155-56	Seguin TX	78839	Crystal City TX	79505	Benjamin TX
77546	Friendswood TX	78201	Balcones Hts TX	78840-42	Del Rio TX	79510	Clyde TX
77547	Galena Park TX	78201-99	San Antonio TX	78852-53	Eagle Pass TX	79512	Colorado City TX
77550-54	Galveston TX	78209	Alamo Hts TX	78861	Hondo TX	79520	Hamlin TX
77563	Hitchcock TX	78213	Castle Hills TX	78873	Leakey TX	79521	Haskell TX
77566	Lake Jackson TX	78219	Kirby TX	78880	Rocksprings TX	79528	Jayton TX
77568	La Marque TX	78232	Hollywood Park TX	78934-43	Columbus TX	79543	Roby TX
77571-72	La Porte TX	78233	Live Oak TX	78942	Giddings TX	79548-53	Stamford TX
77573-74	League City TX	78238	Leon Valley TX	78945	La Grange TX	79549	Snyder TX
77575	Liberty TX	78332-42	Alice TX	78957	Smithville TX	79556	Sweetwater TX
77578	Manvel TX	78336	Aransas Pass TX	79007-08	Borger TX	79601-99	Abilene TX
77581	Pearland TX	78343	Bishop TX	79014	Canadian TX	79701-12	Midland TX
77586	El Lago TX	78355	Falfurrias TX	79015-16	Canyon TX	79714	Andrews TX
77586	Seabrook TX	78357	Freer TX	79018	Channing TX	79720-21	Big Spring TX
77586	Taylor Lake Vlg TX	78359	Gregory TX	79019	Claude TX	79731	Crane TX
77587	S Houston TX	78361	Hebbronville TX	79022	Dalhart TX	79734	Fort Davis TX
77590-92	Texas City TX	78362	Ingleside TX	79027	Dimmitt TX	79735	Fort Stockton TX
77611	Bridge City TX	78363-64	Kingsville TX	79029	Dumas TX	79738	Gail TX
77619	Groves TX	78368	Mathis TX	79035	Friona TX	79739	Garden City TX
77625	Kountze TX	78374	Portland TX	79045	Hereford TX	79745	Kermit TX
77627	Nederland TX	78375	Premont TX	79056	Lipscomb TX	79754	Mentrone TX
77630	Orange TX	78377	Refugio TX	79059	Miami TX	79756	Monahans TX
77640-43	Port Arthur TX	78380	Robstown TX	79065-66	Pampa TX	79760-68	Odessa TX

ZIP	CITY	ZIP	CITY	ZIP	CITY	ZIP	CITY
79772	Pecos TX	80813	Cripple Creek CO	82520	Lander WY	83835	Hayden ID
79778	Rankin TX	80817	Fountain CO	82601-15	Casper WY	83837	Kellogg ID
79782	Stanton TX	80821	Hugo CO	82633	Douglas WY	83843	Moscow ID
79821	Anthony TX	80828	Limon CO	82636	Evansville WY	83854	Post Falls ID
79830-31	Alpine TX	80829	Manitou Spgs CO	82637	Glenrock WY	83861	St Maries ID
79843	Marfa TX	80863	Woodland Park CO	82701	Newcastle WY	83862-65	Sandpoint ID
79848	Sanderson TX	80901-99	Colorado Spgs CO	82716-17	Gillette WY	83873-74	Wallace ID
79851	Sierra Blanca TX	80911	Security CO	82729	Sundance WY	84003	American Fork UT
79855	Van Horn TX	81001-19	Pueblo CO	82801	Sheridan WY	84004	Alpine UT
79901-99	El Paso TX	81036	Eads CO	82834	Buffalo WY	84010-11	Bountiful UT
80001-05	Arvada CO	81050	La Junta CO	82901-02	Rock Springs WY	84014	Centerville UT
80010-45	Aurora CO	81052	Lamar CO	82930-31	Evanston WY	84015	Clearfield UT
80020-21	Broomfield CO	81054	Las Animas CO	82935	Green River WY	84015	Clinton UT
80022	Commerce City CO	81063	Ordway CO	82937	Lyman WY	84015	Sunset UT
80026	Lafayette CO	81067	Rocky Ford CO	82941	Pinedale WY	84017	Coalville UT
80027	Louisville CO	81073	Springfield CO	83001	Jackson WY	84020	Draper UT
80030-36	Westminster CO	81082	Trinidad CO	83101	Kemmerer WY	84021	Duchesne UT
80033-34	Wheat Ridge CO	81089	Walsenburg CO	83201-06	Pocatello ID	84025	Farmington UT
80104	Castle Rock CO	81101	Alamosa CO	83202	Chubbuck ID	84029	Grantsville UT
80110	Cherry Hills Vlg CO	81129	Conejos CO	83211	American Falls ID	84032	Heber City UT
80110	Sheridan CO	81130	Creede CO	83213	Arco ID	84037	Fruit Hts UT
80110-55	Englewood CO	81132	Del Norte CO	83221	Blackfoot ID	84037	Kaysville UT
80117	Kiowa CO	81144	Monte Vista CO	83226	Challis ID	84040-41	Layton UT
80120-62	Littleton CO	81147	Pagosa Spgs CO	83252	Malad City ID	84041	Syracuse UT
80121	Greenwood Vlg CO	81149	Saguache CO	83261	Paris ID	84042	Lindon UT
80201-95	DENVER CO	81152	San Luis CO	83263	Preston ID	84043	Lehi UT
80214	Edgewater CO	81201	Salida CO	83274	Shelley ID	84046	Manila UT
80215	Lakewood CO	81211	Buena Vista CO	83276	Soda Springs ID	84047	E Midvale UT
80221	Federal Hts CO	81212	Canon City CO	83301-03	Twin Falls ID	84047	Midvale UT
80222	Glendale CO	81226	Florence CO	83316	Buhl ID	84047	Union UT
80229	Thornton CO	81230	Gunnison CO	83318	Burley ID	84050	Morgan UT
80233	Northglenn CO	81235	Lake City CO	83322	Fairfield ID	84054	N Salt Lake UT
80301-99	Boulder CO	81252	Westcliffe CO	83330	Gooding ID	84057-59	Orem UT
80401-19	Golden CO	81301-02	Durango CO	83333	Hailey ID	84060	Park City UT
80424	Breckenridge CO	81321	Cortez CO	83336	Heyburn ID	84062	Pleasant Grove UT
80427	Central City CO	81324	Dove Creek CO	83338	Jerome ID	84064	Randolph UT
80440	Fairplay CO	81401	Montrose CO	83350	Rupert ID	84065	Riverton UT
80444	Georgetown CO	81416	Delta CO	83352	Shoshone ID	84065	S Jordan UT
80451	Hot Sulphur Spgs CO	81427	Ouray CO	83401	Ammon ID	84066	Roosevelt UT
80452	Idaho Spgs CO	81433	Silverton CO	83401-15	Idaho Falls ID	84067	Roy UT
80461	Leadville CO	81435	Telluride CO	83422	Driggs ID	84074	Tooele UT
80477-88	Steamboat Spgs CO	81501	Orchard Mesa CO	83423	Dubois ID	84078-79	Vernal UT
80480	Walden CO	81501-06	Grand Junction CO	83440	Rexburg ID	84084	W Jordan UT
80501-02	Longmont CO	81521	Fruita CO	83442	Rigby ID	84087	W Bountiful UT
80513	Berthoud CO	81601	Glenwood Spgs CO	83445	St Anthony ID	84087	Woods Cross UT
80517	Estes Park CO	81611-15	Aspen CO	83467	Salmon ID	84090-94	Sandy UT
80521-26	Fort Collins CO	81623	Carbondale CO	83501	Lewiston ID	84101-99	
80537-39	Loveland CO	81625-26	Craig CO	83530-31	Grangeville ID		SALT LAKE CITY UT
80550	Windsor CO	81631	Eagle CO	83543	Nezperce ID	84107	Murray UT
80601	Brighton CO	81639	Haydon CO	83544	Orofino ID	84115	S Salt Lake UT
80615	Eaton CO	81641	Meeker CO	83605-06	Caldwell ID	84119-20	W Valley City UT
80620	Evans CO	81648	Rangely CO	83611	Cascade ID	84302	Brigham City UT
80621	Fort Lupton CO	81650	Rifle CO	83612	Council ID	84319	Hyrum UT
80631-39	Greeley CO	81657	Vail CO	83616	Eagle ID	84321	Logan UT
80645	La Salle CO	82001-09	CHEYENNE WY	83617	Emmett ID	84332	Providence UT
80651	Platteville CO	82057-71	Laramie WY	83642	Meridian ID	84335	Smithfield UT
80701	Fort Morgan CO	82201	Wheatland WY	83647	Mountain Home ID	84337	Tremonton UT
80720	Akron CO	82225	Lusk WY	83650	Murphy ID	84401	Riverdale UT
80723	Brush CO	82240	Torrington WY	83651-87	Nampa ID	84401-99	Ogden UT
80734	Holyoke CO	82301	Rawlins WY	83661	Payette ID	84403	S Ogden UT
80737	Julesburg CO	82401	Worland WY	83672	Weiser ID	84403	Washington Trc UT
80751	Sterling CO	82410	Basin WY	83701-99	BOISE ID	84404	N Ogden UT
80758	Wray CO	82414	Cody WY	83704	Garden City ID	84404	Pleasant View UT
80759	Yuma CO	82435	Powell WY	83731	Idaho City ID	84501	Price UT
80807	Burlington CO	82443	Thermopolis WY	83805	Bonners Ferry ID	84511	Blanding UT
80810	Cheyenne Wells CO	82501	Riverton WY	83814	Coeur d'Alene ID	84513	Castle Dale UT

ZIP	CITY	ZIP	CITY	ZIP	CITY	ZIP	CITY
84526	Helper UT	85701-99	Tucson AZ	88301	Carrizozo NM	90501-99	Torrance CA
84532	Moab UT	85704	Oro Valley AZ	88310-11	Alamogordo NM	90502	W Carson CA
84535	Monticello UT	85713	S Tucson AZ	88345	Ruidoso NM	90601-10	Whittier CA
84601-06	Provo UT	85901	Show Low AZ	88352	Tularosa NM	90605	S Whittier CA
84627	Ephraim UT	85936	St Johns AZ	88401	Tucumcari NM	90606	Los Nietos CA
84631	Fillmore UT	85937	Snowflake AZ	88415	Clayton NM	90620	Buena Park CA
84642	Manti UT	85938	Springerville AZ	88435	Santa Rosa NM	90623	La Palma CA
84648	Nephi UT	86001-18	Flagstaff AZ	89005-06	Boulder City NV	90630	Cypress CA
84651	Payson UT	86025-29	Holbrook AZ	89013	Goldfield NV	90631	La Habra CA
84660	Spanish Fork UT	86034	Kearns Canyon AZ	89014-16	Henderson NV	90631-33	La Habra Hts CA
84663	Mapleton UT	86040	Page AZ	89030	N Las Vegas NV	90637-39	La Mirada CA
84663-64	Springville UT	86045	Tuba City AZ	89043	Pioche NV	90640	Montebello CA
84701	Richfield UT	86047	Winslow AZ	89049	Tonopah NV	90650	Norwalk CA
84713	Beaver UT	86301	Prescott AZ	89101-99	Las Vegas NV	90660-61	Pico Rivera CA
84720-22	Cedar City UT	86314	Prescott Vly AZ	89301	Ely NV	90670	Santa Fe Spgs CA
84740	Junction UT	86322	Camp Verde AZ	89310	Austin NV	90680	Stanton CA
84741	Kanab UT	86323	Chino Valley AZ	89316	Eureka NV	90701	Artesia CA
84747	Loa UT	86326	Cottonwood AZ	89406	Fallon NV	90701	Cerritos CA
84759	Panguitch UT	86331	Jerome AZ	89415-16	Hawthorne NV	90706-07	Bellflower CA
84761	Parowan UT	86401-45	Kingman AZ	89419	Lovelock NV	90711-16	Lakewood CA
84770-71	St George UT	86403		89423	Minden NV	90716	
84780	Washington UT		Lake Havasu City AZ	89431-36	Sparks NV		Hawaiian Gardens CA
85001-99	PHOENIX AZ	86430	Bullhead City AZ	89440	Virginia City NV	90717	Lomita CA
85201-16	Mesa AZ	87002	Belen NM	89445	Winnemucca NV	90720-21	Los Alamitos CA
85217-19	Apache Junction AZ	87004	Bernalillo NM	89447	Yerington NV	90723	Paramount CA
85222	Casa Grande AZ	87016	Estancia NM	89501-99	Reno NV	90740	Seal Beach CA
85224-27	Chandler AZ	87020	Grants NM	89701-21	CARSON CITY NV	90745	Carson CA
85228	Coolidge AZ	87021	Milan NM	89801	Elko NV	90745-899	Long Beach CA
85231	Eloy AZ	87031	Los Lunas NM	89820	Battle Mountain NV	90806	Signal Hill CA
85232	Florence AZ	87048	Corrales NM	90001	Florence CA	91001-02	Altadena CA
85234	Gilbert AZ	87068	Bosque Farms NM	90001-199	Los Angeles CA	91006	Arcadia CA
85237	Kearny AZ	87101-99	Albuquerque NM	90022	E Los Angeles CA	91010	Duarte CA
85250-71	Scottsdale AZ	87124	Rio Rancho NM	90025	W Los Angeles CA	91011	La Canada CA
85253	Paradise Valley AZ	87301-10	Gallup NM	90040	Commerce CA	91016	Monrovia CA
85273	Superior AZ	87401	Farmington NM	90044	Westmont CA	91020	Montrose CA
85281-89	Tempe AZ	87410	Aztec NM	90069	W Hollywood CA	91024	Sierra Madre CA
85283	Guadalupe AZ	87413	Bloomfield NM	90201	Bell CA	91030	S Pasadena CA
85292	Winkelman AZ	87501-09	SANTA FE NM	90201	Bell Gardens CA	91101-99	Pasadena CA
85301-12	Glendale AZ	87532	Espanola NM	90201	Cudahy CA	91118	San Marino CA
85321	Ajo AZ	87544	Los Alamos NM	90209-13	Beverly Hills CA	91201-99	Glendale CA
85323	Avondale AZ	87571	Taos NM	90221-24	Compton CA	91224	La Crescenta CA
85326	Buckeye AZ	87575	Tierra Amarilla NM	90222	Willow Brook CA	91301	Agoura Hills CA
85335	El Mirage AZ	87701	Las Vegas NM	90230-33	Culver City CA	91303-09	Canoga Park CA
85338	Goodyear AZ	87732	Mora NM	90240-42	Downey CA	91340-46	San Fernando CA
85344	Parker AZ	87733	Mosquero NM	90245	El Segundo CA	91350	Saugus CA
85345	Peoria AZ	87740	Raton NM	90247-49	Gardena CA	91359-67	Thousand Oaks CA
85345	Surprise AZ	87801	Socorro NM	90250	Hawthorne CA	91361	Westlake Vlg CA
85350	Somerton AZ	87830	Reserve NM	90254	Hermosa Beach CA	91500-10	Burbank CA
85353	Tolleson AZ	87901		90255	Huntington Pk CA	91702	Azusa CA
85358	Wickenburg AZ		Truth or Consequences NM	90255	Walnut Park CA	91706	Baldwin Park CA
85363	Youngtown AZ	88001-08	Las Cruces NM	90260	Lawndale CA	91708-10	Chino CA
85364-69	Yuma AZ	88023	Bayard NM	90262	Lynwood CA	91711	Claremont CA
85372-75	Sun City AZ	88030-31	Deming NM	90264-65	Malibu CA	91718-20	Corona CA
85501-02	Globe AZ	88045	Lordsburg NM	90266	Manhattan Beach CA	91722-24	Covina CA
85533	Clifton AZ	88061-62	Silver City NM	90270	Maywood CA	91729-30	
85539	Miami AZ	88063	Sunland Pk NM	90274			Rancho Cucamonga CA
85541	Payson AZ	88101-03	Clovis NM		Palos Verdes Ests CA	91731-34	El Monte CA
85546	Safford AZ	88119	Fort Sumner NM	90274		91733	S El Monte CA
85552	Thatcher AZ	88130	Portales NM		Rancho Palos Verdes CA	91740	Glendora CA
85602	Benson AZ	88201-02	Roswell NM	90274	Rolling Hills Ests CA	91744	S San Jose Hills CA
85603	Bisbee AZ	88210-11	Artesia NM	90274	Rolling Hills CA	91744	Valinda CA
85607-08	Douglas AZ	88220-21	Carlsbad NM	90277-78	Redondo Beach CA	91744	W Puente Vly CA
85613	Sierra Vista AZ	88231	Eunice NM	90280	South Gate CA	91744-49	La Puente CA
85621	Nogales AZ	88240-41	Hobbs NM	90301-99	Inglewood CA	91745	Hacienda Hts CA
85638	Tombstone AZ	88252	Jal NM	90304	Lennox CA	91748	Rowland Hts CA
85643-44	Wilcox AZ	88260	Lovington NM	90401-99	Santa Monica CA	91750	La Verne CA

ZIP	CITY	ZIP	CITY	ZIP	CITY	ZIP	CITY
91752	Mira Loma CA	92334-36	Fontana CA	93221	Exeter CA	93940-44	Monterey CA
91754-56	Monterey Pk CA	92343-44	Hemet CA	93222-23	Farmersville CA	93950	Pacific Grove CA
91760	Norco CA	92345	Hesperia CA	93230-32	Hanford CA	93955	Seaside CA
91761-62	Ontario CA	92346	Highland CA	93234	Huron CA	93960	Soledad CA
91763	Montclair CA	92354	Loma Linda CA	93235	Ivanhoe CA	94002	Belmont CA
91765	Diamond Bar CA	92359	Mentone CA	93241	Lamont CA	94005	Brisbane CA
91765-69	Pomona CA	92363	Needles CA	93245	Lemoore CA	94010	Hillsborough CA
91770	Rosemead CA	92370	Perris CA	93247	Lindsay CA	94010-11	Burlingame CA
91773	San Dimas CA	92373-75	Redlands CA	93250	McFarland CA	94014-17	Daly City CA
91775-78	San Gabriel CA	92376-77	Rialto CA	93257-58	Porterville CA	94019	Half Moon Bay CA
9178-89	Walnut CA	92383	San Jacinto CA	93263	Shafter CA	94022	Los Altos Hills CA
91780	Temple City CA	92387-88	Morneno Valley CA	93268	Taft CA	94022-24	Los Altos CA
91785-86	Upland CA	92388	Sunnymead CA	93274-75	Tulare CA	94025	Atherton CA
91790-93	W Covina CA	92392-94	Victorville CA	93277-79	Visalia CA	94025	Portola Valley CA
91800-99	Alhambra CA	92399	Yucaipa CA	93280	Wasco CA	94025-28	Menlo Park CA
92008-09	Carlsbad CA	92401-99	San Bernardino CA	93286	Woodlake CA	94030	Millbrae CA
92010-13	Chula Vista CA	92501-99	Riverside CA	93300-89	Bakersfield CA	94039-43	Mountain View CA
92014	Del Mar CA	92509	Rubidoux CA	93305	Bakersfield East CA	94044	Pacifica CA
92019-22	El Cajon CA	92621-22	Brea CA	93306	Hillcrest Ctr CA	94061	Woodside CA
92024	Encinitas CA	92624		93308	Oildale CA	94061-65	Redwood City CA
92025-27	Escondido CA		Capistrano Beach CA	93401-12	San Luis Obispo CA	94066	San Bruno CA
92028	Fallbrook CA	92626-28	Costa Mesa CA	93402	Baywood Park CA	94070	San Carlos CA
92032	Imperial Beach CA	92631-35	Fullerton CA	93420-21	Arroyo Grande CA	94080	S San Francisco CA
92037-38	La Jolla CA	92640-45	Garden Grove CA	93422-23	Atascadero CA	94086-89	Sunnyvale CA
92040	Lakeside CA	92646-49	Huntington Bch CA	93433	Grover City CA	94101-99	San Francisco CA
92041-44	La Mesa CA	92651-54	Laguna Beach CA	93434	Guadalupe CA	94244-899	
92045	Lemon Grove CA	92653	Laguna Hills CA	93436-38	Lompoc CA		SACRAMENTO CA
92050	National City CA	92658-63	Newport Beach CA	93442-43	Morro Bay CA	94301-09	Palo Alto CA
92054-56	Oceanside CA	92664-69	Orange CA	93446-47	Paso Robles CA	94303	E Palo Alto CA
92064	Poway CA	92667	Villa Park CA	93448-49	Pismo Beach CA	94401-99	San Mateo CA
92065	Ramona CA	92670	Placentia CA	93454-56	Santa Maria CA	94404	Foster City CA
92069	San Marcos CA	92672	San Clemente CA	93501	Mojave CA	94501	Alameda CA
92071	Santee CA	92675		93505	California City CA	94507	Alamo CA
92075	Solana Beach CA		San Juan Capistrano CA	93512	Bishop CA	94509	Antioch CA
92077-78	Spring Valley CA	92680	Tustin Foothills CA	93517	Bridgeport CA	94510	Benicia CA
92083-84	Vista CA	92680-81	Tustin CA	93526	Independence CA	94513	Brentwood CA
92101-99	San Diego CA	92683-84	Westminster CA	93534-39	Lancaster CA	94515	Calistoga CA
92118	Coronado CA	92686	Yorba Linda CA	93550-51	Palmdale CA	94517	Clayton CA
92201-02	Indio CA	92691	Mission Viejo CA	93555	Ridgecrest CA	94518-24	Concord CA
92220	Banning CA	92701-99	Santa Ana CA	93560	Rosamond CA	94523	Pleasant Hill CA
92223	Beaumont CA	92708	Fountain Valley CA	93561	Tehachapi CA	94526	Danville CA
92225-26	Blythe CA	92713-18	Irvine CA	93610	Chowchilla CA	94530	El Cerrito CA
92227	Brawley CA	92801-25	Anaheim CA	93612-13	Clovis CA	94533	Fairfield CA
92231-32	Calexico CA	93001-07	Ventura CA	93615	Cutler CA	94536-39	Fremont CA
92233	Calipatria CA	93010-11	Camarillo CA	93618	Dinuba CA	94540-46	Hayward CA
92234-35	Cathedral City CA	93013	Carpinteria CA	93620	Dos Palos CA	94546	Castro Valley CA
92236	Coachella CA	93015	Fillmore CA	93622	Firebaugh CA	94547	Hercules CA
92240	Desert Hot Spgs CA	93020-21	Moorpark CA	93630	Kerman CA	94549	Lafayette CA
92243-44	El Centro CA	93022	Oak View CA	93631	Kingsburg CA	94550-51	Livermore CA
92250	Holtville CA	93023	Ojai CA	93635	Los Banos CA	94553	Martinez CA
92251	Imperial CA	93030	El Rio CA	93637-39	Madera CA	94556	Moraga CA
92253	La Quinta CA	93030-35	Oxnard CA	93640	Mendota CA	94558-59	Napa CA
92260-61	Palm Desert CA	93041-43	Port Hueneme CA	93646	Orange Cove CA	94560	Newark CA
92262-64	Palm Springs CA	93060	Santa Paula CA	93648	Parlier CA	94563	Orinda CA
92270	Rancho Mirage CA	93062-65	Simi Valley CA	93654	Reedley CA	94564	Pinole CA
92277-78		93101-90	Santa Barbara CA	93657	Sanger CA	94565	Pittsburg CA
	Twentynine Palms CA	93108	Montecito CA	93662	Selma CA	94566	Pleasanton CA
92301	Apple Valley CA	93116	Goleta CA	93701-99	Fresno CA	94568	Dublin CA
92310-12	Barstow CA	93117	Isla Vista CA	93725	Calwa CA	94571	Rio Vista CA
92311	Lenwood CA	93202	Armona CA	93901-15	Salinas CA	94574	St Helena CA
92315	Big Bear Lake CA	93203	Arvin CA	93921-23	Carmel CA	94577-79	San Leandro CA
92316	Bloomington CA	93204	Avenal CA	93924	Carmel Valley CA	94580	San Lorenzo CA
92320	Calimesa CA	93210	Coalinga CA	93926	Gonzales CA	94583	San Ramon CA
92324	Colton CA	93212	Corcoran CA	93927	Greenfield CA	94585	Suisun City CA
92324	Grand Terrace CA	93215-06	Delano CA	93930	King City CA	94587	Union City CA
92330-31	Lake Elsinore CA	93219	Earlimart CA	93933	Marina CA	94589-92	Vallejo CA

ZIP .... CITY	ZIP .... CITY	ZIP .... CITY	ZIP .... CITY
94593-98 .. Walnut Creek CA	95401-09 ...... Santa Rosa CA	96120-21 .... Corning CA	97458 .... Myrtle Point OR
94601-62 .... Oakland CA	95422 .... Clearlake CA	96122 .... Portola CA	97459 .... N Bend OR
94608 .... Emeryville CA	95425 .... Cloverdale CA	96130 .... Susanville CA	97463 .... Oakridge OR
94611 .... Piedmont CA	95437 .... Fort Bragg CA	96706-07 .... Ewa Beach HI	97467 .... Reedsport OR
94701-10 .... Berkeley CA	95448 .... Healdsburg CA	96720 .... Hilo HI	97470 .... Roseburg OR
94706 .... Albany CA	95453 .... Lakeport CA	96761 .... Lahaina HI	97477-78 ...... Springfield OR
94801-08 .... Richmond CA	95472-73 ...... Sebastopol CA	96766 .... Lihue HI	97479 .... Sutherlin OR
94803 .... El Sobrante CA	95476 .... Sonoma CA	96786 .... Wailuku HI	97496 .... Winston OR
94806 .... San Pablo CA	95482 .... Ukiah CA	96801-99 .... Honolulu HI	97501-04 .... Medford OR
94901-15 .... San Rafael CA	95490 .... Willits CA	97013 .... Canby OR	97502 .... Central Point OR
94904 .... Greenbrae CA	95501-02 .... Eureka CA	97027 .... Gladstone OR	97520 .... Ashland OR
94904 .... Kentfield CA	95521 .... Arcata CA	97030 .... Gresham OR	97524 .... Eagle Point OR
94920 .... Tiburon CA	95531 .... Crescent City CA	97031 .... Hood River OR	97526-27 ...... Grants Pass OR
94925 ...... Corte Madera CA	95540 .... Fortuna CA	97034-05 .. Lake Oswego OR	97540 .... Talent OR
94927-28 .. Rohnert Park CA	95603-04 .... Auburn CA	97038 .... Molalla OR	97601-03 .. Klamath Falls OR
94930 .... Fairfax CA	95608-09 ...... Carmichael CA	97039 .... Moro OR	97630 .... Lakeview OR
94931 .... Cotati CA	95610-11 .... Citrus Hts CA	97045 .... Oregon City OR	97701-09 .... Bend OR
94941-42 ...... Mill Valley CA	95616-18 .... Davis CA	97051 .... St Helens OR	97720 .... Burns OR
94943 .... Larkspur CA	95620 .... Dixon CA	97055 .... Sandy OR	97741 .... Madras OR
94947-49 .... Novato CA	95628 .... Fair Oaks CA	97056 .... Scappoose OR	97754 .... Prineville OR
94952-54 .... Petaluma CA	95630 .... Folsom CA	97058 .... The Dalles OR	97756 .... Redmond OR
94957 .... Ross CA	95632 .... Galt CA	97060 .... Troutdale OR	97801 .... Pendleton OR
94960 .... San Anselmo CA	95642 .... Jackson CA	97062 .... Tualatin OR	97814 .... Baker OR
94965-66 .... Sausalito CA	95648 .... Lincoln CA	97068 .... W Linn OR	97820 .... Canyon City OR
95003 .... Aptos CA	95660 .... N Highlands CA	97070 .... Wilsonville OR	97823 .... Condon OR
95008-09 .... Campbell CA	95662 .... Orangevale CA	97071 .... Woodburn OR	97828 .... Enterprise OR
95010 .... Capitola CA	95667 .... Placerville CA	97075-76 .... Beaverton OR	97830 .... Fossil OR
95012 .... Castroville CA	95670	97103 .... Astoria OR	97836 .... Heppner OR
95014-16 .... Cupertino CA	.........Rancho Cordova CA	97113 .... Cornelius OR	97838 .... Hermiston OR
95020-21 .... Gilroy CA	95673 .... Rio Linda CA	97116 .... Forest Grove OR	97850 .... La Grande OR
95023-24 .... Hollister CA	95677 .... Rocklin CA	97123-24 .... Hillsboro OR	97862 ....
95030 .... Monte Sereno CA	95678 .... Roseville CA	97128 .... McMinnville OR	....Milton-Freewater OR
95030-32 ...... Los Gatos CA	95687-88 .... Vacaville CA	97132 .... Newberg OR	97882 .... Umatilla OR
95035-36 .... Milpitas CA	95691 ...... W Sacramento CA	97138 .... Seaside OR	97913 .... Nyssa OR
95037-38 .... Morgan Hill CA	95694 .... Winters CA	97140 .... Sherwood OR	97914 .... Ontario OR
95041 .... Felton CA	95695 .... Woodland CA	97141 .... Tillamook OR	97918 .... Vale OR
95050-55 ...... Santa Clara CA	95705-08 .. S Lake Tahoe CA	97201-99 .... Portland OR	98001-03 .... Auburn WA
95060-66 ...... Santa Cruz CA	95821 ...... Arcade-Arden CA	97222 .... Milwaukie OR	98002 .... Camelot WA
95066 ....Scotts Valley CA	95825 .... Arden CA	97223 .... Tigard OR	98002 ...... Newport Hills WA
95070-71 .... Saratoga CA	95825-26 .... Rosemont CA	97225 .... W Haven OR	98004 .... Clyde Hill WA
95076-77 .... Watsonville CA	95828 .... Florin CA	97266 .... Errol Hts OR	98004-09 .... Bellevue WA
95101-99 .... San Jose CA	95901 .... Marysville CA	97301-09 .... SALEM OR	98011 ....
95127 .... Alum Rock CA	95926-29 .... Chico CA	97303 .... Keizer OR	....Alderwood Manor WA
95201-13 .... Stockton CA	95932 .... Colusa CA	97321 .... Albany OR	98011 .... Juanita WA
95240-42 .... Lodi CA	95936 .... Downieville CA	97330-33 .... Corvallis OR	98011 ...... Martha Lake WA
95249 .... San Andreas CA	95945-46 .... Grass Valley CA	97338 .... Dallas OR	98011.....Queensborough WA
95301 .... Atwater CA	95948 .... Gridley CA	97351 .... Independence OR	98011-12 .... Bothell WA
95307 .... Ceres CA	95953 .... Live Oak CA	97355 .... Lebanon OR	98020 .... Edmonds WA
95320 .... Escalon CA	95959 .... Nevada City CA	97361 .... Monmouth OR	98022 .... Enumclaw WA
95322 .... Gustine CA	95963 .... Orland CA	97362 .... Mount Angel OR	98027 .... Issaquah WA
95326 .... Hughson CA	95965-66 .... Oroville CA	97365 .... Newport OR	98031 .... Park Orchard WA
95334 .... Livingston CA	95969 .... Paradise CA	97367 .... Lincoln City OR	98031 .... Timberlane WA
95336 .... Manteca CA	95971 .... Quincy CA	97370 .... Philomath OR	98031-32 .... Kent WA
95338 .... Mariposa CA	95988 .... Willows CA	97381 .... Silverton OR	98033 .... Rose Hill WA
95340-44 .... Merced CA	95991-93 ...... Yuba City CA	97383 .... Stayton OR	98033-34 .... Kirkland WA
95350-56 .... Modesto CA	96001-03 .... Redding CA	97386 .... Sweet Home OR	98036 ....
95360 .... Newman CA	96007 .... Anderson CA	97391 .... Toledo OR	........Alderwood Manor WA
95361 .... Oakdale CA	96019 .... Central Vly CA	97401-05 .... Eugene OR	98036 .... Brier WA
95363 .... Patterson CA	96025 .... Dunsmuir CA	97415 .... Brookings OR	98036 .... N Lynnwood WA
95365 .... Planada CA	96067 .... Mount Shasta CA	97420 .... Coos Bay OR	98036 ...... Stickney Lake WA
95366 .... Ripon CA	96080 .... Red Bluff CA	97423 .... Coquille OR	98036-37 ...... Lynnwood WA
95367 .... Riverbank CA	96093 .... Weaverville CA	97424 ...... Cottage Grove OR	98039 .... Medina WA
95370 .... Sonora CA	96094 .... Weed CA	97439 .... Florence OR	98040 ...... Mercer Island WA
95376 .... Tracy CA	96097 .... Yreka CA	97444 .... Gold Beach OR	98043 ....
95380-81 .... Turlock CA	96101 .... Alturas CA	97448 ...... Junction City OR	........Mountlake Terrace WA
95386 .... Waterford CA	96120 .... Markleeville CA	97457 .... Myrtle Creek OR	98052-53 .... Redmond WA

ZIP .... CITY	ZIP .... CITY	ZIP .... CITY	ZIP .... CITY
98055 ...... Cascade Vista WA	98362 .... Port Angeles WA	98660 .... Hazel Del WA	99324 .... College Place WA
98055-58 .... Renton WA	98366 .... Port Orchard WA	98660-86 ...... Vancouver WA	99327 .... Othello WA
98101-99 .... Seattle WA	98368 .... Port Townsend WA	98671 .... Washougal WA	99328 .... Dayton WA
98118 .... Valley Ridge WA	98370 .... Poulsbo WA	98801-07 ...... Wenatchee WA	99336-37 ...... Kennewick WA
98126 .... White Center WA	98371-74 .... Puyallup WA	98816 .... Chelan WA	99347 .... Pomeroy WA
98155 .... North City WA	98373 .... South Hill WA	98823 .... Ephrata WA	99350 .... Prosser WA
98155 .... Ridgecrest WA	98382 .... Sequim WA	98837 .... Moses Lake WA	99352 .... Richland WA
98155 .... Sunnydale WA	98388 .... Steilacoom WA	98840 .... Okanogan WA	99352 .... W Richland WA
98160 ...... Richmont Bch WA	98390 .... Bonney Lake WA	98841 .... Omak WA	99362 .... Walla Walla WA
98166 .....Normandy Park WA	98390 .... Sumner WA	98848 .... Quincy WA	99402 .... Asotin WA
98178 .... Skyway WA	98397-499 .... Tacoma WA	98858 .... Waterville WA	99403 .... Clarkston WA
98188 .... Des Moines WA	98444 .... Midland WA	98901-99 .... Yakima WA	99501-40 .... Anchorage AK
98188 ...... McMicken Hts WA	98466 .... Fircrest WA	98903 .... Union Gap WA	99559 .... Bethel AK
98188 .... Saltwater WA	98501 .... Tanglewilde WA	98926 .... Ellensburg WA	99574 .... Cordova AK
98188 .... Tukwila WA	98501	98930 .... Grandview WA	99576 .... Dillingham AK
98201 .... Silver Lake WA	.......Thompson Place WA	98942 .... Selah WA	99603 .... Homer AK
98201-08 .... Everett WA	98501-07 ...... OLYMPIA WA	98944 .... Sunnyside WA	99611 .... Kenai AK
98221-22 .... Anacortes WA	98502 .... Tumwater WA	98948 .... Toppenish WA	99615 .... Kodiak AK
98223 .... Arlington WA	98503 .... Lacey WA	98951 .... Wapato WA	99645 .... Palmer AK
98225-27 ...... Bellingham WA	98520 .... Aberdeen WA	99004 .... Cheney WA	99664 .... Seward AK
98233 .... Burlington WA	98531 .... Centralia WA	99016 .... Greenacres WA	99686 .... Valdez AK
98239 .... Coupeville WA	98532 .... Chehalis WA	99022 .... Medical Lake WA	99701-16 .... Fairbanks AK
98248 .... Ferndale WA	98541 .... Elma WA	99027 ...... Otis Orchards WA	99723 .... Barrow AK
98250 ...... Friday Harbor WA	98550 .... Hoquiam WA	99109 .... Chewelah WA	99740 ....Fort Yukon AK
98264 .... Lynden WA	98563 .... Montesano WA	99111 .... Colfax WA	99741 .... Galena AK
98270 .... Marysville WA	98577 .... Raymond WA	99114 .... Colville WA	99752 .... Kotzebue AK
98272 .... Monroe WA	98584 .... Shelton WA	99122 .... Davenport WA	99762 .... Nome AK
98273 ...... Mount Vernon WA	98586 .... South Bend WA	99156 .... Newport WA	99801-03 .... JUNEAU AK
98277-78 .... Oak Harbor WA	98604 ...... Battle Ground WA	99163-65 .... Pullman WA	99833 .... Petersburg AK
98284 ...... Sedro Woolley WA	98607 .... Camas WA	99166 .... Republic WA	99835 .... Sitka AK
98290 .... Snohomish WA	98612 .... Cathlamet WA	99169 .... Ritzville WA	99840 .... Skagway AK
98310-15 ...... Bremerton WA	98620 .... Goldendale WA	99201-99 .... Spokane WA	99901 ....Ketchikan AK
98321 .... Buckley WA	98626 .... Kelso WA	99211 .... Parkwater WA	99929 .... Wrangell AK
98331 .... Forks WA	98632 .... Longview WA	99214 .... Opportunity WA	
98354 .... Milton WA	98648 .... Stevenson WA	99301-02 .... Pasco WA	

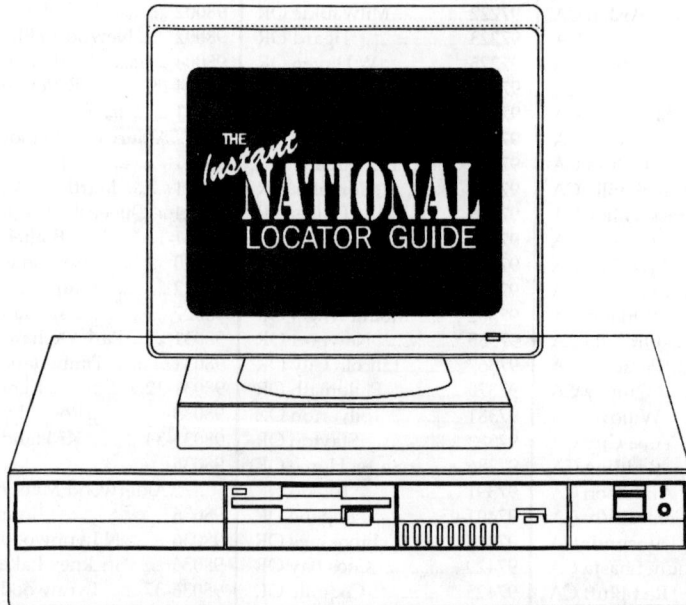

Ask About Our Book on Disk!

Creighton-Morgan
Publishing Group

P.O. Box 470862, San Francisco CA 94147-0862, (415) 922-6684

Area Codes

ALABAMA	205
ALASKA	604, 907
ARIZONA	602
ARKANSAS	501
CALIFORNIA	209, 213, 408, 415, 510, 619, 707, 714, 805, 818, 916
COLORADO	303, 719
CONNECTICUT	203
DELAWARE	302
DISTRICT OF COLUMBIA	202
FLORIDA	305, 407, 813, 904
GEORGIA	404, 912
HAWAII	808
IDAHO	208
ILLINOIS	217, 309, 312, 618, 708, 815
INDIANA	219, 317, 812
IOWA	319, 515, 712
KANSAS	316, 913
KENTUCKY	502, 606
LOUISIANA	318, 504
MAINE	207
MARYLAND	301, 410
MASSACHUSETTS	413, 508, 617
MICHIGAN	313, 517, 616, 906
MINNESOTA	218, 507, 612
MISSISSIPPI	601
MISSOURI	314. 417, 816
MONTANA	406
NEBRASKA	308, 402
NEVADA	702
NEW JERSEY	201, 609, 908
NEW YORK	212, 315, 516, 518, 607, 716, 718, 914
NEW MEXICO	505
NEW HAMPSHIRE	603
NORTH DAKOTA	701
NORTH CAROLINA	704, 919
OHIO	216, 419, 513, 614
OKLAHOMA	405, 918
OREGON	503
PENNSYLVANIA	215, 412, 717, 814
RHODE ISLAND	401
SOUTH DAKOTA	605
SOUTH CAROLINA	803
TENNESSEE	615, 901
TEXAS	214, 409. 512, 713, 806, 817, 903, 915
UTAH	801
VERMONT	802
VIRGINIA	703, 804
WASHINGTON	206, 509
WEST VIRGINIA	304, 614
WISCONSIN	414, 608, 715
WYOMING	307

AREA CODES & THIER STATES

201	New Jersey
202	District of Columbia
203	Connecticut
205	Alabama
206	Washington
207	Maine
208	Idaho
209	California
212	New York
213	California
214	Texas
215	Pennsylvania
216	Ohio
217	Illinois
218	Minnesota
219	Indiana
301	Maryland
302	Delaware
303	Colorado
304	West Virginia
305	Florida
307	Wyoming
308	Nebraska
309	Illinois
312	Illinois
313	Michigan
314	Missouri
315	New York
316	Kansas
317	Indiana
318	Louisiana
319	Iowa
401	Rhode Island
402	Nebraska
404	Georgia
405	Oklahoma
406	Montana
407	Florida
408	California
409	Texas
410	Maryland
412	Pennsylvania
413	Massachusetts
414	Wisconsin
415	California
417	Missouri
419	Ohio
501	Arkansas
502	Kentucky
503	Oregon
504	Louisiana
505	New Mexico
507	Minnesota
508	Massachusetts
509	Washington
510	California
512	Texas
513	Ohio
515	Iowa
516	New York
517	Michigan
518	New York
601	Mississippi
602	Arizona
603	New Hampshire
604	Alaska
605	South Dakota
606	Kentucky
607	New York
608	Wisconsin
609	New Jersey
612	Minnesota
614	Ohio
614	West Virginia
615	Tennessee
616	Michigan
617	Massachusetts
618	Illinois
619	California
701	North Dakota
702	Nevada
703	Virginia
704	North Carolina
707	California
708	Illinois
712	Iowa
713	Texas
714	California
715	Wisconsin
716	New York
717	Pennsylvania
718	New York
719	Colorado
801	Utah
802	Vermont
803	South Carolina
804	Virginia
805	California
806	Texas
808	Hawaii
809	Caribbean Islands
812	Indiana
813	Florida
814	Pennsylvania
815	Illinois
816	Missouri
817	Texas
818	California
901	Tennessee
903	Texas
904	Florida
906	Michigan
907	Alaska
908	New Jersey
912	Georgia
913	Kansas
914	New York
915	Texas
916	California
918	Oklahoma
919	North Carolina

CREIGHTON-MORGAN PUBLISHING GROUP
P.O. Box 470862, San Francisco CA 94147 (415) 922-6684

Reader-Friendly Computer Books

How to Understand and Buy Computers is an easy to read, in-depth book that explains how computers work in simple, understandable terms. **ISBN** 0-945776-09-8 Pages: 200, $7.95

How to Understand and Buy Software explains the different types of software available, and shows you how to select the software that best suits your needs.
ISBN 0-945776-04-7 Pages: 200, $7.95

DOS Secrets will help you organize, gain control of, and maximize the power of your personal computer. **ISBN** 0-945776-12-8 Pages: 178 pages, $7.95

How to Get Started With Modems is a comprehensive introduction to the world of electronic communications; everything from purchase, to installation, to use.
ISBN 0-945776-05-5 Pages: 140, $7.95

Public Records Primer

A complete listing of all public access informational sources in the state of California, including addresses and phone numbers for all County, State, City and Federal offices. **ISBN** 0-938717-05-9 Pages: 126, $14.95

Take the Money & *Strut!*

Now, for the first time, a private investigator risks being torn apart by other p.i.s to share the secrets professionals use to legally separate a man from his money. This witty & informative how-to has been featured on *Larry King Live!* , *Good Morning America,* and in *Entrepreneur Magazine.* **ISBN** 0-9620096-0-1 Pages: 96 $9.95

Credit Power Handbook

This step-by-step guide shows how to legally erase bad credit; establish good credit; get major credit cards (even with bad or no credit); increase your credit limit; and make money using credit. **ISBN** 0-929148-00-2 Pages: 204 $14.95

Ask About Our Book on Disk!

Instant NATIONAL LOCATOR GUIDE

To Order:

Order from your book store, or use the handy form below.

Quantity	Title	Unit Price	Total

Postage & Handling:
1st book: $3.50
add'l books: $1.50ea.
Sales Tax:
California only - 7%

Subtotal_____
Tax_____
Postage &
Handling_____
Total_____

Please allow 2 - 4 weeks for delivery.

Name_____
Address_____

Phone_____